Accountable Governance
Problems and Promises

Edited by Melvin J. Dubnick
and H. George Frederickson

Foreword by David Mathews

Kettering
Foundation

M.E.Sharpe
Armonk, New York
London, England

Library of Congress Cataloging-in-Publication Data

Accountable governance : problems and promises / edited by Melvin J. Dubnick
and H. George Frederickson.
   p. cm.
 Includes bibliographical references and index.
 ISBN 978-0-7656-2383-6 (hardcover : alk. paper)—ISBN 978-0-7656-2384-3 (pbk. : alk. paper)

 1. Government accountability 2. Government accountability—United States.
I. Dubnick, Melvin J. II. Frederickson, H. George.

 JF1351.A25 2011
 352.3′5—dc22   2010022587

Printed in the United States of America

The paper used in this publication meets the minimum requirements of
American National Standard for Information Sciences
Permanence of Paper for Printed Library Materials,
ANSI Z 39.48-1984.

∞

| IBT (c) | 10 | 9 | 8 | 7 | 6 | 5 | 4 | 3 | 2 | 1 |
| IBT (p) | 10 | 9 | 8 | 7 | 6 | 5 | 4 | 3 | 2 | 1 |

CONTENTS

Foreword
David Mathews.. vii
Acknowledgments.. xi
Introduction: The Promises of Accountability Research
Melvin J. Dubnick and H. George Frederickson xiii

Part I. Complex Challenges 1

1. The Challenge of Multiple Accountability: Does Redundancy Lead to Overload?
   Thomas Schillemans and Mark Bovens... 3
2. The Tangled Web of Accountability in Contracting Networks: The Case of
   Welfare Reform
   Barbara S. Romzek 22
3. Accountability Challenges in Public Sector Contracting for Complex Products
   Trevor L. Brown, Matthew Potoski, and David M. Van Slyke................ 42
4. Accountability for Global Governance Organizations
   Jonathan G.S. Koppell 55

Part II. Obstacles to Accountability 79

5. Performance Blight and the Tyranny of Light? Accountability in
   Advanced Performance Measurement Regimes
   Christopher Pollitt.. 81
6. Does Performance Measurement Actually Improve Accountability?
   Beryl A. Radin 98
7. The Accountability Environment of U.S. Counties
   Bonnie J. Johnson, John C. Pierce, and Nicholas P. Lovrich, Jr............... 111

Part III. Assessing Accountability 127

8. Accountability Institutions and Information in the Policy-Making Process
   Paul L. Posner and Robert Schwartz.. 129
9. Accountability and Information-Technology Enactment: A Cross-National Perspective
   Richard K. Ghere 146

Part IV. Adapting to Accountability **165**

10. Blame Avoidance and Accountability: Positive, Negative, or Neutral?
    Christopher Hood.. 167
11. The Challenges of Accountability for International Nongovernmental and
    Civil-Society Organizations
    Margaret P. Karns, Timothy J. Shaffer, and Richard K. Ghere 180
12. Accountability in the Nonprofit Sector: Abandoning the One-Size-Fits-All Approach
    Kevin P. Kearns 197

Part V. Strategies.. **211**

13. Watching the Watchers
    Sally Wheeler... 213
14. Accountability and Voluntary Programs
    Matthew Potoski and Aseem Prakash.. 225

Part VI. Rethinking Accountability... **239**

15. Accountability in Two Non-Western Contexts
    Sara R. Jordan... 241
16. Accountability and a Theory of Representation
    Ciarán O'Kelly.. 255
17. Emergent Accountability and Structuration Theory: Implications
    Kaifeng Yang.. 269
18. Rethinking the Obsession: Accountability and the Financial Crisis
    Melvin J. Dubnick and Justin O'Brien 282

Conclusion: Taking Stock and Moving Forward
    Melvin J. Dubnick and H. George Frederickson 302

About the Editors and Contributors 304
Name Index 309
Subject Index 319

FOREWORD

To What Kind of Democracy Is Accountability Accountable?

DAVID MATHEWS

The Kettering Foundation became drawn into this book's critique of the accountability movement through its studies on democracy—democracy as seen from the perspective of citizens who want a stronger hand in shaping their future. A stronger hand can come from deciding and acting collectively with other citizens on common problems as well as from acting through the governmental and nongovernmental institutions that people believe have been created by and for them.

The Foundation assumes that the ubiquitous emphasis on accountability is prompted by laudable objectives—to demonstrate that institutions are doing their jobs effectively and to show that they are open and responsive to the public. The more we saw of the actual consequences of pursuing these goals, however, the more we became aware of troubling implications for a democratic citizenry. Unintended consequences came from the way accountability objectives have been implemented through standards, benchmarks, performance measures, and evaluation protocols.

Although we had been hearing about accountability for some time in conversations with educators, government officials, and foundation staff, we got insights into how the public understood accountability from a 2001 study done with Doble Research Associates (Doble 2001). We asked John Doble to follow up on earlier research on the lack of a public for the public schools (Mathews 1996). We had found many Americans moving away from these schools; they had little sense of ownership or responsibility, which was a result of feeling that they couldn't bring about the changes in the schools that they wanted.

School officials, on the other hand, believed that they were very responsive and accountable, citing the voluminous test-score data they provided. And educators believed performance measures were in line with the public's demand for higher standards. Doble found, however, that although people might appreciate the information, they weren't persuaded that the schools were doing a good job or being responsive to them. This was a very small study, but only one of the thirty-five people in the focus groups mentioned performance measures as a means of accountability, and she was a school-board member (Doble 2001, 8). Citizens felt students should be held to high expectations but that test scores were only one indicator and didn't reflect other concerns they had, such as the character and values of students. Furthermore, citizens felt that they and their communities should be held responsible for what happened to young people, not just the teachers.

Four years later, a study Kettering did with Mid-Continent Research for Education and Learning (McREL) reinforced what we learned from the Doble report (McREL 2004; Arens 2005). The McREL research suggests that who should be accountable—and for what—is an issue that needs to be decided through public deliberations. When accountability is externally defined, it tends to disenfranchise those most directly affected by it. These two studies are not extensive enough to be cited as definitive proof, but they led us to look further at the way the public understood accountability.

Kettering also encountered accountability in working with grant-making foundations and nongovernmental organizations interested in building civic capacity in communities (Scully and Harwood 1997; *Accountability* 2003; London 2005). Most grant makers were being held accountable through benchmarks that judged the impact of their funding. These benchmarks were then translated into performance measures by the nongovernmental organizations that received their grants. This all seemed unexceptional until we began to get reports of unintended consequences. Some foundation officials were aware that externally imposed objectives (and the performance measures based on them) might undermine building the capacity for self-determination they were intending to promote. Grant recipients, for their part, complained that the indicators being prescribed were often irrelevant and diverted time and energy away from the important work they hoped to do. However, they said they needed the money and had to "play the game," if necessary. Sometimes foundation officers admitted that the criticisms were valid but explained that their boards required proof of impact.

Perhaps the most problematic of all the unintended consequences of the accountability movement for the work of citizens is the effect on collective or civic learning. One of the most telling characteristics of high-achieving communities—those that are adept at bringing citizens together to solve problems—is the way these communities learn collectively from their efforts, including those that fail (Morse 2004; Mathews 2006). This type of learning involves evaluating both outcomes and goals. And it involves assessing both results of projects and the community itself—the way it performs. Accountability protocols, however, typically use objective (outside) evaluators to measure outcomes against predetermined goals. While such evaluations have merit, they are quite different from evaluation that goes on in civic learning.

The untoward effects of accountability measures, we learned, fell not just on grant recipients; they touched the organizations using the measures as well. A recent study done with the Harwood Institute for Public Innovation shows that the pressure to demonstrate accountability with measurable impact has been turning the focus of grant makers inward to concentrate on professionally defined expectations and away from the groups and communities they aim to benefit (Harwood 2008). Furthermore, the need to demonstrate that grants are successful is creating a disincentive to invest in local civic capacity building. Investments in capacity building make it more difficult to prove that external influences, not indigenous ones, have brought about changes (Ellerman 2006).

Accountability measures can have a particularly ironic effect on one of the most cherished objectives of philanthropy, which is to foster innovation. Research done with Kettering by George Frederickson titled *Easy Innovation and the Iron Cage* found that the benchmarks used in demonstrating impact could have a deadening effect on innovation (Frederickson 2003). Inventive enterprises that communities undertake to strengthen their civic capacity don't always produce the definitive outcomes that performance measures impose. And the direction that the enterprises take may change as experience dictates. The people involved usually have to make the road by walking it. Certainly, the civic entrepreneurs involved in these exploratory ventures recognize the need for clarity of purpose, and they want to know if their efforts have had good effects. Still, preordained accountability measures, particularly those externally imposed, can inhibit experimentation. Consequently, rather than play the game, some civic inventors refuse to work with outside funders, which not only imposes a hardship on them, but also is problematic for grant makers who pride themselves on supporting innovation.

Much of what we have heard from grant makers and grantors echoes what we heard from government officials and those who receive support from government funding. The information we have is suggestive, not definitive, but requirements for accountability don't always improve performance or result in greater confidence in the institutions involved. Brian Cook's explanation of what is going awry seems plausible. Cook observes that "an increasingly vicious circle has emerged in which anxiety about control and accountability . . . has led to more extensive, more complex controls, which in turn have increased the bureaucratic distance between administrators and the public they are expected to serve. This distance then raises new worries about control and accountability and brings about the introduction of another layer of controls" (Cook 1996, 134–35). Cook goes on to argue that the result has been the opposite of what the accountability reforms intended, which is greater effectiveness in serving the public.

What, we wonder, might prevent or at least mitigate the unintended consequences that undermine democratic self-rule? A frontal assault on accountability seems ill-advised. After all, the movement has benefits, and it is deeply entrenched. And while criticizing the overreliance on quantitative measures as indicators may be justified, it likely just adds to the existing debate over qualitative versus quantitative measures.

On reflection, it seems to us that the accountability movement is powerful because it serves its own kind of politics, which is as entrenched as the movement. If that is so, nothing will change until there is some reconsideration of the dominant mode of politics. While the accountability movement would likely claim to be serving democracy, we would like to know what kind of democracy; specifically, we would like to know what concept of citizenship is implied in accountability practices. Our system tends to sideline citizens as occasional voters and consumers of political fare but not recognize them as people capable of producing public goods by their collective efforts. So, if the prevailing concept of who citizens are (or should be) is the central issue, we reason, any corrective has to begin there.

More and more, we suspect that there are significant differences in the way citizens understand accountability and the way officeholders and institutional officials (governmental and nongovernmental) understand it. We don't think one understanding is necessarily better than another but that the differences may be responsible for much of the frustration of both institutional leaders and "the people." *A very tentative hypothesis is that institutions think of accountability primarily in informational terms while citizens think of it more in relational terms.* Of course, we recognize that, given the appeal of just being a consumer, people don't always think of their own responsibility. But we have some indications that, under certain circumstances, people do, indeed, recognize that they should be accountable. We would like to know more about what those circumstances are. For instance, in public deliberations on closing the achievement gap, participants came to see multiple gaps, not just the academic one in the schools. When that happened, people began to talk about what they could and should do through their communities (Flono 2010).

When citizens think about the kind of relationship that fosters accountability, we don't think they have in mind a pleasant, personal relationship with officials but rather a candid exchange in which officials would account for what they consider valuable, as well as what they do. We would like to know more about what they envision, and we would also like to know more about how citizens view their own accountability. We suspect that what they see as their responsibility is closely tied to what they think they can and should do. It is difficult to accept responsibility and hold ourselves accountable for things we can't change.

As we pursue these questions, we are very pleased to have this book's account of how scholars in public administration see the accountability movement. It provides an indispensable context for us as we continue our exchanges with educators, government officials, the staff of nongovernmental organizations and, most certainly, citizens.

REFERENCES

Accountability, Community, and Philanthropic Practice: Report on a Session at the 52nd Annual Conference of the Council on Foundations, May 1, 2001. 2003. Dayton, OH: Kettering Foundation.

Arens, Sheila A. 2005. *Examining the Meaning of Accountability: Reframing the Construct.* Aurora, CO: Mid-Continent Research for Education and Learning (McREL).

Cook, Brian J. 1996. *Bureaucracy and Self-Government: Reconsidering the Role of Public Administration in American Politics.* Baltimore, MD: Johns Hopkins University Press.

Doble Research Associates. 2001. *Reframing "Accountability": The Public's Terms.* Report to the Kettering Foundation. Dayton, OH.

Ellerman, David. 2006. "Good Intentions: The Dilemma of Outside-In Help for Inside-Out Change." *The Nonprofit Quarterly* 13 (3): 46–49.

Flono, Fannie. 2010. *Helping Students Succeed: Communities Confront the Achievement Gap.* Dayton, OH: Kettering Foundation.

Frederickson, H. George. 2003. *Easy Innovation and the Iron Cage: Best Practice, Benchmarking, and the Management of Organizational Creativity.* Dayton, OH: Kettering Foundation.

Harwood, Richard C., and John A. Creighton. 2008. *The Organization-First Approach: How Programs Crowd Out Community.* Dayton, OH: Kettering Foundation and Bethesda, MD: Harwood Institute for Public Innovation.

London, Scott. 2005. *Investing in Public Life: A Report from the 2003–2004 Dialogues on Civil Investing.* Dayton, OH: Kettering Foundation and Pew Partnership for Civic Change.

Mathews, David. 1996. *Is There a Public for Public Schools?* Dayton, OH: Kettering Foundation Press.

———. 2006. *Reclaiming Public Education by Reclaiming Our Democracy.* Dayton, OH: Kettering Foundation Press.

Mid-Continent Research for Education and Learning (McREL). 2004. "Examining the Meaning of Accountability: Reframing the Construct." A Report on the Perceptions of Accountability. Dayton, OH: Report to the Kettering Foundation.

Morse, Suzanne. 2004. *Smart Communities: How Citizens and Local Leaders Can Use Strategic Thinking to Build a Brighter Future.* San Francisco, CA: Jossey-Bass.

Scully, Patrick L., and Richard C. Harwood. 1997. *Strategies for Civil Investing: Foundations and Community-Building.* Dayton, OH: Kettering Foundation.

ACKNOWLEDGMENTS

Thirty of the world's leading scholars specializing in accountability in governance gathered in late May 2008 at the Kettering Foundation in Dayton, Ohio. Each had been working for months leading up to the meeting in Dayton on the paper they would give at the Symposium on Accountability. We gathered at the Kettering Foundation at the invitation of David Mathews, President of the Foundation. We thank him and the staff of the Foundation for their support and encouragement. We particularly thank John R. Dedrick, Vice President and Director of Programs, and his staff, who brilliantly facilitated the Dayton side of the Symposium.

The editors especially thank the Kettering Foundation for its support while we continue our work on accountability.

At the University of Kansas we thank Katherine Jennings Logan who managed many of the details of the Symposium and the evolution of the Symposium papers into this volume.

We particularly thank M. E. Sharpe Publishers and especially Harry M. Briggs, executive editor, for his encouragement and gentle prodding. Thanks to Stacey Victor, production editor, at M.E. Sharpe, who deftly managed the production of this book.

Finally, we thank the chapter authors who cheerfully endured seemingly endless rounds of manuscript evaluations, revisions, updating, and proof checking. We thank them and their academic institutions for their support, as we thank our own institutions.

Melvin J. Dubnick   H. George Frederickson
University of New Hampshire   University of Kansas

INTRODUCTION: THE PROMISES OF ACCOUNTABILITY RESEARCH

Melvin J. Dubnick and H. George Frederickson

In listening to the rhetoric surrounding discussions of government in its various forms, one soon becomes aware of a collective obsession with accountability. Accountability emerges in almost every assessment of the way public agencies, nongovernmental organizations (NGOs), and corporations are governed, and as a normative standard, it is central to discussions of how those entities and their associated programs and markets ought to be governed. When it comes to related issues of governance, critics contend there is either too little or too much of it. Accountability, in short, is perceived almost everywhere as both cause and cure.

The question that follows is obvious: the cause of and cure for *what*? Responses will reference a long list of problems, from the corruption and poor performance of public agencies, to the collapse of firms and entire markets, to the injustices and evil acts of bureaucracies and regimes. With so much influence attributed to accountability as both cause and cure, even the most casual observer must conclude that accountability is a major factor in our political and economic lives. Moreover, we assume such a pervasive factor must be the subject of careful analysis and study—which indeed it has been over the past decade or so. Yet given the centrality of accountability in the way we think about governance in the public, private, and nonprofit sectors, it is surprising that so little systematic thought had been given to the subject.

That is not to say that scholars have been blind or indifferent to the role of accountability in the past. On a normative level, the demand for responsible and responsive (i.e., accountable) governance has been addressed in an extensive literature generated in a range of disciplines. In political science, debates over the nature of representation and electoral accountability fill many volumes, and among students of law questions related to liability and fiduciary obligations are topics taking up hundreds of pages in law journals as well as the professional curriculum (Dodd 1935; Scott 1949; Clark 1996). Students of the modern corporation have been debating the implications of management control and accountability to shareholders since at least the early 1930s, when Berle and Means published their observations (1932; McCraw 1990), and in public administration the Friedrich-Finer debate of the early 1940s established the parameters of an ongoing (and often contentious) discussion related to administrative discretion and oversight (Friedrich 1940; Finer 1941; e.g., Harmon 1995; Bertelli and Lynn 2003; Dubnick 2003a).

Yet for all the attention paid to accountability in these discipline-bound studies and academic exchanges, until recently few scholars had tackled the issues surrounding the generic concept of accountability on a theoretical, empirical, or practical level. That changed in the 1980s as more attention was paid to accountability as a factor in decision making (Romzek and Dubnick 1987), and by the late 1990s accountability-related management tools (e.g., performance measurement) attracted a growing number of scholars to the subject (e.g., Thompson 1993; DuPont-Morales and Harris 1994; Gore 1994, 1995; Osborne et al. 1995; Smith 1995). While we have paid more attention to accountability per se, those of us engaged in its study have become increasingly aware of the work that still needs to be done. Approaching accountability as a distinct, cross-disciplinary topic has proven problematic in at least three respects.

First, it has become clear that growing interest in accountability is closely related to the problems of governance, but we have yet to develop a useful theoretical framework within which to examine both. While traditionally viewed as the process by which governments exercise authority, governance is now viewed as a core function of most organized efforts, including networks and the growing number of similar, loosely structured and informal relationships through which we take collective action. It is widely acknowledged that accountability arrangements central to governance functions no longer can be viewed as strictly formalized in either jurisdictional or hierarchical terms (Rhodes 1996; Stoker 1998); still, we have yet to establish even the rudimentary foundations for a theoretical framing of how accountability relates to this broader view of governance.

Second, while a growing number of empirical studies focus on accountability arrangements, no consensus has developed regarding precisely what we are looking for or looking at (Dubnick 1998, 2002; Bovens 2007, 2008). Accountability remains a conceptually amorphous idea that eludes our empirical grasp. Just when we think we have a means for providing an operational definition of the term, we realize that much of the meaning of accountability tends to be lost in empirical translation. Narrowing the concept to answerability, performance, or the management of diverse expectations pays off by yielding insights into some aspects of accountability, but we have yet to develop a conceptually distinct definition or model that captures what it means to be accountable or to hold someone to account.

Third, we have yet to make practical sense of what we do know about accountability. To paraphrase Aaron Wildavsky's observation about planning (1973), if accountability is everything, then perhaps it is nothing. As students of governance, what drives our growing interest in accountability is not an urge to frame some grand theory or develop a comprehensive definition, but rather the need to enhance our understanding of accountability as a means for improving the human condition through more effective governance. It is that motivating urge for practical wisdom that characterizes the purpose of this volume.

FRAMING THE KETTERING SYMPOSIUM

The articles in this collection were presented at a symposium held in April 2008 at the Kettering Foundation near Dayton, Ohio. Invitations to Dayton were extended to individuals known to be engaged in research on accountability; beyond the shared interest in the topic, no formal thematic frame or common thread linked the various presenters at Kettering.

This open approach reflected the assumption that the study of accountability had not advanced to the point where such a gathering would benefit from a clearly focused theme. At best, the embryonic field of accountability studies is at a stage closer to Dwight Waldo's characterization of organization theory in his classic 1961 overview of that emerging field. Reviewing a "round hundred" or so entries in several volumes, he reflected on the view of one contributor who recalled the fable of several blind individuals attempting to describe an elephant. "In point of fact," Waldo remarked, "it is not clear that all the contributors . . . are talking about the same elephant, or even members of the same species. . . . In view of the inclusiveness, the diversity, the amorphousness of the materials put under Organization Theory heading nowadays, one must conclude that, if they all concern the same elephant, it is a very large elephant with a generalized elephantiasis" (Waldo 1961, 216).

Fortunately, the Kettering sessions included several individuals who were able to see the subject well enough to provide some guidance as our exploration of the accountability elephant began. Of special note were comments from Mark Bovens, who offered a distinction (integrated into his co-authored article with Schillemans in this volume) between the American and European approaches to accountability. Put briefly, Bovens posited that while Europeans attach instrumental value to accountability, Americans tend to view accountability as a virtue. The intriguing nature of that distinction proved attractive, and reference was made to it intermittently throughout the rest of the symposium.

The distinction also proved somewhat useful to the editors during the post-symposium period as we considered alternative ways for framing the diverse contributions in preparing this volume. Although we found the geographic characterization of the two perspectives to be exaggerated (some notable work on instrumental approaches to accountability has been done in the United States), the insight that there are at least two very different approaches to accountability proved fruitful in our efforts to frame the range of presentations at the Kettering sessions.

A second theme evident in many of the presentations was the existence of "multiple accountabilities" in almost every arena of governance. With roots in the study of organization and management, the idea of multiple accountabilities first found explicit expression in explanations of accountable governance in work published in the 1980s by Day and Klein (1987) and Romzek and Dubnick (1987). To govern was, in a very real sense, to constantly contend with the multiple, diverse, and often conflicting expectations generated through various systems of accountability. Ironically, the most effective way to govern under those conditions was to develop still more systems of accountability.

A third theme emerging from the conference—and for that matter from much of the recent writing on accountability—is the focus on accountability mechanisms rather than on accountability as an ethical or empirical condition. In the present collection, only three contributions (Jordan, O'Kelly, and Yang) touch explicitly on the meaning of accountability. The relative dearth of attention to what it actually means to be accountable could be explained, in part, by the lack of a theoretical context or conceptual clarity about the subject. The emphasis on accountability mechanisms also reflects the agendas of the authors who—for the most part—come to this research from fields such as public administration and law, where questions related to the efficacy of administrative or legal mechanisms take center stage.

The focus on accountability mechanisms provided an attractive and useful thematic frame for comprehending and focusing the research. The very notion of accountability mechanisms implies their relevance as administrative tools and policy instruments, and in that regard they can be analyzed from a variety of tool-focused frameworks that have been developed over the past three decades. But there are limitations to such an approach. In her analysis of policy solutions and policy instruments, Deborah Stone notes that some of these labels are misleading because they make policies seem too mechanistic (2002). She advocates viewing them instead as "ongoing strategies for structuring relationships and coordinating behavior to achieve collective purposes" (262). The image of policy mechanisms (instruments, tools) implies the presence of resources and strategies that can be applied, changed, manipulated, or managed with the intention of having an impact on the behavior or condition of some target population. What distinguishes accountability mechanisms from other policy instruments is the use of resources and strategies to generate acts of account giving or to create expectations regarding the need for giving accounts.

So what is an accountability mechanism, and how does it differ from other policy instruments? Rather than rely on a definition derived from the characteristics of policy tools conventionally associated with accountability (e.g., Ebrahim 2003a), we posit one that builds on the basic assumptions underlying the existence of a particular social act: account giving.

The act of account giving is a "speech act" typically associated with social rituals such as excuse making, face-saving, or acts of rationalization or justification. Involved in each of these is the capacity of one party in any social relationship to offer an account of their actions to other parties (cf. Mulgan 2003, Bovens 2007, and Schillemans and Bovens, this volume). That assumed capacity for account giving provides the foundation for both *acts* of account giving and the establishment of *expectations for* account giving. What makes the account-giving act attractive as a basis for designing policy instruments is its reliance on the human ability and inclination to account for one's actions (or inactions). Although rarely made explicit in policy debates surrounding accountability-based reforms, accountability mechanisms are designed to take advantage of that implicit social inclination.

Another way to view account giving is as an alternative to the exercise of power in social relationships. In lieu of the direct use of force (or threats of coercive action), the manipulation of incentives (or promises of rewards or sanctions), or even the application of persuasion (reasoned or otherwise), account giving is assumed to bring about appropriate behavior through internal reflections on what one is expected to do.

The role of account-giving capacities and acts has been approached differently by a range of scholars. For Harold Garfinkel and other ethnomethodologists, reflective accountability is a fundamental aspect of social interactions of everyday life (Garfinkel 1967, 1988). For others it is central to the structured relationships created through communicative action (e.g., Habermas 1984a, 1984b) or structuration (e.g., Giddens 1984; Yang in this volume). Institutionalists see account-giving relationships manifested in the culture of rules that emerge over time as markets, hierarchies, and other forms of governance (Ostrom 1990, 2005; Williamson 1998, 2002, 2005). Most relevant for our present purposes, account-giving capacities can be regarded as mechanisms individuals mobilize to bring about desired conditions (e.g., Benoit 1995; Lerner and Tetlock 1999).

Surprisingly, studies focused on the mechanisms of governance have rarely paid account-giving relationships the attention they deserve, given the important role that accountability plays in policy debates and design. For example, in their comprehensive examination of governance mechanisms underlying the globalization of regulatory policies, Braithwaite and Drahos (2000) focus on what they call the "lower-order mechanisms" that reflect "concrete specifications" of higher-order (abstract) forms suggested in the work of Jon Ester and others (Ester 1989; Hedström and Swedberg 1998; Schelling 1998). At the abstract level are mechanisms such as reinforcement, rational choice, coercion; at the concrete level are economic reward systems, reciprocal agreements, military or economic coercion, and so forth. Applying an inductive approach, Braithwaite and Drahos determine that seven governing mechanisms stand out: military coercion, economic coercion, systems of reward, modeling, reciprocal adjustment, nonreciprocal coordination, and capacity building. And although the term accountability is applied throughout their analysis of governance, they give no explicit recognition to the important role played by the mechanisms of accountability and account-giving relationships.

Following the approach of Braithwaite and Drahos, a higher-order view of accountability would regard it as *a set of governance mechanisms that encompasses the propensity of individuals to act in accordance with what they perceive to be the legitimate expectations of others (or the expectations of others whose claims are regarded as legitimate).* This perspective begs for explication on three key points: who are the relevant others; what renders their expectations legitimate; and how are those expectations perceived? Each of those points has been the subject of examination by philosophers, psychologists, sociologists, economists, and game theorists, and when drawn together in an integrative framework, that literature might constitute the foundation for a potentially viable theory of accountability. For present purposes, however, we can use this view of accountability as a working premise to assist in our framing of the contributions to this volume.

Figure I.1 **The Promises of Accountability**

		Accountability mechanism valued:	
		A. Instrumentally	B. Intrinsically
Focus on:	1. Inputs	A1: Control Use of account-giving mechanisms to directly determine acquisition, use, and disposition of material and human resources	B1: Integrity Account-giving mechanisms applied to create culture of competence and trust in those who control material and human resources.
	2. Processes	A2: Appropriate Behavior Account-giving mechanisms applied to promote and ensure actions that meet standards of operations within organized effort.	B2: Democratic Legitimacy Establishment and sustainability of procedures associated with "democraticness."
	3. Outputs	A3: Performance Account-giving mechanisms designed to improve performance by focus on outputs and outcomes.	B3: Justice/Fairness Use of account-giving mechanisms that are symbolically and culturally associated with just and equitable treatment.

Moving to the lower level of concrete mechanisms, accountability manifests itself in policy and program designs as account-giving relationships that take a number of forms under the category of "speech acts." Underlying those designs and related "contrivances" (Braithwaite and Drahos 2000, 15–17) is the idea that governance can be enhanced by facilitating or requiring account-giving behavior—that is, by creating, instilling, fostering, nurturing, sustaining, and otherwise promoting behavior driven by the expectations of relevant and significant others.

THE PROMISES OF ACCOUNTABILITY

We attempt to capture this last view of accountability mechanisms in a framework (see Figure I.1) that stresses the promises of accountability—that is, those beliefs held by policy makers that these particular account-giving mechanisms can serve to enhance certain objectives they seek from the governance process, whatever its context (public, private, and nonprofit). These promises of accountability help determine the design of organizations and strategies for implementing policies and programs, and they energize reorganization and reform efforts within and across all sectors.

In offering this framework, we make no claims for its potential as either paradigm or theory. Rather, we view it as an analytical tool reflecting the range of meanings that policy actors—especially those deliberating on the design and assessment of governance—apply in their approach to accountability mechanisms. One strength of this framework is that it encompasses two of the major themes that emerged from the Kettering sessions.

On the one hand, the framework highlights the multiple accountabilities theme by differentiating among factors that provide the focal points of accountability mechanisms. What attracts policy makers to accountability is the belief that account-giving mechanisms can fulfill some promise. But the nature of the promise which emerges as the focus of policy activity is an open, empirical question. To help simplify the options, we adopt a simple systems model that highlights the general input, processing, and output functions of any organized activity. For analytical purposes, the logic behind this approach is simple as well: Accountability mechanisms are typically characterized by how they render an actor or agent responsible to some other actor or agent for what takes place at various stages of the input-process-output sequence. Thus, accountability mechanisms are designed to address real or potential issues related to the acquisition, maintenance, and disposition of resources (inputs) used in the organized effort, as well as to ensure that appropriate actions (processes) are being applied and intended outputs or outcomes are achieved. At their most basic level, these inputs, processes, and outputs are the raison d'etre for accountability mechanisms in the eyes of those who deliberate and apply them in various contexts.

On the other hand, the framework addresses the idea raised by Bovens at the symposium that accountability mechanisms are valued for different reasons. In some contexts, these mechanisms are valued for what they can accomplish directly. That is, they are perceived as instruments or tools and are valued as such. In other contexts these mechanisms have assumed an intrinsic value within a political or administrative culture, which fosters a preference for their use because they are perceived as legitimate and defining characteristics of the promised condition.

The cells generated by crossing a function with a mechanism reflect the various promises of accountability that can help us frame the articles in this collection. For example, organized endeavors—whether public programs, corporate operations, or nonprofit activities—require the effective (and perhaps efficient) use of scarce resources, and a common problem is how to structure, manage, and monitor the problematic situation that results (Ouchi 1977, 1979). In this framework the promise of control (cell A1) draws upon some of the most basic mechanisms associated with accountability—textbook approaches, ranging from the design of hierarchical and lateral reporting structures to the establishment of production metrics, record-keeping procedures, auditing standards and procedures, oversight and supervision protocols, communications networks, and so forth.

The relationship between accountability and control is conceptually and empirically complex. The assumption about human nature underlying the promise of control is that individual agents, once situated organizationally (e.g., within a bureaucratic hierarchy) or legally (e.g., through legal mandate or contractual obligation), ought to behave according to the role requirements of that situation. It is the promise of control that provides the normative foundation for principal-agent relationships (Ross 1973; Eisenhardt 1989; Broadbent et al. 1996), and the inherent flaws in that position have provided the material for a substantial body of scholarly work (Banfield 1975; Petersen 1993; Brehm and Gates 1997; Besley 2006).

Empirically, accountability mechanisms are perceived in three ways. At times they are regarded as alternatives to approaches that rely on direct control. Thus, the use of incentives based on account giving (e.g., making agents answerable only for poor performance; see the work of Tetlock and colleagues) or the design of what behavioral economists call "choice architectures" (see Thaler and Sunstein 2008) are increasingly perceived as means to impose control through accountability while avoiding the application of direct control. In other situations, accountability mechanisms are perceived as necessary complements to direct control, either with mechanisms requiring some form of oversight based on account giving (e.g., reporting), or as account-giving relationships backed up by the threat of imposing additional controls. A third approach takes a broader view of control, seeing accountability mechanisms not as alternatives or complements, but as one among a number of means applied with the intent of controlling behavior and choices. This approach reflects the classic view of Chester Barnard (1968) that the exercise of authoritative control calls for the creation of a "zone of indifference."

The input stage is also the point at which policy makers believe account-giving mechanisms may be called upon to facilitate and foster responsible, trustworthy, and virtuous behavior—that is, to achieve the promise of integrity (B1; Dobel 1990, 1999; Zauderer 1992). In the public sector, stories of moral exemplars and unsung heroes among public-service professionals are complemented by laws, rules, and norms that serve to protect the integrity of their actions (Riccucci 1995; Rugeley and Van Wart 2006; cf. O'Leary 2006). Ethics codes, civil-service and whistleblower protections, and human-resources practices and policies fostering professional commitment are designed, in part, to support the promise of integrity in public agencies. In the private sector, market rules and legal regulations (e.g., the Sarbanes-Oxley Act) related to the behavior of high-level corporate executives and directors are intended to prevent and punish both malfeasance and misfeasance (Dubnick 2007). Mounting pressures to enforce corporate responsibility, emanating from both within and outside the firm, also promote accountability (Vogel 2005). Donor demands for transparency as well as government regulations work to the same effect for third-sector (nonprofit) organizations (Brown and Moore 2001; Jordan and Tuijl 2006).

At first view, the promise of appropriate (ethical) behavior (A2) seems to be the same as the promise of integrity (B1). After all, those who act with integrity are likely to be ethical by definition. There is, however, an important difference between behavior based on "doing the right thing," which is valued for its own sake and which we often call *integrity,* and behavior that is based on "doing the correct thing," which is defined by one's job or role in an organization (Phillips and Margolis 1999; Weaver et al. 1999; Barker 2002). Regarding the latter, how does one ensure that those engaged in such an effort act (or decide) correctly or appropriately in an instrumental sense? This question was central to Barnard's *The Function of the Executive* (1968) and was at the core of Herbert Simon's conception of organization and decision making throughout his career (Simon 1957, 1987). As a means for dealing with this set of problems arising from "doing the correct thing," accountability has taken a variety of forms—from the articulation and sanctioning of standard operating procedures to the fostering of norms stressing rule following, loyalty, and other forms of organizational citizenship behaviors (Podsakoff et al. 2000). In the public sector, these account-giving mechanisms are linked to "red tape" (Thompson 1975; Benveniste 1977; Kaufman 1977; Bozeman 1993; Niland and Satkunandan 1999; Bozeman 2000), and can be associated with ethical behavior by highlighting the need for individuals to actively uphold "regime values" (Rohr 1989) or demonstrate "constitutional competence" in their actions (Rosenbloom 1983, 1987; Rosenbloom et al. 2000).

The promise of democratic legitimacy (B2) is related to the view that accountability is a core, if not defining, characteristic of regimes that meet contemporary standards for good governance (e.g., Purchase and Hirshhorn 1994; Organisation for Economic Co-operation Development, Public Management Committee 2000; Weiss 2000). Most often these standards will be perceived as open, democratic, and representative governance. Just as divine designation or inspiration once determined the legitimacy of any governing arrangement, today "democraticness" is a prerequisite to any claim to govern in the public sphere (Buchanan 2002; Held 2004, 2006; O'Donnell 2004; see also Matheson 1987), and quite often in the private and third sectors as well. Given the range of accountability mechanisms associated with democraticness—from representation to election to transparency to participation—their application is regarded as intrinsically warranted. The value placed on democratic legitimacy underlies the transparency agenda pursued by government reformers at every level of governance, from local to global (Hood and Heald 2006; Florini 2007; Fung et al. 2007), and it is also central to the "democratic-deficit" critique that has generated national and global calls for more accountability (Durant 1995; Cerny 1999) and effectively put the brakes on efforts to expand the authority and jurisdiction of the European Union (Dahl 1994; Majone 1998; Schmidt 2004).

Of the six types of mechanisms highlighted here, perhaps the promise of performance (A3) has had the greatest impact on the reform of public sector agencies in recent years, although it has been perceived as a common dimension of corporate accountability for decades. Based on the assumption that accountability is instrumentally linked to improved performance (Dubnick 2005), this promise has had global impact and has launched thousands of projects and programs designed to secure the anticipated benefits. The promise of performance has, for a long time, been applied in the private sector as much as for control purposes as for enhancing productivity. The approach has been advocated for third-sector organizations (Kaplan 2001) and embraced by the public sector worldwide with an ideological fervor rarely seen. Assessments of these efforts are starting to emerge (e.g., Propper and Wilson 2003; Frederickson and Frederickson 2006; Radin 2006), but for the moment this mechanism has the power of a movement that seems unstoppable.

The idea that the very act of "bringing to justice" is a form of justice itself is increasingly central to viewing accountability as the promise of justice (B3). This promise has deep roots in beliefs about the basic value of retribution and restitution in the law (Hart 1968; Foucault 1977; Hibbert 2003), but these beliefs regard accountability as a means to the traditional ends of criminal or civil law. In those legal regimes that have established a high degree of legitimacy—that is, where most of the population assumes that the justice system is capable and likely to handle cases in a fair and just manner (Tyler and Huo 2002)—the value of bringing someone to justice (to be held "accountable" in the juridical sense) becomes highly valued for its own sake.

Since at least the middle to late 1980s, the role of accountability as the promise of justice has become a core issue in several of the most prominent cases involving "transitional justice," as regimes the world over became more democratic and sought to deal with past abuses of authority and human rights violations (Minow 1998; Bass 2000). The stark choices typically ranged from collective acquiescence (e.g., Portugal, post-Pinochet Chile) to harsh legal justice meted out by the victors (e.g., post-invasion Iraq, following what is known as the "Nuremberg Paradigm"; Park 2001).

But in several jurisdictions both political realities and moral leadership resulted in the application of alternative approaches, from truth commissions that focused on establishing a record of what took place under the prior regime, to various forms of reconciliation mechanisms that stopped short of juridical sanctions (e.g., the Garaca process in Rwanda), to combination approaches, such as the South African Truth and Reconciliation Commission that offered amnesty in return for confessions of involvement. While few of these processes generated outcomes that proved satisfactory to victims and others seeking more severe punishments for violations of human rights and dignity, in most instances they did satisfy accountability's promise of justice in the sense described here (Sarkin 2000; Roche 2003; Syring 2006).

Whether accountability in this (or any sense) actually delivers real justice is perhaps an unanswerable empirical question. The point here is that the cathartic value of the notion of accountability has significance and a utility tied to the concept's promising nature. This is the case locally as well as globally, for all firms and agencies (public and private) have developed a variety of mechanisms to foster the sense that misbehavior or malfeasance can be brought to account. The very existence of such mechanisms is often perceived as a measure of accountability, even in the absence of evidence that complaints and concerns are actually addressed.

THE CONTRIBUTIONS

As noted earlier, a salient theme among many of the symposium presentations was the existence of multiple accountabilities. Often articulated as an operational or management problem from the perspective of the accountable agent or agency (see Schillemans and Bovens, this volume), the multiple model can also be characterized as an inherent and unavoidable characteristic of the modern democratic administrative state—that is, another manifestation of a political system where public agencies often find themselves subject to the pressures of many and varied interests. The dilemmas and tensions generated by the strong demand for accountability mechanisms and the costs they impose are magnified and multiplied in the increasingly complex environment of today's governing arrangements. To call these situations "challenging" might be an understatement.

Just how challenging is, of course, both an analytical and empirical question. The contributions to the first section of this volume share a common focus on the nature of the accountability challenge in different contexts. Thomas Schillemans and Mark Bovens put to the test the view that creating multiple accountabilities has negative impacts on agency operations. Their context is a relatively common form of accountability in parliamentary systems—ministerial responsibility. The traditional logic is well known: government agencies are accountable to a cabinet minister who is ultimately responsible to parliament. The new public-management forms of the past several decades have, of course, altered that logic by pushing responsibility and accountability downward. Underlying the strong case for such reforms is the promise of improved performance, but long-standing traditions die hard. The general frame of ministerial responsibility remains a powerful standard that has considerable influence on the design of accountability mechanisms.

Schillemans and Bovens examine five Dutch agencies that went through a particular type of reform that applied a governing-board model derived from large private corporations, while empowering agency managers and maintaining general ministry responsibility. The resulting hybrid would seem to be a nurturing environment for a variety of the dysfunctional consequences feared by critics of multiple accountabilities, but what the authors found instead was a relatively positive adaptation by relevant agency actors. In assessing their findings, Schillemans and Bovens focus on the benefits of the redundancy created by this particular reform approach, but they also note the more general lesson: multiple accountabilities may in fact be suitable and appropriate for an increasingly pluralistic approach to governance.

Barbara S. Romzek's chapter deals with multiple accountabilities in a substantially different context. The accountability mechanisms designed to fit hierarchical governing arrangements would be inappropriate for the interorganizational networks that characterize social services in the United States and elsewhere, especially where outsourcing and other forms of contracting have become the modus operandi of governments (Smith 1975; Hood 1997; Bezdek 2001). As key service-delivery mechanisms in the new public administration (Hood 1991) and reinventing government (Osborne and Gaebler 1992; Osborne 1993) movements, contracting and related forms of outsourcing have emerged as arrangements with significant accountability problems—an ironic development considering that the legal (common law) and conceptual (Hobbesian) roots of contracts are found in their use as accountability mechanisms. Placed in a network milieu where various accountability mechanisms seem like promising responses to a range of issues, from coordination and control to performance and program integrity, what emerges is what Romzek terms a "tangled web" of relationships. Romzek offers us some perspective on how that tangled web operates within the child welfare and social services arena, and she takes a critical view of the "accountability craze" that seems to make matters worse rather than better. Unless we are able to engage in some serious untangling, the problem will remain intractable.

There is a note of optimism implied in that last statement, for the tangled web can be regarded as something we have created through our institutional and policy choices—and it follows that (at least theoretically) we can achieve the promises of accountability by undertaking some radical disentangling. Here is where a belief in the promises of accountability has its greatest influence, for the presumption that account-giving mechanisms can prove effective in achieving greater control, performance, and so forth, carries considerable weight in our political culture and fuels that accountability craze. It is the same logic observed by Herbert Kaufman in his classic exploration of another tangled web—government "red tape." In attempting to make sense of red tape, Kaufman applied what he termed the "Pogo theory": "We have met the enemy and he is us" (Kaufman 1977).

But the problems associated with multiple accountabilities would not disappear if we were to set aside any irrational exuberance for accountability associated with current reform movements. Well before the political obsession with accountability took hold in the 1980s, account-giving mechanisms were an essential part of the continuous effort by public sector managers to improve the operations of our administrative state. This was particularly true in the area of defense procurement during the Cold War, which was so significant by 1960 that it warranted a somber warning about the "military-industrial complex" in President Eisenhower's farewell address. The nation's annual expenditures on defense had become a matter of concern within government by 1953, and in response efforts were made to establish a strategic systems approach to bring some order to this expansive arena. Contract-based accountability mechanisms played a major role in the systems approach, with contracts often regarded as the vehicle through which the promises of cost control, performance improvement, integrity, and even equity could be achieved (Miller 1955; Williamson 1967; Hiller and Tollison 1978; Karpoff et al. 1999).

As the analysis of Trevor L. Brown, Matthew Potoski, and David M. Van Slyke indicate, there are major limitations to the use of contracts to achieve even more narrowly defined accountability objectives when dealing with complex products in an uncertain environment. The authors apply the logic of game theory to the case of the U.S. Coast Guard's Project Deepwater—a major multiyear, multibillion-dollar procurement program designed to upgrade and modernize the service's systems. The sophisticated equipment and systems procured through that program are central to their analysis, as are the various uncertainties that surround the task environment over time. The challenges to accountability become even more evident when the relationships among the various parties to the contract are viewed through a "prisoners' dilemma" lens. Time, cost factors, and political pressures have added to the difficulties and created a situation where program managers have become inclined to a more perfunctory approach to applying accountability mechanisms.

The pressure to compromise on the application of accountability when faced with dilemmas created by multiple and diverse expectations is central to Jonathan Koppell's approach to the work of global governance organizations (GGOs). Here we have rather distinct actors on the international stage, each empowered by the support of their creators/members, but operating in a global arena where both the organization's legitimacy and authority are without the firm foundations that protect it from potential challenge. While the development and adoption of specific accountability mechanisms may hold the promise of promoting both legitimacy and authority, the nature of particular mechanisms makes the choice between alternate accountability paths quite tricky. Koppell maps the choice as a "Morton's Fork" dilemma in which GGOs must contend with two "unappealing" options, and he regards a third path (i.e., attempting to use both) as a recipe for "multiple accountability disorder."

The next three contributions deal with major contextual factors that prove to be formidable obstacles to the adoption and implementation of reforms aimed at enhancing accountability. Establishing political accountability as his principle measure, Christopher Pollitt critically examines the contested proposition that performance measurement mechanisms will improve agency accountability to citizens and their elected representatives. While accountability's promise of performance can be rationalized on a number of grounds (cf. Fried 1976; Wholey 1983, 1999; Miller 1984; Holzer and Yang 2004; Dubnick 2005; Yang and Holzer 2006), this particular benefit is a salient theme in the rhetoric of administrative reform. Using two case studies—the United Kingdom's National Health Service and the World Bank's World Governance Indicators—Pollitt concludes that whatever other positive benefits (e.g., managerial and technical) have emerged from the use of performance measurement, enhanced political accountability has not stood out as a result. Until and unless the measured performance of agencies becomes a serious concern among the citizenry and their representatives, this will remain an unfulfilled promise.

Beryl A. Radin is also concerned with how performance measurement reforms live up to their rhetorical promises of improving accountability. Her focus is on the two major efforts to apply performance measurement in U.S. federal agencies: the Government Performance and Results Act (GPRA) and the Program Assessment Rating Tool (PART). Given the complex nature of the U.S. political and administrative systems, one would assume that a well-designed performance measurement system would reflect the multiple and diverse expectations generated by that institutional milieu. Positing the accountability frame first presented by Romzek and Dubnick (1987; also Dubnick and Romzek 1991, 1993), Radin argues that both GPRA and (especially) PART failed to address the complexity of the American political system and took on narrowly bureaucratic forms. If the promises of accountability are going to be achieved, the mechanisms we apply must deal with the institutional realities within which they are expected to operate.

Accepting the argument that accountability reforms need to be adapted to the complex political environments in which they are expected to operate effectively, we are naturally led to ask about the impact that different "accountability environments" (Kearns 1996) might have on efforts to achieve the promises of accountability. We get some insight into that question in the study of U.S. county governments offered by Bonnie J. Johnson, John C. Pierce, and Nicholas P. Lovrich, Jr. Taking into consideration both institutional and cultural factors, they conclude that there are indeed significant variations in how political accountability (defined primarily as access to governmental policy-making activities) manifests itself in different contexts. This finding implies that efforts to meet the promises of accountability are likely to require considerable attention to contextual factors by those engaged in the design and implementation of reforms based on account-giving mechanisms.

However well designed, accountability mechanisms must themselves eventually be held to account for their impacts. Most of the papers delivered at the Kettering sessions can be regarded as evaluative in some sense, but two focus explicitly on questions related to the impacts of these mechanisms on the governing environment in which they are put to use. Paul L. Posner and Robert Schwartz, for example, consider the roles that three major account-giving mechanisms (performance measurement, performance auditing, and program evaluation) play in the policy-making process. Applying Kingdon's "policy streams" approach (1984; see also Mucciaroni 1992), the authors' assessment highlights the fact that accountability mechanisms should be evaluated not merely for their contribution to the development of more open and transparent policy processes (the policy stream), but also for their roles in defining and delineating the problems and solutions of the policy-making process. The authors' examination of the literature associated with the three mechanisms indicates that researchers need to devote greater attention to how each mechanism affects the different streams.

For Richard K. Ghere, the issue is whether a particular set of reforms often touted as enhancing accountability really lives up to those promises—and, if so, how. He focuses on the claims made about the value of adopting e-government and related information-technology (IT) systems and puts them to the test through a secondary analysis of case studies from thirteen countries drawn from twenty-nine articles. Informed by Jane Fountain's enactment theory of digital government (Fountain 2001), Ghere finds that the potential for digital government reforms to work as account-giving mechanisms depends on organizational norms and other contextual factors. The implications of this finding are important well beyond the specific arena of IT reform, for it points to the need for reformers and managers to appreciate that the promise of any accountability mechanism depends on its social enactment in different contexts.

The next three chapters reinforce that point in various ways. Christopher Hood's exploration of the different ways blame-avoidance strategies can be used to deal with the pressures for account giving is a fascinating approach to understanding the logic and implications of the enactment process. Of special note is Hood's point that efforts to deal with the pressures of accountability (in this case, through blame avoidance) do not necessarily generate only negative outcomes.

The enactment thesis is also relevant in the case of PROSHIKA, an NGO designed to serve the needs of the poorer communities in Bangladesh. Margaret P. Karns, Timothy J. Shaffer, and Richard K. Ghere apply the managed expectation frame and the distinctive conditions faced by NGOs operating in the developing world, and the story that emerges is how PROSHIKA adapted to the political and social realities of Bangladesh as well as to the pressures of donors and programmatic (e.g., microcredit) expectations. The conclusion reached by the authors—that efforts to deal with the pressures of accountability in the distinctive political and cultural milieu of Bangladesh—have transformed the organization strategically and operationally and are not surprising in light of what we have learned about the promises of accountability and their enactment.

The lessons learned from the experience of NGOs like PROSHIKA and other nonprofits are reflected in Kevin P. Kearns's effort to counter the one-size-fits-all approach to accountability with a more nuanced view that considers the life-cycle stage of an agency as a factor in strategic approaches to addressing the core issues NGOs face over time: accountability "for what," "to whom," and "how" (which mechanisms). Years of studying and advising nonprofits inform Kearns's model, and his insights complement and reinforce the themes of several symposium presentations.

While public sector and nongovernmental organizations have turned increasingly to strategic views of accountability, the private sector has been preoccupied with the strategic implications of accountability in matters of corporate governance and corporate social responsibility for decades. A foundational premise of the modern public company is that the corporation's managers ought to serve the interests of (and thus be accountable to) the shareholders, and the key mechanism to do so has been the company's board of directors. But the weakness of that mechanism over the years has led to various reforms designed to ensure greater accountability. Among these have been requirements for the appointment and empowerment of outside directors who are supposed to act as an external check on management. Sally Wheeler considers the logical and empirical flaws of this approach as it has been applied under company law in the United Kingdom. If anything results from further pursuit of this strategy, it is likely to be a "thickening" of the network ties that render the idea of outside directors more myth than reality.

Another strategic approach to corporate accountability is the establishment of voluntary programs within and among corporate and industrial sectors. Matthew Potoski and Aseem Prakash perceive these agreements/arrangements as accountability mechanisms that "complement" regulatory regimes, and their specific focus is on global programs such as the International Organization for Standardization's (ISO) 14001 environmental program. The promise of programs such as ISO 14001 is found in the incentives they offer complying entities for providing information to "mitigate information asymmetries" and thereby enhance the capacity of citizens, stakeholders, consumers, and governments to hold firms to account. The authors find ISO 14001 to be an effective mechanism, but their analysis also highlights factors that have rendered similar programs less successful as accountability mechanisms.

The final four contributions to this volume are distinct from the rest in that they address what it means to be accountable. While the number of accountability studies has increased over the past quarter century, the core concept remains an elusive one for both researchers and practitioners (Dubnick 2002). Some studies deal with this problem by avoiding the issue entirely and adopting a particular perspective; for example, the work of Tetlock and colleagues views accountability as answerability (Tetlock 1985; Tetlock and Boettger 1989; Lerner and Tetlock 1999). Others acknowledge the conceptual issue but resolve it through descriptive typologies or, ultimately, by acceptance of one type or version of accountability that can provide the operationalized focus of their study (e.g., studies of "electoral" accountability; see Fearon 1999; Hellwig and Samuels 2004; Stokes 2005; Samuels 2008). Both approaches are conducive to (and commonplace in) the study of accountability mechanisms. Nevertheless, the conceptual problem has to be confronted if we are to make progress in our efforts to make sense of accountability and its role in governance.

Sara R. Jordan takes on the challenge by exploring what being accountable means in different historical and cultural contexts (2006), and in the present volume she contrasts notions of accountability in the mainstream Western liberal tradition with those derived from two non-Western traditions. Her analysis shows the deep ontological and epistemological foundations that shape social and political understandings of what it means to be accountable in the "ritual" (East Asian) and "affective" (African) sense, and in the process shows us that accountability is truly a "situated" construct.

While Jordan finds insights about what it means to be accountable in cross-cultural comparison, Ciarán O'Kelly turns to some of the basic themes of political theory and philosophy. Focusing on the work of Hobbes, Burke, and Darwall, he finds accountability embedded in theories of representation that rely on a "thicker" conception of agency than is traditionally applied in the principal-agent model in the study of accountability. Under the mainstream model (see Besley 2006, especially Chapter 3), being accountable means being engaged in a continuous game in which you, the agent, are subject to the demands and interests of some principal. Under O'Kelly's representation frame, however, the settings for being accountable are moral communities and institutionalized relationships rather than games. He views these settings as "conduits of representation" where members of the moral community are involved in an ongoing political contest over how the community is to be represented. An accountable agent is one who assumes the role of representative in that political struggle, with the nature of the role being determined by the characteristics of the office occupied. From this perspective, accountability mechanisms are established as means for ensuring that accountable agents sustain their roles as representatives. The logic and rationale for much of British Company Law, O'Kelly contends, makes greater sense when viewed from this perspective.

Complementing O'Kelly's effort to reconnect accountability to its roots in political theory and philosophy is Kaifeng Yang's call for more attention to the work of Anthony Giddens and (by implication) other social theorists who also address the role of accountability in modern social relationships. Yang is much more direct in his critical assessment of the unsophisticated treatment of agency that characterizes contemporary studies of accountability, and he sees considerable potential in adopting Giddens's framing of social life to enhance our understanding of how accountability operates in contexts of governance. His article addresses a problem that Ebrahim has termed "accountability myopia" (2005), which afflicts both researchers and practitioners who take too narrow a view of what constitutes accountable relationships. It is perhaps time to rethink our own treatment of accountability by exploring the works of Giddens (1984), Habermas (1993, 1996), Boudieu (1977, 1990), and others.

In the final selection, Melvin J. Dubnick and Justin P. O'Brien take still another approach to understanding what it means to be accountable by focusing on the role accountability has played in the various discourses on the financial crisis that emerged in 2007. What the authors find is a gap between the rhetoric of accountability reform (which stresses the need for more responsible behavior among actors in the financial markets) and the proposals for reform that rely on traditional mechanisms of account giving. From this case study they derive a framework for policy options that reflects the range of meanings of what policy makers proposed to do when faced with the demand for reforms that would "enhance accountability."

THE STATE OF ACCOUNTABILITY RESEARCH

At the very end of this volume we briefly discuss some of the insights and lessons derived from these articles, but at this point we address what this collection implies about the state of accountability research.

First, although issues related to accountability are hardly new (e.g., the Freidrich-Finer debate of the early 1940s), over the past two decades we have witnessed the growth of a body of work specifically devoted to the topic. While not yet constituted as a field of study, such a development seems likely when one considers that some key ingredients are in place. Past studies of accountability have focused on individual behavior and social relationships (e.g., excuse making) or on the functions of specific institutions (e.g., elections or checks and balances), but more recent work has approached the subject within the more generic frame of governance. Related to this is the acceptance of accountability as a phenomenon that is trans-sectoral—that is, as relevant in the governance of corporations and NGOs as in organizations in the public sector. Similarly, analyses of accountable governance transcend national borders and can be applied to regimes of all shapes, sizes, and ideological dispositions. Perhaps most significantly, the literature on accountability is emerging as diverse, cross-disciplinary, and increasingly self-referential—all indications that accountability studies might be emerging from an embryonic stage and on the path to becoming a field.

Second, whether we are witnessing the creation of a distinct field devoted to accountability-relevant studies, we seem to have entered a period of intellectual ferment where critical issues related to the study of accountability are no longer being set aside or taken for granted. While we have yet to reach a paradigmatic consensus on the core concept itself, greater care is now given to defining and elaborating on the various types of accountability addressed in specific studies. We are also less likely to accept at face value the various assumptions and claims or promises of reformers and other policy makers about the utility and value of accountability mechanisms. Such claims are increasingly perceived as empirical questions that must be tested. We also seem more willing to challenge, qualify, and/or supplement our long-standing reliance on principal-agent models as surrogates for relevant theories on accountability.

Third, despite the wide range of issues and topics addressed by students of accountability, some important aspects of the topic remain insufficiently examined and beg for more attention. For example, applying the framework used earlier in the chapter, many of the assumptions underlying the promises of accountability remain unexplored, as do the symbolic and rhetorical uses of accountability. The role of accountability in governance systems has been approached in various ways (Considine and Lewis 1999; Considine 2000, 2002; Wallach 2002), but there is still a need for a more systematic perspective that builds on current discussions of how account-giving mechanisms relate to regulatory and welfare regimes. Given the prominent place of accountability mechanisms in most proposals for reform of governance, there is also need for greater attention to policy design issues. In the public sector, this calls for greater attention to what Michael Barzelay terms "public-management policy" (2001), while in the nonprofit sector the work of Kevin Kearns (1996, 2000;

and this volume), Alnoor Ebrahim (2003a, 2003b, 2005, 2006), and others has already made accountability policies a key factor in strategic management. In the private sector, the recent crisis in domestic and global financial markets has highlighted the vulnerability of regulatory regimes and drawn attention to the need to redesign and reinvigorate the core accountability systems upon which they depend. For now, however, one key lesson can drawn from the Kettering sessions: It is an exciting time to be a student of accountability and accountable governance.

REFERENCES

Banfield, Edward C. 1975. "Corruption as a Feature of Governmental Organization." *Journal of Law and Economics* 18 (3): 587–605.

Barker, Richard A. 2002. "An Examination of Organizational Ethics." *Human Relations* 55 (9): 1097–16.

Barnard, Chester I. 1968. *The Functions of the Executive.* Cambridge, MA: Harvard University Press.

Barzelay, Michael. 2001. *The New Public Management: Improving Research And Policy Dialogue.* Berkeley: University of California Press/Russell Sage Foundation.

Bass, Gary Jonathan. 2000. *Stay the Hand of Vengeance: The Politics of War Crimes Tribunals.* Princeton: Princeton University Press.

Benoit, William L. 1995. *Accounts, Excuses, and Apologies: A Theory of Image Restoration Strategies.* Albany: State University of New York Press.

Benveniste, Guy. 1977. *Bureaucracy.* San Francisco: Boyd and Fraser Publishing.

Berle, Adolf Augustus, and Gardiner Coit Means. 1932. *The Modern Corporation and Private Property.* New Brunswick, NJ: Transaction Publishers.

Bertelli, Anthony M., and Laurence E. Lynn. 2003. "Managerial Responsibility." *Public Administration Review* 63 (3): 259–68.

Besley, Timothy. 2006. *Principled Agents? The Political Economy of Good Government.* Oxford: Oxford University Press.

Bezdek, Barbara L. 2001. "Contractual Welfare: Non-Accountability and Diminished Democracy in Local Government Contracts for Welfare-to-Work Services." *Fordham Urban Law Journal* 28: 1559–1610.

Bourdieu, Pierre. 1977. *Outline of a Theory of Practice.* Cambridge, UK: Cambridge University Press.

———. 1990. *The Logic of Practice.* Stanford: Stanford University Press.

Bovens, Mark. 2007. "Analysing and Assessing Accountability: A Conceptual Framework." *European Law Journal* 13 (4): 447–68.

———. 2008. *Two Concepts of Accountability.* The Netherlands: Utrecht School of Governance.

Bozeman, Barry. 1993. "A Theory of Government 'Red Tape.'" *Journal of Public Administration Research and Theory* 3 (3): 273–303.

———. 2000. *Bureaucracy and Red Tape.* Upper Saddle River, NJ: Prentice Hall.

Braithwaite, John, and Peter Drahos. 2000. *Global Business Regulation.* New York: Cambridge University Press.

Brehm, John, and Scott Gates. 1997. *Working, Shirking, and Sabotage: Bureaucratic Response to a Democratic Public.* Ann Arbor: University of Michigan Press.

Broadbent, Jane, Michael Dietrich, and Richard Laughlin. 1996. "The Development of Principal-Agent, Contracting and Accountability Relationships in the Public Sector: Conceptual and Cultural Problems." *Critical Perspectives on Accounting* 7 (3): 259–84.

Brown, L. David, and Mark H. Moore. 2001. "Accountability, Strategy, and International Nongovernmental Organizations." *Nonprofit Management and Leadership* 30 (3): 569–87.

Buchanan, Allen. 2002. "Political Legitimacy and Democracy." *Ethics* 112 (4): 689–719.

Castells, Manuel, and Gustavo Cardoso, eds. 2005. *The Network Society: From Knowledge to Policy.* Washington, DC: Johns Hopkins Center for Transatlantic Relations.

Cerny, Philip G. 1999. "Globalization and the Erosion of Democracy." *European Journal of Political Research* 36 (1): 1–26.

Clark, Kathleen. 1996. "Do We Have Enough Ethics in Government Yet: An Answer from Fiduciary Theory." *University of Illinois Law Review* 1996 (1): 57–102.

Considine, Mark. 2000. "Contract Regimes and Reflexive Governance: Comparing Employment Service Reforms in the United Kingdom, the Netherlands, New Zealand and Australia." *Public Administration* 78 (3): 613–38.

———. 2002. "The End of the Line? Accountable Governance in the Age of Networks, Partnerships, and Joined-up Services." *Governance* 15 (1): 21–40.

Considine, Mark, and Jenny M. Lewis. 1999. "Governance at Ground Level: The Frontline Bureaucrat in the Age of Markets and Networks." *Public Administration Review* 59 (6): 467–80.

Dahl, Robert A. 1994. "A Democratic Dilemma: System Effectiveness Versus Citizen Participation." *Political Science Quarterly* 109 (1): 23–34.

Day, Patricia, and Rudolf Klein. 1987. *Accountabilities: Five Public Services.* London: Tavistock Publications.

Dobel, J. Patrick. 1990. "Integrity In The Public Service." *Public Administration Review* 50 (3): 354–66.

———. 1999. *Public Integrity.* Baltimore, MD: Johns Hopkins University Press.

Dodd, E. Merrick Jr. 1935. "Is Effective Enforcement of the Fiduciary Duties of Corporate Managers Practicable?" *University of Chicago Law Review* 2 (2): 194–207.

Dubnick, Melvin J. 1998. "Clarifying Accountability: An Ethical Theory Framework." In *Public Sector Ethics: Finding and Implementing Values,* ed. Charles J.G. Sampford, Noel Preston and Carol-Anne Bois. Leichhardt, NSW, Australia: The Federation Press/Routledge.

———. 2002. "Seeking Salvation for Accountability." Paper read at American Political Science Association in Boston, MA, August 29–September 1.

———. 2003. "Accountability and Ethics: Reconsidering the Relationships." In *Encyclopedia of Public Administration and Public Policy,* ed. J. Rabin. New York: Marcel Dekker, 1–14.

———. 2005. "Accountability and the Promise of Performance: In Search of the Mechanisms." *Public Performance & Management Review* 27 (3): 376–417.

———. 2007. "Sarbanes-Oxley and the Search for Accountable Corporate Governance." In *Private Equity, Corporate Governance and the Dynamics of Capital Market Regulation,* ed. J. O'Brien. London: Imperial College Press, 265–93.

Dubnick, Melvin J., and Barbara S. Romzek. 1991. *American Public Administration: Politics and the Management of Expectations.* New York: Macmillan.

———. 1993. "Accountability and the Centrality of Expectations in American Public Administration." In *Research in Public Administration,* ed. J.L. Perry. Greenwich, CT: JAI Press, 37–78.

DuPont-Morales, M. A., and Jean E. Harris. 1994. "Strengthening Accountability: Incorporating Strategic Planning and Performance Measurement into Budgeting." *Public Productivity & Management Review* 17 (3): 231–39.

Durant, Robert F. 1995. "The Democratic Deficit in America." *Political Science Quarterly* 110 (1): 25–47.

Ebrahim, Alnoor. 2003a. "Accountability in Practice: Mechanisms for NGOs." *World Development* 31 (5): 813–29.

———. 2003b. "Making Sense of Accountability: Conceptual Perspectives for Northern and Southern Nonprofits." *Nonprofit Management and Leadership* 14 (2): 191–212.

———. 2005. "Accountability Myopia: Losing Sight of Organizational Learning." *Nonprofit and Voluntary Sector Quarterly* 34 (1): 56–87.

———. 2006. "Placing the Normative Logics of Accountability in 'Thick' Perspective." In *Hauser Center Working Paper Series.* Cambridge, MA: Hauser Center for Nonprofit Organizations, Harvard University.

Eisenhardt, Kathleen M. 1989. "Agency Theory: An Assessment and Review." *Academy of Management Review* 14 (1): 57–74.

Elster, Jon. 1989. *Nuts and Bolts for the Social Sciences.* Cambridge, UK: Cambridge University Press.

Fearon, James D. 1999. "Electoral Accountability and the Control of Politicians: Selecting Good Types Versus Sanctioning Poor Performance." In *Democracy, Accountability, and Representation,* ed. A. Przeworski, S. C. Stokes, and B. Manin. Cambridge, UK: Cambridge University Press, 55–97.

Finer, Herman. 1941. "Administrative Responsibility in Democratic Government." *Public Administration Review* 1 (4): 335–50.

Florini, Ann. 2007. *The Right to Know: Transparency for an Open World.* New York: Columbia University Press.

Foucault, Michel. 1977. *Discipline and Punish: The Birth of the Prison.* New York: Vintage Books.

Fountain, Jane E. 2001. *Building the Virtual State: Information Technology and Institutional Change.* Washington, DC: Brookings Institution Press.

Frederickson, David G., and H. George Frederickson. 2006. *Measuring the Performance of the Hollow State.* Washington, DC: Georgetown University Press.

Fried, Robert C. 1976. *Performance in American Bureaucracy.* Boston, MA: Little Brown.

Friedrich, Carl J. 1940. "Public Policy and the Nature of Administrative Responsibility." In *Public Policy: A Yearbook of the Graduate School of Public Administration, Harvard University,* ed. C.J. Friedrich and E.S. Mason. Cambridge, MA: Harvard University Press, 3–24.

Fung, Archon, Mary Graham, and David Weil. 2007. *Full Disclosure: The Perils and Promise of Transparency.* New York: Cambridge University Press.

Garfinkel, Harold. 1967. *Studies in Ethnomethodology.* Cambridge, UK: Polity Press.

———. 1988. "Evidence for Locally Produced, Naturally Accountable Phenomena of Order, Logic, Reason, Meaning, Method, Etc. In and as of the Essential Quiddity of Immortal Ordinary Society (I of IV): An Announcement of Studies." *Sociological Theory* 6 (1): 103–9.

Giddens, Anthony. 1984. *The Constitution of Society: Outline of the Theory of Structuration.* Berkeley: University of California Press.

Gore, Albert. 1995. "Common Sense Government: Works Better and Costs Less—Third Report of the National Performance Review." Washington, DC: National Performance Review.

———. 1994. "Creating a Government That Works Better and Costs Less: Status Report." Washington, DC: National Performance Review.

Habermas, Jürgen. 1984a. *The Theory of Communicative Action,* Vol. 1: *Reason and the Rationalization of Society.* Translated by T. McCarthy. Boston, MA: Beacon Press.

———. 1984b. *The Theory of Communicative Action,* Vol. 2: *Lifeworld and System: A Critique of Functionalist Reason.* Translated by T. McCarthy. Boston, MA: Beacon Press.

———. 1993. *Justification and Application: Remarks on Discourse Ethics.* Translated by C.P. Cronin. Cambridge, MA: MIT Press.

———. 1996. *Between Facts and Norms: Contributions to a Discourse Theory of Law and Democracy.* Translated by W. Rehg. Cambridge, MA: MIT Press.

Harmon, Michael M. 1995. *Responsibility as Paradox: A Critique of Rational Discourse on Government.* Thousand Oaks, CA: Sage.

Hart, H.L.A. 1968. *Punishment and Responsibility: Essays in the Philosophy of Law.* New York: Oxford University Press.

Hedström, Peter, and Richard Swedberg. 1998. "Social Mechanisms: An Introductory Essay." In *Social Mechanisms: An Analytical Approach to Social Theory,* ed. P. Hedström and R. Swedberg. Cambridge, UK: Cambridge University Press, 1–31.

Held, David. 2004. "Democratic Accountability and Political Effectiveness from a Cosmopolitan Perspective." *Government & Opposition* 39 (2): 364–91.

———. 2006. *Models Of Democracy.* 3d ed. Malden, MA: Polity Press.

Hellwig, Timothy, and David Samuels. 2008. "Electoral Accountability and the Variety of Democratic Regimes." *British Journal of Political Science* 38 (1): 65–90.

Hibbert, Christopher. 2003. *The Roots of Evil: A Social History of Crime and Punishment.* Stroud: Sutton.

Hiller, John R., and Robert D. Tollison. 1978. "Incentive Versus Cost-Plus Contracts in Defense Procurement." *Journal of Industrial Economics* 26 (3): 239–48.

Holzer, Marc, and Kaifeng Yang. 2004. "Performance Measurement and Improvement: An Assessment of the State of the Art." *International Review of Administrative Sciences* 70 (1): 15–31.

Hood, Christopher. 1991. "A Public Management for All Seasons?" *Public Administration* 69 (1): 3–19.

———. 1997. "Which Contract State? Four Perspectives on Over-Outsourcing for Public Services." *Australian Journal of Public Administration* 56 (3): 120–31.

Hood, Christopher, and David Heald, eds. 2006. *Transparency: The Key to Better Governance?* Oxford: Oxford University Press.

Jordan, Lisa, and Peter van Tuijl, eds. 2006. *NGO Accountability: Politics, Principles and Innovations.* Sterling, VA: Earthscan.

Kaplan, Robert S. 2001. "Strategic Performance Measurement and Management in Nonprofit Organizations." *Nonprofit Management and Leadership* 11 (3): 353–70.

Karpoff, Jonathan M., D. Scott Lee, and Valaria P. Vendrzyk. 1999. "Defense Procurement Fraud, Penalties, and Contractor Influence." *Journal of Political Economy* 107 (4): 809–42.

Kaufman, Herbert. 1977. *Red Tape: Its Origins, Uses, and Abuses.* Washington, DC: Brookings Institution Press.

Kearns, Kevin P. 1996. *Managing for Accountability: Preserving the Public Trust in Public and Nonprofit Organizations.* San Francisco: Jossey-Bass.

————. 2000. *Private Sector Strategies for Social Sector Success: The Guide to Strategy and Planning for Public and Nonprofit Organizations.* San Francisco: Jossey-Bass.

Kingdon, John W. 1984. *Agendas, Alternatives, and Public Policies.* Boston, MA: Little Brown.

Lerner, Jennifer S., and Philip E. Tetlock. 1999. "Accounting for the Effects of Accountability." *Psychological Bulletin* 125 (2): 255–75.

Majone, Giandomenico. 1998. "Europe's 'Democratic Deficit': The Question of Standards." *European Law Journal* 4 (1): 5–28.

Matheson, Craig. 1987. "Weber and the Classification of Forms of Legitimacy." *British Journal of Sociology* 38 (2): 199–215.

McCraw, Thomas K. 1990. "Berle and Means." *Reviews in American History* 18 (4): 578–96.

Miller, Arthur S. 1955. "Government Contracts and Social Control: A Preliminary Inquiry." *Virginia Law Review* 41 (1): 27–58.

Miller, Trudi C., ed. 1984. *Public Sector Performance: A Conceptual Turning Point.* Baltimore, MD: Johns Hopkins University Press.

Minow, Martha. 1998. *Between Vengeance and Forgiveness: Facing History after Genocide and Mass Violence.* Boston, MA: Beacon Press.

Mucciaroni, Gary. 1992. "The Garbage Can Model & the Study of Policy Making: A Critique." *Polity* 24 (3): 459–82.

Mulgan, R. G. 2003. *Holding Power to Account: Accountability in Modern Democracies.* Houndmills, Basingstoke, Hampshire, UK: Palgrave Macmillan.

Niland, Carmel, and Shalini Satkunandan. 1999. "The Ethical Value of Red Tape! The Role of Specialised Institutions in Ensuring Accountability (the NSW Experience)." *Australian Journal of Public Administration* 58 (1): 80–86.

O'Donnell, Guillermo A. 2004. "Why the Rule of Law Matters." *Journal of Democracy* 15 (4): 32–46.

O'Leary, Rosemary. 2006. *The Ethics of Dissent: Managing Guerrilla Government.* Washington, DC: CQ Press.

Organisation for Economic Co-operation Development Public Management Committee. 2000. *Trust in Government: Ethics Measures in OECD Countries.* Paris: Organisation for Economic Co-operation and Development.

Osborne, David. 1993. "Reinventing Government." *Public Productivity & Management Review* 16 (4): 349–56.

Osborne, David, and Ted Gaebler. 1992. *Reinventing Government: How the Entrepreneurial Spirit Is Transforming the Public Sector.* Reading, MA: Addison-Wesley.

Osborne, Stephen P., Tony Bovaird, Steve Martin, Mike Tricker, and Piers Waterston. 1995. "Performance Management and Accountability in Complex Public Programmes." *Financial Accountability & Management* 11 (1): 19–37.

Ostrom, Elinor. 1990. *Governing the Commons: The Evolution of Institutions for Collective Action.* Cambridge, UK: Cambridge University Press.

————. 2005. *Understanding Institutional Diversity.* Princeton: Princeton University Press.

Ouchi, William G. 1977. "The Relationship Between Organizational Structure and Organizational Control." *Administrative Science Quarterly* 22 (1): 95–113.

————. 1979. "A Conceptual Framework for the Design of Organizational Control Mechanisms." *Management Science* 25 (9): 833–48.

Park, Stephen Kim. 2001. "Dictators in the Dock: Retroactive Justice in Consolidating Democracies: A Comparative Analysis of Chile and South Korea." *Fletcher Forum of World Affairs* 25 (1): 127–42.

Petersen, Trond. 1993. "The Economics of Organization: The Principal-Agent Relationship." *Acta Sociologica* 36 (3): 277–93.

Phillips, Robert A., and Joshua D. Margolis. 1999. "Toward an Ethics of Organizations." *Business Ethics Quarterly* 9 (4): 619–38.

Podsakoff, Philip M., Scott B. MacKenzie, Julie Beth Paine, and Daniel G. Bachrach. 2000. "Organizational Citizenship Behaviors: A Critical Review of the Theoretical and Empirical Literature and Suggestions for Future Research." *Journal of Management* 26 (3): 513–63.

Propper, Carol, and Deborah Wilson. 2003. "The Use and Usefulness of Performance Measures in the Public Sector." *Oxford Review of Economic Policy* 19 (2): 250–67.

Purchase, Bryne, and Ronald Hirshhorn. 1994. "Searching for Good Governance: Government and Competitiveness Project," Final Report. Kingston, Ontario: School of Policy Studies, Queen's University.

Radin, Beryl. 2006. *Challenging the Performance Movement: Accountability, Complexity, and Democratic Values.* Washington, DC: Georgetown University Press.

Rhodes, R.A.W. 1996. "The New Governance: Governing without Government." *Political Studies* 44 (3): 652–67.

Riccucci, Norma M. 1995. *Unsung Heroes: Federal Execucrats Making a Difference.* Washington, DC: Georgetown University Press.

Roche, Declan. 2003. *Accountability in Restorative Justice.* Oxford: Oxford University Press.

Rohr, John A. 1989. *Ethics for Bureaucrats: An Essay on Law and Values.* 2d ed. New York: Marcel Dekker.

Romzek, Barbara S., and Melvin J. Dubnick. 1987. "Accountability in the Public Sector: Lessons from the Challenger Tragedy." *Public Administration Review* 47 (3): 227–38.

Rosenbloom, David H. 1983. "Public Administrative Theory and the Separation of Powers." *Public Administration Review* 43 (3): 219–27.

———. 1987. "Public Administrators' Liability: Bench v. Bureau in the Contemporary Administrative State." *Public Administration Quarterly* 10 (4): 373–86.

Rosenbloom, David H., James D. Carroll, and Jonathan D. Carroll. 2000. *Constitutional Competence for Public Managers: Cases and Commentary.* Itasca, IL: F.E. Peacock.

Ross, Stephen A. 1973. "The Economic Theory of Agency: The Principal's Problem." *American Economic Review* 63 (2): 134–39.

Rugeley, Cindy, and Montgomery Van Wart. 2006. "Everyday Moral Exemplars." *Public Integrity* 8: 381–94.

Samuels, David. 2004. "Presidentialism and Accountability for the Economy in Comparative Perspective." *American Political Science Review* 98 (3): 425–36.

Sarkin, Jeremy. 2000. "Promoting Justice, Truth and Reconciliation in Transitional Societies: Evaluating Rwanda's Approach in the New Millennium of Using Community Based Gacaca Tribunals to Deal with the Past." *International Law Forum Du Droit International* 2 (2): 112–21.

Schelling, Thomas C. 1998. "Social Mechanisms and Social Dynamics." In *Social Mechanisms: An Analytical Approach to Social Theory,* ed. P. Hedström and R. Swedberg. Cambridge: Cambridge University Press, 32–44.

Schmidt, Vivien A. 2004. "The European Union: Democratic Legitimacy in a Regional State?" *Journal of Common Market Studies* 42 (5): 975–99.

Scott, Austin W. 1949. "The Fiduciary Principle." *California Law Review* 37 (4): 539–55.

Simon, Herbert A. 1957. *Administrative Behavior: A Study of Decision-Making Processes in Administrative Organization.* 2d ed. New York: Free Press.

———. 1987. "Making Management Decisions: The Role of Intuition and Emotion." *Academy of Management Executive* 1 (1): 57–64.

Smith, Bruce L.R., ed. 1975. *The New Political Economy: The Public Use of the Private Sector.* New York: Halstead Press.

Smith, Peter. 1995. "Performance Indicators and Outcome in the Public Sector." *Public Money & Management* 15 (4): 13–16.

Stoker, Gerry. 1998. "Governance as Theory: Five Propositions." *International Social Science Journal* 50 (155): 17–28.

Stokes, Susan C. 2005. "Perverse Accountability: A Formal Model of Machine Politics with Evidence from Argentina."*American Political Science Review* 99 (3): 315–25.

Stone, Deborah A. 2002. *Policy Paradox: The Art of Political Decision Making.* Rev. ed. New York: Norton.

Syring, Tom. 2006. "Truth Versus Justice: A Tale of Two Cities?" *International Legal Theory* 12: 143–210.

Tetlock, Philip E. 1985. "Accountability: A Social Check on the Fundamental Attribution Error." *Social Psychology Quarterly* 48 (3): 227–36.

Tetlock, Philip E., and Richard Boettger. 1989. 'Accountability: A Social Magnifier of the Dilution Effect." *Journal of Personality and Social Psychology* 57 (3): 388–98.

Thompson, Victor A. 1975. *Without Sympathy Or Enthusiasm : The Problem Of Administrative Compassion.* Tuscaloosa: University of Alabama Press.

Thompson, Frank J., ed. 1993. *Revitalizing State and Local Public Service: Strengthening Performance, Accountability, and Citizen Confidence.* San Francisco: Jossey-Bass.

Tyler, Tom R., and Yuen J. Huo. 2002. *Trust in the Law: Encouraging Public Cooperation with the Police and Courts.* New York: Russell Sage Foundation.

Vogel, David. 2005. *The Market for Virtue: The Potential and Limits of Corporate Social Responsibility.* Washington, DC: Brookings Institution Press.

Waldo, Dwight. 1961. "Organization Theory: An Elephantine Problem." *Public Administration Review* 21 (4): 210–25.

Wallach, Lori M. 2002. "Accountable Governance in the Era of Globalization: The WTO, NAFTA, and International Harmonization of Standards." *University of Kansas Law Review* 50 (4): 823–66.

Weaver, Gary R., Linda Klebe Trevino, and Philip L. Cochran. 1999. "Corporate Ethics Programs as Control Systems: Influences of Executive Commitment and Environmental Factors." *Academy of Management Journal* 42 (1): 41–57.

Weiss, Thomas G. 2000. "Governance, Good Governance and Global Governance: Conceptual and Actual Challenges." *Third World Quarterly* 21 (5): 795–814.

Wholey, Joseph S. 1983. *Evaluation and Effective Public Management.* Boston, MA: Little Brown.

———. 1999. "Performance-Based Management: Responding to the Challenges." *Public Performance & Management Review* 22 (3): 288–307.

Wildavsky, Aaron. 1973. "If Planning Is Everything, Maybe It's Nothing." *Policy Sciences* 4 (2): 127–53.

Williamson, Oliver E. 1967. "The Economics of Defense Contracting: Incentives and Performance." In *Issues in Defense Economics,* ed. R.N. McKean. New York: National Bureau of Economic Research, 217–78.

———. 1998. "The Institutions of Governance." *American Economic Review* 88 (2): 75–79.

———. 2002. "The Theory of the Firm as Governance Structure: From Choice to Contract." *Journal of Economic Perspectives* 16 (3): 171–95.

———. 2005. "The Economics of Governance." *American Economic Review* 95 (2): 1–18.

Yang, Kaifeng, and Marc Holzer. 2006. "The Performance-Trust Link: Implications for Performance Measurement." *Public Administration Review* 66 (1): 114–26.

Zauderer, Donald G. 1992. "Integrity: An Essential Executive Quality." *Business Forum* 17 (4): 12–16.

PART I

COMPLEX CHALLENGES

A common theme among those who study accountability mechanisms is the challenges and dilemmas these mechanisms pose for those seeking fulfillment of this promising approach to problems of governance. Accountability mechanisms can be viewed as a collection of tools sharing a common characteristic: they all rely on the use of account-giving relationships to achieve some central objectives of governance. In theory, the major task of accountability is to construct and operationalize a governance system using the appropriate mechanisms found in the accountability toolbox.

Several views of accountability challenges were presented at the Kettering-sponsored sessions. The multiple-accountabilities challenge was initially raised by Romzek and Dubnick in their 1987 examination of the diverse and conflicting expectations that emerged from several major institutional sources (i.e., legal, professional, bureaucratic, and political). In the first chapter Thomas Schillemans and Mark Bovens further elaborate on the multiple-accountability challenge by analyzing five Dutch cases. While finding that such conditions can be dysfunctional in a variety of ways, the authors also recognize the positive aspects of redundancies generated by these seemingly adverse conditions. Perhaps we have more to lose than gain by attempting to resolve the dilemmas posed by the multiplicity of expectations we have for these mechanisms.

Barbara Romzek's study of accountability in the expanding arena of outsourced and networked social services highlights the contemporary challenges of efforts to construct and sustain an effective system of accountable governance in a public sector where multiple and diverse expectations emerge from a "tangled web" of contractual and networked relationships. Central to her study is the greatly expanded role of contracting, a factor that is even more markedly problematic in the complex environment described by Trevor Brown, Matthew Potoski, and David Van Slyke in their study of the Coast Guard's Project Deepwater procurement process. While the source of complexity in the social services area is rooted in the relationships among the parties involved, it is the very nature of the "product" (or service) involved in the procurement process that generates the accountability challenges for Deepwater. Both studies help us better understand why the problem of multiple accountabilities in government proves such an elusive objective in a wide range of programs.

While multiple accountabilities pose a challenging context for those engaged in governance, not all demands for accountability are equal weight. Those linked to major regime values are perhaps the most problematic, especially when they are incompatible and create fundamental dilemmas for those being held to account. The tradeoffs between efficiency and equality in both the design and implementation of public policies and programs have been a concern in the United States where both are perceived as core values in historical waves of administrative reform. A similar dilemma faces those who administer the increasingly significant number of global governance organizations (GCOs) that are the focus of Jonathan Koppel's contribution to this volume. Some of these agencies (e.g., the Universal Postal Union) have been in existence for more than a century; others (e.g., ICANN) are less than two decades old. What they have in common is that today they operate within an international regime that puts a premium on both effectiveness and democratic responsiveness. The challenge of multiple accountabilities in this context requires strategic choices in order to deal with the inherent dilemma emerging from the demands for simultaneous achieving authority and legitimacy in an increasingly dynamic global setting.

THE CHALLENGE OF MULTIPLE ACCOUNTABILITY

Does Redundancy Lead to Overload?

THOMAS SCHILLEMANS AND MARK BOVENS

In the early years of World War II, Friedrich and Finer engaged in a seminal dispute on how to organize responsibilities in modern democratic government (Friedrich 1940; Finer 1941). Their dispute is often referred to as one of the defining moments in the development of the concepts of administrative responsibility and political accountability (Romzek 1996, 97; Dubnick 2005, 1). According to Finer, clear lines of command and control are the basis of any democratic system of ministerial responsibility. He thus proposed what has come to be seen as the conventional approach to accountability: democracy is best served by an unambiguous division between politics and administration and a clear hierarchy, with comprehensive goals and substantial sanctions through which unwanted conduct is punished. Friedrich, on the other hand, claimed that, given the obvious growth in size and complexity of contemporary government, the conventional hierarchical system would not suffice to ensure responsible behavior on the part of government. Simply executing already formulated policies was no longer an option, since important aspects of policy making had shifted from the hands of politicians to administrative agencies (Friedrich 1940, 5). This meant that the conventional, unilateral model of political responsibility and administrative accountability no longer fit the evolving reality of public government. In his view, a firm emphasis on professional norms and a sense of individual administrative responsibility, accompanied by additional accountability mechanisms, were now needed.

This aspect of the Friedrich-Finer debate—how to organize accountability in an era of complex government—is more salient than ever. Accountability almost by definition seems to call for simplicity: clear divisions between oversight and execution of tasks, straightforward criteria and measurements for performance, and a logical hierarchy between agents and principals. Yet at the same time the world of public administration employs a growing number of dispersed and complex practices of governance (Day and Klein 1987, 10; Posner 2002, 545). Salamon describes the tension created by this diverse approach as the accountability challenge. "[M]any of the newer tools of public action vest substantial discretionary authority in entities other than those with ultimate responsibility for the results," he argues. The result is that

> Many new forms of governance require others doing the job, with substantial discretion. This poses an accountability challenge: we need to loosen up traditional notions of political accountability, and develop more pluralistic conceptions (2002, 38).

This chapter examines the accountability challenge through the lens of an empirical analysis of Dutch agencies held accountable to a board of commissioners, as well as to a department in a traditional, hierarchical model. First we will review two perspectives on accountability and look at the negative expectations for using a multiple-accountability model. Then we will discuss our empirical analysis of multiple accountability, which was based on qualitative research done on a number of Dutch agencies. Our purpose is to learn what these cases teach us for situations of multiple accountability, generally. Many authors have associated a large number of problems with multiple accountability. Almost by definition, multiple accountability is seen as too much of a good thing or a burdensome overload. However, following others (for example, Braithwaite 1999; Scott 2000), we will argue that the imminent redundancy of multiple accountability also can contribute positively to the good governance of executive agencies.

ACCOUNTABILITY AS A VIRTUE VERSUS ACCOUNTABILITY AS A MECHANISM

Anyone studying accountability will soon discover that the term has many different meanings. Accountability is used as a synonym for many loosely defined political desiderata, such as transparency, equity, democracy, efficiency, responsiveness, responsibility, and integrity (Mulgan 2000, 555; Behn 2001, 3–6; Dubnick 2005). Such shifting meanings may serve the purpose of political spinning, policy rhetoric, or white papers, but they have been a strong impediment to systematic, comparative, scholarly analysis.

Moreover, much of the academic literature on accountability is disconnected, as many authors set out to produce their own specific definition of accountability. Every newly edited volume on accountability—and even worse, each of the individual chapters within these edited volumes—uses its own concepts, conceptualizations, and frames for studying the subject. (Dowdle 2006; Ebrahim and Weisband 2007). Some use the concept of accountability very loosely, while others produce a more narrow definition, but few of these definitions are fully compatible, which makes it very hard to produce cumulative and commensurable research. In addition, few papers move beyond conceptual and theoretical analyses and engage in systematic, comparative empirical research, with the exception of a series of studies in the narrow field of social psychology (Adelberg and Batson 1978; Tetlock et al. 1989; Lerner and Tetlock 1999). The result of this disjointed accountability talk is that accountability seems to be an ever-expanding concept, which "has come to stand as a general term for any mechanism that makes powerful institutions responsive to their particular publics" (Mulgan 2003,8). However, there is a pattern to the expansion.

Particularly, but not exclusively, in American academic and political discourse, accountability is used mainly as a normative concept, as a set of standards for the evaluation of the behavior of public actors. In this type of discourse the adjective "accountable" often is used as in: "We want public officials to be accountable" or "government has to behave in an accountable manner." In this discourse accountability or, more precisely, being accountable is seen as a virtue or positive feature of organizations or officials. Accountability in this very broad sense is used to positively qualify a state of affairs or the performance of an actor. It comes close to "responsiveness" and "a sense of responsibility," a willingness to act in a transparent, fair, and equitable way. Accountability, used in an active sense as a virtue, refers to substantive norms for the behavior of actors—in this case public officials or public organizations. Hence, accountability studies in this vein often focus on normative issues or the assessment of the actual and active behavior of public agents (O'Connell 2005, 86; Considine 2002, 22; Koppell 2005).

On the other side of the Atlantic, in British, continental European (as well as Australian) scholarly debates, accountability is often used in a more narrow, descriptive sense. Staying close to its etymological and historical roots, scholars define accountability as a specific social relation or *mechanism* that involves an obligation to explain and justify conduct (Day and Klein 1987, 57; Scott 2000, 40; Pollitt 2003, 89; Mulgan 2003, 7–14; Bovens 2007. See also Romzek and Dubnick 1998, 6; Lerner and Tetlock 1999, 255). Explanations and justifications of accountability are not made in a void, but vis-à-vis a significant other. This implies a relationship between an actor (the "accountor"), and a forum (the account-holder, or "accountee"; Pollitt 2003, 89). The accounting process usually involves not just the provision of information about conduct and performance, but also the possibility of debate, of questions by the forum and answers by the actor, and eventually of judgment of the actor by the forum. Judgment also implies the imposition of formal or informal sanctions on the actor in case of poor performance or, for that matter, of rewards in case of adequate performance.

Accountability mechanisms normally exhibit three phases (Mulgan 2003; Bovens 2007). In the first phase, the actor renders an account of his conduct and performance to the accountability forum. This may be coined the information phase. In the second phase, the actor and the forum engage in a debate about this account. The forum may ask for additional information, and the actor will answer questions and, if necessary, justify and defend his course of action. This is the debating phase. Then the forum may pass judgment on the conduct of the actor, by approving an annual account, denouncing a policy, or publicly condemning the behavior of an official or agency. In passing a negative judgment the forum frequently imposes sanctions of some kind on the actor. This is the sanctions or consequences phase. Sanctions may vary from formal disapproval to tightened regulations, fines, discharge of management, or even the termination of the organization. Many authors notice that a hierarchy of sanctions exists. As Hood et al. indicate: "It emanates with the 'ability to shame,' escalates to lighter weapons such as certificates or formal (dis) approvals and culminates in the 'nuclear weapon' of liquidation" (1999, 47).

This model can be called passive accountability because actors are held to account by a forum, ex post facto, for their conduct. Elsewhere (Bovens 2007) we have defined accountability in this more narrow, passive sense as *a relationship between an actor and a forum, in which the actor has an obligation to explain and to justify his or her conduct, and in which the forum can pose questions and pass judgment, and the actor may face consequences.* Hence, the locus of this type of accountability study is not the behavior of public agents, but the way in which these institutional arrangements operate. And the focus is not whether the agents have acted in an accountable way, but whether they are or can be held accountable ex post facto by accountability forums.

Again, the Friedrich-Finer debate is illustrative here; both not only advocated different notions of administrative responsibility, but also used different concepts. Finer predominantly focused on mechanisms that ensure responsibility and accountability, whereas Friedrich on the other side of the Atlantic looked upon accountability as a virtue, as was clearly observed by Finer:

> My chief difference with Professor Friedrich was and is my insistence upon distinguishing responsibility as an arrangement of correction and punishment even up to dismissal both of politicians and officials, while he believes in reliance upon responsibility as a sense of responsibility, largely unsanctioned, except by deference or loyalty to professional standards. (Finer 1941, 335)

Both concepts, the active one, in which accountability is seen as a personal or organizational virtue, and the passive one, in which accountability is defined as an arrangement or mechanism, are very useful for the study of and the debate about democratic governance. However, the two concepts should be distinguished, since they address different sorts of issues and imply very different sorts of standards, frameworks, and analytical dimensions. In this chapter we use accountability in the latter sense, as a mechanism that involves an obligation to explain and justify one's conduct. (The distinction between these two concepts of accountability is treated at length in Bovens 2010.)

NEGATIVE EXPECTATIONS FOR MULTIPLE ACCOUNTABILITY

Growing complexity has been one of the central issues in the literature on accountability since the seminal Friedrich-Finer dispute. The complex structures of contemporary public sectors pose difficulties for both academics and practitioners. A leading question is: how can a system of multiple, overlapping, and more or less competing forms of accountability operate? The accountability literature has identified some key problems and issues in such an approach.

Issue 1: Conflicting Expectations

The most general and most logical expected effect of multiple accountability is that it will result in conflicting expectations for agencies. This may cause considerable confusion among employees and the management of agencies. Stakeholders may find it difficult to combine different expectations, prioritize among differing expectations, or anticipate the actions and actual priorities of various accountability forums. Most difficult is for an agency to behave as an accountable entity if the criteria of accountability are contested. It is this issue of overlapping and conflicting expectations that Romzek and Dubnick refer to as the *accountability dilemma*: "the essence of this dilemma is the inability of 'accountable' entities to resolve the problem of many masters and manage the government's business under conditions of multiple accountability relationships and systems" (1998, 100).

The complex reality of multiple accountability has been described by Klingner et al. (2002), among others. Klingner et al. argue that accountability relationships constitute the institutional arena in which public administrators have to manage diverse expectations (119) and describe a case of policy reform in the area of contracting for foster care. This reform was infused with different expectations, which resulted in multiple, diverse, changing, and conflicting pressures on the participants. The conflicting expectations followed from the fact that a new combination of politics with administration and market elements was sought after. The authors conclude that politics, administration, and marketing are different worlds that produce different expectations of accountability, often at odds with each other.

Issue 2: Transaction and Opportunity Costs

As already noted, processes of account giving can be divided into three phases: the information, debating, and consequences phases. All of these phases require time and effort from the senior level of agencies, because information has to be produced, and they have to engage in dialogue with the accountability forums. Agencies must draft reports that provide hard and soft data on their goals, operations, and achievements. In the debating phase, a substantial amount of time and attention is spent discussing and evaluating the conduct of the actor. The accountability forums on their part also require resources, such as wages and staff, to perform their duties. In short, accountability involves substantial transaction costs.

An increase in the number and variety of accountability arrangements naturally implies an increase in the costs of accountability. The transaction costs of multiple accountability arrangements may be excessive, as some authors have pointed out (Pollitt 2003, 95). Others point at the relative weight of the opportunity costs (Halachmi 2002, 233); accountability demands time and attention of the highest-ranking officials who have the least of these resources at their disposal.

Issue 3: Negativity

In situations of multiple accountability there are multiple forums demanding information from one actor. The inherent logic of this process is that the accountability forums are urged to look for flaws, faults, and other forms of failure. Accountability easily evolves into fault-finding missions that derail into a climate of negativity (Mulgan 2003, 29) or in sheer scapegoating (Mulgan 2003, 4). A potential risk of multiple accountability is that the different forums outbid one another in their negative attention to public agencies. Their quest to find fault and guilty persons may divert attention from the more fundamental question of how to improve public services. Negativity can also be detrimental to the performance of organizations: too stringent accounting and fault finding impairs the inclination of public managers to take risks and to seek improvements (Behn 2001, 15).

Issue 4: Blame Games

As a logical consequence of the preceding issue, multiple accountability may in times of crisis evolve into a blame game with multiple players. In general, delegation is often seen as a form of blame shifting (Hood 2002; Thatcher and Sweet 2002, 141). In many situations of governance, there are numerous parties who carry at least some responsibility for the outcomes that are produced, but none of them is single-handedly responsible for the full outcome. This is the problem of many hands (Bovens 1998). In complex organizations and networks, it is often quite impossible to identify even one actor whose contribution is substantial enough to hold him or her directly responsible for the unwanted outcome. But in the same vein, numerous candidates carry at least a little bit of guilt, and buck passing is then a likely result. If the accountability process devolves into a negative and blame-oriented process, the parties concerned may focus their energy on putting the blame on the shoulders of others. Where this strategy helps to clarify responsibilities, it is a positive development, but very often blame games rather tend to obscure responsibilities and narrow the scope of attention in policy debates to the use of sanctions only.

Issue 5: Multiple Accountabilities Disorder

For some accountability is such a good thing that the more we have of it the better it is. However, too much accountability may impede agencies from actually making decisions, and the conflicting demands from different accountability forums may have a paralyzing effect on agents. Koppell (2005) refers to the problem as "multiple accountabilities disorder" and notes:

> Organizations trying to meet conflicting expectations are likely to be dysfunctional, pleasing no one while trying to please everyone. Ironically this may include failures of accountability—in every sense imaginable [. . .] this article describes this phenomenon and labels it *multiple accountabilities disorder* (MAD). The novel typology of accountability concepts is employed to show the challenges for an organization attempting to be accountable in multiple senses. The contention is that the organization suffering from MAD oscillates between behaviors

Table 1.1

Seven Expectations for Multiple Accountability

Information phase		Transaction and opportunity costs	
Debating phase	Conflicting expectations	Negativism	Blame games
Consequences	Multiple accountabilities disorder	Loss of control	Symbolic accountability

consistent with conflicting notions of accountability. The organization will sometimes empha-size the directives of principals while at other times try to focus on "customers." In the long run, overseers and constituents are displeased and the organization struggles. (95)

Issue 6: Loss of Control

The sixth issue is the reverse of the preceding issue of MAD. With MAD the agency more or less collapses under the weight of multiple accountabilities, but the practical implication of loss of control is that various accountability demands nullify one another. Actors may experience *more autonomy* because the plurality of accountability claims leave them more room to maneuver. Agency theorists are often quite explicit about the fact that the addition of principals makes it more difficult to control agents (Moe 1984, 769; Miller 2005, 211). The problem with multiple accountability in this respect is that it provides actors with the opportunity to shift forums. If actors are accountable to different "significant others," they have the opportunity to make strategic choices to forge alliances with forums most sympathetic to their causes (see Mulgan 2003, 218). Multiple accountability may therefore also result from strategic action: increasing the number of forums is a suitable reaction to external pressures (Day and Klein 1987, 170–1). Keohane underlines the subtle Machiavellianism inherent in such a strategy: "In a democratic era, it is difficult for an agent to say, 'the public be damned' and explicitly to dismiss accountability claims. It may be more feasible, and more clever, to multiply the number of principals to whom one is responsible—and principals on the basis of which one is responsible—so that accountability is eroded in practice" (2002, 15).

Issue 7: Symbolic Accountability

If the cumulative weight of conflicting demands is too heavy we end up with either multiple account-abilities disorder (issue 5) or loss of control due to conflicting demands canceling out one another (issue 6). However, a third option is also possible: the added accountability arrangements may have no positive or negative effects at all. In that case it is likely that the accountability mechanisms have a purely symbolic role—they are mere rituals (Halachmi 2002, 230). Sometimes it may be important to pay lip service to some ideal or constituency without granting it real influence.

The seven negative expectations for multiple accountability are summarized in Table 1.1. The different issues can be situated in the different phases of accountability. In the next section we will provide an empirical analysis of the accountability of agencies to boards in order to assess whether these different expected negative outcomes actually occurred.

MULTIPLE ACCOUNTABILITY FOR DUTCH AGENCIES

Since the late 1980s, boards of commissioners at arm's length from the central government have been introduced to a number of large Dutch agencies. Public policy makers copied the board

Figure 1.1   **Multiple Accountability for Agencies**

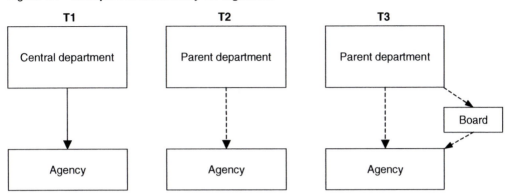

structure from large private corporations when redesigning the management of large public agencies. According to statements issued by the government, the two-tier system had proven its worth in the private sector. In the public sector, these boards tend to have a hybrid character. To start with, they can be seen as parts of the agency, since they have to approve all major decisions the management board makes. They also play an important role in hiring the management board. However, the boards of commissioners are not officially superior to the managers. The boards themselves are selected and installed by the ministry and periodically discuss the operations of the agencies with the ministry, and for these reasons they are connected to the ministry. Finally, they operate independently and may neither seek nor accept instructions in the performance of their duties. For some agencies, the members of the board are liable in person for financial losses to others that stem from a neglect of their duties.

Because of their hybrid character, boards of commissioners add to the complexity of governing executive agencies. The difficulty in controlling agents increases when the governance system in which they operate becomes increasingly complicated (see Przeworski et al. 1999; Strøm 2000). This is precisely what has happened in contemporary democratic governance in general, and is exemplified here by the introduction of boards of commissioners to the governance of agencies. Figure 1.1 depicts three consecutive periods in time. T1 describes the original situation, when government agencies were part of larger ministries and were situated under direct ministerial control. Particularly in the 1990s, many public-service organizations were then granted substantial autonomy (see van Thiel 2000; Pollitt et al. 2004). Crucial to *agentification* is that governmental organizations are placed outside of departmental hierarchies. Their autonomy limits the possibilities for ministerial control. This resulted in a much-diagnosed "gap" or "deficit" in the accountability regime of arm's-length governance (see van Thiel 2000, 167; Flinders 2001, 41; Mulgan 2003, 74; Pollitt 2003). This situation is described through the use of a dotted line in T2.

For many Dutch agencies the relative loss of central control was compensated by the introduction of boards of commissioners operating as independent overseeing bodies. They are installed by the ministry, yet they neither seek nor accept instructions in the performance of their duties. This third situation is illustrated by T3, where the lines of accountability are doubled, and neither renders full control. The control of the agencies is dispersed among different actors.

Our analysis is of the boards of five agencies: the Forest Authority; the Dutch Land Registry Office (Kadaster); the Netherlands Vaccine Institute; and two social security agencies: the Centre for Work and Income and Social Security Agency (UWV). These are all relatively large agencies, employing between 400 (Netherlands Vaccine Institute) and almost 20,000 employees (UWV).

Table 1.2

Five Boards of Commissioners

Phase of accountability	Duties/powers board of commissioners	Land Registry Office (Kadaster); State Forest Authority	Centre Work & Income; UWV; Vaccine Institute
Information phase	Integral overview. Receives all required information.	X	X
	Possibility to "hear" employers and managers. Access to all buildings and books.	X	—
Debating phase	Duty to see to a proper execution of legal duties	X	X
	May neither seek nor accept instructions in the performance of their duties	X	X
Consequences phase	Meets with minister	X	Reports
	Hire, fire, and reward management board	X	Advice
	Sets tariffs	X	No tariffs
	Sets annual plan, budget, major financial decisions	X	Advice
	Decides on external collaborations and internal governance structure	X	Advice

Their boards of commissioners of these different agencies have different formal tasks and powers. By and large they can be divided into two types: boards with substantial formal powers (those of Kadaster and the Forest Authority) and boards with limited powers. Table 1.2 provides an overview.

MULTIPLE ACCOUNTABILITY IN ACTION

The last part of this chapter describes the effects on five major arm's-length agencies in the Netherlands, of adding an extra layer of board accountability to the hierarchical accountability already owed to the ministry. Our findings are based on qualitative research of accountability of the agencies to the boards and parent departments. Since accountability is defined as communicative interaction between two parties, our analysis aimed to reconstruct the content of agency and board communication. This included an analysis of agendas and minutes of board meetings, annual reports, strategic plans, audits and evaluations, policy documents of the ministries, and reports and letters to Parliament. In addition, interviews were held with managers and senior officials of the agencies, members of boards of commissioners, and senior officials of parent departments. In total some 90 interviews were held. (See Schillemans 2007, 2008, for full research.) Respondents are quoted anonymously here by referring to them by number. We sought to uncover in the cases we studied which unintended, mostly negative consequences had materialized in the application of multiple accountability. Our description is organized along the three phases of accountability we distinguished earlier: the information, debating, and consequences. Our analysis shows that, although traces of most of the expected negative effects surfaced, the overall picture of multiple accountability was much more positive than might be predicted.

Information Phase

Agencies primarily account for their conduct and behavior toward boards in regular, official meetings. The five boards of commissioners that were studied hold four to seven official meetings every year, where they discuss major strategic issues with the board of managers. All these boards are able to call upon a secretary who works for the agency. These secretaries are selected from the highest-ranking employees of the agency, and in some cases the same person also works as a secretary of the management board. This mode of selection ensures the seniority of the secretaries and ensures that they have sufficient access within the agencies. The potential drawback, however, is their limited independence that may result in conflicts of loyalty: should the secretary be loyal to his or her formal employer, the agency, or the board as the factual principal?

According to one of our respondents the agendas of the official meetings are strongly influenced by what he calls "the drill of the annual planning and control (P&C) cycle" (R71). Boards are to monitor the entire operations of the agencies; their oversight covers all the activities and decisions of agencies (R73). In order to implement this broad perspective, boards are informed about the conduct of the agencies through a series of reports that are grounded in the P&C cycle of the agencies. Particularly the annual plans, budget, annual accounts, and annual reports are discussed with the boards. As one respondent pragmatically put it: "We simply discuss all the important issues with our board" (R74).

On the basis of the official documentation of the agendas and minutes of meetings, the following indicative typology of different boards can be made. Figure 1.2 indicates the central topics treated by the different boards.

The figure clarifies that general operations is the most important issue that boards address; this topic covers 38 percent of the agendas. Subtopics include organizational changes, information and communication technology (ICT) investments, and financial reporting. The second major issue is the "major annual documents" (24 percent), which include subtopics such as annual plans, annual accounts, and annual reports. Political-strategic issues are in the third group. These are issues that address departmental inquiries into the future of agencies, formal evaluations of the agency, and other issues in which politicians are involved (17 percent). In the fourth group are issues regarding the governance of the agencies, including issues about the management and administrative task divisions (also 17 percent).

In addition to the above picture of the central issues treated by the different boards, respondents indicate that boards devote more time to the political-strategic issues than could be distilled from the minutes and agendas of their meetings. Many respondents indicate that a lengthy general discussion on the current affairs of the agency usually precedes the formal agenda. The board is then informed about "all important issues" (R75). This general discussion treats the inner world of the organization as well as the outer world of the relevant political-strategic environment. The balance between inner and outer world is estimated to be fifty–fifty (R77). Some respondents consider the general discussion to be the real climax of meetings. One of the managers states it thus:

> The most important part is usually our opening discussion. This is the start of our agenda and I usually report on everything that we have experienced and all the important issues. This leads to various discussions. At some point, the chairman of the board of commissioners will raise his voice and suggest to move on to the formal agenda. (R78)

Thus, central management assesses their most important strategic issues, which then become the issues that agencies must account for to their boards.

Figure 1.2 **Topics Accounted for to the Boards**

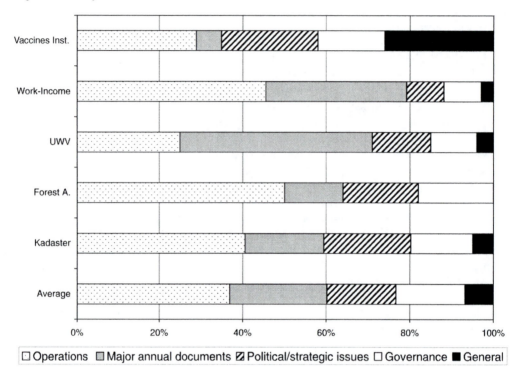

Evaluation: Limited Transaction and Opportunity Costs

We have stated that one of the potential negative effects of multiple accountability can be the increasing transaction and opportunity costs of accountability. The easiest measure for the transaction costs of boards is the size of their fees. For all of the five studied boards, the annual costs in fees is approximately 100,000 euro, in total. It is difficult to say exactly what is "purchased" for this sum. Members of boards estimate that they invest between 50 and 100 hours every year as members of boards. This is less than one sixth of the total salaries for the executive board. If we consider that the salary costs increase with a little less than one sixth, and that boards are informed through documents and reports that are usually available anyhow, it could be stated that the total costs of this added form of accountability are not excessive.

If there is a problem with the costs of boards, it is rather a problem of opportunity costs. The total amount of money or time invested in accountability to boards seems not to be excessive, but board management is done by senior officials who have relatively little time at their disposal. As boards are important accountability forums, maintaining the relationship is complicated because only the highest officials of the agency are permitted to interact with the board. These officials say that they have too little time at their disposal for the board (R190). One of the secretaries states:

> We have our own system of planning and control. And if we had been an ordinary organization that would have been enough. Because this provides necessary information to our management, with all the plans and all our contracts. They can check our operations and draft all the necessary reports. But as a government agency, we have to translate the

outcomes of our system of planning and control to outsiders. This means we have to make a second loop. We are confronted with our parent department. They want to obtain certain information and want to receive this information in specific ways. And *then* you have our board of commissioners, somewhere between an external and an internal entity. They also demand to receive information in specific ways. Our department (central staff) sees some documents come around three times. The board is the last—and at that point we may be quite through with it! (R189)

A secretary adds that his role is "with all respects, only a side run" (R191). A colleague adds: "It is not my hobby" (R192). Respondents also indicate that it requires time to learn how to deal with a board. If either the board or the secretary is new, they need some time to arrive at a fruitful working partnership (R188).

The above quotes from respondents all point in the same direction: there are some opportunity costs involved with the management of the boards of commissioners, but the real transaction costs of the additional form of accountability to boards should not be a problem for these large agencies. However, sometimes there are considerable opportunity costs since the accountability relationship must be maintained by the naturally scarce highest-ranking officials of agencies.

Debating Phase

In the second phase of the accountability process, agencies and boards engage in a dialogue on the issues and documents that have been brought forward in the information phase.

We asked our respondents if they could describe what sort of debate ensues. The respondents were quite unambiguous in their responses and indicated that boards generally choose not to operate as tough investigators looking for breaches of norms, but rather choose to operate in more reflective ways, trying to stimulate the reflexivity of the managers. Most respondents also spoke warmly about the interaction between the boards of commissioners and the boards of managers. They indicate that the discussion is "a real pleasure; very open" (R155), "open and sympathetic" (R156), and that boards and managers "treat each other with a lot of respect" (R157). The interviews thus indicate that boards generally operate as "cooperative entities" (R158) who aim to further the interests of the agencies and aspire to help them improve.

In many accountability processes, the actions of actors are measured according to specific, sometimes rather detailed, standards. In our cases, however, neither the parent department, the board itself, nor the agency has felt inclined to bring forward strict standards of operation and quantifiable expectations. The boards assess the accountability information of agencies on a very pragmatic basis. As one of (the older) members of a board indicates: "you verify the information on the basis of your experience and common sense" (R138). This may be a viable option, as the members of boards always carry a wealth of experience in the public sector and are often highly experienced in the specific policy field as well. The members of boards speak about their roles with a lot of confidence. One member states: "I am familiar with these types of organizations so I know beforehand what to expect" (R139). And another member adds: "With our experience . . . we are certainly able to provide solid advice on these kinds of issues" (R140).

However, the oversight of the boards is not solely based on personal preferences and professional experiences. In addition, boards often verify whether decisions by the managers or specific outcomes of policies are in accordance with the plans of the agency. Boards then operate on the basis of the strategic plans that agencies have drafted themselves. In this way, they perform a reality check and test whether the agency lives up to its own policy ambitions and aspirations as articulated in white papers. The advantage of this perspective is that the boards take the agenda and goals of the agencies as a point of departure. The accountability process is then directed toward the goals that were set by the agency itself.

What is somewhat remarkable about the role of the boards is that they do not act as representatives of the interests of the minister. It is remarkable because, after all, it is the minister who has appointed them. Nevertheless, board members do not perceive themselves as his representatives. Quite the contrary seems to happen, as boards usually choose the side of the agency in cases of policy conflicts with the parent department. The members are quite outspoken on their role in this respect. They state: "I am not here to help the minister" (R122) or "I do not in the least bit represent the minister" (R123). And a third member of a board adds: "As a member of this board, it is my first and foremost obligation to serve the interests of the agency" (R124).

Evaluation: Blame Games Rather than Conflicting Expectations and Negativity

The preceding discussion of the debating phase shows that, as predicted, the introduction of boards makes it necessary for agencies to strike a balance between the conflicting demands and expectations from different significant others. The introduction of boards indeed increases the number of expectations with which agencies have to deal. However, this balancing act is not a cumbersome challenge. As boards basically operate on the basis of a combination of common sense and the agenda of the agency itself, they do not create an unbearable tension for agencies to balance different expectations.

It was also predicted that situations of multiple accountability might invoke cynicism and negativity and that accountability processes are primarily directed at fault finding. But reports from board members indicate that they do not operate in an atmosphere of negativity and instead primarily focus their attention on improving the conduct of agencies. It is a long way from their reflective role to the sort of negativity that has been described in some of the literature (see Behn 2001).

Blame games, however, the third expected effect for multiple accountability, is indeed a phenomenon that can sometimes be found when boards are present. The introduction of boards creates a three-sided relationship where a two-sided relationship used to exist. Sometimes two parties side together, and boards often side with the agencies if they have a conflict with their parent department. During our interviews, the members of boards and managers of agencies pointed out that some of the policy problems they experienced were created by the parent department. They targeted particularly its tendency to produce laws that are too complicated and the tendency to cut the budgets of agencies.

Conversely, some of the respondents also experienced that ministries used boards as lightning rods after policy crises. Three of the investigated agencies were caught up in highly public and politicized policy affairs during the research. In these instances, some of the blame of failures was in retrospect ascribed to the board. In one situation, a departmental respondent admitted that some of the blame was wrongly ascribed to the board:

> "After this situation, we sent a letter to Parliament that was signed by a civil servant. That was not the best of letters. An unfortunate letter. It really put it too strongly. The letter more or less stated that the board should have done its work better. That was really untrue. We knew that ourselves, it really was not their fault." (R348)

To conclude, in the debating phase of accountability to boards, the dialogue between the actor and the forum focuses on how to improve the conduct of agencies. In this dialogue, boards do not focus their attention on breaches of specified external norms, but rather, they follow the agenda and the goals the agency has specified in advance. In this way, they do contribute to the fact that agencies have to deal with different expectations, but without causing worrisome dilemmas for the agencies. Also, there were no traces of the expected negativity. However, the situation of multiple accountability did create some room for blame games. On the one hand agencies and boards often shared the conviction that the parent department was to blame for important flaws; on the other hand, parent departments sometimes used boards as lightning rods that were held responsible for policy crises.

Consequences

In the third phase of the accountability process, boards pass judgment on the conduct of agencies. Their judgment may have consequences, either through the use of formal sanctions or via informal channels, for instance "naming and shaming." Different respondents were asked if and how boards made use of their available sanctions. The minutes of meetings and other formal documents also were scanned for evidence of the use of formal sanctions by boards. This lead to a very clear conclusion: boards are reluctant to use their formal sanctions. The respondents indicated that sanctions hardly ever played an explicit role and that members of boards prefer to use informal methods such as persuasion or perhaps threats to steer agencies. Hood et al. (1999, 53) already noted that accountability forums prefer the use of lighter and informal sanctions above stronger and more formalized sanctions. However, the availability of stronger sanctions leaves forums the possibility to escalate, and actors and forums are fully aware of this possibility. Our research suggests that the same mechanism applies to the cases of boards of agencies: the boards with more far-reaching prerogatives (boards of Kadaster and Forest Authority) seemed to be more influential than the other boards.

Even though formal sanctions were scarcely used, our respondents still consider the relationship between agency and board as an accountability relationship. When asked, almost all respondents indicated that accountability was an important aspect of the role of boards. They thought accountability was an appropriate term because "the agency does have to defend its course of action" (R112), "they had to account for their actions" (R113), and managers "felt an obligation to account to the board" (R114).

The accountability to boards was thus understood to be important. At the same time, it was difficult to pinpoint the exact consequences of their role. The influence of boards is not always apparent. Respondents indicated that boards in general were influential. They were seen as important stakeholders of the organization whose advice was always accepted and implemented. When asked to give examples of the influence of boards, respondents were at a loss. Even though they insisted upon the importance of the boards they were not able to provide convincing examples to substantiate this belief.

This apparent inconsistency might be due to a number of causes. The first reason is that boards often meet with managers in the process of decision making. At that stage, decisions and documents are not finalized, and different concerned parties have their say on the nature of problems and the desirability of various courses of action. If boards are influential in the course of such processes, as indeed our respondents claim they are, it is very hard afterward to reconstruct when and where they were decisive. As one respondent said: "Their impact is difficult to measure as their work is not very visible for outsiders. If they do their job well, they will have influence on the ways our managers think, but this influence is hardly visible" (R86). This difficulty is further complicated because the dialogue managers and boards engage in is directed at reaching "agreement" (R86) or a "consensus" (R87). In the aftermath it is difficult to reconstruct who has been most influential in reaching a specific consensus. A final reason for the apparent difficulty to pinpoint the influence of boards is the fact that they do not operate on the basis of clearly specified norms. They rather prefer, as was described earlier, to stick to the agenda that agencies have laid out for themselves. As a result, the content of their oversight is experienced as a "reinforcement of what we already do" (R89). Put another way, "The bandwidth of their advice is usually quite close to the plans that were already developed" (R90).

Evaluation: Symbolic Accountability Rather than Loss of Control or Paralysis

In the evaluation of the consequences of multiple accountability through the addition of accountability to boards, three possible negative situations were predicted. To begin with, multiple accountability might paralyze decision makers. As there is no one course of action that satisfies all the relevant expectations from the multitude of accountability forums, decisions could be blocked. This is close to what Koppell has termed *multiple accountabilities disorder* (MAD). The accountability to boards of agencies, however, does not qualify as a case of MAD. As indicated earlier, the boards do not operate on a specified external agenda, and they have little inclination to contend with the board of management over decisions that are to be taken. The strongest risk for paralysis stems from the fact that boards sometimes antagonize the ministry over decisions. One respondent noted that this seems to be a "natural development, where we say: 'we are running this agency and the ministry shouldn't interfere so much'" (R230). Members of boards often express the view that the ministry is too deeply involved with the agency and that Parliament asks too detailed questions on the operations of the agency. This antagonism between board and ministry could in theory result in paralysis, as they both need to approve of all major decisions. In practice however, boards are not equipped to compete with ministries, and ministries are able to enforce their will on the agencies. The research shows a number of situations where there was a conflict between ministry and board (and agency) over a specific issue. In all of these cases the ministries won the conflict. In one case, for instance, an agency felt it was being forced by the ministry to make a risky investment in stock. The board clearly and strongly opposed this decision, of which it had to approve. Both the minutes of the meetings on the subject and the recollection of the involved respondents are very clear on this issue. However, in the end the agency did buy the property with the formal approval (yet personal disapproval) of the board. The powers of persuasion of the ministry had clearly been effective.

If boards do not block decisions by imposing accountability requirements on agencies that are too onerous, the opposite problem can occur: the additional accountability, paradoxically, can open up more space for strategic and "unaccountable" action for agencies. Our research finds some, though not very strong, evidence for this. Boards see it as their obligation to serve the interests of the agency, not the minister. This means, as noted earlier, that they usually side with the agency in times of conflict with the parent department. They sometimes operate as spokespersons of the agencies to the outside world. The managers of agencies are aware of this possibility and find it to be a positive thing. One general manager of an agency states: "It is really in our interest that the members of the board act as ambassadors of our organization in important external policy cycles. It is important that they say positive things about our organization and strengthen our image" (R117). The parent departments are also aware of this role of boards. One respondent says: "They also serve as elements of the lobby from these agencies" (R118). Boards thus sometimes operate as spokespersons on behalf of the agencies and try to create room to maneuver for agencies. In this respect, boards actually do contribute to lessening the burdens of agency accountability. However, as noted before, parent departments are fully capable to enforce their will on agencies if they prefer to do so. So the extra space for agencies through multiple accountability opens up only if the principals allow this to happen.

The final potential negative effect of multiple accountability is that it becomes purely symbolic and exhibits all of the external features of accountability but does not play a significant role in the governance of agencies. It would be harsh to conclude that the boards are only of symbolic value. As boards are evaluated in positive terms by most respondents, and boards do have influence on decisions, they are also significant. However, the fact that parent departments are willing and able to overrule boards if they find this necessary indicates that boards always run the risk of becoming symbolic and insignificant.

In the literature on multiple accountability there are many and sometimes contradictory accounts of the potential negative effects of multiple accountability. In the case of arm's-length agencies that are accountable to boards, this does not seem to be the case, perhaps due to the fact that in this specific setting there is a clear hierarchy of different forums. The powers and resources of the parent department are definitely stronger than those of the boards, and the boards fulfill a secondary role in the accountability regime of agencies—they operate in the shadow of hierarchy (Schillemans 2008).

MULTIPLE ACCOUNTABILITY AND THE BENEFITS OF REDUNDANCY

If multiple accountability may have positive *and* negative effects, the important follow-up question is: with which intellectual framework can we asses the practices of multiple accountability in order to address Salamon's (2002) accountability challenge: to develop a more pluralistic conception of accountability?

The preceding description of our cases shows that agencies account for the same topics and documents to their parent departments as they do their boards of commissioners. The multiple accountability forums thus assess the same issues and may come up with conflicting demands and have conflicting expectations. In addition, the different forums are also concerned with each other's actions. Parent departments regularly want to know how boards operate and how they assess specific situations, whereas boards display a keen interest in the political-strategic issues concerning the agencies. In sum, where a conventional perspective would hope for a division of labor among the different accountability forums in order to arrive at a balanced system, our findings suggest that overlap—redundancy—is what actually happens. And it is our contention that this is a result that also will be found in other situations of multiple accountability.

Redundant Accountability

In the past, some authors have argued that redundancy could be an important clue to understanding accountability in an age of fragmented governance (Braithwaite 1999; Scott 2000). The literature on redundancy is based on the classic research by Landau (1969), Wildavsky (1973), and Bendor (1985). Landau (1969) paved the way by arriving at a highly surprising positive answer to the question of whether it is possible to build reliable systems from unreliable parts. Landau argued that this was already the case in different levels of American public administration. The central argument for redundancy is that the reliability of systems increases when parts of the system compensate for flaws in other parts. As such, redundancy is a substitute for perfect parts. In later years, many authors argued that redundancy is vital in high-risk situations. They showed how redundancy is a key to the security systems of nuclear plants (Carroll 2004), the rapid recovery of the central offices of multinationals after the September 11 attacks (Stein 2002), or the "success" of the Manhattan Project (Bendor 1985). Overall, redundancy is often used as a device to protect that which is most valuable or vulnerable (Stein 2002).

The literature on redundancy clarifies that its importance grows in the face of complexity and insecurity; it provides an operational basis that creates possibilities of more flexible approaches (Landau 1969, 352; Bendor 1985, 54). It is for these reasons that some authors have underlined the significance of redundancy as a means to address the complexity and insecurities of accountability in situations of dispersed governance (Scott 2000; Mulgan 2003, 219). There may be some overlap or even competition between the different forums that cast a watchful eye on agencies, and the different forums may demand accountability from each other (Braithwaite 1999, 92). Behn (2001, 197–201), for instance, pleads for a regime of 360-degree accountability, in which every actor in a policy field may at some point account for his contribution to all of the others.

The Advantages of Redundancy

A number of advantages come to the fore if we apply the concept of redundancy to our case of multiple accountability for agencies at arm's length from central government. First, redundancy may be the most pragmatic option, as actors apparently find it difficult to restrict their oversight to a limited number of topics. There is always a tendency to broaden their perspective: ministries demand to be informed about all sorts of operational details that no longer should be a concern, whereas boards want to be informed about political developments in which they formally should not be involved. The members of boards indicate that it is always "tempting" (R299) to discuss any pressing issue with which an agency is confronted, whether or not the board has a formal position on the subject. As the respondents indicated: "We simply discuss all the important issues." Such an expansion in perspective has also been described for other forums. Pollitt et al. (1999) describe how different national courts of audit have expanded their focus by developing "performance auditing." The tendency of forums to expand their focus seems to be a natural development. Accepting this tendency diminishes the costs of coordination among different forms of accountability. The advantage is that redundancy may actually be a cheaper option than the conventional approach that aims at a balanced system (Wildavsky 1973, 143).

A second and arguably more important advantage of redundant accountability is that it mitigates the inherent information asymmetry between actors and forums. As actors naturally have more information on themselves than others have, information asymmetry is one of the archetypical problems of accountability (Strøm 2000). Forums are often partially dependent on information that is controlled by actors. But if there is a multiplicity of information demands, with overlap and some competition among the different sources of information, more information is "pressed" from agencies (Bendor 1985, 257), and this has a reassuring effect on accountability forums (Carroll 2004).

Each of the above advantages was found in our case. The boards are indeed seen as reassuring devices by departmental respondents, who stated that boards were "early warning systems." They were expected to help signal problematic developments as soon as they occurred by broadening the informational basis of the ministries. As one departmental respondent said: "For our minister, the board is an extra safeguard that enhances his trust in the agency" (R98). In addition, boards produce additional information on the agencies through oral and informal communications and through their formal policy advice, which increases the available information on the conduct of the agencies. Particularly significant is the fact that they have to approve of certain important decisions and give advice on other issues. A departmental respondent states:

We would consider a negative advice from the board as a very serious signal. Because we expect the agencies to do everything they can to prevent such a thing to happen, so if it in fact does happen, this should be a situation that we must consider very seriously. (R35)

A third advantage of a redundant accountability regime is that it provides the opportunity to incorporate different values that are embodied in many public policies. If we look at the tasks of different agencies, it is clear that diverse and possibly conflicting values are relevant to their work. Monolithic structures are ill adapted to deal with conflicting values and conflicting interests (Bendor 1985, 255). A redundant multiple accountability regime creates the possibility to embody diverse and important values within a regime. As Scott argues: "We should not iron out conflict, but exploit it in order to hold regimes in appropriate tension" (2000, 57).

Our research shows a number of situations where redundant, multiple accountability created the opportunity to express multiple, relevant values. The most telling example is provided by the State Forest Authority. In past years, the Forest Authority has repeatedly been criticized for the deaths of cattle and wild horses in one of their nature reserves. In the specific area, Parliament had ordered the Forest Authority to create a natural environment that was to be maintained without human intervention (clearly a contradictory order). As a result, natural selection was left to regulate the life spans of animals in the reserve. When animals actually die in larger numbers, which occurs in cold winters, the Forest Authority is scorned by environmentalist groups *and* members of Parliament. In their accountability to the minister, the Forest Authority also has to explain why the unwanted outcomes occur. As a contrast to this incident-oriented form of accountability, the accountability to the board on this issue is of a very different nature. The board accepts the policy of human abstention as a point of departure, but urges the agency to find methods of communication that increase the public acceptance of their policy.

BALANCING OVERLOADS AND REDUNDANCY

In recent years, many authors have acknowledged multiple accountability as a salient and problematic issue. Multiple accountability is often seen as a challenge to the promises of accountability and is often almost a synonym for *accountability overload*. An examination of the practices of multiple accountability of large, executive agencies in the Netherlands, however, warrants a more nuanced perspective. Our empirical research did indeed point at a number of problems, notably opportunity costs, blame games, and symbolic accountability, but these problems were found to be rather moderate. In addition, a number of benefits through redundancy came to the fore. Specifically, the increased level of information through multiple accountability is beneficial, as was the fact that redundant accountability mechanisms provide the possibility to embody several legitimate values. We therefore conclude that under conditions such as those found in our cases, where hierarchical control of professional bureaucracies is challenged and multiple, competing values are at issue, and redundant accountability is probably valuable. It is a partial answer to Salamon's accountability challenge with which we started. It provides a more pluralistic perspective on accountability that aims to tackle the more pluralistic practices of contemporary governance.

REFERENCES

Adelberg, S. and C.D. Batson. 1978. "Accountability and Helping. When Needs Exceed Resources." *Journal of Personality and Social Psychology* 36: 343–50.

Behn, R.D. 2001. *Rethinking Democratic Accountability*. Washington, DC: Brookings Institution Press.

Bendor, J. 1985. *Parallel Systems: Redundancy in Government*. Berkeley: University of California Press.

Bovens, M. 1998. *The Quest for Responsibility: Accountability and Citizenship in Complex Organisations.* Cambridge, UK: Cambridge University Press.

———. 2007. "Analysing and Assessing Accountability: A Conceptual Framework." *European Law Journal* 13 (4): 447–68.

———. 2010. "Two Concepts of Accountability: Accountability as a Virtue and as a Mechanism." *West European Politics* 33 (5): 946–67.

Braithwaite, J. 1999. "Accountability and Governance Under the New Regulatory State." *Australian Journal of Public Administration* 58: 90–3.

Carroll, J.S. 2004. "Redundancy as a Design Principle and an Operating Principle." *Risk Analysis* 24 (4): 955–57.

Considine, M. 2002. "The End of the Line? Accountable Governance in the Age of Networks, Partnerships, and Joined-Up Services." *Governance* 15 (1): 21–40.

Day P., and R. Klein. 1987. *Accountabilities: Five Public Services.* London: Tavistock Publications.

Dowdle, M. 2006. *Public Accountability: Designs, Dilemmas and Experiences.* Cambridge, UK: Cambridge University Press.

Dubnick, M.J. 2005. "Seeking Salvation for Accountability." Paper presented at the Accountable Governance International Research Colloquium at the Institute of Governance, Queen's University Belfast, Ireland, 20–22 October.

Ebrahim, A.S., and E. Weisband. 2007. *Global Accountabilities: Participation, Pluralism, and Public Ethics.* Cambridge, UK: Cambridge University Press.

Finer, H. 1941. "Administrative Responsibility in Democratic Government." *Public Administration Review* 1: 335–50.

Flinders, M. 2001. *The Politics of Accountability in the Modern State.* Burlington, VT: Ashgate.

Friedrich, C.A. 1940. "Public Policy and the Nature of Administrative Responsibility." In *Public Policy,* ed. C.J. Friedrich, and E.S. Mason. Cambridge, MA: Harvard University Press: 3–24.

Halachmi, A. 2002. "Performance Measurement: A Look at Some Possible Dysfunctions." *Work Study* 51 (5): 230–39.

Hood, C. 2002. "The Risk Game and the Blame Game." *Government and Opposition* 37 (1): 15–37.

Hood, C., O. Scott, O. James, G. Jones, and T. Travers. 1999. *Regulation Inside Government: Waste-Watchers, Quality Police, and Sleazebusters.* Oxford: Oxford University Press.

Keohane, R.O. 2002. "Political Accountability." Paper presented at the Conference on Delegation to International Organizations, Park City, UT, 3–4 May.

Klingner, D.E., J. Nalbandian, and B.S. Romzek. 2002. "Politics, Administration and Markets: Conflicting Expectations of Accountability." *American Review of Public Administration* 32 (2): 117–44.

Koppell, J.G. 2005. "Pathologies of Accountability: ICANN and the Challenge of 'Multiple Accountabilities Disorder.'" *Public Administration Review* 65 (1): 94–109.

Landau, M. 1969. "Redundancy, Rationality and the Problem of Duplication and Overlap." *Public Administration Review* 29: 346–58.

Lerner, J.S., and P.E Tetlock. 1999. "Accounting for the Effects of Accountability." *Psychological Bulletin* 125 (2): 255–75.

Miller, G.J. 2005. "The Political Evolution of Principal-Agent Models." *Annual Review of Political Science* 8: 203–25.

Moe, T. 1984. "The New Economics of Organization." *American Journal of Political Science* 28: 739–77.

Mulgan, R. 2000. "Accountability: An Ever Expanding Concept?" *Public Administration* 78: 555–73.

———. 2003. *Holding Power to Account. Accountability in Modern Democracies.* Basingstoke, England: Palgrave MacMillan.

O'Connell, L. 2005. "Program Accountability as an Emergent Property: The Role of Stakeholders in a Program's Field." *Public Administration Review* 65 (1): 85–93.

Pollitt, C. 2003. *The Essential Public Manager.* London: Open University Press/McGraw-Hill.

Pollitt, C., X. Girre, J. Lonsdale, R. Mul, H. Summa, and M. Waerness. 1999. *Performance or Compliance? Performance Audit and Public Management in Five Countries.* Oxford: Oxford University Press.

Pollitt, C., C. Talbot, J. Caulfield, and A. Smullen. 2004. *Agencies: How Governments Do Things through Semi Autonomous Organisations.* Basingstoke, England: Palgrave MacMillan.

Posner, P.L. 2002. "Accountability Challenges of Third-Party Government." In *The Tools of Government: A Guide to the New Governance,* ed. L.M. Salamon. Oxford: Oxford University Press, 523–51.

Przeworski, A., S. Stokes, and B. Manin. 1999. *Democracy, Accountability, and Representation.* Cambridge, UK: Cambridge University Press.

Romzek, B.S. 1996. "Enhancing Accountability." In *Handbook of Public Administration,* ed. J.L. Perry. San Francisco: Jossey-Bass, 97–114.

Romzek, B.S., and M.J. Dubnick. 1998. "Accountability." In *International Encyclopedia of Public Policy and Administration,* Vol. 1: A–C, ed. J.M. Shafritz. Boulder, CO: Westview Press.

Salamon, L.M. 2002. "The New Governance and the Tools of Public Action: An Introduction." In *The Tools of Government: A Guide to the New Governance,* ed. L.M. Salamon. Oxford: Oxford University Press, 1–47.

Schillemans, T. 2007. *Verantwoording in de schaduw van de macht. Horizontale verantwoording bij zelfstandige uitvoeringsorganisaties.* Den Haag: Lemma.

———. 2008. "Accountability in the Shadow of Hierarchy: The Horizontal Accountability of Agencies." *Public Organization Review* 8 (2): 175–94.

Scott, C. 2000. "Accountability in the Regulatory State." *Journal of Law and Society* 27: 38–60.

Stein, J.G. 2002. "Bad Translation or Double Standard? Productivity and Accountability Across the Private, Public and Voluntary Sectors." *The Review of Economic Performance and Social Progress* 2: 259–75.

Strøm, K. 2000. "Delegation and Accountability in Parliamentary Democracies." *European Journal of Political Research* 37: 261–89.

Tetlock, P.E., L. Skitka, and R. Boettger. 1989. "Social and Cognitive Strategies for Coping with Accountability: Conformity, Complexity and Bolstering." *Journal of Personality and Social Psychology* 57: 632–40.

Thatcher, M., and A. S. Sweet. 2002. "Theory and Practice of Delegation to Non-Majoritarian Institutions." In *West European Politics* 25 (1): 1–22.

van Thiel, S. 2000. *Quangocratization: Trends, Causes, Consequences.* Utrecht, Netherlands: Interuniversity Center for Social Science Theory and Methodology.

Wildavsky, A. 1973. "If Planning Is Everything, Maybe It's Nothing." *Policy Sciences* 4: 27–153.

2

THE TANGLED WEB OF ACCOUNTABILITY IN CONTRACTING NETWORKS

The Case of Welfare Reform

BARBARA S. ROMZEK

WELFARE REFORM AND CONTRACT NETWORKS

The confluence of several broad trends in government reform and welfare policy in the United States presents significant challenges for governance and accountability. These trends include privatization, welfare reform, and a heightened concern for accountability. Reform of the U.S. welfare system in the mid-1990s gave American states greater flexibility in providing welfare services to needy clients, by allowing many states to adopt social-services contracting as part of their expanded discretion.[1] Contracts for welfare services typically involve extended networks across the public, nonprofit, and for-profit sectors. Of course, while the exact nature of welfare reform considered in this chapter may be unique to the United States, the trends of attention to government reform and heightened interest in accountability are not limited to the American context. Privatization as a government reform strategy has enjoyed support around the globe (Considine 2002; Entwistle and Martin 2005; Hodge and Greve 2005; Mulgan 1997; Young 2000).

Providing effective services to clients is especially complex in the context of welfare reform, where clients' needs are multifaceted and involve complicated interdependencies. The range of services needed is typically beyond the scope of any one nongovernmental organization, which is why service providers tend to rely on networks (Agranoff and McGuire 1998; Freundlich and Gertzenzang 2002; Johnston and Romzek 2008; Lamothe and Lamothe 2008; Meyers et al. 2001; Milward and Provan 2000; Van Slyke 2003).[2] Networks are "structures of interdependence involving multiple organizations or parts thereof, where one unit is not merely the formal subordinate of the others in some larger hierarchical arrangement" (O'Toole 1997, 45). The focus of organizational networks is to accomplish complex tasks collectively where "more than one organization is dependent on another to perform a task" (McGuire 2002, 600). In theory, contracts for social services hold great promise of accountability because they rely on market forces and contract designs that stipulate in advance roles, deliverables, performance standards, and reporting obligations, all of which provide a source of contractor discipline. In fact, arguments for contracting often are couched in terms of improving accountability. In practice, accountability is a challenge under the simplest administrative arrangements. Thus, the challenges of accountability are especially complex when administrative structures include a networked policy arena.

Successful contracting requires effective network structures (which specify how organizations are linked in their task responsibilities) and effective interpersonal interactions among managers across organizational boundaries. These interpersonal interactions, what O'Toole and Meier (2004) call managerial networking, are essential to make the network structures function successfully. The reliance on contracting and on networks to deliver services results in a tangled web of accountabilities involving numerous actors, who must deal with multiple expectations from several stakeholders, as well as with many overlapping accountability relationships. The result is an arena characterized by a series of bilateral and multilateral ties at both organizational and individual levels that involve a tangled web of accountability relationships. This web is characterized by multiple vertical and horizontal accountability structures, which reflect both formal and informal accountability relationships. Network actors in contract arrangements must navigate this web of accountability, while seeking to reconcile diverse and occasionally conflicting performance expectations and especially challenging performance outcomes and monitoring activities. The reliance on networks of service providers and the presence of both formal and informal accountability ties makes it even harder for both the monitoring agencies and service recipients to pinpoint responsibility and achieve the transparency needed for effective accountability. The discussion that follows provides an overview of the complexity of the tangled web of accountability present for contracts in a networked policy arena.

ACCOUNTABILITY AND CONTRACT NETWORKS

While the concern for accountability is a perennial one in American government, accountability of public officials and public managers has been a matter of heightened interest and rhetoric in the past few decades. This trend has been characterized as an "accountability craze," leading scholars to the observation that some of the new "beefed up" accountability regimes are so complex that they defeat the very purpose they were intended to accomplish and increase the possibility of unintended, negative effects (Bovens and 't Hart 2005). The accountability dynamics in the child-welfare policy arena are illustrative of such complexity.

The variety of conceptual approaches to accountability that has emerged reflects strategic and/ or instrumental definitions of the term (Dubnick 2005). One approach emphasizes accountability as answerability, with the notion of a principal-agent relationship as the fundamental anchor, and recognizes the possibility of differing logic and compounded agency problems (Bovens et al. 2008; Brehm and Gates 1997; Trailer et al. 2004). Another approach emphasizes accountability as reflecting a variety of institutional contexts, involving the management of expectations from numerous sources, and utilizing a range of reporting relationships and mechanisms (Dicke and Ott 1999; Kearns 1996; Klingner et al. 2002; Romzek and Dubnick 1987; Weber 1999). While both approaches can shed light on accountability dynamics, the latter approach best captures the complexity of accountability in networked policy arenas.

Accountability dynamics include the challenge of "many hands" in administrative processes; often it is difficult to identify who has contributed—and how—to the relevant performance, and who should be answerable for the outcomes (Thompson 1980). This challenge is even more complicated in network contracting situations because of the many institutional and individual hands (contractors and subcontractors) involved across multiple sectors. This situation creates the potential for "compounded agency problems," where the public organization and the contracting firm may each benefit from contract arrangements, but at the "expense of consumer welfare;" in such cases, the cost may be in diminished service quality to the target clients or higher cost to the general public paying for the services through taxes (Trailer et al. 2004, 314; Frederickson and Frederickson 2006). The "many hands" problem can exacerbate perceptions of accountability shortcomings for stakeholders located outside the focal network. For example, in Kansas, officials report that legislators continue to hear the same complaints about child-welfare services that they heard before contracting but that it is harder now to pin down an accountable agent. Unlike earlier times, when an agency head was the obvious focus, "legislators don't feel that they have anyone to hold accountable when they get complaints . . . [because] there are a lot of actors in child welfare, by design. So there's no one person who can impose his or her own mode. There is not one person who can jerk kids out of a home without good cause . . . [because] we have many hands involved. . . ."

A variety of factors make accountability difficult to accomplish. Some reasons are related to the structure of accountability relationships (Light 1995; Radin 1998, 2006); others have to do with the clarity and consistency of expectations for performance of the numerous stakeholders (Dubnick and Romzek 1993). Some challenges are associated with the appropriateness of the match between the performance expectations/responsibilities and the mechanisms/relationships used to accomplish accountability (Romzek and Dubnick 1987). And other challenges have to do with the effective implementation of accountability mechanisms/relationships and the political will to impose consequences (Romzek and Johnston 2005; Van Slyke 2007).

To fully understand the dynamics of accountability within contracted network arrangements, one must consider the institutional context within which accountability structures and behaviors are embedded. Contract networks function within both formal and informal accountability relationships, and network actors face the challenge of reconciling the needs of multiple stakeholders, diverse expectations, and varying organizational missions and roles, while implementing complex service-delivery protocols. Network members who succeed at this reconciliation can develop a culture of mutual accountability reflected in congruent goals and shared values, as well as a recognition of interdependencies, reciprocity, and trust among contract network actors.

Institutional Context

Several key institutional features affect the prospects for accountability of contract networks in the child welfare policy arena. These include market conditions, the clarity of contract design, and the multiplicity of key actors and stakeholders within a network.

Market Conditions

The degree of market competition is a key environmental condition for contracting (Sclar 2000). Contracting with nongovernmental entities is based on an assumption that market competition will act as a brake on opportunistic behavior on the part of contractors and function as a force for accountability. Unfortunately market competition in social services cannot be taken for granted (Lamothe and Lamothe 2008; Prager 1994; Sclar 2000; Van Slyke 2003). Competitive, truly private markets typically do not exist for social services. The lack of competition makes effective accountability more difficult than usual because a lack of alternative providers leaves governmental agencies with little latitude to change contractors if performance is unacceptable (Johnston and Romzek 2000).

Moreover, the presence of market competition is not a guarantee that competition will enhance accountability or result in quality services. For example, in Florida, the presence of competitors did not result in greater pressure for contractors to adhere to contract terms (Lamothe and Lamothe 2008). And situations where there are competitive, market-like environments can lead to contract churning—when contractors are replaced in subsequent bid cycles (Romzek and Johnston 2005). Changes in contractors typically result in significant transition costs and often disrupt service continuity and outcomes for clients (U.S. Department of Health and Human Services 2007).

Clarity of Contract Design

The nature of welfare services and the interdependencies of client needs are such that it is often difficult to design contracts that stipulate performance standards clearly and concisely (U.S. Department of Health and Human Services 2007).[3] Clearly delegated responsibilities, as well as carefully stipulated performance measures and the monitoring of protocols can facilitate accountability, but these measures may be difficult to achieve in child welfare services. Evidence of difficulties can be seen in the frequent revisions to program design and performance standards that are made (often through negotiation) after social service contracts have been awarded (Romzek and Johnston 2005). As state administrators and contract officials get more experience with the service-contract area, they are better able to align service objectives and performance rewards and target services to clients (Heinrich and Choi 2007).

Multiple Key Actors, Stakeholders, and Expectations

Networks involve a multitude of participants who bring a wide range of roles, interests, and expertise to the contract arena. The network structure provides a framework for the interaction of these participants.

Multiple Key Actors. The contracting arena relevant to child welfare policy involves several levels of government as well as nonprofit and for-profit contractors who constitute the key actors. The federal government mandates the terms and conditions of welfare policy for the states, provides funding, and grants states waivers to established policy. The states, in their turn, petition the federal government for waivers, cost share with the federal government, and design and implement contracts for welfare services. Services are then delivered by third-party organizations who contract to serve as designated agents of the states; these can include local governments, nonprofits, and for-profit organizations. In each instance, there is formal accountability reporting relationships at work: states reporting to federal government, nonprofit contractors reporting to the state, and subcontractors reporting to contractors. These networks tend to involve numerous partners and/ or subcontractors with different but complementary missions, organizational agendas, and service delivery protocols. For example, in the state of Kansas (with a small population of 2.1 million) five different contracts are awarded for foster care and adoption services, each with a multitude of subcontractors; any one child/client could conceivably require services from as many as seven different subcontractors. In some instances, subcontractors (those with larger geographical reach or specialized services) participate in several contract networks (see Figure 2.1). In the more populous state of Florida (18 million), the state employs twenty lead contractors for child welfare and over 500 subcontractors (Armstrong et al. 2007).

Multiple Stakeholders and Diverse Expectations. Each key actor in the contracting arena operates within an institutional context of numerous stakeholder groups who have an interest in the policy arena. Stakeholders vary for different key actors, of course, but they typically include elected officials, other government agencies within the policy arena, child welfare advocacy groups, professional associations in the relevant fields (e.g., health care, mental health, public safety, education, social welfare), network employees, other organizations in the contract network, and the families and children who are the targeted clientele. Each stakeholder group has expectations for how the key actors should carry out their conferred responsibilities. The multitude of stakeholders in the pluralistic American context ensures that the expectations of these stakeholders will be diverse

Figure 2.1   **Examples of Accountability Ties Among Foster Care and Adoption Service Contracting Network for One Child-Client in Kansas.***

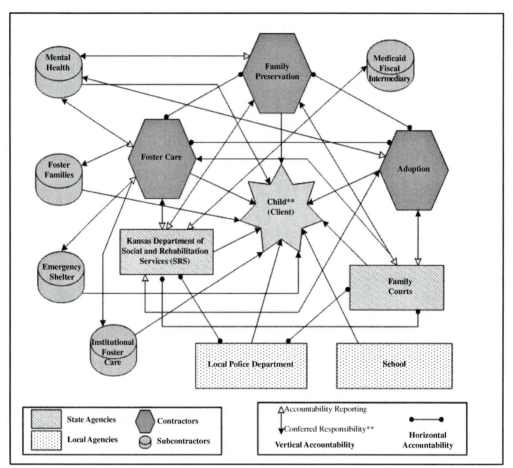

Typical Sequence of Action:

SRS receives initial complaint, investigates, and makes recommendation regarding removal from the home.

- Local police take custody of child for the state.
- Family Court judges review and decide whether to accept recommendation for removal from the home. Courts monitor child's case management by child welfare contractors until child is reintegrated into family, adopted, or reaches the age of majority (18 yrs.).
- Primary child welfare contractor (foster care, family preservation, or adoption) accepts custody of the child within 24 hours of removal from the home, decides on placement (either emergency shelter, institutional foster care of family foster care setting), assesses mental and physical health needs, and arranges for the necessary services to be provided, either in house or through subcontracts.
- SRS monitors overall performance of primary child welfare contractors.
- Medicaid Fiscal Intermediary, through separate contract with SRS, reimburses subcontractors for physical and mental health services.
- Child-client's school will interact with all state agencies, contractors, and subcontractors, as necessary.
- In this diagram, connections between Foster Care contractor and other service providers are illustrative of case in which child-client requires all available services. Some of these connections (especially for physical, mental health, and family preservation services) could also exist for other contractors (Family Preservation and/or Adoption).

* Adapted from Johnston and Romzek, 2008.

** State agencies, contractors and subcontractors each are expected to be attentive to the needs and rights of clients, reflecting a responsiveness standard under political accountability (Dubnick and Romzek, 1987).

***Conferred responsibilities in contract stipulations.

and often conflicting (Dubnick and Romzek 1993). The accountability challenge for network key actors at each level of the contract regime is to manage their accountability reporting and conferred responsibilities. They must accommodate diverse and conflicting expectations while pursuing their separate organizational missions and goals as well as their collective network missions and goals (Kenis and Provan 2007; Provan and Milward 2001; Radin and Romzek 1996). These dynamics are most important when ambiguity exists about service provision (Whitaker et al. 2004), a circumstance that often is present in social services.

Network Structure. The presence of so many key actors necessitates administrative arrangements to structure the interaction among these separate entities. Sometimes a state agency will make a conscious decision to create a network, for example, when it chooses to "bundle previously separate but interrelated service contracts into a few lead agency contracts" (Lamothe and Lamothe 2008, 2). Contracting networks for child welfare services typically are structured around two kinds of lead organizations: lead state agencies and lead contractor organizations.[4] A lead state agency's role is to manage the contract in all its aspects, which includes developing pre-contract cost estimates, contract design and award processes, and post-award contract monitoring and accountability. In other instances, networks are created by nongovernmental contractors who recognize the need for partners to construct a competitive bid in response to a Request for Proposal. In such cases, contractors enter into subcontracts with numerous local service providers and become lead contractors of networks of service providers (Kenis and Provan 2007). Cooperating organizations in a child welfare contracting network typically include local service providers in the areas of education, housing, welfare, mental health, juvenile justice, substance abuse, and the courts.

Management of Interorganizational Behaviors

Structures that identify network roles and responsibilities make accountability possible, but the behavior of network participants, especially the management of network relationships (O'Toole and Meier 2004), is another essential component of the accountability dynamic. The intra- and interorganizational behaviors of individual network participants play a significant role in effective network service delivery and accountability, especially those behaviors within participants' respective zones of discretion that address conferred responsibilities.

As with bilateral relations, effective network collaboration includes mutual articulation and mapping of expectations, monitoring and measuring progress and performance, and adapting as circumstances warrant. The interorganizational task is to have network members embrace network relations and measure organizational performance by their separate and collective service outcomes for clients. This approach enables them to reach beyond their home organizational boundaries without threatening existing administrative arrangements (Radin and Romzek 1996).

Trust is key to maintaining good relationships in contracting networks (Edelenbos and Klijn 2007; Isett and Provan 2005; Van Slyke 2007); it serves as the basis for decision making within agencies that strive for effective collaboration. Trust is both an important precondition for interorganizational cooperation as well as an outcome of it. Trust facilitates network success and creates norms of reciprocity and social capital for future collaboration (Roberts 2002; Romzek et al. 2009).

Network actors use skills that complement those required in direct-service operations. Network actors engage in collaboration, negotiation, conflict resolution, cultivation of trust, and management of tensions between member and collective network goals (Agranoff and McGuire 1998,

2004; Frederickson and Frederickson 2006; Kettl 2002; Klijn and Koppenjan 2000; O'Toole and Meier, 2004). Network actors must be able to sustain relationships and negotiate successfully in an environment of multilateral ties and shifting responsibilities and roles. The management challenge of networks is to find common ground among the separate organizational missions, cultures, and service delivery protocols of network members (Kenis and Provan 2007; Milward and Provan 2006; Svennson et al. 2008).

The management challenges in networks include cultivating shared goals, developing trust, and fostering a culture of collaboration (Ansell and Gash 2008). Shared goals enable organizations to reconcile their separate and collective missions. Goal congruence is especially difficult when organizational systems are as complex as welfare service networks tend to be (Meyers et al. 2001).[5] Successful collaboration in a network depends upon commitment of network members to the joint effort (as individuals and/or as organizations), through contributions of time, information, resources, creative strategizing, and collaborative efforts. Goal congruence, shared values, recognition of mutual interdependence, reciprocity and trust will foster a culture of mutual accountability; such accountability will be based upon dialog that determines responsibilities, authorizes discretion, establishes reporting procedures, and creates review processes (Whitaker et al. 2004). The resulting collaboration can foster creative problem solving when clients present particularly difficult cases (Bardach and Lesser 1996).

Market conditions, contract design, network structures, and network behaviors are key features of contract regimes. Each contributes to operations along the chain of conferred responsibilities and network dynamics that are characteristic of accountability within contract networks in the child welfare arena. These complex dynamics make it clear that accountability is not self-executing. Purposeful effort must be expended if accountability is to be achieved. And both formal and informal accountability relationships are inevitably at work in such settings. Sometimes they reinforce each other, but at other times they can undermine each other.

TANGLED WEB OF ACCOUNTABILITY RELATIONSHIPS

Accountability relationships in social service contracting constitute a web of multiple and overlapping accountabilities that are even more complex than the service delivery networks themselves. There are numerous stakeholders, diverse and conflicting expectations, delegations of complex responsibilities, multiple accountable actors, a varied assortment of accountability reporting structures and relationships, and a diverse range of potential consequences (rewards and/or sanctions). For example, the list of accountability reporting ties among key actors in a contract network of service providers is fairly lengthy; it typically includes ties between the federal government and the states, the lead state agencies and their various lead contractors, the lead state agencies and the contractor network as a whole, the lead contractors and each of their numerous subcontractors. In addition, ties exist among network subcontractors (peers or partners) and between the lead state agency and various subcontractors. Each of these key actors brings his or her separate stakeholder expectations and organizational agendas and assumes different responsibilities within the contract regime.

Some of these accountability ties are based on formal agreements and reflect vertical and horizontal accountability structures, such as contracts and memoranda of understanding. Other ties are based on informal mutual, reciprocal accountability resulting from shared bilateral and multilateral expectations and obligations (Romzek et al. 2009). The picture that emerges is a tangled web of accountability. The very presence of so many accountability ties makes it difficult to identify transparent relationships, responsibilities, and performance.

When contracting involves networks of service providers, it is a challenge to map the tangled web of accountability relationships. To illustrate this complexity visually, Figure 2.2 depicts a highly simplified scenario of both vertical and horizontal accountability relationships when a hypothetically few (four) lead contractors maintain networks of subcontractors to provide services for clients within separate geographically defined areas. For visual parsimony the diagram does not map all the potential horizontal accountability relationships that could exist among subcontractors.

Formal Accountability

Formal accountability relationships are the kind of accountability mechanisms that are most familiar. They can include both vertical and horizontal structures and are manifested in reporting relationships and conferred responsibilities outlined in contract stipulations about the roles, responsibilities, and performance expectations of relevant parties. Such ties typically involve principal-agent relationships based on contracts and subcontracts that specify roles, performance expectations, and obligations. Conferred responsibilities (to provide services on behalf of the contract principal) constitute the basis for expectations of answerability for performance through established reporting structures.

Most manifestations of formal vertical accountability structures are well recognized in the literature. For example, research has identified several types of accountability in use in contracting situations, including legal, professional, political, and hierarchical relationships (Bardach and Lesser 1996; Johnston and Romzek 1999; Moon and Welch 2000; Romzek and Johnston 2005). Legal accountability, in the form of audits and other means of external monitoring, are the preferred methods for government agencies to maintain accountability of nonprofit contractors (Dicke and Ott 1999), such as an audit for compliance with conditions for receipt of federal funds.[6] Other examples of external monitoring include legislative oversight hearings, periodic detailed case reviews, monitoring of staff certifications, reviews of client event reports, verification that the provider has national accreditation, and conduct of client surveys (Shively 2006; U.S. Department of Health and Human Services 2008). Professional accountability is manifested in the concerns about professional certification of staff and reliance on contract service delivery protocols that defer to case managers to develop plans of care and deliver appropriate services for child welfare clients. Political accountability is reflected in efforts to measure contractor responsiveness to client needs, sometimes through client-satisfaction surveys. Hierarchical accountability is evident in contracts that stipulate the internal operations of the contractor or subcontractors, such as in prescribed service delivery protocols and/or staffing ratios. In a social service contracting milieu contract-network actors often have direct accountability ties with the target clients. The lead state agency, contractors, and subcontractors are each expected to be attentive to the needs and rights of clients and in doing so they reflect another accountability "tie," this one based upon the responsiveness standard of political accountability (Romzek and Dubnick 1987).

Examples of formal horizontal accountability structures include partnership agreements and memoranda of understanding that stipulate commitments for cooperation. These can address matters such as the sequencing of services to clients, interorganizational referral protocols, expectations regarding documentation, information sharing, and other collaborative activities that facilitate each organization's ability to provide appropriate services for clients. As agreements among network peers, accountability expectations and options for redress often involve negotiation and, in extreme circumstances, withdrawal from the collaborative arrangement. Such agreements can have considerable significance in facilitating collaboration and clarifying responsibilities. This latter task is an especially important one when breakdowns in collaborations result in service shortfalls

Figure 2.2 Illustration of Vertical and Horizontal Accountability Relationships for One Contract Program with Multiple Contractors

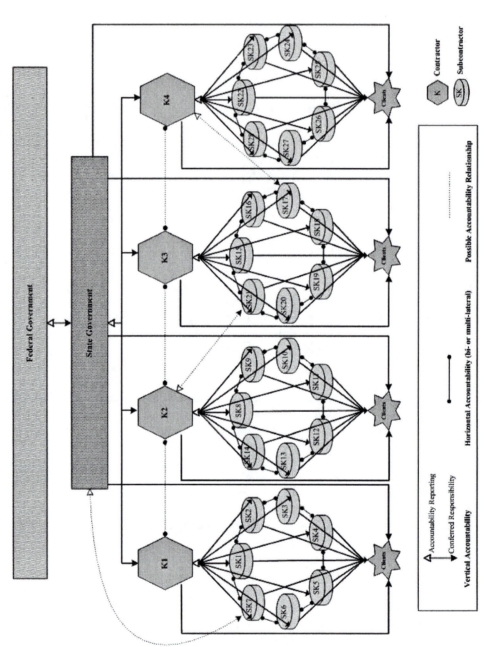

to a client. Then such agreements often become the basis for documenting (after the fact) which party had responsibility for the performance in question.

The likelihood of contractor accountability is enhanced if the terms of contract obligations and performance expectations of all relevant parties are clearly articulated in advance. In the area of social services contracting, client needs are sufficiently complex and interdependent that it is often difficult to write contracts with sufficient specificity regarding expectations, obligations, and performance standards (Behn and Kant 1999; Heinrich and Choi 2007; Lynn et al. 2000). As a result, the terms of social services contracts often require renegotiation after the contracts are awarded and once contractors have some experience working under the contract (Romzek and Johnston 2002; Sclar 2000; Schwartz 2005).

The record of success in imposing accountability based upon formal ties has been uneven because of inadequate performance monitoring and a lack of contract management expertise, often due to staff cutbacks (Frederickson and Frederickson 2006; Kettl 1993; Posner 2002; Van Slyke 2003). Government agencies' contract-management staff often lacks sufficient substantive knowledge of the policy arena to do an effective job monitoring contractor performance. Shortcomings in administrative capacity to monitor contracts in four cities in New York State resulted in poor monitoring, backlogs in accounting, and inadequate assessments of contractor expenditures and performance (Sanger 2003). Similar concerns have been raised about the quality of subcontractor monitoring in the State of Florida's system of contracting for child welfare services. Florida's state oversight agency noted the need for training for contract-monitoring staff, greater oversight of lead agencies to ensure compliance with contract provisions, and the need for lead-agency contractors to take on more responsibility for monitoring subcontractors (State of Florida 2006).

In some instances, program specialists with expertise in the policy arena have been asked to shift to contract management duties, sometimes with little training in contract management (Johnston and Romzek 2000). Often these duties are unwelcome as reflected in the following comment:

> Many of the people serving as CORs (contracting officer representatives) were hired by the government as scientists, logisticians and engineers, but are now being asked to manage contractors, . . . Too often CORs do not see this role and responsibility as the job they were hired to do, instead viewing it as a collateral duty or even worse. "It is not as valued inside their organizations, and thus not seen as a desirable role for federal managers to take on. Government has not put a premium on this job." (U.S. Government Accountability Office 2007, GA007–45SP, 14)

Such circumstances lead to a method of contract management that tends to focus on procedural and compliance issues rather than substantive performance or outcomes (Kettl 1993).

Contract monitoring can also be achieved by third parties. States often use other contractors to monitor contractor-network performance as a way to tap substantive expertise and capacity that the state agency lacks. Third-party monitoring to provide external assessments of contractors' performance allows states to acquire documentation regarding the quality of contractor performance, delivery of services to clients, and viability of performance measures. For example, the State of Florida outsourced oversight of its community-based child welfare contracts and created a pilot program that used a third-party contractor to develop outcome measures to assess contractors' performance and monitor it accordingly (State of Florida 2007b). As sometimes happens, the outside reviewer encountered significant problems getting the necessary data to perform the assessment. This in turn affected the oversight contractor's ability to meet its own contractual obligations.[7] The State of Kansas also used third-party contractors to evaluate its social service contracts. The contract evaluators encountered similar problems because of their reliance on service-delivery contractors to provide the evaluators with data to assess the Medicaid managed-care social service contract (State of Kansas 1999; Romzek and Johnston 2005).

Research indicates that when evidence exists of failure to meet performance expectations states infrequently impose sanctions. In both Florida and Kansas, the lead state agency made changes in contractors only in extreme circumstances, when financial difficulties compromised contractor performance (Armstrong et al. 2007; Romzek and Johnston 2005).[8] In short, while some of the difficulty in holding contractors accountable may be due to lack of effective monitoring, at other times it is due to lack of political will (Johnston and Romzek 1999; Posner 2002).

Informal Accountability

The relationships among network members are the most complicated and least transparent accountability terrain in networked settings. These relationships are created through formal vertical and horizontal contractual arrangements (contracts between lead contractors and subcontractors within the network) and informal interorganizational dynamics. Figure 2.3 provides a diagram of typical vertical and horizontal accountability ties within a contract network. While formal accountability relationships are the easier to map, informal and norm-based accountability can be a significant complement to formal accountability relationships. Informal accountability relationships are at least as important to effective network operations as formal accountability structures. Van Slyke's (2007) research on social welfare contracts found accountability relationships evolving from principal-agent relationships (with an emphasis on more formal accountability ties) toward more informal stewardship relationships over time. This pattern suggests that, in stable networks, informal accountability can play an increasingly significant role over time.

State agencies and nongovernmental contractors can develop a range of informal accountability relationships among key actors within the network through shared norms about organizational and individual working relationships and administrative practices. Network norms emerge when constructive engagements among professional or network peers result in recognition of interdependencies and the need for mutual accommodation to shared professional and institutional expectations (Acar et al. 2008; Bardach and Lesser 1996; Bottom et al. 2006; Huang and Provan 2007; Isett and Provan 2005; Whitaker et al. 2004).[9] Informal norms and interorganizational dynamics lead to the development of reciprocal relationships and a sense of partner accountability (Bardach and Lesser 1996; Whitaker et al. 2004; Romzek et al. 2009). Bardach and Lesser (204) "conjecture that professional norms, interpersonal loyalties, and a shared desire to work together in the future do more to promote peer accountability among partners than do more formal agreements." Partners can hold each other to account for performance by supplying or withholding network resources, such as frequent communication, reputation, cooperation, and leadership.

Intranetwork communication and collaboration are not always easy. There are often possibilities of intranetwork tension over organizational turf, conflicting expectations, disparate organizational agendas and administrative cultures, and tensions over performance standards and monitoring (Romzek and Johnston 1999). Sometimes partners do not collaborate, even though consultation is a widely held informal expectation in contracting arrangements and an important contributing factor in the development of a sense of partnership among network agencies. For example, the State of Kansas made changes in its foster care contract model, which had significant implications for contractor performance expectations, without consulting many of key stakeholders (i.e., judges, child-welfare workers, and families; Humphrey et al. 2006). While the state was well within its formal contractual authority to make these changes, the lack of consultation resulted in a significant

Figure 2.3 **Vertical and Horizontal Relationships Reflecting Formal and Informal Accountability Within One Contractor Network**

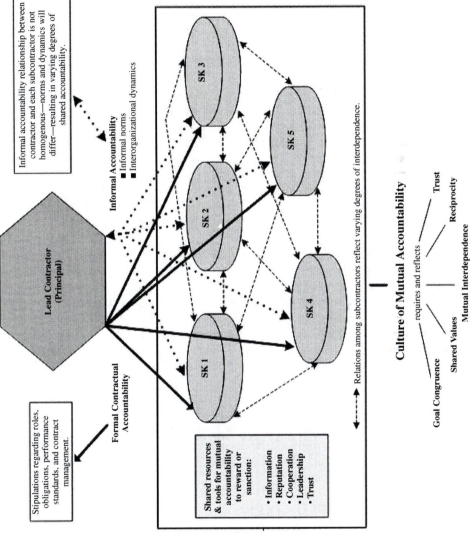

erosion of the sense of shared purpose among network members. To this date many state judges remain unconvinced that the system is an improvement over the precontract days.

The shared commitments and trust that help network members work together successfully can be subject to strain when mutual expectations are not met or when networks encounter membership turnover. When organizations join the contract network, time and effort must be spent integrating the new members into the shared norms and culture of the network as well as the relevant service protocols. When partners are not able to perform at an acceptable level, or when contracts are up for rebid, the sense of shared purpose and collaboration can be severely strained if not abandoned altogether. For example, relationships among network members can be disrupted by changes in contract roles in subsequent contract rebids. In Kansas some lead contractors failed to win lead contract renewals during a rebid cycle. As a result, lead contractors (in round one) became subcontractors (in round two) to network members who had been long-time peers or competitors. This shift in role significantly disrupted informal and formal network relationships, affecting interorganizational patterns of communication, collaboration, and dependence (Johnston and Romzek 2008).

Sometimes entrenched professional norms can undermine collaboration—for instance, when traditional thinking on the part of state administrators or entrenched professional monopolies work against informal collaboration (Considine 2002). Preexisting organizational cultures and network relationships occasionally are disrupted by contracts; when this happens informal norms can be counterproductive to network accountability. For example, in Kansas, a leading state administrator at the welfare agency observed that the state uses the language of collaboration in its communication with network contractors, but does not practice what it preaches: "Even ten years after the reform, most long-time staff members [at the lead state agency] do not really feel as though they are partners with the contractors. Instead they cling to the perspective that they are overseers of the contractors. They are most comfortable focusing on process rather than outcomes."

Many informal relationships among network actors (e.g., state agencies, contractors, and subcontractors) predate the creation of the contract network, and as a result continue to be relevant even when contract network arrangements put a lead contractor between the lead state agency and the subcontractor. Many subcontractors are able to sustain access to policy makers in the lead state agency and often retain the potential to contribute to deliberations regarding the relevant contracts.[10]

Clearly the organizational structures and interorganizational behaviors among network members reflect formal and informal relationships that result in a complex and tangled web of accountabilities. Together these various ties offer the potential for fulfilling the promise of accountability as both an external check on performance and an internal guide for ethical behavior in the exercise of discretion. But fulfilling that potential remains a significant challenge in contract networks due to the complexity of accountability ties.

TANGLED ACCOUNTABILITY IN CONTRACT NETWORKS

States have downsized their cumbersome, rule-bound public-welfare bureaucracies and created extensive networks of nongovernmental contractors delivering services on behalf of government. The pattern has been to implement contracting and work out the details of accountability as the programs are implemented. This approach is ironic in light of the current obsession with accountability, which has made transparency a popular buzzword in both political and administrative circles, and the fact that a key argument in support of contracting is greater accountability.

Accountability in government contracting requires careful monitoring when the contracts entail straightforward principal-agent relationships for goods or services that are easily measured. The accountability challenge increases significantly when the services under contract are social services to be delivered through multiparty networks of contractors and subcontractors. Some have argued that the drive toward contracting and market-driven modes of governance has worsened conditions of accountability and resulted in declining levels of trust (Haque 2001).

Welfare contracting networks operate within a tangled web of accountability ties encompassing formal agreements and informal ties, multiple actors, diverse expectations, shifting participants, changing roles, and challenging performance-measurement issues. These separate formal and informal accountability ties themselves are not really new on the scene. Rather, in contract networks, they are more dense and overlapping because of the service delivery interdependencies. Although the philosophy of American government embraces the notion that one can never have too much accountability, the reality is that multiple accountability relationships are not always conducive to transparency and effective performance, which are key characteristics of any successful accountability strategy. These complex network arrangements have the potential to undermine the very accountability they were designed to enhance (Bovens et al. 2008). Not only are "many hands" active in these networks, but there are also many strands of accountability within which the hands are expected to operate.

The challenges to effective accountability are greater in networks because of the potential for accountability to get "lost in the cracks of horizontal and hybrid governance" (Bovens et al. 2008, 240; Milward and Provan 2006) and because network settings provide "more opportunities for free riding as well as free wheeling, fewer reliable reporting mechanisms for political overseers and less overall clarity regarding expectations" (O'Toole 2000, 28). While the language of contracts for network service delivery may suggest bounded responsibilities and clear accountability expectations regarding delivery of client services, the boundaries for individual and organizational responsibility within those networks are often blurred.

The extensive use of contracting networks for welfare services has made transparency an even more elusive feature of welfare services delivery for clients and contracting principals (government monitors). This is an ironic outcome, since much of the campaign to shift to government contracting has been promoted under the banner of greater efficiencies and transparency. Without greater transparency, there is little basis for concluding that contracting has provided greater accountability. The picture that emerges from this overview of child welfare contract networks suggests that complexity in contract networks makes it difficult to document greater efficiencies and also compromises transparency and clarity about performance.[11]

While states have been persistent in their efforts to design and implement contracts that specify contractor performance and impose accountability, these efforts have fallen short, especially in the areas of measurement of performance, transparency of operations, and consequences for contractor performance shortfalls. Because the operations of these contracting networks are less transparent than earlier direct service delivery arrangements, they risk undermining the legitimacy of contracting and provide opportunities for other accountability shortcomings to emerge. For example, in his research on social-services contracting in the state of New York, Van Slyke (2003, 303) found close working relationships between state agency managers and nonprofit providers that "bordered on incestuous, implying that agency managers were so connected with nonprofit personnel that the contracting relationships were anything but competitive and objective."

The prevalence of tangled accountability relationships in networks of service providers makes it difficult to identify which agencies and/or individuals are responsible for which outcomes. This presents a challenge for practitioners as well as scholars. The operations of contract networks of multiple service providers linked through extended chains of contracts and subcontracts make the transparency of provider roles, obligations, and performance especially difficult to discern. As a result, contract-management challenges continue to be significant. Staffing patterns are such that oversight agencies often lack the necessary expertise to manage contracts, especially in areas of performance specification and contract monitoring. To the extent that contractors adopt a stewardship perspective toward their contract obligations and clients, government agencies may get the outcomes they seek in contract arrangements. But the tangled accountability picture makes it difficult for those government agencies to know whether that indeed is the case.

The usual response to concerns about accountability is to call for more precise measures of performance outcomes of contractors and subcontractors—for example, creating more structured relationships. Such an approach is valuable for understanding the formal aspects of accountability but will do little to shed light on the tangled web of accountability that includes both formal and informal accountability ties. There has been much fine work on formal accountability structures by scholars in the field; less attention has been devoted to informal accountability in the public management literature. A next step in this direction is to expand the focus on informal accountability to identify the behaviors of network organizations as well as individual network actors that facilitate a shift to a partner approach to pursue collective network goals. Such a shift would emphasize shared values, expectations, and outcomes and should lead to informal ties that promote mutual accountability for network outcomes (Austin, 2003; Romzek et al. 2009).

The dynamics of network accountability are still relatively opaque and warrant more focused research attention than they have received to date. The tangled web of network accountability presents both individuals and organizations within networks with cross-pressures of accountability that are more complicated than those experienced within traditional hierarchical organizations. It is important to recognize and map the complexity of this accountability terrain.

NOTES

The author is grateful for the research assistance provided by Jeannette Blackmat.

1. The Personal Responsibility and Work Opportunity Reconciliation Act (PRWORA) enacted major reform of the federal/state welfare system in 1996. It is also known as the 1996 Welfare Reform Act.

2. Two states that have been fairly ambitious in their effort to privatize child welfare services, Kansas and Florida, have used lead agencies to manage their child welfare networks. In each case the state social welfare agency awards contracts to a number of nonprofit entities for delivery of a complex array of child welfare services in their designated service areas. In Kansas, the number of child welfare contractors varies between three and five across five geographic service areas. In Florida the number has varied between 20 and 22. In turn these contractors develop extensive networks of service providers for their service catchment areas through a series of subcontracts.

3. Extensive research on performance measurement and performance management explores the complexities of this enduring challenge (Frederickson and Frederickson 2006; Radin 2006).

4. These organizations correspond to what Kenis and Provan (2007) identify as lead organization governed networks; they also identify two others types: participant governed networks and network administrative organizations.

5. Examples of tactics that can contribute to goal congruence and trust include holding regular meetings with local providers and state agencies involved in the service delivery network (such as children's mental health, juvenile justice, substance abuse, child welfare legal staff, and guardians ad litem). Such meetings can facilitate work on communication issues, conflict resolution, and proactive reviews of system-level challenges and individual cases (State of Florida 2007a).

6. For example, the Florida Department of Children and Families used an assessment that reviewed "organizational, operational, and program performance factors, each with established benchmarks for performance based on contractual, statutory, regulatory, or general industry standards. The assessments processes and procedures will establish an integrated approach to performance analysis and review, beginning at the

district/zone level. Standardized criteria for additional review or intervention will be established based on each provider's performance against established benchmarks" (State of Florida 2005, 12).

7. The State of Florida sought to help contractors and increase the likelihood of compliance by creating a multipurpose instrument called the Child Welfare Integrated Quality Assurance Tool (CWIQA) for child welfare programs (State of Florida 2005). Network contractors had not conducted the necessary and expected quality-assurance internal reviews nor had they conducted quality-assurance reviews of their subcontractors. These assurance reviews were to provide the data stipulated to be the basis for the third-party review (State of Florida 2008).

8. Two (of 22) lead contractor agencies in Florida lost their contracts due to financial difficulties; these changes did not result in any significant disruption of services because the lead agencies were not providing direct services (Lamothe and Lamothe 2008). To minimize chances these problems would arise in the future, the Florida Department of Children and Families developed a viability profile-screening tool for lead agencies based on performance measures that address the agency's ability to sustain oversight, community participation, staffing, program performance, financial position, and risk management (State of Florida 2005). When Kansas contractors experienced financial trouble, the effects cascaded onto other contract relationships. When one contractor went bankrupt, the state appealed to another contractor to take over the service contract for the bankrupt organization. The second contractor subsequently encountered financial difficulties as well, which in turn led to difficulties in service delivery for clients (Freundlich and Gertzenzang 2002; Legislative Division of Post Audit 2001; Romzek and Johnston 2005).

9. Network actors attest that occasionally the best faith efforts to accommodate network partner expectations can be for naught. For example, a contractor in Kansas voluntarily sought to align its organizational processes (employee incentives) and service delivery protocols to state contract expectations. The effort caused significant disruption for the contractor agency but it was seen as a way to maximize good service under the contract. Unfortunately, this example of an attempt to align organizational processes was for naught. Just as the contractor implemented changes in its reimbursement system to mirror contract expectations (at the start of the new fiscal year), the state unilaterally changed its contract terms (it reverted to an earlier model) to terms that were inconsistent with the newly implemented contractor incentive system. The effort caused significant disruption for the contractor and its workforce; and, of course it undermined the effort of the contractor to align its organizational procedures and incentives with the state contract.

10. Sometimes the best of intentions to find common ground are outstripped by a rapidly changing environment. Network actors attest that occasionally the best faith efforts to accommodate partner expectations can be for naught.

11. Globerman and Vining (1996) assert that an underlying premise for pursuing contracts should be to make clients better off than they were in the pre-reform era. Available evaluation research indicates that this goal is being met in child welfare contracting. Limited assessments available to date indicate that clients in these networks are reasonably well served, with contractors having met or exceeded outcome goals (Freundlich and Gertzenzang 2002). For example, the State of Kansas's welfare agency noted that "In the nine contract years of operating this very complex program, CWCBS [Child Welfare Community Based Services—foster care] providers have met or exceeded outcome goals related to child safety, minimizing placement moves, maintaining siblings together in placement, and maintaining placement in or close to the child's home community" (State of Kansas, Department of Social and Rehabilitation Services, Business Plan, January 2006, 84). Others have found evidence of consistent improvements in the well-being of children and families that correlate with the duration, focus, and intensity of family-friendly services and local collaboration (Page 2005). The Kansas foster-care contracts included a well-designed process for monitoring contractors' performance (Legislative Division of Post Audit 2008), evidenced by the fact that in 2006 the State of Kansas was recognized as a national leader for the quality of its child welfare program and service delivery by the Child Welfare League of America (State of Kansas 2006).

REFERENCES

Acar, Muhittin, Chao Guo, and Kaifeng Yang. 2008. "Accountability When Hierarchical Authority Is Absent: Views from Public Private Partnership Practitioners." *The American Review of Public Administration* 38 (3): 3–23.

Agranoff, Robert, and Michael McGuire. 1998. "Multinetwork Management: Collaboration and the Hollow State in Local Economic Policy." *Journal of Public Administration Research and Theory* 8: 67–91.

————. 2004. *Collaborative Public Management: New Strategies for Local Government.* Washington, DC: Georgetown University Press.

Ansell, Chris, and Alison Gash. 2008. "Collaborative Governance in Theory and Practice." *Journal of Public Administration Research and Theory* 18: 543–71.

Armstrong, Mary I., Amy C. Vargo, Neil Jordan, Tara King-Miller, Stephen Roggenbaum, Cathy Sowell, and Svetlana Yampolskaya. 2007. *Semi-Annual Progress Report: IV-E Waiver Demonstration Evaluation,* submitted to the Department of Children and Families, April 4, 2007, University of South Florida.

Austin, Michael J. 2003. "The Changing Relationships Between Nonprofit Organizations and Public Social Service Agencies in the Era of Welfare Reform." *Nonprofit and Voluntary Sector Quarterly* 32 (1): 97–114.

Bardach, Eugene, and Cara Lesser. 1996. "Accountability in Human Services Collaboratives: For What? And to Whom?" *Journal of Public Administration Research and Theory* 6 (2): 197–224.

Behn, Robert D., and Peter A. Kant. 1999. "Strategies for Avoiding the Pitfall of Performance Contracting." *Public Productivity & Management Review* 22 (4): 470–89.

Bottom, William P., James Holloway, Gary J. Miller, Alexandra Mislin, and Andrew Whitford. 2006. "Building a Pathway to Cooperation: Negotiation and Social Exchange between Principal and Agent." *Administrative Science Quarterly* 51: 29–58.

Bovens, Mark, and Paul 't Hart. 2005. "Evaluating Public Accountability." Internal Research Colloquim Accountable Governance, Queens University, Belfast: October.

Bovens, Mark, Thomas Schillemans, and Paul 't Hart. 2008. "Does Public Accountability Work? An Assessment Tool." *Public Administration* 86 (1): 225–42.

Brehm, John, and Scott Gates. 1997. *Working, Shirking and Sabotage: Bureaucratic Response to a Democratic Public.* Ann Arbor: University of Michigan Press.

Considine, Mark. 2002. "The End of the Line? Accountable Governance in the Age of Networks, Partnerships, and Joined-Up Services." *Governance: An International Journal of Policy, Administration, and Institutions* 15 (1): 22–40.

Dicke, Lisa A., and J. Steven Ott. 1999. "Public Agency Accountability in Human Service Contracting." *Public Productivity & Management Review* 22: 502–16.

Dubnick, Melvin J. 2005. "Accountability and the Promise of Performance." *Public Performance & Management Review* 28 (3): 376–417.

Dubnick, Melvin J., and Barbara S. Romzek. 1993. "Accountability and the Centrality of Expectations in American Public Administration." *Research in Public Administration* 2: 37–78.

Dubnick, Melvin J., and Jonathan B. Justice. 2004. "Accounting for Accountability." Paper presented at annual meeting of the American Political Science Association, September.

Edelenbos, Julian, and Erik-Hans Klijn. 2007. "Trust in Complex Decision-Making Networks: A Theoretical and Empirical Exploration." *Administration & Society* 39 (1): 25–50.

Entwistle, Tom, and Steve Martin. 2005. "From Competition to Collaboration in Public Service Delivery: A New Agenda for Research." *Public Administration* 83 (1): 233–42.

Frederickson, David. G., and H. George Frederickson. 2006. *Measuring the Performance of the Hollow State.* Washington, DC: Georgetown University Press.

Freundlich, Madelyn, and Sarah Gertzenzang. 2002. *An Assessment of the Privatization of Child Welfare Services: Challenges and Successes.* New York: Children's Rights.

Globerman, Steven, and Aidan R. Vining. 1996. "A Framework for Evaluating the Government Contracting-Out Decision with an Application to Information Technology." *Public Administration Review* 56 (6): 577–86.

Haque, M. Shamsul. 2001. "Diminishing Publicness of Public Service Under the Current Mode of Governance." *Public Administration Review* 61 (1): 65–78.

Heinrich, Carolyn, and Youseok Choi. 2007. "Performance-Based Contracting in Social Welfare Programs." *American Review of Public Administration* 37 (4): 409–35.

Hodge, Graeme, and Carsten Greve. 2005. *The Challenge of Public-Private Partnerships: Learning from International Experience.* Northampton, MA: Edward Elgar.

Huang, Kun, and Keith G. Provan. 2007. "Resource Tangibility and Patterns of Interaction in a Publicly Funded Health and Human Services Network." *Journal of Public Administration Research and Theory* 17: 435–54.

Humphrey, Kristen, Ann P. Turnbull, and H. Rutherford Turnbull III. 2006. "Perspectives of Foster-Care Providers, Service Providers, and Judges Regarding Privatized Foster-Care Services." *Journal of Disability Policy Studies* 17 (1): 2–17.

Isett, Kimberley Roussin, and Keith G. Provan. 2005. "The Evolution of Dyadic Interorganizational Relationships in a Network of Publicly Funded Nonprofit Agencies." *Journal of Public Administration Research and Theory* 15: 149–65.

Johnston, Jocelyn M., and Barbara S. Romzek. 1999. "Contracting and Accountability in State Medicaid Reform: Rhetoric, Theories, and Reality." *Public Administration Review* 59 (5): 383–99.

———. 2000. *Implementing State Contracts for Social Services: An Assessment of the Kansas Experience.* PricewaterhouseCoopers Endowment for the Business of Government, Washington, DC, May.

———. 2008. "Social Welfare Contracts as Networks: The Impact of Network Stability on Management and Performance." *Administration and Society* 40 (2): 115–46.

Kearns, Kevin. 1996. *Managing for Accountability: Preserving the Public Trust in Public and Nonprofit Organizations.* San Francisco: Jossey-Bass.

Kenis, Patrick, and Keith G. Provan. 2007. "Modes of Network Governance: Structure, Management, and Effectiveness." *Journal of Public Administration Research and Theory* 18: 229–52.

Kettl, Donald. 1993. *Sharing Power: Governance and Private Markets.* Washington, DC: Brookings Institution Press.

———. 2002. "Managing Indirect Government." In *The Tools of Government: A Guide to the New Governance,* ed. L.M. Salamon. New York: Oxford University Press, 523–64.

Klijn, Eric-Hans, and Joop F.M. Koppenjan. 2000. "Public Management and Policy Networks: Foundations of a Network Approach to Governance." *Public Management* 2 (2): 135–58.

Klingner, Donald E., John Nalbandian, and Barbara S. Romzek. 2002. "Politics, Administration, and Markets: Conflicting Expectations and Accountability." *The American Review of Public Administration* 32 (2): 117–44.

Lamothe, Meeyoung, and Scott Lamothe. 2008. "Beyond the Search for Competition in Social Service Contracting: Procurement, Consolidation, and Accountability." *The American Review of Public Administration:* 1: 25.

Legislative Division of Post Audit. 2001. Performance Audit Report: *The State's Adoption and Foster Care Contracts: Reviewing Selected Financial and Services Issues.* A Report to the Legislative Post Audit Committee, State of Kansas, Topeka: January.

———. 2008. *Foster Care: Reviewing Selected Issues Related to State Contracts for Foster Care and Family Preservation Services. A Report to the Legislative Post Audit Committee, State of Kansas.* Performance Audit Report 08PA04, Topeka, KS, April.

Light, Paul. 1995. *Thickening Government: Federal Hierarchy and the Diffusion of Accountability.* Washington, DC: Brookings Institution Press.

Lynn, Laurence E., Carolyn J. Heinrich, and Carolyn J. Hill. 2000. "Studying Governance and Public Management: Challenges and Prospects." *Journal of Public Administration Research and Theory* 10 (2): 233–61.

McGuire, Michael. 2002. "Managing Networks: Propositions on What Managers Do and Why They Do It." *Public Administration Review* 62 (5): 599–609.

Meyers, Marcia K., Norma M. Riccucci, and Irene Lurie. 2001. "Achieving Goal Congruence in Complex Environments: The Case of Welfare Reform." *Journal of Public Administration Research and Theory* 11 (2): 165–201.

Milward, H. Brinton, and Keith G. Provan. 2000. "Governing the Hollow State." *Journal of Public Administration Research and Theory* 10: 359–80.

———. 2006. A *Manager's Guide to Choosing and Using Collaborative Networks.* IBM Foundation for the Business of Government, Washington, DC.

Moon, M. Jae, and Eric W. Welch. 2000. "Managerial Adaptation through the Market in the Public Sector: Theoretical Framework and Four Models." *International Review of Public Administration* 5 (2): 129–41.

Mulgan, Richard. 1997. "Contracting Out and Accountability." *Australian Journal of Public Administration* 56 (4): 106–16.

O'Toole, Laurence J. Jr. 1997. "Treating Networks Seriously: Practical and Research-based Agendas in Public Administration." *Public Administration Review* 57: 45–52.

———. 2000. "Different Public Managements? Implications of Structural Contexts in Hierarchies and Networks." In *Advancing Public Management: New Developments in Theory, Methods, and Practice,* ed. Jeffrey L. Brudney, Laurence J. O'Toole, Jr., and Hal G. Rainey. Washington, DC: Georgetown University Press, 19–32.

O'Toole, Laurence J. Jr., and Kenneth J. Meier. 2004. "Public Management in Intergovernmental Networks: Matching Structural Networks and Managerial Networking." *Journal of Public Administration Research and Theory* 14 (4): 469–94.

Page, Stephen. 2004. "Measuring Accountability for Results in Interagency Collaboratives." *Public Administration Review* 64 (5): 591–606.

———. 2005. "What's New about the New Public Management? Administrative Change in the Human Services." *Public Administration Review* 65 (6): 713–27.

Posner, Paul, 2002. "Accountability Challenges of Third-Party Government." In *The Tools of Government: A Guide to the New Governance,* ed. L.M. Salamon. New York: Oxford University Press, 523–64.

Prager, Jonas. 1994. "Contracting out Government Services: Lessons from the Private Sector." *Public Administration Review* 54 (2): 176–84.

Provan, Keith G., and H. Brinton Milward. 2001. "Do Networks Really Work? A Framework for Evaluating Public-Sector Organizational Networks." *Public Administration Review* 61 (4): 414–23.

Radin, Beryl. 1998. "The Government Performance and Results Act (GPRA): Hydra-Headed Monster or Effective Policy Tool?" *Public Administration Review* 58: 307–16.

———. 2006. *Challenge the Performance Movement: Accountability, Complexity, and Democratic Values.* Washington, DC: Georgetown University Press.

Radin, Beryl A., and Barbara S. Romzek. 1996. "Accountability Expectations in an Intergovernmental Arena: The National Rural Development Partnership." *Publius: The Journal of Federalism* 26 (2): 59–81.

Roberts, Nancy C. 2002. "Keeping Public Officials Accountable through Dialogue: Resolving the Accountability Paradox." *Public Administration Review* 62 (6): 658–69.

Romzek, Barbara S., and Jocelyn M. Johnston. 1999. "Reforming Medicaid Through Contracting: The Nexus of Implementation and Organizational Culture," *Journal of Public Administration Research and Theory* 9 (1): 107–39.

———. 2002. "Effective Contract Implementation and Management: A Preliminary Model." *Journal of Public Administration Research and Theory* 12 (3): 423–53.

———. 2005. "State Social Services Contracting: Exploring the Determinants of Effective Contract Accountability." *Public Administration Review* 65 (4): 436–47.

Romzek, Barbara S., and Melvin J. Dubnick. 1987. "Accountability in the Public Sector: Lessons from the Challenger Tragedy." *Public Administration Review* 47: 227–38.

Romzek, Barbara S., Kelly LeRoux, and Jeannette Blackmar. 2009. "The Dynamics of Informal Accountability in Networks of Service Providers." Paper presented at National Public Management Research Conference, Ohio State University, Columbus, OH.

Sanger, Mary Bryna. 2003. *The Welfare Marketplace: Privatization and Welfare Reform.* Washington, DC: Brookings Institution Press.

Schwartz, Robert. 2005. "The Contracting Quandary: Managing Local Authority-VNPA Relations." *Local Government Studies* 31 (1): 69–83.

Sclar, Elliott. 2000. *You Don't Always Get What You Pay for: The Economics of Privatization.* Ithaca, NY: Cornell University Press.

Shively, Candy. 2007. *Update on Foster Care: Integrated Service Delivery.* Testimony before State of Kansas, Joint Committee on Children's Issues, October 30.

State of Florida, Florida Department of Children and Families. 2007a. *Evaluation of the Department of Children and Families Community-based Care Initiative Fiscal Year 2005–2006.* Submitted by Vargo, Amy C., Mary I. Armstrong, Neil Jordan, Stephanie Romney, Svetlana Yampolskaya, and Tara King-Miller. University of South Florida, Tampa, FL, January 15, 2007,

———. 2007b. *Semi-Annual Progress Report: IV-E Waiver Demonstration Evaluation,* Submitted by Armstrong, Mary I, Amy C. Vargo, Neil Jordan, Tara King-Miller, Stephen Roggenbaum, Cathy Sowell, and Svetlana Yampolskaya, Tallahassee, FL. April 4, 2007.

State of Florida, Office of Program Policy Analysis & Government Accountability. 2005. *Child Welfare Transition Nearly Complete; Budget Allocation and Oversight Systems Need Strengthening.* Publication Report No. 05–12. Tallahassee, FL.

———. 2006. *Additional Improvements Are Needed as DCF Redesigns Its Lead Agency Oversight Systems.* Publication Report No. 06–05. Tallahassee, FL.

———. 2007. *CBC Pilot Project Implementation Delayed But Proceeding; Other Initiatives Implemented.* Publication Report No. 07–03. Tallahassee, FL.

———. 2008. *Pilot to Outsource CBC Program Oversight Encountered Setbacks: Effectiveness Unknown.* Office of Program Policy Analysis & Government Accountability Publication Report No. 08–09. Tallahassee, FL.

State of Kansas Department of Social and Rehabilitation Services. 1999. *External Evaluation of the Kansas Child Welfare System, Year End Report (January-December 1999).* Contract #98–59, submitted by Bell Associates, Topeka, KS, November 15.

———. 2006. *Business Plan.* Topeka, KS.

———. 2007. *2007–2008 Business Plan.* Topeka, KS.

State of Kansas, Joint Committee on Children's Issues. 2006. *Update on Foster Care: Integrated Service Delivery.* Testimony by Candy Shively, October 30. Topeka, KS.

Svennson, Jorgen, Willem Trommel, and Tineke Lantink. 2008. "Reemployment Services in the Netherlands: A Comparative Study of Bureaucratic, Market, and Network Forms of Organization." *Public Administration Review* 68 (3): 505–15.

Thompson, Dennis. 1980. "Moral Responsibility of Public Officials: The Problem of Many Hands." *American Political Science Review* 74: 905–16.

Trailer, Jeff W., Paula L. Rechner, and Robert C. Hill. 2004. "A Compounded Agency Problem: An Empirical Examination of Public-Private Partnerships." *The Journal of American Academy of Business, Cambridge* 5(1–2): 308–15.

U.S. Department of Health and Human Services. 2007. *Program and Fiscal Design Elements of Child Welfare Initiatives,* Topical Paper #2, U.S. Health and Human Services Publication. Washington, DC: U.S. Department of Health and Human Services, December.

———. 2008. *Final Report: Kansas Child and Family Services Review.* U.S. Health and Human Services Publication. Washington, DC: U.S. Department of Health and Human Services, March.

U.S. Government Accountability Office. 2007. *Federal Acquisition Forum,* GAO-07–45SP. Washington, DC: U.S. Government Printing Office.

Van Slyke, David M. 2003. "The Mythology of Privatization in Contracting for Social Services." *Public Administration Review* 63 (3): 296–315.

———. 2007. "Agents or Stewards: Using Theory to Understand the Government-Nonprofit Social Service Contracting Relationship." *Journal of Public Administration Research and Theory* 17: 157–87.

Weber, Edward P. 1999. "The Question of Accountability in Historical Perspective: From Jackson to Contemporary Ecosystem Management." *Administration and Society* 31: 451–94.

Whitaker, Gordon P., Lydian Altman-Sauer, and Margaret Henderson. 2004. "Mutual Accountability between Governments and Nonprofits: Moving Beyond 'Surveillance' to 'Service.'" *American Review of Public Administration* 34 (2): 115–33.

Young, Dennis R. 2000. "Alternative Models of Government-Nonprofit Sector Relations: Theoretical and International Perspectives." *Nonprofit and Voluntary Sector Quarterly* 29 (149): 149–72.

3

ACCOUNTABILITY CHALLENGES IN PUBLIC SECTOR CONTRACTING FOR COMPLEX PRODUCTS

TREVOR L. BROWN, MATTHEW POTOSKI, AND DAVID M. VAN SLYKE

The U.S. federal government spent over $419 billion in fiscal year 2006 for procurement—almost doubling 2001 procurement expenditures (Hutton 2008). The rationale for this level of buying is to lower costs through scale or market efficiencies, spark service-delivery improvements or innovation through competition, and access expertise or capacity unavailable in-house (Kelman 2002). The risks of so much buying are that cost savings through contracting are sometimes illusory, quality suffers, and delivery is delayed (Sclar 2000). Some fear that such large-scale procurement undermines accountability: when government purchases rather than produces, the chain of accountability is extended even further and perhaps is weakened. People working for government are more easily held accountable than people working for organizations that sell to the government. When contracting fails, responsibility is muddled. Does fault lie with the seller, the buyer, or unforeseen circumstances that nature delivered?

Contracting produces low risk win-win outcomes when markets function well: markets need enough buyers and sellers, buyers and sellers need to be well informed about products and each others' preferences, and actors must be able to easily enter and exit the market and exchange resources at low costs.[1] Market discipline provides its own accountability by revealing who is responsible for deals in which agreed-upon goals are not achieved and then sanctioning those parties. Accountability is compromised when buying and selling is more complex: when the market is thin, and where the few buyers and sellers are uncertain about the terms of exchange. This makes the future unpredictable. And unpredictability increases costs for both parties to the contract. Moreover, complex circumstances threaten the win-win gains from market exchanges and obfuscate responsibility when exchanges turn out badly.

Contracting in complex circumstances does not guarantee problems, but it does make them more likely. Buyers and sellers can no longer rely on market discipline, but instead must manage their relations to ensure the exchange bears fruit. This chapter will investigate accountability issues raised when governments purchase complex products. Our inquiry uses the simple but powerful heuristic of game theory to show the complexities of accountability questions in public-sector contracting. The outcome of a complex contract exchange is the result of the buyer's and seller's efforts as well as luck: sometimes participants make good faith efforts to maximize the mutual gain the contract can generate, and sometimes unforeseen circumstances make difficult tasks easier or harder. Because the effects of these factors are generally unknown, it is difficult to determine whether the outcome of a complex contract was due to the efforts of the parties or the fortunes of changing circumstances. Our theoretical inquiry highlights how buyers and sellers can improve the chances of win-win outcomes and make the contracting process more accessible and accountable.

Our discussion is divided into four sections. In the first section we distinguish between simple and complex products and then highlight the risks and rewards of contracting for complex products. In the second section we describe the basic bilateral contracting game and then use it to identify accountability challenges in contracting for complex products. We show the challenges of trying to determine whether outcomes result from the behavior of the two parties in the exchange or exogenous factors. In the third section we provide an illustration of an accountability challenge—the Coast Guard's Project Deepwater, a multiyear, multibillion dollar procurement. In the fourth and concluding section we summarize our arguments by highlighting important implications for contracting practice and accountability.

COMPLEX PRODUCTS AND COMPLEX CONTRACTING

Successful contracting promises a win-win exchange between the buyer and seller. Buyers seek goods or services that meet their expectations for quality at a price lower than the value they attribute to the product, while sellers want compensation that exceeds their costs for producing the good or service. Buyers and sellers can easily define cost, quality, and quantity parameters for simple products that exist in a vibrant market with many exchanges and clear price, quantity, and quality signals. In a market exchange for simple products, the buyer (in our case a government agency) can describe with a high degree of detail what it wants the seller (a private firm, a nonprofit organization, or even another government) to do or produce.

The market for simple products is its own accountability mechanism. If the seller (or the buyer) fails to live up to her contractual obligations—if the product quality is substandard or delivery is late—the transgression is quickly and easily revealed, and a richly competitive market provides a ready replacement partner seeking similar terms. The transgressing seller loses the buyer's business and that of future buyers as her reputation for bad business spreads through the market. With an effective market disciplining buyers and sellers to live up to contract obligations—as clearly spelled out in their contract—buyers and sellers of simple products can be reasonably confident of achieving the mutual gains from successful win-win exchanges.

Optimistic win-win scenarios are less likely in contracting for complex products. For complex products, neither buyers nor sellers know the products' cost, quality, and quantity parameters.[2] An executable contract defines each party's obligations and responsibilities, including the price, qualities, and quantities of the product.[3] Contract completeness is the degree to which the contract defines buyers' and sellers' rights and obligations across all contingencies (Hart and Moore 2008; Tirole 1999; Bajari and Tadelis 2001; Heinrich 1999; Martin 2004; O'Looney 1998). All contracts are incomplete to some degree because the future contains an infinite number of scenarios, not all of which can be specified in advance. The effect of nature is random, since the parties do not know all the possible events and the probabilities that could occur. Not surprisingly, complex products lead to highly incomplete contracts. At some point the costs of writing contract terms for all future scenarios exceed the mutual gains from the trade.

In areas where the contract is vague, the buyer and seller's behavior can be either *perfunctory* or *consummate* (Hart and Moore 2008; Williamson 1975). Perfunctory behavior conforms to the bare minimum "letter" of the contract as enforceable by a court of law. Consummate behavior, on the other hand, is performance that, in the win-win spirit of the contract, goes beyond the bare minimum of what is required. For example, the complete portion of a contract can specify the number of jokes a hired comedienne must tell, but it is impractical to specify how funny she should be when she tells them. A consummate comedian would strive for big laughs while a perfunctory comedian would be satisfied with mild giggles. It is cheaper to perfunctorily follow the letter of a contract, but doing so reduces the value the other side receives. Consummate behavior requires more effort and expense but increases the value for the other side.

THE CONTRACTING GAME AND ACCOUNTABILITY CHALLENGES

Viewing complex contracting through the prisoners' dilemma lens helps us understand why the failure risk is so high for these contracts and also sheds light on how to manage these contracts to transform lose-lose conflict into win-win cooperation. In a PD game, two (or more) players choose whether to cooperate or defect (join the enemy or the other team), with the payoff of their choices jointly determined. Figure 3.1 depicts the payoffs for consummate behavior (cooperation) and perfunctory behavior (defection) as a two-person prisoners' dilemma game. If both choose consummate behavior, each receives a moderately high payoff (3 each in Figure 3.1) and if both choose perfunctory behavior, each receives a moderately lower payoff (2 each in Figure 3.1). If one elects to cooperate and the other to defect, the defector receives a very high payoff (4) and the cooperator a very low one (1). Consummate behavior means forgoing a large unilateral gain in exchange for a smaller individual payoff from a potentially larger mutual gain. Perfunctory behavior means accepting greater individual gain, but an almost certainly smaller mutual payoff. The contract produces the most gains for the buyer and seller when both perform consummately, and the smallest gains when both perform perfunctorily. The upshot is that no matter what the other player chooses, each player can improve his own payoff by choosing perfunctory behavior, even though mutual defection (perfunctory behavior) generates the lowest net payoff and mutual cooperation generates the highest net payoff for both players.

Achieving the promise of win-win exchanges of complex products requires some mechanism for holding the buyer and seller accountable so that each performs consummately despite the incentives to behave perfunctorily. One might expect the market for complex products to hold buyers and sellers accountable by punishing them for their perfunctory behavior. What buyer would want to do business with a seller that would take advantage of contract ambiguities for her own gain, at the buyer's expense? A buyer would clearly want to replace a seller performing perfunctorily with another whose behavior would be more consummate. Unfortunately, market discipline may not effectively hold buyers and sellers accountable in transactions for complex products. Two sources of this inability are lock-in problems stemming from asset-specific investments and uncertainty about how much unpredictable events and the players' strategies will affect outcomes of the exchange.

Asset-Specific Investments

Negotiating and executing a contract for a complex product often requires the buyer and seller to make asset-specific investments. Expenditures are asset specific to the extent that they have no economic value outside the product being produced (Williamson 2005). For example, some research in the U.S. space program produced economic value outside the contract (e.g., Tang), while other research produced little value outside the contract (e.g., spacesuits). Asset-specific investments in complex contracting may include the buyer and seller customizing production processes to suit each other's idiosyncrasies. Since asset-specific investments are lost if the contract is not executed, they create the classic "lock-in" problem (Williamson 1996). A party becomes locked into a contract because it cannot deploy its asset-specific investments to other profitable endeavors. For the buyer,

Figure 3.1 **The Complex Contract Dilemma**

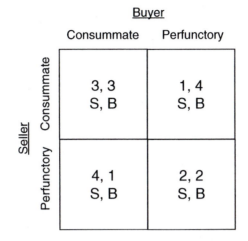

the "lock-in" risk is that once a seller has been selected, no other potential sellers have made the necessary investments. Thus the advantaged seller may seek to opportunistically exploit contract ambiguities, perhaps by perfunctorily "gold plating" the product with costly features that increase his profits but add little value for the buyer and considerable expense. Alternatively, because the seller has only one buyer for his products, the buyer may also opportunistically exploit contract terms for her own favor. The buyer may force a seller, for example, to make changes to a product that increase costs above the agreed-upon price, even though she knows that a much cheaper product would meet her needs almost as well. In these circumstances, the exploiter's gains can be smaller than the exploited party's losses, leading to a prisoners' dilemma problem.

Future Uncertainty

Changing the payoff structure of the game increases the possibility of cooperation for complex contracting. But external uncertainty, or ambiguity about the impact of future events or states (Heide and Miner 1992), can undermine the prospects of cooperation. After the buyer and seller negotiate terms of a complex contract, leaving some portion incomplete, each makes asset-specific investments. Each one then chooses whether to behave consummately or perfunctorily in areas where the contract is incomplete. The payoffs the actors receive are a result of their own behavior, the other party's behavior, and unforeseen events. The buyer and seller do not necessarily know how nature affected them or the other party. Perhaps the product was happily cheaper to produce for the seller and more valuable to the buyer than anticipated. Or, perhaps the seller's production costs were much higher and the product turned out to be less valuable to the buyer. If the buyer and seller do not know each other's strategy or whether circumstances were favorable, neither will know the extent to which the payoff was due to the other party's strategic choice or the vagaries of natural fortune. Moreover, without credible verification, neither side can reliably claim it was cooperating.

Bilateral and Vertical Accountability

Not surprisingly, the lock-in problem and uncertainty about the effects of unforeseen events weaken market discipline as an accountability mechanism in the exchange of complex products.

But as the complex contracting prisoners' dilemma shows, some accountability mechanism is necessary to transform lose-lose conflicts into win-win exchanges. Achieving win-win outcomes in complex contracting requires changing the buyer's and seller's incentives to elicit consummate performance (cooperation). The challenge is to change the payoff structure to another type of game (Lichbach 1996).

Bilateral and vertical accountability mechanisms can promote consummate behavior in these circumstances. Bilateral accountability refers to mechanisms or norms embedded in the relationship—sometimes directly into the contract—that reflect the two parties' credible commitments to cooperate. Bilateral accountability promotes win-win outcomes by rewarding consummate behavior and penalizing perfunctory behavior. An example of a bilateral accountability mechanism might be third-party certification, often referred to in formal contracts as independent validation and verification (IV&V) and combined with a sanction. Under IV&V, an independent third party first validates the need for a proposed product and then verifies that it has been designed and produced correctly. An example of a bilateral norm might be a public commitment by both parties to cooperate. While not contractually formalized like IV&V, such a commitment does more than simply signal good faith behavior; it creates a reputational penalty should the party choose perfunctory behavior. A party that performs perfunctorily becomes a less attractive partner for future complex contracts. Bilateral accountability mechanisms and norms work well when the criteria for what constitutes consummate and perfunctory behavior are easily identified and verified, and the sanctions are well specified and significant. Bilateral mechanisms and norms work less well when criteria for consummate and perfunctory behavior are not mutually agreed upon and verified, and sanctions are unspecified or insignificant.

Vertical accountability refers to contract management systems, processes, and practices that affect interactions between the two parties and promote win-win outcomes by framing a cooperative relationship. In the federal contracting arena, there is typically an array of vertical accountability overseers, including the Government Accountability Office and the Office of Inspector General on the legislative side; the Office of Management and Budget on the executive side; oversight actors within the agency's home department; and committees and subcommittees of the House and Senate. Congress in particular, through the oversight powers of its committees, can promote cooperative behavior, such as allowing the use of alternative dispute-resolution techniques or placing minimal restrictions on the use of different types of contracting arrangements. Alternatively, Congress can inhibit consummate behavior by mandating more formalized contracting practices (e.g., binding arbitration) or by using its oversight powers aggressively to search for malfeasance (i.e., hearings, investigations). These vertical systems, processes, and practices are likely to have their most powerful impact when contracting occurs in multiple stages. In our theoretical perspective, a multistage contracting process is analogous to a collective action game played over multiple rounds. Cooperation can be achieved through a "tit-for-tat strategy," in which both sides initially cooperate and then mirror the other party's behavior from the previous round. The vertical accountability systems in place essentially frame the rules of the game for iterative play.

COMPLEX CONTRACTING AND THE COAST GUARD'S DEEPWATER PROGRAM

The Coast Guard's Project Deepwater illustrates the accountability challenges inherent in contracting for complex contracts. The Deepwater program is an effort to upgrade and overhaul the Coast Guard's air and sea vessels and the command and control links among them. In 1998, the Coast Guard issued a Request for Proposal for a system of air and sea assets, evaluated three industry proposals, and selected a design from Integrated Coast Guard Systems (ICGS—a Lockheed Martin and Northrop Grumman consortium). Under the ICGS proposal, the Coast Guard's Deepwater air and sea assets would be integrated in a state-of-the-art command, control, communications, computers and intelligence, surveillance, and reconnaissance system (commonly referred to as C4ISR). ICGS received the first installment of the Deepwater contract in June 2002.

Deepwater negotiations occurred in a context of high uncertainty and lock-in fears, and the resulting contract was incomplete. The Coast Guard and ICGS each claimed to pursue cooperative contracting behavior, although these claims were difficult to verify. The contract's initial payoffs were lower than anticipated, although it is difficult to determine whether this was the result of contract strategies or an environment that turned out to be less favorable than anticipated.

Deepwater as a Complex Product

Prior to Deepwater, the Coast Guard's practice was to separate purchases for individual classes of assets—ships, cutters, planes, and helicopters—as each asset reached the end of its life. By the early 1990s, it became clear that the Coast Guard needed a more targeted approach to upgrade its rapidly aging assets. The Coast Guard leadership lobbied Congress for a long-term acquisition strategy to upgrade and modernize the fleet with a stable funding stream. In 1998, Congress and the Clinton administration committed to a multiyear procurement at approximately $500 million a year, significantly more than the Coast Guard's historical acquisition expenditures (U.S. Department of Transportation, 1999). The Deepwater program was a complex product, and the Coast Guard was highly uncertain about its value. Of course, the Coast Guard understood its objectives—maritime security (upholding the law), maritime safety (rescuing the distressed), protection of natural resources (protecting the environment), maritime mobility (ensuring safe marine transportation), and national defense (operating in coordination with the U.S. Navy)—and the basic components that would ultimately comprise its asset fleet (small and large boats, planes, and helicopters, tied together through communication and integration technologies). But the Coast Guard did not know the exact mix of boats, planes, and helicopters to purchase, their performance specifications, and how they would operate in a system. The Coast Guard was not well positioned to assess alternative system portfolios and components. For example, how many fewer aircraft would be needed if the large cutters were 20 percent faster? ICGS also faced uncertainty. The Coast Guard had established a hard cap on overall costs ($500 million annually), but ICGS did not know the cost of producing these assets in a system that met the Coast Guard's objectives. Full cost information for each asset would not be available until the Coast Guard either specified more exact performance standards or designed the first unit.[4]

Asset-Specific Investments and Lock-In Risks

The Deepwater contract required specific investments. On the high end of asset specificity was the development of new assets or system elements for which the Coast Guard is one of only a few potential buyers, if not the only buyer. To build the National Security Cutter (NSC), Northrop Grumman—the lead subcontractor on the NSC—had to develop a relatively specialized production process because of the unique performance attributes requested by the Coast Guard. The Coast Guard's asset-specific investments included the creation of a Deepwater acquisition office that was designed exclusively for engaging with ICGS; Coast Guard staff had to have special clearance to work on the Deepwater acquisition (e.g., access to the actual contract documents). As processes and staff become embedded with a single seller, it becomes more difficult to adapt to alternative sellers. As a result, there is greater reliance on bilateral accountability relationships.

Asset-specific investments create lock-in risks. For the Coast Guard the risk was that ICGS would eventually gain an information advantage as it began to design and build products. If ICGS elected to abuse its information advantage (e.g., by "gold plating" the product), the Coast Guard would have limited options on where to go to acquire alternatives. ICGS had substantial research, development, modification, and adaptation costs to meet the Coast Guard's needs. To secure a return on its investment, ICGS had a strong incentive to make this system as proprietary as possible so that the Coast Guard would have to rely on ICGS for costly capability enhancements, training, technical assistance, maintenance, and upgrades. For ICGS, the principal lock-in risk was that it may not recoup its investments if the Coast Guard chose to stop buying those system elements for which ICGS had made asset-specific investments.

Incomplete Contracts

In designing and producing an aerial or sea vessel, let alone an interoperable system of such assets, there was an almost infinite set of product specifications over which the buyer and seller could have negotiated. Fully specifying many of these product attributes required forecasting unpredictable future conditions. Given such uncertainty and the mutual risk of lock-in, the Coast Guard and ICGS parties entered into a contract that specified only some aspects of the system. The Coast Guard and ICGS balanced specificity against the uncertainty inherent in buying a complex product by specifying three layers of contract arrangements.

The top layer was a performance-based indefinite delivery, indefinite quantity (IDIQ) contract. An IDIQ does not specify a firm quantity of products or the tasks required to produce them. Instead, it specifies a minimum or maximum number of products and some endpoint for termination of the agreement. The Deepwater IDIQ contract allowed the Coast Guard to buy a specified set of system components without competitively bidding each one. In a sense, the IDIQ acts like a menu with the base costs for various items (e.g., a $20,000 automobile), but where the add-ons are neither specified nor priced (e.g., roof rack, spoiler, performance rims and tires, and high-output speakers).

The middle layer of the contract set the broad terms of exchange. Each individual purchase under the IDIQ was negotiated through a task order between the Coast Guard and ICGS that specified basic terms, such as the number of units to be purchased in a class of assets and their delivery schedule, but left many dimensions indeterminate, such as the exact design and performance specifications, cost schedules, and the evaluation metrics.

Specifying many of the details of each task order occurred through a final contract layer of Integrated Product Teams (IPTs) that were intended to facilitate cooperation through the process of designing, testing, and building the asset. The IPTs brought together ICGS personnel, subcontractors, and Coast Guard officials to decide the important details about the asset, so that once production was underway, rather than fully renegotiate each task order the Coast Guard and ICGS could use Undefinitized Contract Actions (UCAs). UCAs are a legal vehicle that allows production to continue after a design change, even though the parties have not formally negotiated the full price and terms of that change. UCAs require that the parties formally resolve the specification and price within 180 days. UCAs place the cost risk on the buyer because the seller has considerable discretion over the price charged for each revision. Once these items become "definitized" they operate like fixed-cost contracts.

These three contractual layers specified the terms of the exchange and established a process for the Coast Guard and ICGS to negotiate uncertainty. Still, these arrangements did not fully specify the contract. The task orders and even UCAs could not specify every design and performance requirement for each asset in the system and how they would fit together. Part of the specification challenge was the interoperability requirement—and hence interconnectedness—of the system. Each performance specification (e.g., the speed of a boat) carried implications for other system elements (e.g., the range of helicopters and planes). The Coast Guard and ICGS were unable to formally specify all relevant details in task orders because doing so would cement performance specifications for all later assets, which had not yet been specified or fully designed. As a result, the incompleteness of the contractual arrangements left substantial room for the behavior, or strategy, of both the Coast Guard and ICGS to impact outcomes.

Strategy

At the outset of the contract, ICGS and the Coast Guard pledged to pursue consummate, cooperative strategies, often invoking "partnership" language to describe the relationship they were entering into as one of strong bilateral accountability. Harkening back to our theoretical terms, a partnership implies that each party was prepared to forgo an advantage for itself in favor of a larger benefit for the other side. With so much of the Deepwater contract incomplete, much of the contract's payoff would be determined by the parties' behavior.

Here we return to the delivery of the NSC to illustrate the importance of strategy. The NSC presented lock-in risks; the task order was incomplete, since it left many performance requirements indeterminate and did not identify the decision-making rights and obligations of either ICGS or the Coast Guard over these unspecified elements. For example, the task order did not identify which party had decision-making authority over structural-design specifications and the conditions under which independent third-party assessment of the design would be necessary. These gaps left both parties with a wide berth to behave consummately or perfunctorily. Moreover, the lack of inclusion and specificity in the contract about third-party assessments, such as those that could be conducted by organizations such as the U.S. Navy's Surface Warfare Division, weakened the power of bilateral accountability mechanisms. The contract could have specified which organization would perform validation and verification of the NSC's design and production, as well as which criteria would be used to determine when sanctions could be imposed for failure to perform.

ICGS had discretion to openly discuss and jointly agree with the Coast Guard on the remaining unspecified decisions for the final design of the NSC. Such an approach would be consummate behavior because it would produce win-win outcomes for the Coast Guard and ICGS. Alternatively, the contract allowed ICGS to specify design standards unilaterally. This would be perfunctory behavior because although it was easier for ICGS to decide standards on its own, the Coast Guard bore the risk of buying assets whose performance abilities did not meet its needs. If ICGS chose consummate behavior, it would use the Integrated Product Teams (IPTs) to jointly develop design and performance standards that met the Coast Guard's goals. For example, these discussions might include an explanation on the part of ICGS that would clearly articulate that an additional investment of "x" dollars would yield an increase in "y" days at sea, or conversely that accepting some alternative would lead to a "z" percent decline in days at sea, but potentially lower costs by "x" dollars or increase the lifespan of the cutter by "y" years. This would have been an appropriate implementation of bilateral accountability with the inclusion of third parties validating alignment between the contracting partners.

This cooperative approach would increase ICGS's costs, because orchestrating an open conversation with the Coast Guard about alternative-design specifications would be costly and might not produce benefits for ICGS that exceeded its costs. However, supplying more complete information would provide more value to the Coast Guard than it would cost ICGS because the Coast Guard would be more likely to receive an asset—the NSC in this case—better aligned with its mission. Conversely, ICGS could choose to make minimal investments in providing comparative information to the Coast Guard, or simply make decisions itself, which would be less costly. However, because the Coast Guard would receive a product that might not meet its performance requirements, it would then be forced to pay even more to modify the asset, and its costs would be higher than if ICGS and the Coast Guard negotiated through the IPTs.

The Coast Guard faced a similar decision. It could reduce ICGS's costs by inviting ICGS to provide comparative information on alternative performance specifications and then expeditiously respond to the consortium's presentations. Such an approach would be consummate behavior. Alternatively, the Coast Guard could eschew collaboration and instead unilaterally process task orders. If the Coast Guard chose consummate behavior, it would actively participate in the IPT by providing technical and operational staff to suggest ways the proposed assets might be designed or modified to fulfill mission requirements before production moved too far along. Collecting relevant performance requirements and translating them for ICGS would increase the Coast Guard's costs. However, specifying performance requirements would provide more value for ICGS, because it would both produce a satisfied customer more inclined to renew existing task orders and process new ones, as well as lower the costs of designing and producing subsequent interoperable assets. Conversely, if the Coast Guard chose perfunctory behavior, it would save costs for itself because it would not devote resources to acquiring performance-requirement information for specifying incomplete design standards. However, ICGS's costs would increase by more than the Coast Guard's saving, since it would have to devote its own resources to gather such information.

Together ICGS and the Coast Guard found themselves on the horns of a collective-action problem. Both the Coast Guard and ICGS would be better off if each behaved consummately. The costs of cooperation—the resources devoted to reducing the other party's uncertainty—would be high, but not as high as their mutual gains. The benefits of cooperation were jeopardized because the Coast Guard and ICGS each risked losing their investments if the other party opted not to reciprocate. If the Coast Guard behaved consummately and ICGS perfunctorily, the Coast Guard would receive an NSC that met basic contractual requirements (i.e., adhered to the "letter" of the contract) but failed to meet expectations in areas not specified in the contract, with ICGS still receiving its full payment. If ICGS behaved consummately and the Coast Guard perfunctorily, ICGS would have devoted resources to deliver an NSC to meet its best guess of the Coast Guard's mission requirements but perhaps still miss the mark, thereby subjecting itself to the risk of not receiving full payment and/or putting contract renewal and future task orders at risk. Finally, if both parties behaved perfunctorily by avoiding costly collaboration in an IPT, the result would be an NSC that failed to meet Coast Guard's expectations and the prospect of the IDIQ not being renewed.

Nature and Outcomes

On May 8, 2008, ICGS delivered the first-in-class NSC—the *Bertholf*—255 days after the projected delivery date and over double the projected cost baseline.[5] The boat was seaworthy and met most contractual performance requirements, and the Coast Guard accepted delivery. However, both ICGS and the Coast Guard received less than anticipated from this task order and are generally unhappy with the outcomes from the contract. A series of studies have questioned the leadership actions and decisions, and cast blame on each for the cost overruns, poor quality, and delays (GAO 2008, 2008a, 2007, 2007a, 2005, 2005a, 2004; O'Rourke 2008; DHS OIG 2007; DAU 2007). The Coast Guard received criticism for the delays and for accepting higher costs and a flawed asset. ICGS received Congressional scrutiny, damage to its reputation, and lost future task orders under the IDIQ.

Our framing of the Deepwater contract as a prisoner's dilemma suggests a possible explanation for these outcomes is that both the Coast Guard and ICGS defected by behaving perfunctorily. Some evidence is consistent with this explanation. The Coast Guard has been criticized for not actively participating in the NSC IPT, thereby leaving many important design decisions to ICGS, and for unilaterally changing other NSC specifications through UCAs and then failing to "definitize" them within the required 180-day time period (GAO 2008a). Likewise, ICGS has been criticized for not providing the Coast Guard with sufficient information about the NSC's value-cost tradeoffs, for overbilling the Coast Guard for modifications and alterations, and in some cases for improperly exercising independent decision authority in the IPT by specifying design standards without sufficient input from the Coast Guard (DHS OIG 2007; GAO 2008a, 2007, 2007a, 2007b). The lack of market accountability and failure to implement bilateral accountability mechanisms may have led each party to pursue a course misaligned with the overall partnership and collaborative goals of the contract.

Recall that one of the implications of our complex-contracting theory is that it is particularly difficult to sort out the independent impact of strategy and nature on final outcomes. A negative turn of events outside the control of the parties may make the outcomes of even a cooperative contract disappointing. In the case of the NSC, unpredicted external events may have contributed to the deleterious outcomes and thus potentially masked what might have been cooperative, consummate contracting practices. First, the terrorist attacks of September 11, 2001, which occurred in the midst of the NSC's design and production phases, spurred the assignment of the Coast Guard to the newly created Department of Homeland Security and expanded its mission responsibilities. The Coast Guard's enhanced mission drove a series of significant changes to the design of the NSC, notably an increase in its size, deployment duration, military capabilities, and durability in the case of another terrorist attack.[6] Given the speed of events and the Coast Guard's desire not to derail production of the NSC, the Coast Guard made these decisions unilaterally. ICGS, perhaps interpreting the receipt of major changes to an agreed upon design as perfunctory behavior, did not invest in explaining the cost implications of these changes to the Coast Guard.

The second unforeseen event was Hurricane Katrina, which struck the Gulf Coast in 2005, damaging Northrop Grumman's Ingalls shipyard in Pascagoula, Mississippi, where the NSC was being constructed. The damage was sufficient enough to delay the delivery of the cutters and increase their production costs. Contingencies such as a hurricane had not been anticipated in the task order. As ICGS felt that the calamity was not its fault, it opted to pass some of the cost increase on to the Coast Guard. At the time of billing, ICGS submitted a Request for Equitable Adjustment (REA), which included modifications to meet the mission changes resulting from the terrorist attacks and the costs associated with Hurricane Katrina.

Although the exact impacts of these unforeseen events remain unknown, the Coast Guard and ICGS believe the other's perfunctory behavior is largely to blame for the NSC's outcomes. As a result, in the most recent rounds of task-order contracts, the Coast Guard and ICGS have now clearly adopted perfunctory strategies that meet the letter of the contract, without the spirit of co-operation. The pretense of collaboration has been abandoned as the Coast Guard has set up its own acquisition directorate, has assumed an increasing number of the responsibilities delegated to ICGS under the original IDIQ contract, is exercising greater authority over decision making (in and out of the IPTs), and is seeking to buy assets outside the IDIQ. The promise of a win-win partnership has deteriorated into a lose-lose transaction as each party pursues a perfunctory strategy.

Bilateral accountability mechanisms, like the use of IV&V, can help promote win-win outcomes.

In the Deepwater Program, the utilization of third parties (e.g., American Bureau of Shipping), consultants (e.g., Acquisition Solutions), and technical experts (e.g., the U.S. Navy's Naval Surface Warfare Center) can facilitate alignment between the buyer and seller. The use of IV&V as a bilateral accountability mechanism was successful for some of the Deepwater assets. Notably, third-party experts were effectively deployed in the construction of the NSC, though perhaps not as early or as frequently as external overseers might have desired. While the NSC was late in delivery and over budget, it is a seaworthy craft that meets the basic performance criteria. Bilateral accountability mechanisms were not effectively used across all of the assets, however. For example, in the upgrade of the Coast Guard's primary patrol boat, the P-123, ICGS had difficulty communicating the extent of asset deficiencies, and the Coast Guard did not draw upon third-party experts early enough to evaluate structural flaws to the boat's hull and initiate processes for resolving quality and performance conflicts. While the contract included some language about drawing on third parties for external evaluation and oversight, specificity was lacking with regard to conditions under which such experts should be used, which experts were qualified to provide services, and which party had the authority to request external monitoring.

The Deepwater program also had vertical accountability measures in place to promote win-win outcomes. In particular, the contracting process was governed by an array of executive (e.g., Department of Homeland Security) and legislative branch (e.g., GAO) overseers. An example in which vertical accountability by overseers had positive outcomes for the Deepwater contract was the substantial effort made by the GAO to encourage Coast Guard officials to formalize and specify a range of tools to improve contract governance. Through investigations, testimony, and reports, GAO officials provided Coast Guard officials with guidance on how to clearly delineate the governance procedures of the IPTs and effectively use performance reporting tools, such as earned-value management. This had the effect of institutionalizing decision-making processes and guidelines. However, vertical-accountability mechanisms were sometimes unsuccessful in creating alignment among the parties around the desired performance outcomes. Specifically, the fragmentation of the House and Senate committees and subcommittees with jurisdiction over the Coast Guard created a confusing oversight environment. In the case of the disputed P-123 boat, the Coast Guard had difficulty sorting out differing guidance it received from Congressional reports, testimony, and resolutions about how to address procurement problems. This confusion and the overall intensity of oversight scrutiny contributed to more antagonistic negotiations between the Coast Guard and ICGS over the P-123's flaws.

CONCLUSION

The theories we have outlined and the illustration of the Coast Guard's Project Deepwater suggest that complex contracting raises important accountability issues. Complex contracts are highly uncertain, costly to negotiate and execute, and prone to obfuscation in the realm of accountability. Lose-lose "defection" is individually more attractive than win-win cooperation, despite cooperation's higher mutual gains. Uncertainty about nature's contributions to payoffs means that even the parties in the contract do not know whether contract outcomes stem from misfortune, the other party's malfeasance, or their own mismanagement. In the case of Deepwater, both the Coast Guard and ICGS assumed the other defected. While bilateral and vertical accountability mechanisms have contributed positively in some cases, they have not fully delivered on the promise of a win-win outcome. For one, overseers, notably Congressional oversight committees, have determined that one or both parties defected, even though there is credible evidence to suggest that nature's role in Deepwater's early stages had been strong. As a result, Congress has taken steps to push the Coast Guard into a more perfunctory contracting approach.

Because complex contracts are prone to renegotiation, the "shadow of the future" opens a wealth of cooperative strategies to foster norms of reciprocity and trust and thus allow contract parties to turn lose-lose conflict into win-win cooperation (e.g., Axelrod 1984; Heide and Miner 1992). Moreover, these cooperative strategies enhance the overseer's ability to hold the exchange parties accountable in the contract process. In the case of Deepwater, the multistage architecture of the contracting process allows for this kind of renegotiation. While experts have estimated that it will take 25 years to deliver all the component Deepwater assets, the Coast Guard and ICGS did not formally commit to a 25-year agreement. Instead the IDIQ contract is structured in five, five-year increments. The asset-specific nature of some of the system components means that the Coast Guard faces a thin market of alternative suppliers for some assets, but at a minimum the overall contract arrangement allows for both exit and renegotiation. In moving forward, the default response should not necessarily be to position the Coast Guard and whatever sellers it engages into a rigid, perfunctory posture, but to develop accountability mechanisms and processes that are understood and easily verified by the contracting parties and the designated oversight bodies. Consistent and balanced oversight that is transparent can promote accountability and encourage parties to engage in consummate behavior toward win-win outcomes.

NOTES

This research is funded by the IBM Business of Government Foundation, the Smith Richardson Foundation, the Navel Postgraduate School Acquisition Research Program, and the Department of the Navy.

1. The view on why markets fail varies, and failure may be attributed to incomplete property rights, transaction costs, and information asymmetries. Goods may be noncompetitive or nonexcludable so that transferable property rights cannot be established and enforced without transaction costs swamping gains from trade (Weimer and Vining 1999). Historical accident may inefficiently lock in path-dependent technologies such as the QWERTY keyboard (David, 1985). Information asymmetries between buyers and sellers may create a "lemon market" where inferior products keep good products off the market (Akerloff 1970).

2. A lot has been written about "lemons" markets, where buyers are uncertain about the product but sellers are not (Akerloff 1970). This discussion focuses on contracts where both buyers and sellers are initially uncertain.

3. Fixed-price contracts set compensation on the seller's outputs, while cost-reimbursement contracts set compensation on inputs, such as time and materials. These terms specify who generally bears cost risk: fixed-price contracts place more of the risk on sellers and cost-plus (a cost-reimbursement contract with an award fee motivator) contracts place more of the risk on buyers (Bajari and Tadelis 1999). The contract may also include terms that grant or limit each party's discretion and reference public law for default rights and obligations (Brown et al. 2006).

4. First-in-class designs typically encounter cost overruns and schedule delays as the buyer and seller work out the precise specifications for the product. Cost-plus contracts are often used for the prototype design where the buyer bears greater cost risk. This puts the burden on the buyer to determine what it is exactly that it wants to buy. Once the first-in-class asset is completed, parties often switch to fixed-price contracts for subsequent assets. In this case, the seller bears greater cost risk.

5. Preliminary testing of the Bertholf revealed 2,800 issues (trial cards) to be addressed, but only eight issues (starred trial cards) that required addressing before acceptance (U.S. Coast Guard, 2008).

6. For example, the Department of Homeland Security mandated that the NSC have the ability to detect environmental hazards at sea and enter a nuclear-biological-chemical exposure-containment environment (DHS OIG 2007).

REFERENCES

Akerloff, G. 1970. "The Market for Lemons: Qualitative Uncertainty and the Market Mechanism." *Quarterly Journal of Economics* 84 (3): 488.

Axelrod, R. 1984. *The Evolution of Cooperation*. New York: Basic Books.

Bajari, P., and S. Tadelis. 2001. "Incentives versus Transaction Costs: A Theory of Procurement Contracts." *Rand Journal of Economics* 32 (3): 387–407.

———. 1999. "Procurement Contracts: Fixed Price vs. Cost Plus." Available at http://ssrn.com/abstract=156470 (March 15, 1999).

———. 2006. "Managing Public Service Contracts: Aligning Values, Institutions, and Markets." *Public Administration Review* 66 (3): 55–67.

Brown, T., M. Potoski, and D. Van Slyke. 2008. "Trust and Contract Completeness in the Public Sector." *Local Government Studies* 33 (4): 607–23.

David, P.A. 1985. "Clio and the Economics of QWERTY." *The American Economic Review* 75 (2): 332–37.

Defense Acquisition University. 2007. Quick Look Study: United States Coast Guard Deepwater Program. February.

Department of Homeland Security Office of Inspector General. 2007. Acquisition of the National Security Cutter: U.S. Coast Guard. OIG-07–23, January.

Government Accountability Office. 2004. Contract Management: Coast Guard's Deepwater Program Needs Increased Attention to Management and Contractor Oversight. GAO-04–380, March 9.

———. 2005. Coast Guard: Progress Being Made on Addressing Deepwater Legacy Asset Condition Issues and Program Management, but Acquisition Challenges Remain. GAO-05–757, July 22.

———. 2005a. Coast Guard: Preliminary Observations on the Condition of Deepwater Legacy Assets and Acquisition Management Challenges. GAO-05–307T, April 20.

———. 2007. Coast Guard: Preliminary Observations on Deepwater Program Assets and Management Challenges. GAO-07–446T, February 15.

———. 2007a. Coast Guard: Status of Efforts to Improve Deepwater Program Management and Address Operational Challenges. GAO-07–575T, March 8.

———. 2007b. Coast Guard: Challenges Affecting Deepwater Asset Deployment and Management and Efforts to Address Them. GAO-07–874, June.

———. 2008. Coast Guard: Deepwater Program Management Initiatives and Key Homeland Security Missions. GAO-08–531T, March 5.

———. 2008a. Coast Guard: Changes in Course Improves Deepwater Management and Oversight, but Outcome Still Uncertain. GAO-08–745, June.

Hart, O., and J. Moore. 2008. "Contracts as Reference Points." *The Quarterly Journal of Economics* 123 (1): 1–48.

Heide, J., and A. Miner. 1992. "The Shadow of the Future: Effects of Anticipated Interaction and Frequency of Contact on Buyer-Seller Cooperation." *Academy of Management Journal* 35 (3): 265–91.

Heinrich, C.J. 1999. "Do Government Bureaucrats Make Effective Use of Performance Management Information?" *Journal of Public Administration Research and Theory* 9 (3): 363–94.

Hutton, J. 2008. "Presentation on Contracting to MPA Students." Delivered at the Maxwell School of Citizenship and Public Affairs, Syracuse University, New York, April 2. Data based on GAP analysis of data from the Federal Procurement Data System.

Kelman, S.J. 2002. "Contracting." In *The Tools of Government: A Guide to the New Governance,* ed. Lester M. Salamon. New York: Oxford University Press.

Lichbach, M.I. 1996. *The Cooperator's Dilemma.* Ann Arbor, MI: University of Michigan Press.

Martin, L.L. 2004. "Performance-Based Contracting for Human Services: Does It Work?" *Administration in Social Work* 29 (1): 63–77.

O'Looney, J.A. 1998. *Outsourcing State and Local Government Services: Decision-Making Strategies and Management Methods.* Westport, CT: Quorum Books.

O'Rourke, R. 2008. Coast Guard Deepwater Acquisition Programs: Background, Oversight Issues, and Options for Congress. Congressional Research Service Report for Congress, June 5.

Sclar, E.D. 2000. *You Don't Always Get What You Pay For: The Economics of Privatization.* Ithaca, NY: Cornell University Press.

Tirole, Jean. 1999. "Incomplete Contracts: Where Do We Stand?" *Econometrica* 76 (4): 741–81.

U.S. Coast Guard. 2008. "First National Security Cutter Delivered to the Coast," Press Release, May 8. http://www.piersystem.com/go/doc/786/201676/.

U.S. Department of Transportation. 1999. "Coast Guard Deepwater Acquisition Project Designated as Government Reinvention Laboratory." Press Release, June 24. http://govinfo.library.unt.edu/npr/library/news/062999.html.

Weimer, D., and A. Vining. 1999. *Policy Analysis: Concepts and Practice.* Upper Saddle River, NJ: Prentice Hall.

Williamson, O. 1975. *Markets and Hierarchies, Analysis and Antitrust Implications: A Study in the Economics of Internal Organization,* New York: Free Press.

———. 1996. *The Mechanisms of Governance.* New York: Oxford University Press.

———. 2005. *The Economics of Governance. American Economic Association Paper and Proceedings* 95 (2): 1–18.

4

ACCOUNTABILITY FOR GLOBAL GOVERNANCE ORGANIZATIONS

Jonathan G.S. Koppell

The language of legitimacy and authority is abstract. People rarely discuss these ideas explicitly in the course of daily affairs. But they do, in fact, talk about them. A lot. Both concepts are subsumed in a word amorphous enough to encompass them both, and then some. The word, of course, is *accountability,* and it has become a catch-all for all that is good in administration and governance. One can never have too much accountability. No one will ever be criticized for excessive emphasis on accountability. Democrats and Republicans, conservatives and liberals, Big Enders and Little Enders, all can agree that accountability is a good thing, worthy of our attention and pursuit.

But all this bonhomie masks some critical disagreement. What is meant by accountability varies with the values of the person using the word and also the context in which it is being applied. To be accountable in the governmental context, for example, is not the same as it is in a for-profit firm. And, even more specifically, to be accountable as an elected official is not the same as being accountable as a bureaucrat, a regulator, or a judge. Although not as precise as we ought to be in the formulation of accountability expectations, we nonetheless have an intuitive understanding of the variations. It is understood, for example, that an accountable judge need not agree with the person who appointed her, though this expectation may apply to appointees in other contexts. Uncertainty regarding accountability expectations dramatically increases the likelihood of an individual or organization being branded "unaccountable."

So it is with global governance organizations (GGOs), entities that promulgate rules with the goal of global adoption and implementation. GGOs are frequently maligned as unaccountable precisely because there is no shared intuition regarding the meaning of accountability for such bodies. Even more problematic, global governance organizations elude even self-conscious efforts to formulate an applicable notion of accountability

THE ACCOUNTABILITY DILEMMA OF GLOBAL GOVERNANCE ORGANIZATIONS

Global governance organizations (GGOs) have been simultaneously accused of irrelevance and illegitimacy. They are irrelevant, it is charged, because GGOs lack the coercive tools so crucial to compelling obedience from the governed and thus depend on the good will of those they ostensibly control. At the same time, GGOs are called unjust because they do not live up to contemporary norms of democratic governance. They suffer chronically from a "democratic deficit" (Keohane and Nye 2003; Falk and Strauss 2001; Verweij and Josling 2003). And, more pertinently from the perspective of those gathered here, they are accountability-challenged (Bovens 2007).

The persistence of both critiques of GGOs is not trivial. For GGOs to be effective and escape the charge of irrelevance they must deviate significantly from the accepted normative models of democratic governance. These adaptations are not merely unfamiliar; they are at odds with some core beliefs about the requirements of legitimate democratic governance—for example, equity, fairness, and disinterestedness. Indeed, the undemocratic practices of GGOs clash even with expectations adapted to the transnational setting, such as those offered by Dahl (1999) or Keohane (2002): accountability, participation, and transparency. Meeting the demands of effective global governance can be fundamentally inconsistent with norms of democratic administration—and is problematic for those who call for more transnational democracy. Any democratic legitimacy achieved in the realm of global governance will never *fully* meet expectations cultivated in a domestic context. Conversely, any global governance organization that *does* meet traditional norms of democratic legitimacy will likely never possess meaningful authority. This conclusion is based on an empirical examination of 25 global governance organizations that develop, promulgate, and implement rules on a global scale (see Table 4.1). The study, which took an evolutionary perspective, sought to understand GGOs' approach to organizational structure, rule making, adherence, and interest-group participation. Inferences are drawn from the collective characteristics of the surviving population.

The pages that follow explore variation in accountability expectations of GGOs. This variation is not random and in fact is a function of the blended aspirations for organizational legitimacy and authority that bedevil GGOs. Emphasis on either of these sometimes conflicting qualities will lead to different types of accountability and, unavoidably, different unmet accountability expectations. I argue that achieving the legitimacy/authority balance and resolving conflicts among aspects of accountability represent a single struggle. Understanding why some global governance organizations tilt toward *responsibility* notions of accountability while others lean in the direction of *responsiveness* hinges on the same distinction that drives organizations to emphasize legitimacy or authority. The explanation lies in the publicness and constrictiveness of each GGO's activities. These two dimensions of each GGO's purpose determine the salience of legitimacy and authority, respectively, and, in turn, explain the accountability patterns we observe.

The first section of the chapter briefly describes the tension between legitimacy and authority and summarizes the typology of notions of accountability and the claims regarding the pathological consequences of achieving all five accountability types. The second section then links accountability types with legitimacy and authority. As the demands of legitimacy and authority permeate all five accountability notions to some extent, this analysis focuses on the two most distinctive associations: legitimacy-responsibility and authority-responsiveness. Finally, the third section develops the core claim of the essay, that the lines from GGO publicness and constrictiveness are drawn to accountability demands through the variation in emphasis of legitimacy and authority.

The set of organizations studied includes well-known entities such as the World Trade Organization, World Health Organization, and International Atomic Energy Agency, as well as many others that toil in relative obscurity because their actions are remote from the lives of the typical individual—for example, the World Customs Organization, the Marine Stewardship Council, and the Universal Postal Union. Some have the additional cloak of anonymity that comes from operating in highly specialized spheres like accounting (International Accounting Standards Board, or IASB) and the engineering of computer code (World Wide Web Consortium [W3C or the Unicode Consortium]). The empirical findings are based on an examination of a dataset created by the coding of structural and procedural elements and complemented by a qualitative investigation that revealed the organizational dynamics within and surrounding each GGO. The study's conclusions are neither defeatist nor a rationalization of undemocratic structures. Rather,

Table 4.1

Global Governance Organizations Studied

	Acronym	Name
1	ASTM	ASTM International (American Society for Testing and Materials)
2	BCBS	Basel Committee on Banking Supervision
3	CITES	Convention in the Trade of Endangered Species
4	FLOI	Fairtrade Labeling Organizations International
5	FATF	Financial Action Task Force on Money Laundering
6	FSC	Forest Stewardship Council
7	IASB	International Accounting Standards Board
8	IAEA	International Atomic Energy Agency
9	ICAO	International Civil Aviation Organization
10	IEC	International Electrotechnical Commission
11	ILO	International Labor Organization
12	IMO	International Maritime Organization
13	ISO	International Organization for Standardization
14	ISA	International Seabed Authority
15	ITU	International Telecommunications Union
16	IWC	International Whaling Commission
17	ICANN	Internet Corp for Assigned Names and Numbers
18	MSC	Marine Stewardship Council
19	UC	Unicode Consortium
20	UPU	Universal Postal Union
21	WCO	World Customs Organization
22	WHO	World Health Organization
23	WIPO	World Intellectual Property Organization
24	WTO	World Trade Organization
25	W3C	World Wide Web Consortium

I attempt to paint a portrait of global governance organizations that highlights common features and crucial differences—and that is realistic in its evaluation of GGOs against a backdrop that accurately reflects the constraints they face.

Legitimacy-Authority Tension in Global Governance

Accountability is thought to be a necessary if not sufficient element of legitimacy in the context of democratic governance, but this seemingly straightforward connection is certainly not applicable in the realm of global governance. In fact, the dynamic relationship among accountability, legitimacy, and authority provides the key for deciphering the observed variation in GGO structure and process. Previously I have argued that a five-part schema can be used to differentiate among different accountability types—*liability, transparency, controllability, responsibility,* and *responsiveness* (Koppell 2005a). This typology reflects that notions of accountability are sometimes incompatible with one another, a complication that sometimes poses vexing challenges to leaders of organizations caught in the crosshairs. Organizations in this position are diagnosed as suffering from "Multiple Accountabilities Disorder" (MAD). But the ongoing study of global governance organizations suggested that another struggle is at play—the conflict between legitimacy and authority (Koppell 2008).

Like the dimensions of accountability which, when pried apart, reveal their internal tension, the notions of legitimacy and authority are typically treated as constant allies. Legitimacy is the basis of authority. "Power with legitimacy" is often offered as the very definition of authority. But this perspective does not take into consideration the reality of authority; obedience and the institutionalization of power *may* be grounded in legitimacy but oftentimes it is not. The coerciveness of a state, to take one example, can bring authority even in the profound absence of legitimacy. Coverage of the aftermath of the catastrophic flood in Burma showed a regime with authority that is utterly lacking in legitimacy in either political terms (sham elections notwithstanding) or practical terms (the shameful failure to care for victims of the recent cyclone undermines such claims).

Prying apart legitimacy and authority reveals that these two concepts do not necessarily go hand-in-hand. And in this chapter I argue that the publicness and constrictiveness of each GGO's activities will determine whether the organization is primarily concerned with one or the other.

Publicness → Legitimacy → Responsibility. Public concerns are shared and reflect common welfare and matters that affect us collectively or our fundamentally shared rights. As a result the more public an organization's activities, the more amplified will be concerns regarding the justness of that GGO's assumption of its role and the manner in which its mission is carried out. Note that not everything a governmental organization does is equally public by this definition.

Constrictiveness → Authority → Responsiveness. When a governance organization approaches monopoly in a given sphere, when it is unconstrained by structures or rival claims, when its jurisdiction expands to cover more people, territory, or substantive issues and thus excludes the possibility of exit, its constrictiveness grows. Essentially, its power demands become less avoidable and the implicit call for authority is more likely to be questioned.

A wide variation exists across the entire population of organizations studied on both publicness and constrictiveness. Postal services in the United States are neither highly public nor constrictive by the terms laid out here. The state's monopoly on violence is not invoked, and civil liberties are not in peril. The postal service does not impose a high degree of constraint either. It does reach an enormous number of people and provide an important service, but it is highly constrained itself by regulation, oversight, and competitors who limit its ability to dominate the markets in which it faces substitutes (i.e., email) or rivals (e.g., United Parcel Service). Thus it is not surprising that neither the legitimacy nor the authority of the USPS is terribly salient notwithstanding the fact that the selection (hiring) of postal workers is beyond the direct influence of the citizenry.

Now consider a different type of organization: private prison operators. These have transformed the correctional systems of many states by assuming responsibility (by contract) for locking up those convicted of violating our laws. In this case, the organization's function is highly public and thus raises legitimacy as a concern. The prison operators also impose a high degree of constraint (albeit on a relatively small population), and their power is only loosely constrained in daily exercise. Not surprisingly, the delegation of authority to such firms is of heightened concern. As GGOs rise on both dimensions—publicness and constrictiveness—the pressures that create conflicts manifest as clashing accountability expectations. Conflicting accountability expectations—echoes of the tension between legitimacy and authority—are the byproduct and, at worst, the immediate sources of GGO dysfunction.

DIFFERENT TYPES OF ACCOUNTABILITY

Layering every imagined meaning of "accountability" in a single definition would render the concept effectively meaningless. To address this persistent problem, scholars have offered typologies of accountability to help us articulate the value emphasis for different accountability approaches to public administration. The five-part schema we have aleady mentioned (Koppell 2005a) emphasizes the "virtues of accountability," rather than the mechanisms constructed to achieve it (a distinction explained by Schillemans and Bovens in this volume). The reason for presenting yet another typology is to facilitate the clearest possible discussion about account-ability in the global governance context. In the political context, one's conception of account-ability is tied to beliefs regarding the nature of a just government, the role of the citizenry in setting policy, and the interaction between elected officials and career civil servants. In other contexts, one's definition of accountability reflects beliefs about the ideal distribution of power. The definition of an "accountable chief executive," for example, depends upon one's vision for the relationship among the board of directors, management, and shareholders. For nonprofits, accountability reflects ideals for the relationship between leaders and contributors (living and dead), the community, and society.

The five categories of accountability offered—transparency, liability, controllability, responsi-bility, and responsiveness—are broad and not mutually exclusive. Organizations can be account-able in more than one sense. Indeed, transparency and liability can be thought of as foundations, supporting notions that underpin all accountability manifestations. Greater tension exists among controllability, responsibility, and responsiveness. The last two notions of accountability in particu-lar seem to pull GGOs in different directions. This reflects the relationship between these notions of accountability and the legitimacy-authority tension in global governance.

Transparency

Transparency is the literal value of accountability. An accountable organization cannot obfuscate its mistakes to avoid scrutiny. Transparency is important for its instrumental value in assessing organizational performance, but belief in the openness of government is so firmly ingrained in our collective psyche that it has innate value. Transparency requires that bureaucrats be subject to regular review and questioning. Alleged wrongdoing or perceived failure must be investigated and explained. A transparent public organization grants access to the public, the press, interest groups, and other parties interested in an organization's activities.

Liability

Individuals and organizations must face consequences attached to performance—punishment for malfeasance and rewards for success—to be accountable in this sense. Seemingly alien in the public sector, this notion is quite familiar with respect to elected officials. They are said to be ac-countable because they can be "punished,"—removed from office by voters, unlike bureaucrats and judges who are said to be unaccountable for this reason (Goodin 2000). Unelected persons can be punished in other ways, of course. Both public and private bureaucrats are criminally li-able for misappropriating resources; even organizations can be held criminally liable for illegal activities. One example is the indictment and plea bargain of the Arthur Andersen accounting firm for its actions related to Enron. Negative consequences do not have to involve criminal penalties to create "liability." Poor performance evaluations with consequent impact on compensation are consistent with this dimension of accountability. Rewarding managers based on their individual or organizational performance is consistent with the liability vision of accountability. Employees in a host of jobs are compensated based on performance (e.g., sales personnel that are paid on a com-mission system) or receive bonuses tied to their performance. Government agencies now provide cash rewards for exemplary performance. New York City school superintendents, for example, are eligible for bonuses (New York City Department of Education 2002). This approach also has been adapted by governments. The 1996 welfare reform provided for grants of $20 million to five states based on their ability to reduce the rate of out-of-wedlock births (Healy 1999).

Controllability

The dominant conception of accountability revolves around *control*. If X can induce the behavior of Y, it is said that X controls Y—and that Y is accountable to X. The plausibility of "bureaucratic control" has been the subject of debate from the early days of public administration (Barnard 1938; Selznick 1957). Wilson (1887) and Goodnow (1900) offered the normative ideal of a politics/administration dichotomy: elected officials should reach consensus on public-policy objectives and rely upon bureaucrats for implementation. Thus the accountability of an organization depends on the answer to this key question: Did the organization do what its principal) commanded?

The well-known schema of accountability types initially offered by Romzek and Dubnick (1987) elaborates on the idea of control. They characterize "accountability relationships" on two dimensions, "the source of control (internal or external) and the degree of control (high or low)" (1987, 61) which yields four accountability types—hierarchical, legal, professional, and political—each of which is associated with a different "value emphasis" (Dubnick and Romzek 1991, 1993; Radin and Romzek 1996; Romzek and Ingraham 2000). But this leaves some ambiguity. "Political accountability," for example, is marked by an expectation of "responsive[ness] to key stakeholders" (Romzek and Dubnick 1987). This conflates an organization's responsiveness to entities that have formal authority (e.g., Congress) and those that have informal influence (e.g., interest groups). In my view these are distinct conceptions of accountability, one upward and one outward.

Controllability is especially ambiguous in the context of global governance, since it is not clear who *ought* to have control. One naturally looks to the members, but it is the tension among members that GGOs inevitably struggle with. Moreover, the relationships between GGOs and their members vary by context. In the discussion of organizational structure, for example, the members are seen as "principals" who delegate to and oversee their "agents." The control notion seems to fit naturally (notwithstanding the difficulty in figuring out whose preferences are operative). But in the adherence context, the roles are reversed. Members are now the de facto agents of the GGO, adopting and implementing rules to give them meaning. This doesn't reduce the need for control-type accountability. Indeed, the adherence relationship underscores the importance of maintaining members' enthusiasm for the rules promulgated by the GGO. In its absence, adherence will suffer dramatically. But the control arrow seems to be constantly spinning rather than pointing in one direction.

Responsibility

Bureaucrats and organizations can be constrained by laws, rules, or norms rather than commands. This is labeled responsibility, a notion broad enough itself to accommodate alternative visions. Moe and Gilmour (1995) stress legal requirements regarding organizational behavior, incorporation of policy and program objectives into legislation, and elimination of plural executives (e.g., commissions) and other novel institutional arrangements that confuse lines of authority and diminish accountability (Leazes Jr. 1997; Moe 1994, 2000). Responsibility can also take the form of formal and informal professional standards or behavioral norms. Such standards set expectations against which bureaucrats can be evaluated (DiIulio 1994; Kearney and Sinha 1988; McKinney 1981). Accountable bureaucrats ought not simply follow orders, Carl Friedrich (1940) argues, but utilize their expertise, constrained by professional and moral standards. In retort, some have argued that professional standards can in fact hinder control by substituting professional interests for public concerns (Tullock 1965; Piven and Cloward 1971; Mladenka 1980; Hummel 1987).

Responsibility can pertain to internal standards of behavior and performance not set by legislators. For example, Bernard Rosen (1989) outlines responsibilities to "make laws work as intended," to "initiate changes in policies and programs," and to "enhance citizen confidence in the administrative institutions of government." All variations on responsibility boil down to a core question quite different than the one at the heart of controllability. Did the organization follow the rules?

Responsiveness

Another alternative to the hierarchical controllability approach to accountability is, in a sense, more horizontal. Responsiveness differentiates an organization's attention to direct expressions of the needs and desires of its constituents (or clients) from the orders of elected officials. This element of accountability is emphasized in the customer-oriented approach suggested by reforms aimed at "reinventing government" (Sensenbrenner 1991; Osborne and Gaebler 1992). Note that responsiveness is often used to connote the sense of accountability described above as controllability (e.g., Rourke 1992; Romzek 1987). Responsiveness, as used in this typology, turns accountability outward rather than upward.

An organization can be responsive to the demands of the governed in different ways. It might poll "customers," solicit input through focus groups, or establish advisory councils with representation of key constituent groups. Organized interest groups aggregate and articulate preferences of affected communities. The core question of responsiveness: did the organization meet expectations?

ACCOUNTABILITY, LEGITIMACY, AND AUTHORITY

Cataloging alternative notions of accountability does not explain why an organization emphasizes one type of accountability or another. But this question dovetails with another issue for global governance organizations: the tension between legitimacy and authority. All types of accountability can be traced to both legitimacy and authority. Legitimacy is most intimately tied to responsibility, while authority is strongly associated with responsiveness.

Legitimacy and Responsibility

Accountability that emphasizes responsibility focuses on rules and norms in carrying out organizational functions. This approach resonates powerfully with the tenets of normative legitimacy. Legitimate government bodies—particularly in the democratic context—are expected to be run in accordance with established principles either enshrined in law or encapsulated in social, cultural, and professional norms. The process by which the leaders are chosen and the procedures followed in the exercise of state power are keys to democratic legitimacy. Hallmarks of a legitimate process include transparency, predictability according to a set of well-known rules, equality before the law or in any governmental proceeding, professionalism, objectivity, and disinterestedness in the arbitration of disputes. An irresponsible GGO, one that fails to meet these expectations, is not legitimate.

Fidelity to rules as a feature of normative legitimacy can also be seen in nongovernmental contexts. The legitimacy of a scientist or a scientific institution, for example, depends in large measure on demonstrable consistency with norms regarding the scientific method. Failure to follow accepted practices regarding collection of data, research design, and so on, will impugn results as illegitimate. In the realm of public policy making, procedural legitimacy is shaped by political *and* scientific considerations. Legitimacy requires that the process be open and in accordance with legal requirements (e.g., Administrative Procedures Act in the United States). Transnational governance organizations struggle with norms because there is no agreed upon procedural standard to which they can refer (Esty 2007). But if the analysis informing policy decisions is not carried out in a fashion consistent with professional norms or appears to be manufactured to support a predetermined outcome, the resulting policy will also lack legitimacy.

Authority and Responsiveness

The demands of authority for GGOs reflect the distinctive dynamics of global governance. Lacking coercive tools, GGOs are missing a core mechanism by which obedience is compelled. Legitimacy is often framed as a basis of authority—we obey institutions because they are legitimate—but this is not the end of the story. In some circumstances we obey institutions because we must or because it is in our interests to so. An organization's power to coerce enhances its authority precisely because it has the ability to manipulate the interests of the potential subject. Some global governance organizations do have coercive tools. A small set of GGOs effectively controls access to some valued resource that offers an analogous tool. For example, the Internet Corporation for Assigned Names and Numbers (ICANN) can effectively deny access to the "root servers" of the Internet to those entities unwilling to comply with its rules on domain-names usage and dispute resolution. Several GGOs have agents that effectively wield such a cudgel. The World Customs Organization (WCO), for instance, sees its rules backed by the threat of exclusion by import authorities. Market-driven governance organizations try to approximate this power by creating a comparative market advantage to compliance. The Forest Stewardship Council, for example, promotes its standards in the retail marketplace and controls use of its distinguishing mark. This strategy is different than the prototypical governmental sanction (e.g., fine, imprisonment), but it is intended to alter the interest calculus of potential subjects.

Lacking the ability to enforce their will, global governance organizations seek alternative means to make obedience serve the interests of potential subjects. In a nutshell, some GGOs rely on responsiveness-type accountability, or satisfying the demands of subjects so that the institutionalization of power is in their best interests. In the absence of such benefits, nations or companies may simply walk away, thus denying the GGO authority, regardless of any normative legitimacy it may have achieved through the structure and process. Every time another member walks away, the benefit of accepting the GGO's authority is further reduced for remaining members, because the rules created are that much less universal. Put into stark relief, all GGO members are not created equal, and their preferences must be treated accordingly. As explained in previous work (Koppell 2008), the GGO must place the interests of key parties first. In real terms this hard fact means that responsiveness is not universal but focused on those entities whose obedience is most critical to the authority of the organization—a clear violation of responsibility.

UNDERSTANDING THE ACCOUNTABILITY EQUATION FOR GGOS

If concern with organizational legitimacy and authority were fixed, observation of the legitimacy-responsibility and authority-responsiveness linkages would not add much insight. But variation exists in the degree to which we care who has acquired authority and whether an organization is legitimate. The neighborhood supermarket and coffee shop don't spend much time on legitimacy, for example. Many nonprofit organizations are untroubled by legitimacy or authority. Is the Junior League legitimate? Does the American Cancer Society wield inordinate authority? Clearly something can be learned from an examination of the variation in the importance of legitimacy and authority, which speaks directly to the accountability problem of GGOs.

Varying Salience of Legitimacy and Authority

Legitimacy is most frequently raised as an issue in the governmental context. Following the 2000 U.S. presidential election, for example, some speculated that George W. Bush's ability to govern might be impaired by the controversy surrounding the election (Woodlief 2000; Apple 2000). For fledgling democracies, the approval of outside election monitors confers legitimacy on new leaders, which increases their credibility not only with their own people but also with the international community. But we are not equally concerned with the legitimacy of all governmental entities. The legitimacy of the king (or the president) is of concern, but the legitimacy of the dogcatcher or the mail carrier generally is not.

Outside the governmental sphere legitimacy is questioned less frequently. The legitimacy of some nongovernmental entities has been broadly critiqued. In recent years, for example, heavy-handed tactics of some NGOs in the name of environmental goals has prompted critics to question their role as environmental defenders (e.g., Koch-Mehrin 2006). For-profit prison operators have been criticized as illegitimate holders of power over inmates (Schmidt 2006; *St. Petersburg Times* 2001; *Washington Post* 1998). Companies that misrepresent themselves to customers or engage in exploitative business practices are often called "illegitimate" in ways that stretch beyond any dictionary definition of illegality (e.g., Siegel 2004).

The salience of authority as a concern is similarly variable. The authority of an organization with rather modest ability to compel behavior, say, a pet-grooming establishment, is far less controversial than a regulatory organization with the ability to assess substantial fines. Identifying the drivers of variation in the salience of legitimacy and authority unravels the connection between these theoretical constructs, along with the practical demands faced by GGOs. Contemporary questions about the legitimacy and authority of GGOs (articulated as demands for greater accountability) indicate that something has changed. Global governance organizations have been with us for over one hundred years in transportation and telecommunications, for example, and yet their critics are only recently loud enough to be heard (Murphy 1994). Either a new set of expectations has arisen, or the context in which such entities operate has evolved.

Publicness and Legitimacy

Publicness and constrictiveness are keys to the salience enigma. The term "publicness" is intended to capture the extent to which different organizations draw upon, invoke, and affect the common and shared interests of all members of a society. Publicness is more than "governmentality" although government organizations are, by and large, more public than nongovernmental organizations. Indicators of organizational publicness are:

An *exclusive hold on tools of sanction:* Weber famously differentiated states by their monopoly on the legitimate use of force (Weber 1965 [1918]). State coerciveness is on a continuum, and we can see state violence—capital punishment and incarceration—as on the far end. Any organization with coercive force at its disposal is more public. Other coercive powers, including seizing property, levying fines, or imposing other penalties, also are indicators of heightened publicness of an organization.

Pursuit of common/collective goods: The more an organization serves a common interest, the more public the organization should be regarded. Indivisible public goods are in this sense more public than individually consumed goods that everyone needs or wants. Thus, to illustrate with a rather extreme comparison, the United Nations High Commission on Refugees is a more public organization than Coca-Cola, even though the beverage company provides a good to a large percentage of the world's population. It follows that control of a common good—by a private or governmental organization—renders an organization more public.

Effect on the public side of the individual: State violence is public not only because it strikes at the core of the government's distinctive place in society, but also because it gives the state power to deprive individuals of civic guarantees. By depriving individuals of their rights of citizenship, an organization is directly impinging on the public side of the individual. Some effects on individuals are essentially public—those that lie at the core of an individual's citizenship—while others are more private. Organizations are therefore differentiated based upon the sphere of their effects on individuals. Organizations that affect individuals' purely private interests—their income or product choices—are less public than those that affect civic interests such as voting ability or right to purchase property. Organizations that pursue profits for shareholders are less public than those endeavoring to maintain collective goods such as security. Organizations that rely upon market mechanisms widely available are less public than those wielding the exclusive power to levy fines or impose penalties.

On each dimension of publicness, there is variation for every organization, but assigning a numerical score on each dimension as a means of establishing an aggregate "publicness" measure would yield a highly subjective result. A solution to this problem is to rate organizations on a continuum from "high" to "medium" to "low publicness." Table 4.2 provides a sense of the range of possibilities in the total population of organizations.

As the publicness of an organization's activities increases, the legitimacy of that organization becomes an increasingly salient consideration. Our concern for the legitimacy of the police department, for example, a government agency with the authority to deprive many people of their fundamental rights, is higher than our concern about a municipal sanitation department. Even a governmental entity without the power of violence, such as a municipal zoning board, raises significant legitimacy concerns because of its ability to curtail enjoyment of property rights. Few have trouble seeing the work of such governmental bodies as public in character. Yet there are also private organizations with a high level of publicness that arouse legitimacy concerns.

One such organization is the Educational Testing Service (ETS). The Princeton, New Jersey–based nonprofit company creates and administers a range of academic tests (including the SAT) which are crucial to thousands of students seeking admission to American universities every year. ETS exams are offered around the world and constitute a gateway to U.S. higher education. Thus the role performed by this private company is public in its effect (and its nonprofit status accords special privileges under U.S. law). It is not surprising that the legitimacy of this organization has been called into question by teachers, students, parents, and concerned interest groups (Nordheimer and Franz 1997; Jackson 1986). Critics have objected to the unchecked power of the testing agency, the manner in which it produces its exams, and the fees it charges test takers.

Other nongovernmental organizations have a higher level of publicness because they are engaged as government contractors. The numerous charges of malfeasance aimed at Halliburton, the massive defense company carrying out billions of dollars of work in Iraq, raise legitimacy questions for the company and the government (e.g., Gibbons 2004). Private prison operators, companies that have assumed increasing responsibility for housing the nation's inmates, also raise legitimacy concerns because of the intrinsically public nature of the role they are performing and the delegation of responsibility from a governmental body. Indeed, the legitimacy of even allowing private organizations to assume this responsibility has been questioned (e.g., Morris 1998).

The organizational profile considers three aspects of publicness, (Table 4.2) to arrive at an overall composite—which is more art than science. One might take issue with the assessment of a particular organization, and certainly good arguments could be made for adjusting the characteriza-

Table 4.2

Variation in Publicness of Sample Organizations

Organization	Sanction	Collective Good	"Public Side of the Individual"	Overall Publicness
Real estate appraiser	L	L	L	L
Hair stylist	L	L	L	L
Hot dog vendor	L	L	L	L
Elks Club	L	L/M	L	L
Little League	L	L/M	L	L
Wal-Mart	L/M	L	L	L
Microsoft	L	M	L	L/M
W3C (World Wide Web Consortium)	L	H	L	M
Educational Testing Service	M	M	L/M	M
International Organization for Standardization	L	M	L	M
Prison contractor	H	H	H	H
International Accounting Standards Board	M	H	L	M
ICANN	H	H	L	M
Zoning board	M	H	L	M
World Health Organization	M	H	M	H
President of the United States	H	H	H	H
U.S. Supreme Court	H	H	H	H
UN General Assembly	M	H	M	H
Police department	H	H	H	H
Grammar school principal	M	M	M	M
Housing authority	M	M	M	M
UNICEF	L	H	M	M
NASDAQ	L/M	M	L	M
NH Economic Development Commission	L	H	L	M/L
U.S. Postal Service	L	H	L	M/L
Fannie Mae and Freddie Mac	L	M	L	L/M
Licensing agency	M	H	H	H/M
Animal control	M	H	L	M

tion of several of the organizations. The use of very broad categories is intended to keep the focus on the essential point instead of getting caught up in the characterization of one organization or another. This hypothesized account of the salience of legitimacy and authority is confirmed mostly by intuition. When we consider organizations along the spectrum of publicness, legitimacy is more likely to be an issue with greater publicness, which suggests that the demands for responsibility-centered accountability will grow correspondingly louder as well.

Constrictiveness and Authority

The salience of authority as an issue naturally reflects the nature of the power being institutionalized. Differentiating organizations based upon the "amount of power" required to achieve their objectives makes sense, but such a concept is difficult to measure. The focus is on a discrete dimension of power, here called "constrictiveness." Individuals and organizations are most concerned with the limitations placed on them by rulemaking bodies. The more constraint, the greater the concern people will have about that organization's assumption of authority.

Differentiating organizations based on constrictiveness is analogous to the treatment of publicness in our discussion of legitimacy. We would expect organizations seeking more constrictive authority to encounter more resistance. Thus assertions of greater constrictiveness increase the salience of authority as an issue. A composite picture of an organization's constrictiveness extends from classic differentiations of power.

Extent and Scope

Dahl's explication of the concept of power differentiates two aspects (1957). Extent of power refers to the likelihood of compliance or the probability that an organization gets what it wants. The higher the probability, the more powerful we consider the organization. An organization seeking a high level of compliance is more constrictive than one which provides greater latitude to "the governed."

Scope can be seen from two perspectives. It refers to the number of people or entities over which an organization has influence as well as to the range of substantive areas in which it has influence. The latter is similar to the "spheres" described by Michael Walzer (1983). An organization with influence in more spheres is regarded as being more powerful. Organizations seeking dominion over a global population (of people or organizations) make a prima facie significant assertion of power in this sense.

Latitude

The limitations on an organization's power can include formal encumbrances associated with a constitutional regime and informal restrictions borne of dependence on allies, interest groups, and so forth. More constrained organizations are less constraining themselves. An organization that is subject to significant pressure in shaping its preferences has less latitude than one immune to such influence. So the "latitude" enjoyed by a GGO (or any other governing body) is intended to broadly capture ways in which an organization may be limited.

Concentration

Highly concentrated power ought to be distinguished from widely distributed power. This consideration extends from the previous point. Unrivaled power deprives affected parties of any recourse and thus is more constrictive. The World Trade Organization, for example, is the only venue for adjudication of many disputes within its substantive domain. Parties have no alternative available in its sphere. The International Electrical Commission, on the other hand, faces competitor organizations (e.g., International Organization for Standardization, International Telecommunications Union) that promulgate some overlapping standards in its sphere of specialization. This provides potentially constrained organizations an alternative to submission.

An organization facing a great deal of competition in a market environment should be regarded differently than the monopolist because its options are more proscribed. Michael Porter captured this dynamic well with his model describing the "forces" that constrain businesses (1998). Outside forces—suppliers, investors, customers—can limit a firm's power in the marketplace.

As Table 4.3 indicates, many of the more constrictive organizations are governmental. But nongovernmental organizations also rise on this dimension, which illustrates the notion that constrictive power is not the exclusive property of the government. It is important to understand what makes a nongovernmental entity constrictive. Consider Microsoft, a semi-monopolist that has driven out competitors and dominates the market for PC operating systems. Microsoft controls

Table 4.3

Variation in Constrictiveness of Sample Organizations

Organization	Extent and Scope	Lack of Constraint	Concentration	Overall Constrict
Real estate appraiser	L	L	L	L
Hair stylist	L	L	L	L
Hot dog vendor	L	L	L	L
Elks Club	L	L	L	L
Little League	L	L/M	L	L
Wal-Mart	M	M	M	M
Microsoft	H	M/H	M	H
W3C (World Wide Web Consortium)	H	H	H	H
Educational Testing Service	H	H	H	H
International Organization for Standardization	H	M	M	M
Prison contractor	M	M	M	M
International Accounting Standards Board	H	H	M	H
ICANN	H	H	H	H
Zoning board	M	M	H	M
World Health Organization	H	M	M	M
President of the United States	H	H	H	H
U.S. Supreme Court	H	H/M	H	H

a valuable commodity with few alternatives available. As such it imposes significant constraints on its users or even those who choose *not* to use its product. One would expect its authority to be questioned as it has been. On the other hand, Salvatore the Hot Dog Man, a vendor who competes with many comparably priced substitutes in an evenly divided market, receives little scrutiny or objection. Unlike the hot dog man, Microsoft's power is not as constrained by competitive forces. Thus the institutionalization of power in Redmond arouses concern, but Sal's position at a prime intersection does not.

The potential for assertion of highly constrictive power by private-sector organizations is exemplified by the "company town," a disappearing model that saw a single firm as the sole source of employment and the sole provider of all goods and services for an entire community. Residents had almost no ability to disobey the company. Outside critics questioned the moral and political acceptability of such towns in a democratic society, but the authority of the company was essentially absolute.

It's important to see gradations among governmental organizations rather than treat the state as one all-powerful monolith at the high end of the constrictiveness scale. Legislatures have the ability to make and abolish laws within structural and procedural constraints and subject (in most cases) to the electoral consequences of their actions. Some governmental bureaucracies can seize land, freeze assets, and issue or withdraw licenses vital to the operation of businesses. Of course, the police and other law-enforcement agencies have the ability to arrest and detain individuals. Courts can send individuals to prison or even to their death if the accused are found guilty according to prescribed processes. In summary, the power of the state is quite awesome—seemingly unconstrained—and the delegation of this authority is of the highest salience.

But other governmental bodies are not so powerful. As mentioned earlier, the U.S. Postal Service (USPS) provides an important function, but its power is limited in important ways. It is overseen by Congress and constrained in its ability to make key management decisions—such as raising rates—without approval of outside entities. Moreover, it faces competition in significant portions

Table 4.4

Overview of Publicness/Constrictiveness of Sample Organizations

Organization	Publicness	Constrictiveness
Real estate appraiser	Low	Low
Hair stylist	Low	Low
Hot dog vendor	Low	Low
Elks Club	Low	Low
Little League	Low/medium	Low
Wal-Mart	Low	Medium/high
Microsoft	Low	High
W3C (World Wide Web Consortium)	Medium	High
Educational Testing Service	Medium	High
International Standards Organization	Medium	Medium
Prison contractor	High	Medium
International Accounting Standards Board	Med	High
ICANN	Med	High
Zoning board	Med	High
World Health Organization	High	Med
President of the United States	High	High
U.S. Supreme Court	High	High
UN General Assembly	High	High/med
Police Department	High	Medium
Grammar school principal	Med	Low/medium
Housing authority	Med	Low/medium
UNICEF	High	Low
NASDAQ	Medium	Medium
NH Economic Development Commission	High/medium	Low
U.S. Postal Service	Medium	Low
Fannie Mae and Freddie Mac	Medium	Medium
Licensing agency	Medium/high	Medium
Animal Control	Medium	Low

of its business from private rivals such as FedEx. Finally, technological innovation—notably the rise of the Internet—has reduced the dependence on the USPS for significant portions of the population. Not surprisingly, no one is terribly concerned with the authority of the USPS or its accumulation of power. Similarly, sanitation services are undoubtedly important public functions performed by government agencies, but these organizations are not terribly powerful and thus their authority is generally not an issue.

A word of caution about "banal" government agencies: some seemingly innocuous governmental bodies are quite coercive by virtue of their ability to constrain. A state professional licensing agency serves as the unilateral gatekeeper (albeit to a significantly smaller population than many other bodies). There may be little recourse or appeal to decisions of such a body or few options to nonconformance to its norms (Glaberson 2006). Not surprisingly, objections to such panels' actions—and the authority they possess—are voiced regularly, generally by those who are rejected (e.g., Green 2004).

Taken together these determinants of an organization's constrictiveness provide a profile that is helpful in predicting the salience of authority. Some examples used to illustrate publicness and constrictiveness provide a sense of variation that is intuitively apparent, if difficult to quantify (Table 4.4). The reader is left to determine whether this limitation undermines the argument. Facing a highly constrictive regime, individuals and organizations will be warier of any voluntary delega-

Figure 4.1   **Mapping Organizations on Publicness and Constrictiveness**

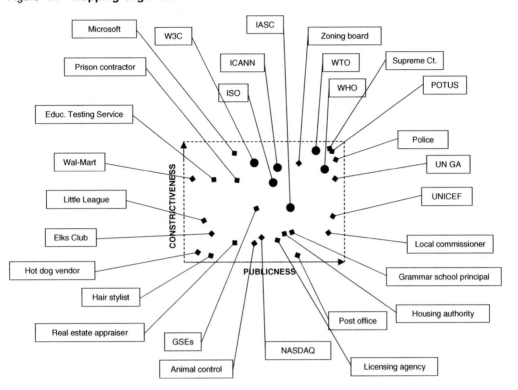

tion of authority. Organizations rising on multiple dimensions of power (e.g., absolute unrivaled control over a sizeable population) are most likely to face rigorous examination and questioning by potential subjects. In terms of accountability, this manifests itself as concern with responsiveness. Imposition of constraint begets demands for the satisfaction of interests.

Drawing a Two-Dimensional Map

The two dimensions of publicness and constrictiveness are mapped in Figure 4.1. This map calls visual attention to the variation on both dimensions and the relationship between them. Interpretation of the picture consistent with the logic of this discussion attributes rising salience of legitimacy as the placement of an organization moves from left to right and rising salience of authority as the placement of an organization moves from bottom to top. GGOs are circular points on the map of organizational legitimacy in Figure 4.1.

A haphazard collection of organizations is distributed across the map revealing the range of combinations. Some organizations are highly public but do not assert much power in their typical activities. One such visible organization is the United Nations Children's Fund (UNICEF). UNICEF runs a wide variety of programs intended to serve and advocate on behalf of the world's poor children (http://www.unicef.org/whatwedo/index.html). With support from the governments of the world and strong dedication to the achievement of a collective good, UNICEF is a highly public organization. Still it neither possesses nor asserts constraining power in any of the ways suggested.

In contrast, organizations with low levels of publicness nevertheless assert a remarkable power in almost every sense. Both Microsoft and Wal-Mart are private companies selling commodities that are consumed privately by millions. Through their remarkable domination of markets, however, both companies impose significant constraints on suppliers, employees, communities, and even customers. Market power does not limit them to the extent that it does many other firms.

Organizations that rise on both the power and constrictiveness dimension raise special concerns precisely because they seek relatively unfettered power in arenas at the core of our shared interests. These organizations face demands associated with both legitimacy and authority, a combination that can prove problematic. Along the central axis of the map, running from the center to the upper right are organizations characterized as medium to high on both dimensions. This area of heightened salience for legitimacy and authority might be called the "Accountability Hot Zone." This tongue-in-cheek label is applied because denizens of the Hot Zone face intense responsibility and responsiveness-accountability demands due to the high salience of legitimacy and authority.

The Hot Zone is not an especially lonely place. Many organizations find themselves occupying this part of the map. The American Presidency and Supreme Court are both in the upper right hand corner of the map. Several organizations find themselves along the central axis of the map—indicating both heightened legitimacy and authority considerations—without the dramatically high publicness and constrictiveness of these institutions. One example is Fannie Mae, a government-sponsored enterprise (GSE) created by the U.S. federal government to expand availability of credit to American homebuyers. Fannie Mae is privately owned with its shares traded on the New York Stock Exchange. And yet it maintains connections to the government (and high levels of publicness) in the form of special privileges and regulatory exemptions granted to facilitate expansion of homeownership. By virtue of its access to relatively inexpensive capital, the two GSEs (Fannie Mae and Freddie Mac) maintain a duopoly in the American secondary mortgage market. Direct competition with the GSEs is effectively impossible given the companies' highly constrictive power over other market participants.

With publicness and constrictiveness in the upper middle range, the salience of Fannie Mae's legitimacy and authority is quite high. Compelling evidence lies in the time and energy being devoted by Congress to an overhaul of the regulatory infrastructure for the GSEs and a reconsideration of their responsibilities (Hilzenrath 2008). Objections to the management of Fannie Mae and Freddie Mac, the compensation of leaders, the fulfillment of public responsibilities, and other matters have led to questions regarding the fundamental appropriateness of their corporate form. Legitimacy is in question in the most basic sense; should the company continue to exist?

Another interesting organization in the middle of the map is NASDAQ, a private company that runs a global equity market based in New York. Listing on NASDAQ is extremely valuable to companies seeking equity capital. NASDAQ provides access to millions of investors around the world and clearly offers a public good, a venue that provides for liquidity and serves as an engine for economic growth. NASDAQ is itself limited and heavily regulated by the federal government and, in recent years, by New York State. It also faces competition from other markets such as the venerable New York Stock Exchange and other exchanges that now compete globally. The legitimacy of NASDAQ, including the appropriateness of its enormous authority to set rules and standards that influence the fortunes of millions of stockholders and employees, has been questioned (and promoted; e.g., Posner 2005).

Mapping Global Governance Organizations

The heterogeneous population of global governance organizations is clustered in the Accountability Hot Zone. Unlike many entities that also reside in this area, GGOs are ill-equipped to navigate the stormy waters of the Hot Zone. The conflicting demands of accountability (responsibility and responsiveness) pose challenges that GGOs struggle to resolve. Table 4.5 compares publicness and constrictiveness dimensions of the GGOs studied.

Most GGOs are *at least* in the medium range on the publicness dimension. GGOs provide public goods, establish and maintain rules and, to some extent, enforce regimes. The Universal Postal Union (UPU), for example, among the most venerable global governance organizations, sets standards and procedures for interaction of the world's postal agencies. UPU created and maintains a system that allows the efficient flow of letters and packages across borders. Other GGOs support subsequent generations of global communications technology, including the International Telecommunications Union (ITU) and the Internet Corporation for Assigned Names and Numbers (ICANN).

With nation-states as members, many GGOs have a governmental quality that underscores their publicness. This is true of ITU and UPU as well as other UN-affiliated entities such as the World Health Organization (WHO), the World Intellectual Property Organization (WIPU), and the International Labor Organization (ILO). They are funded through governments, and their representative bodies are comprised of officials appointed by national governments. All together these features indicate a significant collective investment and interest in their performance.

Global governance organizations are also typically medium to high in terms of their constrictiveness. The geographic scope of GGO activities is, by definition, global. In most substantive areas, a single global governance organization is dominant, and this dominance enhances the constrictiveness of the organization. In shipping, trade, accounting, banking, and aviation there is little choice of a forum for those interested in global rules: opt in to the system as structured, or choose not to participate. Many of the organizations included in this study have deep penetration. The WTO, for example, has 150 nations as members. The ITU not only has 191 member countries, but nearly 700 firms have joined as associates with the implicit intention to adopt existing ITU standards and influence the creation of new ones.

By definition, the substantive scope of activities for GGOs examined is relatively narrow compared with national governments but broader than one might expect. The International Organization for Standardization (ISO) has standards in a wide range of areas, from building materials to medical devices to pollution control. It is currently contemplating standards in the field of corporate social responsibility that push the envelope even further than two recent efforts, ISO 9000 on management controls and ISO 14000 on management of environmental impact. ASTM International, a competing standard setter, also has offerings in a wide range of areas (although its offerings are not as extensive as ISO's). GGOs are continuously surveying the landscape for areas of potential expansion. The International Labor Organization (ILO) recently produced a comprehensive maritime labor treaty, in cooperation with the International Maritime Organization, that would supersede many existing treaties in the field, including several not created by ILO.

Global governance skeptics might argue that speaking of their constrictiveness is nonsensical. GGOs' lack of coercive tools has already been touched upon, although their power is growing each day—perhaps explaining why the salience of GGO legitimacy is rising (Barnett and Finnemore 2004). For example, the World Health Organization's declarations regarding the lack of safety in certain cities during the SARS (severe acute respiratory syndrome) outbreak had severe economic effects in China and Canada. ISO's standards on environmental and management quality are guiding production and investment around the globe and are potentially steering millions of dollars of capital investment to and from compliant and noncompliant firms.

The realities of organizational life in the Accountability Hot Zone are reflected in the commonplace accountability failures of GGOs. Indeed, it seems that concerns regarding legitimacy

Table 4.5

Publicness and Constrictivess of Global Governance Organizations

				Publicness			Constrictiveness		
	Org	Publicness	Constrict	Sanction	Collective goods	Public individual	Extent/scope	Latitude	Con-centration
ASTM International	ASTM	**M**	L	L	M	L	M	L	L
Basel Committee on Banking Supervision	BCBS	M	**H**	H	H	M	H	H	H
Convention in the Trade of Endangered Species	CITES	M	**H**	H	H	L	M	H	H
Financial Action Task Force on Money Laundering	FATF	H	H	H	H	M	H	H	H
Forest Stewardship Council	FSC	M	M	L	H	L	M	M	M
International Accounting Standards Board	IASB	M	**H**	M	H	L	H	M	M
International Atomic Energy Agency	IAEA	H	H	H	H	L	H	H	H
International Civil Aviation Organization	ICAO	H	H	M	H	L	H	H	M
International Electrotechnical Commission	IEC	M	M	L	M	L	M	M	H
International Labour Organization	ILO	**H**	M	L	H	M	H	M	H
International Maritime Organization	IMO	**H**	M	M	H	L	H	M	H
International Organization for Standardization	ISO	M	M	L	M	L	L	M	M
International Seabed Authority	ISA	**H**	L	L	H	L	L	L	M
International Telecommunications Union	ITU	M	M	M	M	L	M	M	M
International Whaling Commission	IWC	M	M	M	H	L	M	M	M
Internet Corporation for Assigned Names and Numbers	ICANN	M	**H**	H	H	L	H	H	H
Unicode Consortium	UC	H	H	L	H	L	H	H	H
Universal Postal Union	UPU	M	M	M	H	L	H	M	M
World Health Organization	WHO	**H**	M	M	M	M	H	M	M
World Intellectual Property Organization	WIPO	M	**H**	M	H	M	H	H	H
World Trade Organization	WTO	H	**H**	H	H	M	H	H	H
World Wide Web Consortium	W3C	M	**H**	L	H	L	H	H	H
World Customs Organization	WCO	M	**H**	M	H	M	H	H	H
Fairtrade Labelling Organizations International	FLOI	M	M	L	M	L	M	L	M
Marine Stewardship Council	MSC	M	M	L	H	L	M	M	H

Note: Bold letters indicate a differential in salience.

and authority interact. Organizations with fairly high publicness and higher levels of constrictiveness seem to have higher levels of salience of legitimacy than one would expect on the basis of publicness alone. GGOs get caught oscillating between demands or choosing to satisfy one and consistently come up short on the other.

The Internet Corporation for Assigned Names and Numbers (ICANN) provides a perfect example of the former approach. Considered on either single dimension, ICANN does not seem likely to arouse deep concerns. ICANN is an entity created to administer the Domain Name Registry, essentially the Internet's phonebook and switchboard. ICANN is incorporated as a private nonprofit corporation, but it was created under the direction and with the consent of the U.S. government, with its power derived from its control over the Domain Name System (which is actually operated on government computers). ICANN is indirectly overseen by Congress through the government agency with which it has a contractual relationship. Within its relatively narrow substantive sphere, ICANN has significant power. It controls the creation of new domains (e.g., ".com") and the approval of registrars for new domain names, a lucrative business. The combination of relatively uncontested power and responsibility for a public space and resource such as the Internet raises the legitimacy stakes quite high. Not surprisingly, ICANN's legitimacy and accountability have been questioned for its entire history (Koppell 2005b).

Buffeted by criticism of its closed structure and decision-making process, ICANN was the first international organization to experiment with direct elections. Internet users around the world participated and selected several directors (including ICANN critics). This was unsettling to many vested parties, and the elections were quickly scrapped by fiat and replaced with an indirect system of representation. The organization is now reforming again and seemingly pivoting back toward responsibility in the face of more criticism.

Another GGO in the Hot Zone is the International Accounting Standards Board (IASB).[1] This body is a nonprofit organization that creates the International Financial Reporting Standards (IFRS), a global accounting standard. Although IASB lacks any enforcement power and cannot sanction governments that do not adopt its standards, questions regarding the authority of the IASB reflect the importance of its rules. Its standards are used around the world and are the official standards in the European Union; in coming years even the American securities markets will accept IFRS accounting (Twarowski 2008). The mission and the widespread acceptance of IFRS give the nongovernmental IASB a medium to high level of publicness. IASB is attempting to create and regulate a commons, a shared set of principles and expectations for financial statements. Thus it is hardly surprising that the IASB arouses legitimacy concerns alongside authority considerations (e.g., Tyrall 2005; Peel 2001).

Unlike ICANN, however, the IASB has historically leaned in the authority direction rather than attempting to satisfy both authority and legitimacy expectations. The board of the organization is not representative of nation-states and gives no formal guarantee of representing any constituency. The rulemaking process is fairly accessible to those in the industry who have the knowledge and wherewithal to track developments and participate in working groups, but noncommercial groups would find participation challenging. Requirements fall short of what one might expect of a government rulemaking effort in a constitutional democracy. As one harsh critic judged, "The simple truth is that accounting rules are the outcomes of politics and bargaining among corporate elites populating the IASB. . . . Ordinary people suffering from dubious accounting and losing their jobs, savings, investments, pensions and homes are not in any position to shape IASB standards" (Sikka 2007). The European Parliament issued official complaints calling for a "public oversight body involving all public stakeholders, including legislators and supervisors, and a body representing market participants" (European Parliament 2008). It also demanded more European representation on the board, given the EU's commitment to IFRS.

Interestingly, the IASB has been cited for its *exemplary* accountability by one international organization. Still the leaders of this global governance organization have responded to critics with a reform proposal. The two biggest changes involve an expansion of the board (with formalized geographic distribution requirements) and creation of a monitoring group that includes the head of the U.S. Security and Exchange Commission, the World Bank, the European Commission, the International Monetary Fund, the International Organization of Securities Commissioners, and the Japan Financial Services Agency (IASB 2008). It is hard to see such a change as an abandonment of responsiveness-centered accountability. Rather, these changes formalize the organizational commitment to keeping the key constituents satisfied.

Did You Ever Have to Make Up Your Mind?

Global governance organizations appear to be confounded by the challenge of accountability. If they make a definitive choice, to emphasize responsiveness or responsibility, most GGOs are likely to come up short (at least sometimes) on the other dimension. This is a serious matter. Failures of responsiveness can lead to abandonment of the organization and ultimate ruin as parties grow leery of ongoing support for an organization that does not serve their interests. Alas, failures of responsibility can lead to the same outcome. GGOs that cater assiduously to the interests of key members risk alienation of those that are not among the chosen. Pushed beyond an unknown limit, these aggrieved parties can paralyze the organization and ultimately bring it down with their defection.

Imperfect though it may be as a solution, the "make-a-choice" strategy seems more effective than the alternative: trying to be accountable in all senses. This is true for two reasons. First, many GGOs have resources to overcome deficits in legitimacy or authority, thus providing some leeway in terms of accountability. Second, attempts to meet all accountability expectations generally leave all constituencies unsatisfied and keep the organization in a state of perennial confusion in which they suffer from Multiple Accountabilities Disorder. Some GGOs appear to grasp this dynamic and make a calculated decision to tilt in the direction of accountability linked with the more immediate vulnerability. That is, organizations seem to emphasize responsibility when legitimacy is of greater salience and responsiveness when authority concerns are dominant. An examination of the organizations with a differential between publicness and constrictiveness is indicative.

Seven of the 25 organizations present constrictiveness as a greater concern than publicness. This group includes the Basel Committee on Banking Supervision, the Convention on Trade in International and Endangered Species, the International Accounting Standards Board, the Internet Corporation for Assigned Names and Numbers, the World Intellectual Property Organization, the World Wide Web Consortium, and the World Customs Organization. This collection includes several entities regarded as GGOs with the most bite. It follows that maintaining this authority requires a high level of responsiveness.

Observations are consistent with this hypothesis. The BCBS is a closed-membership organization—meaning it is open to a limited set of members—with a relatively secretive rulemaking process affording opportunities to the most powerful players to ensure acceptable outcomes. Similarly, the IASB is careful to coordinate its standards development with key markets to ensure adoption. ICANN, by virtue of its unusual contractual relationship with the United States, must keep this particular constituent happy.

Among organizations with a seemingly greater need to satisfy legitimacy considerations due to a differential emphasis on publicness, the emphasis is opposite (as one would expect). The International Seabed Authority and International Labour Organization, to take two examples, have adopted processes and organizational norms that do not emphasize the special influence of powerful players. The International Seabed Authority, for example, is the only GGO that did not grant guaranteed membership in its intermediate body (an executive council or gathering of a subset of members) to the United States. Although this was begrudgingly altered, the United States has still not joined the organization. This is consistent with other observations. Emphasis on responsibility over responsiveness seems to be reflected (not surprisingly) in the ambivalence of influential nations regarding participation in these GGOs. The ILO too has seen a turbulent past with some members—again including the United States—who have even withdrawn from the organization at times.

In conclusion, the core argument drawn from my study of global governance organizations is that each inevitably faces a Morton's Fork (or choice between two unappealing alternatives). They can maintain fidelity to the norms of democratic legitimacy and sacrifice authority by failing to reassure the most powerful actors that participation in a GGO regime will never result in an outcome worse than the status quo. Or they can compromise the legitimacy of the process in order to ensure the ongoing participation of key nations/organizations. Either way the organization will likely be cited for a lack of accountability.

The third option—not choosing and trying to satisfy all demands—often creates problems that undermine the organization and leave everyone disappointed as well (i.e., Multiple Account-abilities Disorder). Choosing one or the other seems preferable. Whether the emphasis ends up on responsibility or responsiveness reflects the nature of the organization and its needs. Based on their location within the Accountability Hot Zone, GGOs will lean toward responsibility (legitimacy) or responsiveness (authority). The IASB case shows that the choice is dynamic. As the organizations increases its publicness, demands on the legitimacy side find new prominence.

International organizations offered accountability solutions by problem solvers are being led down a garden path. One sense of accountability may be achieved, but the demands of other dimensions are masked by the ambiguity of a word so amorphous that scholars can gather for two days (and then some) of examination with little prospect of resolution. Global governance organizations are better advised to determine which sort of accountability to pursue notwithstanding the inevitable failures.

NOTE

Versions of material appearing in this chapter are largely drawn from *World Rule: Accountability, Legitimacy and the Design of Global Governance* (University of Chicago Press, 2010), and "Global Governance Organizations: Legitimacy and Authority in Conflict," *Journal of Public Administration Research and Theory,* 2008.

REFERENCES

Apple, R.W., Jr. 2000. "A Shaky Platform on Which to Build." *The New York Times,* December 13, A1.
Barnard, Chester I. 1938. *The Functions of the Executive.* Cambridge, MA: Harvard University Press.
Barnett, Michael, and Martha Finnemore. 2004. *Rules for the World: International Organizations in Global Politics.* Ithaca, NY: Cornell University Press.
Bovens, Mark. 2007. "New Forms of Accountability and EU-Governance." *Comparative European Politics* 5 (1): 104–20.
Dahl, Robert. 1957. "The Concept of Power." *Behavioral Science* 2: 201–15.
———. 1999. "Can International Organizations Be Democratic? A Skeptic's View." In *Democracy's Edges,* ed. I. Shapiro and C. Hacker-Cordon. Cambridge, UK: Cambridge University Press.
DiIulio, John D., Jr. 1994. "Principled Agents: The Cultural Bases of Behavior in a Federal Government Bureaucracy." *Journal of Public Administration Research and Theory* 4 (3): 277–318.

Dubnick, Melvin J., and Barbara S. Romzek. 1991. *American Public Administration: Politics and the Management of Expectations.* New York: Macmillan.

———. 1993. "Accountability and the Centrality of Expectations in American Public Administration." In *Research in Public Administration,* ed. J. L. Perry. Greenwich, CT: JAI Press, 37–78.

Esty, Daniel C. 2007. "Good Governance at the World Trade Organization: Building a Foundation of Administrative Law." *Journal of International Economic Law* 10 (3): 509–27.

European Parliament. 2008. "More Transparency and Accountability Needed in Bodies Setting International Accounting Standards." Press release, April 24. http://www.europarl.europa.eu/sides/getDoc.do?language=EN&type=IM-PRESS&reference=20080423IPR27465.

Falk, Richard, and Andrew Strauss. 2001. "Toward Global Parliament." *Foreign Affairs* 80 (1): 212–220.

Financial Times. 2004. "Facing Down the Bear: Putin Should Realise Ukraine is not a Zero-Sum Game." November 27, 12.

Finer, Herman. 1940. "Administrative Responsibility in Democratic Government." *Public Administration Review* 1:335–50.

Friedrich, Carl J., 1940. "Public Policy and the Nature of Administrative Responsibility." *Public Policy* 1: 3–24.

Gibbons, James Howard. 2004. "Kuwaiti Gratitude? More Like a Rip-off." *The Houston Chronicle,* January 12, 16.

Glaberson, William. 2006. "How a Reviled Court System Has Outlasted Many Critics." *The New York Times,* September 27, 1.

Goodin, Robert E. 2000. "Accountability—Elections as One Form." In *The International Encyclopedia of Elections,* ed. R. Rose. Washington, DC: Congressional Quarterly Press.

Goodnow, Frank J. 1900. *Politics and Administration: A Study in Government.* New York: Macmillan.

Green, Ashbel S. 2004. "University Sues Oregon, Says Degrees Are Legitimate." *The Oregonian,* August 3, B01.

Healy, Melissa. 1999. "State Posts Drops in Births to Single Women; Welfare: California Leads the U.S. in Reducing Unwed Motherhood, Which Is Linked to Dependence on Aid." *Los Angeles Times,* September 14, 3.

Hilzenrath, David S. 2008. "U.S. May Loosen Reins on Fannie, Freddie; Deal Would Reduce Companies' Required Amount of Capital, Allowing More Mortgage Purchases." *The Washington Post,* March 18, D03.

Hummel, Ralph P. 1987. *The Bureaucratic Experience.* 3d ed. New York: St. Martin's Press.

International Accounting Standards Board (IASB). 2008. "Trustees Publish Proposals on Enhancements to Public Accountability and to IASB Composition." Press release, July 21. London. http://www.iasb.org/News/Press+Releases/Trustees+publish+proposals+on+ enhancements+to+public+accountability+and +to+IASB+composition.htm.

Jackson, Dan. 1986. "Student Testing Comes Under Fire." *New York Times,* June 1, 5.

Kearney, Richard C., and Chandan Sinha. 1988. "Professionalism and Bureaucratic Responsiveness: Conflict or Compatibility." *Public Administration Review* 48 (1): 571–79.

Keohane, Robert O. 2002. *Power and Governance in a Partially Globalized World.* London: Routledge.

Keohane, Robert O., and Joseph S. Nye. 2003. "Redefining Accountability for Global Governance." In *Governance in a Global Economy: Political Authority in Transition,* ed. M. Kahler and D.A. Lake. Princeton: Princeton University Press.

Koch-Mehrin, Silvana. 2006. "NGOs Lack Transparency and Should Face Regulation." *Financial Times,* February 11.

Koppell, J.G.S. 2005. "Pathologies of Accountability: ICANN and the Challenge of Multiple Accountabilities Disorder." *Public Administration Review* 65 (1): 94–108.

———. 2008. "Global Governance Organizations: Legitimacy and Authority in Conflict."*Journal of Public Administration Research and Theory* 18 (2): 177–203.

Leazes, Francis J., Jr. 1997. "Public Accountability." *Administration & Society* 29 (4): 395–412.

McKinney, Jerome B. 1981. "Process Accountability and the Creative Use of Intergovernmental Resources." *Public Administration Review* 41: 144–9.

Mladenka, Kenneth R. 1980. "The Urban Bureaucracy and the Chicago Political Machine: Who Gets What and the Limits to Political Control." *American Political Science Review* 74: 991–8.

Moe, Ronald C. 1994. "The Reinventing Government Exercise: Misinterpreting the Problem, Misjudging the Consequences." *Public Administration Review* 54 (2): 111–22.

———. 2000. "Government Reinvention Revisited." *The Public Manager* 29 (3): 37.

Moe, Ronald C., and Robert S. Gilmour. 1995. "Rediscovering Principles of Public Administration: The Neglected Foundation of Public Law." *Public Administration Review* 55 (2): 135–46.

Morris, Phillip. 1998. "Is Ohio's Private Prison Safe, Legal?" *Plain Dealer* (Cleveland, Ohio), February 17, 9B.

Murphy, Craig N. 1994. *International Organization and Industrial Change: Global Governance Since 1850.* Oxford: Oxford University Press.

New York City Department of Education. 2002. "Chancellor Klein Announces First Performance-Based Bonus Program for Community and High School Superintendents." NYC Department of Education, September 24 [cited April 12, 2003]. http://www.nycenet.edu/press/02–03/n29_03.htm.

Nordheimer, Jon, and Douglas Franz. 1997. "Testing Giant Exceeds Roots, Drawing Business Rivals' Ire." *New York Times,* September 30, 1.

Osborne, David, and Ted Gaebler. 1992. *Reinventing Government: How the Entrepreneurial Spirit Is Transforming the Public Sector.* Reading, MA: Addison-Wesley.

Peel, Michael. 2001. "The Touchy Rule-Maker: The International Accounting Standards Board Has a Worthy Goal. But It Should Be More Prepared to Listen to Its Critics." *Financial Times,* November 15, 2.

Piven, Frances Fox, and Richard A. Cloward. 1971. *Regulating the Poor: The Functions of Public Welfare.* New York: Pantheon Books.

Porter, Michael E. 1998. *Competitive Strategy: Techniques for Analyzing Industries and Competitors: With a New Introduction.* New York: Free Press.

Posner, Elliot. 2005. "Sources of Institutional Change: The Supranational Origins of Europe's New Stock Markets." *World Politics* 58 (1): 40.

Radin, Beryl A., and Barbara S. Romzek. 1996. "Accountability Expectations in an Intergovernmental Arena: The National Rural Development Partnership." *Publius* 26 (2): 59–81.

Romzek, Barbara S., and Melvin J. Dubnick. 1987. "Accountability in the Public Sector: Lessons from the Challenger Tragedy." *Public Administration Review* 47 (3): 227–38.

Romzek, Barbara S., and Patricia Wallace Ingraham. 2000. "Cross Pressures of Accountability: Initiative, Command, and Failure in the Ron Brown Plane Crash." *Public Administration Review* 60 (3): 240–53.

Rosen, Bernard. 1989. *Holding Government Bureaucracies Accountable.* 2d ed. New York: Praeger.

Rourke, Francis E. 1992. "Responsiveness and Neutral Competence in American Bureaucracy." *Public Administration Review* 52 (6): 539–46.

Scales, Ann. 1999. "Bush Raps Rivals, Own Party on Education; Urges Accountability for Schools; Rues Democrats' Despair." *Boston Globe,* October 6, 29.

Schmidt, Steve. 2006. "Exporting State's Inmates; Packed Prisons Get Some Relief; Critics Want Reforms." *The San Diego Union-Tribune,* November 19, A1.

Selznick, Philip. 1957. *Leadership in Administration.* New York: Harper and Row.

Sensenbrenner, Joseph. 1991. "Quality Comes to City Hall." *Harvard Business Review* 69 (2): 64–70.

Siegel, Judy. 2004. "Pfizer Fights On-line Sales of Fake Viagra." *The Jerusalem Post,* August 5, 16.

Sikka, Premm. 2007. "There's No Accounting for Accountants." *The Guardian* (Comment Is Free), United Kingdom, August 29.

St. Petersburg Times. 2001. "No-Protection Prisons." December 5.

Tullock, Gordon. 1965. *The Politics of Bureaucracy.* Washington, DC: Public Affairs Press.

Twarowski, Christopher. 2008. "SEC Opens Debate on Adopting International Accounting Rules." *Washington Post,* August 28, 2.

Tyrall, David. 2005. "Can Accountants Figure a Way to Global Standards?" *Financial Times,* March 17, 42.

Verweij, Marco, and Timothy E. Josling. 2003. "Special Issue: Deliberately Democratizing Multilateral Organization." *Governance* 16 (1): 1–21.

Walzer, Michael. 1983. *Spheres of Justice: A Defense of Pluralism and Equality.* New York: Basic Books.

Washington Post. 1998. "The Problem with Private Prisons." *Washington Post,* November 1, 1998.

Weber, Max. 1965 [1918]. *Politics as a Vocation.* Minneapolis: Fortress Press.

Wilson, Woodrow. 1887. "The Study of Administration." *Political Science Quarterly* 2: 197–222.

Woodlief, Wayne. 2000. "Divine Inspiration Needed; VP Choice Key to Post-election Unity." *Boston Herald,* December 3, 23.

PART II

OBSTACLES TO ACCOUNTABILITY

As promising as accountability may be, there are many obstacles to overcome in bringing about the desired results—and some of those obstacles may be insurmountable.

Christopher Pollitt examines the assumed connection between accountability and the promise of enhanced agency performance and finds the link problematic at best. Until and unless a wider segment of the lay public becomes more concerned about and engaged in assessments of agency performance, the effectiveness of such measurement regimes remain limited.

Beryl Radin's analysis of the U.S. federal government's experience with two major performance measurement initiatives—GPRA (Government Performance and Results Act) and PART (Program Assessment Rating Tool)—stresses the role of the United States' complex institutional context and how multiple expectations have limited the impact of these accountability mechanisms.

The study by Bonnie Johnson, John Pierce, and Nicholas Lovrich, Jr. shifts our attention in a number of ways. First, in contrast to the other studies in this volume, they focus on accountability in a general governmental jurisdiction: the American county. Second, while most contemporary studies of accountability reflect the current bias toward the promise of performance, they highlight the standards associated with political accountability—for example, government openness and responsiveness. But most significant is their exploration of the role played by what Kevin Kearns termed the "accountability environment." Conceptually, the accountability environment constitutes an array of external factors that scholars find intriguing. But for those engaged in the practice of enhancing political accountability in real world situations, the environment also imposes constraints and obstacles.

5

PERFORMANCE BLIGHT AND THE TYRANNY OF LIGHT?

Accountability in Advanced Performance Measurement Regimes

Christopher Pollitt

Advanced performance-measurement regimes—core features of the "new public management" (NPM) in several countries—are supposed to increase the quality and degree of accountability to citizens and their elected representatives. According to NPM theory and many official pronouncements, sophisticated systems of performance measurement considerably enhance public accountability. It seems obvious that more information—especially information about outputs and outcomes rather than inputs and internal organizational processes—will sharpen the sense of responsibility of those service providers who are being measured and will simultaneously empower those who hold them to account.

Contrary to this view, however, there are at least three arguments in the literature that are skeptical of the likelihood of such rational outcomes. First, there is the long-standing psychological work on decision making (e.g., Hammond 1996; Hibbard et al. 1997), which identifies many barriers and diversions liable to prevent the lay public or their representatives from making accurate and warranted interpretations of performance data. Second, developing public administration literature documents possible perversions and pathologies of performance measurement (e.g., Bevan and Hood 2006; De Bruijn 2001; Meyer and Gupta 1994; Radin 2006; Smith 1996). One might refer to these problems collectively as "performance blight," a disease that sets in as soon as one plants the performance-measurement saplings. A third view suggests that, irrespective of gaming or cheating, advanced measurement systems tend to become more and more abstruse over time and may, eventually, actually reduce public trust. This phenomenon is described by Tsoukas (1997) as the "tyranny of light." The idea is that the yearning for fully transparent and objective measures paradoxically leads to complexity, elitism, and popular distrust in the numbers.

The aim of this chapter is to consider these competing claims with respect to the relationship between performance measurement and accountability: does intensive and sophisticated performance measurement improve public accountability and, if so, under what conditions? We first look at arguments emerging from the general literature and then test these against two case studies. The first of these concerns one of the oldest and most sophisticated performance-improvement systems—that covering the UK National Health Service. The second comprises the decade-long development of "world governance indicators" (WGIs) by the World Bank. We will focus on *public* accountability, meaning the ways in which public officials (both elected and appointed) describe, explain, and justify the activities of governments to their wider audiences of legislatures and citizens. This categorization heavily overlaps with Romzek's "political accountability," though it may sometimes also include elements of her "legal accountability" (Romzek 2000, 24). We are interested in reports and statements placed in the public domain—with at least one of their objectives being that of informing legislatures and citizens. By such reports and statements, it is supposed, the people and their representatives can come to judgments about the effectiveness, frugality, fairness, legality, and so forth, of their elected governments. Therefore, we are less concerned with various other aspects of accountability, such as professional accountability or internal hierarchical accountability (Romzek 2000, 24; Pollitt 2003, 93).

COMPETING INTERPRETATIONS OF THE RELATIONSHIP BETWEEN PERFORMANCE MEASUREMENT AND ACCOUNTABILITY

Position A: Performance Measurement Promotes Public Accountability

This position is taken in many government documents. Thus in the United Kingdom we find a Conservative minister praising the performance targets set for executive agencies because they have "enhanced the exercise of accountability through clearer public definition of roles" (Chancellor of the Duchy of Lancaster 1997, v). A Labour white paper written a few years later speaks enthusiastically of "new accountability arrangements, such as . . . cross-cutting performance measures and appraisal systems which reward team-working across traditional boundaries" (Prime Minister and Minister for the Cabinet Office 1999, 18). New Labour's Public Service Agreements (PSAs), festooned with performance targets, were described by the then Chancellor (now Prime Minister) as a "contract with the people." Meanwhile, in the United States, the 1993 Government Performance and Results Act (GPRA) declared that the new performance-oriented regime would:

> improve the confidence of the American people in the capability of the federal government by systematically holding federal agencies accountable for achieving program results . . . [and] improve federal program effectiveness and public accountability by promoting a new focus on results, service quality, and customer satisfaction. (U.S. Congress, Committee on Governmental Affairs, section 2)

In 2002, the No Child Left Behind Act prescribed an ambitious testing and scoring regime and was "rooted in the premise that instruments such as high-stakes testing will promote accountability, which in turn will improve the performance of public schools" (Gormley and Balla 2004, 2). These examples could be multiplied from many other countries (Bouckaert and Halligan 2008; Boyne et al. 2008; Ministry of Finance 2006, 19; Pollitt and Bouckaert, 2004, chapter 4). This positive stance has also long been adopted by many consultants and quite a few academics. For example, a handbook on public productivity states:

> Performance measurement can help improve accountability of:
>
> - Governments to the citizens they serve
> - Public service providers to their service clients, users, or customers
> - Public service executives to their elected bodies or appointed governing boards of their organizations
> - Lower-level managers and staff to higher-level managers and executives of public service organizations

- Public service contractors and grantees (public and private, for-profit and non-profit organizations) to the government organizations that fund and regulate their services
- Governments and public authorities to their taxpayers, ratepayers, bondholders, bond rating agencies, and other users of public reports, including financial reports (Epstein 1992, 162, original italics)

Another accountability proponent says that "by producing results—by achieving specific, pre-established performance goals—public agencies may begin slowly to convince the citizens that government performance is not an oxymoron" (Behn 2001, 119).

Position B: Tension Exists Between Accountability and Performance Improvement Through Measurement

The more emphasis is put on measurement, the more help lay decision makers will need to make sense of the data, and the more the subjects of the measurement may be tempted to game and pervert the system. Several different, though overlapping, bodies of research address this problems of improving performance through measurement.

First is the study of how individuals—both lay and expert—acquire and process information to make decisions or create interpretations. Most of this research has been conducted by psychologists, and some has been specifically focused on the use of performance information. Second is the public-management and public-policy literature, which looks at a series of specific cases to determine whether performance data have been used to make decisions. Third is Tsoukas's "tyranny of light" thesis.

Hibbard et al. (1997) summarize the position of the researchers in the first group:

Evidence shows that people can process and use only a limited number of variables. However, when asked, consumers will often say that they want more information rather than less. (397)

Making "trade-offs" in order to integrate conflicting dimensions into an overall choice is a very difficult task. When faced with these trade-offs, individuals tend to make compromises and take heuristic shortcuts that may undermine their own interests. (399)

A basic assumption of rational theories of choice is that preferences or beliefs about one's self-interest are stable. However, a large body of research shows that preferences are remarkably labile and sensitive to the way a choice is described or framed, even in the absence of intervening time or events. (402)

The following are just some of the hurdles that psychological studies have found standing between the availability of performance information and its rational use:

- It is difficult to attract attention for it—much performance information is simply ignored (Pollitt 2006a). This is true for politicians in England (Johnson and Talbot 2007), the United States (Gormley and Balla 2004, 18), Canada (Treasury Board of Canada Secretariat 1996, 21), and the Netherlands (Ter Bogt 2004). With similarly few exceptions, this lack of attention is even more true for citizens (Marshall et al. 2000; Mannion and Goddard 2003). When the British government put 100,000 copies of its annual performance report into supermarkets only 12,000 were purchased (at £2.99), and under the terms of the contract many thousands had to be bought back by the government (BBC News 1999, 2000).

- Citizens' capacities to process new information are often very limited—they quickly give up or resort to vast and arbitrary simplifications (Hibbard et al. 1997).
- Citizens' soundness of judgment declines dramatically when the information concerns a service or condition of which that particular citizen does not have direct or recent experience (Van Ryzin 2007). "In general . . . judgments mediated by perception (e.g., the visual perception of objects and events) have been found to be remarkably good but to become less so as judgment moves from *perceptual* to *conceptual* tasks and materials" (Hammond 1996, 110; original italics). Across many experiments, a wide range of common biases have been identified (Tversky and Kahneman 1974).
- Handling complex information that involves trading off positives and negatives is often done in an "irrational" (logically incoherent) way (Hibbard et al. 1997).

Decision and policy analysts who have identified these hurdles have not drawn entirely pessimistic conclusions. Rather, they have emphasized that several factors will need to be in place significantly to increase the probability that lay people will sensibly use performance information (Coulter et al. 2002; Hibbard et al. 1997, 406–411; Pollitt 2006a, 49–50). These factors are as follows:

- Information arrives at the time it is needed for consequential decisions, which is usually somewhere near the beginning of the active decision-making process (Pollitt 2006a). Information is neither too early (low interest) nor too late (minds already made up).
- Information is presented in a concise, simple, nontechnical way, and in language that the decision maker can understand and deal with (Hibbard et al. 1997; Pollitt 2006a).
- Information comes from someone trusted and/or known to the citizen/politician, i.e., through a trusted intermediary (Hibbard et al. 1997; Pollitt 2006a).
- Information is standardized and a decision aid/method is explained and made available to citizens/politicians (Hibbard et al. 1997).
- More time is made available and more discussion is conducted when the issue is one the decision maker has not confronted before (e.g., how to deal with a cancer or HIV/AIDS diagnosis—Hibbard et al. 1997).
- All aspects of the process take place within the current norms, probably localized and specific, of the jurisdiction in question, i.e., decision support in Birmingham will not be the same as in Bejing or Bahgdad (Pollitt 2006a).

In the second body of literature on the use of performance measurement, many scholars have noted the possibilities for, or actualities of, perversions in performance-measurement systems, either through "gaming" or outright cheating by the subjects of the measurement (e.g., Bevan and Hood 2006; De Bruijn 2001; Hood 2007; Radin 2006; Smith 1996). This work points to a problem of "performance blight," meaning that, as soon as intensive performance measurement for control and accountability begins, its subjects wriggle and twist every which way rather than show a poor result. They may "perform" the performance rather than substantively achieving it (Clarke 2005). The energies and ingenuity thus devoted to "looking good" are siphoned off from activity devoted to real service improvement.

Perhaps the most fundamental criticism of the effects of performance measurement on public accountability is Tsoukas's notion of the "tyranny of light" (Tsoukas 1997). Tsoukas argues that attempts to create measurement systems which will reassure the public that organizations and services are performing well eventually become self-defeating. This is because the process of measurement inevitably becomes a domain of experts, and a deep asymmetry of knowledge develops between these "insiders" and the citizen and politician "outsiders." Ultimately, the strenuous efforts of the experts to cast light on the strengths and weaknesses of public policies has the paradoxical effect of *increasing* citizen distrust (Tsoukas 1997, 834). This effect tends to be amplified rather than reduced by the intervention of the mass media, with their partiality for stories of calamity, corruption, and failure:

> Mass media that are characterised by a combination of political-economic antagonism towards public services and journalistic cynicism about politics form a difficult setting for the publication and celebration of "success stories." (Clarke, 2005, 226)

CASE STUDY: THE UK NATIONAL HEALTH SERVICE (UK NHS)

The UK NHS is a rich and early example of an organization with "measurementitis." The first national set of performance improvements (PI) was instituted in 1983. The systems in place since the late 1990s are probably among the most sophisticated and ambitious anywhere in the world of public-service performance measurement. An entire industry—involving dozens of different organizations and hundreds of experts, including civil servants, epidemiologists, clinicians, statisticians, social scientists, health-service managers, and management consultants—has grown up around health-service performance measurement. The analysis in this section is drawn mainly from research funded by the UK Economic and Social Research Council; the analysis compares the evolution of PI systems in the UK NHS with the Dutch health-care sector since the 1980s (Pollitt et al. 2010; see also Pollitt et al. 2007).

A Potted History

Next is a brief selection of the major developments, with particular emphasis on those that have implications for public accountability.

1983   First national package of NHS PIs (seen as being mainly for management purposes) is produced by the Department of Health and Social Security (see Pollitt 1985). Seventy indicators for each District Health Authority are grouped into clinical, financial, manpower, support services, and estate management.

1988   Department of Health develops a new PI package based on the "Korner minimum data set." (The Korner enquiry had recently reviewed NHS data needs.) The PI package includes roughly 2,500 indicators. In the same year the health minister asks health authorities to produce commentaries on their PI scores to be available to newspapers.

1991   Conservative government publishes Patients' Charter (as part of the wider Citizen's Charter program), which includes standards for waiting times, ambulance calls, and so forth, although the standards have no legal force. Initially the Charter is not much connected with the main NHS PI system, but is intended to be, inter alia, a mechanism for *public* accountability.

1994   NHS Executive publishes the first set of comparative league tables of institutions intended explicitly for public use (for a slightly later example, see NHS Executive, 1996). Five stars are awarded to the best-performing institutions.

1997   New Labour Government publishes white paper, *New NHS: Modern, Dependable.* White paper includes the announcement that new PIs will be developed under six headings:

- Health improvement
- Fair access
- Effective delivery of appropriate health care
- Efficiency
- Patient/carer experience
- Health outcomes of NHS care

1998   Public Service Agreements (PSAs) are introduced as part of the government's Comprehensive Spending Review. The PSA objectives for the NHS include cutting waiting lists by 100,000.

2000   Two journalists establish Dr. Foster Intelligence, a company that subsequently became a major source of consumer-oriented information about hospital quality. By now there are several sets of NHS PIs produced by different institutions, not just one national set. By 2008 Dr. Foster's main customer is the NHS itself.

2001   The "star system" is introduced, a draconian regime in which NHS trust hospitals are scored on various PIs, and these scores are aggregated into a composite judgment. (Ratings are from zero to three stars.) The star scores are given wide publicity in national and local media. Top managers at most zero-rated institutions are removed.

2004   The Healthcare Commission announces that it will move to a "balanced scorecard" system with 24 "core" and 10 "developmental" standards.

2004   The Quality and Outcomes Framework (QoF) is introduced and ties a large part of the income of general practitioners (GPs) to the achievement of specific targets. The Department of Health seems to have underestimated how efficient GPs already are, and the result is a much larger expenditure/much higher salaries than expected.

2007   Society of Cardiac Surgeons publishes risk-adjusted mortality data for individual cardiac surgeons.

2007   Comprehensive Spending Review announces a reduced set of PSA with a smaller number of PIs. However, whether a genuine reduction has been effected is not clear; in any case, many different sets of PIs are now produced by many different bodies.

Changes Over Time

Even the most diligent model citizen or attentive Member of Parliament (MP) would have found it hard to follow progress in the medium or long term, because the definitions, measures, and presentation were themselves constantly on the move (the history provided here reflects only a few of these changes). Stability in PI sets is unlikely for many reasons. A first and major reason is that the various parties involved in the creation of PI sets almost always have multiple objectives (Behn 2003; Hood 2007). As the bargaining and debate goes on between these actors, certain objectives rise in importance and others fall. Public accountability is only one of these objectives and, according to our interviewees, seldom the most important one. The main objectives mentioned by our interviewees were:

- To encourage the more efficient use of scarce resources
- To inform local clinicians and managers so that they can better identify local weaknesses and problems, and devise plans for addressing them
- To influence resource allocation to specific services or organizations (if you score better, you will receive more generous resources, or greater organizational and financial autonomy—a favorite policy of the Blair government)
- To serve as the basis for a performance pay system for individual clinicians (as in the case of the NHS Quality and Outcomes Framework [QoF] of 2003)
- To serve as a criterion for judging management performance (and, if necessary, sacking managers of low-scoring organizations, as in the NHS hospital "stars" system of 2001–5)
- To enable inspectorates to focus on those organizations that appear to perform badly on performance indicators
- To enable members of the public to see how the performance of their local health organizations compared with national standards and the performances of other organizations in other parts of the country (see, e.g., Healthcare Commission 2006, 4)

A number of other factors are responsible for the frequent change in PI measures. Experts learn from their attempts to measure and frequently want to replace an existing measure with one that is technically better. Shifts in public and political attention may lead to new indicators being added (an example that was mentioned to us was child obesity). New procedures or technologies are introduced that require new measures. An indicator may at some point become embarrassing, and is altered or dropped. Commercial companies take publicly available data and refashion its presentation to sell it to specific customers in more tailored, user-friendly formats. This has clearly happened in both the United Kingdom and the United States. The periodic desire to curb the proliferation of different indicators and somehow get back to a small number of understandable, key indicators is also a factor in continual change in PI indicators. This seems to be a cyclical phenomenon and has also been observed in other sectors and other countries (Pollitt 2008). Last but not least, deliberate changes in indicator sets can help curb the growth of gaming—if healthcare providers are not sure what they will be measured on next year they are less able to prepare to "look good" (Bevan and Hood 2006).

Note that such "churn" in PIs tends to privilege synchronic over diachronic comparisons. Long, stable time series are made less likely by this tendency of PI sets constantly to evolve. Moreover, the sources of change are both endogenous and exogenous—any system in the public domain is open to the exogenous influences of politics, the media, and public opinion.

Indicators in the Public Domain

Once an indicator exists somewhere within the system, it is hard to prevent its existence from eventually becoming known to the public. The pressures of an inquisitive media industry and the opportunism of elected politicians combine to make a policy of secrecy look like an admission of guilt. This also means that once PIs exist it is quite hard to abolish them completely—to try to do so usually leads to accusations of a "cover-up." There have been a few examples of public disclosure being diminished or abandoned in certain jurisdictions (e.g., Wales), but this is the exception rather than the rule, and a comprehensive retreat is hard to imagine. "Public reports are here to stay"—on both sides of the Atlantic (Marshall et al. 2003, 143). The original indicator packages of the mid-1980s contained very few measures of clinical outcomes, and on the whole the medical profession wanted to keep it that way. But gradually doctors lost that battle (as they also did in the United States), and by the late 1990s more and more clinical outcomes were being included in the published data.

Once the data are in the public domain, professional and expert groups can no longer expect to control how they are formatted and used. Thus, for example, even if the originators of the system were opposed to the idea of league tables, some newspaper or website or commercial consultancy will rearrange the data to rank hospitals or practices against one another. There is also often a temptation to aggregate indicators into one composite number that then appears to summarize everything for easy consumption by the general public (Hood 2007). The result is often an indicator that is far from clear or transparent.

The NHS Case as an Example of the "Tyranny of Light"?

The NHS story gives little support for Position A, that performance measurement promotes accountability. There seems to be no evidence of systematic use by either MPs or citizens. On the other hand, there is considerable evidence for Position B, that tension exists between accountability and performance measurement. This includes evidence of each of the three problems identified in the general literature: first, lack of interest and misunderstanding when performance measurement is attempted (Coulter et al. 2002); second, gaming (e.g., Bevan and Hood 2006; Pitches et al. 2003); and, third, a lack of public trust in the official figures.

As the NHS performance regime has evolved over time it has become more sophisticated. The number of indicators—and sets of indicators—has expanded. Data-collection systems are constantly being refined. The procedures for making allowances for case mix and other contextual factors are becoming more elaborate. The community of experts spending their time improving and refining the system grows. These normal processes of the evolution of a "performance industry" bring paradoxical results. On the one hand they produce not only more measures (potentially useful when one is dealing with such a multifaceted process as the delivery of health care), but also more valid and reliable measures. On the other hand, the growth in the size and sophistication of the measurement community effectively, if unintentionally, excludes the general public. At the same time, as hundreds of person years are being invested in the continuous refinement of NHS PIs, "evidence on what type of information British patients want, if any, and what they might use it for, is sparse" (Coulter 2002, 22; see also Mannion and Goddard 2003, 284).

Thus the PI system has come to be seen by many as something created and manipulated by "them"—the experts and insiders (or just "the government"). This seems very close to Tsoukas's general point:

> Transparency [of expert systems] presupposes a subject: transparent to *who?* . . . one realizes that what the outsiders see (and the significance they attach to what they see) is not the same with what [sic] the insiders see (and the significance they attach to their experiences). There is an important knowledge asymmetry between the two parties that cannot be removed with generating more information, for information needs to be interpreted and it is precisely the terms of interpretation that are contested. (Tsoukas 1997, 834)

CASE STUDY: THE WORLD BANK'S WORLD GOVERNANCE INDICATORS

Since 1996 the World Bank has published a regular (now annual) series of World Governance Indicators (WGIs). They have six main dimensions, each a composite index of many separate individual measures, and each of which is given a single score:

- Voice and accountability
- Political stability and the absence of violence
- Government effectiveness
- Regulatory quality
- Rule of law
- Control of corruption

The sheer weight of data going into these aggregate indicators is impressive. For the 2006 round, data were taken from 33 different sources provided by 30 organizations, adding up to 310 individual variables (Kaufmann et al. 2007, 4).

WGIs are one of a large number of sets of internationally comparative governance indicators—in 2006 Arndt and Oman estimated that there were 140 user-accessible sets to choose among (2006, 30; see also Besançon 2003, 11–32). WGIs are, by common consent, the most carefully conceived and presented set of indicators, and one of the most widely cited and used (Arndt and Oman, 2006, 28; Van de Walle 2005, 439; Van Roosbroek, 2007).

But when it comes to the purpose of the WGIs, we encounter a curious reticence. The official web site carefully states that "The WGI are not used by the World Bank Group to allocate resources or for any other official purpose" (http://info.worldbank.org/governance/wgi2007/). The authors themselves have produced a lot of supporting technical literature, but this contains only a few statements about purpose(s) (e.g., Kaufman et al. 1999; 2007). Here are two of the somewhat small number of direct claims on this point:

> A useful role of the aggregate indicators is that they allow us to summarize in a compact way the diversity of information on governance available for each country, and to make comparisons across countries and over time. (Kaufmann et al. 2007, 16)

> . . . these aggregate governance indicators are useful because they allow countries to be sorted into broad groupings according to levels of governance, and they can be used to study the causes and consequences of governance in a much larger sample of countries than previously. (Kaufmann et al. 1999)

Swarming around each year's new scores, the media praise and blame individual governments for their positions in the WGI league tables. More seriously, perhaps, is that despite the fact that the World Bank says it does not use WGIs in its official decision making, some aid donors—including the U.S. Millenium Challenge Account—clearly do (Arndt and Oman 2006, 41–46; Johnson and Zajonc 2006). Overall, one might say that WGIs differ from NHS PIs insofar as they are purported to be of no direct use to individual citizens. Rather, they appear to be directed at aid agencies, nongovernmental organizations (NGOs), investors, and the media—a more knowing and more organized set of audiences than the general public.

Table 5.1

WGI Government Effectiveness: "Best," "Worst" and Selected Intermediate Scores in 2006

Denmark	+2.29
Finland	+2.08
United Kingdom	+1.83
United States	+1.64
Italy	+0.38
Afghanistan	−1.39
Somalia	−2.19

Source: World Bank.
Note: Worldwide Governance Indicators: scores range from approximately +2.5 to −2.5.

The Dimension of Government Effectiveness

The full scope and content of WGIs are too vast to be analyzed here. For illustrative purposes we will, therefore, concentrate on one of the six dimensions—government effectiveness—as seen in Table 5.1.

The World Bank defines government effectiveness as a mixed bag of characteristics and includes data relating to government instability; the quality of government personnel; progress with e-government; the quality of bureaucracy and the amount of excessive red tape; the composition of public spending; the quality of general infrastructure; the quality of public schools; satisfaction with public transportation roads and highways, and the education system; and policy consistency and forward planning (Kaufmann et al. 2007, 72). Kaufmann et al. define government effectiveness as "measuring the quality of public services, the quality of the civil service and the degree of its independence from political pressures, the quality of policy formulation and implementation, and the credibility of the government's commitment to such policies" (2007, 3).

Critique

WGIs have always been somewhat controversial, among both academics and practitioners. What follows is a summary of the main lines of criticism, with an emphasis on those aspects that have particular salience for accountability.

No Theory of Governance. Ideally, any indicator set measuring government effectiveness grows out of a theory of governance. The theory would predict which factors were most likely to improve or undermine governance, and the measures would then chart changes in these factors. It seems there is no such theory behind the WGIs (Arndt 2008).

No Definition of Good Governance. The WGIs are not based on an explicit, coherent definition of good governance. Their authors speak of governance as "the traditions and institutions by which authority in a country is exercised" (Kaufmann et al. 2004, 3), but that is so broad as to embrace almost everything (Rothstein and Teorell 2008, 168). The lack of a good overall definition might not be a problem if the concept in question was one on which there was already broad agreement about its meaning within the relevant community of discourse. Notoriously, this is not the case for governance (Bovaird and Löffler 2003; Frederickson 2005).

Lack of Clarity of Meaning. Each of the six dimensions gives rise to a composite index figure. The complexity of this process is such that it is virtually impossible to give a clear meaning to any of the indicators. This holds true for our chosen indicator of government effectiveness. Thus it is not at all clear what Finland = 2.08 actually means. If one looks back at the definition of government effectiveness one can see that it includes inputs (the quality of personnel), processes (time spent by senior management dealing with government officials), and outcomes (public satisfaction with roads and highways). The definition covers some policy sectors, but not others. It includes measures that attempt to capture complex and ambiguous concepts (the quality of bureaucracy, the quality of public schools) and then submerges them in a weighted, composite index of even greater complexity. Even if these composite indicators were highly valid and reliable, their precise meaning could be understood only by a few experts.

A possible set of problems also needing consideration is differing cultural responses to survey questionnaires. Different understandings may exist of some of the keywords or concepts (Van de Walle 2007, 171–202). Furthermore, it may well be that respondents from different cultures behave in different ways when faced with the choice of "extreme" or "middle" box markings. Varying cultural predispositions may affect the use of the "don't know" category. As yet little work seems to have been done on the multicultural aspect of gathering information.

Lack of Transparency. Although the World Bank authors have done much to improve transparency, they are ultimately limited by the fact that some of the data from some of the commercial sources they use are not freely accessible (indeed, some are very expensive). Furthermore, no comprehensive listing exists of the criteria all the sources have used to arrive at their own country scores (Arndt and Oman 2006, 72).

Possible Bias Toward Business and Away from Ordinary Citizens. Many critics note that the aggregation procedure seems routinely to give greater weight to the opinions of business experts and commercial risk-rating agencies than to the perceptions of ordinary citizens. The technical detail of this debate is dense, but admirably summarized in Arndt and Oman (2006, chapter 4). If we look specifically at the indicator for government effectiveness we find that, of the 1845 data points included in the measure, 46 percent come from "commercial business information providers," 20 percent from "surveys of firms or households," and 17 percent from "public sector organizations" (Kaufmann et al. 2007, 28). What is more, the complicated weighting system used for the aggregation gives a preponderance of the aggregate score to business-sourced data. Thus, for example, in the composition of government effectiveness, the data from Global Insight Business Conditions and Risk Indicators is accorded a weight of 0.148, while the main household survey (Gallup World Poll) is weighted at 0.005 (Kaufmann et al. 2007, 29). Moreover, WGIs are constructed using a technique ("unobserved components model") that gives less weight to perception data that diverges from the dominant majority perceptions. Arguably this devalues the very variance that we should be interested in, as extreme values may well express different perspectives or concepts or values.

Changes over Time. Despite the originators' claims to the contrary, WGIs "cannot reliably be used for monitoring changes in levels of governance over time" (Arndt and Oman 2006, 67). This is partly because the sources used to compose each indicator vary from one year to the next. More generally, a change in a particular index figure over time may imply one or more of the following possibilities (Arndt 2008, 281):

1. There has been an actual change in "government effectiveness," "voice and accountability" or other measure.

2. Perceptions held by the people surveyed have changed, but this does not reflect an underlying change (and the key people—for reasons indicated above—will usually be business advisers and risk experts).
3. The ratings of other countries have changed. Because WGIs are designed so that the global average and standard deviation remain constant, changes in one or more countries' ratings usually changes all countries' ratings.
4. The number and composition of the sources from which the data are drawn have changed.

Kaufmann et al. react to these criticisms by arguing that large changes in the index scores are likely to reflect that something real is going on (Kaufmann et al. 2007, 18–21). From an accountability perspective, however, it matters hugely which of the above possibilities is responsible for which share of any apparent change.

Discussion

To this list of criticisms one might add the point made earlier—that it is not at all clear who the World Bank expects to use the WGIs, or for what. These indicators deliver complex and highly normative data into the wider world of aid agencies and multiple media. Yet the vision of the accountability system that the data are supposed to feed remains obscure.

It is hard to think of a specific assessment or choice for which a WGI would or should be the crucial piece of evidence. Yet WGIs may encourage decision makers to think they need not spend much time probing the detail of particular cases, because a reliable general yardstick is ready to hand. It is certainly difficult to imagine how one could credibly disentangle specific causes and consequences from the hyper-composite WGIs. Imagine applying the idea to a developed rather than a developing country. Could indicators of this kind contribute significantly to the assessment of the big public-management reforms of the Blair administrations in the UK—Public Service Agreements, joined-up government, Best Value, foundation hospitals, city academies? Definitely not. Why, then, does anyone suppose that they could be used to make a similar assessment in any of the developing countries?

The organization producing these PIs is well known for having its own problems of accountability. Although powerful, the World Bank is an object of suspicion from the developing world and from many groups in the developed world (e.g., Stiglitz 2003; Woods 2001). The WGIs strive to clothe what are, in effect, huge judgments of merit and demerit of particular states and societies in a cloak of confidence-enhancing statistical methods (for a fascinating historical treatment of this tactic, see Porter 1995, 200). Yet there is large-scale resistance to WGIs. In 2007 nine of the World Bank's 24 executive directors wrote to its president to object to the very idea that the Bank would produce these kinds of figures (Guha and McGregor 2007).

The WGI story also raises the issue of contextualization. The WGIs have a strong decontextualizing effect. Tsoukas sees this as a general problem in late modern societies:

> In the information society, the abundance of information tends to overshadow the phenomena to which the information refers: the discussion of crime easily slips to debating crime rates and spending on police; the debate about quality in education more often than not leads to arguing about league tables; the concern with the performance of hospitals leads to debating readmission rates and other indicators. In short, the more information we have about the world, the more we distance ourselves from what is going on and the less able we become in comprehending its full complexity. (1997, 833)

Thus some people may be misled into thinking that they can know something about specific countries simply by reading their WGI scores.

Reflections on WGIs and Public Accountability

The World Bank draws the data for the WGIs from a disparate range of sources but has no direct control of how the data are collected. Overall, there appears to be a heavy weighting accorded to sources devoted to the needs of business relative to those of the common citizen. The Bank subsequently assembles the data into a limited number of highly aggregated, composite indicators, the meaning of which is often obscure, even to experts. Then the Bank publishes the indicators, usually with extensive accompanying publicity. *Then* it partially disowns them, saying that "the data and research reported here do not reflect the official views of the World Bank, its Executive Directors, or the countries they represent" (http://info.worldbank.org /governance/wgi2007/). As in the NHS case, evidence of rational use by elected politicians or citizens themselves (Position A) either does not exist or has not been reported. With respect to Position B, WGIs certainly exemplify the first layer of problems, in the sense that the sheer complexity of the six composites means that their correct use by ordinary, cognitively fallible mortals must be highly improbable. Curiously, though, WGIs may be less vulnerable to the second danger—gaming. That is because their very complexity means that it would be hard for even a government to manipulate events or reporting in order to "look good" (Arndt and Oman 2006; Johnson and Zajonc 2006, 19–20). Finally, WGIs seem to personify the "tyranny of light." Their complexity guarantees that they will be understood only by a small group of experts—as the voluminous technical literature put out by their authors amply demonstrates (e.g., Kaufmann et al. 1999; Kaufmann et al. 2007).

CONCLUSIONS

We are now well into the third decade of intensive public-sector performance measurement in a number of countries. Yet it seems that, so far as the use of performance information for public-accountability purposes is concerned, governments are just beginning. We have little systematic evidence about what politicians and the public do with the data, and there is small indication that most governments have been very concerned about acquiring such knowledge. Predictably, perhaps, the main effort has been to use PIs for managerial and technocratic purposes, in a series of attempts to better control and direct (Boyne et al. 2008). These kinds of internal uses may be highly beneficial in a number of different ways, but they don't have much to do with external accountability.

Certain conclusions follow. First, despite the frequent rhetoric to the contrary, governments in fact have had very limited interest in using performance measurement to engage the citizens or legislatures. Second, the presumptions of Position A—that performance measurement promotes public accountability—are rarely born out by the evidence. In addition to our survey of the general literature we have looked at two cases of long-lasting performance measurement systems which, prima facie, would appear to be of wide public and political interest. Both neglect several of the considerations that would help promote responsible public debate. Although (respectively) twenty-five and twelve years old at the time of writing, neither case can show much evidence of having seized public attention, and neither can show any evidence of increasing public trust.

Thus it would appear Position B accurately describes the relationship between performance measurement and accountability. There is strikingly little evidence that the makers of PI systems are particularly concerned about their usefulness to legislators and citizens, as opposed to ministers and managers. Position A—that simply providing performance data will serve a rationally exercised form of public accountability—appears naïve. On the contrary, it is very hard work to make the performance data valid and reliable, and it is equally hard (and uncertain) work to ensure that politicians and the public notice and make sensible use of data.

So far, so bad. Yet the final conclusion is not necessarily so pessimistic. The preceding analysis may be accurate for the period up until now—the first twenty-five years of intensive public-service performance measurement (at least in some countries, though hardly at all in others). But that does not mean that the situation must remain the same. The health-care field seems to be the most promising with regard to performance measurement. This statement has been made about the UK and the United States: "A consistent finding in both countries is the lack of public interest in quality reports. This may change in the future, as the public becomes better informed and more assertive and (in the United Kingdom) enjoys greater choice" (Marshall et al. 2003).

While less optimistic than this particular group of authors, I do share their overall observation of "incremental progress" (over decades). For the determined few there is already much more that can be discovered about our health and education services than ten or twenty years ago. While the "tyranny of light" may well set some outer, eventual limits to such progress, much can be done within those limits.

The psychologists and policy analysts have some strong suggestions about what would be required for a performance-measurement system that actively engages a wider audience. The problem is that very few existing performance-measurement systems remotely meet these requirements. To move toward a more relevant system for the wider public would require many changes and a considerable redirection of resources. The crafting of texts and displays and reports written for specific lay audiences is only the first step. The provision of a network of intermediaries—trusted, independent, local, well-informed—would probably be the most challenging and expensive element in such an approach. Yet there are some precedents. Problems with vulnerable patients in hospitals, skilled-nursing facilities, and other care homes have provoked a literature on "patient advocates," which rehearses a number of points that are also highly relevant to performance improvement. The education sectors in both the UK (with school league tables) and the United States (with school report cards) offer extensive natural laboratories for learning more about how and when parents and their associations use performance information. In fact we have many clues about what could be done, even if these are scattered over several disciplines and sectors. Performance-measurement systems can be made better to serve the objective of public accountability, but only if they are specifically and carefully designed to do so.

ACKNOWLEDGMENT

The material on the NHS has been drawn from the project "Performance Indicators in Health Care: A Comparative Anglo-Dutch Study," financed by the UK Economic and Social Research Council (award No. RES 166–25–0051). My colleagues in this project were Steve Harrison (Principal Investigator), George Dowswell (University of Manchester), and Roland Bal and Sonja Jerak (Erasmus Medical School, Erasmus University, Rotterdam).

REFERENCES

Arndt, C. 2008. "The Politics of Governance Ratings." *International Public Management Journal* (11) 3: 275–97.

Arndt, C., and C. Oman. 2006. "Uses and Abuses of Governance Indicators." Paris: OECD, Development Centre Studies.

BBC News. 1999. "UK Politics: Government Puts a Gloss on its Goals." July 26. http://bbc.co.uk/1/hi/uk_politics/403993.stm.

———. 2000. "Annual Report: A Hostage to Fortune?" July 13. http://bbc.co.uk/1/hi/uk_ politics/831585.stm.

Behn, R. 2001. *Rethinking Democratic Accountability.* Washington, DC: Brookings Institution.

———. 2003. "Why Measure Performance? Different Purposes Require Different Measures." *Public Administration Review* 63 (5): 586–606.

Besançon, M. 2003. "Good Governance Rankings; The Art of Measurement." WPF Reports N0.36, Cambridge, MA: World Peace Foundation.

Bevan, G., and C. Hood. 2006. "What's Measured Is What Matters: Targets and Gaming in the English Public Healthcare System." *Public Administration* 84 (3): 517–38.

Bouckaert, G., and J. Halligan. 2008. *Managing Performance: International Comparisons.* London and New York: Routledge/Taylor and Francis.

Bovaird, T., and E. Löffler. 2003. "Evaluating the Quality of Public Governance: Indicators, Models And Methodologies." *International Review of Administrative Sciences* 69 (3): 313–28.

Boyne, G., K. Meier, L. O'Toole, Jr., and R. Walker (eds.). 2006. *Public Service Performance: Perspectives on Measurement and Management.* Cambridge: Cambridge University Press.

Chancellor of the Duchy of Lancaster. 1997. *Next Steps: Agencies in Government Review 1996,* Cm3597. London: The Stationary Office.

Clarke, J. 2005. "Performing for the Public: Doubt, Desire and the Evaluation of Public Services." In *The Values of Bureaucracy,* ed. P. Du Gay. Oxford: Oxford University Press, 211–32.

Coulter, A., R, Fitzpatrick, and L.J. Davis. 2002. "Patient and Public Perspectives on Health Care Performance." Report prepared for the Commission for Health Improvement, Oxford, England, April.

De Bruin, H. 2001. *Managing Performance in the Public Sector.* London: Routledge.

Epstein, P. 1992. "Measuring the Performance of Public Services." In *Public Productivity Handbook,* ed. M. Holzer. New York: Marcel Dekker, 161–93.

Frederickson, G. 2005. "Whatever Happened to Public Administration? Governance, Governance, Everywhere." In *The Oxford Handbook of Public Management,* ed. E.Ferlie, L. Lynn, Jr., and C.Pollitt. Oxford: Oxford University Press, 282–304.

Gormley, W., and S. Balla. 2004. *Bureaucracy and Democracy: Accountability and Performance.* Washington, DC: CQ Press.

Guha, K., and R. McGregor. 2007. "World Bank Directors Test Zoellick." *Financial Times,* July 13. Available at www.ft.com/cms/s/0/fe1d7ece-30d8-11dc-0a81-0000779fd2ac.html.

Hammond, K. 1996. *Human Judgment and Social Policy: Irreducible Uncertainty, Inevitable Error, Unavoidable Injustice.* New York and Oxford: Oxford University Press.

Healthcare Commission. 2006. *The Annual Health Check in 2006/2007: Assessing and Rating the NHS.* London: Healthcare Commission.

Hibbard, J., P. Slovic, and J. Jewett. 1997. "Informing Consumer Decisions in Health Care: Implications from Decision-Making Research." *The Milbank Quarterly* 75 (3): 395–414.

Hood, C. 2007. "Public Service Management by Numbers: Why Does It Vary? Where Has It Come From? What Are the Gaps and the Puzzles?" *Public Money and Management* 27 (2): 95–102.

Hood, C., and C. Beeston. 2005. "How Does Britain Rank and How Do We Know? International Rankings of Public Service Performance." Paper presented to ESRC Conference, Where Does Britain Rank? International Public Service Rankings, London, December 13.

Johnson, C. and C. Talbot 2007. "The UK Parliament and Performance: Challenging or Challenged?" *International Review of Administrative Sciences* (73) 1: 113–31.

Johnson, D., and T. Zajonc. 2006. "Can Foreign Aid Create an Incentive for Good Governance?" Evidence from the Millennium Challenge Corporation, conference paper, Harvard University, Cambridge, MA, April 11.

Kaufmann, D., A. Kraay, and M. Mastruzzi. 2004. "Governance Matters III: Governance Indicators for 1996–2002." Policy Research Working Paper 3106. Washington, DC: World Bank.

———. 2007. "Governance Matters VI: Aggregate and Individual Governance Indicators 1996–2006." Policy Research Working Paper 4280. Washington, DC: World Bank.

Kaufmann, D., A. Kraay, and Zoido-Lobatón. 1999. "Aggregating Governance Indicators." Policy Research Working Paper 2195. Washington, DC: World Bank.

Kettl, D., and S. Kelman. 2007. *Reflections on 21st Century Government Management.* Washington, DC: IBM Center for the Business of Government.

Marshall, M., P. Shekelle, H. Davies, and P. Smith. 2003. "Public Reporting on Quality in the United States and the United Kingdom." *Health Affairs* 22 (3): 134–48.

Marshall, M., P. Shekelle, S. Leatherman, and R. Brook. 2000. "The Public Release of Performance Data. What Do We Expect to Gain? A Review of the Evidence," *Journal of the American Medical Association* 283 (14): 1866–74.

Mannion, R., and M.Goddard. 2003. "Public Disclosure of Comparative Clinical Performance Data: Lessons from the Scottish Experience" *Journal of Evaluation in Clinical Practice* 9 (2): 277–86.

Maxwell School of Citizenship and Public Affairs. 2003. *Paths to Performance in State and Local Government.* Syracuse, NY: Syracuse University, Pew Charitable Trusts.

Meyer, J., and V. Gupta. 1994. "The Performance Paradox." *Research in Organizational Behavior* 16: 309–69.

Ministry of Finance. 2006. *Handbook on Performance Management.* Helsinki: Public Management Department/Ministry of Finance.

NHS Executive. 1996. *The NHS Performance Guide 1995–96.* London: Department of Health.

Pitches, D., A. Burls, and A. Fry-Smith. 2003. "How to Make a Silk Purse from a Sow's Ear—A Comprehensive Review of Strategies to Optimize Data for Corrupt Managers and Incompetent Clinicians." *British Medical Journal* 327: 1436–39.

Pollitt, C. 1985. "Measuring Performance: A New System for the National Health Service." *Policy and Politics* 13 (1): 1–15.

———. 2003. *The Essential Public Manager.* Maidenhead, UK and Philadelphia: Open University Press/McGraw Hill.

———. 2006a. "Performance Information for Democracy: The Missing Link?" *Evaluation* 12 (1): 39–56.

———. 2006b. "Performance Management in Practice: A Comparative Study of Executive Agencies." *Journal of Public Administration Research and Theory* 16 (1): 25–44.

———. 2008. *Time, Policy, Management: Governing with the Past.* Oxford: Oxford University Press.

Pollitt, C., and G. Bouckaert 2004. *Public Management Reform: a Comparative Analysis.* 2d ed., Oxford: Oxford University Press.

Pollitt, C., S. Harrison, R. Bal, G. Dowswell, and S. Jerak. 2007. "Conceptualising the Development of Performance Measurement Systems." Paper presented at the annual conference of the European Group for Public Administration, Madrid, September.

Pollitt, C., S. Harrison, G. Dowswell, S. Jerak-Zuiderent, and R. Bal. 2010. "Performance Regimes in Health Care: Institutions, Critical Junctures and the Logic of Escalation in England and the Netherlands." *Evaluation* (16) 1: 13–29.

Porter, T. 1995. *Trust in Numbers: The Pursuit of Objectivity in Science and Public Life.* Princeton: Princeton University Press.

Prime Minister and Minister for the Cabinet Office. 1999. *Modernising Government,* Cm4310, London: The Stationary Office.

Radin, B. 2006. *Challenging the Performance Movement: Accountability, Complexity and Democratic Values.* Washington, DC: Georgetown University Press.

Romzek, B. 2000. "Dynamics of Public Sector Accountability in an Era of Reform." *International Review of Administrative Sciences* 66 (1): 19–42.

Rothstein, B., and J. Teore. 2008. "What Is Quality of Government? A Theory of Impartial Government Institutions," *Governance* (21) 2: 165–90.

Smith, P. 1996. "On the Unintended Consequences of Publishing Performance Data in the Public Sector." *International Journal of Public Administration* 18: 277–310.

Stiglitz, J. 2003. "Democratizing the International Monetary Fund and the World Bank." *Governance* 16 (1): 111–39.

ter Bogt, H.J. 2004. "Politicians in Search of Performance Information? Survey Research on Dutch Aldermen's Use of Performance Information." *Financial Accountability and Management* 20 (3): 221–52.

Treasury Board of Canada Secretariat. 1996. *Evaluation Report: Improved Reporting to Parliament Project.* Available at www.tbs-sct.gc.ca/rma/eppi-ibdrp/irp, accessed April 25, 2005.

Tsoukas, H. 1997. "The Tyranny of Light: The Temptations and Paradoxes of the Information Society." *Futures* 29 (9): 827–43.

Tversky, A., and D. Kahneman. 1974. "Judgement under Uncertainty: Heuristics and Biases." *Science* 185: 1124–31.

U.S. Congress, Senate, Committee on Governmental Affairs. 1993. *Government Performance and Results Act of 1993*. Report 103–58, 103rd Congress, 1st session. Washington, DC: Government Printing Office.

Van de Walle, S. 2005. "Measuring Bureaucratic Quality in Governance Indicators." Paper presented to the European Group for Public Administration Annual Conference, Bern, Switzerland, August 31–September 3.

———. 2007. "Determinants of Confidence in the Civil Service: An International Comparison." In K. Schedler, and I. Proeller, *Cultural Aspects of Public Management Reform*. Amsterdam: Elsvier, 171–201.

Van Roosbroek 2007. "Re-thinking Governance Indicators: What Can Quality Management Tell Us About the Debate on Governance Indicators?" Paper presented at the European Group for Public Administration Conference, Madrid, September 19–22.

Van Ryzin, G. 2007. "Can Citizens Accurately Judge Public Performance? Evidence from New York City, with Implications for Developing International Bureaumetrics." Paper presented at the European Group of Public Administration Conference, Madrid, September.

Woods, N. 2001. "Making the IMF and the World Bank More Accountable." *International Affairs* 77 (1): 83–100.

6

DOES PERFORMANCE MEASUREMENT ACTUALLY IMPROVE ACCOUNTABILITY?

BERYL A. RADIN

Performance measurement and accountability are two extremely common but very imprecisely defined terms. Moreover, the rhetoric surrounding them clearly suggests that while citizens believe they are linked, they are not able to move much beyond the rhetorical association. An assumption (not always articulated) is that the availability of performance data will provide both those inside the public sector and concerned citizens with information that will lead to more accountable behavior. This assumption appears to support the view that citizens across the globe are skeptical about the ability of their governments to be accountable or able to perform as expected.

The public management literature indicates that more scholarly attention has been given to the various aspects of accountability than to performance measurement. In fact, many of the advocates of performance measurement have rarely moved beyond advocacy of the goals of performance measurement and have not made a significant effort to analyze the appropriate means of achieving those goals. Neither have many of them attempted to offer typologies or categories of reasons why performance-measurement efforts work in some situations and not in others (Frederickson and Frederickson 2007 is an exception). As a result, the problems that have emerged during the implementation of performance activities are not well understood, nor are they examined in a conceptualized framework.

This chapter explores this issue by reviewing the accountability literature and drawing on one conceptual framework (that provided by Romzek and Dubnick 1993) to describe the multiple faces of accountability. The discussion indicates how current views about performance measurement are rooted in just one perspective on accountability and do not include attention to other approaches. This limited scope leads to a range of problems that have been experienced in performance-measurement activities (Radin 2006). The chapter analyzes the recent performance activities in the U.S. federal system (the Government Performance and Results Act [GPRA] and the Program Assessment Rating Tool [PART]) to illustrate this pattern.

THINKING ABOUT ACCOUNTABILITY

Clearly the concept of accountability is fundamental to the design of the American political system. One of the major assumptions of a democratic society is that the institutions and processes of government are designed to be answerable to the citizenry for their performance. But we have not been clear about how to think about that performance (Radin 2002). Much of the literature that deals with accountability actually emphasizes its negative and formal aspects and highlights methods that can limit the ability of both political appointees and career public servants to exert discretion. At least five different forms are found within the literature: legal constraints, fiscal constraints, political constraints, efficiency norms, and forms that flow from attempts by those in formal hierarchical positions to control the bureaucracy (Radin 2002, p. 12). Indeed, the focus on hierarchical control of bureaucracy has been the approach to accountability that dominates the public administration field. The Weberian bureaucratic form—often described through a machine metaphor—is the most typical point of departure for those who focus on the approach to accountability that emanates from the top of an organization. Despite some significant evidence that leads one to question this belief, most federal management reforms have bought into the perspective of Frederick Malek, a former Nixon administration adviser, who said: "If the executive branch of government is to be managed effectively, it clearly needs a system for setting priorities, pinpointing responsibility for their achievement, requiring follow-through, and generating enough feedback that programs can be monitored and evaluated from the top" (Malek 1978).

Alternatives have emerged over the years as scholars have written about the limitations of the hierarchical-control approach. Among those scholars are Louis C. Gawthrop, Martin Landau and Russell Stout Jr., Herbert Kaufman, Mark H. Moore, Bernard Rosen, and Judith Gruber. Romzek and Dubnick provide a broad definition of accountability that is especially relevant to understanding its relationship to performance measurement. They point to the multiple expectations involved in accountability relationships and say that the United States has the pattern of layering one kind of accountability mechanism upon another. These newly designed mechanisms are not substituted for earlier mechanisms; rather, they are added to the mix and result in a pattern of multiple accountability relationships that vary in the source of control (whether it is external or internal to the agency) and degree of control (whether it involves a high degree of control and close scrutiny or a low degree of control and minimal scrutiny (Romzek and Dubnick 1987). Romzek and Dubnick emphasize four different types of relationships: legal, political, professional, and bureaucratic. They argue that the American political system, with its fundamental cultural norm of distrust of concentrated governmental power, has made the accountability task of governance extremely complex. The American system of separation of powers means that legitimate performance expectations and account-ability relationships emerge from diverse sources wishing to promote very different perspec-tives, roles, and often values.

Adding to this structural diversity is the historical tendency in the United States to layer one kind of accountability mechanism upon another (see also Light 1997). As one kind of account-ability problem or scandal emerges, mechanisms are designed in an attempt to ensure that such an event cannot recur. The pattern has resulted in a complex situation in which the four different types of accountability relationships (bureaucratic, legal, professional, and political) included in the Romzek-Dubnick framework intersect (see Figure 6.1).

Bureaucratic Accountability

Bureaucratic accountability relationships are defined internally and exhibit a high degree of control. They are manifested in organizational roles, supervisory relationships, rules, standard operating procedures, and close, detailed scrutiny of employee or agency performance. The relationships are based on an expectation of obedience to organizational directives. This type of accountability emphasizes the approach to control that is found in the traditional approaches to the subject. It assumes that the pyramid that formally describes organizations actually results in controlling relationships.

Figure 6.1   **Types of Accountability Mechanisms: Romzek-Dubnik Framework**

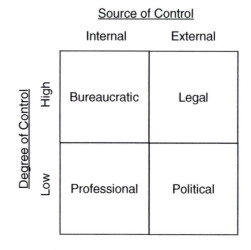

Political Accountability

Political accountability relationships derive from external sources but involve low degrees of direct control. They are manifested in a high degree of discretion for the individual or agency to choose whether or not to respond to the expectations of some key external stakeholder and to face the consequences of that decision. The relationship is based on an expectation of responsiveness to these stakeholders. Some of the stakeholders (for example, those in legislative positions) hold formal positions of authority. These stakeholders are especially relevant to agency leaders because of the influence that they have within the broader political system. For example, interest groups do not have formal authority, yet they often communicate their accountability expectations to agency officials.

Professional Accountability

Professional accountability relationships derive from internal sources but involve low degrees of control and high degrees of discretion to the individual or agency being held answerable for performance. These relationships are manifested in deference to the expertise of the administrator (or agency), who is expected to exercise discretion in a manner consistent with the norms of professional practice relevant to the area of expertise. This source of control emanates from within the organization as internalized professional norms and standards. Rarely do these expectations result in formal accountability requirements. Rather, they are found in informal relationships within many organizations.

Legal Accountability

Legal accountability relationships derive from external sources that exercise a high degree of control and scrutiny. They are manifested in oversight and monitoring activities. Some actor (individual or organization) external to the office or agency has an independent basis for scrutinizing performance, such as an auditor, a legislative oversight hearing, or a court review of administrative practices.

In both legal and bureaucratic accountability relationships, there is little choice about whether to respond to the relevant expectations. The high degree of control and scrutiny leaves little room for discretion; in contrast, both professional and political accountability relationships allow a high degree of discretion on how to respond to expectations for performance. The scrutiny that does occur is less frequent and less detailed.

FEDERAL PERFORMANCE REQUIREMENTS

During the past decade, the concern about performance has taken several different forms. Performance information has been touted as both a basis for future decision making and as a mechanism to evaluate ongoing performance. It is the basis for a federal law, the Government Performance and Results Act (GPRA), enacted in 1993 and implemented several years later with interest by both the Congress and the Executive Branch. It is also the basis for a process undertaken in the federal Office of Management and Budget (OMB) during the Bush administration, called the Program Assessment Rating Tool (PART), which attempt to link executive branch budget and program recommendations to the performance of specific federal programs.

Both GPRA and PART—like a number of earlier federal management reform efforts—do not fit easily into the institutional structures, functions, and political realities of the American system. That system is designed to include multiple values and players, but both of the recent reform efforts focus almost entirely on efficiency values, and PART focuses only on the executive branch (U. S. Government Accountability Office 2004).

Despite the array of management-reform efforts over the years, couched in different guises and forms, few attempts to deal with management have resulted in much or significant change. This is not to say that some achievements have failed to emerge from the range of efforts, but they are modest and usually limited to the concerns of program managers. The reform efforts often do not meet the expectations of actors in a broader government context.

GPRA and PART repeat the tendency of architects of management reform to focus on what have turned out to be fairly ineffective approaches. The time and energy expended in this process have created significant opportunity costs within the federal government. Many of these reforms, based on experience of others, have borrowed ideas from the private sector, local government, the experience of parliamentary systems, or nations with smaller and more homogeneous populations. Moreover, too often these reforms have evoked a compliance mentality and cynicism among individuals in the bureaucracy who are expected to change.

GPRA and PART are prime examples of the difficulty of dealing with federal management as a government-wide strategy and set of generic activities and requirements. The public-administration community has focused on a set of institutions and processes that do not really touch the core of the nation's decision-making processes. They operate largely as rhetorical entities without the ability to influence substantive policy and budgetary processes.

GPRA: THE ORIGINAL AND DRIVING FORCE OF THE FEDERAL PERFORMANCE EFFORT

The Government Performance and Results Act (GPRA), passed by Congress in 1993, requires all federal agencies to develop strategic plans, annual performance plans, and performance reports. These stipulations are implemented within the constraints and realities of the annual budget process. All of these requirements are supposed to elicit a focus on the outcomes that have been achieved in the use of federal resources and to justify requests for dollars in terms of both promised and actual outcomes.

On its face, the GPRA legislation seems quite straightforward—indeed, almost innocuous. It clearly follows the tradition of past reform efforts within the federal government. In a report on the historical antecedents of the performance budgeting movement, the Government Accountability Office concluded that GPRA "can be seen as melding the best features of its predecessors. . . . Nonetheless, many of the challenges which confronted earlier efforts remain unresolved and will likely affect early GPRA implementation efforts" (U.S. Government Accountability Office 1997, p. 7).

There are a number of assumptions embedded in GPRA that have established quite difficult pathways to attain implementation. First, the Act assumes that a single piece of information will be able to meet the complex decision-making needs of both the executive and legislative branches. Second, GPRA's focus on outcome performance measures (and the avoidance of process and output measures) denigrates the role of the federal government in many program areas. Third, GPRA assumes that it is possible to directly link planning, management, and budgeting processes through performance information. Fourth, the Act assumes that it is possible to avoid partisan political conflicts and the differences in policy constructs among programs (programs that range from efforts that are delivered directly by the federal government to those that are hands-off block grants delivered to others, particularly state and local governments). Finally, the Act's imposition of performance measures establishes a set of expectations and processes that, according to a number of observers, moves agencies to emphasize more centralized relationships than were anticipated.

PART—THE EXECUTIVE BRANCH PERFORMANCE EFFORT

Most presidential administrations seem to put their own imprint on management reform efforts. In this respect, the George W. Bush administration was no different from many that preceded it. While some believed that the passage of GPRA in 1993 established an approach to management reform that involved both Congress and the White House and was bipartisan in nature, the Bush administration actually created its own approach to performance management within the executive branch. This approach was implemented by the Office of Management and Budget alongside the GPRA requirements.

The Bush administration's effort was called the Program Assessment Rating Tool (PART) and was viewed as a part of the Bush management agenda—to integrate the budget and performance assessments. The effort was described as including four purposes:

1. To measure and diagnose program performance
2. To evaluate programs in a systematic, consistent, and transparent manner
3. To inform agency and OMB decisions with regard to management, legislative or regulatory improvements, and budget decisions
4. To focus program improvements and measure progress compared with prior year ratings

PART started as a small-scale effort and reported information on 67 programs as a part of the presidential budget for fiscal year (FY) 2003. Following that, PART expanded the process to include 20 percent of all federal programs within the FY-2004 budget document (231 programs) and included an additional 20 percent of programs each subsequent year. Some changes were made in the requirements, but the general format remained fairly consistent. Unlike GPRA, which focused on agencies and departments, the PART analysis focused on specific programs. The OMB budget examiner for each program played the major role in evaluating the assessments.

Each program included in a special volume of the president's budget document was rated along four dimensions: program purpose and design (weight 20 percent); strategic planning (weight 10 percent); program management (weight 20 percent); and program results (weight 50 percent). Questionnaires were available to agencies (but completed by the OMB examiners), which were theoretically fine-tuned to respond to the program type. Thus different questionnaires were given for competitive grant programs, block/formula grant programs, regulatory-based programs, capital-assets and service-acquisition programs, credit programs, direct federal programs, and research-and-development programs. Five categories of ratings were used: effective, moderately effective, adequate, results not demonstrated, and ineffective. Of the programs included in the FY-2004 budget document, 14 were rated as effective, 54 moderately effective, 34 adequate, 11 ineffective, and 118 results not demonstrated. In the FY-2005 budget document, 11 percent of the programs were rated effective, 26 percent rated moderately effective, 21 percent adequate, 5 percent ineffective, and 37 percent results not demonstrated (U.S. Office of Management and Budget 2004).

The patterns of rating programs were not very clear regarding the FY-2004 process, largely because of variability among the OMB examiners. This variability was pointed out by GAO in its assessment of the process. Little attention was given to equity issues within the rating process. Rather, ratings emphasized issues dealing with efficiency values. OMB noted that every program should have an efficiency measure or be in the process of developing one. There is no discussion of equity in the instructions (U.S. Office of Management and Budget 2004). The more than 300-page document that was issued as a part of the White House budget does not give attention to protected groups (such as specific racial or ethnic groups or women's groups) within the society.

TWO PERFORMANCE EFFORTS: SIMILARITIES AND DIFFERENCES

The rhetoric of performance is a predominant language of the public sector at the end of the twentieth and beginning of the twenty-first centuries. This rhetorical style employs a vocabulary that highlights outcomes rather than inputs, processes, or even outputs. It focuses on the benefits derived from the use of public sector funds and seeks to establish a framework that moves away from traditional incremental decision making in which budgets are created largely on the basis of past allocation patterns. This rhetoric has been used as a way to counter the public's disillusionment with government as well as the government bashing that has been employed by political figures at both ends of the political spectrum. But while the concern about performance is pervasive, it is not expressed consistently, takes many different forms, and is attached to diverse efforts that involve all levels of government.

A number of aspects of the American institutional setting have an impact on the implementation of reform efforts such as GPRA and PART. These include the institutional conflict between the legislative and executive branches, the fragmentation of responsibilities within the legislative branch, intergovernmental relationships, and tension between OMB and departments and agencies.

Institutional Conflict Between Legislative and Executive Branches

Because GPRA established a shared set of expectations for both the legislative and executive branches, this reform effort directly collided with the institutional design of separation of powers. And PART did not deal with that conflict at all since it essentially ignored the role of Congress. The U.S. institutional structure rarely provides the means for a smooth path from one institutional setting to another. The system of shared powers within the context of a national political setting creates tensions and frequently leads to conflict between the two ends of Pennsylvania Avenue.

The American system assumes a complex society with very diverse players with multiple and often conflicting agendas. The GPRA legislation did establish a formal set of shared responsibilities for the two branches of government with a few words in the legislation that called for the involvement of Congress in the strategic plan development.

The Fragmentation of Responsibilities within the Legislative Branch

Although we have a tendency to speak of Congress as if it operated as a unified, monolithic institution, the fragmentation in the structure of the legislative branch does not allow it to speak with a single voice. It is difficult to expect a body with a combined membership of 535 individuals to operate in lock step, particularly in a country where political party discipline is usually quite weak. The roles of the authorizing and appropriations committees are perhaps the most formal expression of the reality of multiple voices. Despite the increased role of the appropriations committees over the past decades, the authorizing committees often look at programs and policies in different ways (and continue to have reauthorizing and oversight responsibilities) than do the appropriators.

GPRA was designed to establish close linkages to the budget process in both the executive branch and the Congress, while PART focused only on the executive branch's budget process. In at least a few instances, agency and department officials have actually pleaded with Capitol Hill appropriations staffers to use GPRA performances plans in their decision-making process, but had very little success in that setting. Some appropriations committee staff believed that GPRA could potentially provide them with information that they could use to minimize the power of interest groups who do not tend to talk about the effectiveness of programs they are supporting. However, there was little indication that Congress used the PART information; this is not surprising, since OMB did not include the various congressional perspectives on the programs.

Intergovernmental Relationships

In addition to the horizontal separation of powers defined by the separate branches of government, the U.S. system is designed to minimize the power that is lodged in the national government. Debate over the appropriate role of the federal government has been a constant since the early days of the nation. While often this discussion takes place in the context of specific policies and programs, it is also a part of the overall rhetoric about the role of government in this country. During the past decade, increasing attention has been paid to the devolution of responsibilities for the implementation of programs that are partially or mainly funded with federal dollars. Fewer and fewer federal domestic programs are entirely implemented by federal staff. Instead, responsibility for making allocation decisions and actually delivering services has been delegated to state and local governments or to other third parties, who are often nonprofit organizations (Beam and Conlan 2002).

Both GPRA and PART moved against this tide. The rating of block grants as "results not demonstrated" did not give attention to the limited ability of the federal government to require states and localities to report specific information about program implementation. Many block grants were created to minimize or eliminate the role of the federal government and, instead, to give significant amounts of discretion to state or local governments. Efforts to hold federal government agencies accountable for the way that programs are implemented actually assumes that these agencies have legitimate authority to enforce the requirements that are included in performance measures. The imposition of federal performance requirements is often viewed as an attempt by the federal government to take away the discretion that was designed within the program. In some cases, federal agencies have worked closely with these other partners to devise a set of performance measures that are mutually agreed upon. More often, however, these other partners—especially states—have worked to protect their discretion in programs that are politically sensitive such as Medicaid and Temporary Assistance for Needy Families (TANF).

Thus third-party perspectives create a major problem in the performance context and determine which party defines the outcomes that are expected (Frederickson and Frederickson 2007). States that already have performance measurement systems in place also do not want to shift to a national system if their current activities provide them with information that is useful to them. In this sense, if performance information is taken very seriously, it can lead to centralization—an increase in the federal role.

Tension Between OMB and Departments and Agencies

Historically, federal, government-wide management reform has been concentrated in the management staff at the Office of Management and Budget, which reflects the effort from the White House to approach management issues from the perspective of the government as a whole. Although the management side of OMB was effectively eliminated (or at least drastically reduced) since the reorganization of the agency early in the first Clinton term, there continues to be a small staff within OMB that has lead responsibility for GPRA and PART. PART actually relied on budget examiners to evaluate program information from the agencies. The theoretical relationship between the performance information and the budget process provides OMB with an opportunity to make tradeoffs across programs and organizational units and to deal with management issues as an aggregate.

OMB's niche in the process is built around the budget process—a process that has always involved a tension between the Executive Office of the President and individual departments and agencies. The budget process provides limited opportunities for the discussion of specific aspects of programs and policies. The shorthand discussion of numbers is not conducive to capturing the detailed nuances of program operations and tends to accentuate questions of efficiency—using limited resources—rather than issues related to program effectiveness or equity concerns. In addition, OMB itself is actually quite decentralized. Budget examiners within OMB have been given both budgetary and management responsibilities for a specific set of programs and have significant autonomy to deal with agencies. As a result, some OMB staff gave serious attention to the GPRA submissions while others have dealt with them in a broad-brush fashion. The budget examiners played a crucial role in assessing the PART submissions and varied considerably in the way they applied the requirements. Some OMB staffers describe the agency as the preeminent government agency that already uses performance information in the process of developing the budget.

THE LIMITED REACH OF FEDERAL PERFORMANCE MEASUREMENT

This short description of GPRA and PART suggests that neither performance measurement effort reaches very far into the complex picture offered by the Romzek-Dubnick accountability framework. Indeed, this is not the first time that federal management reforms exhibited this limitation. Neither effort was constructed around the reality of the structure of the U.S. system. This structure formally creates a system of diverse actors who not only have different perceptions of what programs and agencies are attempting to accomplish but have legitimate authority to impose their perceptions on those who implement programs. In addition, the system creates policies and programs that frequently have multiple goals that are often not consistent with one another. Given those realities, how does one go about defining performance measures? What are the measures, who defines them, and what information is used to document them? Each of the accountability mechanisms offered by Romzek and Dubnick provides its own answer to those questions.

Bureaucratic Accountability Mechanisms

These mechanisms generally belong to the executive branch and exhibit an agenda of direct control (Rosenbloom 1983, pp. 219–220). Traditionally the measures that come from the bureaucracy emphasize efficiency values and have much in common with measures that would emerge from the private sector. They are defined internally and often emphasize classic administrative functions (e.g., POSDCORB—planning, organizing, staffing, directing, coordinating, reporting, and budgeting), particularly the budgeting process. This approach tends to assume that measures should be similar across agencies and moves toward a one-size-fits-all approach. Measures often are constructed under the assumption that federal agencies actually control the delivery of services.

The bureaucratic approach looks to the top of the hierarchy to define its measures. The process takes place inside of the executive branch. In the case of GPRA, measures were often nominated by program units, but the officials at the top of the agency or the department actually signed off on them. In the case of PART, the authority for agreeing to measures was found inside OMB and rested with budget examiners. If the budget examiner for a program did not agree with those measures nominated by agencies or departments, he or she had the ability to impose these measures on the unit. This generates significant resistance inside the agency affected. Top political officials in the Bush Environmental Protection Agency (EPA) were actually publicly critical of the measures imposed by OMB on EPA research programs.

Despite the argument that both GPRA and PART focus on program outcomes (and not outputs), the bureaucratic approach often emphasizes output data to document its measures because it is the type of information that is produced inside agencies. Such information would include data that document the speed of agency action, the number of individuals who receive a service, and descriptions of attempts to eliminate duplication or overlap between several programs.

Political Accountability Mechanisms

The Romzek-Dubnick framework characterizes these mechanisms as emerging from external sources but involving low degrees of direct control. However, in applying the framework to performance measurement, it is useful to think of political actors as those with authority, control, and influence.

Because of the multifaceted nature of congressional authority (involving both appropriations and authorizing responsibilities in both the House and the Senate), measures can take many different forms. The political process emphasizes responsiveness to public concerns and, as a result, can emphasize the values of representativeness, political responsiveness, and accountability through elected officials (Rosenbloom 1983, p. 221). The measures that emerge from this process reflect the nature of political pluralism and have, at times, included some managerial efficiency measures as well as questions related to distribution of services and equity. The type of measure used also can differ in terms of the form of the program at hand. Congress sometimes enacts programs to support a symbolic rather than actual agenda.

The multiple actors within the U.S. democracy play a part in defining performance measures. Formal congressional authority can produce measures both through the budget process and through the enactment/authorization of programs and policies. Clearly, interest groups have a role in both processes and have strong influence on the process of crafting programs and policies. In addition, external stakeholders that emerge from the construct of the federal system can influence the process. This is particularly important in program areas in which third parties (state and local actors as well as for-profit and nonprofit organizations) are major players in the implementation process. Because political actors are likely to trade off conflicting values in their decision-making process, they often include elements drawn from effectiveness, equity, and efficiency goals. This can put them at odds with those measures defined only by bureaucratic perspectives.

When Congress crafts a program that gives these third parties significant discretion in determining how to implement the effort, it often expects those parties to be able to define their own measures appropriate for the needs of a particular jurisdiction or setting. For example, when Congress enacted the Community Development Block Grant program, it gave state and local governments authority to define the needs in their communities. However, through the PART process, OMB sought to impose a single performance-measurement system on grantees which eliminated that discretion.

Unlike the bureaucratic frame, which emphasizes formal data, the political approach is often open to a range of information sources to document its measures. Agencies such as the National Institutes of Health (NIH) may present their performance information through what they call "stories of discovery." These presentations before congressional committees are qualitative accounts of multiyear efforts to explore complex issues. NIH officials are comfortable providing information about the important findings from negative research findings. In other program areas, political officials are particularly interested in hearing how federal programs have had an impact on individuals and families who reside in their districts. In still other areas, Congress uses information that is generated by both the Congressional Research Service and the Government Accountability Office. The latter frequently emphasizes issues related to managerial efficiency in its reports.

Professional Accountability Mechanisms

The Romzek-Dubnick framework describes these relationships as expectations that emerge from internal sources in the organization but involve low degrees of control. They are particularly relevant in those areas where specific professional groups are given extensive discretion in the implementation of a program.

The performance measures that flow from the professional accountability perspective are rooted in the norms of a specific profession charged with responsibility for implementing programs. Measures are built into the internalized norms and standards of a field and its defined expertise. Frequently these measures deal with issues of program quality as well as concern about who is served by the program; they can collide with the efficiency expectations of those in charge of bureaucracies (Radin 2006).

The professionals within an organization expect to be involved in the measurement definition process, but they are often ignored. If they come into the process they are likely to bring the advice of their professional organizations to the table and justify their measurement choices in terms of the norms of the profession. Their exclusion from the measurement definition process can contribute to perverse responses to the requirements that are imposed on them. At the same time, those who do impose such requirements have difficulty creating compliance, since they do know that the programs and policies cannot be implemented without the professionals. The inability of the federal government to successfully implement the No Child Left Behind program is a stark example of what happens when performance measures are defined without interaction or involvement of representatives of teachers' organizations.

The information that professionals like to use to document measures would likely emerge from the range of behaviors exhibited by those charged with carrying out a program. Information would be derived from the desire of professionals to maximize their discretion and protect their ability to innovate. They would be wary of information systems that suggested that there is one best way to achieve a program goal. For example, reliance on standardized tests as the only measure of performance in education is criticized by most professional education organizations because it ignores learning processes and achievement gains that fall outside the scope of the tests.

Professionals are comfortable with information presented as a combination of both quantitative and qualitative data. They would include information that documents issues related to quality of services and the complexity and variety of settings in which they work. In many cases, such information is not already available, and a dispute may arise within the program about determining the balance between achieving multiple goals and providing the information required.

Legal Accountability Mechanisms

According to Romzek and Dubnick, these mechanisms come from external sources that are able to exercise a high degree of control and scrutiny. They note that legal requirements provide little discretion for the organization and are expressed in oversight and monitoring activities.

The measures that can emerge from the legal accountability frame completely depend on the expectations of those who have the authority to make demands on the program or organization. Measures could be specific quantitative requirements or process requirements; they could involve any aspect of the decision-making process (from inputs and processes to outputs and outcomes). Measures may include a focus on due process, fairness, and equity. Participants in this category have their own perspective on the type of measures that are relevant and important.

Legal accountability expectations can come from any group that has an independent basis for scrutinizing performance; thus the actors in this frame can include auditors and legislative oversight committees, as well as action from courts. The oversight and monitoring function often includes Inspector General (IG) offices, the GAO, and CRS. GAO and CRS are organs of the Congress. while IG offices have dual responsibility to the executive and legislative branches. Court action can occur at various points within the decision-making process.

Conflict often arises between the executive branch and the players involved in this frame. During the PART process the Consumer Product Safety Commission, Occupational Safety and Health Administration, and Mine Safety and Health Administration were all penalized by OMB for failing to use economic analysis in their rulemaking processes—even though they are forbidden by law and Supreme Court precedent from doing so.

While the players in this frame have the ability to document, question, criticize, and sometimes penalize the executive branch's choices about performance measurement, their ability to create their own information sources is constrained by their own resources and perspectives. The oversight function attached to the Congress through the committee structure, GAO, and CRS all produce some independent assessment, but most of it occurs when problems are already identified. Even then, it took an outside group to point out that the PART assessment by OMB of the Consumer Product Safety Commission (CPSC) specifically clashed with congressional directives. CPSC was instructed by Congress not to use cost-benefit analysis when issuing rules specifically required by law, yet the agency was criticized in the PART assessment for not using cost-benefit analysis.

CONCLUSION

An examination of the two recent federal performance-measurement activities through the Romzek-Dubnick accountability framework helps explain why there is significant discomfort with the approach found in GPRA, and especially in PART. The promises of improved accountability that have been made—at least rhetorically—by advocates of the performance movement have failed to acknowledge the complexity of accountability expectations.

It is clear that both federal initiatives focus almost exclusively on the perspective of the bureaucratic accountability mechanism. The efforts are defined almost entirely within the executive branch. In the case of PART, the control was in the hands of the White House and OMB and expresses a strong command-and-control approach that often overrules the perspective of program officials. The executive branch ignores the multiple perspectives raised in the complex congressional structure that is the main player in the political frame. The executive branch approaches the performance-assessment task as if the federal government had complete control over the implementation of programs despite the increasing strength of third-party government.

The perspectives of professionals have frequently been ignored or actually overridden because of executive-branch distrust of their discretion and autonomy. Requirements are often imposed on professionals charged with implementing the programs that violate their professional norms. And we have increasingly operated as if the U.S. system is a parliamentary structure without the overlapping and shared power arrangement detailed in our Constitution. This is particularly problematic as one sees how the executive branch has ignored the perspective of the legal frame.

As a result, both GPRA and PART have created cynicism both inside the federal government and within the broader society. Critics of current policies have been labeled advocates of the status quo. In truth, the debate that has ensued has often confused the ends of performance activity with the means that have been put in place to accomplish those goals. Critics of the means are sometimes accused of opposing the idea of performance assessment, defending the status quo, and—worst of all—wasting public funds. Advocates of efforts like PART (and to some extent GPRA) do not want to acknowledge the flaws in these approaches, which contribute to their failure to significantly influence those in Congress who both appropriate funds and authorize policies and programs. The requirements attached to these programs too often ask agencies to develop analyses that they know will not be used; this can create a cynical, compliance-driven mentality that moves an agency far from the goals of performance assessment. Even advocates of PART, for example, find it difficult to find examples of the impact that data have made on decisions.

A new administration in Washington now has the challenge of creating a performance-assessment system that acknowledges the complexity of the American system, respects multiple perspectives, moves away from the one-size-fits-all view of the bureaucratic frame, and finds ways for the executive branch to respond realistically and modestly to the almost impenetrable structure of the U.S. system.

REFERENCES

Beam, David R., and Timothy J. Conlan. 2002. "Grants." In *The Tools of Government: A Guide to the New Governance*, ed. Lester M. Salamon. New York: Oxford University Press.

Dubnick, Melvin J., and Barbara S. Romzek. 1993. "Accountability and the Centrality of Expectations in American Public Administration." *Research in Public Administration* 2: 37–78.

Frederickson, David G., and H. George Frederickson. 2007. *Measuring the Performance of the Hollow State*. Washington, DC: Georgetown University Press.

Light, Paul C. 1997. *The Tides of Reform: Making Government Work, 1945–1995*. New Haven: Yale University Press.

Malek, Frederick V. 1978. *Washington's Hidden Tragedy: The Failure to Make Government Work*. New York: Free Press, 148.

Radin, Beryl A. 2002. *The Accountable Juggler*. Washington, DC: CQ Press.

———. 2006 *Challenging the Performance Movement: Accountability, Complexity and Democratic Values*. Washington, DC: Georgetown University Press.

Romzek, Barbara S., and Melvin J. Dubnick. 1987. "Accountability in the Public Sector: Lessons from the *Challenger* Tragedy." *Public Administration Review* 47 (May/June): 227–38.

Rosenbloom, David H. 1983. "Public Administration Theory and the Separation of Powers." *Public Administration Review* 43 (May/June): 219–20.

U.S. Government Accountability Office. 2004. *Performance Budgeting: Observations on the Use of OMB's Program Assessment Rating Tool for the Fiscal Year 2004 Budget.* GAO-04–174, January 30. Washington, DC.

———. 1997. *Performance Budgeting: Past Initiatives Offer Insights for GPRA Implementation.* GAO/AIMD-97–46, March. Washington, DC.

U.S. Office of Management and Budget (OMB). 2004. "Performance and Management Assessments." *Budget of the United States Government,* Fiscal Year 2004.

———. 2004 "PART Frequently Asked Questions." Available at http://www.whitehouse.gov/omb/rewrite/part/2004_faq.html.

7

THE ACCOUNTABILITY ENVIRONMENT OF U.S. COUNTIES

BONNIE J. JOHNSON, JOHN C. PIERCE, AND
NICHOLAS P. LOVRICH, JR.

This chapter examines the "accountability environment" (Kearns, 1996) of American counties. In particular, the study focuses on contextual sources of variations in what Romzek and Dubnick (1987) have termed "political accountability." Political accountability refers to how open and accessible government is to the public. We examine the degree to which variations in this political accountability are associated with differences in the political and cultural environments of county governments, including social capital levels (trust, networking), diversity, political competitiveness, form of county government, and state influence. Looking at county governments and accountability is important because there is little research in this area (Streib et al. 2007), while at the same time, counties are becoming essential regional partners in providing all types of public services from airports and solid waste disposal (Benton 2002) to economic development (Leland and Thurmaier 2005).

J.E. Benton has noted that "we still know very little about counties as laboratories of democracy" (2005, 467). Once thought of as "corrupt, wasteful, unaccountable, and unprofessional" (Streib et al. 2007, 968), counties now provide city-level services and are often the only hope for regional planning and coordination. Counties also are unique among local governments because they provide redistributive services (Benton 2002). Despite their importance, observers continue to lament that "little is known about the mechanisms used by county governments to encourage citizen input and other forms of participation" (Streib et al. 2007, 971). Indeed, in setting an agenda for future county research, Streib et al. issue a call for "studies that will assist in improving the efficiency, effectiveness, responsiveness, and accountability of county government and its officials" (2007, 979).

Krislov and Rosenbloom (1987, 529) discuss the challenge "of effectively integrating bureaucratic power into democratic government" when bureaucracies are characterized by "hierarchy, specialization, and formalization." Essential to that "effective integration" is accountability, "the measures by which public agencies and their workers manage the diverse expectations generated within and outside the organization" (Romzek and Dubnick 1987, 228). To manage those expectations, Romzek and Dubnick (1987) suggest the presence of four types of accountability systems: bureaucratic (hierarchical), legal, professional, and political. Measuring accountability in these different systems can take the form of what Roberts (2002, 659) calls direction-based accountability (goals and objectives), performance-based accountability (outputs and outcomes), or procedure-based accountability (managerial reporting). Along these lines, scholars have typically focused on budgets and finance (Willoughby 1987; Wang 2002) and how responsive administrators are to elected officials (Wood & Waterman 1991; West 2004) while this study focuses on "political accountability."

COUNTIES AND POLITICAL ACCOUNTABILITY

This study centers on what Romzek and Dubnick characterize as "political accountability," as seen in "open meetings laws, freedom of information acts, and 'government in the sunshine' statutes" (1987, 229–30). Political accountability reflects Frederickson's (1991, 410) notion that the term "public" in public administration means attending to mechanisms in which public administrators hear not only from interest groups, but also from the "inchoate public." Likewise, Roberts (2002) emphasizes the importance of "dialogue" as an accountability mechanism, and Wang (2002) argues that accountability can come from public hearings and community meetings, which allow for information sharing and public input. Within this democratic context, Gormley and Balla (2004, 5) stress the importance of "fairness" exhibited by "all parties desiring to participate in particular decision-making processes. . . . [being] given the opportunity to make their preferences known." In this regard, knowing that they may be reluctant to take the time and energy to genuinely engage the public, Etzioni (1975, 279) cautions administrators to avoid "accountability as gesture." He emphasizes the need for "fixed, 'institutionalized' opportunities for communication" that "constitute a vital element of any effective accountability system" (Etzioni 1975, 285). These perspectives lead us to measure accountability by counting the number of public-participation opportunities that county governments offer. Just as Romzek and Dubnick (1987) highlight the complex internal and external forces structuring accountability, Etzioni (1975, 283) makes clear that "accountability is based on a variety of interacting forces, not one lone attribute or mechanism." In this context, we find Kevin Kearns's concept of the "accountability environment" quite useful, in which he defines it as "a constellation of forces—legal, political, sociocultural, and economic—that place pressure on organizations and the people who work in them to engage in certain activities and refrain from engaging in others" (1996, 29). Our sense of the county accountability environment includes (but is not limited to) the following forces: sociocultural (diversity and political culture in the form of social capital), legal (indirect state requirements, form of government), and political (competitive elections).

This study also draws on the analytical model Benton (2002) developed to predict county government service levels. He explores the influence of region and culture, state financial aid, metropolitan status, amount of growth, and form of government. Benton (2002) finds that services provided by counties in the New England, Mid-Atlantic, and North Central regions continue to follow traditional patterns, while counties in the South have expanded their roles. Benton also shows that growing counties, metropolitan counties, and those with more modern forms of government are most likely to provide higher levels of "city services." In the context of this study, the presence of political accountability might be construed as a significant form of service to the public.

THE STUDY

The analysis presented here is based on data gathered from three different sources. The main source is a 2006 ICMA (International City/County Management Association) survey that featured information on political accountability activities for 241 participating counties (ICMA 2006; Moulder and O'Neill, Jr. 2007). The second source contains social-capital data at the county level in the form of networking/organizational opportunities from various aggregate data sources, as described in Rupasingha et al. (2006). Moreover, for a subset of the 241 counties (n = 59–67), survey results are available for citizen views on a series of items related to social capital, like levels of trust (see Pierce, Lovrich, and Moon 2002). Measures of political accountability, diversity, political competitiveness, and form of government are available for all 241 counties in the ICMA data set.

Political Accountability Measures

Political accountability is conceptualized as the presence of political processes and mechanisms through which civic influence and public oversight can be exercised. We include four measures of political accountability constructed from the ICMA data set.

1. *Number of accountability opportunities.* A count was made of reported established opportunities for citizen participation through each of the following six mechanisms: commission meetings, town meetings, neighborhood meetings, citizen participation processes, ad hoc task forces, and other channels of citizen access (mean = 3.03; sd = 1.42; alpha = .58). The alpha reported here is the coefficient alpha, which is a measure of a scale's reliability. It ranges in value from 0 to 1 with 1 meaning perfect reliability.

2. *Publicizing accountability opportunities.* A count was made of county reports of ways counties publicize political accountability opportunities: newspaper notices, newsletters, email, cable TV, local-government website, and other (mean = 2.48; sd = 1.40; alpha = .56).

3. *Ways citizens are informed about upcoming council agenda.* A count was made of the ways citizens are informed about an upcoming commission meeting agenda: newspaper notices, newsletters to all residents, email, cable TV, local government website, and other (mean = 2.27; sd = 1.25; alpha = .45).

4. *Overall summary index of citizen engagement.* An additive scale created by summing the three previous measures was calculated for a composite measure (mean = 7.78; sd = 3.48; alpha = .76).

POLITICAL CULTURE AND COUNTY ACCOUNTABILITY

We begin exploring county accountability environments by looking at political culture and then moving on to other aspects, such as diversity, political competition, form of government, and state effects. Sharp recently noted a "'renaissance' of attention to the concept of culture in political science" (2005, 132; see also Miller et al. 2006). Daniel Elazar, a pioneer in this area of research, has defined political culture as "the particular pattern of orientation to political action in which each political system is embedded" (1994, 9). One question explored in this study is whether political culture is central to Kearns's accountability environment (1996). For this analysis, political culture is conceptualized as social capital (e.g., Putnam 2000), which is defined by types of networks and levels of trust.

Social capital is the resource that emerges from "the norms and social relations embedded in the social structure of societies that enable people to coordinate action to achieve desired goals" (Borgada et al. 2002, 126). Coordinated collective action is based on trust that facilitates the formation of networks, which are in turn capable of producing purposive civic activity (Coleman 1988, 1990; Halpern 2005; Putnam 2000). Thus political culture can be characterized by the degree to which trust is exhibited among citizens. Previous research has shown substantial variation across urban areas in the levels of social capital (Putnam 2000; Putnam and Feldstein 2003) and have noted that the variations are associated with differences in the quality of government performance (Knack 2002; Pierce et al. 2002).

In this study our expectations were that differences in county government political accountability would be systematically associated with variations in aggregate trust levels and with types of network relationships. Consistent with the findings of Knack (2002), however, we anticipated contrasting patterns in the impact of levels of trust when compared to the effects produced by networks. Thus, our hypotheses were that greater accountability would be associated with greater aggregate trust levels, but not with the greater relative presence of networks, because the quality of the network relationship is what matters (Claibourn and Martin 2007; Price 2002). As Knack notes in this regard, "Many or even most social interactions may not contribute to public-spiritedness or generalized trust and reciprocity. Depending on the composition, activities, and goals of these networks, some of them may reduce trust and cooperation between members and nonmembers" (2002, 783).

In the study of social networks the distinction often is made between networks that are based in bonding trust and those that are characterized by bridging trust (Putnam 2000, 22–24). Trust that bonds generally is directed at others who are part of the same set of social connections or networks. In contrast, trust that "bridges" is directed at individuals who are outside of one's own immediate social and organizational circles. Social capital based in bridging trust is believed to be more likely to help individuals of different backgrounds take collective action (networking) across diverse social/ethnic/economic groups for the accomplishment of shared or reciprocal interests. The type of network (bridging vs. bonding) is important when looking at how government responds to different groups.

Political Culture Measures

Two types of social capital relate to political culture: trust-based social capital and network-based social capital.

Trust-based social capital. This measure is drawn from a set of surveys conducted among residents in 75+ American urban areas. Leigh Stowell & Company of Seattle donated to Washington State University more than 350 major media market studies conducted from 1989 through 2003 in both the United States and Canada. The principal clients of the firm are the television network affiliates of CBS, NBC, and ABC, and major newspapers. The telephone surveys (n = from 750 to 2000) were computer assisted with random digit dialing and conducted by experienced interviewers. In addition to information on media-use habits, consumer preferences, and demographic attributes, most of these studies also included a variety of social/psychological items. Among those items are some relating to political and social trust. Nearly all of the media markets surveyed included multiple counties. For this present study, 59 counties in the Stowell data set included all five of the questions below and co-occur in the ICMA survey data set and in the networking/organizational data set. The following questions were employed to assess levels of trusting versus cynical outlook (with the trusting-response direction in parentheses):

1. Too many people are getting a free ride in today's society (disagree).
2. As a rule, I don't believe in taking risks (disagree).
3. It is always better to stay with something familiar, rather than something new (disagree).
4. Most public officials today are only interested in people with money (disagree).
5. I often feel that my opinions are not taken seriously (disagree).

For each of the 59 counties, the mean (average) individual responses to these five questions are used as an aggregate measure of trust levels. While these data are useful in our analysis, several important caveats must be noted. First, the small number of counties available constrains the analyses that can be conducted. Second, the number of cases for aggregation within each county sometimes ranges as low as n = 59. Third, the sampling frame is the media market area and not the counties, so no claims can be made with regard to the actual representation of the county

Table 7.1

Statistically Significant Correlations Between Trust-Based Social Capital Survey Items and Organizational/Network Social Capital Measures (n = 59–241)

Network/organization per capita	Trust-based Stowell survey items				
	Free ride	No risks	Stay with familiar	Opinions ignored	Public officials money interests
Civic/social					
Bowling					
Fitness	−.32**			−.41**	−.29**
Golf	.25*			.20*	
Religious	.22*			.22*	
Sports					
Membership sports	−.23*				
Political	−.27*				
Professional					
Business	−.38**				−.28*
Labor					
Other			−.34*		
Overall association					−.22*
Overall association (no religious)	−.27**				−.24**

*$p \leq .05$; **$p \leq .01$.

populations. Fourth, while the survey items can be interpreted to relate to trusting versus cynical outlooks, the term "trust" is not in the specific questions.

Network-based social capital. The 1997 data from the website for the Rupasingha et al. study (2006) of social capital in U.S. counties are used to calculate the county network-based social-capital measures used here. Rupasingha et al. (2006) gathered data on many different kinds of associations and establishments that might foster network-based social capital ranging from bowling centers and religious establishments to political organizations and civic and social associations. The per-capita number of associations or establishments in each county for 12 different types of organizations or facilities are used here, along with a per capita measure of the aggregate number of all such associations and establishments (See Table 7.1 for the complete list).

Table 7.1 displays the statistically significant relationships between the network-based and the trust-based social-capital measures. The perception that too many people are getting a free ride has a positive relationship with the greater presence of golf and religious networks, and a negative set of relationships with fitness, membership sports, political and business networks, and the overall association measure (excluding religious groups). Likewise, disagreement with the belief that "public officials don't pay attention to what people like me think" is associated with fitness networks, business networks, the overall association network measure, and the total association network measure exclusive of religious groups. Thus, as the work of Knack (2002) and others suggests the trust-based environment for network-based social capital does indeed depend on the substantive content of the networks. To be sure, while these findings are not uniformly consistent, there is considerable evidence that a coherent nexus exists between network-based social capital on the one hand, and patterns of social trust on the other.

Findings: Political Culture and Accountability

Table 7.2 shows the bivariate correlations (r) between the political accountability indexes and network-based social-capital measures. Several noteworthy findings are presented in Table 7.2. First, consistent with our expectation based in the prior work of Knack (2002), most of the significant relationships are negative, the most powerful ones of which are linked to the measure for religious organizations. Why would accountability mechanisms be greatest in those counties with the lowest levels of social capital as measured by the associations/establishments that: (1) presumably are based in or generate interpersonal trust; and (2) would be available for mobilization to enact sanctions or influence public officials? One might reasonably expect them to press for formal and public processes through which they can ensure accountability. Instead, it might well be the case that the associations/establishments with a broad (and perhaps bridging) social-membership base act as substitutes for formal accountability mechanisms, displacing the demand for such mechanisms, as suggested by Hero (2007, 133–150). A second possibility, particularly in the case of the religious organizations, is that these may be largely bonding-based rather than bridging-based organizations. If so, their often inwardly focused trust and their congregation-based activity may generate less motivation to focus on civic affairs and/or less need to press for formal mechanisms. Also, religious organizations may prefer pressing claims through informal mechanisms. These findings may relate to observations by Hill and Matsubayashi (2005) that communities with greater levels of bonding group membership have lower levels of agreement between the preferred policy agendas of the mass public and those of governing elites.

Adding to the plausibility of these conclusions are connections found when looking at the 64 counties for which we have both social capital network data and survey data. In the survey data, there is an item that reads: *I believe the world was created in six days, just like the Bible says.* The county-level mean agreement with that statement on biblical literalism has a very strong and statistically significant (p) correlation (r) with the number (n) of religious establishments per capita in the county (r = .64; p = .000; n = 64). Thus if, as some suggest, more fundamentalist religious organizations are inward-looking with more bonding rather than bridging social capital than mainline denominations (Coleman, 2003; see also, Schneider, 2006), one might expect them to be concerned with informal network-based access to accountability. They would be less comfortable with the inclusivity and visibility of formal accountability processes.

Significant positive correlations of network-based social capital and the summary index of civic accountability are in evidence only for professional associations. Why is it that counties with a greater presence of professional organizations, rather than groups like bowling leagues, are more likely to have formal accountability mechanisms? Along with three other types of organizations (political, business, and labor) Rupasingha (2006) and his colleagues assign professional organizations to the "rent-seeking" organizational category (see also, Knack and Keefer 1997; Krueger 1974). As Tulloch puts it, rent-seeking is when " . . . people use their votes or other political means" to gain benefits exclusively for themselves (2005, 92). Non–rent-seeking organizations, in contrast, press claims that result in collective community benefits. A further plausible distinction can be drawn between rent-seeking organizations that are altruistic and those that are not. In addition to rent-seeking benefits, altruistic rent-seeking organizations may seek distributions not only for themselves but also for "free riders," or those who do not actively participate in obtaining the benefits (for related discussions, see Gradstein 1993; Baron 2003; Folbre and Nelson 2000). But the effects of professional and

Table 7.2

Correlations (r) Among Accountability Measures Present and Network Social Capital Measures (n = 241)

Network measures	Accountability measures			
	Accountability opportunities	Publicize accountability opportunities	Ways informed re: agenda	Summary index
All associations	−.39**	−.31**	−.34**	−.40**
Associations (not religious)	−.16**	−.11*	−.13**	−.16*
Establishments				
Civic/social	−.10	−.08	−.10	−.11*
Bowling	−.16**	−.10	−.10	−.15*
Fitness	.04	.05	.09	.07
Golf	−.16**	−.12*	−.12*	−.16**
Religious	−.38**	−.31**	−.33**	−.40**
Sports	.05	.02	.07	.05
Membership sports	−.08	−.07	−.14**	−.11*
Political	.05	.08	.13*	.10
Professional	.06	.10	.16**	.12*
Business	−.01	−.01	.06	.02
Labor	−.01	−.08	−.14**	−.11*
Other	−.11	−.09	−.16**	−.14**

*$p \le .05$; **$p \le .01$.

political organizations on accountability are positive, while labor organizations have a negative correlation. One possibility to consider is that the professional and political networks are altruistic rent-seeking organizations or bridging networks. Unlike pure rent-seeking organizations, they may seek to influence public policy within their area of expertise and create benefits for everyone, regardless of whether those benefiting are members of their organizations or not. Also, professional groups may be the most comfortable with formal mechanisms and speaking out in public.

Similarly, the four accountability indexes are often correlated with county mean responses on the five trust items. The results of this analysis are reported in Table 7.3. One of the trust items ("As a rule, I don't believe in taking risks") demonstrates a consistent effect across all four accountability indexes. A trustful response to the item is a low score, so the negative correlations in the results reflect trust associated with greater formal political accountability. It may be that a greater tolerance for risk facilitates greater comfort in dealing with the openness and uncertainty of public political accountability processes. This finding is consistent with recent research showing that city-planning departments with entrepreneurial, risk-tolerant atmospheres are associated with planners who feel comfortable with actively promoting open, democratic processes (Johnson 2006).

The other trust item with several significant correlations with the accountability measures, including the summary index, is "I often feel that my opinions are not taken seriously." The mean level of citizen disagreement with that item is associated with greater accountability. Again, greater trust in others' attentive response to the expression of one's opinions may reflect the presence of bridging trust in the form of greater support for public and open political accountability processes.

Table 7.3

Correlations (r) of Accountability Measures with Trust Measures of Social Capital ($n = 59 - 68$)

Trust measures	Accountability measures			
	Accountability opportunities	Publicize accountability opportunities	Ways inform re: agenda	Summary index
Free ride	.03	−.01	.01	.01
No taking risks	−.30**	−.27*	−.33**	−.36**
Stay with familiar	.00	.00	−.02	−.06
Public officials money interests	.18	.07	.05	.13
Opinions not taken seriously	−.08	−.11	−.28**	−.18*

* $p \le .05$; ** $p \le .01$.
Note: The n for the correlations ranges from 59 to 68 counties because not all of the county data contains all of the trust survey items.

OTHER EFFECTS ON ACCOUNTABILITY: DIVERSITY, PARTISAN COMPETITION, FORM OF COUNTY GOVERNMENT, AND THE STATE

Several other possible environmental influences on variations in county political accountability levels were also investigated; these included the racial/ethnic diversity of the county population, the extent of partisan competition present, the form of county government, and presence of particular state effects.

Competitive Elections and Diversity

Competitive elections are broadly viewed as a necessity for citizens to control their governments (Schattschneider, 1960/1975). In this specific regard, Hill and Matsubayaski (2005) find that the presence of democratic processes promoting competitiveness is more important to representation than the presence of bridging social capital. Research shows that city planners have more motivation to promote community dialogue and involve the public when local elections are not competitive (Johnson 2006). This finding may be due to two factors. Noncompetitive elections may mean a lack of conflict, a condition that makes it more comfortable and less risky for planners to reach out. Another factor may be that planners compensate for noncompetitive elections. When elections are not competitive there is limited public debate, which results in public servants having little information on citizen preferences. Thus, we expect accountability to be negatively correlated with the level of competitiveness.

We expect that greater ethnic diversity, with its presumed accompanying variety of competing interests, may enhance the overall sense that there is a need for public venues to press claims on behalf of different interests. Public officials may believe it is simply "the right thing to do" or in their political best interest to make certain that various racial and/or ethnic interests have equal access to the workings of government. Also, they may see the benefits of heading off complaints that certain groups were shut out of the process. Largely based in the work of Hill (1994), Hero clearly has established that social diversity helps explain democratization scores at the state level (1998, 48). We consider the presence of political accountability processes to be a significant component of the formal democratic character of county governments. The ethnic diversity of the county population is calculated using Hero's formula (1998, 158, footnote 44). Party competition

Table 7.4

Correlation (r) of Diversity and Partisan Competition with Political Accountability Indexes ($n = 241$)

	Accountability measures			
	Accountability opportunities	Publicize accountability opportunities	Ways inform re: agenda	Summary index
Partisan competition	−.14*	−.08	−.12*	−.10**
Ethnic diversity	.11*	.14*	.14*	.13*

*$p \le .05$; **The statistical significance level for this correlation is .059.

may be measured by applying the Hero diversity formula to the division of the 1996 vote for U.S. president in each county. Table 7.4 shows the zero-order correlations of diversity and competitiveness with the four accountability measures.

Both partisan competition and ethnic diversity exhibit significant zero-order correlations with the accountability measures. The relationships for level of party competition are negative (the greater the competition, the less the presence of formal political accountability processes), while those for ethnic diversity are positive (the greater the diversity, the greater the presence of formal accountability processes). As suggested above, the presence of partisan competitiveness may perform much the same function as the formal accountability processes, given that those who are in disagreement with the decisions of public officials have a realistic opportunity to sanction them—hold them accountable—at the next election. While the pattern with regard to ethnic diversity and political accountability has been observed in prior studies (e.g., see the review of studies presented in Hero 1998), the explanation for this pattern is less clear. It may well be that significant diversity accommodation is a function of the democratic attitudes and actions of public officials and public servants in creating more formal accountability processes. Moreover, the diversity of interests may produce greater demand for open public venues in which to press racial and ethnic group claims.

Form of Government

Similar to the council-manager form of government adopted by cities, some counties are moving toward strengthening executive authority. Some counties use an appointed executive, while others have created an elected executive. It is widely believed that "both the appointed administrator and elected executive forms provide for stronger leadership, accountability, professionalism, and . . . a single focus for daily administration" (Benton 2002, 9–10). Thus we looked at the impact of the form of government on political accountability. Data on the form of government in each county was obtained from the 2006 ICMA data set. The variable code identified three forms: commission, council administrator, and council-elected executive. However, the 241 counties responding to the survey had only the two latter categories of government. We conducted a series of simple one-way analyses of variance to determine the effects of form of government on accountability, the results of which are shown in Table 7.5.

Even in this restricted analysis the form of county government results in a clear difference in the formal accountability processes available to the public. When compared to the council-elected executive counties, those with council-administrator forms of government had a greater

Table 7.5

Analysis of Variance of Effects of Form of Government on Political-Accountability Indexes in U.S. Counties ($n = 241$)

Form of government	Accountability opportunities	Publicize accountability opportunities	Ways inform re: agenda	Summary index
Council-administrator	3.29	2.59	2.41	8.3
Council-elected executive	2.73	2.34	2.11	7.2
F	9.75	2.04	3.55	6.4
Sig.	.002	.16	.061	.01

Note: The entry in each cell is the mean score for counties with that form of government on that particular political accountability index.

average number of formal accountability options, used more ways to inform the public about the upcoming council agenda, and, on the average, scored higher on the summary measure. We also calculated a special type of correlation for ordinal measures (tau-beta) between the form of government variable and the several dependent variables (not shown). We found much the same pattern.

Why is it that commissions with an appointed executive provide more political-accountability opportunities than those with an elected executive? We speculate that elected executives may feel that the competitive electoral process itself has provided the opportunity for them to be held accountable (see the previous findings on party competition). The competition among candidates and the exposure of the candidates to diverse political interests in the county (electoral accountability) may reduce the need for what might be viewed as redundant formal processes. In contrast, appointed executives are not directly vetted by the public through elections. Thus, the appointed executive (perhaps more likely to be a professional administrator) may feel a greater need to put in place formal accountability processes in order to meet the demands of accountability or, due to personal or professional ethics (Nalbandian 1991), feel an obligation to establish such democratic processes.

State Effects

Because of their status as administrative arms of states, what counties can and cannot do are subject to the availability of state funding and the dictates of state statutes. Streib and Waugh (1991, 140) note that little is known about the relationships between states and counties, other than there is "substantial state-to-state variance in county governmental forms, responsibilities, and authorities." Moreover, American states often are contrasted in terms of their political cultures (Elazar 1984, 1994; Hero 2007), and key dimensions of those cultures may produce particularly distinctive accountability environments.

State effects were investigated by creating a dummy variable for each state (a dummy variable is a variable with a value of "1" meaning it is in a particular category or "0" meaning it is not in that particular category) (with Michigan omitted as required for statistical analysis). Zero-order correlations (r) between the state dummy variables and the four accountability dependent variables were then calculated. Table 7.6 highlights those states with a significant positive correlation with the specific accountability indexes shown in the column headed by (+), while states with a negative correlation are shown under the columns headed by (−). Several states stand out as distinctive in

Table 7.6

Zero-Order Correlations of Accountability Indexes and State Dummy Variables: The Significant (*p* = .05) Positive and Negative Outcomes

Accountability measures							
Accountability opportunities		Publicize accountability opportunities		Ways inform re: agenda		Summary measure	
(+)	(−)	(+)	(−)	(+)	(−)	(+)	(−)
CA	ILL	FLA	ILL	CA	ILL	FLA	ILL
FLA	IA	OR	IA	WA	IA	WA	IA
OR	ND	VA			KY		ND
VA		WA					

their accountability-index positions. California, Florida, Oregon, Virginia, and Washington counties emerge on the high accountability end, while Illinois, Iowa, and Kentucky counties are least likely to exhibit the accountability processes featured in our indexes.

What accounts for these state effects? There are several possible answers to this question. One possibility may be different state political cultures; another may be the particular state-level requirements for sunshine or open-government policies to be followed at the county level, which themselves may grow out of the states' political cultures. However, state-level scores on various social capital indices (Putnam 2000) show little systematic relationship of social capital levels to the magnitude and direction of state effects. Four of the six states with positive effects have social capital scores below the mean, while two of the four states with negative effects do.

More similarities are found when we look at how amenable states are to allowing counties either home-rule authority or elements of self-rule. California was the first state to allow home rule in 1911. Washington followed in 1948, Oregon in 1958, and Florida in 1968 (Salant 1991). On the other hand, the four states with negative effects were later in allowing home rule or permitting counties to choose optional forms of government—Illinois in 1970, Iowa in 1988, Kentucky in 1974, and North Dakota in 1985. Virginia, one of the six states with positive effects, did not allow home-rule authority until 1985. However, Virginia is highly amenable to city-county consolidations, which have resulted in independent cities such as the City of Virginia Beach (Jeffery et al. 1989, 109). Home-rule authority influences a county's ability to choose its own structural, functional, and fiscal authority (Jeffrey et al. 1989). Home rule authority may be a proxy for state culture, and the freedom counties have to choose how much or how little citizen participation to pursue.

Through multiple regression analysis (ordinary least squares) we also looked at the cumulative and relative impact on the accountability measures of state dummy variables with significant zero-order correlations when combined with the diversity and party competition measures (see Table 7.7). The set of independent variables produced a significant R^2 for each of the dependent variables. For example, the highest R^2 value was .27 indicating that the model accounted for 27 percent of the variation in county accountability opportunities. Clearly, the greater the level of party competition, the fewer accountability processes present. Most noteworthy, though, is the observation that when diversity is combined with the state dummy variables, the impact of diversity disappears altogether. Three state dummy variables (Florida, Maryland, and Washington) exhibit a significant impact on all four of the accountability dependent variables; and three state dummy variables (California, Illinois, and Virginia) have a significant impact on three of the dependent variables, including the summary index.

Table 7.7

Regression of County Accountability Measures on County Diversity, County Partisan Competition and State Dummy Variables (*n* = 241)

	Accountability measures			
	Accountability opportunities	Publicize accountability opportunities	Ways inform re: agenda	Summary measure
Independent Variables (b)†				
Party competition	−.18**	−.12	−.13*	−.17**
Diversity	−.06	.01	.02	−.01
California	.18**	.07	.19**	.17**
Florida	.26**	.23**	.15*	.25**
Illinois	−.16**	−.11*	−.11	−.16*
Iowa	−.18**	−.10	−.11	−.15*
Kentucky	−.09	−.06	−.13*	−.11
Maryland	.14*	.13*	.15*	.16**
North Dakota	−.13*	−.10	−.10	−.13*
Oregon	.10	.20**	.08	.15**
Pennsylvania	−.14*	−.11	−.01	−.10
Virginia	.11	.17**	.15*	.17**
Washington	.15*	.22**	.19**	.22**
R²	.27	.23	.20	.26
F	6.5	5.2	4.3	7.4
Sig.	.000	.000	.000	.000

*$p \le = .05$; **$p \le .01$; †Standardized regression coefficient.

In the subsample of counties for which we have the social trust measures, one of the items stands out as the most powerful in terms of zero-order prediction of U.S. county accountability scores—the "no risk" question. We conducted a second multiple regression analysis (not shown) which predicts county variations on the accountability measures using the "no risk" trust item and the party competition and diversity measures. The "no-risk" item had a significant effect on each of the accountability variables, but the other two variables became statistically nonsignificant. Thus, in this analysis of a limited subsample, variations in the trust dimension of social capital seem to produce different levels of formal accountability processes. But how does risk hold up in the context of using selected network-based social capital measures? For at least the summary accountability measure, the no risk social trust item retains its significant effect even when controlling for party competition, diversity, and form of government as well as for labor, professional, political, and religious networks. Because of the small number of cases (60) we conducted a series of single variable regressions rather than a multiple regression taking out the "no risk" item and each of the other independent variables one at a time in the regressions. In each case, only the no-risk item survived.

SUMMARY MODEL

One final look at the data attempts to sort out the relative effects of the variables with significant effects when they are taken together in a multiple regression analysis predicting the political accountability measures (see Table 7.8). The independent variables are as follows: the cumulative association measure without religious organizations in it, religious organizations (as the

Table 7.8

Multiple Regression of Political Accountability Measures on Selected Network and Environmental Variables ($n = 241$)

	Accountability measures			
	Accountability opportunities	Publicize accountability opportunities	Ways inform re: agenda	Summary measure
Independent variables (b)†				
Associations (not religious)	−.03	.02	−.06	.00
Religious associations	−.30**	−.23**	−.27**	−.28**
Professional associations	.02	.06	.13†	.09
Form of government	−.10	.00	−.07	−.04
Party competition	−.15*	−.09	−.09	−.10
Diversity	.00	.08	.06	.08
Florida	.12	.13*	.02	.09
Oregon	.07	.18**	.05	.13*
Washington	.11	.18**	.14*	.18*
Illinois	−.15*	−.14*	−.11	−.15*
Iowa	−.13*	−.07	−.08	−.09
R^2	.26	.22	.20	.25
F	7.4	5.8	5.1	6.8
Sig.	.000	.000	.000	.000

Note: The entries in the cells are the standardized regression coefficients for the effect of the independent variables in the left column on each the four accountability measures.
  $*p \leq .05; **p \leq .01; †p = .062.$

non-rent-seeking exemplar), professional organizations (as the altruistic rent-seeking exemplar), form of government, party competition, diversity, and the state dummy variables for Florida, Oregon, Washington, Illinois, and Iowa. The state effects remained strong, but the only significant impact by networks continued to be that for religious organizations. Level of partisan competition maintained its significant negative effect on the number of accountability mechanisms in the presence of other variables.

CONCLUSION

The general proposition on which the study was based holds, namely that county political accountability processes are systematically linked to variations in distinct elements of what Kearns calls an accountability environment. That environment is indeed complex, and the forces in it are clearly intertwined. It also is clear that state effects are very strong; they likely reflect statewide accountability environments (cultural or legal) that are pervasive across counties. Likewise, the negative public accountability impact of the presence of religious organizations is clearly in evidence. We have speculated here that this negative effect may be a consequence of bonding social capital that focuses activity within the faith-based organizations (Wellman 2004). We also have suggested here that in environments with many religious organizations the accountability of government agencies may be addressed through informal linkages rather than through those that are public (Wuthnow 2002). A similar explanation may account for the level of partisan competition, which is likewise negatively linked to the range of opportunities for open access to the operation of county governments. For many county officials, the presence of partisan competition may make the formal access processes seem redundant, since officials can be sanctioned through the electoral process. However, the benefits of elections can be blunted by groups high in bonding social capital. As Hill and Matsubayaski note, the danger is in bonding groups "transmitting" their "exclusive rather than general values" to the "political elite," and thus short-circuiting the accountability benefits of elections (2005, 216).

The impact of political culture in creating an accountability environment appears more starkly when one revisits the zero-order relationships explored at the very start of this inquiry. Within a subsample of counties for which a range of relevant information was available, the degree to which citizens in the county on average are inclined to tolerate risk is linked to multiple-accountability processes. The formal public nature of those processes surely increases the risk for particular interests pressing claims or monitoring the actions of county government. Advocacy in such forums certainly entails considerable uncertainty and anxiety, and the willingness to act in public despite the risk of failure or embarrassment creates an environment amenable to more public participation. American counties differ in the extent to which their citizens are risk-tolerant, and these differences relate systematically to the range and character of formal channels of public access to county government.

Likewise, the zero-order relationships between the network-based measures and accountability indexes reveal intriguing differences among non–rent-seeking, traditional rent-seeking, and altruistic rent-seeking networks. The religious networks are apparent exemplars of the non–rent-seeking organizational networks, and their relative presence is strongly related to the presence of fewer formal political accountability processes. We hypothesize that the informal networks produced by non–rent-seeking organizations either allow for a sense of informal access and accountability in the absence of formal processes, or constitute an isolating factor showing a lack of concern with those processes. In contrast, rent-seeking organizational networks may want open processes in which they can legitimize their claims, which may be for monopolistic and self-serving benefits. We speculate that altruistic rent-seekers, in addition to their own selective income-producing benefits, are also seeking public-good distribution; the altruistic benefits they ask government to distribute are neither restricted to their own members nor to those citizens who have contributed to their achievement.

In general, these findings point to the significant influence of information and risk in the accountability environment. If the county is rich in information from informal channels (e.g., networks) or partisan competition, then it appears that relatively few formal participatory opportunities are created. Having active, altruistic rent-seeking groups, such as political and professional associations, may give rise to a relatively comfortable, low-risk environment for public participation. In contrast, a political environment with few such networks and noncompetitive elections may leave public servants with a paucity of information, thereby highlighting the need for open accountability processes. Overall, it is clear that external forces (the accountability environment) influence the need for and the comfort level with political accountability mechanisms in county government.

After exploring the accountability environments of American counties we now know more about "counties as laboratories of democracy" (Benton 2005, 467). We have made use of both Kearns's (1996) model of an accountability environment and Romzek and Dubnick's (1987) accountability typology, which in combination clearly point to the "internal and external" forces acting upon public organizations and public servants as they decide "to engage in certain activities and refrain from engaging in others" (Kearns 1996, 29). Within the parameters of this study we have focused on external forces (state and local cultures, social capital, ethnic diversity, political competitiveness, and form of government) acting upon the degree to which county governments provide channels for formal access to their workings. The results reveal how differences in a county's "accountability environment" can lead to more or less public access to county government policy making.

REFERENCES

Baron, J. 2003. "Value Analysis of Political Behavior. Self-Interested: Moralistic: Altruistic: Moral." *University of Pennsylvania Law Review* 151: 1135–67.

Benton, J.E. 2002. *Counties as Service Delivery Agents: Changing Expectations and Roles.* Westport, CT: Praeger.

———. 2005. "An Assessment of Research on American Counties." *Public Administration Review* 65 (4): 462–74.

Borgada, E., J.L. Sullivan, A. Oxendine, M.S. Jackson, E. Riedel, and A. Gangl. 2002. "Civic Culture Meets the Digital Divide: The Role of Community Electronic Networks." *Journal of Social Issues* 58 (1): 125–41.

Claibourn, M., and P.S. Martin. 2007. "The Third Face of Social Capital: How Membership in Voluntary Associations Improves Policy Accountability." *Political Research Quarterly* 60 (2): 192–201.

Coleman, J.A. 2003. "Religious Social Capital: Its Nature, Social Location, and Limits." In *Religion as Social Capital: Producing the Common Good,* ed. C.E. Corwin. Waco, TX: Baylor University Press, 33–48.

Coleman, J.S. 1988. "Social Capital in the Creation of Human Capital." *The American Journal of Sociology* 94: 95–120.

———. 1990. *Foundations of Social Theory.* Cambridge: Harvard University Press.

Elazar, D.J. 1984. *American Federalism: A View from the States.* 3rd ed. New York: Harper and Row.

———. 1994. *The American Mosaic: The Impact of Space, Time, and Culture on American Politics.* Boulder, CO: Westview.

Etzioni, A. 1975. "Alternative Conceptions of Accountability: The Example of Health Administration." *Public Administration Review* 35 (3): 279–86.

Folbre, N., and J. Nelson. 2000. "For Love or Money—or Both?" *The Journal of Economic Perspectives* 14: 123–40.

Frederickson, H.G. 1991. "Toward a Theory of the Public for Public Administration." *Administration and Society* 22 (4): 395–417.

Gormley, W.T. Jr., and S.J. Balla. 2004. *Bureaucracy and Democracy: Accountability and Performance.* Washington, DC: CQ Press.

Gradstein, M. 1993. "Rent-seeking and the Provision of Public Goods." *The Economic Journal* 103: 1236–43.

Halpern, D. 2005. *Social Capital.* Malden, MA: Polity Press.

Hero, R.E. 2007. *Racial Diversity and Social Capital.* Cambridge: Cambridge University Press.

———. 1998. *Faces of Inequality: Social Diversity in American Politics.* New York: Oxford University Press.

Hill, K.Q. 1994. *Democracy in the Fifty States.* Lincoln, NE: University of Nebraska Press.

Hill, K.Q., and T. Matsubayashi. 2005. "Civic Engagement and Mass-Elite Policy Agenda Agreement in American Communities." *American Political Science Review* 99 (2): 215–24.

International City and County Management Association (ICMA). 2006. *State of the Profession 2006* (Survey of U.S. Cities and Counties). Washington, DC: International City and County Management Association.

Jeffery, B.R., T.J. Salant, and A.L. Boroshok. 1989. *County Government Structure: A State by State Report.* Washington, DC: National Association of Counties.

Johnson, B.J. 2006. "Civic Bureaucracy: An Affirmative Role for City Planners in Building Civic Capital and Representing Communities." PhD. diss., University of Kansas, Lawrence.

Kearns, K.P. 1996. *Managing for Accountability: Preserving the Public Trust in Public and Nonprofit Organizations.* San Francisco: Jossey-Bass.

Knack, S. 2002. "Social Capital and the Quality of Government: Evidence from the States." *American Journal of Political Science* 46 (4): 772–85.

Knack, S., and P. Keefer. 1997. "Does Social Capital Have an Economic Payoff? A Cross-Country Investigation." *Quarterly Journal of Economics* 112 (4): 1251–88.

Krislov, S., and D.H. Rosenbloom. 1987 [1981]. "Representative Bureaucracy and the American Political System." In *Classics of Public Administration,* 2d ed., ed. J.M. Shafritz and A.C. Hyde. Pacific Grove, CA: Brooks/Cole Publishing, 529–38.

Krueger, A.O. 1974. "The Political Economy of the Rent-Seeking Society." *American Economic Review* 64 (2): 291–303.

Leland, S., and K. Thurmaier. 2005. "When Efficiency Is Unbelievable: Normative Lessons from 30 Years of City-County Consolidations." *Public Administration Review* 65 (4): 475–89.

Moulder, E.R., and R.J. O'Neill Jr. 2007. *Citizen Engagement and Local Government Management. The Municipal Yearbook 2007.* Washington, DC: International City and County Management Association.

Miller, D.Y., D.C. Barker, and C.J. Carman. 2006. "Mapping the Genome of American Political Subcultures: A Proposed Methodology and Pilot Study." *Publius* 36 (2): 303–15.

Nalbandian, J. 1991. *Professionalism in Local Government.* San Francisco: Jossey-Bass.

Pierce, J.C., N.P. Lovrich Jr., and C.D. Moon 2002. "Social Capital and Government Performance: An Analysis of 20 American Cities." *Public Performance and Management Review* 25 (4): 381–97.

Price, B. 2002. "Social Capital and Factors Affecting Civic Engagement as Reported by Leaders of Voluntary Organizations." *The Social Science Journal* 39 (1): 119–27.

Putnam, R.D. 2000. *Bowling Alone: The Collapse and Revival of American Community.* New York: Simon and Schuster.

Putnam, R.D., and L.M. Feldstein. 2003. *Better Together: Restoring the American Community.* New York: Simon and Schuster.

Rupasingha, A., Goetz, S.J., and Freshwater, D. 2006. "The Production of Social Capital in US Counties." *The Journal of Socio-Economics,* 35 (1): 83–101.

Roberts, N.C. 2002. "Keeping Public Officials Accountable through Dialogue: Resolving the Accountability Paradox." *Public Administration Review* 62 (6): 658–69.

Romzek, B.S., and M.J. Dubnick. 1987. "Accountability in the Public Sector: Lessons from the Challenger Tragedy." *Public Administration Review* 47 (May/June): 227–38.

Salant, T.J. 1991. "County Governments: An Overview." *Intergovernmental Perspective* 17 (1): 5–9.

Schattschneider, E.E. 1975 [1960]. *The Semisovereign People: A Realist's View of Democracy in America.* New York: Harcourt Brace Jovanovich College Publishers.

Schneider, Jo Anne. 2006. *Social Capital and Welfare Reform: Organizations, Congregations, and Communities.* New York: Columbia University Press.

Sharp, E.B. 2005. "Cities and Subcultures: Exploring Validity and Predicting Connections." *Urban Affairs Review* 41 (2): 132–56.

Streib, G., J.H. Svara, W.L. Waugh Jr., K.A. Klase, D.C. Menzel, T.J. Salant, et al. 2007. Conducting Research on Counties in the 21st Century: A New Agenda and Database Considerations. *Public Administration Review* 67 (6): 968–83.

Streib, G., and W.L. Waugh Jr. 1991. "The Changing Responsibilities of County Governments: Data from a National Survey of County Leaders." *American Review of Public Administration* 21 (2): 139–56.

Tulloch, G. 2005. *Public Goods, Redistribution and Rent-Seeking.* Cheltenham, UK: Edward Elgar.

Wang, X. 2002. "Assessing Administrative Accountability: Results from a National Survey." *American Review of Public Administration* 32 (3): 350–70.

Wellman, J.K. 2004. "The Churching of the Pacific Northwest: The Rise of Sectarian Entrepreneurs." In *Religion and Public Life in the Pacific Northwest: The None Zone,* ed. P. Killen and M. Silk. New York: Alta Mira Press, 79–106.

West, W.F. 2004. "Formal Procedures, Informal Processes, Accountability, and Responsiveness in Bureaucratic Policy Making: An Institutional Policy Analysis." *Public Administration Review* 64 (1): 66–80.

Wood, B.D., and R.W. Waterman. 1991. "The Dynamics of Political Control of the Bureaucracy." *American Political Science Review* 85 (3): 801–28.

Willoughby, W.F. 1987 [1918]. The Movement for Budgetary Reform in the States. In *Classics of Public Administration,* 2d ed., ed. J.M. Shafritz and A.C. Hyde. Pacific Grove, CA: Brooks/Cole Publishing, 33–37.

Wuthnow, R. 2002. "Reassembling the Civic Church: The Changing Role of Congregations in American Civil Society." In *Meaning and Modernity: Religion, Polity and the Self,* ed. R. Madsen, W. Sullivan, A. Swidler, and S. Tipton. Berkeley: University of California Press, 166–75.

PART III

ASSESSING ACCOUNTABILITY

It is one of the ironies of accountability that it is rarely held to account. Implied in the "promises of accountability" perspective is the need for us to determine the impacts, consequences, and implications of accountability. But such efforts require framing accountability within a context of criteria, measures, and metrics—in essence, developing or adopting an appropriate theory of governance within which such assessments can occur.

Paul Posner and Robert Schwartz use John Kingdon's policy-streams framework to describe and assess the many ways that accountability can and has been applied in various governance contexts. Their focus is on three "accountability institutions" (or mechanisms) designed to play important roles in the policy process: performance measurement, performance auditing, and program evaluation. They find that the role and significance of each varies depending on which policy stream (i.e., problem, solution, or politics) is being examined. Reviewing the limited empirical evidence, they find that these mechanisms are playing significant roles in all three streams, and perhaps are most involved in the problem stream, despite the expectation that they would be of greatest value in the solution stream. It is also clear that, despite efforts to keep out of the political realm, these institutions or mechanisms invariably get drawn into partisan debates by the very nature of their work.

Richard Ghere takes on the task of assessing the claims by advocates of e-government technologies that IT (information technology) and related innovations are accountability-enhancing (and performance-improvement) mechanisms. Grounding his analysis in Jane Fountain's examination of technology "enactment" and Dubnick's 2005 critique of the assumed relationship between accountability and performance found in the New Public Management literature, Ghere examines 28 case studies (found in 27 articles) and finds the assumed connection between IT-based accountability reforms and performance to be contingent on a "normative" dynamic that alters the form of—and reshapes expectations about—both accountability and performance. Under the right conditions and with strategic acumen that is attentive to the power and role of norms, he concludes, accountability's promise of performance can be achieved.

8

ACCOUNTABILITY INSTITUTIONS AND INFORMATION IN THE POLICY-MAKING PROCESS

PAUL L. POSNER AND ROBERT SCHWARTZ

In many member nations of the Organisation for Economic Co-operation and Development (OECD), the term "accountability" has grown to an iconic status that permits this chameleon-like term to be attached to a wide range of causes and agendas (Dubnick and Justice 2004). This expansive role is reflected and reinforced by the growing use of accountability institutions (mechanisms). National audit offices have expanded their purview beyond traditional financial and compliance auditing to focus on performance auditing and assessments. Performance auditing has become a central feature of the national audit offices of most advanced nations, and this auditing has often been replicated by inspectors general offices located inside agencies. Indeed, some offices have been pushed into ever more expansive policy roles in which they are introducing new issues to policy agendas and adjudicating budget forecasts. Policy evaluation has taken its place as a management discipline in many governments, along with expectations for periodic studies and program assessments or reviews. Performance measurement has become institutionalized in most OECD nations, and most advanced nations have worked to integrate performance information into their budget formulation processes. While earlier attempts foundered, most nations have retained their performance budgeting systems for over ten years (OECD 2005).

Understanding how accountability mechanisms affect decisions in democratic organizations is, thus, essential as their role and importance in public management grows. When, how, why, and to what extent do accountability mechanisms further accountability outcomes? Salient accountability objectives are improved performance, fairness in delivering public services, and proper stewardship of finances (Behn 2001). In order to achieve these positive outcomes, the products of accountability activity need to influence agenda formation and policy formulation. Alongside expectations for positive accountability outcomes, observers identify potential for several negative, unintended consequences, including inhibition of innovation and risk taking, tunnel vision (teaching to the test), focus on short-term objectives, focus on more easily quantifiable measures, and diversion of resources from core work (Smith 1995; Anechiarico and Jacobs 1996; Power 1997; Behn 2001; Dubnick 2005).

There is a dearth of conceptual modeling and empirical research about accountability mechanisms when it comes to which factors create positive outcomes and which create unintended negative consequences (Halachmi 2002; Dubnick and Justice 2004). Leading scholars of policy evaluation have come to pessimistic conclusions—which apply to accountability institutions— about the impact of analysis on policy making. For instance, in her survey of congressional committee staff Carol Weiss found that it is highly unlikely for analysis to be used in setting the broad direction of public policy (Weiss 1989). Although the social-science community has conducted a prodigious amount of research on many leading policy issues, Sheldon Danziger summed up the results by noting, "so much social science, so little impact" (Hird, 2005, 12). This pessimistic outlook is in distinct contrast with the hopes and dreams of many advocates of accountability institutions and reforms. The experts in the policy-analysis community as well as political leaders sometimes have unrealistic expectations of policy analysts, which necessarily lead to self-proclaimed failures. For instance, many analysts harbor expectations that specific reports will have immediate and concrete impact on legislation and when that does not happen, they become disillusioned and cynical about the role of analysts.

This chapter applies the "policy streams" model (Kingdon 2003) as a primary lens for understanding the role of accountability information in the policy-making process. We have chosen to focus on three prominent accountability mechanisms—performance measurement, performance auditing, and program evaluation. We endeavor to provide a conceptual framework and review of knowledge about the extent to which prominent accountability mechanisms result in desired outcomes, and we explore the contexts under which accountability information is more or less likely to result in desired outcomes. The first section of the chapter outlines a conceptual framework for understanding how accountability mechanisms and information influence agenda and policy formulation through problem, solution, and politics streams. The second section reviews the literature and assesses the state of evidence about impacts of accountability mechanisms and information. Gaps in evidence are identified and an empirical research agenda outlined.

OVERVIEW OF THE POLICY STREAMS APPROACH

Kingdon's policy-streams model was a seminal contribution to the literature on agenda setting and policy formation. Following Deborah Stone (1989), Kingdon noted that the portrayal of conditions as problems mobilizes apathetic stakeholders to become involved. However, the portrayal of conditions as problems is a necessary but insufficient condition of policy change. Unless there are perceived viable solutions, coherent advocacy coalitions (Sabatier 1993; Wilson 2000, p. 250), policy entrepreneurs (Kingdon 2003, or favorable political climates, policy change is unlikely (Kingdon 2003; Birkland 1997).

As Kingdon notes, analysis can enter the problem or solution stream but must often wait for a window of opportunity to open to become relevant for decision making. In some cases this can take many years. For instance, a GAO report done in the late 1980s on lessons learned from federal bailouts of such entities as New York City and Lockheed was anxiously pulled from the shelf in the wake of the 9/11 terrorist attacks by congressional and administrative staff pressed to enact the new Airline Stabilization Board providing temporary financial assistance to affected airlines (Governmental Accountability Office 1984).

The structure of this chapter follows that of the policy-streams model. Within each of the problem, solution, and politics streams we have identified a number of contexts that influence the likelihood of information from each of the mechanisms—performance measurement (and performance budgeting), performance auditing, and evaluation—impacting accountability outcomes. By outcomes we mean policy changes intended to promote improved performance, fairness, and stewardship of finances. Following the stream-by-stream analysis is a section on stream interactions.

PROBLEM STREAM

The role of accountability mechanisms looms larger in the problem stream than in either the solutions or politics streams. Indeed, a primary focus of accountability is to identify gaps between actual behavior and standards. Performance-measurement systems compare current to past performance or to benchmarks set by similar organizations. Auditors compare administrative processes and outcomes to laws, rules, regulations, and outcome measures set up as standards. And evaluators compare actual effects to desired effects.

In most cases, auditors and evaluators define problems with current programs and operations of government. After all, that is the essence of program evaluation and certainly the primary mission of performance auditing. Increasingly, accountability mechanisms have become tools for problem analysis. For example, the General Accountability Office (GAO) has identified problems in the readiness of chemical plants to deal with terrorist attacks and in the condition of schools' physical plants throughout the country.

Problem Identification Roles

Not all problems identified by accountability institutions receive equal public attention or end up being rectified through policy or management change decisions. We have identified several contextual factors that contribute to understanding when problems raised by accountability institutions are more and less likely to lead to change. These include the problem-identification role played by the accountability institution, the nature of the problem, the quality of the evidence, and institutional legitimacy.

Nature of the Problem

Following a line of research that started with Theodore Lowi's 1964 classic formulation of policy types, political scientists have long been interested in the influence of attributes of different policy areas on policy making (Lowi 1964; see Anderson 1997 for a review). Only recently has this framework been adapted to studying differences amongst policy types in the use and impact of data (Oh 1996; Lavis et al. 2002). Lavis et al. find that professional or technical "content-driven" problems may be more amenable to the influence of research than large-scale decisions concerned with, for example, jurisdictional considerations. Schwartz and Rosen (2004) find that differences among problems—to the extent to which data are used in the policy-making process—are largely explained by the political salience of those problems. Policy decisions with jurisdictional-turf or larger budgetary implications have high political salience and tend toward data immunity despite the conscious effort to rationalize decision making. More technical and professional policy decisions with low political salience tend to be more data driven. Apparently contrasting findings suggest that accountability information on high-profile issues is more likely to receive parliamentary attention. In a systematic review of Israeli audit reports over an eleven-year period, Schwartz (2000) found that audits of high-profile issues received greater attention from Parliament. It is possible that high-profile problem reports are more likely to reach the public agenda, while policy change may be another matter.

A subset of high-profile problems are issues that are highly sensitive to the public, such as tangible safety and health risks. Accountability information on such problems is very likely to not only reach the agenda, but also to generate policy change. One example is the Israeli Comptroller General's reports on gas masks issued to civilians during the first Iraq war:

> During the first Gulf War, the Government of Israel distributed gas masks to the civilian population for protection against the threat of Iraqi chemical and biological missile heads. Shortly after the end of the war the State Comptroller issued a dramatic report revealing that the 'one

size fits all' gas masks provided inadequate protection for one third of the adult population and that the protective tent for small children was ineffective (State Comptroller's Office, 1991).

The findings relied on Israel Defense Force experiments and implied that senior officials and the Minister of Defense knowingly allowed for the distribution of the ineffective equipment. The report identifies a policy of inadequate budget allocation as partially responsible for the ineffective protective equipment. Less than a year after the audit report, in a major policy shift, the Government allocated over 100 million dollars for a five-year plan designed to solve the problems outlined by the Comptroller (State Comptroller's Office 1994).

Quality of Evidence

Increasing attention is being paid to the quality of accountability information, which includes reliability, validity, credibility, legitimacy, functionality, timeliness and relevance (Streib and Poister 1999; Schwartz and Mayne 2005; Lonsdale in Schwartz and Mayne 2005). Accountability information that lacks these characteristics stands little chance of legitimately enhancing performance and other accountability outcomes.

Low-quality evaluative information is commonly cited as one cause of the failure of rational budgeting systems like the Program Planning Budget System (PBBS). In assessing the failure of PPBS, for example, Wildavsky (1983) notes: "Since the advice was for 'them' and not for 'us,' it was either doctored to appear impressive or ignored because nothing could be done about it."

Institutional Legitimacy

Accountability institutions are part of the generic landscape of analytic ideas and inputs influencing the policy process. Many policy advocates and analytic organizations outside of government work tirelessly to transmit information to policy makers by either putting new issues on the table or providing oversight and insight on existing programs or operations. We might call these processes the informal accountability system, which has an important role in framing accountability for these areas by defining implicit standards for performance, expectations for implementation, types of information considered to be legitimate and necessary, and actions to be taken in response to perceived problems. Actors involved in this informal system include interest groups, media, and central executive reviewers such as budget officers, legislative committees, and other observers/ researchers with an interest in the program area—what Heclo (1978) called "issue networks." In what Lindblom (1968) termed the partisan mutual-advocacy model, performance metrics and data are transmitted through political competition among advocates who have learned that analysis and performance information have become a new currency of debate and legitimacy.

While formal governmental accountability institutions face similar opportunities and challenges, as does policy analysis in general, there are clear differences in their prospects for influence. In general, we would argue that analysis and information produced by accountability institutions of government have both brighter prospects for impact on policy makers as well as unique challenges in preserving analytic boundaries and independence.

The institutional legitimacy of accountability institutions depends largely on their actual and perceived independence from political pressures and administrative officials. State auditors and program evaluators seek to fulfill their role as nonbiased bystanders able to produce objective and useful reports. This role might be perceived as crucial when agency-controlled evaluation efforts are considered to be swayed by political considerations.

In the United States, institutional trends are mixed. The politicization of the U.S. bureaucracy has contributed to an erosion of professionalism in the ranks of senior managers. Williams' (1998) classic work chronicles the decline of influence of policy-analysis offices in federal agencies in recent years; this decline stems from the eclipse of neutral competence as a central value in executive agencies. Nonetheless, there has been a veritable flowering of analytic support in the Congress, thanks to the development of institutions with high credibility and strong norms of neutral competence. The Congressional Budget Office (CBO) and the Government Accountability Office (GAO) have become leading producers of primary research on major policy and programmatic issues across the entire range of governmental functions. These institutions have survived, even thrived, in highly politicized institutions, to become respected suppliers of data and analysis with presumptive credibility and influence across a wide range of issue networks. These trends have been replicated at the state level as well, as many state governments have developed staff members working in the legislature who do high-level policy analysis and evaluation during this period of renaissance in state governance capacity (Hird 2005).

Solutions Stream

While accountability institutions are most active in the problem stream, they do often become involved in recommending solutions to the problems that they or others have identified or raised with regard to the public agenda. Institutions vary in the extent of involvement in discussing solutions. In the United States, the GAO generally strives to develop recommendations as part of its reports, while the CBO studiously avoids recommendations. For the most part, however, audit institutions worldwide are concerned that involving themselves in policy solutions limits their capacity to be truly independent critics of the policies' implementation (Sharkansky 1991). They do not see it as their job to offer solutions, and Sharkansky (1991) suggests that auditors want to avoid dealing with "hot potatoes." Nevertheless, accountability reports do focus on government policies and how effectively they are implemented. A fine line exists between auditing and advocating policy change. Several studies observe that effectiveness audit can place auditors at the heart of policy debate (Sutherland 1986; Gray et al., 1992; Roberts and Pollitt 1994; Broadbent and Laughlin 1997; Barzelay 1997; Schwartz 1999, 2000). Even backward looking and narrowly focused reports can have broader relevance and the potential to influence future policy decisions (e.g., on approaches to funding major government projects). In finding particular programs ineffective in achieving policy objectives, accountability reports often require change in programs and in policies.

In the United States, analytic input has been critical in setting the agenda and in developing policy alternatives across a range of issues that Brown (1974) would characterize as rationalizing in nature. Whether it be Medicare reimbursement formulas, formulas allocating billions in grant dollars, financial reforms of federal-deposit and pension-insurance programs, analysts from GAO, CBO, federal agencies, and think thanks have played vital roles in solution development. Student-loan reform provides an excellent example of this dynamic. As loan defaults rose to exceed 20 percent, the student-loan program earned the dubious distinction of being named a "high-risk area" by the GAO, which prompted attention from the administration and the Congress. With the assistance of staff from GAO and the Education Department, the Congress developed a wide-ranging set of reforms targeted at reversing the incentives facing the key actors in this elaborate system of third-party government—the banks, the state guarantee agencies, the trade schools generating much of the defaulting students, and the former students themselves. As a result, the default rate was lowered to less than 10 percent.

Table 8.1

The Four "Pathways" of Power (with Prototypical Examples Listed)

		Scope of Mobilization	
		Narrow	Broad
Form of Mobilization	Interests	Pluralist	Partisan
	Ideas	Expert	Symbolic

To what extent do accountability mechanisms and other forms of expert-based policy making constitute a compelling new strategy for policy development, and have they come to actually supplant other, more traditional modes of policy formation? The growing role of experts calls for a reassessment of traditional models of pluralist and party politics in the policy process (Beam et al. 2002a).

We have found it useful to characterize the politics of policy reforms by referring to two dimensions—the scope and scale of mobilization (whether specialized or mass) and the method of mobilization (principally whether interests or ideas are at play). We found a fourfold typology of "pathways to power" developed previously helped to capture the more diverse ways that new issues reach the agenda and take policy form: pluralist, partisan, expert, and symbolic (Beam et al. 2002b; Table 8.1). Each of these strategies draws on different political resources, appeals to particular actors, and elicits its own unique strategies, language, and styles of coalition building.

The traditional methods of mobilization constitute the two paths relying on organization and interests. In the pluralist path, policy making is driven principally by the process of adjustment among contending interest groups. When policy monopolies dominate an area, policy making might proceed consensually with relatively low levels of visibility and involvement by broader publics or other actors. In the partisan pathway, policy making is characterized by major involvement by party leaders either in the White House or the Congress. As noted above, traditional models in political science envisioned major policy change as occurring primarily when presidents rallied the party faithful and the public behind it.

Emergent methods of mobilization use ideas and values as key independent factors to drive the placement of proposals on the agenda and push them through to enactment. Experts and their professional knowledge have come to play growing roles in policy making in our system. When issues fall into the expert pathway, professional knowledge and technical feasibility become the source of legitimacy against which all proposals are based. When issues are on this track, we would expect their salience for the public to be relatively low and the level of consensus within the political community to be relatively high in deference to the professional consensus purveyed by experts. Brown (1974) defines the typical policy focus of the expert path as "arcane, complex, bloodless, managerial, technocratic, [and] reasonable" but he also acknowledges how party leaders adopt these policies by elevating the rhetorical stakes and justifying these policy reforms as major policy breakthroughs.

Finally, ideas and values of broad public appeal have come to play a growing role in defining and legitimizing issues and actions in what we call the symbolic pathway. Unlike the expert path, ideas in the symbolic path are advanced not for their technical adequacy but for their potential to appeal to widely shared values and moods held by the public. Unlike pluralist or partisan pathways, the advocates need not assemble coalitions of interests or bargain with others through compromise; rather, ideas in the symbolic path can take the system by storm in what some have described as the bandwagon effect.

We found that the expert pathway was characterized by distinctive modes of problem definition and conflict when compared to other policy pathways. While feedback from clients and monitoring by interest groups constitute principal ways that problems were defined in the pluralist pathway, problems in the expert path, by contrast, were defined based on indicators and data and policy research. For instance, the need for farm reform ultimately passed by the Congress in 1996 was informed by economic studies showing the impacts of the web of federal subsidies on consumer prices and the federal budget. Bills on the expert and symbolic pathways largely steered clear of high levels of conflict as well. Once the expert frame became the primary frame for addressing the issue, both parties steered clear of outright opposition to expert-driven proposals. Both parties sought to either endorse the proposal or work out differences in bargaining among experts from different factions, parties, and branches. While policies on the partisan pathway prompted the most extensive policy changes, expert-based policies also showed the potential to yield significant reforms over a relatively short amount of time to major areas thought at one time to be locked down in a pluralistic pathway—the 1986 Tax Reform Act of 1986, the 1996 Federal Agricultural and Improvement Act and the 1983 Social Security Amendments are cases in point.

The pathways model can help us understand the contingent and differential influences of accountability institutions for different policy areas over differing periods. When the expert pathway is engaged, audit, evaluation, and performance information can be influential. However, when the process is locked in on the pluralist or partisan pathway, accountability information often falls on deaf ears.

For instance, as noted above, the student loan defaults were turned around when policy makers turned to auditors and analysts for answers to complex and vexing problems that had become politically embarrassing to the federal agency and to members of Congress. On the other hand, in the United States, GAO has not been welcome in such areas as farm and veterans policy where pluralist interest-group pathways dominate the policy process. Moreover, when GAO took on issues such as the federal deficit and health-care reform that had become firmly planted on the partisan pathway, it came under political attack and criticism for becoming too involved in inherently political matters.

POLITICS STREAM

Irrespective of the dominant policy-formulation pathway, the potential for impact of accountability information is dependent on the existence of a political environment that is conducive to change. Even with no strong partisan or pluralist pressures, expert information offered by accountability institutions will fall on deaf ears unless policy makers perceive that recommended solutions are necessary and feasible in respect to economic and political acceptability.

One useful way to assess the relative difference across analytic and accountability institutions is to use the framework developed by political scientists Matthew McCubbins and Thomas Schwartz (1984). They differentiate between police-patrol and fire-alarm oversight. Under police-patrol oversight, government officials actively use information to highlight problems and change programs. By contrast, under fire-alarm oversight, government officials establish the infrastructure of information and provide open doors for others to raise alarms, which officials may act on at their own discretion. Political environments more conducive to change are more likely to dominate when accountability information is provided to a police patrol rather than to fire-alarm oversight.

We would argue that formal and informal accountability institutions can be arrayed along a continuum corresponding to these concepts, as shown in Figure 8.1.

Active police-patrol oversight is associated with the engagement of audit institutions and evalu-

Figure 8.1   **Formal and Informal Accountability Institutional Continuum**

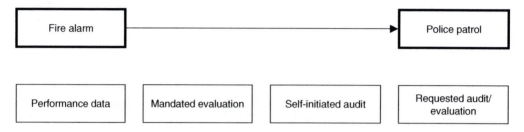

ation units by policy makers who have already decided that a program or problem is of sufficient concern to warrant a position on their formal agenda. In the case of the GAO, for instance, most of their audit and evaluation work is driven by requests from Congressional committees, either chairs or ranking minority members.

Not all of the work of accountability institutions has the eager attention of top policy makers. Many audit offices throughout the world initiate many studies with the hope and expectation that they will prompt timely action by policy makers. Even the GAO initiates some of its work to address important but not necessarily urgent issues that need audit or evaluation attention, but which have not ripened to the point of warranting attention on the formal agenda. These studies are in the middle of our continuum. When compared to more informal accountability information provided by nongovernmental groups and analysts, formal governmental agencies have greater potential to have their issues gain traction and agenda status. Auditors often have sufficient credibility to make powerful claims on the agenda, often prompting government officials to modify their agendas to address the issues raised in reports. At the very least, most governments have formal requirements for agencies to provide comments on audit reports, which are often made public in the report itself. In some parliamentary systems, the auditor general is provided with formal opportunities to testify before oversight committees chaired by the minority party.

Government-performance information is found on the left-hand side of the continuum. Although established by governmental leaders, performance information is a more passive tool of accountability that requires actors in or out of government to actually use it to impact policy and management decisions. As such we would categorize performance information as one of the tools of fire-alarm oversight. Government leaders have gone to considerable lengths in many OECD nations to institutionalize a continuous infrastructure of information on program performance and financial management. While some get discouraged when this information is not routinely used to drive decisions, the fire-alarm model tells us that decision makers will use the data only when and if they decide to examine particular programs and operations in the future. In the United States, periodic initiatives have built more active oversight and review programs on the information base established by performance-management reforms. In the latest iteration, the Bush administration established the Program Assessment Rating Tool (PART) to apply the growing base of performance data established by agencies under the earlier Government Performance and Results Act (GPRA). This tool was used to actively assess all program activity in the federal budget on a regular schedule over five years.

Program evaluation can and is conducted at varying points on the oversight continuum. Often evaluation work is conducted in order to meet formal top-down accountability requirements set by legislatures or by central-government agencies—often finance departments. These evaluations rarely meet a political environment that is conducive to generating the identified needs for change. Utilization-focused evaluation approaches beseech evaluators to undertake evaluation work only when they are assured that people in positions of authority are on board and will be willing and able to facilitate needed change as a result of evaluation findings.

As the accountability institutions move along the continuum from fire alarm to police patrol, greater prospects for policy impact are coupled with greater risks to independence and autonomy. Audit institutions must delicately steer between responding to these legitimate information needs while sustaining their independence in developing findings and reports. The independence of audit institutions is fortified through career nonpolitical staffs and appointment of agency leaders with exceptionally long tenure. However, even with such institutional protections, these agencies can become a magnet for criticisms when their studies veer too closely to partisan or pluralist pathways. The involvement of accountability institutions in reviews of program results and effectiveness carries obvious political risks. For this reason many audit institutions have charters that limit their coverage of these issues and constrain them from making recommendations on matters of policy and program design (Schwartz 2000).

Regardless of the specific role of accountability institutions, their impact will ultimately be determined by the interests of political principals. What are the specific dynamics that lead political and administrative officials to address the findings and data presented through accountability institutions? Surprisingly little research has been done on this important question, but several factors seem to be relevant.

Shame

At times, expert ideas gain compelling political status, rising to the level of a valence issue. As will be noted in the next section, ideas grounded in a consensus by mainstream experts can gain credibility, which can move agendas and prompt the embrace of those ideas in the face of opposition by interest groups. Whether it be free trade, second-hand smoking bans, or trans fat prohibition initiatives, expert-based recommendations can shake agendas and enable leaders to more easily blunt opposition by narrow interests that heretofore had hegemonic influence over these areas. The disclosure of problems by experts can prompt members to shift positions and at least appear to embrace findings and recommendations, partly due to the potential exploitation of these issues by prospective opponents. Anxiety about shame prompts agencies and congressional committees alike to adopt most GAO recommendations, notwithstanding the fact that the agency has no formal power to force responses to its suggestions. GAO's "high-risk list" is a particularly powerful shaming device that includes the specific programs and operations that the agency feels are at high risk of fraud, waste, and abuse. Agencies go to considerable lengths to avoid such designations when they are coupled with extensive media publicity.

Competition

Competition can be a particularly powerful incentive within bureaucracies. Agencies may be motivated to adopt recommendations or initiate their own expert-based ideas either to compete with fellow bureaus or to compete with central actors, such as agency leaders and budget offices. The PPBS introduced by Secretary McNamara to the Pentagon in the early 1960s became deeply rooted in the bureaucracy of the Department of Defense, when the military services realized that they had to acquire the capacity to do systems analysis and evaluations to stay competitive with the secretary's "whiz kids." Similarly, the Bush Administration's PART assessed programs throughout the agencies, and inspired some to improve their evaluation information to be able to compete with the Office of Budget and Management (OMB) in budget debates in Congress and the public (U.S Government Accountability Office 2004). The movement to create report cards assessing agencies and programs in an open, public process constitutes a strategy to jump-start competition among bureaucratic actors for public approbation and the high ground (Gormley and Wiemer 1999). The foregoing suggests that multiple actors in competitive policy-making environments can inspire a "race to the top" among other actors, which can serve to ratchet up attention and resources devoted to accountability reforms and enhancements. Multiple accountability actors within the Congress, the executive branch, and even the public sphere can serve to trigger a mutually reinforcing process in this model.

Principal Agency

A major rationale for the creation of the GAO in 1921 was to provide Congress with a tool to contest the president for control over the bureaucracy. Accountability institutions provide political principals—whether they be the GAO for Congress or the Inspectors General for cabinet departments—a resource to compete with bureaucratic agents who have leverage owing to their control over information. By utilizing its experts in agencies like the GAO and relying on other independent evaluation reports, Congress can come to its own conclusions about program implementation and results freed from exclusive reliance on self-interested agency data and reports.

Conflict Management

Reliance on policy research also can help policy makers channel and contain conflict by providing a credible base of information that is considered by all contestants as setting the parameters for debates. Rather than debate the veracity of information, the presence of credible institutional information can help leaders focus debates on broader issues. The independence and respect accorded to the Congressional Budget Office (CBO) is an example of how much legislators need an independent referee to resolve fact-based questions, thereby controlling the scope of conflicts. Although some conservatives have called for CBO to open up the "black box" to deploy dynamic scoring for tax-policy changes, the validity and assumptions about specific CBO cost estimates are rarely challenged openly. It is conceivable that political actors observe norms of reciprocity, knowing that a challenge by one side will precipitate corresponding challenges by competing actors on other estimates, thereby throwing the entire process into disarray.

Collaboration

While underemphasized in the literature, audit agencies often gain influence through collaboration with internal champions of change within executive agencies. Far from competitors, policy experts and advocates inside executive agencies can adroitly exploit external audit and other accountability information to place pressure on political leaders to institute reforms and other changes. For instance, cooperation replaced confrontation in accounting and financial management shortly after World War II with the Joint Financial Management Improvement Program—a collaborative effort between GAO, OMB, and The Department of the Treasury to engage in common projects to improve the state of practice at the federal level.

The Contingent Nature of Accountability Impacts

Notwithstanding these political incentives, the impact of accountability institutions on the policy process is highly contingent—influenced by institutional, political, and environmental factors. In his provocative book about auditing in the United Kingdom, Michael Power (1997) introduces the notion of decoupling. Accountability information may be ignored, or only ritualistically adhered to, because it lacks credibility, is seen as demanding too high a standard, or is not perceived as significant to core organizational operation. Decoupling is associated with lack of senior-management engagement and buy-in for promoting the use of accountability information. Studies of internal auditing, for example, have found that senior-management engagement is crucial to its success. In an Israeli study, Schwartz and Sulitzeanu-Kenan (2002) found internal audits to be largely decoupled in almost all government departments, with the exception of two ministries in which senior management was strongly committed to using internal auditors to improve efficiency and effectiveness of operations.

Even when accountability information instigates policy debate that leads to policy change, accountability institutions bear little responsibility for policy making. Rather, politicians and senior public officials decide to change policy when they perceive that the political climate is conducive to change. There are numerous examples where despite the severity of problems outlined in accountability reports no policy change occurred due to the absence of a conducive political climate, an organized advocacy coalition, or a policy entrepreneur.

More often, audit reports that highlight problems in need of solution are insufficient to create policy-change windows if feasible solutions are not available and political climates are not conducive to change. In these cases, advocacy coalitions or policy entrepreneurs may push for particular policy solutions and for the development of more conducive policy climates.

Specific features of accountability institutions themselves limit their role in policy making. For example, traditionally, many audit agencies have not engaged in policy advocacy. They have been closed organizations concerned about their independence and reluctant to work with others. If outsiders supported them, it was unlikely that this would be acknowledged by the audit organization. They have not, therefore, looked to form coalitions. Such closed organizations have kept their draft reports to themselves for fear of leaks and have privileged access to information that they cannot share. And they generally chose not to speak publicly on issues or to get involved with others. When giving press briefings, auditors stick to the facts and tend to be understated in approach. Many auditing organizations rotate their staffs when they become too familiar with the programs they are reviewing, which preserves independence but often at the expense of expertise. This institutional insulation and isolation has the price of diminishing the roles such institutions can play in the issue networks that are responsible for policy development and change in most systems.

Israel's State Comptroller's Office does little to promote the utilization of its reports, or even their dissemination—preferring to maintain the image of not being a policy actor. Some aspects of this have changed in recent years in other countries. In the United Kingdom, for example, auditors have sought ways of spreading the message more widely, including through conferences related to reports and by publishing summaries to reach managers (Lonsdale 2001). UK auditors have also sought to combat some of the negative perceptions of civil servants by taking a more proactive role—for example, by contributing to the work of government committees. In a similar vein, the U.S. GAO takes a very active role in working with congressional clients in developing oversight agendas, publicizing their results, and working with congressional and other staff in issue networks to publicize report findings and recommendations. Generation-three and generation-four evaluation approaches aimed at increasing utilization have encouraged evaluators to actively pursue strategies to open windows of opportunity for policy change. The current explosion of knowledge exchange is in large part a reaction to the phenomenon of decoupling. Recognizing the gaps between the availability of knowledge and its use, proponents have encouraged government and knowledge-production agencies to commit substantial resources to a two-way flow of knowledge, to promote production of knowledge on issues of relevance to the policy and practice fields, and then to encourage use of this knowledge. To the extent that evaluation, audit, and performance measurement are supported by knowledge-exchange functions, they are more likely to impact agenda formation and policy formulation.

THE STATE OF EMPIRICAL RESEARCH ON THE IMPACTS OF ACCOUNTABILITY INSTITUTIONS

In the first half of this chapter, we applied the policy-streams model to conceptualize how and why accountability information is likely to influence agenda formation and policy formulation under a variety of contexts. Using examples drawn from the United States and other countries, we demonstrated that performance audit, performance measurement, and program evaluation can and do play roles in all three of the policy (problem, solution, and politics) streams. More recently, some accountability actors have become more active in attempting to open windows of opportunity for stream interactions. The next section explores what systematic empirical research can tell us about if, when, how, and why accountability information has influenced agenda formation and policy formulation.

Performance Measurement

There is a substantial literature about performance measurement, but little knowledge about the impacts of performance measurement on accountability outcomes—improving performance, fairness, and financial stewardship. A recent review of the literature on performance measurement found 4,879 articles in four indices and eight core journals; however, only 21 of these reported on empirical studies of utilization or impacts (Schwartz, 2010).

A content analysis of the 21 studies enabled extraction of underlying theoretical frameworks, even when these were not explicitly mentioned. In this way the findings of the studies were classified as being connected with either public-choice or rational-actor theories. Findings classified as being associated with the rational-actor theory included those that looked at the utilization and impact of performance measurement on decision making, strategic planning, budgeting, program prioritization, and resource allocation. Public-choice/principal-agent related findings address program management, efficiency, program monitoring, managerial accountability, rewards for good performance and sanctions for poor performance, and coordination. Findings from eight articles addressed rational-actor theory. Similarly, findings from eight articles addressed public-choice/ principal-agent theories. Some studies contributed findings to both theoretical frameworks, while others contributed only to one or the other.

To address our questions for each theoretical framework, findings were categorized either as positively supporting the theoretical assumptions or negatively refuting them. From this analysis it becomes immediately clear that the study findings are not black and white. A substantial number of findings lend credence to the rational-actor basis for engaging in performance measurement, while a similarly substantial number of findings raise questions about engaging in performance measurement with the hope of making decisions more rational. To further complicate the matter, many studies reveal both positive findings in support of the theory and negative findings against the theory. Moreover, almost all of the findings (both positive and negative) are equivocal in that they refer to averages of positive (or negative) responses ranging from just over 50 percent to about 80 percent.

The analysis suggests that greater empirical support exists for use of performance measurement as a means to improving the control of principals over agents. Only two of the eight studies with findings related to the principal-agent model offer any refutation of this theory. Melkers and Willoughby (2005) find that performance measurement is not generally used to reward good performance or sanction poor performance. Similarly, Julnes and Holzer (2001) found relatively few instances where performance-measurement systems were used for monitoring or managing efficiency and effectiveness. If poor, inefficient, and ineffective performance is not attended to or sanctioned, the agent is unlikely to improve his or her efforts to promote the interests of the principal. While seven of the eight studies in this grouping contained findings in support of the principal-agent basis for using performance measurement, once again these positive findings are equivocal—where percentages are given, they tend toward the 70 percent mark.

In the realistic-synthesis approach, equivocal findings are not necessarily a bad thing. On the contrary, they offer potential for learning about the contexts that promote or hinder the success of interventions, such as performance measurement. The next step in the inquiry was to comb through the relevant articles in search of findings and discussions about contexts, that is, what works better and worse, for whom, under which circumstances, and why.

Realistic synthesis of the findings from these studies reveal equivocal and often conflicting conclusions about the use and influence of performance measurement in decision making and management (Streib and Poister 1999; Wang 2000, 2002b; Willoughby and Melkers 2000; Bernstein 2001; Julnes and Holzer 2001; Melkers and Willoughby 2005). The synthesis raises some hypotheses for further research: Performance measurement is more likely to improve rational decision making when it has the strong support of governmental stakeholders, senior management, and internal interest groups. When performance measurement is conducted in order to comply with top-down mandated or legislated requirements, it is less likely to reap either rational-actor or principal-agent benefits (Alford and Baird 1997; Cavalluzzo and Ittner 2004).

This realistic synthesis of evaluation research reveals large gaps in knowledge about if, when, and how performance-measurement information is used in policy making and management decision making. Relatively few studies explore the contexts under which performance measurement works better or worse. The small number of evaluation studies with contextual findings and the generally weak methodologies employed prevent significant theory development.

Performance Audit

In comparison with the sizable empirical literature on performance measurement, performance audit has received very little attention from empirical researchers. A recent literature review identified only seven studies (see Table 8.2).

Analyzing this table we see that five studies identify some positive effects of state audit—generally meaning that audit reports were perceived by auditors or those audited as having improved financial stewardship, fairness, or performance. Of the five, two report low effects. None of the studies looked seriously into the black box to ascertain what it was about the audit reports that led to positive effects. In fact, very little attention is paid to variance among audit reports. An exception is Schwartz's 2000 study, which found that audits of effectiveness and of high-profile issues received greater attention from Parliament, and were perceived by those who were audited as contributing to greater performance. Only two of the studies addressed negative unintended consequences, but again without explicitly looking into the black box to figure out the causes. To conclude, the empirical study of state audit tells us little about the influence of this important administrative accountability mechanism on finances, fairness, and performance. We

Table 8.2

Empirical Research on State Audit and Accountability

State Audit	Intended and positive effects	Unintended and negative effects	Methods: Open black box? Underlying theory?
Pollitt et al. 1999 (Europe)	Yes		Anecdotal
Barzelay 1996, 1997 (Comparative)			
Schwartz 2000 (Israel)	Low		
Morin 2004 (Quebec)	Yes	Low	Some
Power 1997 (UK)		Yes	Anecdotal
Lapsley and Pong 2000 (Scotland)	Yes		
Morin 2001	Low		

don't know how much of what type of state auditing is more or less productive and under which circumstances.

Program Evaluation

There is a substantial literature on evaluation use and utilization and several reviews of this literature have been conducted (Alkin 1975; Cousins and Leithwood 1986; Hofstetter and Alkin 2003; Johnson 1998; Kirkhart 2000; Leviton and Hughes 1981; Leviton 2003; Shulha and Cousins, 1997). Factors identified as affecting use include users and use characteristics; the evaluation itself; the evaluator; organizational (internal contextual) factors; environmental (external contextual) factors; and interpersonal and interaction characteristics. Critical analysis suggests that the methodological quality of evidence for associating these factors with evaluation use is quite poor. Studies of the impacts of evaluation have been largely limited to examining use or utilization and fall short of looking at influence or impact on performance and other accountability objectives. Leading evaluation researchers have recently called for the generation of systematic knowledge about the mechanisms and outcomes of evaluation influence (Mark and Henry 2004).

DISCUSSION

As we have seen, accountability institutions have substantial influence in policy making and management in democratic systems. While by no means straightforward, accountability institutions and the information they produce have become a more systematic and institutionalized feature of public-policy processes in all advanced nations. However, accountability institutions achieve their influence in highly contestable systems, rife with competing values. Far from hegemonic influence, these systems appear to veer from accountability deficits to accountability excesses, depending on such variables as the strength of accountability offices and the receptivity of the broader political system (Bovens 2005).

The policy-steams model has proven to be a useful framework for approaching the challenging question of how accountability information gets used to influence desired accountability outcomes. The model serves to temper the enthusiasm of those who expect immediate and tangible policy change and resource reallocation upon the publication of accountability information. The analysis reminds us that in democratic regimes, identification of problems, even when coupled with feasible solutions, does not translate into automatic policy change.

There is evidence that the influence of accountability institutions pervades all stages of the process. While agenda formation is perhaps most prevalent in many OECD nations, auditors and analysts also play roles in policy formulation. In the United States, David Whiteman's (1995) study of congressional-information searches shows that policy analyses and information produced by these offices played a surprisingly central role in the substantive development of legislative policy proposals as well as in policy argumentation. From the perspective of his garbage-can model, Kingdon 2003> suggested that policy analysts and accountability institutions would have their greatest role in articulating alternatives for the solution stream. However, policy research and audits are increasingly being marshaled to assess and validate the legitimacy of problems presented in the problem stream for policy makers' attention. While the political stream is generally regarded as being off limits, even here accountability institutions have been known to open political windows of opportunity through findings and reports on corruption in public office. The Canadian Auditor General's reports on the Martin government's pattern of influence peddling were widely viewed as the most important event triggering the government's downfall.

The analysis of the policy streams suggests how accountability institutions are achieving their influence. Such an approach is productive in generating hypotheses for further research. However, comparatively little is known about the actual effects that accountability institutions are having on public management and policy outcomes. The review of the literature on impacts of accountability information begs for more empirical study. A disconnect exists between the large investments in time and money and the considerable demand for accountability, as compared to the dearth of systematic research on the results of accountability.

REFERENCES

Alford, J., and J. Baird. 1997. "Performance Monitoring in the Australian Public Service: A Government-Wide Analysis." *Public Money and Management* 17 (2): 49–58.

Alkin, M. 1975. "Evaluation: Who Needs It? Who Cares?" *Studies in Educational Evaluation* 1 (3): 201–12.

Anderson, J.L. 1997. "Refocusing the Lowi Policy Typology." *Policy Studies Journal* 25 (2): 266–82.

Anechiarico, F., and J. Jacobs. 1996. *The Pursuit of Absolute Integrity. How Corruption Control Makes Government Ineffective.* Chicago: University of Chicago Press.

Barzelay, M. 1997. "Central Audit Institutions and Performance Auditing: A Comparative Study of Organizational Strategies in the OECD." *Governance* 10: 253–60.

Baumgartner, F.R., and B. Jones. 1993. *Agendas and Instability in American Politics.* Chicago: University of Chicago Press.

Beam, D.R., Timothy J. Conlan, and Paul L. Posner. 2002a. "The Politics That Pathways Make." Paper presented at annual meeting of the American Political Science Association, Boston, September 1.

———. 2002b. "The Pathways to Power: A Framework for Contemporary Federal Policymaking." Paper presented at the annual meeting of the American Political Science Association, Boston, September 1.

Behn, Robert. 2001. *Rethinking Democratic Accountability.* Washington, DC: Brookings Institution Press.

Bernstein, D.J. 2001. "Local Government Measurement Use to Focus on Performance and Results." *Evaluation and Program Planning* 24 (1): 95–101.

Bovens, Mark. 2005. "Analysing and Assessing Public Accountability: A Conceptual Framework." Paper read at Accountable Governance: An International Research Colloquium, Queen's University, Belfast, October 20–22.

Broadbent, J., and R. Laughlin. 1997. "Evaluating the 'New Public Management' Reforms in the UK: A Constitutional Possibility." *Public Administration* 75 (Autumn): 487–507.

Brown, L. 1974. *New Politics, New Policies: Government's Response to Government's Growth.* Washington, DC: Brookings Institution Press.

Cavalluzzo, K.S., and C.D. Ittner. 2004. "Implementing Performance Measurement Innovations: Evidence from Government." *Accounting Organizations and Society* 29 (3–4): 243–67.

Cousins, J.B., and K.A. Leithwood. 1986. "Current Empirical Research on Evaluation Utilization." *Review of Educational Research* 56 (3): 331–64.

Dubnick, M. 2005. "Accountability and the Promise of Performance." *Public Performance and Management Review* 28 (3): 376–417.

Dubnick, M., and J. Justice. 2004. "Accounting for Accountability." Paper read at annual meeting of the American Political Science Association, Chicago, IL: September 2–5.

Gormley, W.T., Jr., and David L. Weimer. 1999. *Organizational Report Cards.* Cambridge, MA: Harvard University Press.

Government Accounting Office (GAO). 1996. *School Facilities: America's Schools Report Differing Conditions,* GAO/HEHS-96-103. Washington, DC: June.

———. 2005. *Protection of Chemical and Water Infrastructure: Federal Requirements, Actions of Selected Facilities, and Remaining Challenges,* GAO-05-327.Washington, DC: March. 28.

Gray, A., B. Jenkins, and J. Glynn 1992. "Auditing the Three Es: The Challenge of Effectiveness." *Public Policy and Administration* 7 (Winter): 56–69.

Halachmi, A. 2002. "Performance Measurement, Accountability, and Improved Performance." *Public Performance and Management Review* 25 (4): 370–74.

Heclo, H. 1978. "Issue Networks and the Executive Establishment." In *The New American Political System,* ed. Anthony King. Washington, DC: AEI Press.

Hird, J.A. 2005. *Power, Knowledge and Politics: Policy Analysis in the States.* Washington, DC: Georgetown University Press.

Hofstetter, C.H., and M.C. Alkin. 2003. "Evaluation Use Revisited." In *International Handbook of Educational Evaluation,* ed. T. Kellaghan and D.L. Stufflebeam. London: Kluwer Academic, 197–222.

Johnson, R.B. 1998. "Toward a Theoretical Model of Evaluation Utilization." *Evaluation and Program Planning* 21: 93–110.

Julnes, P., and M. Holzer. 2001. "Promoting the Utilization of Performance Measures in Public Organizations: An Empirical Study of Factors Affecting Adoption and Implementation." *Public Administration Review* 61(6): 693–708.

Kingdon, John. 2003. *Agendas, Alternatives, and Public Policies,* 2d ed. New York: Longman.

Kirkhart, K.E. 2000. "Reconceptualizing Evaluation Use: An Integrated Theory of Influence." In *New Directions for Evaluation,* ed. V.J. Caracelli and H. Preskill. San Francisco: Jossey-Bass, 5–23.

Lavis, J.N., S.E. Ross, J.E. Hurley et al. 2002. "Examining the Role of Health Services Research in Public Policymaking." *The Milbank Quarterly* 80 (1): 125–54.

Leviton, L.C. 2003. "Evaluation Use: Advances, Challenges and Applications." *American Journal of Evaluation* 24 (4): 525–35.

Leviton, L.C., and E.F.X. Hughes. 1981. "Research on the Utilization of Evaluations: A Review and Synthesis." *Evaluation Review* 5 (4): 525–48.

Lindblom, C.E. 1968. *The Policy-Making Process.* Englewood-Cliffs, NJ: Prentice Hall.

Lonsdale J. 2001. "Auditing in a Changing World: Developments in the Work of the National Audit Office 1997–2001." Paper presented to the seminar on Advances in the Public Management of Information and Control, European Institute of Public Administration, Maastricht, The Netherlands, October.

Lowi, T.J. 1964. "American Business, Public Policy, Case Studies and Political Theory." *World Politics* 16: 677–715.

Mark, M.M., and G.T. Henry. 2004. "The Mechanisms and Outcomes of Evaluation Influence." *Evaluation* 10 (1): 35–57.

McCubbins, M., and T. Schwartz 1984. "Congressional Oversight Overlooked: Police Patrols Versus Fire Alarms." *American Journal of Political Science* 28: 16–79.

Melkers, J., and K. Willoughby. 2005. "Models of Performance-Measurement Use in Local Governments: Understanding Budgeting, Communication, and Lasting Effects." *Public Administration Review* 65 (2): 180–90.

Oh, C.H. 1996. *Linking Social Science Information to Policy-Making.* Greenwich, CT: JAI Press.

Organization of Economic Cooperation and Development (OECD). 2005. *Performance Information in the Budget Process: Results of the OECD 2005 Questionnaire.* Paris, France: OECD.

Power, Michael. 1997. *The Audit Society: Rituals of Verification.* Oxford: Oxford University Press.

Roberts, S., and C. Pollitt. 1994. "Audit or Evaluation? A National Audit Office VFM Study." *Public Administration* 92 (4): 527–49.

Sabatier, P. 1993. *Policy Change and Learning: An Advocacy Coalition Approach.* Boulder, CO: Westview Press.

Schwartz, R. 1999. "Coping with the Effectiveness Dilemma: Strategies Adopted by State Auditors." *International Review of Administrative Sciences* 65 (4): 511–26.

———. 2000. "State Audit—Panacea for the Crisis of Accountability? An Empirical Study of the Israeli Case." *International Journal of Public Administration* 23 (4): 405–34.

———. 2010. "Public Management Theory, Evaluation and Evidence-based Policy." In *Mind the Gap: Perspectives on Policy Evaluation and the Social Sciences,* ed. F. Leeuw F,and J. Vassen J. *Transaction,* 21–140.

Schwartz, R., and J. Mayne. 2005. "Assuring the Quality of Evaluation: Theory and Practice." *Evaluation and Program Planning* 28 (1): 1–14.

Schwartz, R., and B. Rosen. 2004. "Bringing Data to Bear: The Politics of Evidence-Based Health Policymaking." *Public Money and Management* 24 (2): 121–28.

Schwartz, R., and R. Sulitzeanu-Kenan. 2002. "The Politics of Accountability: Institutionalising Internal Auditing in Israel." *Financial Accountability and Management* 18 (3): 211–31.

Sharkansky, I. 1991. "The Auditor as Policymaker." In *State Audit and Accountability,* ed. A. Friedberg, B. Geist, N. Mizrahi and I. Sharkanksy. Jerusalem: State of Israel, State Comptroller's Office, 74–94.

Shulha, L.M., and J.B. Cousins. 1997. "Evaluation Use: Theory, Research, and Practice Since 1986." *Evaluation Practice* 18 (3): 195–208.

Smith, Peter. 1995. "On the Unintended Consequences of Publishing Performance Data in the Public Sector." *International Journal of Public Administration* 18 (2–3): 277–310.

State Comptroller's Office (SCO). 1991. "Gas Masks for the Civilian Population." SCO, Jerusalem.

———. 1994. "Protective Kits for the Civilian Population." SCO, Jerusalem.

Streib, G.D., and T.H. Poister. 1999. "Assessing the Validity, Legitimacy and Functionality of Performance Measurement Systems in Municipal Governments." *American Review of Public Administration* 29 (2): 107–23.

Stone, D. 1989. "Causal Stories and the Formation of Policy Agendas." *Political Science Quarterly* 104: 281–300.

Sutherland, S. 1986. "The Politics of Audit: The Federal Office of the Auditor General in Comparative Perspective." *Canadian Public Administration* 29 (Spring): 118–48.

Tierney, C.E. 2000. *Federal Accounting Handbook: Policies, Standards, Procedures, Practices.* New York: Wiley, 58–59.

U.S. Government Accountability Office. 1984. *Guidelines for Rescuing Large Failing Firms and Municipalities.* GAO/GGD-84–34, March 29. Washington, DC: U.S. Government Printing Office.

———. 2004. *Observations on the Use of OMB's Program Assessment Rating Tool for the Fiscal Year 2004 Budget.* GAO-04-174. Washington, DC: U.S. Government Printing Office.

Wang, X. 2000. "Performance Measurement in Budgeting." *Public Budgeting and Finance* 20 (3): 102–18.

———. 2002b. "Assessing Performance Measurement Impact: A Study of U.S. Local Government." *Public Performance and Management Review* 26 (1): 26–43.

Weiss, C. "Congressional Committees as Users of Analysis." *Journal of Policy Analysis and Management* 8 (3): 411–31.

Whiteman, David. 1995. *Communication in Congress.* Lawrence: University Press of Kansas.

Wildavsky, A. 1983. *The Politics of the Budgetary Process* 3d ed. Boston: Little Brown.

Williams, W. 1998. *Honest Numbers and Democracy.* Washington, DC: Georgetown University Press.

Willoughby, K., and J. Melkers. 2000. "Implementing PBB: Conflicting Views of Success." *Public Budgeting and Finance* 20: 105–20.

Wilson, C. 2000. "Policy Regimes and Policy Change." *Journal of Public Policy* 20 (3): 247–74.

9

ACCOUNTABILITY AND INFORMATION-TECHNOLOGY ENACTMENT

A Cross-National Perspective

Richard K. Ghere

In October 2005, some twenty-five members of the America Society for Public Administration attended a conference held at the University of Electronic Science and Technology of China in Chengdu. Among the 191 papers presented, more than 40 focused upon some aspect of e-government, mostly within local governments in China. Current Chinese interest in e-government follows a broader stream of public-management research on the effects of computers in government dating back three decades (particularly to the prolific work of Kenneth Kraemer and colleagues at the University of California at Irvine as well to as the efforts of others). That research in turn stemmed from earlier attention to sociotechnical systems by mid-twentieth-century organization theorists.

Yet the current Chinese interest in e-government appears theoretically salient for a variety of reasons. First and foremost among them is that the interest emerged amid national governmental and "free-market" economic reforms during the 1990s that paralleled the New Public Management (NPM) movement in the United States (Lan 2005, 9); thus information technology's place in business-based appeals for governmental reform extends globally. Second, e-government's implicit commitment to democracy raises speculation about the authenticity of motives within traditionally authoritarian settings. In a study of openness among nations using e-government, Katchanovski and La Porte find evidence of "high-tech façades that create the impression of government openness" among nations lacking Western traditions (2005, 677). Other researchers, however, refute such assertions, claiming that they are based on the false premise that nations can be dichotomized simply as democratic or undemocratic (see Yang 2003). And the third reason, presuming some authenticity in government-reform efforts, is that Chinese experiences with e-governments raise broader questions about public-sector uses of information technology (IT) and the quality of governance in national settings, particularly regarding causality. In short, does public IT use affect (improve) governance or the other way around?

This chapter focuses on IT use in government and its possible impact on governance as an accountability issue. It is a question obscured by IT's role in legitimizing the ideology of New Public Management. From a "managerialist" (NPM) perspective, IT can be viewed as "the stick" that imposes accountability upon otherwise unresponsive public bodies. Such thinking even supports the premises of some scholarly research. For example, an article surveying international developments in e-government published by two management professors rests on the following assertion: "Government departments and procedures are commonly held to be inefficient because they have little motivation to please the citizen, and the citizen does not have an alternative provider available to him for these services. The increase in technology and communication has changed some of these attitudes on the part of the government. A more enlightened view has begun in the ranks of government to treat the citizen like a consumer whose transaction satisfaction is important" (Evans and Yen 2006, 235).

By contrast, Jane Fountain's *Building the Virtual State* (2001) characterizes bureaucratic responses to information technology in entirely different terms. Recognizing that NPM ideology is often packed into advocacy for IT, Fountain develops a theory of *technology enactment* (in essence, bureaucratic behaviors reacting to IT) and then applies that framework in three case studies. Stuart Bretschneider highlights three components of Fountain's enactment argument: (1) that the intended (or objective) forms of IT can be manipulated (or "bent") within the bureaucratic setting, (2) that the relationship between IT and bureaucracy is non-recursive, that is, the causal arrow points in both directions, and (3) that "enacted technology" can change organizations and institutions (2003, 738).

Fountain's technology enactment can then be interpreted as an improvisational form of account giving that would typically be dismissed as error or bias within the managerialist's accountability of factual reporting and compliance (Tetlock 1991, 451). Nonetheless, how bureaucrats use the technology designed for them essentially amounts to a contemporary issue of administrative discretion. This inquiry examines governmental IT enactment in various global settings to determine (1) where and how this improvisational account giving occurs, and (2) what (if any) effect enactment has upon governance in particular settings.

The next section translates the enactment issue and its potential to affect governance into an accountability conversation initiated by Melvin Dubnick about accountability and the "promise of performance" (2005). The sections that follow report on a study of how cases of technology enactment were accessed along with observations emerging from the study. A concluding discussion reviews those observations within Dubnick's accountability conversation as supplemented by a norms-dynamic framework developed by international-relations scholars.

ACCOUNTABILITY IN THE VIRTUAL STATE

Jane Fountain's discussion of the "virtual state" provides an intriguing lens through which to examine the accountability and performance rhetoric in the New Public Management (NPM) ideology and how it affects behavior in various governance settings. Whether as basic as a public-agency web site or complex as a multiagency network system, these behavior-influencing technologies direct attention not merely to the costs or benefits of compliance but also to opportunities for improvised action—"technology enactment"—to affect governance. In particular, these possibilities can arise in administrative environments where regime and/or managerial values compete with other norms (for example, transparency or human rights) associated with a global outlook.

Thus, this inquiry treats information-technology enactment as an accountability issue that is fundamental to the prospect of norms development, particularly as related to globalization. To begin within the managerialist perspective that Dubnick critiques (2005), the assumed relationship between accountability and performance (A=>P) appears deeply rooted in NPM expectations that IT will yield substantial cost efficiencies, enhanced government-to-citizen and government-to-business responsiveness, and tighter coordination that "connects the dots" in interagency program areas such as international trade and military logistics (Fountain 2001, 4–6; 107–128; and 167–192).

In differentiating "objective technology" from "enacted technology," that is, between the behavior intended by system design and actual human responses, Fountain focuses upon IT's potential to elicit bureaucratic account giving that deviates from or circumvents system compliance (2001, 10–14). Thus, enactment (E) can be understood as negating accountability (E=>A) or engendering alternative forms of accountability designated as A-prime (E=>A)? This latter possibility corresponds with Dubnick's discussions of "mitigating" (particularly, account-giving that justifies actions or explains one's role) and "reframing" (transforming how the problem should be perceived) as contrasted with compliant reporting (2005, 386–391). In essence, discussion of IT's potential to transform institutional behavior and alternatively to be transformed by that behavior, extends conversation of accountability beyond the managerialist perspective into the realm of "thick" social relationships associated with institutional norms—what Dubnick calls the "social-mechanisms approach" to accountability.

Cross-national contexts presumably stretch a social understanding of accountability even further by entertaining the possibility that agents' accounts may promote values that are fundamentally different from those of their regime principals. In cross-national comparison, IT systems (S) imposed on bureaucracies could be expected to reflect regime values (R), such that those systems are intended to yield accountability (A)—and/or performance (P)—behaviors in furtherance of those regime values—as can be expressed as SR=>AR and/or SR=>PR. Yet system enactment could elicit improvisational responses that champion other (O) values—perhaps global transparency or beneficence to marginalized subpopulations—different than regime values designed into the system (SR). Thus AO can be substituted for A-prime in the notation scheme, signifying that IT systems–designed enforce regime values can be enacted in pursuit of other values (SR=>E=>AO or PO). where "other" could reflect values related to a global outlook, democratic responsibility, or even self-serving bureaucratic entrepreneurism, among other concerns that might compete with regime values.

THE STUDY

In search of information regarding bureaucratic experiences related to IT systems, inquiry here depended on a five-year (2003–7 inclusive) review of fourteen academic journals in the areas of public administration, development administration, technology and society, government information, and public finance.[1] This literature search was intent on locating specific case study material that could be gleaned to assess bureaucratic dynamics related to IT-system experiences in government. At minimum, these articles needed to comment on how bureaucrats (or in some cases, other policy actors) were affected by the technology and/or how they responded to it. In all, twenty-nine articles were located relating to various types of public agency IT systems in thirteen national settings. It is difficult to determine if this sample is representative of IT uses generally.

The difficulties and limitations encountered in this information-gathering effort are important to note. First, some journals included (particularly those from outside the social-science areas) are understandably focused upon system description or advocacy rather than upon the political implications of technology in government. In a similar vein, some authors focused their commentary on description or advocacy more so than on critical analysis.

Notwithstanding these limitations, various efforts to classify these technologies are found in Appendix 9.1, Table 9.1, and Table 9.2. Table 9.1 breaks out twenty-eight systems by the IT-system typology that Fountain introduces, wherein types range from basic agency web sites to complex cross-agency integration systems (2001, 100). Most of the technologies accessed in this study fall into either the agency web site (10) or agency internal-network (12) category. It should be noted, however, that each type in Table 9.1 includes a wide variation of IT systems. This becomes more

Table 9.1

Public[a] Information Technology (IT) Systems Surveyed

System type[b]	N	Descriptions (national settings)
Agency web sites	10	Municipal e-government ([3] China, South Korea, Taiwan, U.S.); Federal-Level e-government ([2] U.S); Web sites supporting relevant political community[a] ([2] Egypt, U.S.); Other ([3] India, Taiwan[c], U.S.)
Interagency web sites	3	Municipal e-government ([3] China)
Agency internal networks	13[c]	Various functions (India [2], Mozambique, Malaysia, Netherlands [2], South Africa, South Korea [2], Tanzania, UK [2], U.S.)
Cross-agency integration and systems	2	National-level multiagency Management Information Systems (Jordan); Municipal-level capital planning/budgeting system (U.S.)
Total	28[c]	

[a]Two studies of IT systems used by political communities making demands on government (Copts in Egypt [Brinkerhoff 2005] and health care advocates in the United States [Brainard 2003]) are included with those of governmental entities. Also, Taipei City (Taiwan) system described in two studies (Chen et al. 2003; 2006).

[b]IT types introduced by Fountain theoretically associated with varying degrees of institutional change and operational change (2001, 100).

[c]South African and Tanzanian systems compared in same article (de Vreede et al. 2003); thus, 28 systems discussed in 27 articles (as listed in Appendix 9.1; see system A-15).

Table 9.2

IT System Cases Surveyed by System Type and Performance Type

Type of system	Type of performance[a]			
	Production	Competence	Results	Productivity
Agency web site[b]	3	0	3	2
Interagency web site	1[c]	0	1	0
Agency internal network	10	0	2	0
Cross-agency integration and system	2	0	0	0
N = 24	16	0	6	2
Percent	67%	0%	25%	8%

[a]See Dubnick (2005, 391–4).

[b]Two studies of IT systems used by political communities making demands on government (Brinkerhoff 2005; Brainard 2003) are excluded here.

[c]Taipei City (Taiwan) system described in two studies (Chen et al. 2003, 2006) counted as one here.

apparent in the Appendix, which also classifies systems by Fountain's four types, but in addition provides brief descriptions of each IT system examined (along with type of performance). These variations are especially noticeable within the agency web site category that includes systems in municipal agencies, national-level bureaucracies, and even (two) citizen-interest groups seeking access to government (Brainard 2003; Brinkerhoff 2005).

Although instructive, the difference among technological devices (shown in Table 9.1) is not necessarily indicative of variations in what IT systems have been designed to accomplish in managing public organizations. In that IT looms so prominently in the performance rhetoric of the NPM, it is helpful to classify systems in terms of particular performance objectives they are intended to achieve. As Dubnick asserts, it is not always easy to extract meaning from conversation about "performance"—a highly symbolic but often ambiguous term in the context of public-agency management. Attempts herein to differentiate IT systems according to performance design are guided by two questions (paraphrased here) Dubnick asks to coax meaning out of performance rhetoric:

1. [Is design concern] high or low with regard to performance actions?
2. [Is design concern] high or low with regard to performance achievement? (2005, 391–4)

Together, these criteria leave Dubnick with four possible definitions of performance: production (low on both), competence (low on actions, high on achievement), results (high on actions, low on achievement), and productivity (high on both). As Table 9.2 shows, two-thirds (67 percent) of the IT systems found in this search appear best categorized as designed for production, rather than for competence, results, or productivity. Elaborating on performance as production, Dubnick comments:

> The most basic form of performance focuses attention on tasks being carried out by the performing agent. It is the view of performance associated with the process of "production" in the broadest and narrowest senses of that term. For example, we speak of theatrical "productions" as the staging of performances. We also speak to manufacturing forms of production that are associated with the design and operation of machinery and foster a machine view of work . . . While few of the major performance measurement systems associated with the NPM rely explicitly on this view of performance, it is a pervasive presence within organizations at the level where job design . . . , personnel selection . . . , and performance appraisal systems . . . are put to regular use. (2005, 392; see this chapter for complementary explanations of competence, results, and productivity)

Table 9.2 then conveys that designs for two-thirds (18 of 24) of IT systems[2] in this study most appropriately align with production in the sense of either reinforcing or reorienting how work is done—in essence, reengineering bureaucratic structures and procedures according to technologically imposed standards—rather than by upgrading competence, outputs, or outcomes per se. Even where systems are described as facilitating shared (or integrated) information the stronger performance rationale seems to be that of coordinating work through technologically programmed channels.[3] The prevalence of an apparent production orientation (as performance) in most IT designs in this study supports accountability comparisons among what otherwise could be taken as an "apples-and-oranges" assortment of disparate systems.

A cross-national comparison of the public accountability–IT enactment relationship needs to tap nation-specific indicators of governance quality. This inquiry applies the World Bank's Worldwide Governance Inventory (WGI) covering 212 nations in eight reports issued between 1996 and 2006 (see Kaufmann et al. 2007). The six governance dimensions (voice and accountability, political stability, government effectiveness, regulatory quality, rule of law, and control of corruption) are formulated as aggregates (each) of eight to nine data sources maintained by thirty different organizations (2006).

Data sources for the WGI fall into four categories: commercial-business providers, surveys of firms or households, nongovernmental organizations (NGOs), and public-sector organizations.

Analysis in this study draws upon the voice-and-accountability (VaA) indicator to reflect governance differences among the national settings of the IT systems surveyed. Specifically, VaA "measure[s] the extent to which a country's citizens are able to participate in selecting their government, as well as freedom of expression, freedom of association, and a free media" (2006, 3). It should be noted that this indicator is heavily weighted toward NGOs (and away from commercial-business) sources, more so than the other indicators—indeed, only three of nineteen data sources for this indicator are provided by business organizations (2006, 28–29). The WGI authors state that this inventory can be appropriately used both to compare nations on particular governance dimensions and to monitor a particular nation's progress or decline over time (2006, 6–7).

OBSERVATIONS

The scope of inquiry here encompasses possible interactions among three variables: the IT system, enactment behavior in response to the system, and the nature of governance in the system's national setting. (Actually, more issues are involved since these variables subdivide into more specific component issues—for example, attention to IT focuses on design and implementation, as well as intent, of the system.) Although logic offers several combinations of conceivable interactions, five possible causal relationships surface as pertinent to the question of IT enactment as it pertains to national governance.

The first two possibilities posit governance as a determinant both of the nature (as well as design and implementation) of IT systems and how they are enacted by bureaucrats or other government actors.

> P1: Current governance status determines IT-system enactment as a form of discretionary behavior.

With this possibility, more pronounced forms of enactment might be expected in nations with more established democratic traditions that allow administrative actors discretion in how they achieve public goals. A second possibility stresses the nature of the system more so than the link between governance and discretion (assumed in the first).

> P2: National governance determines the function and role of the IT system that in turn evokes particular patterns of enactment behavior.

For both possibilities 1 and 2, interactions are presumed as nonrecursive—that is, governance stimulates behaviors that in turn have the potential to reshape governance.

Alternatively, governance can be viewed as a dependent variable affected by the impacts of IT systems and/or its enactment. This presumes that particular system designs provoke enactment behaviors with capabilities to reshape governance:

> P3: IT-system use, design, and implementation evoke enactment responses that impact governance.

A variation on this third proposition might qualify enactment impacts on governance as occurring only in certain settings (depending upon conditions specific to the national setting)—in other words, IT systems affect governance in certain situations (requiring contextual explanations specific to the setting).

Fourth and fifth possibilities discount IT-system enactment (beyond intended system behavior) as a factor affecting governance:

P4: IT systems affect governance, but merely as intended by design and function.

This implies that any institutional change brought about by the virtual state is a function of design and intention. Finally, it could be the case that neither systems nor the behaviors they evoke significantly affect the status of national governance:

P5: Neither the IT system nor how it is enacted has any bearing on the character of national governance.

Eighteen of the articles reviewed offer sufficient descriptions to determine enactment behavior. Table 9.3 orders brief enactment descriptions according to the World Bank's 2006 VaA indicator ranging from –2.50 to +2.50. Table 9.3 also shows changes (up or down) in this governance measure as the difference between 2006 and 1996 scores—the earliest and most recent indicators available (this "change" variable turns out not to be significant), as well as "performance type" based on Dubnick's typology (2005, 391–394).

With regard to causal possibilities 1 and 2, no discernable patterns emerge from the ordering in Table 9.3 to support the case that governance has a determining influence on how IT systems are enacted. To the contrary, similar variations of behaviors (system-resisting, opportunistic, and norms-promoting) appear both at the low and high ends of the VaA scale. Similar orderings emerge in arraying system-enactment summaries against the government-effectiveness and control-of-corruption scales (not shown), with only two and three ordering differences, respectively—thus, it is doubtful that patterns from any of the World Bank governance indicators would emerge supporting governance as an independent variable.

Nonetheless, some of the individual summaries shown in Table 9.3 convey enactment behaviors[4] that appear formative in changing governance norms in their respective societies. At the low end of the scale, for example, municipal information bureaus in China (see Table 9.3, 3–1) use e-government systems intended to promote transparency, but also to establish privacy norms that protect citizens from "transparency"—that is, the exposed two-way flow of information to and from government. And in Mozambique (3–5), India (3–6), and South Korea (3–9), policy actors use IT systems as platforms for advancing democratic norms that have the potential to improve governance. Alternatively, at the high end of the VaA scale, two IT systems related to health care—monitoring nurses in the United Kingdom (3–15) and physicians in the Netherlands (3–17)—engender professional resistance with the potential to bring about institutional change in national ministries. Further, enactment in response to some systems in the United States (3–11, 3–12, and 3–14) appear to position public agencies well in relation to their private-sector counterparts.

Table 9.3 then includes a number of assessments suggesting that human enactment behavior (apart from that intended by IT systems) either contributes to governance or at least affects how norms evolve in significant bureaucratic institutions. Perhaps it is telling that these systems, along with all the others on the lower half of the governance scale, appear to emphasize production (as indicated in Table 9.3)—which is performance through explicit control. This suggests that, even under these constraints, bureaucrats and other public actors can reframe managerial compliance designs in ways that reflect different norms. The analytical challenge is to hone in on plausible explanations that account for why and how human responses to IT systems can bring about these institutional changes.

It is instructive to determine if any of these IT systems are essentially "designed to be enacted,"

Table 9.3

System Enactments by Voice-and-Accountability Governance Indicator

Voice-and-Accountability Scale (all system enactments found)

Low   **China: –1.66 (no change)[a]**

(3–1) At a decentralized level, local agencies decide what information the public "owns;" and rightful dissemination procedures on behalf of citizens amid national imperative for "open, transparent" government—production[b]

Jordan: –0.62 (down .23)

(3–2) Ministry officials resist systems; don't support technology management—production

Malaysia: –0.34 (down .07)

(3–3) System works against the creativeness of more experienced editors in government publishing house—production

Tanzania: –0.26 (up .44)

(3–4) System facilitates citizen participation through anonymity—production

Mozambique: –0.06 (down .04)

(3–5) Use the system as argument for improving local conditions; network provides agenda for "counternetworks"—production

India: 0.35 (up .27)

(3–6) System reform provides policy maker a means to champion large-scale policy issues (Andrah Pradesh)—production

(3–7) Low-cost access to information infrastructure helps grass-roots intermediaries interpret system information in a local context—production

South Africa: 0.60 (down .23)

(3–8) Manager-facilitators of citizen participation lose "face," control of dialog—production

South Korea: 0.71 (up .24)

(3–9) System strengthens political leader spearheading anticorruption reform—production

United States: 1.08 (down .25)

(3–10) agencies establish barriers to resist IT-driven citizen participation processes—productivity

(3–11) Bibliographic Reference Service seen as an incursion into the private index-citation market—results

(3–12) IRS uses e-file as a means to strengthen collaborative alliances with the tax preparation industry—production

(3–13) IT communications systems in human services make network more exclusive, as it constructed barriers to participation by some organizations—production

(3–14) Budgeting and planning officials use system as a means of political positioning for upcoming bond elections—production

United Kingdom: 1.42 (up .38)

(3–15) Nurses use system with resistive compliance; the system doesn't de-skill, but facilitates professional conversation—results

(3–16) Hospital system enhances middle management in synthesizing system information for top-management decision making—results

Netherlands: 1.67 (up .19)

(3–17) 50% of physicians resist prescription; adverse to professional culture—production

(3–18) IT control systems obscure discretion (not destroy it); induce employees into
High   interpretation that mediates human practice and system information—production

Source: Kaufmann et al. 2007.

[a]Change, up or down shows comparison of 2006 measure against that of 1996, the first year these indicators were used.

[b]Performance type (see Table 9.2; Dubnick, 2005, 391–4).

and if so, how those cases differ (in terms of design, use, and/or implementation) from those that clearly are not. The "open government" system in Shanghai (3–1) stands out as a case where the system has been intentionally designed to incubate openness norms not only to promote a global trade image, but also to protect citizens against government misuse of transparency. A participant on the municipal-information committee describes the system by focusing upon the good faith of city government in establishing such a system. In particular, this author elaborates on intentions to sustain ongoing collaborative processes within various departments to make necessary adjustments needed to support openness norms:

> In terms of channels for disseminating information, we have stressed putting the people first, and providing convenience and benefits for the people. In addressing different types of information, we have tried to guide all departments to choose the public dissemination channels and methods most suited for the characteristics of each type of information . . . In terms of establishing mechanisms with long-term effects, we have stepped up efforts. These mechanisms include a Guide to Open Government Information Norms, organizational training, supervision and inspection, dispute resolution, effectiveness evaluations, and other necessary mechanisms. All departments take open information as an opportunity to combine daily updating and maintenance of information with the management of internal documents, construction of E-government, the reform of administrative approvals and other types of work, and to explore ways to create lasting efficiencies in our work mechanisms. (Qiao 2006, 30)

Designs that promote adjustment and adaptability can be found as well within prominent nongovernmental organizations. A founding staff member of Transparency International (TI) explains, "Indeed, a key element of TI's success has been its choice of changing underlying structures— legal and institutional frameworks . . . This policy is uniquely adapted to aspects of the corruption scene. It is not the tool itself, but its finely tuned adaptability to the given context that makes it so effective" (Galtung 2001, 198–199). In a similar vein, Amnesty International's accountability statement implies methodological adaptability: "Methodologies such as impact assessment and stakeholders' analysis enable us to ensure Amnesty International is delivering real and positive change for those people for whom we work."[5] Perhaps some government agencies guided by IT systems "designed to be enacted" can be said to take on "NGO-like" attributes—particularly, the capability to mitigate according to context in championing norms.

By contrast, the Netherlands Ministry of Health adopted an electronic prescription system (to be used during patient consultation—see 3–17) that was clearly *not* designed to afford physicians flexibility to adapt the technology to a patient's particular situation. Since the system was not compulsory, many physicians abandoned it. Authors reporting on this system provide the following reactions from physicians: "I studied medicine to help patients as well as I can. I feel that systems like these invade my relation with patients; so I want to determine effective therapies on my own," and "I feel that the system leads to impersonal contacts, it reduces involvement. I have a lot of experience with different therapies and I want to use that" (Boonstra et al. 2004, 136–137).

The Shanghai open-government and Dutch electronic-prescription cases appear as extremes in system design, particularly with regard to agency (or agent) capabilities to work the technology and adjust to context. The former might be said to resemble a "mini–Transparency International" with considerable autonomy to use its authority on behalf of openness norms. No such autonomy was possible in the Dutch case, short of physicians' opting out of the system.

If it makes sense that some government agencies can take on NGO-like authority, perhaps they engage in something akin to what David Weimer calls "private rulemaking." Directing attention to how life-saving human organs are allocated for transplantation, Weimer differentiates the rulemaking processes of the Organ Procurement and Transportation Network from the standard regulatory rule procedures under the Administrative Procedures Act of 1946. In essence, private rule making comes about when policy makers permit a public entity to circumvent the standard procedures in favor of rule adoption through stakeholder negotiation. Weimer explains, "Private rulemaking involves the delegation of authority to an NGO for the rules governing the allocation of things of value. Private rulemaking provides an alternative to public rulemaking for developing the substantive content of rules" (2006, 578). Further, he offers three conditions under which policy makers are likely to grant this self-regulating authority (579–80):

1. "Blame avoidance"—motivation to remove delicate issues from the political agenda
2. "Technical efficiency"—the imperative for stakeholders to encompass the expertise needed to make decisions
3. The extent that "the policy area must involve changing circumstances that demand frequent adjustment of the rules"

Weimer's conditions for private rule-making authority may have applicability to the linkage between IT system design and agency operations affected by the system. In both contexts, trust and social capital emerge as the common elements that support collaboration—an asset unlikely to evolve solely from the generation of technical information (see Fountain 2001, 76–79). In turn, it is reasonable to associate the trust necessary for social capital with strong peer-accountability bonds within these institutional settings. Thus commentaries in some of the articles reviewed allow for rough estimates of where the IT-enactment cases plot against two of Weimer's three conditions—encompassed expertise and adjustment capability—but lack information about political motivations such as blame avoidance.

Figure 9.1 shows estimated plots[6] of the IT cases on an axis of system expertise encompassed against design capability to make adjustments. Cases on the low ends of both (in the top left) exact either compliant or resistant behaviors, while those at the high ends (bottom right) are associated with varying degrees of self-regulatory operations. The resulting differences appear more dichotomous than scalar. One of the UK cases (3–16) involving an IT system monitoring patient diagnoses in hospital settings yields somewhat ambiguous findings (system enhances middle-management discretion but reduces flexibility in treating patients). The plot of that case (in-between the two clusters) is more representative of this ambiguity than of a "true" middle position between the clusters. Especially noticeable in Figure 9.1 is the clustering of comparatively self-regulating (or NGO-like) organizations in nations scoring low on the governance scale. Generally speaking, the systems in these cases are built upon low-end, user-friendly technology that is widely accessible as compared to the more complex systems (for example, the Dutch electronic prescription system in the top-left cluster).

It can be said that the seventeen[7] organizations plotted across a spectrum of enactment behaviors shown in Figure 9.1 exhibit reactions to IT systems that embody regime values aligned with NPM objectives (e.g., encouraging agency coordination, promoting transparency, etc.). With one exception, systems in the top-left cluster elicit various forms of agent resistance. As mentioned earlier, the Dutch electronic prescription system (3–17) elicits outright resistance from physicians deciding to opt out rather than compromise their professional norms (Boonstra et al. 2004). Response to a system in Jordan appears more nuanced. In that country national-level bureaucrats are willing to use an imposed interagency system for informational purposes, but they will not incorporate it into

Figure 9.1 **IT Systems Plotted by Agency (Agent) Technical Expertise and System-Adjustment Capability**

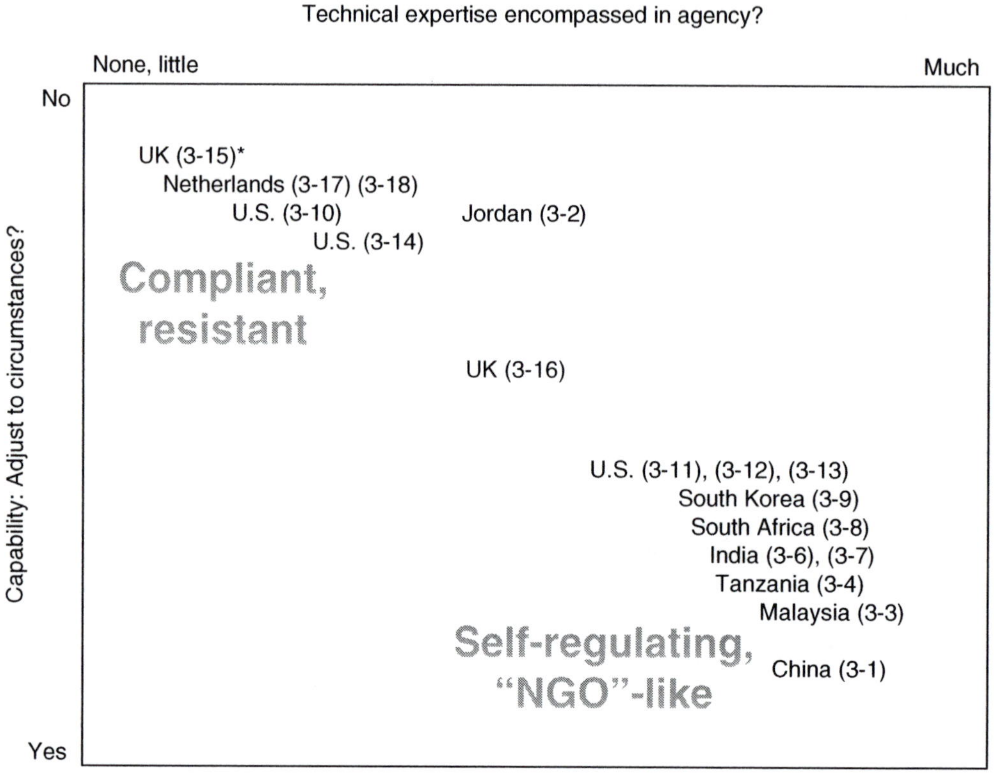

Technical expertise encompassed in agency?

None, little   Much

No

UK (3-15)*
    Netherlands (3-17) (3-18)
        U.S. (3-10)   Jordan (3-2)
            U.S. (3-14)

Capability: Adjust to circumstances?

Compliant,
resistant

UK (3-16)

U.S. (3-11), (3-12), (3-13)
South Korea (3-9)
South Africa (3-8)
India (3-6), (3-7)
Tanzania (3-4)
Malaysia (3-3)

Self-regulating,
"NGO"-like   China (3-1)

Yes

Source: Adapted from David L. Weimer, "The Puzzle of Private Rulemaking: Expertise, Flexibility, and Blame Avoidance in U.S. Regulation." Public Administration Review 66 (4) (July–August 2006): 569–82.
Note: Placement of systems based on rough estimates; the ordering of plots within clusters is arbitrary.
*Enactment behaviors described by corresponding entries in Table 9.3 and in the text.

ministry decision making (Kulchitsky 2004). It is instructive that this author stresses the "need for behavioral training" to surmount this "obstacle" (a presumably managerialist interpretation). In a second Dutch case (3–18), IT control systems are characterized as not eliminating bureaucratic discretion but instead obscuring it. This implies that reliance upon IT as a means of standardization in actuality increases (rather than reduces) the frequency of operational "blind spots" that require more (rather than less) discretion (Jorna and Wagenaar 2007)—a paradox of sorts.

In the UK case (3–15), nurses comply with the standardization logic of a work-surveillance system, but in so doing they scale back on work to the bare minimum demanded as a means of protest (Timmons 2003). Likewise, in one U.S. case of a system designed to enrich citizen participation (3–10), reported political and financial constraints keep municipal bureaucrats in Los Angeles from using the system beyond the perfunctory posting of public meeting notices (Musso and Weare 2005). In these four cases, regime values reflecting NPM ideology encountered enactment behaviors of resistance (SR=>E). However, one system in this cluster did garner compliance. The integrated eCAPRIS system in Austin, Texas (3–14), provides standardized capital-budget information needed for planning decisions in many affected departments—here, regime values elicited conventional accountability (SR=>AR; Canally and Neitsch, 2005). Yet even these compliant responses constitute significant enactment behaviors, since generated information is used for political advantage in subsequent city elections involving bond financing.

By contrast, IT systems clustered in the bottom right in Figure 9.1 elicit a wider range of enactment responses, a few of which appear to stretch beyond regime values. With regard to compliance, accommodation with NPM ideology in two U.S. cases serves the entrepreneurial interests of the Department of Energy (DOE) and Internal Revenue Service (IRS). In one case (3–11), the DOE's Office of Scientific and Technical Information creates an electronic bibliographic citation system in competition with private, scientific reference services (Salem 2003). In the other (3–12), the e-file system provides the IRS leverage to partner advantageously with private-sector tax preparers (Holden and Fletcher 2005). In a similar vein, research on a number of human-service agencies in the United States (3–10) finds that Internet systems tend to spawn exclusive networks of politically influential, system-user stakeholders rather than expand agency access (Rethemeyer 2007, 270). In each of these U.S. cases, it appears that system responses are generally in line with NPM-induced regime values (SR=>AR).

Yet in some of the international contexts, systems built on rather low-end technologies were indeed effective in expanding government access, particularly to marginalized subpopulations. In the Indian case, focusing on the state of Andrah Predash (3–6), a top-level ministry official uses a "planned information system" to develop stakeholder partnerships among government agencies, private consultants, and marginalized groups to work effectively in a number of social as well as technical areas (Krishna and Walsham 2005). In a similar discussion of IT systems (3–7) in rural India, authors stress that these technologies can offer "grassroots intermediaries" access in advocating for their groups at a comparatively low cost (Cecchini and Scott 2003). From a different perspective, IT systems support the involvement of the marginalized in Tanzania (3–4) and in South Africa (3–8) by providing them the cover of anonymity in their communications with bureaucrats. Authors indicate that beneficial system impacts were more pronounced in the Tanzanian case, as government officials there were originally more reticent in extending electronic participation (de Vreede et al. 2003).

E-government systems were enacted in South Korea (3–9) and in Shanghai (as discussed earlier 3–1) in line with NPM objectives to make government transparent. In the former case, e-government provided the platform for "the right leader at the right time" for the Seoul Metropolitan Government to launch a war on corruption (Cho and Choi 2004, 733). In Shanghai the NPM objective for transparency in government elicited the opportunity for municipal information committee members to enlist the cause of protecting citizens from government misuse of personal information (Qiao 2006). If the design intents in these international contexts were to disseminate NPM ideals, it can be said that they also facilitated other social objectives in ways that impacted governance for the better (SR=>AO and PO). One outlier case in this cluster concerns an IT system used in a Malaysian government printing house that takes discretion away from more experienced editors (Mohmud and Sackett 2007). Yet outside of the U.S. and Malaysian cases, the IT systems in this bottom-right cluster generally contribute to the self-regulatory capacities of agencies and tend to promote democratic social norms.

Finally, it is important to note that the various IT systems are shown in Figure 9.1 as gross approximations rather than precise calibrations, and that the ordering of cases within the two clusters are for the most part arbitrary. And, as indicated earlier, not all of the articles reviewed focus directly on the human responses to IT systems (although some in fact do). Nonetheless, this arrangement of IT cases provides modest support for the assertion that government IT-system design and use can evoke human behaviors (or in Fountain's terminology, "be enacted"; 2001, 83–103) in ways that impact upon governance. Weimer's criteria for private rule making (2006) appear helpful in probing the link between IT systems and human response—yet there may be other factors not uncovered in this study that could explain this relationship with more clarity.

"OUGHTNESS" AND ACCOUNTABILITY IN VIRTUAL STATES

This study has examined interactions among government IT systems, behavioral responses to (or enactment of) those systems, and governance in various national settings. Assuming IT-system enactment as an accountability issue, this study finds theoretical guidance in Dubnick's critique on accountability and the promise of performance in public management (2005). Nonetheless, this inquiry ultimately drifts into another theoretical domain—that of developing or changing norms more closely tied to the field of international relations (IR). This concluding discussion therefore integrates a norms-dynamic framework from IR into conversation about a social-mechanisms approach to accountability in public institutions. Specifically, such integration can place the observations from this study in a more cogent perspective. Yet more generally, norms dynamics can lend some analytical precision to what has been called "thick accountability" (for example, see Dubnick and O'Kelly 2005)—the dense entanglement of normative claims on and in public organizations.

"Oughtness" is the term IR scholars Martha Finnemore and Kathryn Sikkink use to "set norms apart from other kinds of rules" (1998, 891). These scholars guide norms conversation discriminately to avoid confusing specific norms with collections of norms, rules, and practices that constitute institutions: "Used carefully, norms language can steer scholars toward looking inside social institutions and considering the components of social institutions as well as the way these elements are renegotiated into new arrangements over time to create new politics" (1998, 891).

Finnemore and Sikkink's framework can contribute to Dubnick's critique on accountability by assigning temporality among the normative (account) warrants on public organizations. They understand norm dynamics in terms of evolution along a "life cycle" of three stages—norm emergence, norm cascade, and internalization:

> The first two stages are divided by a threshold, or "tipping" point, at which a critical mass of relevant state actors adopt the norm . . . The characteristic mechanism of the first stage, norm emergence, is persuasion by norm entrepreneurs. Norm entrepreneurs attempt to convince a critical mass of states (norm leaders) to embrace new norms. The second stage is characterized more by a dynamic of imitation as the norms leaders attempt to socialize other states to become norm followers. The exact motivation for this second stage where the norm "cascades" through the rest of the population (in this case, of states) vary, but we argue that a combination of pressure for conformity, desire to enhance international legitimization, and the desire for state leaders to enhance their self-esteem facilitate norm cascades. At the far end of the norm cascade, norm internalization occurs; norms acquire a taken-for-granted quality and are no longer a matter of broad public debate. (1998, 895)

It is suggested here that (1) this social-mechanisms approach to norm emergence parallels that of Dubnick's account giving and (2) "thick accountability" derives from competing loyalties to norms at different life-cycle stages. Regarding the latter, the diffusion of NPM norms appears to reflect a cascading ideology that challenges previously internalized (for example, professional) norms. Further, its managerialist advocates ("Y is imperative"—see Figure 9.2) need to protect it against other conceptions of "oughtness" that might arise. On the defensive, those loyal to previ-

Figure 9.2   **Three Life-Cycle Stages of Norms Development[a] Related to Account-Giving Patterns[b]**

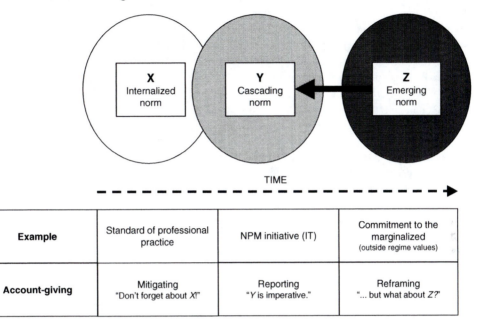

	Example	Standard of professional practice	NPM initiative (IT)	Commitment to the marginalized (outside regime values)
Account-giving		Mitigating "Don't forget about *X*!"	Reporting "*Y* is imperative."	Reframing "... but what about *Z*?"

[a]Finnemore and Sikkink (1998).
[b]Dubnick (2005).

ously internalized norms couch their account giving in mitigating tones that imply "You say Y is imperative, but don't forget about X!" On the other hand, norm entrepreneurs attempt to reframe with questions like "You say Y is important, but what about Z?" Or (insinuating that Z is a logical extension of Y) "If Y is important, then why isn't Z as well?" Figure 9.2 uses a Venn diagram to show how the three stages of norm evolution relate to alternative types of account giving in Dubnick's social-mechanisms model. Note that the temporal sequence in the diagram reverses the order in which Finnemore and Sikkink presented the norm-development stages in the previous passage.

So how then does IT play into these contests within the thick context of institutional accountability? It facilitates the cascading (or recently cascaded) NPM agenda in at least four different ways:

1. By legitimizing the rhetoric simply by its inclusion in the "sales pitch"
2. By providing the electronic architecture for imposed production methods
3. By narrowing the formats from account giving to reporting
4. By enhancing the public roles of private consultants who design technological constraints on government operations

Yet this study indicates there is more to this story. The observations here also suggest that through technology, norm entrepreneurs can access information for discovery, verification, and dissemination in pursuit of reaching that tipping point of legitimacy.

Several cases reviewed in this study depict norm entrepreneurs (individual or collective) who in essence reframe the appropriate use of IT. Among some U.S. cases, IT is enacted to agency advantage in collaboration or competition with private businesses—and one could debate whether NPM ideology actually embraces such bureaucratic enterprises. Yet more germane to governance concerns, other commentaries report on how government agencies and/or policy actors have used IT systems to promote norms that further democratic government and serve the marginalized (see bottom-right cluster in Figure 9.1). These response behaviors appear accommodated within a specific pattern of IT enactment corresponding to the "what about Z?" question (previously discussed)—the logic of account-giving that challenges more prevalent uses of IT in governance.

A second pattern of enactment can be found among cases where those loyal to established, internalized norms resist the powerful role of technology in supporting the cascade of managerialism (top-left cluster in Figure 9.1). Although frequently discredited as obstructionist, biased, or "out of touch," these behaviors—at least from the point of view of Finnemore and Sikkink's norms dynamic—can forthrightly be attributed to professionals fending off the deleterious effects of a technology-based managerialism in fields like medicine and nursing. In two of the cases reviewed, professional resistance leads to a paradoxical outcome when strict system reporting amounts to substantially diminished (bare minimum) performance.

In conclusion, it is worth noting that both of these social-mechanism approaches (Finnemore and Sikkink's norms dynamics and Dubnick's accountability and performance promises) start from similar premises—the need to refute rationalists who discredit the roles of norms in institutional life—and end with the same conundrum of not being able to identify which particular factors in context actually drive these respective social mechanisms. Applying the latter to observations in this study, for example, it is not possible to predict if e-government designed to bring about transparency in various settings will in turn motivate officials to protect citizens' privacy, as in Shanghai. Nor can we necessarily expect marginalized groups from different rural locales to recognize low-end technology as a means of accessing government anonymously, as in Tanzania. Thus the observations support a situational qualification on the third causal alternative presented earlier: "IT-system use, design, and implementation can evoke enactment responses that impact upon governance," but predicting where those impacts will occur is beyond our efforts here. Yet there is good reason to speculate from the cases reviewed that people can and do enact (or react to) technology on behalf of normative causes with strategic acumen—and that appears impressively rational.

NOTES

1. Journals reviewed include the following: *Administration and Society; American Review of Public Administration; Government Finance Review; Government Information Quarterly; Information Technology for Development; International Journal of Public Administration; Journal of Public Administration Research and Theory; New Technology, Work and Employment; Perspectives on Global Development and Technology; Public Administration; Public Administration and Development; Public Administration Review;* and *Technology for Development.*

2. Two systems used by political communities making demands on government (Brainard 2003; Brinkerhoff 2005) are excluded. The Taipei City (Taiwan) system described in two studies (Chen et al. 2003; 2006) counted as one here. Thus, number of systems is reduced to 24.

3. Such is the essence of Fountain's case about "the virtual military organization" included in *Building the Virtual State.* This case chronicles an infantry division's experiences in relying upon an IT control system to guide logistical decision making. She finds that in this "high-tech" army division, lesser-experienced, enlisted personnel (referred to as "button pushers") had more impact on decisions due to their data-entry function than did their mid-level managers and top commanding generals (whom the system was intended to serve). The generals subsequently complained that the system had usurped their traditional autonomy in leading military operations (2001, 167–192).

4. Particular enactment behaviors could be ascertained for 18 of the 24 IT systems included in Table 9.2.

5. Text taken from the accountability statement, Amnesty International Web page at http://www.amnesty. org/en/who-we-are/accountability.

6. Plot estimates based on a code sheet that tracks pertinent article text to Weimer's two dimensions: "technical expertise encompassed in agency" and "capability to adjust to circumstances" (2006). The code sheet is available from the author.

7. The Mozambique case (3–5) is omitted from Figure 9.1 because that commentary lacks sufficient detail for plotting.

REFERENCES

Boonstra, Albert, David Boddy, and Moira Fischbacher. 2004. "The Limited Acceptance of an Electronic Prescription System by General Practitioners: Reasons and Practical Implications." *New Technology, Work and Employment* 19 (2): 128–44.

Brainard, Lori. A. 2003. "Citizen Organizing in Cyberspace: Illustrations from Health Care." *American Review of Public Administration* 33 (4): 384–406.

Bretschneider, Stuart. 2003. "Information Technology, E-Government, and Institutional Change." *Public Administration Review* 63 (6): 738–41.

Brinkerhoff, Jennifer M. 2005. "Digital Diasporas and Governance in Semi-Authoritarian States: the Case of the Egyptian Copts." *Public Administration and Development* 25 (3): 193–204.

Canally, Greg, and Bruce Neitsch. 2005. "Using Technology to Enhance Capital Planning and Budgeting: Austin's E-Capris Project Reporting and Information System." *Government Finance Review* (December): 37–41.

Cecchini, Simone, and Christopher Scott. 2003. "Can Information and Communications Technology Applications Contribute to Poverty Reduction? Lessons from Rural India." *Information Technology for Development* 10 (2): 73–84.

Chen, Don-yun, Tong-yi Huang, and Naiyi Hsaio. 2003. "The Management of Citizen Participation in Taiwan: A Case Study of Taipei City Government's Citizen Complaints System." *International Journal of Public Administration* 26 (5): 525–47.

———. 2006. "Reinventing Government Through On-Line Citizen Involvement in the Developing World: A Case Study of Taipei City Mayor's E-Mail Box in Taiwan." *Public Administration and Development* 26 (5): 409–23.

Cho, Yong Hyo, and Byung-Dae Choi. 2004. "E-Government to Combat Corruption: The Case of Seoul Metropolitan Government." *International Journal of Public Administration* 27 (10): 719–35.

Currie, Graeme, and Stephen Proctor. 2002. "Impact of MIS/IT upon Middle Managers: Some Evidence from the NHS." *New Technology, Work and Employment* 17 (2): 102–18.

de Vreede, Gert-Jan, Rabson J. Mgaya, and Sadja Qureshi. 2003. "Field Experiences with Collaboration Technology: A Comparative Study in Tanzania and South Africa." *Information Technology for Development* 10 (3): 201–19.

Dubnick, Melvin. 2005. "Accountability and the Promise of Performance: In Search of the Mechanisms." *Public Performance and Management Review* 28 (3): 376–416.

Dubnick, Melvin, and Ciarán O'Kelly. 2005. "Accountability Though Thick and Thin: Moral Agency in Public Service." In *Ethics in Public Management,* ed. H. George Frederickson and Richard K. Ghere. Armonk, NY: M.E. Sharpe.

Evans, Donna, and David C. Yen. 2006. "E-Government: Evolving Relationship of Citizens and Government, Domestic and International Development." *Government Information Quarterly* 23: 207–35.

Finnemore, Martha, and Kathryn Sikkink. 1998. "International Norms Dynamics and Political Change." *International Organizations* 52 (4): 887–917.

Fountain, Jane E., 2001. *Building the Virtual State: Information Technology and Institutional Change.* Washington, DC: Brookings Institution Press.

Gaitlung, Fredrik. 2001. "Transparency International's Network to Curb Global Corruption." In *Where Corruption Lives,* ed. Gerald E. Caiden, O.P. Dwivedi, and Joseph Jabbra, 189–206. Bloomfield CT: Kumarian Press.

Holden, Stephen H., and Patricia D. Fletcher. 2005. "The Virtual Value Chain and E-Government Partnership: Non-Monetary Agreements in the IRS E-File Program." *International Journal of Public Administration* 28 (7/8): 643–64.

Jorna, Frans, and Pieter Wagenaar. 2007. "The Iron Cage Strengthened? Discretion and Digital Discipline." *Public Administration* 85 (1): 189–214.

Katchanovski, Ivan, and Todd La Porte. 2005. "Cyberdemocracy or Potemkin E-Villages? Electronic Governments in OECD and Post-Communist Countries." *International Journal of Public Administration* 28 (7/8): 665–81.

Kaufmann, Daniel, Aart Kraay, and Massimo Mastruzzi. 2007. "Governance Matters VI: Governance Indicators for 1996–2006." World Bank Policy Research Working Paper No. 4280 (July). http://ssrn.com/abstract=999979.

Kim, Hyun Jeong, Gary Pan, and Shan Ling Pan. 2007. "Managing IT-Enabled Transformation in the Public Sector: A Case Study on E-Government in South Korea." *Government Information Quarterly* 24 (2): 338–52.

Kim, Soonhee, and Hyangsoo Lee. 2006. "The Impact of Organizational Context and Information Technology on Employee Knowledge-Sharing Capabilities." *Public Administration Review* 66 (3): 370–85.

Krishna, S., and Geoff Walsham. 2005. "Implementing Public Information Systems in Developing Countries: Learning from a Success Story." *Information Technology for Development* 11 (2): 123–40.

Kulchitsky, D. Roman. 2004. "Computerization, Knowledge, and Information Technology Initiatives in Jordan." *Administration and Society* 36 (1): 3–37.

Lan, Z. 2005. "Administrative Reform after 1978." In *China Today: An Encyclopedia of Life in the People's Republic,* ed. J. Luo. Westport, CT: Greenwood Press.

Liao, Shu-hsien, and Huey-pyng Jeng. 2005. "E-Government Implementation: Business Contract Legal Support for Taiwanese Businessmen in Mainland China." *Government Information Quarterly* 22 (3): 505–24.

Ma, Lianjie, Jongpil Chung, and Stuart Thorson. 2005. "E-Government in China: Bringing Economic Development Through Administrative Reform." *Government Information Quarterly* 22 (1): 20–37.

Mahmood, Rumel. 2004. "Can Information and Communication Technology Help Reduce Corruption? How So and Why Not: Two Case Studies from South Asia." *Perspectives on Global Development and Technology* 3 (3): 347–73.

Mohmud, Dahlina D., and Peter Sackett. 2007. "Malaysia's Government Publishing House: A Quest for Increased Performance Through Technology." *Public Administration and Development* 27 (1): 27–38.

Mosse, Emilo L., and Sundeep Sahay. 2003. "The Role of Communication Practices in the Strengthening of Counter Networks: Case Experiences from the Health Care Sector of Mozambique." *Information Technology for Development* 11 (3): 179–99.

Musso, Juliet A., and Christopher Weare. 2005. "Implementing Electronic Notification in Los Angeles: Citizen Participation Politics by Other Means." *International Journal of Public Administration* 28 (7/8): 599–620.

Qiao, Zhigang. 2006. "Exploration and Practice in Promoting Shanghai Municipal Open Government Information." *Government Information Quarterly* 23 (1): 28–35.

Rethemeyer, R. Karl. 2007. "Policymaking in the Age of Internet: Is the Internet Tending to Make Policy Networks More or Less Inclusive?" *Journal of Public Administration Research and Theory* 17 (2): 259–84.

Salem, Joseph A. 2003. "Public and Private Sector Interests in E-Government: A Look at the DOE's Pub-SCIENCE." *Government Information Quarterly* 20 (1): 13–27.

Timmons, Stephen. 2003. "A Failed Panopticon: Surveillance of Nursing Practice via New Technology." *New Technology, Work and Employment* 18 (2): 143–53.

Weimer, David L. 2006. "The Puzzle of Private Rulemaking: Expertise, Flexibility, and Blame Avoidance in U.S. Regulation." *Public Administration Review* 66 (4): 569–82.

Xuhui District People's Government. 2006. "On the Implementation of Open Government Information in Xuhui District, Shanghai." *Government Information Quarterly* 23 (1): 66–72.

Yang, Kaifang. 2003. "Neoinstitutionalism and E-Government." *Social Science Computer Review* 21 (4): 432–42.

163

Appendix 9.1

Intended IT System Impacts on Organization

System type	Institutional setting	IT system impacts	Performance type
Agency web sites	Agencies in two Indian states (Andrah Predash and Bangladesh)	Web-based e-government reduces corruption (bribery) (Mahmood 2004)	Production
	Agencies in Seoul, South Korea metropolitan government	Web-based e-government reduces chances of bribes (Cho and Choi 2004)	Production
	Agencies in Los Angeles (U.S.) city government	Enhance citizen participation (Musso and Weare 2005)	Productivity
	U.S. DOE Office of Scientific and Technical Information Bibliographic Reference Service	Serve science community with web-based bibliographic service (Salem 2003)	Results
	National-level Ministry of Economic Affairs web site, Taiwan	Provide informational support for Taiwanese business representatives in China (Liao and Jeng 2005)	Results
	Taipei municipal e-government	System facilitates citizen complaints; exerts pressure on bureaucrats to establish "knowledge-based" feedback" (Chen 2004; Chen et al. 2003)	Production
	U.S. Federal Agency (e.g., FDA, USDA, Commerce, EEOC) web sites	Solicit comments that inform legislation-drafting conversation (Mahler and Regan 2005)	Results
	U.S. Internal Revenue Service E-File Program	Allows taxpayers to submit tax returns via the Internet (Holden and Fletcher 2005)	Production
	Citizen cyber-organization around two health issues—DES (diethylstilbestrol) exposure and HIV infection[a]	Promotes public policy discussions and public agency interaction (Brainard 2003)	N/A
	Copt community web site in Egypt[a]	Web technology to mobilize and empower the dispersed Egyptian copt community in relation to the Egyptian government (Brinkerhoff 2005)	N/A
Interagency web sites	Shanghai (China) municipal government	Web-site technology to implement open and transparent city government (Qiao 2006)	Production
	A Shanghai (China) municipal district	Web-site technology to encourage open municipal government (Xuhui District 2006)	Production
	E-government in various Chinese municipalities	IT used to to drive efforts both to accelerate and decentralize public administration but also enhance government's ability to oversee key activities (Ma et al. 2005)	Results

(continued)

Appendix 9.1 *(continued)*

System type	Institutional setting	IT system impacts	Performance type
Agency internal networks	Primary health care sector, Mozambique	Health information system (HIS) as a key strategy to improve health care delivery (Mosse and Sahay 2005)	Production
	Electronic community meetings in Tanzania and South Africa (compared)	IT systems intended to facilitate citizen participation (de Vreede et al. 2003)	Production
	State-level computer-aided registration department, Andhra Pradesh, India	Implementation of IT public information system in an underdeveloped state (Krishna and Walsham 2005)	Production
	State-level computer-aided registration department, Andhra Pradesh, India	Information and communications technology (ICT) to reduce poverty by improving poor people's access to education, health, government and financial services (Cecchini and Scott 2003)	Production
	Electronic prescription system, Netherlands	To control the cost of drugs prescribed by general practitioners (Boonstra et al. 2004)	Production
	UK national health IT surveillance, Hospital Nursing	To institute electronic surveillance of nursing practices in hospitals (Timmons 2003)	Results
	IT communication systems in U.S. state-level adult education and mental health networks	To facilitate interorganizational communication (Rethemeyer 2007)	Production
	UK national health service patient administration system	To institute organizationwide IT intervention in hospitals that coordinate clinical information at the ward level (Currie and Proctor 2002)	Results
	Electronic publishing, government publishing house, Malaysia	To increase efficiency in a government enterprise for book publishing (Mohmud and Sackett 2007)	Production
	IT systems in national-level ministries, South Korea	To enhance employee knowledge-sharing capability, the ability of employees to share their work-related experience (Kim and Lee 2006)	Production
	IT control systems in two subsidy (housing and farming) programs, the Netherlands	Institutionalizing information systems in two national-level government programs (Jorna and Wagenaar 2007)	Production
	E-government in supreme court registry office, South Korea	To promote unrestricted and flexible communications between citizenry and 43 court registry offices (Kim et al. 2006)	Production
Cross-agency integration and systems	Information systems in national-level ministries, Jordan	To integrate knowledge sharing and decision processes (Kulchitsky 2004)	Production
	Capital planning and budgeting system, city of Austin TX	To integrate financial and project information for municipal capital improvement projects (Canally and Neitsch 2005)	Production

[a]Both Brainard (2003) and Brinkerhoff (2005) studies involve political communities using IT to mobilize and place demands on government.

PART IV

ADAPTING TO ACCOUNTABILITY

As promising and attractive as accountability mechanisms seem to those seeking to resolve the problems of governance, the reality of our political and organizational worlds inevitably frustrates even the most dedicated reformers. The situated nature of accountability begs for a more informed and nuanced approach to applying accountability where sectoral, temporal, or even spatial factors can make or break such efforts. It is evident that we need to pay greater attention to the process of adapting to the circumstances and pressures generated by accountability expectations.

Christopher Hood takes note of the existence of a stream of writing in political science that is relevant to these issues. He shows that study of "blame avoidance" in all its forms provides a potentially rich source of ideas about the strategic responses emerging from the circumstances that characterize governance and political life. His essay only touches the surface, but it furthers the general discussion of how the analytic treatment of accountability can be enhanced by thinking both more broadly and in-depth about its place in political studies.

The context of accountability is evident as well in the chapter by Margaret Karns, Timothy Shaffer, and Richard Ghere, who offer a study of PROSHIKA, an NGO dedicated to improving the economic opportunities and well-being of the poor of Bangladesh through microcredit programs. The complex circumstances shaping the work of PROSHIKA go well beyond the organization's task of dealing with multiple, diverse, and often conflicting expectations. Working within the context of the modern state, NGOs such as PROSHIKA that are dedicated to bringing about social change form a special challenge to the legitimacy of the regime within which they operate. To succeed in light of the inherent state-NGO tensions requires adaptations that often constrain and frustrate—and such strategic choices impact NGO priorities and operations and may require the organization to fall short of expectations in the eyes of other stakeholders.

But surrendering to dysfunction and frustration may not be inevitable or the only option for NGOs. Building on years of study and direct observation of accountability in the nonprofit sector, Kevin Kearns posits a life-cycle framework for comprehending—and dealing with—the different challenges that accountability poses over time for third-sector organizations.

10

BLAME AVOIDANCE AND ACCOUNTABILITY

Positive, Negative, or Neutral?

Christopher Hood

ACCOUNTABILITY AND BLAME AVOIDANCE: TWO SEPARATE TABLES IN POLITICAL SCIENCE?

Other chapters in this volume give an account of the developing literature on accountability in executive government (hereafter referred to as AEG), with its exploration of the dimensions and trade-offs of accountability (see, for instance, Bovens 2005). And over the past two decades (at least since Kent Weaver's seminal paper on the subject in 1986), a literature has also grown up on the subject of "blame avoidance" by politicians and bureaucrats (hereafter referred to as BA). But, as so often happens in political and bureaucratic science, those two literatures tend to sit at separate tables in the epistemic dining room (Almond 1988), and the relationship between the two has mostly been left implicit.

So how are AEG and BA related, if at all? It seems hard to dismiss the idea that BA is to some extent independent of formal arrangements for AEG. After all, psychologists see BA as a common human trait linked to negativity bias, part of a normal human imperative to be liked and respected by others.[1] So it seems implausible to argue that BA would disappear altogether even in some imaginary world where AEG did not exist at all.

However, it would also be hard to posit no causal relationship at all between BA activity and AEG. After all, officeholders who do not have to account for their actions to effective legislatures or other public forums, such as Kim Jong Il of North Korea or the late Saparmurat Niyazov of Turkmenistan, can be expected to have less incentive to avoid blame in the eyes of the public at large than those who do have to account for their behavior to such forums.

Moreover, the intensity and form of officeholders' accountability environment may shape their behavior as well. For instance, at about the same time that Kent Weaver published his well-known paper on blame avoidance, in a different part of the political-science forest McCubbins and Schwarz (1984) produced their now famous "fire-alarm" analysis of legislative strategies for controlling bureaucracies and keeping them accountable. For McCubbins and Schwarz, the way for principals such as legislative committees to keep tabs on their potentially wayward bureaucratic agents is to behave more like a fire brigade than a police patrol and wait for the equivalent of fire alarms to sound and then concentrate on bureaucracies in trouble, rather than do the equivalent of patrolling the streets on the off chance of finding something amiss. The advantage of the former strategy over the latter is that it focuses the legislator principals' inevitably limited monitoring capacity and directs it into areas where someone is claiming there are problems.[2]

McCubbins and Schwarz's analysis stops there, but it would be strange if that much-discussed fire-alarm strategy did not ramp up the drive toward blame avoidance on the part of officeholders under scrutiny, by creating further asymmetry between the incentives to avoid standing out as a problem case (thereby liable to attract the full attention of the political fire brigade), and the incentives to stand out because of excellent performance (thereby destined to be ignored by the fire brigade).[3] Many other AEG strategies, such as transparency rules, may also have the effect of shaping blame-avoidance behavior on the part of officeholders. An example is Andrea Prat's (2005) case of the "wrong kind of transparency," in which he claims principals can be worse off as a result of being more informed about their agents' behavior in certain circumstances, if the information leads to blame-avoiding herd behavior.

On the other side of the equation, BA strategies by officeholders can lead to AEG responses, when efforts to avoid blame by delegation lead legislatures (or law courts) to pay more attention to scrutinizing apparently independent bodies. So the potential causal connections between BA and AEG can run in several ways. The aim of this chapter is to examine those interconnections by discussing three kinds of BA strategies that are commonly discussed in the literature and then by briefly exploring their relationship, positive or negative, with AEG strategies and with broader governance issues. Accordingly, the next section discusses agency, presentational, and policy approaches to BA. The section following considers the positive and negative AEG effects of those strategies.

THREE TYPES OF BLAME AVOIDANCE: AGENCY, PRESENTATIONAL, AND POLICY STRATEGIES

To date, political science has not developed a general theory of blame avoidance or a systematic classification of types of blame avoidance that would correspond to the effort put into categorizing and classifying forms of persuasion in the traditional study of rhetoric. And though the term "blame avoidance" has been in currency in political science and some other fields for twenty years or more, the literature on the subject remains patchy. But in that literature we can identify at least three main strategies for deflecting or avoiding blame (see Hood 2002; Sulitzeanu-Kenan and Hood 2005): agency strategies, presentational strategies, and policy strategies (Table 10.1).

Blame has numerous dimensions (Hood 2002; Sulitzeanu-Kenan and Hood 2005), including at least some perception of avoidable loss or harm caused by a particular actor or institution at a particular time. Agency strategies, as that term implies, deal mainly with the agency dimension of blame, but they also may be directed at the time element, for instance by using revolving-door systems for moving officeholders on so that by the time blame comes home to roost, someone else is in office. Policy strategies also deal mainly with the agency and time dimensions, but through different means, namely the architecture of policy and operating routines rather than the distribution of responsibility in an organizational structure. Presentational strategies deal mainly with the loss-perception dimension, but may also involve the time dimension. Table 10.1 spells out some of the basic features of each of these three types of strategy, sets out some examples, and identifies some of the assumptions associated with each type of strategy.

Agency strategies involve various ways of trying to avoid blame by the way lines of formal responsibility are drawn in government and public services. The agency strategist aims to work on the directional (agency) dimension of blame and focuses primarily on government's organogram (organizational chart) and on who occupies which position within it at what time. In a tradition that goes back to Machiavelli's early sixteenth-century maxim that "princes give rewards and favours

Table 10.1

Three Types of Blame-Avoidance Strategy

	Aspect of blame dealt with	Works on	Example	Assume
Agency strategies (Slogan: "Find a scapegoat")	Agency and time	Distribution of formal responsibility, competency, or jurisdiction among institutions and officeholders in space or time	Formal delegation of potentially blame-worthy tasks to "lightning rods"	Formal allocation of organizational responsibility is sufficiently credible and salient to last through blame firestorms
Presentational strategies (Slogan: "Spin your way out of trouble")	Loss perception and time	Arguments for limiting blame (excuses) or turning blame into credit (justifications) and other methods of shaping public impressions	Shaping of public perceptions through news management	Presentational activity will limit or deflect rather than exacerbate or attract blame
Policy strategies (Slogan: "Don't make contestable judgments that create losers")	Agency and time	Selection of policies or operating routines to minimize risk of institutional or individual liability or blame	Protocolization and automaticity to remove or minimize the exercise of individual discretion by officeholders	There is a low- or no-blame option (e.g., in choosing between errors of commission and errors of omission or between opting for automaticity and opting for discretion)

Source: Developed from Hood (2002).

with their own hands but death and punishment at the hands of others (1961, 106)," agency strategists aim to delegate the activities that will attract blame while retaining in their own hands the activities that will earn credit. For example, they may seek to diffuse blame by working through partnerships or multiagency arrangements or institutional machinery so complex that blame can be shuffled about or made to disappear. Agency strategists may use reorganizations, rotations, or reshuffles to move officeholders in time, so that by the time blame for their mistakes is firmly pinned down in the AEG process, the relevant individuals have moved out or on, leaving no heads available to stick on spikes.

The analysis of agency strategies takes us into that part of political science that is concerned with all the recondite details of how executive government is organized, including its use of private and independent organizations in partnership or delegation arrangements. Indeed, the blame-avoidance perspective may be one way of making sense of the much-remarked development of so-called quangos (quasi nongovernmental organizations) and more and more complex multilevel governance and partnership arrangements, and also of explaining why elected politicians and senior bureaucrats often seem to spend so much time on the fine print of organizational design while usually professing that all they are interested in is "results."

In contrast, presentational strategies, as Table 10.1 indicates, involve various ways of trying to avoid blame by spin, stage management, and argument. The presentational strategist works on the loss-perception dimension of blame, for example, by "accentuating the positive" to counter negativity bias and focusing primarily on what kind of information to offer, when, and how. Presentational strategists aim to find ways of showing that what might be perceived by their detractors as blameworthy is in fact a blessing in disguise—for instance, short-term pain in the service of long-term gain. These strategists may offer excuses to mitigate blame on the part of particular officeholders, at the point where loss perception and agency meet. They may actively create diversions or time potentially blame-attracting announcements when they will receive minimal public attention; for example, increases in politicians' pay or abandonment of once-cherished flagship policies may be sneaked out on public holidays or at a time when media attention is focused on some other major event.

The analysis of presentational strategies takes us into that part of political science that is concerned with the framing of arguments, the rhetorical dimension of politics and management, and the links between media and politics. Such strategies have attracted much attention in the current age of "spinocracy," with its so-called media class, its swelling armies of flak-catchers and public-relations (PR) professionals, and its PR bureaucrats, often in influential positions in government and public organizations (see Kurtz 1998; Jones 1996 and 1999; Oborne 1999). And after a crisis has struck, presentation is typically the main strategy for blame avoidance for beleaguered officeholders, since agency and policy strategies normally require defensive action to be taken in advance of the blame event.

Policy strategies, also noted on Table 10.1, can also include ways of trying to avoid blame by using the substance or content of what officeholders do to put them in the best light, rather than spinning a presentation or putting a scapegoat in the front line of responsibility. Policy strategists aim to work on the agency and time dimensions of blame by means of the policies or routines they choose to follow so that officeholders' judgments are hard to contest or even identify. For instance, when it comes to potentially blame-attracting policies such as taxation, officeholders may rely heavily on policies they have inherited, so that blame attaches as much to their predecessors as to themselves (see Rose 1990). They may seek to replace human judgment and the blame it can attract by following automatic formulas, such as formula-driven rather than discretionary budget allocations. For example, two decades ago Kent Weaver (1988) pointed to a decline in the proportion of the U.S. federal budget devoted to nonmandatory spending, and that trend has continued since then (see U.S. Congressional Budget Office 2004, Table A.1). Other forms of nondiscretionary procedures include protocols rather than professional judgment in casework decisions and tick-box approaches rather than qualitative assessment, such as computer-marked, multiple-choice tests rather than essays judged in the round by teachers. Or officeholders may simply abandon activities that may attract blame (such as advice or the provision of recreational facilities to the public) rather than relying on being able to spin their way out of trouble or shifting the responsibility around.

The greater the real or perceived negativity bias in the population at large, the more public discourse is likely to be dominated by such defensive approaches all along the food chain of executive government. And indeed policy strategies may be the blame-avoidance strategy of choice when agency strategies are not available—for example by those at the bottom of the pile in government and public services who are on the receiving end of such strategies from those above them.

BA AND AEG: POSITIVE, NEUTRAL, OR NEGATIVE?

Blame avoidance of the three types presented here become fairly familiar in the workings of executive government in many developed countries, with much discussion of the growth of spin doctors, delegated bodies, and defensive policy stances of various kinds. Much of the political-science writing on BA tends to treat it as a kind of realpolitik, and BA often gets bad press in popular writing and even some academic writing as an unsavory mixture of political or administrative chicken-heartedness and manipulation. But is the link between BA and AEG as simple as that?

A parallel can perhaps be drawn with "defensive medicine," the practice of medicine to reduce the risk of malpractice suits. While most of the popular discussion of defensive medicine tends to be negative in tone, and defensive medicine tends to be deplored as a prime source of high costs and indeed some of the harm to patients in the U.S. health-care system, some have pointed out conditions in which defensive medicine can cut costs or raise health-care quality, and even do both in some cases (see U.S. Congress, Office of Technology Assessment 1994: 22–24). Can we say the same for BA and AEG? After all, BA strategies will be neutral for AEG if they are simply discounted or seen through by others. They will be negative for AEG if they successfully undermine the efforts of legislatures and other actors to hold executive government to account. And they will be positive for AEG if, intentionally or otherwise, they make lines of responsibility clearer, clarify or balance accountability arguments, or (more tenuously for orthodox definitions of AEG) simply make the actions of officeholder "agents" conform more closely to the wishes of their "principals" in a democracy. The next three subsections explore each of these three possibilities.

BA as Neutral for AEG?

BA will simply be neutral for AEG if presentational, policy, and agency strategies are ineffective in achieving their intended effects of dodging accountability and shaping the way blame is allocated—that is, if BA strategies are discounted or ignored by legislators or voters in the same way that courts sometimes "look through" certain types of contracts. The old British civil-service joke that nothing should ever be believed until it has been denied by several government departments reflects such a view. And if we add time into the reckoning, there are plausible mechanisms by which a definite effect (positive or negative) of BA on AEG in one time period might be followed by neutrality, or vice versa. A definite effect followed by a null effect can be brought about through the process of recognition and disillusion followed by more critical scrutiny or other forms of counteraction. Howard Kurtz (1998) claims this was what happened to the propaganda machine of the Bill Clinton presidency in the United States (and the same can be said for the Blair government's spin operation in the United Kingdom, which was modeled on the tactics used by the Clinton machine). Or alternatively, a null effect followed by a definite effect can come about through processes of gradual adaptation, as voters and legislators eventually adapt to new systems after a time lag, as reformers have expected of delegation to agencies by ministers in Westminster-model systems (that is, in governments that follow the British parliamentary system).

Social scientists and historians very often find the effectiveness of social interventions and strategies to be remarkably elusive and hard to pin down. But casual evidence suggests that BA activities such as delegation and spin doctoring often fail to protect officeholders from the force of accountability. Attempts at more systematic analysis often tells the same story as well. For instance, an impact-intervention analysis that studied the responses of ministers and bureaucrats to media blame over fiascos in the operation of the public examination system of Scotland in 2000 and England in 2002 showed that presentational strategies adopted by ministers were wholly ineffective in reducing the level of blame in the following day's newspapers in the Scottish case, and only minimally effective in the English case (Hood et al. 2009). Moreover, some strategies in the English case seem to have been effective in the wrong direction, by pouring gasoline rather than water on the flames of the media firestorm. So the possibility of neutrality or null effect can never be dismissed from discussions of blame avoidance.

Blame Avoidance as Positive for AEG?

Just as there are some circumstances in which defensive medicine can cut health-care costs or raise quality, BA will be positive for AEG when it succeeds—intentionally or otherwise—in sharpening the accountability of officeholders in government. Despite the bad press that they get, "blame games" and BA can in principle be positive for AEG in some conditions.

For example, agency strategies of delegation may well be intended to shield the delegator from blame for the activities being delegated to flak-catchers or lightning rods. But in the process—and in the ensuing blame games between the delegator and originator of the action—it may become clearer who is responsible for what in the complex structure of executive government. As a result those who make the key decisions can become directly answerable to legislatures or other accountability forums. So a positive outcome can come about when delegation of operational tasks to agencies forces elected politicians to account for setting targets reflecting their perceptions of what voters want, as well as trade-offs over the conflicting values to be balanced in the actions of government. On their part, the experts and managers have to account for weighing up abstruse technical evidence and for the conduct of detailed project management and implementation. It could be argued that AEG arrangements are improved by making each of those players answer for the actions for which they have direct responsibility. And that is the standard argument against the traditional doctrine of ministerial responsibility in Westminster-model parliamentary democracies, as an AEG system that is seen by its critics as making ministers over-accountable to the legislature and bureaucrats and experts under-accountable. So arrangements that require each of those parties to account for the tasks they have a comparative advantage in performing could be considered a formula for a marriage (if not of love, at least of convenience) between blame avoidance and effective AEG.

Presentational strategies of spin and public debate are similarly intended to put the conduct and decisions of officeholders in the most favorable light to those to whom they have to answer. Often such efforts to "control the story" can be seen as attempts by spin doctors to get media and other watchdogs off the backs of the officeholders they work for, by fair means or foul, and in that sense can be seen as an escape from AEG. Nevertheless, there are conditions in which such BA activity can be positive for AEG. As already mentioned, it can happen unintentionally when such activity turns government's spin-doctoring machine itself into the story, as happened under both the Clinton presidency and the Blair premiership, leading the legislature, the media, and the public to apply greater scrutiny to the government's propaganda machine itself and thus producing heightened accountability of information activity. In some conditions BA can happen intention-ally too, for instance, when BA presentational activity serves as an effective counterweight to the negativity bias that would otherwise go unchallenged in public and media debate. After all, AEG is hardly enhanced if no officeholder or official spokesperson is ever on hand to counter accusa-tions of incompetence or corruption.

The potentially positive effects of presentational BA strategies for AEG roughly parallels the so-cial case for advertising, as put forward by authors like John Hood (2005). Well-framed excuses and justifications can in some circumstances better inform voters and legislators about the complex issues, trade-offs, and judgment calls that government involves. In that sense presentational BA activity can provide the basis for more sophisticated AEG over issues such as politicians' rewards or their private lives. And beyond that, presentational activity by officeholders designed to avoid blame can serve to balance the politics of AEG when it works to counterbalance the spin put on hot political issues by nonelected media, NGOs, or unrepresentative but well-funded pressure groups with particular and often concealed axes to grind. In that sense, government spin doctoring can reflect Georg Hegel's classic argument for a bureaucracy that was not a captive to any one interest group in society (1896).

To the extent that BA policy strategies (of focusing officeholder and government activity into courses designed to minimize public blame) can be positive for AEG, it would seem to be through processes of anticipation of AEG effects that align officeholder activity with the assumed prefer-ences of voters and legislators. For example, if the fear of AEG encourages officeholders to put the stress on avoiding harm rather than producing positive benefits, that would be counted by philosophers such as Shrader-Frechette (1991) as likely to more closely approximate the prefer-ences of voters at large than the opposite kind of risk bias.[4]

Shrader-Frechette is concerned with the balance in public policy between "precautionary" and "science-based" approaches to the handling of risks, and makes the case for the former kind of bias. If BA considerations lead officeholders to adopt policy strategies that incorporate that type of bias, Shrader-Frechette's perspective would suggest this is a positive result for AEG, in the sense that she claims precautionary policy stances tend to be less biased toward unrepresentative producer interests and thus more likely to reflect the preferences of voters at large. But that understanding of AEG goes beyond the definitions used by most authors in this volume.

To see BA strategies as universally positive for AEG, even if only through unintended conse-quences, might be an excessively optimistic view of the world. The more general point is that BA may deserve credit rather than blame in discussions of AEG, at least some of the time.

BA as Negative for AEG?

Turning to the negative side of the story, BA strategies will be negative for AEG if they succeed in blunting or deflecting accountability by allowing officeholders to escape the answerability they would otherwise face from legislatures or other forums. And those negative effects can also come about in several ways.

Agency strategies for BA can undermine AEG if they succeed in their intended aim of taking officeholders out of the front line of blame for anything bad that happens. While simple delegation might in some circumstances clarify responsibility and thereby sharpen AEG, messier and more plastic processes of delegation will not necessarily have that effect, and the associated blame-game processes may simply make responsibility disappear in unresolved claim and counter-claim. Moreover, there are several agency strategies for BA that do not involve delegation in the ordinary sense—for example, where partnerships across the public and private sectors or complex multi-agency arrangements are used to create structures in which any actor in the complex can blame others for failure, which makes the accountability trail go cold.

Presentational strategies for BA can undermine AEG if they do not counterbalance what would otherwise be the one-sided picture coming from unrepresentative interests or clarify the complexities of the policy issues—and thus keep potentially embarrassing issues off the agenda altogether. An example of this scenario would involve "burying bad news" by creating or exploiting diversions that dodge or divert the awkward questions rather than using persuasive excuses or justifications. Presentational BA strategies can also work against AEG when they involve backdoor pressures on news media rather than open engagement in policy arguments, when they involve an iron grip over any information that could be potentially embarrassing, and when they involve bullying of whistleblowers or others whose uncontrolled actions or views could put the officeholders concerned in a bad light.

Policy strategies for BA can undermine or negate AEG when they turn into a preoccupation with box-ticking or formulaic types of transparency that can undermine the sort of two-way communication that effective AEG requires, according to theorists such as Onora O'Neill (2002), who see defensive transparency as undermining real accountability. The outcome then is box-ticking bureaucracy rather than positive AEG (see McGivern and Ferlie 2007). Policy BA strategies that involve abandonment of potentially blame-attracting services that are nevertheless valued by voters can mean misalignment of government decisions with voters and legislator preferences. Policy strategies that are primarily designed to produce back-covering alibis or get-out-of-jail clauses for providers and decision makers—such as insisting on collective decision making at every point—can also have the effect of making individual answerability disappear.

As noted already, BA tends to get a bad press, and it is not difficult to identify a potentially dark side to BA strategies for the operation of effective AEG. Many of the negative effects mentioned here are not far to seek in executive government today. How should we therefore see the overall picture?

LOOKING FOR THE BALANCE: GOOD AND BAD BLAME AVOIDANCE?

This discussion suggests—as so often happens with debates about politics, governance, or public management—that we can find prima facie arguments and plausible examples of cases where BA strategies might be positive, negative, or neutral for AEG. That conclusion is reminiscent of Aristotle's argument that each of the three basic types of rule he identified (a millennium and a half before Vincent de Gournay added bureaucracy as a fourth type) could potentially take negative or positive forms. So how can we tell which is which? Here are two ways of thinking about that.

First, following a familiar line of analysis in social science, is to see the link between BA strategies and AEG as mediated by social context or culture. The difference between the positive, negative, or neutral effects would then be sought in the attitudes and beliefs of officeholders and those who hold them accountable, and in the congruence or lack of it between the two. There-

Table 10.2

Good and Bad Blame Avoidance? Some Hypothesized Links between BA and AEG

		Three AEG-related features		
Three broad types of BA strategy	Two variants of each broad type	Sharpening policy argument	Making policy or administrative responsibility clearer	Aligning behavior of officeholder agents with voter and legislator principals
Agency strategies	Hard delegation	? +	+	( )
	Soft/complex delegation	( )	–	( )
Presentational strategies	Winning the argument	+	( )	?+
	Changing the subject	–	( )	?–
Policy strategies	Defensive nonprovision of service	?+	+	?–
	Herd operational tactics	( )	–	( )

Key: Hypothesized links between BA and AEG:
+   Likely to be positive
?+   Possibly positive
–   Likely to be negative
?–   Possibly negative
( )   Probably neutral

fore, identifying "the wrong sort of blame avoidance" takes us into institutional analyses that distinguish between first-order and second-order types of value change in institutions[5] and that explore the effects of the same institutional forms in different social contexts. The idea that culture determines whether the "sign" of BA for AEG is positive, negative, or neutral has much to be said for it, though such an approach is notoriously hard to turn into institutional remedies or policy prescriptions (other than the often unhelpful prescription that the best thing is to have the right kind of culture). After all, Onora O'Neill's (2002, 2006) well-known argument that transparency can undermine AEG when it leads to a check-box mentality and the one-way communication so often found in organizational web sites rests on an assumed culture of blame and fear that produces these outcomes. But such cultures are not necessarily universal.

A second approach, not fully separable from the first, is to hold the cultural conditions constant and think of each of the three domains of BA considered here as containing potentially positive AEG-enhancing variants as well as negative AEG-undermining variants. The analytic task then becomes one of identifying which variants are positive or negative. Table 10.2 offers a simple analysis of that kind, by identifying three possible AEG-related effects of BA behavior discussed earlier. They are: sharpening argumentation over policy and officeholder conduct, clarifying responsibility for action, and—with a more tenuous link to accountability as conventionally defined—aligning the behavior of officeholder agents with voter or legislator principals. Table 10.2 identifies two variants of the three types of BA strategy and explores the relationship between the two.

For agency BA strategies, Table 10.2 distinguishes between the sort of "hard" delegation that involves a clear-cut division of responsibilities and substantial institutional distance between the delegator and the delegate, and "soft" delegation that involves fuzzy or plastic division of responsibilities (e.g., in partnership arrangements) and little institutional distance between the delegator and the delegate. Fuzzy or clear-cut division of responsibilities will depend on the complexity and ambiguity of delegation or task sharing. Institutional distance between delegator and delegate will depend on the ease of revocability of the delegation arrangement and the ease with which the delegator can steer the activity of the delegate by appointments, formal directions, or informal influence.[6] We might expect the former type of BA agency strategy to be more likely than the latter to have positive effects on the second AEG dimension identified in Table 10.2 (making responsibility clearer).

For presentational BA strategies, Table 10.2 distinguishes between variants that focus on winning arguments (by showing that whatever officeholders are being accused of is either bogus or justifiable in some way) and those that focus on changing the subject in order to move attention of voters, legislators, or other accountability forums onto other issues ("losing the tabloids," in the language of British spin doctoring). The first set of variants uses approaches such as problem denial (showing either that there is no problem or that the problem is being exaggerated for some reason); selective presentation of the facts—as in Paul Flynn's quip that under Tony Blair's New Labour regime, the future was always the same, but the past kept changing (1999, 24); excuses offered in mitigation (such as "no one told me"); and justificatory arguments designed to show that what is considered blameworthy is in fact a blessing in disguise. The second set of variants uses approaches such as creating or exploiting diversions (finding good days to bury bad news);[7] putting backdoor pressure on the media; or simply "lying low" or refusing to engage in discussion of the subject in the hope that another issue will soon capture public attention. Whereas the former set of variants can at least sometimes serve to sharpen AEG arguments, the latter seems much more likely to have the opposite effect.

With regard to BA policy strategies, Table 10.2 distinguishes between the defensive approach that concentrates on not operating or providing services that potentially attract blame (for instance advice services or risky leisure or transport services) and defensiveness that concentrates on "herd" policy procedures (such as group styles of working, collective decisions in which individuals are not responsible, or "double blind" grading procedures so often found in the academic world). The former approach involves a decision on whether to operate or offer services based on a calculation of blame avoidance versus credit claiming, whereas the latter involves finding ways of providing potentially blameworthy services in such a way that those making the key decisions are not individually identifiable. Whereas the former variant might in some conditions to be associated with clarity of responsibility (even though in some cases it may run counter to the preferences of voters or legislators), the latter variant seems more likely to have the opposite effect.

CONCLUSION

Three broad conclusions can be drawn from this discussion, limited and tentative as it is. First, the analysis suggests that, indeed, links exist between BA and AEG (even though those topics are typically discussed at "separate tables" in political science, as noted at the outset), and that in spite of the generally bad press BA gets, those links are unlikely to be universally positive, negative, or neutral. Different "signs" are likely to manifest for different kinds of links, which raises questions about what exactly determines the sign of the type of relationship between BA and AEG.

Second, there is much more to be said and known than a short essay can cover. This chapter has been confined to concepts and categories rather than detailed analysis of empirical cases, and even then the conceptual analysis has been kept simple, by looking at only three main types of BA strategies (each of which has itself been quite sketchily described) and only two variants of each of those strategies. Many more variants of each of the three types of strategies exist and can be discussed in a longer account. For instance, for BA agency strategies, we focused mainly on delegation rather than the commonly observed phenomenon of defensive reorganizations. For presentational strategies, we have not discussed the preemptive apology approach that is central to Ed Van Thijn's engaging account of so-called sorry-democracy in the Netherlands in the 1990s (1998), which he sees as negative for "real" AEG. For BA policy strategies, we have not discussed blame-the-victim strategies, such as disclaimers and small print. Even at a conceptual level, a full development of the complex links between BA strategies and AEG would need to consider all of those important variants of BA behavior.

Third, BA strategies may of course have effects—positive or negative—for the conduct of executive government and public services other than their effects on AEG. For instance, if government and policy delivery is organized according to BA agency strategies primarily aimed at muddying the waters of blame when adverse events happen, that delivery can make an organization far more costly and cumbersome than it would otherwise be. Such an organization produces duplication, unnecessarily complex structures that expend their energies in managing the ambiguities of who is responsible for what rather than concentrating on policy delivery, and endless defensive reorganizations that absorb the limited time of managers at the expense of all else. If the conduct of government and public services is dominated by presentational BA strategies that are primarily concerned with controlling the story, the result can be a stultifying centralization that slows up decision making, a blaming, bullying culture that flies in the face of conventional precepts for high-reliability organization, and a diversion of the scarce time of top-level leaders away from other activities in which they might be engaged—such as actually running their organizations.

Likewise, if the conduct of government and public services is dominated by policy strategies designed to avoid the provision of services (such as advice), that could lead to blame over risk or error or to adopting defensive procedures to ensure that any blame is transferred to users or clients. These strategies may result in sacrificing what the most vulnerable individuals want or need in favor of what will protect the service providers, or may transfer responsibility for risk to those who are worst-placed to bear that responsibility on grounds of information and resources.

Such questions are undoubtedly important for matters of justice and efficiency, and indeed are central to modern debates about the conduct and organization of government. But even for those cases where BA strategy is positive for AEG (for example the "protocolization" variant of BA policy strategies that involves playing everything by the book so that there is always an audit trail or alibi when issues of blame arise), it remains an open question as to whether those positive BA-AEG combinations are positive for good government in some broader sense. The problematic link between accountability and the quality of government is the subject of a developing literature of its own (see for instance Dubnick 2005) and is discussed in some of the other chapters in this volume, but such issues go beyond the scope of this essay.

NOTES

1. For negativity bias, see for instance Baumeister et al. 2001 and Lau 1985.

2. Nor is the beguiling logic of such behavior confined to the accountability strategies of legislative committees. Central progress-chasing units within executive government, such as Tony Blair's Prime Minister's Delivery Unit, often find themselves following a similar logic, when they focus their own limited attention on the hard or troublesome organizations at the bottom of league tables or that are "failing" in other ways. Politicians who use media monitoring to hold officeholders accountable will also often tend to be biased toward dramatic examples of failures rather than pay attention to less newsworthy instances of quiet progress or achievement.

3. Politicians who practice the fire-alarm strategy as AEG may well be among those who castigate

bureaucrats for excessive risk aversion, but that is precisely the kind of behavior that their AEG strategies will tend to encourage.

4. This type of risk bias is also more just when viewed from the political-theory viewpoint that sees avoidance of harm as more important than the promotion of other kinds of benefit. That view is reflected in Jeremy Bentham's (1962, vol. 1, 301) famous dictum that: "the care of providing for his enjoyments ought to be left almost entirely to each individual; the principal function of government being to protect him from sufferings."

5. On first- and second-order change in institutions see, for instance, Levy 1986 or Laughlin 1991.

6. Thus institutional distance will depend on whether delegation is to nonelected or nonjudicial bodies whose composition the delegator can readily determine or alter, to agencies with statutory independence in which changes in appointments require legislative time to reverse, or to constitutionally entrenched agencies (such as law courts or elected authorities) that need even bigger legislative coalitions to dislodge or alter them.

7. See Kurtz (1998, 224) on the use of this tactic by the Clinton spin machine in the 1990s and McLean and Johnes (2000, 737–38) for the creation of diversions by the Liberal government of the United Kingdom in 1912 to draw attention away from the role of the British Board of Trade in certifying the *Titanic* as seaworthy in spite of its insufficient number of lifeboats.

REFERENCES

Almond, Gabriel A. 1988. "Separate Tables: Schools and Sects in Political Science." *PS: Political Science and Politics* 21 (4): 828–42.

Baumeister, Roy F., Ellen Bratslavsky, Catrin Finkenauer, and Kathleen D. Vohs. 2001. "Bad Is Stronger than Good." *Review of General Psychology* 5 (4): 323–70.

Bentham. Jeremy. 1962. *The Works of Jeremy Bentham* (Bowring ed), Book II. New York: Russell and Russell.

Bovens, Mark. 2005. "Public Accountability." In *The Oxford Handbook of Public Management,* ed. Ewan Ferlie, Laurence Lynn, and Christopher Pollitt. Oxford: Oxford University Press, 182–208.

Dubnick, Melvin J. 2005. "Accountability and the Promise of Performance: In Search of the Mechanisms." *Public Performance and Management Review* 28 (3): 376–417.

Flynn, Paul. 1999. *Dragons Led by Poodles: The Inside Story of a New Labour Stitch-Up.* London: Politico's.

Hegel, Georg W.F. 1896. *Philosophy of Right, trans. of Grundlinien* der Philosophie des Rechts by Samuel W Dyde. London: George Bell and Sons.

Hood, Christopher. 2002. "The Risk Game and the Blame Game." *Government and Opposition* 37: 15–37.

Hood, Christopher, Will Jennings, Ruth Dixon, and Brian Hogwood, with Craig Beeston. 2009. "Testing Times: Exploring Staged Responses and the Impact of Blame Management Strategies in Two Exam Fiasco Cases" *European Journal of Political Research* 48 (6): 695–722.

Hood, John. 2005. *Selling the Dream: Why Advertising Is Good Business.* New York: Praeger.

Jones, Nicholas.1999. *Sultans of Spin.* London: Gollancz.

———. 1996. *Soundbites and Spin Doctors: How Politicians Manipulate the Media—and Vice Versa.* London, UK: Indigo.

Kurtz, Howard. 1998. *Spin Cycle: Inside The Clinton Propaganda Machine.* New York: Free Press.

Lau, Richard R. 1985. "Two Explanations for Negativity Effects in Political Behavior." *American Journal of Political Science* 29 (1): 119–38.

Laughlin, Richard. 1991. "Environmental Disturbances and Organizational Transitions and Transformations: Some Alternative Models." *Organization Studies* 12 (2): 209–32.

Levy, Amir. 1986. "Second-Order Planned Change: Definition and Conceptualization." *Organizational Dynamics* 15 (1): 5–23.

Machiavelli, Niccolò. 1961. *The Prince, trans.* George Bull. Harmondsworth, UK: Penguin.

McCubbins, Matthew D., and Thomas Schwartz. 1984. "Congressional Oversight Overlooked: Police Patrols versus Fire Alarms." *American Journal of Political Science* 28: 165–79.

McGivern, Gerry, and Ewan Ferlie. 2007. "Playing Tick-Box Games: Interrelating Defences in Professional Appraisal. *Human Relations* 60 (9): 1361–85.

McLean, Iain, and Martin Johnes. 2000. "'Regulation Run Mad': The Board of Trade and the Loss of the Titanic." *Public Administration* 78 (4): 729–49.

Oborne, Peter. 1999. *Alastair Campbell: New Labour and the Rise of the Media Class.* London: Aurum.

O'Neill, Onora. 2006. "Transparency and the Ethics of Communication." In *Transparency: The Key to Better Government,* ed. Christopher Hood and David Heald. Oxford: British Academy/Oxford University Press, 75–90.

———. 2002. *A Question of Trust* (The 2002 Reith Lectures). Cambridge: Cambridge University Press.

Prat, Andrea. 2005. "The Wrong Kind of Transparency." *American Economic Review* 95 (3): 862–77.

Rose, Richard. 1990. "Inheritance before Choice in Public Policy." *Journal of Theoretical Politics* 2 (3): 263–91.

Shrader-Frechette, Kristin. 1991. *Risk and Rationality,* Berkeley: University of California Press.

Sulitzeanu-Kenan, Raanan, and Christopher Hood. 2005. "Blame Avoidance with Adjectives? Motivation, Opportunity, Activity and Outcome." Paper presented at the European Consortium of Political Research Joint Sessions, Granada, Spain, April 14–20.

U.S. Congress, Office of Technology Assessment. 1994. *Defensive Medicine and Medical Malpractice.* OTA-H-602. Washington, DC: U.S. Government Printing Office.

U.S. Congressional Budget Office. 2004. "The Cyclically Adjusted and Standardized Budget Measures," Table A.1. http//www.cbo.gov/Spreadsheet/5163_Data.xls.

van Thijn, Ed A. 1998. *De Sorry-Democratie: Recente Politieke Affaires en de Ministeriële Verantwoordelijkheid (The Sorry Democracy).* Amsterdam: Van Gennep.

Weaver, R. Kent. 1986. "The Politics of Blame Avoidance." *Journal of Public Policy* 6: 371–98.

———. 1988. *Automatic Government: The Politics of Indexation.* Washington, DC: Brookings Institution Press.

11

THE CHALLENGES OF ACCOUNTABILITY FOR INTERNATIONAL NONGOVERNMENTAL AND CIVIL-SOCIETY ORGANIZATIONS

MARGARET P. KARNS, TIMOTHY J. SHAFFER, AND RICHARD K. GHERE

The growth of nongovernmental organizations (NGOs) and NGO networks in the 1990s was a major factor in their increasing activity at all levels of human society and governance from the global to national and local levels. These private, voluntary organizations are generally formed by individuals or associations to achieve a common purpose. Some advocate a particular cause such as human rights, peace, or environmental protection. Others are established to provide disaster relief, humanitarian aid in war-torn countries, or development aid. The literature on NGOs generally distinguishes between not-for-profit groups (the great majority) and for-profit corporations. In reality terrorist and liberation groups, as well as drug cartels and crime syndicates, are also NGOs, but they represent the "dark side" of the phenomenon and, therefore, are usually studied separately. Exclusively national NGOs are estimated to number over 26,000, and grassroots organizations number in the millions. Truly international NGOs (INGOs) are identified by the nature of their membership or their commitment to conduct activities in several countries. The *Yearbook of International Organizations* identifies approximately 6,000 such INGOs currently. Examples of large INGOs include the International Federation of the Red Cross and Red Crescent Societies, Oxfam, CARE, Doctors without Borders, Transparency International, Greenpeace, and Amnesty International.

In some settings, NGOs have taken on many of the public functions in weak, inept, or failed states—in this regard, Bangladesh is a particularly good example. It hosts the largest NGO sector in the world (over 19,000 by one count), responding to what one Bangladeshi describes as "the failure of government to provide public goods and look after the poor, and the failure of the private sector to provide enough gainful employment opportunities" (quoted in Waldman 2003, A8). NGOs have taken on roles in education, health, agriculture, and microcredit, all of which were originally government functions. Some attribute the decline of Bangladesh's poverty rate since 1971 from 70 percent to 43 percent to this non-state sector.

Regarding accountability, NGOs are not necessarily subject to the same provisions and checks that constrain governmental bureaucracies. Nonetheless, they are answerable to an array of stakeholders, such as boards of governors or executive committees; to the general members (if they are membership organizations); to governments in countries where they operate; to the people (both recipients and non-recipients of the benefits and services provided); and to the donors that provide resources. Yet it is important to note that "accountability" has many different connotations and meanings (Karim 1996, 139). Lee (2004, 3) suggests that "their [that is, NGOs'] commitment, values and good intentions . . . [is no longer] a sufficient basis for accountability." Rapid growth, increased funds, and increased power heighten concerns for accountability in NGOs. With the measures to demonstrate accountability, NGOs stand to benefit from an increase in trust and commitment from stakeholders, increased organizational performance and learning, and the ability to counter criticisms that NGOs are secretive and undemocratic (Lee 2004, 7).

This chapter includes a case study of PROSHIKA—a large NGO committed to the social and political empowerment of Bangladesh's poor—to illustrate the accountability environment of the NGO sector. First, we develop an NGO accountability framework that connects a managed-expectations approach (Romzek and Dubnick 1987) with national legitimacy concerns and with subsequent boundary-spanning and decision-making capabilities. Second, we use the case study to illustrate how PROSHIKA's accountability environment changes as that NGO takes on new programmatic missions. Finally, we review the accountability environment of PROSHIKA within the contours of the framework introduced.

MANAGING EXPECTATIONS IN NONGOVERNMENTAL ORGANIZATIONS

This section lays out a framework for understanding NGO accountability as a complex array of diverse expectations converging within the nexus between state legitimacy and NGO activities, particularly those promoting social change.

Romzek and Dubnick's inquiry into the "lessons from the 1986 Challenger tragedy" (1987) focuses on alternative approaches for managing diverse expectations within a public-sector context. These scholars understand that accountability questions—even those appearing to hinge upon narrow technical and managerial questions—need broader scrutiny within the context of a wider social system. To Romzek and Dubnick, accountability in the public sector extends beyond technical and managerial "answerability" to the institutional question "involv[ing] the means by which public agencies and their workers manage the diverse expectations generated within and outside the organization" (228). They identify alternative systems for managing diverse expectations as dependent upon two interrelated control issues: (1) whether the ability to define and control expectations resides within or outside the organization and (2) "the degree of control that entity is given over defining those agency's expectations" (228). Thus, four alternative systems emerge—bureaucratic, legal, professional, and political.

Romzek and Dubnick's institutional perspective appears especially helpful in understanding the cross-pressures of stakeholder demands exerted on NGOs assuming particular roles in a variety of settings. Specifically, this expectation management approach moves past the futility of asking if a particular NGO "is accountable" with a simple "yes" or "no," depending upon the stakeholder, circumstance, definition of accountability, and so forth—to questions of how a diversity of expectations are mediated around the NGO's mission and role. Edwards and Hulme (1996a, 259–260) in fact conclude in their edited book titled *Beyond the Magic Bullet* that the "the management of accountability" is a key theme that emerges in studying NGOs. This approach extends the accountability question beyond reaction to imposed demands, standards, and constraints to proactive initiatives of strategic action. As Biggs and Neame suggest, "It might seem that the more accountable NGOs are, the less autonomy they have. Pure autonomy and multiple accountability are clearly incompatible. However, by increasing the number and types of arenas in which NGOs are accountable, they may create greater room to maneuver as they gain spheres in which to negotiate" (1996, 48–49).

The following assesses some selected topics addressed in an emerging literature on NGO accountability—stakeholders, performance criteria, functional versus strategic accountability, hemispheric region, the New Policy Agenda, internal structure and roles, and self-regulation.

Stakeholders

NGOs need to manage the expectations of a diverse array of constituents, support groups, and regulating authorities—each with varying capacities to demand and appraise reports and information, as well as impose sanctions on NGOs. Edwards and Hulme (1996b, 10) list the following among that stakeholder mix: (1) beneficiaries and members, (2) trustees, (3) private contributors, (4) NGO networks, (5) nations, (6) donors, and (7) other supporting (funding) NGOs. Clearly some of these constituents reside outside the host nation, while others represent regime authorities and beneficiary groups within that setting.

Performance Criteria

Accountability typically presupposes tangible definitions and standards of performance. Nonetheless, ideas about NGO performance can be ambiguous as well as contestable within the cross-pressures of expectations from multiple stakeholders. For example, investors may demand productivity in terms of output-cost ratios; host nations may expect conformity with regime laws and agendas; and beneficiaries and/or mission-committed contributors may seek out evidence of results as desired change or improvement from the status quo. To the extent that improvement is understood as social or political change (for example, democratization), adverse reaction might be anticipated on the part of governmental authorities.

Functional versus Strategic Accountability

According to Avina (1993), NGO accountability can be differentiated between functional reporting on resource use and short-term outcomes and longer-term impacts that affect the wider environment. Performance as impact, as assessed by *strategic accountability,* contends with the reality of pertinent forces outside of NGOs' control. To the extent that strategic accountability informs subsequent NGO action, impact studies imply that the NGO benefits from some "negotiating room [in which] to maneuver" (Biggs and Neame 1996, 40–52) or "insulation" to facilitate learning from the process of being held accountable.

Hemispheric Region

The NGO literature differentiates between Northern and Southern NGOs, a distinction related to the geographic base of most large international NGOs in developed or northern hemisphere countries. First, Northern NGOs (such as Oxfam USA or CARE International) often function as donor agencies that disburse funds for particular projects (for example, rural development) undertaken by Southern NGOs, typically in less developed settings. As Chambers (1996) points out, both the Northern disbursement and the Southern recipient/project implementation suggest actions that presumably attest to "appropriate" performance. For example, Northern donor organizations want to be seen as actively disbursing money, rather than having it languish in banks. Thus, the donor's need to move money places pressure on recipient NGOs to show timely results, irrespective of critical timing and other strategic considerations that impinge on the recipient's program activities. Chambers details how the interplay between donor and recipient performance imperatives result in hierarchical relationships with northern NGOs usually at the top. Nonetheless, recipients may willingly assume this subservient role in seeking out readily available dollars to underwrite their efforts (Edward and Hulme 1996b, 6).

New Policy Agenda

Much as the New Public Management influences contemporary public administration, the New Policy Agenda (NPA) affects the rationales for funding some NGO projects as well as the accountability standards placed upon them. In essence, these Northern donor agencies base their funding decisions on how NGOs contribute to "good governance" and market efficiency. As Edwards and Hulme (1996b) explain, the neoliberal thrust of the NPA encourages NGOs to assume economic roles as "efficient providers of services" and political agents of democratization. In some cases, the NPA attempts to characterize NGOs as "more efficient providers" of services than counterpart governmental agencies. Such a rationale is clearly consistent with an ideological preference by which "leaner" governments are assumed better able to compete in the global market. The NPA's preference for leaner government and its claim that NGOs should act as agents of democratization may complicate Southern NGO project initiatives to promote social and political mobilization in particular settings. From an accountability standpoint, good governance imperatives impose (what Edwards and Hulme refer to as) accountancy standards—in essence, business control systems—rather than impact accountability that assesses project effectiveness (Edwards and Hulme 1996b, 6).

Internal Structure and Roles

Those who serve in organizations are typically held accountable by upper-level managers and executives. Nonetheless, those individuals should be understood as internal stakeholders whose efforts and conduct have direct impacts upon organizational performance and legitimacy. Of particular significance in project-oriented NGOs are fieldworkers who directly interact with those served, often poor and in remote locales. One account characterizes fieldworkers in a southern setting as "underpaid, undervalued, overworked, and unappreciated" (Ahmad 2007, 349). As Ahmad notes, strongly motivated field workers can stimulate client satisfaction. On the other hand, those engaging in corrupt practices or showing indifference to the poor can undermine NGO legitimacy (351).

Self-Regulation

NGO efforts toward self-regulation often involve developing codes of conduct or ethics for individuals and/or organizations either within national settings or partnership associations. Antöv et al. discuss the efforts of the Agency for Research, Education, Economic and Social Development in Indonesia to establish an NGO umbrella organization as a platform for a code of ethics (2007, 157), and Karim tells of the Association of Development Agencies in Bangladesh undertaking similar activities (1996, 134–35). Difficulties in interorganizational consensus building can lead to minimal standards that counteract the intent to gain legitimacy through self-regulation. Callamard chronicles the efforts of Humanitarian Project International (2007, 184–86), which involved identifying the following elements in determining some common principles for self-regulation: Who is accountable? To whom? For what? How? And for what outcome?

Together, these questions coax out an array of institutional pressures on various NGOs that in turn account for diverse expectations placed upon them. Romzek and Dubnick's accountability perspective asserts that public organizations prioritize among alternative accountability mechanisms in accommodating the particular mix of demands they confront. Table 11.1 depicts how the variables discussed above activate varying accountability systems as a means of managing

Table 11.1

Romzek and Dubnick's Four Accountability Systems Related to Selected NGO Issues

Selected NGO variables	Alternative accountability systems			
	Bureaucratic	Legal	Professional	Political
Performance	Investor, donor demands for productivity	Regulation by host (government) regime		Responsiveness to direct program beneficiaries
Functional vs. strategic accountability	Functional: Need to report on resource use and short-term impacts		Strategic: Need to reassess direction to make long-term impacts vis-à-vis forces outside NGO control; need to maintain negotiating room in which to maneuver	
North/South; New policy agenda	Need to impose management control systems to report on services "shed" by government			NGOs pressured to assume "third sector" roles
Internal structure and roles	"Northern" NGOs, top executives in "Southern" NGOs focus on "accountancy," reporting systems	Some roles (particularly in field work) subject to government regulation	Need for codes of conduct, principles of practice (especially for field workers); training important	Employee (especially field worker) conduct a determinant of NGO legitimacy
Self-regulation				Associational consensus on accountability standards; practice supports NGO's legitimacy

Source: Barbara S. Romzek and Melvin J. Dubnick (1987).

expectations. It shows, for example, the underlying tension (particularly acute among Southern, grassroots organizations) between pressures to impose hierarchal (bureaucratic) control systems to satisfy investors or donor organizations and the need for political accountability—that is, the need to be mission responsive to project beneficiaries and other committed constituents. This tension becomes all the more pronounced in an era of good governance (as manifested in the New Policy Agenda) that in some cases expects NGOs to replace supposedly "inefficient" government agencies as direct providers of services. Such pressures to assume loads shed by government agencies are accompanied by expectations that NGOs will institute business-like control systems.

Second, Table 11.1 suggests that program-implementing NGOs need to offset bureaucratic "accountancy" pressures to maintain sufficient "insulation" (Johnson 2008) or "maneuvering room" (Biggs and Neame 1996) for subsequent action in pursuit of mission legitimacy. Although these demands place priority on political accountability, they also direct attention to professionalism, the support for self-regulation, and support for institutionalizing good practices in the field. And third, Table 11.1 stresses legal accountability that, although pertinent generally, takes on primacy where NGO operations potentially conflict with regime values, which can lead to aggressive government regulations and perhaps sanctions. In summary, we assert that Romzek and Dubnick's managed-expectation perspective accentuates the diversity of institutional pressures NGOs confront as well as the various types of accountability systems for managing those pressures.

LEGITIMACY ISSUES AND ACCOUNTABILITY EXPECTATIONS

Since Romzek and Dubnick develop their accountability perspective within a singular sociopolitical context—that is, the American political system—there is little discussion in their work of how accountability systems relate to matters of political legitimacy in varied national settings. As applied to NGOs, their perspective raises questions regarding the linkages between political legitimacy (whether based on national regime values, global good-governance agendas, or some other authority) and priorities among alternative accountability systems. In the introductory chapter of their edited volume, *NGO Accountability,* Jordan and van Tuijl present a "short history of NGO accountability . . . [in terms of] an evolving set of syllogisms that outline the prevailing perception of NGO roles, roughly in the last 25 years" (2007, 9–13).

Table 11.2 characterizes Jordan and Van Tuijl's syllogisms as legitimating varying logics of appropriateness that emphasize certain of Romzek and Dubnick's accountability systems over others. For example, syllogisms 1 and 2 (complementing government and the rise of civil society, respectively), both derived from neoliberal ideology, demand bureaucratic accountability mechanisms, albeit somewhat differently. In the first case, it is reasoned that NGOs (preferable to government agencies) should administer public services shed from government and that their accountability obligations should primarily focus on financial reporting. The second line of neoliberal thinking presumes NGOs are good engines for building democratic capacity and therefore views accountability in the establishment of good-governance structures and processes within NGOs.

In contrast to the second, syllogism 3 emphasizes good-government outcomes more than form and process. As Jordan and van Tuijl note, this thinking provoked "a more heated discourse on NGO accountability" that pitted self-regulation and accreditation (professional accountability systems) against imperatives for management controls and governance structures. "The return to state supremacy" (syllogism 4) constitutes a state-centered reaction to increased NGO autonomy through self-regulation, which thereby imposes legal accountability to governmental authority. Finally, a "rights-based approach" (syllogism 5) focuses on balancing stakeholder interests of

Table 11.2

Contextual Logics of Accountability Legitimizing or Prioritizing Alternative Accountability Systems

Syllogisms	Jordan and Van Tuijl's syllogisms[a] related to Romzek and Dubnick's accountability systems[b]				
	(1) Complementing government (1980–1989)	(2) The rise of civil society (1989–1995)	(3) The rise of good governance (1995–2002)	(4) The return to state supremacy (2002 onward)	(5) A rights-based approach (2002 onward)
Logic of argument	1. Governments are not good at delivering public services.	1. Civil society is necessary for democracy.	1. Good governance is necessary for development.	1. Government is essential to ensure safety and development.	1. There is no democratic global governance supporting universal human rights.
	2. NGOs are closer to the public.	2. NGOs are civil society.	2. NGOs are not different from other organizations in civil society.	2. NGOs' influence is not in proportion to their credentials.	2. NGOs assert and solidify human rights in different political arenas, regardless of governance.
	3. NGOs are good at delivering public services.	3. NGOs are good for democratic development.	3. NGOs need to apply principles of good governance.	3. NGOs need to be kept in check by legitimate government frameworks.	3. NGOs contribute to democratic governance by articulating public policy needs and practicing solutions to resolve public needs.
Alternative accountability system	Bureaucratic		Professional	Legal	Political

[a]Lisa Jordan and Peter van Tuijl (2007).
[b]Barbara S. Romzek and Melvin J. Dubnick (1987).

multiple constituencies, thus stressing political accountability mechanisms as especially vital. In summary, the multiplicity of settings emerging from inquiry into NGO accountability encourage "a step back" from the question of appropriate systems for managing expectations to the consideration of varying logics of legitimacy that support accountability mechanisms.

MANAGING ACCOUNTABILITY AND SUBSEQUENT STRATEGY

Obligations of accountability are typically understood as constraints upon action in the public sector. Although valid to a point, such thinking tends to understate the inherent complexity of public matters, complexity that necessitates successive iterations of adjustment—often referred to as "boundary spanning." This idea implies that program implementation rarely flows from the straightforward execution of tasks in furtherance of a preestablished goal, but rather as a continuous mission-refining process (see Thompson and McEwan 1958). Adjustment depends upon the accurate reading of cues from the environment as stimuli for mission refinement. In this regard, an NGO's assessment of its various accountability obligations constitutes a key step in boundary spanning, or, more specifically, its ongoing strategic-management process. Specifically, accountability matters need consideration as risks (as well as opportunities) in both mission setting and decision making that guides implementation. Such overt political roles necessitate organizational learning processes that factor in accountability dilemmas among stakeholder (the state, donor agencies, beneficiaries) expectations—expectations that pit risks against impact opportunities in the strategic-management process.

Thus, NGO accountability can be assessed in terms of an elongated model of three components:

1. State and/or societal legitimacy as the source or sources of compelling accountability mechanisms
2. The management of expectations and demands among those mechanisms (in essence, the Romzek and Dubnick model)
3. Concern for how management of expectations informs strategy and action

THE CASE OF BANGLADESH AND PROSHIKA

Bangladesh stands out as a comparatively small nation where nearly 23,000 registered NGOs, including some of the largest INGOs in the world, are active in affecting Bangladeshi society. These NGOs must be registered by the NGO Affairs Bureau (NAB), the government agency charged with controlling NGOs operating in Bangladesh with foreign funds (Karim 1996, 133). Since the NGO presence is so pervasive here as to threaten governmental authority (see Haque 2002), Bangladesh offers a particularly good setting for examining diverse accountability expectations placed on NGOs.

Historical Background

Pakistan was formed as a new country when India gained its independence from Great Britain in 1947. Given tensions between Hindus and Muslims, the two states were formed as a compromise, with India remaining populated primarily by Hindus and Pakistan primarily by Muslims. The new Pakistan, however, had two parts—east and west—separated by more than 1,000 miles as well as language and cultural differences. The former East Pakistan gained its independence with India's help following the 1971 war with Pakistan. At independence, Bangladesh became one of the world's poorest nations and was regarded by many at the time as an "international basket case." Many of the issues still being addressed today by NGOs and INGOs operating in Bangladesh have very clear roots in the struggle for independence in 1971. With the creation of this new state, efforts were taken to provide medical and other humanitarian services to refugees across the border in India as well as within the country to help address the suffering of war. Several relief and rehabilitation programs were started both with and without international assistance. This alternative-relief process then led to development initiatives that are still apparent with the tremendous number of both NGOs (local and national) and INGOs operating in Bangladesh. In the mid-1990s, NGOs in Bangladesh operated in "more than 50 percent of all villages in the country, involving over 3.5 million families as beneficiaries of their work" (Karim 1996, 132). The country's geographic location also makes it extremely vulnerable to natural disasters that produce flooding, massive loss of life, and displacement of thousands. This reality has reinforced the continuing need for international relief aid and the presence of relief organizations. In addition, Bangladesh is a vibrant democratic society, and that has encouraged the growth of grassroots groups.

NGOs in Bangladesh are almost totally dependent on foreign financing and have garnered an increasing share of total foreign assistance to Bangladesh as shown in Figure 11.1. The total aid to NGOs rose from an average of $232 million between 1990 and 1995 to $326 million between 1996 and 2004, while the total aid to Bangladesh fell from an annual average of $1.62 billion to $1.35 billion during this period. Thus the share of aid to NGOs as a portion of total aid to Bangladesh has risen from 14.4 percent in the early 1990s to 24.5 percent since then as shown in Figure 11.1 (Zaman et al. 2005). The role of NGOs in Bangladesh therefore continues to expand into areas where typically government would respond, such as education and economic development. Increasingly, some NGOs in Bangladesh are acting as political entities (Ahmed and Potter 2006, 128–30).

The delicate balance of power between governments and NGOs in nations such as Bangladesh highlights the growing influence of the NGO sector in terms of "societal roles, public image, and [the] capacity to command external support" (Haque 2002, 412). While the elected governmental officials are accountable to the Bangladeshi public, large NGOs have obligations "mainly to the multilateral institutions, bilateral agencies, and private foundations financing their activities" (426). Additionally, NGO accountability becomes problematic with the growing monopoly of "a few large NGOs in terms of membership, loans, revenues, and funds." Haque contends that the monopolistic nature of these large NGOs "makes them too powerful for their poor and powerless members to hold their NGOs accountable to them" (426). That is to say, as small NGOs mature into larger entities, the connection with those they seek to serve becomes diminished as heightened attention to internal organizational issues displace member participation as a matter of concern. Building on the work of Hulme and Edwards, Haque notes the importance of not "overemphasizing the contribution of NGOs to society while overlooking the vested interests behind the 'big business' of NGOs" (429). It therefore becomes important for the state to closely scrutinize foreign linkages and funding sources of NGOs and to ensure that NGOs comply with national rules for dealing with external forces such as foreign assistance agencies.

The Inception of PROSHIKA

In 1976, in a few villages in the Dhaka and Comilla districts, PROSHIKA (a center for human development) was established by a group of social workers to (1) reduce poverty, (2) protect and regenerate the environment, (3) improve the status of women, (4) increase participation in public institutions, and (5) enhance people's capacity to gain and exercise their democratic and human rights. To achieve its goals, PROSHIKA has implemented a wide range of activities geared toward

Figure 11.1 **External Aid to Bangladesh**

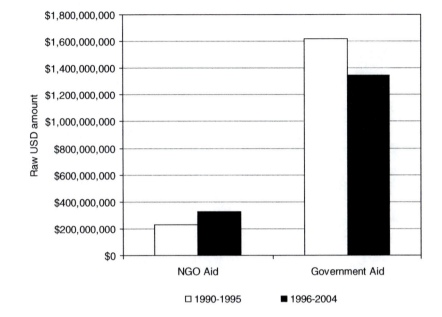

facilitating people's access to public resources, services, and institutions with the hope these steps will lead to self-reliance (Karim 1996, 135). All PROSHIKA programs are rooted in the People's Organization Building Programme, the tactical core of its outreach activities. The poor people living in rural and urban areas are encouraged to organize themselves into primary groups popularly known as samitis and to form group federations at village, union, and upazila (subdistrict) levels, for the purpose of building a broad organizational network. The process constitutes the basis of participatory development and spurs the acquisition and strengthening of human, socioeconomic, and cultural resource bases of the poor. Table 11.3 shows how PROSHIKA attempts to accomplish its goals through the People's Organization Building Programme.

To date, 149,016 primary groups have been formed with 97,562 of these being women's groups. This number of primary groups is up from 41,205 in 1996. There are currently 18,231 group federations. According to statistics reported by PROSHIKA, work is taking place in more than 24,139 villages and 2,108 slums, up from 6,006 villages and 108 slums in 1996—a considerable increase in little more than a decade. Additionally, the number of districts in which PROSHIKA operates has increased from 35 to 59 during the same period (Karim 1996, 135). Clearly, PROSHIKA continues to expand its role in both rural and urban settings by providing empowerment programs for the poor, a universal education program, and disaster-management programs (Ahmed and Potter 2006, 132). These programs are geared toward both adults and children, providing the necessary training to move individuals and families beyond a dependence on PROSHIKA and its funds.

The Internal Structure of PROSHIKA

Ahmad writes that "Although P[roshika] says that it has a democratic management system and has no system of bosses, it was found . . . that there is a hierarchy in the management of P[roshika]." And, while field workers within PROSHIKA call each other and their superiors "bhai" (brother),

Table 11.3

PROSHIKA People's Organization Building Programme

Microcredit and Saving Services: Types of Programs	Social and Natural Resource Development: Types of Programs
1. Employment and income generating	1. Human development training
2. Practical skill development training	2. Extended social and human development
3. Small enterprise development	3. External training division
4. Livestock development	4. Universal education
5. Policies for risk and vulnerability management	5. Good governance and advocacy
6. Fisheries development	6. Social forestry
7. Apiculture development	7. Health
8. Sericulture development	8. Housing
9. Organic agriculture	9. Impact evaluation and research department
10. Irrigation and farm power technology services	10. Development support communication program
11. Collaborative	11. People's culture
12. Research and demonstration project	12. Programme on liberation war
	13. PROSHIKA legal aid services
	14. Integrated multisectoral women's development
	15. Information and documentation resource cell
	16. Computer in development
	17. Disaster management and preparedness
	18. Human resource department

a hierarchical structure is also evident in the field. Specifically, field workers at the lowest level of PROSHIKA's organizational structure have commented that there are few opportunities for promotion and that a change in pay or elevation from one post to another "does not require any examinations, as promotions are on the basis of evaluation of the field workers by the area coordinator" (Ahmad 2002, 23). By contrast, field workers simply seeking a lateral change of duty (e.g., for promotion from economic development worker to training coordinator) "have to sit for a two-hour written test and face an interview." Workers also complained of irregularities in the promotion and posting system. Indeed, PROSHIKA lacked a personnel evaluation system over its first twenty years of existence, only to introduce it in 1996 after years of demands (24).

There is a clear structure within PROSHIKA beginning with field workers, and rising to area coordinators, zone coordinators, and central coordinators based out of the Dhaka office. Each level supervises and monitors the activities of those immediately below within the organization. A clear authority hierarchy can be found within the PROSHIKA organization that fosters ongoing supervision to monitor program missions and responsibilities. This type of control is fundamental in ensuring that all within PROSHIKA are working toward organizational goals and expectations. This hierarchical relationship carries over to the relationship between the field worker and clients.

Nonetheless, the nature of fieldwork and its relationship with the PROSHIKA hierarchy has undergone significant change in recent years. In 2002 Ahmad's study of field worker/client relationships among NGOs in Bangladesh found that PROSHIKA indeed ranked highest—indicating strong field-worker relationships with clients (Ahmad 2002, 120). Since then, however, the recent push for NGOs to become more involved in microcredit (as discussed next) has taken PROSHIKA away from its roots of motivating and organizing the landless poor. This shift has redirected accountability away from client empowerment and toward the financial imperatives associated with implementing its microcredit programs.

Increased Political and Social Activity

In 2002, following the general elections of October 2001, the Bangladeshi government intervened in PROSHIKA's work and halted $50 million in funds from foreign donors. The crackdown on PROSHIKA was over alleged concern that it was engaged in "antigovernment activities." PROSHIKA's president and the vice president were detained along with hundreds of PROSHIKA employees, oftentimes without being charged with any specific crime. Government officials attributed these actions to PROSHIKA's increasing involvement in mobilizing the poor toward political action. The government also charged the organization with alleged financial irregularities. Yet there were serious concerns about the lack of transparency in the investigations. Donors expressed concern to the government that they saw no grounds for blocking PROSHIKA's entire program while this investigation was carried out, as this would cut off thousands of people from assistance, but PROSHIKA's funds were not unblocked.

ROSHIKA was obliged to respond to those charges. Bangladesh's government agencies are key stakeholders in the work of PROSHIKA. In particular, the NAB (regulating NGO activities) functions as a gatekeeper between foreign donors and the NGO itself. And, due to its size and breadth of program missions, PROSHIKA functions more like a governmental entity than do most of the thousands of other grassroots organizations in Bangladesh. Haque comments that in addition to "the varieties of inputs and services related to microfinance, small industry, livestock, fisheries, sanitation, basic education, and health care . . . state monopolies are facing formidable challenges from large NGOs in areas such as printing and computer software. PROSHIKA, for example, has programs dealing with both of these areas" (Haque 2002, 420). PROSHIKA also has developed a transport company of 28 buses at a cost of 30 million taka ($437,000) in addition to a printing press and garment business at a cost of 15 million taka ($219,000) (Ahmed 2002, 13). These types of ventures blur the lines between the tax-exempt work of NGOs and the market-oriented work of private companies.

The government of Bangladesh, not surprisingly, has grown very concerned about the role and influence of PROSHIKA in the political arena. By enlisting police efforts to disrupt the NGO's work, the government can counteract PROSHIKA's efforts in heightening grassroots involvement in the political process. PROSHIKA's most recent annual report for the fiscal year of July 2007 to June 2008 addresses the effects of the government crackdown on its work. The chairman notes,

> The year 2007–2008 has been a challenging one for PROSHIKA due to the continued blockage of funds by the previous governments. Moreover, the abnormal civil rights situation due to the emergency posed serious obstacles to the implementation of some of the activities. The programme activities were implemented with PROSHIKA's own resources, and the targets were set on the basis of the cash-flow situation (PROSHIKA, 2008, Foreword).

The Impact of Microcredit

The ability to provide microcredit to individuals and families is one of the primary methods for addressing societal issues facing Bangladeshis. Indeed, microcredit was invented in Bangladesh by Mohamed Yunis who founded the Grameen Bank. As PROSHIKA has become more involved in microcredit lending, it acts more as a business than a development organization. The growth of microcredit lending requires lenders to become performance-focused to ensure that individuals are repaying their loans in a timely manner. The outcomes sought include meeting goals for the delivery of services as well as maintaining appropriate repayment schedules for microloans (Ahmed 2002, 183).

PROSHIKA has changed its system for accessing funds to safeguard against embezzlement from a group savings account by requiring field worker consent for clients' savings-account transactions—thus clients become increasingly dependent on field workers. This diminishes the empowerment that has been foundational to PROSHIKA's mission (Ahmed 2002, 159). Thus, microcredit's imperative for managerial accountability trumps PROSHIKA's long-standing mission to give the poor the ability to manage their own lives.

DISCUSSION: PROSHIKA AND THE CHALLENGES OF NGO ACCOUNTABILITY

The PROSHIKA case presents a diverse array of expectations placed on an NGO that has assumed key roles in (1) providing basic public services complementing or in lieu of those provided by the government; (2) offering means of integrating and empowering emerging civil society groups in Bangladesh; and, thereby, (3) promoting good governance that obligates PROSHIKA to model principles of transparency, financial discipline, and political responsiveness. Each of these roles raises issues of accountability as related to the broader context of political legitimacy.

Legitimacy and Accountability

PROSHIKA's roles in providing public services, promoting civil-society development, and modeling good governance both enhance and threaten the political order in Bangladesh. Indeed these three roles represent alternative logics of NGO legitimacy based upon Jordan and van Tuijl's syllogisms as represented in Table 11.2 (see columns 1, 2, and 3). To the extent that these activities could be taken as political mobilization, it is apparent that PROSHIKA challenges state supremacy (syllogism 4 in Table 11.2), a traditional interpretation of political legitimacy. Thus PROSHIKA is challenged to manage expectations in ways that recognize that its ongoing activities coincide with new logics of appropriateness that are to an extent welcomed by the state, yet also elicit aggressive state reactions in the form of NGO regulation.

Managing Expectations

Within this national context of crosscutting logics of legitimacy, PROSHIKA confronts numerous pressures. Some of these are internal to Bangladeshi society; others are products of the extensive presence of INGOs and other international donors. These pressures present a serious challenge for managing the diverse expectations of all stakeholders and must be managed by the various accountability systems in the Romzek and Dubnick (1987) typology.

Legal Accountability

PROSHIKA is registered under the Societies Registration Act of 1860 as well as with the NGO Affairs Bureau (NAB), which functions out of the prime minister's office. The NAB is the governmental agency that is charged with controlling activities of NGOs that operate with foreign funds in Bangladesh. As one considers the regulatory role the government plays in the operation of NGOs such as PROSHIKA, there is a need to recognize the power dynamic unfolding within Bangladesh between the government and NGOs with substantial financial support for their initiatives. In short, PROSHIKA is accountable to the state and must satisfy the requests of the government when it comes to issues of accountability and finances.

Professional Accountability: Self-Regulation

In 1993, the Association of Development Agencies in Bangladesh (ADAB) adopted a code of ethics as a step toward self-regulation for its member NGOs. The code was prepared in consultation with its members, which at that stage was viewed as a positive response to many of the problems confronting NGOs. The code provides a detailed framework of nonprofit sector ethics defined at four levels in relation to the poor people for whom the nonprofit sector works: the government and the state; other private, volunteer development organizations in Bangladesh; development partners (or donors); and NGO staff. In terms of commitment, the document promises high standards and practices, including self-regulation, efficiency, transparency, and accountability. It raises the importance of checks against political influences, factionalism, and divisiveness within NGOs. The code also commits NGOs to strong collaboration with the government and to an independent and transparent relationship with donors. The objectives of NGOs laid out in the code are to raise the standard of living of the poor and to help them become worthy citizens of Bangladesh. The code posits that aside from generating their own funds, NGOs can "accept resources and services from the public, the business community, the government of Bangladesh, and external development partners. But these resources are to be used exclusively for the development of the poor and not for any personal profit" (Karim 1996, 134).

Members of ADAB (PROSHIKA included) commit themselves to "working for solidarity among the poor, democratic leadership, and self-reliance, irrespective of caste, creed, religion and gender." The NGOs must also be accountable and transparent to the government with regard to their funds and activities. The code calls for "the highest standards of transparency and honesty" (Karim 1996, 134–35). Yet there are no means of ensuring compliance with all these lofty goals. No incentive system exists within the sector to encourage good practices, nor any mechanism to prevent noncompliance. Any prospect of introducing effective measures to implement such instruments and to promote internal self-governance has suffered a serious setback. Thus the code of ethics that was regarded as a means for the ADAB to have a standard for NGOs in Bangladesh functions in that capacity only as much as each NGO chooses to comply.

Multiple Stakeholders: Performance and Political Accountability

Like other NGOs PROSHIKA needs to prioritize the crosscutting expectations placed on it by its numerous stakeholders. For example, Northern donors include the World Bank, UN development agencies, major INGOs such as CARE and Oxfam, as well as the United States, the United Kingdom, the European Union, Canada, and Japan. PROSHIKA must conform to the goals and procedures of these donors in order to secure funds. Additionally, the restrictions of donor funding require proposals for work on particular issues for a particular period of time (Ahmed and Potter 2006, 136–37). Figure 11.2 illustrates the multiple levels of accountability when dealing with internal and external funding, governmental oversight, and accountability to those who are beneficiaries of the services and programs provided by PROSHIKA.

The complexity of multiple donors is part of what makes PROSHIKA an interesting NGO to probe more deeply. One example of INGOs partnering with PROSHIKA was on a project aimed at addressing the exploitation of women. Since exploitation has a central role in perpetuating poverty, PROSHIKA has a program that provides training for self-help groups as well as microcredit loans. This project included the Canadian International Development Agency (CIDA), the Netherlands Organisation for International Development Cooperation (NOVIB, which is associated with Oxfam), and the British Government's Department for International Development (DFID). Each partner had its own guidelines for how its funds were to be used and reported. This is only

Figure 11.2   **The NGO Chain: PROSHIKA's Accountability to Multiple Stakeholders**

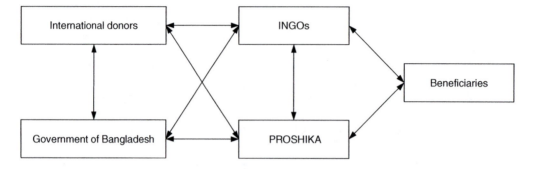

one example of how international donors and INGOs have a stake in the work of PROSHIKA, and it illustrates the challenges of accountability with multiple donors.

One of the most important means by which PROSHIKA accounts to its stakeholders is by publishing its annual report. The most recent report available on the PROSHIKA web site is for July 2007 to June 2008. As Chairman Qazi Faruque Ahmed notes in the foreword, "We take much pleasure in presenting it [the annual report] to the members of PROSHIKA, its development partners, members of civil society and all those who have inspired and stood by us in our fight against poverty" (PROSHIKA 2008, Foreword).

Although PROSHIKA's annual report includes highly detailed information regarding the programs for 2007–2008, it lacks information regarding funding and the organization's relationship with donors. Donors are able to see how financial support was channeled during the year, but they are not provided detail on funding from particular donors. This is not atypical. According to Ahmad, "Most NGOs in Bangladesh maintain a high level of secrecy about their documents, staff salary and budgets" (2002, 11). This is important to note because NGOs tend to identify themselves as participatory grassroots groups. Yet, in reality, this is an illusion (Ahmad, 2002, 11). Without access to this funding information, one can only guess about the relationships that PROSHIKA has with its donors. Still, from the standpoint of performance accountability, the activity report for PROSHIKA shows different levels of measurement for programs, ranging from the amount of income generated for the Employment and Income Generating Programme to the number of bee colonies established for the Apiculture Development Programme.

PROSHIKA is not so forthcoming about the requirements that international donors and IN-GOs place upon it in its available published reports—thus relationships between this NGO and its individual donors appear to escape scrutiny. Nevertheless, donors can track online details on objectives and implementation published by the Information and Documentation Resource Cell within PROSHIKA. That unit also publishes the annual activity report in addition to preparing six-month progress reports for PROSHIKA's governing body, senior management, and donors, detailing the accounts of achievements as well as the reasons for either over- or underachievements of all of the programs (PROSHIKA 2008).

Finally, PROSHIKA is fundamentally accountable to its beneficiaries. Through the field worker/ client relationship, PROSHIKA engages citizens and encourages them to feel empowered in order to help address societal issues that marginalize a considerable portion of the population. Yet, as has been noted, the hierarchical structure of Bangladeshi culture pervades PROSHIKA. The challenge for PROSHIKA is to allow its beneficiaries to take responsibility for their own lives and the health of their communities while also getting the support necessary to make and sustain meaningful impacts.

CONCLUSION: FROM ACCOUNTABILITY TO STRATEGY AND ACTION

Accountability for NGOs, particularly those such as PROSHIKA with many different stakeholders, is clearly challenging. Likewise, the issues may be very different in a developing country where an NGO "conglomerate" comes to be seen as a threat to the legitimacy and authority of the government because of the wide range of services it provides and roles it plays. PROSHIKA's role in promoting microcredit can be taken as a classic example of goal succession in response to several governmental reactions—which is different from its previous efforts to mobilize civil society. In essence, by emphasizing political accountability as responsiveness to program beneficiaries and donors, PROSHIKA has strained its relationship with the government of Bangladesh. The relatively recent microcredit role provides PROSHIKA with opportunities to adjust its strategy in ways that allow some room for subsequent negotiation with the government. Its new role also shifts its priorities away from the political rationales of accountability toward increased emphases on bureaucratic control and professional self-regulation. For some, these developments are troubling since it appears that PROSHIKA has abandoned its programmatic role in serving Bangladesh's poor and marginalized in favor of monitoring microcredit loan repayment. The case, therefore, also illustrates how government actions can force NGOs to reassess their strategies and tactics in reference to their understanding of the need for accountability.

REFERENCES

Ahmad, Mokbul M. 2002. *NGO Fieldworkers in Bangladesh*. Burlington, VT: Ashgate.
———. 2007. "The Careers of NGO Field-Workers in Bangladesh." *Nonprofit Management and Leadership* 17 (3): 349–65.
Ahmad, Mokbul M., and David M. Potter. 2006. *NGOs in International Politics*. Bloomfield, CT: Kumarian Press.
Antöv, Hans, Rustam Ibraham, and Peter van Tuijl. 2007. "NGO Governance and Accountability in Indonesia: Challenges in a Newly Democratizing Country." In *NGO Accountability*, ed. Lisa Jordan and Peter van Tuijl. London: Earthscan, 147–63.
Avina, Jeffrey. 1993. "The Evolutionary Life Cycle of Non-Governmental Development Organizations." *Public Administration and Development* 13 (5): 453–74.
Biggs, Stephen D., and Arthur D. Neame. 1996. "Negotiating Room to Maneuver: Reflections Concerning NGO Autonomy and Accountability Within the New Public Agenda." In *Beyond the Magic Bullet*, ed. Michael Edwards and David Hulme. West Hartford, CT: Kumarian Press, 23–39.
Callamard, Agnes. 2007. "NGO Accountability and the Humanitarian Accountability Project: Toward a Transformative Agenda." In *NGO Accountability*, ed. Lisa Jordan and Peter van Tuijl. London: Earthscan, 183–94.
Chambers, Robert. 1996. "The Primacy of the Personal." In *Beyond the Magic Bullet*, ed. Michael Edwards and David Hulme. West Hartford, CT: Kumarian Press, 241–53.
Edwards, Michael, and Hulme, David. 1996a. "Beyond the Magic Bullet: Lessons and Conclusions." In *Beyond the Magic Bullet*, ed. Michael Edwards and David Hulme. West Hartford, CT: Kumarian Press, 254–66.
———. 1996b. "Introduction: NGO performance and Accountability." *In Beyond the Magic Bullet*, ed. Michael Edwards and David Hulme. West Hartford, CT: Kumarian Press, 1–20.
Haque, M. Shamsul. 2002. "The Changing Balance of Power Between the Government and NGOs in Bangladesh." *International Political Science Review* 23 (4): 411–35.
Johnson, Tana. 2008. "The Importance of Insulation in Intergovernmental Organizations." Paper Presented at annual meeting of the Midwest Political Science Association, April 2–6, Chicago, IL.
Jordan, Lisa, and Peter van Tuijl. 2007. "Rights and Responsibilities in the Political Landscape of NGO Accountability: Introduction and Overview." In *NGO Accountability*, ed. Lisa Jordan and Peter van Tuijl. London: Earthscan, 147–63.

Karim, Mahbubul. 1996. "NGOs in Bangladesh: Issues of Legitimacy and Accountability." In *Beyond the Magic Bullet,* ed. Michael Edwards and David Hulme. West Hartford, CT: Kumarian Press, 132–41.

Lee, Julian. 2004. *NGO Accountability: Rights and Responsibilities.* Geneva: CASIN.

PROSHIKA Information and Documentation Resource Cell (IDRC). 2008. *PROSHIKA: A Centre for Human Development. Activity Report,* July 2007–June 2008. I/1-GA, Section-2, Mirpur, Dhaka–1216, Bangladesh. http://www.proshika.org/03_AR_2008_mcss.pdf.

Romzek, Barbara S., and Melvin J. Dubnick. 1987. "Accountability in the Public Sector: Lessons from the Challenger Tragedy." *Public Administration Review* 47 (3): 227–38.

Thompson, James D., and William J. McEwan. 1958. "Organizational Goals and Environment: Goal Setting as an Interaction Process." *American Sociological Review* 23 (2): 23–31.

Waldman, Amy. 2003. "Helping Hand for Bangladesh's Poor." *New York Times* (March 25): A8.

Zaman, Hassan, Nagavalli Annamalai, Irajen Appasamy, Stephen Rasmussen, Suraiya Zannath, and Frank Matsaert. 2005. "The Economics and Governance of Nongovernmental Organizations (NGOs) in Bangladesh." Poverty Reduction and Economic Management Sector Unit, South Asia Region. Document of the World Bank, consultation draft. www.lcgbangladesh.org/ngos/reports/ngo_report_clientversion.pdf.

12

ACCOUNTABILITY IN THE NONPROFIT SECTOR

Abandoning the One-Size-Fits-All Approach

KEVIN P. KEARNS

Many of the chapters in this book address accountability from the perspective of governmental or quasi-governmental organizations. This chapter explores accountability in the U.S. nonprofit sector, which has grown dramatically in size and influence over the past 25 years.

As the nonprofit sector in America has grown, so has its visibility. And as its visibility has grown, so has public scrutiny of nonprofit operations, finance, governance, and programmatic impacts. The private nonprofit sector is under the microscope of public scrutiny as never before, mostly in a favorable light, but sometimes with very unflattering results.

Large nonprofit organizations have found their way into the public spotlight because of financial and operational scandals involving executive abuse and apparent lack of governance oversight. In the early 1990s the United Way of America suffered through one of the worst public scandals in the history of the nonprofit sector, which involved abuse of executive authority by former president William Aramony (Glaser 1994). More recently, the American Red Cross has been repeatedly criticized for lack of transparency and poor response to national and regional disasters (Brody 2002). Covenant House and numerous Catholic parishes have been rocked by scandals involving sexual abuse of children (Sennott 1992). The U.S. health-care industry, which is dominated by nonprofit hospitals, has been widely criticized for many years for skyrocketing costs, lackluster quality, and inaccessibility to many uninsured citizens (Noble et al. 1998; Mechanic 1996). The list of public lashings that have been suffered by large nonprofit organizations could go on and on and include international NGOs that provide essential aid to countries in need (Gibelman and Gellman 2004). Even small nonprofits have been criticized, sometimes for abuses like those described above, but also for their inability to develop accountability mechanisms to ensure that their services are delivered efficiently and effectively. These controversies are mostly of a local and regional scope and can be found just about any time one opens the local newspaper.

There have been a variety of initiatives locally, nationally, and internationally to hold nonprofits accountable for their actions and their performance. In city halls and state capitals around the country, public officials are debating ways to ensure that nonprofits are acting in accordance with their charitable mandates. In the U.S. Senate, Charles Grassley (R-Iowa) has convened hearings on how to hold the nonprofit sector to higher standards of financial accountability and transparency; his efforts have lead to changes in the IRS Form 990 that nonprofits use to annually supply the government with information about their finances and how much they pay their top executives. Some policy makers have argued that the rigorous standards of financial reporting and internal controls specified by the Sarbanes-Oxley legislation, which now applies only to publicly traded companies, also should apply to nonprofit organizations. Self-appointed watchdog organizations like the Better Business Bureau (2008) and the National Committee for Responsive Philanthropy (2008) have for many years advocated various benchmarks of accountability in the nonprofit sector. Independent Sector, the national advocacy and policy organization for the nonprofit sector, perhaps in a defensive maneuver, recently completed an extensive study that contains a wide variety of recommendations regarding both external and internal oversight of the nonprofit sector (Panel on the Nonprofit Sector 2005, 2007).

Many of these accountability initiatives, while noble in their intentions, make the mistake of treating the nonprofit sector as a monolithic entity when, in fact, it is an almost bewildering menagerie of 1.7 million organizations of different sizes, missions, and resources. This chapter suggests that a one-size-fits-all approach to accountability of nonprofit organizations fails to give sufficient attention to this diversity and may lead to unanticipated consequences. Applying the organizational life-cycle model to the nonprofit sector illustrates that organizations face different accountability challenges and imperatives at various stages in their life cycle. Implications for management, policy, and future academic research are discussed.

A BRIEF DEFINITION OF ACCOUNTABILITY

It is beyond the scope of this chapter to offer a detailed longitudinal analysis of how accountability has been conceptualized and defined through the years. Such analyses are provided elsewhere (Weber 1999) and in other chapters in this book, which document the historical tensions between relatively narrow and relatively broad definitions of accountability. Narrow definitions of accountability tend to focus on compliance with internally or externally imposed laws, regulations, procedures, or other codified standards of performance. For example, in his *Dictionary of American Politics and Government* Shafritz defines accountability as "(1) the extent to which one must answer to a higher authority—legal or organizational—for one's actions in society at large or within one's organization; (2) An obligation for keeping accurate records of property, documents, or funds" (Shafritz 1992, 4).

While compliance is certainly a primary concern for any organization (Mulgan, 2002), this chapter embraces a broader definition of accountability that takes into account the expectations, values, and perceptions of multiple stakeholders who include clients, donors, partner organizations, the general public, and the media, as well as authorities that are legally charged with oversight of nonprofits, such as state attorneys general and the Internal Revenue Service. An outstanding example of a broader definition of accountability is provided by Romzek and Dubnik who state that "accountability involves the means by which public agencies and their workers manage the divers expectations generated within and outside the organization" (Romzek and Dubnik 1987, 228). Similarly, Ebrahim says that "accountability [is] the means through which individuals and organizations are held externally to account for their actions and . . . the means by which they take internal responsibility for continuously shaping and scrutinizing organizational mission, goals, and performance" (Ebrahim 2003, 194).

These broader definitions of accountability are distinguished by several features. While they embrace the fact that legal compliance is a prerequisite for accountability, they also acknowledge that accountability involves more than mere compliance with the letter of the law. Accountability also involves responsiveness to the needs and interests of stakeholders inside and outside of the organization in an effort to maintain the credibility of the organization and sustain public trust in its activities. Not all scholars embrace this broader definition. For example, Mulgan (2002) argues that these broader concepts of accountability divert our attention from the core concept. He says that a person or organizations must be held to "account" in a literal sense for their actions in order for accountability to have meaning. But nonprofits are indeed held to account in many ways, beyond mere reporting and formal assessment by oversight agencies. For example, charitable donors can withhold their charitable support if they are not satisfied with the performance of the organization. The nonprofit organization can lose market share and jeopardize its sustainability if it cannot compete effectively in the marketplace. And negative media publicity can lead to the erosion of public confidence if nonprofit officials behave in a way that is contrary to public expectations or values. In all of these dire circumstances, an individual or an organization is indeed held to account (in Mulgan's terms), but not just through formal mechanisms of reporting and authoritative oversight, but also through the court of popular opinion.

Broader definitions of accountability imply that a major responsibility of the organization's leaders—the executive staff and the volunteer board of directors—is to continuously monitor societal expectations, trace their origins and likely trajectory, and try to strategically position their organizations to respond effectively. In other words, accountability is more than just a reaction to a demand from some internal superior or an external oversight body. Rather, accountability also involves continuous and proactive efforts or strategic moves to anticipate new standards of accountability even before they emerge and position the organization to be ready for them.

Finally, of course, the broader definitions assume that accountability is a dynamic concept. In other words, these broader definitions assume that the standards to which nonprofit organizations are held accountable are constantly shifting and must be continuously monitored as part of the organization's environmental scanning process (Kearns 1996, 35–44).

WHY IS MEANINGFUL DIALOGUE ON ACCOUNTABILITY IN THE NONPROFIT SECTOR SO DIFFICULT?

Discussions about accountability typically emanate from three fundamental questions:

- Accountability for *what?*
- Accountability to *whom?*
- Accountability through which *mechanisms?*

In the nonprofit sector these three core questions about accountability are complicated by the fact that many people don't have a clear idea of *what* actually constitutes the nonprofit sector or *who* it serves or which *mechanisms* nonprofits should use to demonstrate their accountability. The confusion is fueled by the way we label the nonprofit sector, by the diversity of missions pursued by nonprofit organizations, and by the extraordinary asymmetry in the sector in terms of the size of organizations and their corresponding resources.

Naming the Sector

The nonprofit sector in the United States goes by various names, each of which conveys a glimpse of its fundamental character while at the same time contributing to the confusion about the sector. A number of years ago Lester Salamon warned us that these various labels of the nonprofit sector have created confusion and unrealistic expectations on the part of the general public (Salamon 1993). The nonprofit sector is somewhat like the parable of the blind man and the elephant—the sector takes on a totally different shape and identity, depending on where you "touch" it. Here are a few of those alternative identities.

Nonprofit Sector

This name gives the false impression that nonprofit organizations cannot or should not make a profit. In reality, there is nothing in federal or state law governing charitable organizations that forbids them from generating a profit. For example, some nonprofit hospitals and HMOs, especially those that have consolidated into vertically integrated health-care systems, are generating record surpluses at a time when many citizens cannot gain access to even rudimentary health care. To some observers, this market orientation, at odds with what they perceive a nonprofit to be, is especially objectionable given the state of health care in the United States (Eikenberry and Kluver 2004). Yet from a legal perspective these organizations are doing nothing wrong. Indeed, spokespersons for these institutions say that the positive financial results are evidence that they are fulfilling their public trust to protect their charitable assets in perpetuity.

Charitable Sector

This name may give the false impression that nonprofits literally give away their programs and services to people in desperate need and, in turn, rely totally on the charitable largesse of individuals, foundations, and corporations to finance their good works. While this is true of some organizations, it is largely a romanticized notion of nonprofits that has been inaccurate for many years. Today, most nonprofits, including social service organizations, rely on a diverse mix of income streams to fund their missions (Young 2007). Quite often this revenue mix includes some form of earned income, such as fees for service. Fee income is among the fastest growing sources of revenue for certain types of nonprofits. Since 1977 fee income grew by almost 600 percent in social services, nearly 300 percent in arts and culture, and well over 200 percent in civic organizations (James and Young 2007, 94). In fact, private donations, which are presumed by casual observers to be the financial backbone of the nonprofit sector, comprise only 20 percent of total income for the sector (Rooney 2007, 23). Thus, people who still subscribe to the literal meaning of "charitable sector" are likely to be disillusioned by the modern realities of nonprofit finance.

Voluntary Sector

This name suggests that the nonprofit sector is managed and governed completely, or at least primarily, by volunteers—people who generously donate their time, talent, and treasure to the organization. This may have been true for the generation of our great grandparents, but not for today's nonprofit employees. Fundraisers, chief executives, clinical specialists, financial managers, information experts, marketing specialists, and even volunteer coordinators are highly trained professionals. In some cases, they are also highly paid professionals who are being trained not only in schools of social work, as in the past, but in schools of public policy and even in business schools that are offering specialized curricula in nonprofit management and governance. Not long ago there were only a few such academic programs in the United States. Today, over 200 colleges and universities offer specialized training in the art and science of nonprofit management and leadership (Mirabella and Wish 2001). The image of the nonprofit sector relying primarily on the services of well-intended volunteers who have time and money to spare may have nostalgic appeal, but it is no longer accurate.

Third Sector or Independent Sector

These two names imply that the nonprofit sector exists independently of government and business in a free market economy. There was once a time when the activities of the three sectors were distinctly separate—when government provided purely *public goods,* when business provided *private goods,* and when the nonprofit sector provided a hybrid of the two. But today corporations are increasingly involved in activities like running prisons, schools, day-care centers, hospitals, and universities. Even armed-security forces representing the United States around the globe are operated for a profit by private firms. Conversely, nonprofits are engaged in business-oriented entrepreneurial ventures to diversify their income streams while simultaneously advancing their mission, sometimes competing head-to-head with private businesses. Casual observers, including average citizens, may find that this new seamless economy challenges their notions of what a nonprofit organization is and what it does.

So, the basic terminology we use to describe the nonprofit sector creates confusion about the concept of accountability, especially when misunderstandings lead to unrealistic expectations by key constituencies. For example, citizens may be outraged when it is revealed that a nonprofit has accumulated significant surpluses because they presume that *nonprofit* literally means "no profit." Donors may feel betrayed when they discover that a nonprofit is charging clients for its services because they presume that charitable means "free of charge." Legislators may chastise nonprofit CEOs for drawing substantial salaries because they presume that in the voluntary sector employees should be content with low wages, regardless of their professional credentials. Tax payers may be amazed that some nonprofits derive nearly 100 percent of their revenues from government contracts, which makes them the equivalent of quasi-governmental agencies, not independent and autonomous organizations.

Variability of Missions

Adding to the confusion caused by terminology is the bewildering diversity of organizations that comprise the nonprofit sector. Section 501 of the Internal Revenue Code contains over two dozen classes of organizations that are eligible for some type of preferential tax treatment from the federal government. So-called 501c3 organizations are, of course, most familiar to all of us because they provide the prototypical nonprofit services in domains like education, arts and culture, social services, health care, scientific research, and religious services. But the Code also addresses 501c4 (political education organizations), 501c6 (business leagues and chambers of commerce), 501c14 (credit unions) and many other categories of organizations that receive some type of preferential tax treatment.

Even section 501c3 covers a menagerie of various nonprofit organizations. The National Taxonomy of Exempt Entities (NTEE), designed by the National Center for Charitable Statistics (2008), divides charitable organizations into ten categories such as arts, education, and so on. Each group contains many highly specialized subcategories. In the arts category for example, there are over 30 separate subcategories for specialized organizations like culture and ethnic awareness, arts education, children's museums, history museums, natural-history museums, and so forth. Thus there are actually hundreds of different types of 501c3 organizations.

When we try to have a meaningful conversation about accountability in the nonprofit sector, we must be prepared for the fact that each of these different types of organizations will bring to the dialogue its own specialized language, especially with respect to missions and programmatic outcomes, which is a key issue in any discussion of accountability. Some of these organizations pursue relatively vague outcomes like "quality of life," while others continuously monitor precise outcomes dealing with metrics of violence reduction. Some are constrained by codified performance standards imposed on them by accrediting or regulatory bodies, while others pursue idiosyncratic outcomes that they themselves have designed.

So, the problem of holding nonprofits accountable for their performance is exacerbated by the fact that the missions of nonprofit organizations are extremely diverse. Dialogue on account-ability *for what* and accountability *to whom* is challenged by this diversity. There are likely to be as many different answers to these two questions as there are types of nonprofit organizations in the NTEE categorization schema. Schools are accountable for educational outcomes, hospitals are accountable for health outcomes, and human-service agencies are accountable for behavioral outcomes or economic-status outcomes. Arts organizations are accountable to patrons and critics, universities are accountable to students and accrediting agencies, and community-development organizations are accountable to local businesses and residents. This is not to suggest that a dia-logue on accountability is impossible. But we do need to be cognizant of the inherent difficulties when everyone in the conversation is essentially speaking a different language.

Asymmetric (and Limited) Capacity in the Nonprofit Sector

Any realistic discussion of accountability in the nonprofit sector must take into account the vari-ability of size, resources, management sophistication, and general operational capacity among organizations that comprise the sector. By any measure, the nonprofit sector is big and getting bigger. Consider the following 2006 profile of the U.S. nonprofit sector as reported in the 2008 *Nonprofit Almanac* (Wing et al. 2008). In 2006 the nonprofit sector contributed $666.1 billion to the U.S. economy and received $1 trillion in total revenue, an increase of 5.7 percent over 2005. The U.S. nonprofit sector consists of roughly 1.4 million organizations, up from 1.1 million in 1998. The private nonprofit sector accounts for 5 percent of the gross domestic product in the United States, 8.1 percent of the country's wages, and 9.7 percent of the jobs. Total nonprofit employment jumped over 16 percent between 1998 and 2006.

But beneath the aggregate statistics is a more accurate picture of astonishing asymmetry in the nonprofit sector. Over 70 percent of nonprofit organizations in the United States spend less than $500,000 per year. Only 30 percent of the organizations in the sector, primarily hospitals and univer-sities, account for 97 percent of all nonprofit expenditures. Health-care and education organizations account for over 36 percent of all nonprofit assets and nearly 63 percent of all nonprofit employees. Therefore, if we take hospitals and educational institutions out of the picture, we can see that that the vast majority of nonprofit organizations are quite small. The typical nonprofit organization has only a few employees and an annual budget typically well under $500,000. Even these statistics may be inflated because we know almost nothing about the thousands of nonprofits that are not required to file reports with the IRS because their annual revenues are less than $25,000.

Size is an important consideration in holding nonprofit organizations accountable for their per-formance because most nonprofit organizations, being very small, have limited capacity to account for their performance with reasonable levels of confidence. Many of these small organizations do not have even the rudimentary elements of a strong and vibrant infrastructure, such as internal compliance controls, reasonable metrics and methods for tracking performance, reliable information and data-management systems, modern employee-recruiting and employee-development systems, and competent governing boards that provide true stewardship of the mission.

The author has worked intensively with dozens of small nonprofits as president of a foundation, as a consultant, and as a board member. Most of these organizations have not developed even a basic logic model that specifies with some precision the amount of resources (inputs) devoted to a given activity or program. Moreover, small nonprofits have great difficulty documenting and accounting for the fixed and variable costs of their programs. Because they are small, these organizations find it difficult to account with any precision for varying amounts of human capital associated with their programs (Fine et al. 2000; Poole et al 2001; Hoefer 2000; Campbell 2002). Employees and volunteers are constantly multitasking, by sharing space and other resources across program lines in a way that makes traditional fund accounting a challenge. Added to this legitimate accounting challenge is the not-so-legitimate habit of borrowing from Peter to pay Paul, the creative accounting practice used by some small organizations to cover shortfalls in one program category with surpluses in another.

Thus any realistic analysis of accountability in the nonprofit sector must attempt to compare "apples with apples." Only a tiny proportion of nonprofit organizations have the internal capacity and the resources to develop sophisticated methods to monitor their effectiveness on a continuous basis. Very few have the type of capacity to implement and sustain rigorous corporate compliance processes to ensure that they are always operating in accordance with laws and regulations.

True, much of the negative publicity that has been directed to the nonprofit sector has focused on relatively large organizations that do indeed command significant resources and should be expected to maintain accountability systems on a par with those used by the largest corporations in the private sector. But the simple truth is that most nonprofit organizations are the equivalent of storefront businesses and, consequently, they lack the internal-management and governance capacity to police themselves and are severely stretched to comply with standards imposed by outside overseers.

Does this mean that we should allow small nonprofits to get away with sloppy performance, poor governance oversight, self-perpetuating programs, and less than rigorous legal standards for fiduciary accountability? Absolutely not! But as with any teaching strategy, we must first diagnose the "student's" current state of knowledge and capacity to absorb new knowledge before rushing into the most sophisticated material in the course.

THE DANGERS OF A ONE-SIZE-FITS-ALL APPROACH TO ACCOUNTABILITY

The data presented above clearly demonstrate the diversity among organizations in the nonprofit sector in terms of mission, size, capacity, and funding. Yet many proponents of greater accountability in the nonprofit sector wish to apply uniform standards of performance to all organizations. The website for the Better Business Bureau (BBB), for example, has posted "Standards for Charity Accountability." These standards assert that program expenditures for nonprofits should be at least 65 percent of total expenditures and that fundraising costs should be 35 percent or less of total revenue raised by fundraising activities. Moreover, in an effort to discourage nonprofits from accumulating surplus assets, the BBB asserts that net unrestricted assets (minus fixed assets) should be no more than three times the organization's annual budget.

Metrics like these are intuitively appealing and, on initial inspection, seem perfectly reasonable as expectations for all nonprofits. Closer examination, however, reveals some concerns. A nonprofit's ability to comply with these metrics may vary wildly by mission, size, maturity, and internal-management capacity. A community-development organization, for example, engages in a variety of staff-intensive activities such as business development, real-estate management, housing development, and so forth. In such an organization, it is extremely difficult to segment administrative activities from programmatic activities, which thus makes it difficult to allocate a percentage of total expenditures to one or the other. The situation is quite different in, say, a family counseling center in which the administrative staff and their work are clearly separated from the clinical staff and their work.

The stage of the organization's development may also make a difference. In young organizations that are just getting started, administrative costs are likely to be much greater as a percentage of total costs than in mature or sophisticated organizations that can benefit from economies of scale.

Public acceptance of the organization may also impact performance on certain uniform accountability benchmarks. An organization that raises funds for controversial causes, say assistance for gay, lesbian, bisexual, and transgender causes, might reasonably spend more than 35 percent of total monies on fundraising expenses. It is simply more difficult (and more costly) to convince the public to donate to controversial causes than to popular ones.

With regard to the ratio of unrestricted net assets to annual expenditures, it may not be prudent for a nonprofit to cut this ratio as low as possible. In today's volatile economic and political environment, some types of nonprofits may find that a ratio of three-to-one is prudent although the BBB would frown upon this ratio. For example, donations to international-aid organizations are notoriously volatile, or at least cyclical, and depend on public moods and perceptions of international events like ethic conflict, natural disasters, or famine. Organizations that address these issues might legitimately desire a larger financial cushion (a kind of rainy-day fund); organizations in which revenues are more stable and reliable do not need such a fallback.

There are unintended consequences whenever one attempts a universal application of accountability metrics like those advocated by the BBB. For example, a nonprofit might be tempted to classify certain types of fundraising expenses, such as the printing of a prospectus, as educational expenses rather than fundraising expenses. Perhaps the most disturbing feature of these quantitative metrics, applied universally to all nonprofits, is that they do not accommodate the notion of organizational learning and growth (Argyris 1990; Senge 1990). The recommended metric exists as a discreet goal that is either attained or not. It allows no room for testing the validity of the goal relative to the organization's unique mandate, mission, capacity, and context. Such an exercise might lead to new insights suggesting, for instance, that the externally imposed standard is either inappropriate or even not rigorous enough for the organization.

The key point is that a one-size-fits-all approach to accountability will likely encounter problems when applied in the nonprofit sector. Organizations may strive to comply with such measures because they feel they have no choice. But in the long run such approaches will inhibit, not facilitate, intelligent public dialogue on the meaning of accountability in the nonprofit sector and how best to enhance it.

AN ORGANIZATIONAL LIFE-CYCLE APPROACH TO ACCOUNTABILITY IN THE NONPROFIT SECTOR

Like any living organism, a nonprofit organization goes through several stages in its life cycle (Hansenfeld and Schmid 1989).

In *the birth and start-up stage* the founder(s) of the organization sense that there is an unmet need for a good or service, and they develop a vision for an organization to meet that need. Typically, they must enlist the support of others to support the vision, which likely will involve some type of needs assessment, business plan, and/or logic model to convey the rationale and viability of the organization.

If the organization is successful in its initial stage, demand for its goods and services will increase, and it will be confronted with the many challenges that accompany the *growth and development stage* of the organization. Typically at this stage of development we see the organization evolving toward more formal management and governance structures to handle the increased demand and the higher community expectations that accompany growth.

At *the maturity stage* in the life cycle, the organization has become well established in its particular field of service. Typically mature organizations have relatively sophisticated management infrastructure and governance systems. Often mature organizations have a strong culture and sophisticated internal-compliance systems to ensure that the culture tolerates no deviation from an ethical code of conduct.

During the challenging *decline-and-renewal stage* in the life cycle, the leaders of the organization may need to confront the fact that demand for the organization's products or services is falling, either because of poor performance or simply because of changing community needs and market forces. The challenge is to respond to this eventuality by deciding if the organization can renew itself or if it should responsibly divest itself and downsize or terminate operations.

Life-cycle theory also is a very useful framework for identifying different types of accountability challenges and opportunities that typically face nonprofits at each stage of the cycle. It is an approach that can help us begin to disentangle ourselves from the one-size-fits-all approach to accountability in the nonprofit sector, by recognizing at least some aspects of the remarkable diversity that is present in the nonprofit sector.

Tables 12.1 and 12.2 contain a set of propositions regarding some of the accountability challenges and opportunities likely to face nonprofit organizations at each of the four stages of their life cycle.

Birth and Start-Up

At the birth and start-up phase the leaders of the organization need to give attention to the "nuts and bolts" of accountability, focusing largely on compliance issues. They must decide whether to incorporate as a nonprofit organization with state and federal authorities and, if so, how to demonstrate their compliance with the relevant laws and regulations regarding qualification for tax-exempt status. They must design and implement a set of governance structures and policies that will carry them through the crucial formative stages of the organization. These structures and policies will likely grow more elaborate in later stages of the organizational life cycle, but even in their embryonic stage, these policies must contain the seeds for effective and accountable governance (Ott 2001). Finally, even at the initial stage, the organization must establish procedures for accounting for the seed capital that has been invested in the organization to establish itself in the marketplace. These initial financial controls will grow more elaborate with time, but at the beginning stage they need to focus on compliance with donor intent. The organizational prospectus, the logic model, the business plan, and the organization's articles of incorporation are the organization's primary accountability documents at this early stage of development.

Growth/Development and Maturity

At the next two stages in the organizational life cycle, growth and maturity, the focus of the organization's leaders must remain on compliance as a first priority. Indeed, the compliance issues facing organizations at this stage of the life cycle will grow more complex and more onerous. For example, when the annual budget exceeds $300,000 the organization should conduct an independent, external audit. Additional compliance costs will be incurred from various government grants and contracts that the organization might receive (Smith and Lipsky 1993; Dicke and Ott 1999).

Also during the growth and maturity stages of development, the attention of leaders broadens

Table 12.1

Life-Cycle Framework for Accountability

	Birth and start-up	Growth and development	Maturity	Decline and renewal
Accountability for what?	Legal compliance in organizational (corporate) design and operational compliance with the prospectus and business plan	Compliance plus responsible growth management, demonstrated progress on mission accomplishment	Compliance plus responsiveness to changing community needs and demands, significant progress toward mission accomplishment, corporate social responsibility, industry-wide best practices	Compliance plus responsible divestment management
Accountability to whom?	Initial investors, volunteers, board members, founding employees, clients	An increasing large and diverse group of clients, funders, regulators, volunteers and employees, accreditation agencies, the media, partner organizations, vendors	Multiple and increasingly diverse stakeholders in the community and potentially in the industry	Clients, funders, contractors, creditors, regulators, employees, volunteers
Mechanisms of enforcement	Articles of incorporation, business plan, marketing materials, logic model, initial internal financial and operational controls	Strategic plan, more sophisticated internal accountability controls including financial audits, contract management mechanisms, performance management	Strategic plan, sophisticated internal-compliance mechanisms, self-designed standards of performance that meet or exceed industry standards, quality control, crisis-management plan, risk-management plan	Valuation of organizational assets for dissolution or distribution to other comparable organizations

from short-term tactical accountability, defined in relatively narrow terms, to long-term and strategic concerns as well. In these two stages, the organization must be concerned with the perceptions and needs of an ever-widening circle of stakeholders who may have significant power and influence over the organization's accountability strategy, even if they do not necessarily wield legal authority to enforce their desires and expectations. This involves organizational leaders in a continuous process of negotiating with these stakeholders regarding their expectations of the organization and how it should respond (Kearns, 1996). Moreover, if the organization has achieved status as an industry leader, it might be in a position to actually shape and influence the accountability standards for an entire industry through its discretionary actions and its ability to lobby legislators and other policy makers regarding the continuous evolution of the legal-compliance environment.

Table 12.2

Instruments of Accountability

Birth and start-up stage	Medium and growing organizations	Large and mature organizations	Declining organizations
• Articles of incorporation • IRS letter of determination for federal income tax exemption • Comparable letter of determination for state and local tax exemptions • Mission and values statement • Business plan and logic model • Board governance policies • Separating executive and board functions • Proper use of venture capital • Human resource policy including volunteers • Financial management controls (budget, cash flows, balance sheet, audit) • Truthful education of consumers and donors • Financial compilation statements for organizations with revenues of $50–100k • Establishment of conflict-of-interest policies	• Move from business plan to strategic plan • Developing and monitoring financial performance ratios that are meaningful to the organization • Issuing an annual report to the public • Development of more sophisticated governance infrastructure including committees, self-assessment, rotation, and continuous board development activities • Development of compensation plan and benchmarks for key executives • Compliance with IRS and state reporting requirements • Compliance with IRS and state auditing requirements • Avoiding mission drift • Adherence to stricter accounting standards and auditing standards • Development of a procurement policy • Development of an investment policy • More sophisticated methods of contract management • Development of donor-rights policy • Whistle blower protection • Document retention • Confidentiality for clients (HIPPA and other laws) • Developing performance management information systems and infrastructure • Human-resource strategies to ensure compliance and control • EEO and other policies as applicable • Due diligence on collaborations and strategic alliances • Truth in advertising and marketing campaigns • Consumer satisfaction and quality control measures • Media-relations and crisis-management strategy • Code of conduct • Financial reviews for organizations with revenues of $100–300k • Liability and risk management • Continuous needs assessment • Gift policy	• Strategic plan • Control over diversified revenue streams • Unrelated business income tax • Intellectual property • Brand protection • Protection of endowments and restricted funds • Corporate social responsibility • Cost-control strategies • Quality control • Social enterprise • Advocacy • Financial audits for organizations with revenues of $300k or more • Lobbying policy • Setting standards higher than industry • Crisis-management policy • Risk-management policy	• Protection of core assets • Intensify financial controls • Appropriate public communication • Dissolution of assets appropriately valued • Preservation of legal obligations to clients and contracts • Ethical human-resource practices
Tactical/Legal →	Strategic/Proactive →	Strategic/Proactive →	Tactical/Legal

Decline and Renewal

Finally, if the organization confronts the prospect of decline, then it likely will return to a focus on short-term tactical accountability issues, which include how to handle the dire prospect of terminating programs or perhaps even closing the organization. For example, taking stock of the net value of the organization will be important if it is to dispense any surplus assets following its dissolution. Addressing legal obligations to clients and to contractors will be another preoccupation during the decline stage of the organization.

Thus Tables 12.1 and 12.2 present a cycle within a cycle. The central proposition is that any nonprofit organization will begin its life cycle with a strong emphasis on compliance issues and focused on relatively narrow tactical definitions of accountability. During the growth and maturity phases, its focus will broaden to include strategic definitions of accountability as it is bombarded by multiple and sometimes conflicting expectations from a wide range of constituencies. Finally, during the decline and renewal phase, the attention of organizational leaders is likely to return to a tactical orientation toward accountability, as they carefully prioritize their obligations to various constituencies and likely focus again on legal and moral obligations.

IMPLICATIONS FOR RESEARCH AND PRACTICE

The life-cycle model of nonprofit accountability implies a set of testable hypotheses for future research. Surveys and case studies could be used to assess the implementation of various accountability strategies and mechanisms to determine if they are related to the stages of the organizational life cycle. The overarching proposition is that nonprofit organizations will rely more heavily on tactical and compliance-focused accountability mechanisms at both the beginning and end of the organizational life cycle. Organizations that are in the middle stages of the cycle will rely more heavily on broader definitions of accountability and strategic mechanisms to achieve it.

From the perspective of management and governance practice, the life-cycle framework can be used as a strategic-planning tool for executives and board members to scan their environment and develop accountability tactics and strategies appropriate to their current stage of development. The concept can also be used by other stakeholders. For example, grant makers can use the life-cycle model to hold nonprofits to various standards of accountability depending on their stage of development and to target their philanthropic investments where they will have the greatest impacts. For example, a grant maker interested in funding capacity building to enhance the accountability of a nonprofit organization might use the following general guidelines:

- Nonprofits at the start-up stage face the need for venture capital, program development, marketing, and program testing and refinement.
- At the growth stage organizations need help building their internal operating systems, building their board, and going to scale with their programs.
- At the mature stage, nonprofits need help perhaps reinvesting in innovation and learning, or perhaps in preparing for executive transitions.

Tailoring grants to the organization's need at different stages in its life cycle offers grant makers and grant seekers alike a clear set of performance targets—which may involve getting to the next stage in the cycle or improving performance in the current stage.

We have suggested that it is difficult to have a reasonable dialogue about accountability in the nonprofit sector because of the diversity of organizations in the sector. Nonprofit organizations vary wildly in terms of mission, size, and internal-management capacity. Moreover, stakeholder perceptions and expectations of the nonprofit sector are easily distorted by misleading labels and by persistent myths about the sector. Efforts to force fit all nonprofit organizations into a single one-size-fits-all framework of accountability are likely to fail, and may even lead to unanticipated consequences. A life-cycle model of accountability offers some promise as both a research framework and as a tool for better management and governance.

REFERENCES

Argyris, Chris. 1990. *Overcoming Organizational Defenses: Facilitating Organizational Learning.* Needham, MA: Allyn and Bacon.

Better Business Bureau. 2008. *Standards for Charity Accountability.* Arlington, VA: Council of Better Business Bureaus.

Brody, Evelyn. 2002. "Accountability and Public Trust." In *The State of Nonprofit America,* ed. Lester M. Salamon. Washington, DC: Brookings Institution Press.

Campbell, David. 2002. "Outcomes Assessment and the Paradox of Nonprofit Accountability." *Nonprofit Management and Leadership* 12 (3): 243–59.

Dicke, Lisa, and J. Steven Ott. 1999. "Public Agency Accountability in Human Service Contracting." *Public Productivity and Management Review* 22 (4): 502–16.

Ebrahim, Alnoor. 2003. "Making Sense of Accountability: Conceptual Perspectives for Northern and Southern Nonprofits." *Nonprofit Management and Leadership* 14 (2): 191–212.

Eikenberry, Angela M., and Jody D. Kluver. 2004. "The Marketization of the Nonprofit Sector: Civil Society At Risk?" *Public Administration Review* 64 (2): 132–40.

Fine, Allison H., Colette Thayer, and Anne Coghlan. 2000. "Program Evaluation Practice in the Nonprofit Sector." *Nonprofit Management and Leadership* 10 (3): 331–39.

Gibelman, Margaret, and Sheldon Gelman. 2004. "A Loss of Credibility: Patterns of Wrongdoing Among Nongovernmental Organizations." *Voluntas: International Journal of Voluntary and Nonprofit Organizations* 15 (4): 355–81.

Glaser, John S. 1994. *An Insider's Account of the United Way Scandal: What Went Wrong and Why.* New York: John Wiley.

Hasenfeld, Yeheskel, and Hillel Schmid. 1989. "The Life Cycle of Human Service Organizations: An Administrative Perspective." *Administration in Social Work* 13 (3/4): 243–69.

Hoefer, Richard. 2000. "Accountability in Action? Program Evaluation in Nonprofit Human Service Agencies." *Nonprofit Management and Leadership* 11 (2): 167–77.

James, Estelle, and Dennis Young. 2007. "Fee Income and Commercial Ventures." In *Financing Nonprofits: Putting Theory into Practice,* ed. Dennis Young. Lanham, MD: AltaMira Press, 93–119.

Kearns, Kevin. P. 1996. *Managing for Accountability: Preserving the Public Trust in Public and Nonprofit Organizations.* San Francisco: Jossey-Bass.

Mechanic, D. 1996. "Changing Medical Organization and the Erosion of Trust." *The Milbank Quarterly* 74 (2): 171–89.

Mirabella, Roseanne, and Naomi Wish. 2001. "University-Based Education Programs in the Management of Nonprofit Organizations: An Updated Census of U.S. Programs." *Public Performance and Management Review* 25 (1): 30–41.

Mulgan, Richard, 2002. "Accountability: An Ever Expanding Concept?" *Public Administration* 78 (3): 555–73.

National Center for Charitable Statistics. 2008. "National Taxonomy of Exempt Organizations." http://nccs. urban.org/about/index.cfm.

National Committee for Responsive Philanthropy. 2008. *Strategic Plan 2008–2012.* Washington, DC.

Noble, Alice, Andrew L. Hyams, and Nancy M. Kane. 1998. "Charitable Hospital Accountability: A Review and Analysis of Legal and Policy Initiatives." *The Journal of Law, Medicine and Ethics* 26 (2): 11–37.

Ott, Steven. 2001. *Understanding the Nonprofit Sector: Governance, Leadership, Management.* Boulder, CO: Westview Press.

Panel on the Nonprofit Sector. 2005. *Strengthening Transparency, Governance, and Accountability of Charitable Organizations:* A Final Report to Congress and the Nonprofit Sector. Washington, DC: Independent Sector.

———. 2007. *Principles for Good Governance and Ethical Practice.* Washington, DC: Independent Sector.

Poole, Dennis L., Jill Davis, Jane Reisman, and Joan Nelson. 2001. "Improving the Quality of Outcome Evaluation Plans." *Nonprofit Management and Leadership* 11 (4): 405–21.

Romzek, Barbara, and Melvin Dubnick. 1987. "Accountability in the Public Sector: Lessons from the Challenger Tragedy." *Public Administration Review* 47 (3): 227–38.

Rooney, Patrick. 2007. "Individual Giving." In *Financing Nonprofits: Putting Theory into Practice,* ed. Dennis Young, 23–44. Lanham, MD: AltaMira Press.

Salamon, Lester. 1993. *The Nonprofit Sector: A Primer.* New York: The Foundation Center.

Senge, Peter. 1990. *The Fifth Discipline: The Art and Practice of Learning Organizations.* New York: Currency Doubleday.

Sennott, Charles M. 1992. *Broken Covenant.* New York: Simon and Schuster.

Shafritz, Jay M. 1992. *The HarperCollins Dictionary of American Government and Politics.* New York: HarperCollins.

Smith, Steven Rathgeb, and Michael Lipsky. 1993. *Nonprofits for Hire: The Welfare State in the Age of Contracting.* Cambridge, MA: Harvard University Press.

Weber, Edward P. 1999. "The Question of Accountability in Historical Perspective: From Jackson to Contemporary Grassroots Ecosystem Management." *Administration and Society* 31 (4): 451–94.

Wing, Kennard, Thomas Pollak, and Amy Blackwood. 2008. *The Nonprofit Almanac 2008.* Washington, DC: Urban Institute Press.

Young, Dennis, ed. 2007. *Financing Nonprofits: Putting Theory to Practice.* Lanham, MD: AltaMira Press.

PART V

STRATEGIES

A common theme among the several promises of accountability is the desire that those being held to account behave appropriately. That seems simple enough, but in practice it requires decisions about which techniques and strategies are relevant to accountability and are deemed suitable for a given set of problematic relationships and circumstances. The determination of what approaches are "deemed suitable" is unlikely to emerge from carefully considered and rationally designed policies, but rather from the current toolbox of accountability mechanisms that reflect current dominant reform ideologies or common management "best practices." In this section we bring together two contributions that focus on different approaches to a particular arena of accountable governance that has received growing attention in recent years: the effort to hold corporations to account.

In some instances, holding corporations accountable reflects the general sense that stakeholders—and especially shareholders—need to be able to exercise some control or direction over those charged with the day-to-day management of the firm. Sally Wheeler offers a critical examination of efforts to regulate corporate behavior from within the corporate governance structure by empowering outside directors who supposedly would act as a check on the overwhelming power of internal management. As Wheeler shows in "Watching the Watchers," there are some fundamental problems with this strategy as put into practice.

A contrasting strategy for keeping the modern corporation accountable is, of course, the development of a regulatory regime where the watchdogs are placed outside the firm to ensure appropriate behavior—that is, behavior that does not threaten the "public interest." Matthew Potoski and Aseem Prakash offer an analysis of one such approach to render the behavior and choices of corporate actors more accountable. The use of voluntary arrangements ("clubs") to facilitate socially and environmentally responsible corporate behavior is more common than generally acknowledged, and its relative success in certain arenas suggests considerable potential for application in other areas. The authors articulate a model of such arrangements and use the case study of ISO 14001 as a practical demonstration of how such an accountability mechanism works. Focused primarily on creating and promoting international product standards that facilitate international trade, the International Organization for Standardization (ISO) has a long and established history in which it has morphed into a viable vehicle for promoting responsible behavior among thousands of companies from around the globe.

13

WATCHING THE WATCHERS

Sally Wheeler

This chapter focuses on corporate governance and corporate boards in the public, for-profit, sector, and particularly on the role of nonexecutive or outside directors and the ideas of accountability under which they are presumed to operate. Ensuring accurate and trustworthy corporate governance, given the nature of corporate power in the global context, is a broader issue that goes beyond the concerns of individual shareholders and nation-state economic policy (Huse 2003). The world's largest corporations have revenues in excess of the gross domestic product (GDP) of many individual states and have a global presence in the sense that their market listing is not confined to one nationally based exchange. At the domestic level an argument can be made that corporations are no longer private actors. They are public actors in terms of power and influence in areas such as environmental impact, location and relocation decisions, and corporate social responsibility.

WHO IS IN NEED OF GOOD GOVERNANCE?

The most popular and pervasive model of corporate regulation sees the shareholders of the corporation as those most in need of the protection of good governance and naturally emphasizes the private nature of the corporation and its governance structure. Given this model's dominance, it would seem to make sense to accept it for the purposes of this discussion, although vigorous condemnation of this model can be found among commentators in both the United Kingdom and the United States (Mitchell 1995), since it concentrates on financial performance and short-term profits and neglects wider interests. Examining just two points of qualification for the corporation's private nature should make it clear that governance failure has consequences wider than the official model would lead us to believe. The first is that the rise of defined-contribution pension plans in the United Kingdom and the United States makes many employees interested parties in corporate governance through the medium of institutional investment. They are literally arm's-length investors, for their financial well-being after retirement depends on favorable market returns on their personal retirement investment plans. The second is that a key function of boards of directors is the monitoring of the strategic direction of the corporation's business model and its risk-management contingency. Should these functions and the monitoring of them not be exercised properly, it is likely that the pool of those looking for accountability will be wider than simply shareholders. Fannie Mae and Freddie Mac in a U.S. context and Northern Rock in a UK context demonstrate are examples of effects that widely extend beyond shareholder interests. The idea that governance failure in a corporate sense is not always driven by fraud is a point to which I return later. All of these issues make the executive management of the corporation an issue wider than simply the mechanics of private governance.

TWO BOARDS OF DIRECTORS

Boards of directors are "the apex of the internal control system" (Jensen and Meckling 1976) of the corporation. The official narrative in Anglo-American corporate law is that directors are appointed by shareholders and are the representatives of shareholders or owners. Corporate boards are responsible for devising and/or revising corporate strategy; ensuring that management operate effectively in the interests of shareholders; setting performance incentives for managers; and appointing, monitoring, and (if necessary) removing the Chief Executive Office (CEO). Outside or nonexecutive directors form a second layer within the board itself to watch over executive directors carrying out their tasks. The reality is that the appointment of directors, both executive and nonexecutive, is approved by the shareholders without, in the overwhelming majority of cases, any discussion. The board in many ways is a self-perpetuating oligarchy. Its existing members put up new members for election and reelection. Shareholders do not interview directors and rarely even look at their curricula vitae to determine their suitability. These things are done by existing board members who "market" the suitability of new appointees to the shareholders (Davis and Robbins 2004, 292). Directorships are rarely contested. While the recent example of Yahoo! and Microsoft provides a different story, its news value lies in its novelty and hence helps to distinguish between official and realist narratives about the way corporate governance works.

VOLUNTARY CODES OF CORPORATE CONDUCT IN THE UNITED KINGDOM

The strategic and managing function of directors sits alongside the structural requirements of the regulatory framework in which the corporation operates, although both the United States and United Kingdom are characterized in the main *not* by specific regulatory demands but by broad regulatory directives that the corporation, through its directors and managers, interprets and absorbs into internal structures (Edelman 1990). However, the United Kingdom uses this approach to governance on a larger scale than does the United States. In the last fifteen years of the twentieth century, the United Kingdom experienced huge corporate collapses that were thought to be due to poor governance rather than market conditions; the examples of Bank of Credit and Commerce International (BCCI), Polly Peck, and the Maxwell Empire spring to mind. Moreover, an outbreak of executive-salary increases were thought to be "excessive" particularly since they often seemed to be for the executive leadership of recently privatized, formerly publically owned utilities. The United Kingdom, rooted in a "principles" rather than "rules" culture (Kershaw 2005), established a tradition of dealing with pressures on the corporate system by holding a private inquiry, led by a "City" figure (Jones and Pollitt 2002), which lead to the publication of a voluntary regulatory code supported by the listing authority. Corporations that do not either follow the voluntary code or explain why they are not following it will be denied a listing on the London Stock Exchange. The City figure for the first such inquiry was Sir Adrian Cadbury, the recently retired chairman of the then FTSE-100[1] company Cadbury Schweppes PLC and former director of the Bank of England and IBM. Subsequent inquiry chairmen have been just as illustrious within the City of London. The importance of elites and the social capital they generate is something we will return to later in this chapter.

The Code appears as a series of "main principles" with "supporting principles." The philosophy of the Code is that corporations should "comply or explain," that is, comply with the code or offer reasons made public through the channels of corporate reporting for noncompliance—which leaves the market to decide on the appropriateness of any noncompliance. What this means in effect is that if noncompliance is announced, the shareholders will decide on whether they approve of the corporation's decision not to comply for the reasons it gives, by either selling their shares, which results in a share-price drop, or keeping their shares, which results in price stability (MacNeil and Li 2006). A recent example is provided by the governance changes at Marks and Spencer PLC. A key component of the Cadbury report, or Cadbury Code as it came to be called, was the separation of the function of chairman and chief executive. The Code recommended that these positions should be held by different members of the board of directors. In March 2008 Marks and Spencer PLC, a long established FTSE-100 company, announced that upon the retirement of its current chairman later that year the position would be filled by its current chief executive who would then hold both jobs until his scheduled retirement in 2011. Shareholders were issued with individual letters explaining the background to and the reasons for the decision, which amounted to an admission that the corporation had been guilty of succession-planning failure: no insider was ready to take on the job, and bringing in an outsider was thought to be too disruptive. The immediate reaction of the market, assessed by share-price change, was indifference; the share price dropped 3p in that day's trading. At the actual shareholders' meeting some months later in July 2008, holders of 22 percent of the company's equity voted against or abstained from the resolution to appoint the chief executive as chairman. This was accompanied by a share-price drop of 25 percent, but also at the same time an unexpected profits warning.[2] In August 2008 the share price had recovered some of this loss and was on a roughly upward trajectory despite holding its listing in a steadily dropping exchange during this time. From this example we can deduce that either the market is not as responsive to governance issues as those who drafted these ex anteprinciples thought that it would be, or that the market generally did not disapprove of the governance change enough to use the exit option of share sale despite exercise of the voice option in relation to the shareholders' meeting (Shabbir and Padgett 2008). Despite the importance attached to the separation of these roles within the Cadbury report and from practitioner comments (Keenan 2004), there is no empirical evidence to support the idea that this sort of structural independence produces improved financial performance (Dalton and Dalton 2005).

The net result of these inquiries has been an enhanced role for independent or, as they are called in the United Kingdom, nonexecutive directors, and greater accounting disclosure and instructions to the corporate sector to improve its communications with its larger institutional shareholders. This model of governance, with professional board members directing and producing strategy but held in check by the addition of lay members, has in the context of the United Kingdom become a very popular method of governance. It is the preferred method of governance for organizations as diverse as hospital trusts and school governing boards. It is also used for judicial appointments. This model of governance is seen as a mechanism for ensuring compliance and probity for a distant public.

In the context of the corporation this form of governance can be seen as embodying the classic law and economics approach to corporate regulation (Shleifer and Vishny 1997). Regulation is enabling, rather than mandatory, and ultimate judgment on the structures adopted is exercised by the financial market. Otherwise described as the principal and agent approach, it assumes that shareholder value is maximized through the adoption of efficient structures that both police the behavior of potentially errant managers—errant in the sense that they might indulge in "shirking" or other "opportunistic behavior" at the expense of shareholders (Williamson 1985)—and accurate and sufficient information is relayed to shareholders (Fama 1980; Fama and Jensen 1983).

The only suggestion that the "contractarian" approach is not on its own able to tell the story of corporate governance is the recourse to a "City figure" to produce the voluntary code. In essence a system of accountability based on an impersonal financial market could not be imposed without acknowledging that the corporate sector is embedded in social relationships and social networks; in fact no system could be imposed without acknowledging this fact. This system of governance had to be created and endorsed as appropriate by an insider if it were to gain traction. Participants in governance are discriminating about whom they acknowledge as a relevant and meaningful insider in any particular context (Davis and Greve 1997). The Higgs report is an exemplar of this need to acknowledge the power of social and political context. Higgs was an executive director of an FTSE-100 listed corporation, a nonexecutive director of a large PLC, and an institutional director (Jones and Pollitt 2004, 164).

A succession of reports, recommendations, and statements of best practice have followed the initial report, compiled under the auspices of self-regulation, with each communication seeking to improve the standards of corporate governance generally and mechanisms for setting directors' remuneration specifically, for the benefit of shareholders (Cadbury 1992; Greenbury 1995; Hampel 1998; Turnbull 1999). Taken together these codes (generated by the Cadbury, Greenbury, Hampel, Turnbull and Higgs reports) are now known as the Combined Code, the latest iteration produced in June 2008. When a corporation releases its statement of compliance or explains noncompliance, it is doing so against the principles and supporting principles of the 2008 Combined Code.

The Higgs Report (Higgs 2003) was the last in the series of reports that make up the Combined Code and is our main focus of attention. It was commissioned by the UK government specifically to look at how corporate governance in the United Kingdom could be strengthened in the wake of the Enron, WorldCom, and Tyco failures and scandals in the United States. The Higgs Report was proactive in a UK context but also reactive in the sense that it was a direct response to the Sarbanes-Oxley legislation in the United States. The brief of the Higgs report was to look at outside directors with regard to their identity, their independence, and their effectiveness. The first iteration of the voluntary code on corporate governance, the Cadbury Report, had handed a key monitoring role in corporate governance to outside directors. The Higgs report was the first time in over ten years that the role of this group had been subjected to serious scrutiny. The decision to look at outsider/nonexecutive directors was no doubt inspired by the view that they and their independence were thought to be significant in the failure of Enron. Enron looked to have a largely independent board with only two of its directors occupying executive positions within the corporation. However, when industry ties and other factors such as charitable donations were factored in, the board had 43 percent independent directors as opposed to 72 percent in its peer corporations and 63 percent for investment banks (Gillan and Martin 2007).

AMENDMENTS TO THE VOLUNTARY CODE: THE IMPORTANCE OF OUTSIDE DIRECTORS

The results of the Higgs Report, after much debate, were amendments to the voluntary code that included a requirement that outside directors make up a significant portion of the board—the actual phraseology is that "there should be a balance between executive and non-executive directors such that no one group can dominate decision making" (Combined Code Main Principle A3); that letters of appointment of nonexecutive directors be made available through corporate reporting mechanisms (so that shareholders would be able to see the terms on which they had been appointed to the board and for how long); a definition of independence from the board for outside directors, and a requirement that outside directors be declared to be independent and on what grounds their independence is asserted; a designation of one of the outside directors as the senior director; and an identification of one of the outside directors as a communication conduit between investors and the board.

Given that each review of corporate governance has been in the shadow of an actual or feared failure of governance, it is hardly surprising that the thrust of these recommendations should be toward monitoring and control of executive directors by nonexecutive directors through structural reforms and for the benefit of distant shareholders. The test for code amendments is colloquially known as the "Maxwell test," that is, will this stop another Maxwell? By way of explanation, the now deceased Robert Maxwell provides the complete antithesis of the City figures used to suggest and endorse corporate governance codes and amendments to them. He did not come from an established family business background; as part of the East European Jewish diaspora, he was not British by birth and compounded these disadvantages by both serving as a Labour Member of Parliament and remaining a Labour Party activist. He was an outsider in every sense of the word. He had been the subject of Department of Trade and Industry investigation in the early 1970s, which had resulted in the Department declaring that he was an unsuitable person to be involved in the running of a public company. Later in his business career he was found to have used the pension funds of several of his companies to purchase shares in one of his own corporations to prop up its share price. The result was a huge corporate collapse and the personal bankruptcy of several family members. The Maxwell story is being used as a classic atrocity story to create a moral panic against which the need for good governance can clearly be demonstrated (Bromley et al. 1979).

The volatile nature of markets and the boom-and-bust cycles, which it seems are endemic to capitalism, mean that each new set of ex ante rules is set up with the last high-profile business failure or scandal in mind. Failure is not always the result of dishonesty. Northern Rock is a good example of the environment external to the business itself changing and so putting pressure on what had been seen as a successful and innovative business model previously. What is lauded in boom times as creative accounting and innovation becomes in recession the latest loophole to be closed (Clarke 2004). Corporate success is often founded on the use of practices that take compliance with governance regimes to the legal limit, and governance changes merely result in new devices being created (McBarnet and Whelan 1999). Corporate governance regimes then are linked less to performance measurement and more to the policing of periodic market crises. The terms of each intervention in corporate governance are not strictly ex ante, as they are dealing with ex post events. Despite the UK approach of general principles and flexibility as to how the principles are adopted or even if they are to be adopted, the emphasis is still on structural change as a way of creating better governance. The most important tasks that nonexecutive directors are charged with are overseeing the setting of incentives for managers (executive pay), appointing and if necessary removing the chief executive or other nonperforming executives, and assessing strategy and performance of the corporation. This last task is, of course, also the task of executive directors, so this creates a double layer of protection for shareholders.

The seriousness with which these Code reforms have been made should not be underestimated. To soften the legislative impact on those UK-based firms that had a cross-listing in the United States, the UK financial sector needed to convince the U.S. Securities and Exchange Commission (SEC) that the requirements of the UK's corporate-governance code were as strict as those imposed on U.S.-listed corporations by the Sarbanes-Oxley legislation. Higgs himself said in an interview with the *Daily Telegraph* in January 2003: "We want to raise the bar for performance from corporate boardrooms and blow away the last vestiges of perhaps how things were a few decades ago when it was all a bit cosy, a bit familiar, a bit Christmas-ornamenty."

DOES DOUBLE-LAYERED ACCOUNTABILITY RAISE THE BAR FOR GOOD GOVERNANCE?

So how likely is it that this double-layered accountability will "raise the bar for performance," and what is meant by "performance"? Perhaps unsurprisingly, given the nature of the pervasive corporate-governance model, this second question can be answered more easily than the first—performance is financial performance measured in terms of profit levels and dividend declarations for shareholders (Bhagat and Bolton 2008). Agency theorists are unable to agree on whether the presence of outside directors does or does not improve a corporation's financial performance. A number of studies provide conflicting conclusions. For example, Baysinger and Butler (1985) find that the presence of outside directors might have a "mild effect"; Kesner (1987) asserts that it has no effect (although Kesner's primary agenda was to look at questions of gender and board diversity within board committees rather than specifically examine financial performance); and Dalton et al. (1998) use meta-analysis of 54 studies of board composition and 31 studies of board leadership structure to conclude that there is little evidence of a link between a corporation's governance structure and its financial performance.

Conflicting empirically based accounts about the effect of the presence of nonexecutive or outside directors occur throughout the literature on takeover defenses, the composition of board committees, executive composition, and removal of the chief executive (see generally Filatotchev 2007). The equivocal findings in these areas tell us something about using agency theory to explain board behavior. Agency theory can look only at the structural components of board composition and then judge them only against its assumptions about what motivates opportunistic behavior (Davis1997), and agency theory presents a one-dimensional picture of human nature (Daily et al. 2003). It is not our purpose to delineate the failings of agency theory; there are plenty of reviews of this subject elsewhere (e.g., Anderson et al. 2007; Davis 2005). However, once we move away from the formulistic approach applied to board behavior and firm performance offered by agency theory, the model of the outsider director as the ultimate "watcher" begins to come under considerable pressure. If we are testing only the presence of outside directors against fixed variables, such as the presence or absence of shareholder litigation (Kesner and Johnson 1990), for example, then more nuanced questions about role, behavior, and perceptions of status are not on the agenda.

To make any judgment about the strategy and performance-assessment role of outside directors we need to look at a wider picture (Eisenhardt 1989). This takes us into the realm of stewardship theory and resource-dependency theory and to the last, but I think the most significant, part of this discussion for accountability—the potential effect of the presence of elites and networks. We need to open the black box of the boardroom (Leblanc and Schwartz 2007, Pettigrew 1992) and think about the sort of issues that arise when the shareholders' original watchers—executive directors—are themselves being watched by outside directors. The key questions would appear to center on *power, influence, independence,* and *trust.* These issues have to be negotiated within the boardroom itself for board members to have the ability to function as a unit. Once this is achieved the next question is what effect does this successful negotiation have on the accountability function of nonexecutive directors? Or in other words, can distant accountability be maintained in the presence of a locally negotiated functionality?

An extract from the first principle of the Code makes it clear that outside directors are required to engage with and endorse corporate strategy in addition to their monitoring of performance and remuneration. This makes sense in its operational context as it is hard to see how any meaningful monitoring of performance could take place without a reasonably detailed understanding of the corporation's market position, product placement, and expansion strategies. However, the explicit rendition of performance review and endorsement of strategy makes it clear that there has been a considerable expansion of what can be termed internal-service tasks:

A.1 The Board

Main Principle: Every company should be headed by an effective board, which is collectively responsible for the success of the company.

Supporting Principles: The board's role is to provide entrepreneurial leadership of the company within a framework of prudent and effective controls which enables risk to be assessed and managed. The board should set the company's strategic aims, ensure that the necessary financial and human resources are in place for the company to meet its objectives and review management performance. The board should set the company's values and standards and ensure that its obligations to its shareholders and others are understood and met. (Bezemer 2007)

As part of their role, nonexecutive directors should constructively challenge and help develop proposals on strategy. Nonexecutive directors should scrutinize the performance of management in meeting agreed goals and objectives and monitor the reporting of performance. They should satisfy themselves on the integrity of financial information and that financial controls and systems of risk management are robust and defensible. They are responsible for determining appropriate levels of remuneration of executive directors and have a prime role in appointing, and where necessary removing, executive directors, as well as in succession planning.

To provide the sort of input that the Code requires, outside directors must display an awareness of how business works and be able to quickly assimilate information about how the particular business works. They need to understand the dynamics between executive directors. They need to understand how individual strategic decisions will impact on share price and how strategy is formulated within the organization and then packaged to those outside the organization (Stiles 2001). They need to display sufficient knowledge in these areas to garner the *trust* of executive directors, thus enabling their comments and views to have an effect, and yet they must maintain a sufficient distance to avoid capture by executive directors and to remain *independent.* Obviously they will be *influenced* by executive voices around them, but they must not be dwarfed by that *influence.* Trust is a two-way process, as outside directors must feel able to rely on the extent and quality of information they are given by executive directors in order to perform their monitoring function (Hooghiemstra and van Manen 2004). Distrust between the two groups splits the board and results in a "circle of control and counter control" (Daudi 1986). Outside directors are nominated by the board for a five-year term initially, and if they wish to be reappointed they must be considered effective and not divisive or undermining of their executive counterparts. Shareholders must feel that the outside directors have sufficient *influence* within the board dynamic, such that they can get their voice heard. The black box of management process is gradually being opened by empirical work looking at the dynamics of board relationships (Pettigrew and McNulty 1995; Forbes and Milliken 1999; McNulty and Pettigrew 1999).

The Higgs report itself commissioned a piece of research from academics steeped in management-process research (McNulty et al. 2003; Roberts et al. 2005). Their task was to interview corporate chairman and nonexecutive directors to ascertain how they conducted the tasks listed above. The results of this research make fascinating reading. It tells the story of combining control and collaboration in a dialogue that the authors see as creating accountability and setting up intelligent accountability in place of distant accountability. Roberts (one of the authors of the Higgs research) describes in a different context what takes place as the "socializing forms of account-ability" (Roberts 2001, 1554–55, 1567). This form of accountability occurs when two conditions are met: where frequent face-to-face contact takes place between people and when there is no (or relatively no) power differential between the participants. It seems that what actually occurs in board processes is a nondefensive form of local accountability. Thus what nonexecutive directors are doing is ensuring that board processes give rise to reciprocal understanding and dialogue rather than box checking.

Intelligent accountability or socializing forms of accountability may well describe the changes in governance practice that are taking place in the post-Higgs era of boardroom discussions, but what they seem not to acknowledge is that this form of adaption is unlikely to take place without being enmeshed in an elite network that in social-capital terms and network terms encompass both executive and nonexecutive directors. The test of independence within the Code (A3.1) is a test of independence in relation to each particular corporation where office is held. It is not a test of network independence or ties outside that particular boardroom. What occurs is much more accurately described as a negotiation of independence that all parties can live with at this board and every other board rather than a creation of accountability. Dialogues around control and collaboration are in fact an informal sharing of information that may or may not have an effect on delivering distant accountability.

In the United States this translates into research on interlocks, where discussions about the presence and effects of what are termed "interlocked boards" is well-worn ground. The primary concern in the United States seems to be the effect of interlocks on firm behavior rather than on the behavior of those individuals whose appointments form the basis of the interlock. Following Granovetter (1985) the question for those researching interlocks was whether the embedded nature of economic relations resulted in interlocks powering control or communication (Mizruchi 1996). If control over other corporations was the answer in the 1970s, by the 1980s communication through learning from other corporations was the answer presented not least by Useem's (1984) influential study of British and American directors. Interlocks helped in the spread of innovation and contemporary business practices. It is unlikely that what was spread was best governance practice—it was far more likely to be conducive to the spread of McBarnet and Whelan's (1999) creative compliance to boost short-term profitability. More recent studies in the United States have been concerned with corporate donations to political-action committees and the role of interlocks. The same questions are asked of interlocks as are asked of the presence of outside directors—what are the effects on takeover defenses and compensation payments, and so forth. These questions reflect the following: that structural, not behavioral, determinants are what matters for agency theory and that interlocks are caused more often by nonexecutive or outside-director interchange than by executive-director exchange.

In the United Kingdom the concept of the interlocks is something mentioned only by sociologists such as John Scott or Richard Whitley whose interests are primarily in social-network analysis and social stratification (Scott 1991a, 1991b, 1997) and not in governance and account-ability. We could speculate on why this is the case. It is no more difficult to map boardroom elites in the United Kingdom than it is in the United States—all the information needed is publicly available. The dearth of discussion may say something about perceived hierarchies and stability within British society (Bond 2007, 61; Harris and Helfat 2007), but it also may be the influence of the "so what" school (Pettigrew 1992): What does the presence of interlocks actually tell us? The answer to that question depends on which story is being told—the story about firm performance (to which Pettigrew's comments are directed) or the story about the prospects for effective boardroom monitoring.

Recent research by Froud et al. (2008) demonstrates that there is an exchange of executive-director personnel into nonexecutive director personnel on retirement, particularly within the FTSE-250 companies. Fround et al.'s key findings were that 60 percent of FTSE-100 companies had a nonexecutive director who was an executive director at another FTSE-100 company, suggesting the beginnings of a postretirement career, perhaps, but more importantly that in excess of 40 FTSE-100 companies shared a nonexecutive director with another listed company. More or less the same pattern of appointments emerged from empirical work commissioned by the Higgs Review (McNulty et al. 2005); 16 nonexecutive directors drawn from the FTSE-350 held 54 nonexecutive directorships between them. The same duplication of nonexecutive appointments was also found by Bond (2006).

One might have thought that increased burdens of monitoring on nonexecutive directors and recent media messages about potential legal liability (rather than actual liability; see Black et al. 2005) would have severely reduced the number of people prepared to undertake this role. Instead what can be observed is that boardroom members, whether they are executives or nonexecutives, "seem to know one another, seem quite naturally to work together, and share many organizations in common" (Mills 1956, 294). The incentive for individual directors to hold nonexecutive and executive appointments at the same time and for nonexecutive directors to hold more than one appointment at the same time is partly salary uplift, but it is more likely to be the opportunity to observe how others deal with the demands of monitoring, to capture innovation from a range of sources, and to gain general network endorsement (Westphal and Stern 2007). The incentive for boards to recruit existing executive directors or outside directors already serving elsewhere as nonexecutive directors is based upon prior experience—their recruits will know what to expect—skills in the area of shareholder relations, takeover defense strategies, and network endorsement. What we do not know is what the consequences of network membership and reputation have for accountability concerns. The post-Higgs review desire for more nonexecutive directors is likely to result in a thickening of network ties—there is a finite pool of recruits with these skills available.

The corporate governance system itself drafts for interlocks. One of the more interesting features of UK-company law, with its mix of common law and statutes, is that although common law hints that interlocks might not be permitted (because they are difficult to accomplish without a breach of fiduciary duty) successive Companies Acts ignore the issue and remain silent. The Companies Act 2006, which came into force in October 2008, appears to suggest that directorial conflicts of interest must be declared and can then be ratified by nonconflicted directors. However, at the drafting stage of this Act, assurances were given that nothing in this new clause (section 175) was new law; it was merely confirming what the case law had been since 1845 and would not make multiple directorships more difficult.

Code drafters and amenders are well aware that the pool of talent on which to draw for appointments within corporate boards is limited and that little attempt is made to find talent in any other pool. Code drafters and amenders are themselves part of the circularity of boardroom appointments. Reputation within the network is maintained not by being an effective monitor but by negotiating sufficient independence to be associated with success and untainted by failure. Higgs was invited to put a limit on the number of boardrooms in which any one individual could sit in any capacity and declined to do so. When questioned by a journalist about his own portfolio of corporate activity (four nonexecutive directorships and two executive directorships) he answered that "if any of the companies feel that I am not giving the job enough attention they will say so." That comment is an agency theorist's worst nightmare—the group members who are supposed to comment on lack of attention and any consequent monitoring failure are also the shareholders. There is a certain circularity to accountability in the boardroom—the watchers (executive directors) are watched by other watchers (nonexecutive directors), who themselves are watched by shareholders through disclosure to the market. It has the look of a rather unedifying dance.

NOTES

1. The FTSE 100 is a group of 100 companies that are the most highly capitalized of those listed (quoted) on the London Stock Exchange.

2. A profits warning is an alert released by a listed/quoted company via an exchange that indicates profits for the forthcoming quarter will be less than those for the equivalent quarter in the previous year.

REFERENCES

Anderson, D. et al. 2007. "The Evolution of Corporate Governance: Power Redistribution Brings Boards to Life." *Corporate Governance* 15 (6): 780–97.

Baysinger, B., and H. Butler. 1985. "Corporate Governance and the Board of Directors: Performance Effects of Changes in Board Composition." *Journal of Law Economics and Organization* 1 (1): 101–34.

Bezemer, P., et al. 2007. "Investigating the Development of Internal and External Service Tasks of Non-Executive Directors: the Case of the Netherlands (1997–2005)." *Corporate Governance* 15 (5): 1119–29.

Black, B., et al. 2005. "Liability Risk for Outside Directors: A Cross Border Analysis." *European Financial Management* 11 (2): 153–71.

Bhagat, S., and B. Bolton. 2008. "Corporate Governance and Firm Performance." *Journal of Corporate Finance* 14 (3): 257–73.

Bond, M. 2006. *The Effects of Inter-Corporate Networks on Corporate Social and Political Behaviour.* End of Award Report, ref 000–22–0872, Economic Social and Research Council. www.esrc.ac.uk award.

———. 2007. "Elite Social Relations and Corporate Political Donations in Britain." *Political Studies* 55 (1): 59–85.

Bromley, D., et al. 1979 "Atrocity Tales, the Unification Church and the Social Construction of Evil" *Journal of Communication* 29 (3): 447–65.

Cadbury, A. 1992. *The Financial Aspects of Corporate Governance* (The Cadbury Report). Committee on the Financial Aspects of Corporate Governance, December 1. London, UK: Gee Publishing.http://www. econsense.de/_CSR_INFO_POOL/_CORP_ GOVERNANCE/images/cadbury_report.pdf.

Clarke, T. 2004. "Cycles of Crisis and Regulation: The Enduring Agency and Stewardship Problems of Corporate Governance." *Corporate Governance* 12 (2): 153–61.

Combined Code. 2008. The Financial Reporting Council, London.

Daily, C., et al. 2003. "Corporate Governance: Decades of Dialogue and Data." *Academy of Management Review* 28 (3): 371–82.

Dalton, C., et al. 1998. Meta-Analytic Review of Board Composition, Leadership Structure and Financial Performance. *Strategic Management Journal* 19 (3): 269–90.

Dalton, C., and D. Dalton. 2005. "Boards of Directors: Utilizing Empirical Evidence in Developing Practical Prescriptions." *British Journal of Management* 16 (S1): S91–97.

Davis, G.F. 2005. "New Directions in Corporate Governance." *Annual Review of Sociology* 31: 143–62.

Davis, G.F., and H.R. Greve. 1997. "Corporate Elite Networks and Governance Changes in the 1980s." *American Journal of Sociology* 103 (1): 1–37.

Davis, G.F., and G.E. Robbins. 2004. "Nothing but Net? Networks and Status in Corporate Governance." In *The Sociology of Financial Markets,* ed. K. Knorr-Cetina and A. Preda. Oxford: Oxford University Press, 290–311.

Davis, J., et al. 1997. "Towards a Stewardship Theory of Management." *Academy of Management Review* 22 (1): 20–47.

Daudi, P. 1986. *Power in the Organisation.* Oxford: Blackwell.

Edelman, L. 1990. "Legal Environments and Organizational Governance: The Expansion of Due Process in the American Workplace." *American Journal of Sociology* 95 (6): 1401–40.

Eisenhardt, K. 1989. "Agency Theory: A Review and Assessment." *Academy of Management Review* 14 (1): 57–74.

Fama, E. 1980. "Agency Problems and the Theory of the Firm." *Journal of Political Economy* 88 (2): 288–307.

Fama, E., and M. Jensen. 1983. "Separation of Ownership and Control." *Journal of Law and Economics* 26 (2): 301–25.

Filatotchev, I., et al. 2007. *Key Drivers of "Good" Corporate Governance and the Appropriateness of UK Policy Responses.* London: Department of Trade and Industry.

Forbes, D., and F. Milliken. 1999. "Cognition and Corporate Governance: Understanding Boards of Directors as Strategic Decision-Making Groups." *Academy of Management Review* 24 (2): 489–505.

Froud, J., et al. 2008. "Everything for Sale: How Non-Executive Directors Make a Difference." In *Remembering Elites,* ed. M. Savage and K. Williams. Oxford: Blackwell.

Gillan, S., and J. Martin. "Corporate Governance Post-Enron: Effective Reforms or Closing the Stable Door." *Journal of Corporate Finance* 13 (5): 929–58.

Granovetter, M. 1985. Economic Action and Social Structure: The Problem of Embeddedness. *American Journal of Sociology* 91 (3): 481–510.

Greenbury, R. 1995. *Directors' Remuneration: Report of a Study Group Chaired by Sir Richard Greenbury* (The Greenbury Report), July 17. London: Gee Publishing. http://www.econsense.de/_CSR_INFO_POOL/_CORP_GOVERNANCE/images/greenbury_report.pdf.

Hampel, R. 1998. *Final Report. Committee on Corporate Governance* (The Hampel Committee), January. London, UK: Gee Publishing. http://www.econsense.de/_CSR_INFO_POOL/_CORP_GOVERNANCE/images/hampel_report.pdf.

Harris, D., and C. Helfat. 2007. "The Board of Directors as Social Network: A New Perspective." *Journal of Management Inquiry* 16 (3): 227–38.

Higgs, D. 2003. *Review of the Role and Effectiveness of Non-Executive Directors.* The Higgs Report, January 2003. http://www.berr.gov.uk/files/file23012.pdf. Available from the Department of Trade and Industry.

Hooghiemstra, R., and J. van Manen. 2004. "The Independence Paradox: (Im)Possibilities Facing Non-Executive Directors in The Netherlands." *Corporate Governance* 12 (3): 314–24.

Huse, M. 2003. "Renewing Management and Governance: New Paradigms of Governance?" *Journal of Management and Governance* 7 (3): 211–21.

Jensen, M., and W. Meckling. 1976. "Theory of the Firm: Managerial Behaviour, Agency Costs, and Ownership Structure." *Journal of Financial Economics* 3 (4): 305–60.

Jones, I., and M. Pollitt. 2002. "Who Influences Debates in Business Ethics? An Investigation into the Development of Corporate Governance in the UK since 1990." In *Understanding How Issues in Business Ethics Develop,* ed. I. Jones and M. Pollitt. Basingstoke, UK: Palgrave Macmillan, 14–66.

———. 2004. "Understanding How Issues in Corporate Governance Develop: Cadbury Report to Higgs Review." *Corporate Governance* 12 (2): 162–71.

Keenan, J. 2004. "Corporate Governance in UK/USA Boardrooms." *Corporate Governance* 12 (2): 172–76.

Kershaw, D. 2005. "Evading Enron: Taking Principles Too Seriously in Accounting Regulation." *Modern Law Review* 68 (4): 594–625.

Kesner, I. 1987. "Directors' Characteristics and Committee Membership: An Investigation of Type, Occupation, Tenure and Gender." *Academy of Management Journal* 31 (1): 66–84.

Kesner, I., and R. Johnson. 1990. "An Investigation of the Relationship between Board Composition and Stockholder Suits." *Strategic Management Journal* 11 (4): 327–36.

Leblanc, R., and M. Schwartz. 2007. "The Black Box of Board Process: Gaining Access to a Difficult Subject." *Corporate Governance* 15 (5): 843–51.

MacNeil, I., and X. Li. 2006. "'Comply or Explain': Market Discipline and Non-Compliance with the Combined Code." *Corporate Governance* 14 (5): 486–96.

McBarnet, D., and C. Whelan. 1999. *Creative Accounting and the Cross-Eyed Javelin.* New York: Wiley.

McNulty, T., and A. Pettigrew. 1999. "Strategists on the Board." *Organization Studies* 20 (1): 47–74.

McNulty, T., et al. 2003. *Creating Accountability Within the Board: The Work of the Effective Non-Executive.* London: Department of Trade and Industry (DTI).

McNulty, T., et al. 2005. "Undertaking Governance Reform and Research: Further Reflections on the Higgs Review." *British Journal of Management* 16 (S1): S99–S107.

Mills, C. 1956. *The Power Elite.* New York: Oxford University Press.

Mitchell, L. 1995. *Progressive Corporate Law.* Boulder, CO: Westview Press.

Mizruchi, M. 1996. "What Do Interlocks Do? An Analysis, Critique and Assessment of Research on Interlocking Directorates." *Annual Review of Sociology* 22: 271–98.

Pettigrew, A. 1992. "On Studying Managerial Elites." *Strategic Management Journal* 13 (S2): 163–82.

Pettigrew, A., and T. McNulty. 1995. "Power and Influence in and Around the Boardroom." *Human Relations* 48 (8): 845–73.

Roberts, J. 2001. "Trust and Control in Anglo-American Systems of Corporate Governance: The Individualizing and Socializing Effects of Processes of Accountability." *Human Relations* 54 (12): 1547–72.

Roberts, J., et al. 2005. "Beyond Agency Conceptions of the Work of the Non-Executive Director: Creating Accountability in the Boardroom." *British Journal of Management* 16 (S1): S5–S26.

Scott, J. 1991a. *Who Rules Britain.* Oxford: Polity.

———. 1991b. "Networks of Corporate Power: A Comparative Assessment." *Annual Review of Sociology* 17: 181–203.

———. 1997. *Corporate Business and Capitalist Classes.* Oxford: Oxford University Press.

Shabbir, A., and C. Padgett. 2008. *The UK Code of Corporate Governance: Link Between Compliance and Firm Performance.* RP 2/08. Cranfield University School of Management. February. http://dspace.lib.cranfield.ac.uk/handle/1826/3931.

Shleifer, A., and R. Vishny. 1997. "A Survey of Corporate Governance." *Journal of Finance* 52 (2): 737–80.

Stiles, P. 2001. "The Impact of Boards on Strategy: An Empirical Examination." *Journal of Management Studies* 38 (5): 627–50.

Turnbull, N. 1999. *Internal Control: Guidance for Directors on the Combined Code* (The Turnbull Report). London: Institute of Chartered Accountants in England & Wales (ICEAW), September. http://www.icaew.com/index.cfm/route/120907/icaew_ga/pdf.

Useem, M. 1984. *The Inner Circle.* New York: Oxford University Press.

Westphal, S., and I. Stern. 2007. Flattery Will Get You Everywhere (Especially if You Are a Male Caucasian): How Integration, Board Room Behavior And Demographic Minority Status Affect Additional Board Appointments at US Companies. *Academy of Management Journal* 50 (2): 267–88.

Williamson, O. 1985. *The Economic Institutions of Capitalism.* New York: Free Press.

14

ACCOUNTABILITY AND VOLUNTARY PROGRAMS

Matthew Potoski and Aseem Prakash

When companies try to be socially responsible, they are often met with skepticism. After all, the justification for the vast government regulatory apparatus is that profit-seeking firms simply are unwilling to do the right thing. The root cause of public skepticism is not just doubts about firms' motives, but also that their claims are often difficult for outsiders to verify. Is the company that claims to have a "cleaner manufacturing process" really doing anything better for the environment? Many firms make these claims, whether about environmental or other areas of socially desirable behavior, and many people would be happy to recognize and even reward firms, should their claims be true.

An important yardstick for evaluating any governance system is the extent to which it enhances accountability (Pitkin 1967; Dubnick 2005). In public management and government spheres, the criterion is whether governments are accountable to citizens (Behn 2001). In business arenas accountability refers to firms' fiduciary duties (Terlaak and King 2005). Accountability questions are also germane to nonprofits whose primary aim is holding governments and private firms accountable (Fox and Brown 1998). Efforts to improve accountability focus on identifying accountability standards and to whom they apply, ensuring that the rights to evaluate others are appropriately conferred, and establishing proper incentives and sanctions for ensuring subjects adhere to the standards.

In this chapter we investigate voluntary programs as accountability mechanisms by using the International Organization for Standardization's ISO 14001 voluntary environmental program as an illustrative case. We shed light on important but less studied aspects of accountability, which include satisfying information deficits through voluntary institutions that provide information about accountability subjects. Voluntary programs are important elements of governance systems around the world and in many important policy domains. As complements to public regulation, they are designed to induce firms to generate positive social externalities beyond the requirements of government regulations. While these programs aim to induce firms to "do good," their performance has been uneven and has thus left considerable skepticism about their efficacy and whether they improve accountability. Voluntary programs' uneven performance and sometimes impenetrability to outsiders suggest weaknesses when viewed through traditional analytic lenses that focus on questions such as who has the authority to hold accountable the voluntary programs and to whom are the firms joining these programs being held accountable.

We propose that voluntary programs can serve a valuable role in accountability processes, one that raises important but often neglected analytic questions. Voluntary programs can mitigate information asymmetries between firms and their stakeholders. Much of the accountability research has traditionally focused on whether principals have the legitimacy and resources to hold agents accountable. While resources are necessary for ensuring accountability, so too is information about agents' activities. Accountability can break down because principals lack information about agents' behavior. Because resources cannot perfectly substitute for information (though they may help in eliciting information), we believe that accountability scholars need to study how information about firms and their activities is generated and communicated through the governance mechanisms that are designed to hold them accountable. Voluntary programs can help hold firms accountable to government regulators acting on behalf of citizens and directly to citizens in their interactions with firms. In both cases the value added from an effective voluntary program is information about firms' behavior that government regulators and citizens would otherwise have difficulty acquiring.

A second advantage of studying voluntary programs is that they help shed light on why firms sometimes voluntarily submit themselves to formal accountability guidelines enacted by nongovernmental actors. Unlike other notions, such as the "social license to operate" (Gunningham et al. 2003), voluntary programs outline concrete standards with which participating firms are expected to comply. At the same time, these firms are free to choose from multiple programs, each offering its own version of accountability. Instead of a single source of supply for accountability, we can think of a market for accountability institutions and examine how market pressures affect firms' participation in them (Prakash and Potoski 2006b). Firms need accountability institutions to corner reputational benefits, while institutions need participating firms to survive. It is this mutual dependence that makes the study of accountability dynamics so interesting.

This chapter shows how voluntary programs can contribute to governance systems' efficacy. Our analysis of ISO 14001 highlights the importance of information in accountability, identifies institutional features voluntary programs need to serve as effective information providers in governance systems, and illustrates the policy and managerial circumstances in which voluntary programs can add value as accountability mechanisms. Our analysis follows the research tradition summarized in Grant and Keohane (2005, 29), in which accountability is evaluated both as an ends—whether accountability targets behave in desired ways—and as a means—whether the appropriate individuals and groups are able to participate in the accountability process in desired ways.

ACCOUNTABILITY, INFORMATION, AND GOVERNANCE

The governance research tradition takes a broad view of accountability relationships by examining "chains of accountability": whether politicians are accountable to the will of citizens, whether agencies are accountable to their political overseers, and ultimately whether the policy "works" in terms of achieving the outcomes citizens desire. Following Grant and Keohane (2005, 29), by accountability we mean "that some actors have the right to hold other actors to a set of standards, to judge whether they have fulfilled their responsibilities in light of these standards, and to impose sanctions if they determine that these responsibilities have not been met."

Principal-agent theory provides a convenient framework for describing accountability relationships such as those between government regulators and firms and citizens and firms (Nielson and Tierney 2003). In principal-agent lexicon, those looking to hold others accountable are the principals and those being held accountable are called agents. There are two necessary conditions for principals to effectively hold agents accountable. First, the principals must have sufficient resources to induce the agents to change their behavior in desired ways. We use the term *resources* here in a broad sense to include both carrots and sticks that principals can deploy to influence agents, so that resources include legal authority to establish and enforce rules and financial resources to pay a price premium for products produced in desirable ways. Second, principals need information on whether agents are performing in the ways they desire. Both information and resources are necessary for accountability, and neither alone is sufficient. Voluntary programs can contribute to participatory accountability by mitigating information asymmetries, thereby empowering their principals (specifically, regulators and citizen stakeholders) to hold firms accountable. Principals are hampered by information asymmetries in that they do not know enough about agents' behavior. If agents and principals had identical preferences, accountability losses (agency costs) would be small, but to the extent their preferences diverge, the principals look to align their agents' interests with their own, perhaps through accountability mechanisms that monitor agents and sanction them if agents behave contrary to the principals' preferences.

Accountability is important because citizens want firms to do socially "good" things, such as reduce their pollution emissions or adopt fair-labor practices in the developing world. We use the term "social good" to refer to what are sometimes called "positive externalities." In the public-policy lexicon, externalities are negative or positive consequences of actions that are experienced by those not involved in the action; the social costs and benefits of an action differ from the private costs and benefits that actors experience. Actors tend to "underproduce" goods with positive externalities because they cannot capture all the benefits society enjoys, yet they bear all the costs. For example, if I pay all the costs of a street lamp I install at the end of my sidewalk, my neighbors enjoy a safer neighborhood and an easier path to their homes. But I would not install the lamp if its costs exceeded the benefits I would receive, an unfortunate loss to my neighbors whose gains (in addition to my own) would have been more than my costs. Similarly, actors tend to overproduce goods with negative externalities because, while they enjoy the benefits, they only partially bear the costs society suffers, such as when unregulated factories emit pollution. Markets can solve some externality problems without governmental intervention. If the producers and receivers of externalities could bargain easily—that is, with few information asymmetries and low transaction costs of negotiating and writing contracts—receivers of externalities could compensate producers of externalities, which would lead to socially optimal production (Coase 1960).

One goal of the governance research tradition is to find ways to structure firms' behavior so that it is not incompatible with, and perhaps even promotes, public welfare (Dubnick 2005; Behn 2003). The traditional approach to compelling firms to do socially good things and prevent them from doing harm uses government mandates codified in public law, such as taxes or regulations on firms. In the United States, command-and-control regulation, in which the government specifies how firms should behave, has been the traditional approach for compelling firms to do socially good things, particularly in environmental policy.

The efficacy of an accountability mechanism varies with the quality of information in it. If government agencies implementing the laws had complete information, they could write rules that align firms' behavior with public welfare and then monitor firms' compliance with these rules to ensure that firms are behaving in ways that citizens want. But agencies do not have perfect information and, therefore, do not know which firms are complying with laws, and when noncompliance occurs, whether it stems from the firm's deliberate evasion or is an unfortunate accident that occurs despite good intentions (Pfaff and Sanchirico 2000). If regulators could distinguish between the well intentioned and the evaders, they could provide technical assistance and incentives to the former and throw the book at the latter.[1] Without some way to identify which firms were making good-faith efforts to comply with regulation, regulators strictly enforce all rules lest any incentives and assistance be seen as a sign of laxity and an invitation for nefarious firms to shirk their regulatory responsibilities even further. If regulators knew which violations emanated from deliberate malfeasance and which were unfortunate accidents of well- intentioned firms, they could target their limited enforcement resources more effectively. At the same time, firms would have more incentive to invest resources in avoiding environmental mishaps because the regulator would recognize and even reward their good deeds, even in the event of an environmental mishap.

Government regulations are not the only mechanism for holding firms publicly accountable. Citizens also directly interact with firms through their purchases and in extreme cases through their protests and lobbying, or what Baron (2003) calls "private politics." As consumers, citizens might be willing to lobby firms or pay extra for goods from firms that behave in the way they desire, such as making products in environmentally friendly ways. A citizen would reward a firm for such good behavior only after verifying that the firm's behavior is actually good in the ways she wants it to be. But such verification is difficult because so much of what firms do—from their pollution activities to their labor policies in the developing world—is unobservable to outsiders. Firms could unilaterally declare that their goods have been produced in socially responsible ways. Such self-declarations would generally not be very credible and citizens would make their purchases as if no firms were doing anything socially responsible lest they be caught in a "suckers'" scam of paying a price premium for socially responsible products that were in fact produced just like all others.

We thus have two mechanisms for holding firms accountable to citizens—government regulations and private politics—whose efficacy depends on the availability of information about which firms are behaving in socially desirable ways. Information asymmetries where agents have more information about their own behavior than do their principals are problematic, not just for the citizens and the regulators acting on their behalf, but also for firms. Because citizens and regulators cannot identify the firms doing socially good things, all firms are tarred with the same brush, and no firm has much incentive to do social good. Some firms might be willing to do socially good things—in how they produce products or strive to comply with government regulations—but only with assurance that citizens and regulators would reward them for their good deeds, by buying more of their products and not punishing them severely for accidental regulatory violations. The tragedy is that absent information identifying which firms are behaving in socially desirable ways, citizens and regulatory enforcers have little choice but to assume no firms are behaving well, lest they end up rewarding firms' empty claims.

VOLUNTARY CLUBS

We propose that voluntary programs, or "voluntary clubs" as we call them, can improve governance by providing information about firms' behavior that regulators and citizens would not otherwise have. We call the programs "clubs" because they share features with the economic theory of clubs (Buchanan 1965; Cornes and Sandler 1996). Voluntary programs are like clubs in that they offer an excludable benefit that firms receive from their stakeholders (regulators, customers, and suppliers) that nonparticipating firms do not receive. Participating firms receive these benefits because membership in the program signals that the firm is taking progressive environmental action, which allows club sponsors to require members to pay the costs. While command-and-control regulations seek to persuade firms to adopt such policies via the stick of mandatory enforcement, green clubs seek to do so via the carrot of enhancing firms' reputation through their membership in the club. This chapter summarizes our theoretical view of voluntary clubs, drawing on our theoretical (Prakash and Potoski 2006a, 2007) and empirical (Potoski and Prakash 2005a, 2005b) studies of voluntary programs and ISO 14001.

Voluntary programs are rule systems that specify how members are to behave and the public goods they need to produce as program members. Club standards specify what firms need to do to join the program and remain members in good standing, and might specify performance expectations (sometimes called outcome standards) or processes, such as requirements that members adopt a management system or consult with community groups. Lenient club standards require little of their members beyond what government regulations require. Stringent club standards require that members produce high levels of positive social externalities. By "voluntary" we mean behavior that produces positive social externalities beyond what public law requires. Public law is thus the analytic referent for measuring the public value a voluntary program creates: the marginal contribution to public welfare from voluntary programs is the value added from its participants' activities that are beyond the applicable legal requirements.

Firms participating in a voluntary program may have incentives to "free ride" (Olson 1965) and enjoy the benefits of affiliating with the club without paying the costs of adhering to its requirements. An effective voluntary program must mitigate shirking through monitoring and enforcement rules. Third-party monitoring means that firms are required to have their actions audited by accredited, external auditors to verify that they are producing the social externalities that club membership requires. In some cases, program sponsors may require public disclosure of audit information. Finally, the sponsoring organization may itself act upon the audit information and sanction the members that have been found to be shirking their obligations.

For consumers, resources for using a voluntary-program brand are those necessary for private politics, including paying price premiums for products produced through program membership, or having resources to lobby or protest firms on a sufficiently large scale. In developed countries, aggressive "green" consumer-marketing campaigns suggest firms do value a positive public image. Consumers are sometimes willing to pay a price premium for products with credible and tangible environmental benefits (Kotchen and Moore 2007).[2]

The role of government regulators in voluntary programs and firm accountability is more complex. The primary approach is for governments to use voluntary programs to suggest the nature of the regulatory enforcement toward individual facilities. Government regulators can reward voluntary program participation with a cooperative enforcement style in which transgressions and violations are problems to be solved through collaboration rather than a cause for harsh punishment. In some cases, regulators may not have the legal authority to reward firms for their actions as program members (Scholz 1991). Indeed, firms are less likely to join voluntary programs where regulators lack the discretion to flexibly enforce regulations (Potoski and Prakash 2004a). In the United States the Environmental Protection Agency (EPA) has launched many voluntary programs of its own, but has not been receptive to using voluntary program membership in its regulatory enforcement programs. For example, the uneven reception of voluntary programs in the United States, as compared to Western Europe's enthusiasm for these programs, stems from the United States' adversarial regulatory culture and a domestic environmental movement suspicious of government getting to cozy with firms (Kollman and Prakash 2001).

Even if consumers and regulators are able to reward firms for their voluntary-program participation, to hold firms accountable they must also be able to recognize and interpret what a voluntary-program brand signals about its members' behavior. For a voluntary program to improve accountability, its brand must convey useful information about program members' behavior that citizens and government regulators would otherwise be unable to acquire. For citizens, interpreting brand signals can be daunting because club standards do not always translate directly to public-goods production. ISO 14001's requirement that members adopt an environmental management system is not an easily understood message for consumers, even relatively sophisticated ones. Alternatively, citizens could use the identity of the program sponsor to infer information about the stringency of the club standard, although even these inferences require some sophistication. Only well-informed citizens are likely to know the difference between the Nature Conservancy's emphasis on private-sector solutions and Friends of the Earth's more activist approach.

Voluntary-program efficacy hinges on whether several conditions are met. First, the institutional design of voluntary programs must be strong. They must have club standards that require members to produce positive externalities beyond what government law requires, and they must have effective monitoring and enforcement rules to ensure members are complying with club standards. Second, voluntary clubs must provide stakeholders with useful information about the externalities their members produce. Sophisticated stakeholders such as government regulators may be able to interpret the program's club standards and enforcement rules; citizens may need information shortcuts such as inferences based on the reputation of the program sponsor. Third, stakeholders must be able to use this information to reward or punish firms for the action they take (or do not take) as program members.

ISO 14001 AS AN ACCOUNTABILITY SIGNAL

In this section we examine ISO 14001's performance as an accountability mechanism by examining its institutional design, the reputation of its sponsor, and the ability of stakeholders to use ISO 14001 certification. We first describe the ISO's mission, organizational structure, and rule-development processes and evaluate the information the ISO brand conveys as a voluntary-program sponsor. We then outline ISO 14001, ISO's preeminent voluntary environmental program, and describe its club standards and enforcement rules. We conclude with an investigation of the ISO and ISO 14001's performance-as-accountability mechanisms.

The International Organization for Standardization

The mission of the International Organization for Standardization is to reduce transaction costs by providing clear standards and definitions about products exchanged in international markets. Since its inception in the early twentieth century, the ISO had developed over 16,000 international standards in response to demands for international market standards. ISO standards help corporations reduce the transaction costs of dealing with varying standards across their subsidiaries and with their trading partners.[3] Its acronym, ISO, is no accident: *iso* is a Greek word meaning equal. Starting in the 1990s, the ISO began expanding its product menu to codify management systems for quality management (ISO 9000), environmental management (ISO 14001) and, more recently, corporate social responsibility (ISO 26000).

The ISO (2010) is a nongovernmental organization composed of the national standards institutes from each of 163 countries. The American National Standards Institute, the Deutsches Institut für Normun, and the Instituto Argentino de Normalización are examples of national standards bodies. ISO's standards development process is democratic, although participation is limited to "principal" dues-paying members. Each year, ISO convenes a meeting of its General Assembly to vote on various proposed standards, with each full member receiving one vote. Proposals are submitted to the General Assembly by the ISO Council, which serves as the executive committee for the organization. Representation on the ISO Council rotates every three years among full members. The Council itself does not develop the proposed standards. Instead, it forms ad hoc technical committees to develop specific standards and then disbands them once the standards are in place. Technical-committee members represent specific countries. Typically, those on the committee are experts on loan from industry, technical bodies, or governmental agencies. Although nongovernmental organizations (NGOs) or trade associations do not have independent standing in the ISO, they can serve on technical committees as a part of a national delegation. For members to retain voting rights in technical committees, the ISO requires that they regularly attend the meetings. To approve a new standard, the ISO requires a two-thirds majority approval in the technical committee and a three-fourths majority in the General Assembly. The ISO reviews and if necessary revises each standard at least every five years (ISO, 2004b). Once the ISO issues a standard, it becomes a public good in that anyone in any country can adopt it.

Accountability and Standards Development in the ISO

As a nongovernmental organization, ISO's standards-development processes are fairly democratic and transparent. Any country can place its national-standards body as a fully participating member. Still, ISO's standards-development processes have been criticized for being unjust and inequitable. The costs of participating in ISO meetings and the difficulty in supplying technical experts tend to exclude participation by developing countries (Clapp 1998). Consequently, although developing countries account for about 75 percent of ISO's national-standards bodies, they contribute less than 5 percent of the technical rule-making work. The United Nations Conference on Trade and Development has recommended that the ISO provide financial support to facilitate developing countries' participation. ISO's standards-development process also does not grant NGOs independent standing, unlike much public regulation in democracies, particularly in the United States, which receive NGO input through established institutional mechanisms such as sunshine laws and notice and comment hearings on proposed regulations. Despite these criticisms, ISO still enjoys credibility for its technical expertise and its relatively open and fair rule standards development processes.

We should note that the ISO's standards are nonbinding: anyone can choose whether or not to participate in them. However, firms' decisions about using a standard affect other firms' value from using that standard. For example, the size of a voluntary club's membership roster affects the strength and value of its brand to others members of the club, because more members create economies of scale in building the club's reputation (McGuire 1972), a dynamic akin to network effects (Bessen and Saloner 1988). Network effects are the changes in the benefit that an actor derives from a good when the number of other actors consuming the same good changes. Positive network effects create increasing returns to scale: with every additional unit, the marginal cost of production decreases. Having more members helps advertise a voluntary club broadly among stakeholders as one member's socially desirable activities generates positive, goodwill externalities for other members, so that the value of membership increases as others join.

The benefits of voluntary-club membership are noncompetitive because the positive branding benefits one member enjoys can be simultaneously enjoyed by other members. However, at some point, crowding may set in. While a voluntary club with universal membership would do little to identify which firms were producing desirable social goods, industry-sponsored clubs might desire universal membership of the firms operating in their industry, as is the case with the National Ski Areas Association's Sustainable Slopes Program, the American Chemistry Council's Responsible Care Program, and the American Forestry and Paper Association's Sustainable Forestry Initiative. Thus, similar to the traditional club literature on optimal club size (Cornes and Sandler 1996), there are significant opportunities to examine this issue in the context of voluntary clubs.

ISO 14001: Institutional Design

In 1997, ISO launched the ISO 14001 environmental certification program as part of its 14000 series of standards. ISO 14001 has had a tremendous growth rate (International Organization for Standardization, 2002). By October 2004, 74,004 facilities across 130 countries had joined ISO

14001 (International Organization for Standardization 2005).[4] The explicit goal of ISO 14001 is to improve the environmental and regulatory performance of businesses by having participating firms adopt stringent environmental management systems (International Organization for Standardization 2002). The logic is that if appropriate management systems are in place, superior environmental performance will follow.

ISO 14001's club standards specify the management practices a facility must adopt for its environmental operations. To receive ISO 14001 certification a facility must undertake an initial comprehensive review of its environmental practices, formulate and implement an action plan for environmental management with ongoing performance targets, clearly identify internal governance responsibilities for environmental issues, and make necessary corrections to address identified environmental problems. ISO 14001's monitoring and enforcement procedures center on a system of third-party audits to verify that members' environmental management system (EMS) is in compliance (International Organization for Standardization 2002).[5] Certified facilities are expected to receive surveillance audits at least once a year, and a complete reassessment every three years. (The ISO requires that third-party auditors themselves receive accreditation.) The length of audits can range from a few weeks to several months, depending on the size of the facility and the advance work it has done (Registrar Accreditation Board 2004). The ISO recognizes an accreditation authority in each country—such as the United Kingdom Accreditation Service, Comité Français d'Accréditation, Trägergemeinschaft für Akkreditierung GmbH, China National Accreditation Council for Registrars, and the American National Standards Institute-Registrar Accreditation Board (ANSI-RAB)—that certifies which organizations can perform ISO 14001 certification audits (International Organization for Standardization 2004).[6]

Establishing an EMS and having it audited by a third party can cost from $25,000 to over $100,000 per facility (Kolk 2000). In practice, an ISO-certified EMS requires substantial investment beyond the cost of external auditors, including the costs of maintaining paper trails and even hiring additional personnel (Prakash 2000). William Glasser of the EPA estimates that "large facilities spend on average about $1 million in sunk transaction costs to pursue certification."[7]

ISO 14001's Brand Image

Do company stakeholders understand the ISO 14001 brand? According to interviews we conducted with managers at ISO 14001-certified facilities and with government regulatory officials in the United States, the ISO 14001 standard is fairly well known among more sophisticated stakeholders, such as government regulators and trading partners, and less well understood by consumers.[8] Plant managers saw that ISO 14001 had a positive brand identity that could benefit their company, though only one manager noted that certification helped company relations with consumers. Another manager stated that ISO 14001 certification raised awareness among suppliers and vendors that the firm was attentive to environmental issues, though she was skeptical that most consumers were able to recognize ISO 14001. A third manager felt ISO 14001 held considerable value as a marketing tool and was disappointed that her parent corporation did not promote its ISO 14001 certifications more aggressively. ISO 14001's positive brand name is evident in how these facilities advertised their certification locally: one manager reported that the local newspaper reported a favorable article when the facility received ISO 14001 certification, although the facility's earlier pollution-prevention award received more prominent press coverage. A manager at another certified facility reported flying an ISO 14001 flag on the facility flagpole. Although we do not have extensive evidence on this point, the plant manager interviews suggest that consumers generally do not use the ISO 14001 brand in their purchasing choice.

As reported in Prakash and Potoski (2006a), interviews with nine government regulators suggest that ISO 14001 has a strong and positive brand image, as all recognized ISO 14001 as an important voluntary program that indicated members were making a commitment to environmental action. Jeff Smoller and Mark McDermid of the Wisconsin Department of Natural Resources view ISO 14001 as the "gold standard" among EMS-based voluntary regulations.[9] They believe that ISO 14001 reduces regulators' workload in terms of identifying paper trails and elements of management systems within firms. While regulators recognize that the quality of audits and auditors vary, third-party audits by trained and accredited people provide credible assurance about the quality of EMS-based clubs. Of course, Smoller and McDermid recognize that regulators do not give ISO 14001 firms an "auto pass" on issues pertaining to regulatory compliance. Nevertheless, Smoller and McDermid acknowledge that externally verified, EMS-based voluntary programs such as ISO 14001 might indicate that the firm is serious about regulatory compliance.[10] William Glasser of the EPA likewise noted that "ISO certification does signal firms' commitment to better compliance as this is a commitment that is almost always memorialized in the Environmental Policy. ISO is not a compliance tool per se nor should it be construed or used as such. But it does support the emergence of systems thinking vis-à-vis environmental aspects/impacts and that, in turn, supports a greater awareness of and emphasis on compliance."[11] Doug Smith of the EPA, Region 10, noted, "ISO 14001 signals firms' commitment to environmental excellence."[12] Susan Roothaan of Texas Department of Natural Resources (DNR) also noted that ISO 14001 signals firms' intent to better comply with the law.[13] Finally, David Ronald commented that "ISO [14001] requires a commitment to compliance [with government regulations]."[14]

ISO 14001's standing with regulators appears to stem from several factors. First, receiving certification requires firms to outlay a substantial amount of money and other resources. Doug Smith noted "[ISO 14001] requires a lot of work and resources to establish solid EMS and get it audited." [15] Consequently, U.S. firms often cannot simply receive certification with a few slight modifications to their existing practices. Second, several regulators saw considerable value in ISO 14001's third-party auditing. David Ronald, the Executive Director of the Multi-State Working Group, noted that third-party audits are useful to bring about cultural change within companies.[16] This is because no manager wants to look bad to the top management, which eventually gets the audit reports. Susan Roothan also noted that "the largest driver from a psychological perspective is the desire not to fail. If an organization knows it is being audited to a standard, top management will typically do what they can to pass."[17] Finally, several officials suggested that ISO 14001 significantly eases regulators' tasks because the EMS documents firms' environmental activities. As Douglas Smith explained, EPA field inspectors get a list of facilities to inspect from EPA program managers. They spend two to three weeks studying the background information prior to visiting the facility. They typically spend two to three days at the facility and then another week writing their inspection report. A well functioning EMS reduces inspectors' workloads, both prior to and during the inspection. If EMS is in place, inspectors get information they need, and whom to contact for specific pieces of information that is not readily available.[18]

Signaling and ISO 14001

If ISO 14001 is to improve accountability, it must accurately signal that its members have better environmental and regulatory performance than nonmembers. Some research indicates that firms that join ISO 14001 do in fact improve their environmental and regulatory performance. Firms that join voluntary environmental programs, including ISO 14001, are generally cleaner than those that do not join (Potoski and Prakash 2005a; Delmas 2001), although the degree to which members are cleaner varies for different programs, and not all programs lead to environmental and regulatory improvements (Darnall and Carmin 2005). If the role of voluntary environmental programs is to distinguish environmental leaders from laggards, we might be content to know that program members are cleaner and not worry ourselves over whether joining the program caused them to be cleaner. The question of causality is important because if we are to give voluntary programs credit for holding firms accountable, we want to know that the voluntary program was in some way responsible for compelling firms to improve their behavior. Attributing causality in social-science research is generally quite difficult, with the credibility of conclusions often hinging on difficult-to-verify and quite technical assumptions. In the case of ISO 14001's efficacy at improving members' environmental performance, the evidence is mixed, although perhaps a bit stronger in supporting the claim that the program works. In a study of 236 Mexican firms in the food, chemical, nonmetallic minerals, and metal industries (which together generate 75 percent to 95 percent of Mexico's industrial pollution), Dasgupta et al. (2000) find that ISO 14001 adopters show better compliance with government environmental regulations, an important finding given that many developing countries have difficulties enforcing government regulations. In his analysis of 316 U.S. electronics facilities, Russo (2001) finds that ISO 14001 membership is associated with decreased toxic emissions. Our own studies of about 3,000 U.S. facilities regulated under the Clean Air Act indicate that ISO 14001 adopters, in comparison to non-adopters, pollute less (Potoski and Prakash 2005b; see also Toffel 2006) and show better compliance with the law (Potoski and Prakash 2005a). Some other studies which do not employ sophisticated statistical techniques (specifically, controlling for endogeneity—or determining what effect a firm's decision to join ISO 14001 had on performance, as opposed to the effect of ISO 14001 on their performance) suggest that ISO 14001 is ineffective. Dahlstrom et. al (2003) report that ISO 14001 did not improve regulatory performance of British facilities. For the U.S. case, Andrews et al. (2003) suggest that ISO 14001 did not affect firms' environmental performance.

CONCLUSIONS: IMPLICATIONS FOR VOLUNTARY PROGRAMS AND ACCOUNTABILITY

Our brief study of ISO 14001 suggests some lessons about voluntary programs as accountability mechanisms. ISO 14001 can serve as an accountability mechanism by reducing information asymmetries between firms and their stakeholders. ISO 14001 has a strong institutional design with fairly stringent club standards and monitoring and enforcement practices. The program's sponsor, the ISO, has a generally favorable reputation due to its fairly open and accessible standards-development process and its impressive history in the international standards arena. While the evidence is not conclusive, the research suggests that receiving certification reduces members' pollution output and improves their compliance with government regulations. Still, the ISO 14001 signal is complex, perhaps too much so for stakeholders for whom the environment is not central, such as consumers and citizens. The complexity of the ISO 14001 signal suggests that the program works best for sophisticated stakeholders such as government regulators rather than citizens.

It is therefore perhaps not surprising that ISO 14001 certification is seen quite favorably by government regulators, even in the United States where voluntary regulatory approaches have found less fertile ground. ISO 14001 certification requires firms to identify and conform to the applicable government regulations. Any noncompliance that remains is therefore less likely to be the consequence of deliberate neglect or malfeasance but rather noncompliant firms' ignorance or misunderstanding of what regulations require of them. Rather than a deterrence-based enforcement approach that punishes all noncompliance as if it were deliberate, a cooperative approach would offer technical assistance and guidance to solve the compliance problem. Regulators can reward a firm's voluntary-program membership by granting regulatory relief in the form of fewer inspections, fast-tracking permit applications, or reduced fines in the event firms are out of compliance (Potoski and Prakash 2004b; Prakash and Potoski 2006a).

The ISO 14001 case also provides some broader lessons about the role of voluntary programs in improving firms' accountability. Effective voluntary programs can improve firms' public accountability by serving as a credible signaling device, but not all voluntary programs carry such promise. First, not all voluntary programs are effective: some fail to attract any companies to join, and others attract members but appear to do little to induce them to do any more good things than they would otherwise have done, even when in some cases the program's strong standards on paper would appear to suggest otherwise. Beyond ISO 14001, research on the efficacy of voluntary programs—whether they induce members to improve their performance—has produced mixed results (Ramus and Monteil 2005). Rivers and deLeon (2004) report that ski resorts participating in the Sustainable Slopes Program were not greener than nonparticipants. Similarly, King and Lenox (2000) found that chemical firms participating in the Responsible Care program did not reduce the emission of toxic chemicals any faster than nonparticipants, and Delmas and Keller (2005) present a similar weak effect of the U.S. EPA's WasteWise Program. However, Khanna and Damon (1999) report that firms that joined the Environmental Protection Agency's 35/50 voluntary program reduced their emissions of toxic pollutants more than the nonparticipants. An explanation for these disparate findings is that successful voluntary programs have effective monitoring and enforcement mechanisms that prevent shirking among participants.

For voluntary programs to improve accountability they must address some governance gap. There may not be adequate legal means for holding firms accountable, and citizens and regulators may have inadequate information about how firms are behaving. This suggests that the promise of voluntary programs is strongest where accountability through governmental channels is weakest, such as in the developing world. Some measure of caution is in order, however, because effective voluntary programs often rely on third-party monitoring and enforcement whose efficacy may be weakened by the same causes that undermine governments. Voluntary programs also hold the most promise in areas where firms' behavior is difficult for external actors to verify, such as their behavior toward the environment.

NOTES

1. See Potoski and Prakash (2004b) and Scholz (1991) for fuller treatments of these enforcement dynamics.

2. Such action overcomes a collective-action problem: consumers may be willing to pay the private costs of producing social externalities at socially optimal levels (Kotchen 2006).

3. These standards might also be motivated by the desire to preempt the emergence of new national-level regulations and standards—an important issue that undermines ISO's legitimacy among some stakeholders (Prakash and Potoski 2006a).

4. The ISO 14000 series consists of a mandatory guideline for environmental management (ISO 14001), and several non-mandatory guidelines governing environmental labeling (14020 and 14021), environmental performance evaluations (14031), and life-cycle assessment (14040–43, 14048–49).

5. Although firms can self-audit and declare themselves to be in compliance, to receive the actual ISO 14001 certification firms are required to undergo annual third-party audits.

6. In practice, certified auditors are generally for-profit consulting companies. The accreditation authority reviews the paper evidence about the auditors' competencies and performs an on-site audit of the auditors by witnessing how an auditor goes about certifying a facility. To prevent a conflict of interest, the accreditation authorities typically prohibit auditors from performing other consulting work for facilities seeking certification (International Organization for Standardization 2004).

7. Email, January 30, 2004.

8. Plant-manager interviews were conducted during spring of 2003, and government-regulator interviews during fall of 2003 and winter of 2004. Most interviews were conducted by phone; some in-person interviews were also conducted. A few days prior to the interview, we emailed a list of questions we wanted to discuss. After the phone interview, to ensure we correctly noted the responses, we emailed the summary of the conversation. For email responses to our questions, such summaries were not required.

9. Interview with Jeff Smoller and Mark McDermid, September 15, 2003.

10. Ibid.

11. Email, January 30, 2004.

12. Interview with Doug Smith, January 24, 2004.

13. Email response from Susan Roothaan, December 16, 2003.

14. Interview with David Ronald, December 11, 2003. Some regulators do not view ISO 14001 favorably. Chuck Corell of the Iowa Department of Natural Resources said that he does not treat ISO 14001 facilities any differently than non-ISO facilities. For him, the motivation for joining ISO 14001 is "the ability to show that the firm has had some documented level of environmental performance. In my opinion, all of these firms would be much better off developing a strong and honest relationship with their regulators." Email response, March 15, 2004.

15. Interview with Douglas Smith, January 24, 2004.

16. Interview with David Ronald, December 11, 2003.

17. Email response from Susan Roothaan, December 16, 2003.

18. Interview with Douglas Smith, January 24, 2004.

REFERENCES

Andrews R.N.L, D. Amaral, N. Darnall, D. Gallagher, D. Edwards Jr., A. Hutson A, C. D'Amore, and Y Zhang. 2003. Environmental Management Systems: Do They Improve Performance? Chapel Hill: Department of Public Policy, University of North Carolina at Chapel Hill and Environmental Law Institute. Prepared for the U.S. Environmental Protection Agency, Office of Water and Multistate Working Group on Environmental Performance.

Baron, David. 2003. "Private Politics." *Journal of Economics and Management Strategy* 12: 31–66.

Behn, Robert. 2001. *Rethinking Democratic Accountability.* Washington, DC: Brookings Institution Press.

———. 2003. "Why Measure Performance? Different Purposes Require Different Measures." *Public Administration Review* 63 (5): 586–606.

Bessen, S.M., and G. Saloner. 1988. *Compatibility Standards and Private Property.* New York: Harcourt, Brace & World.

Bovens, Mark. 1998. *The Quest for Responsibility: Accountability and Citizenship in Complex Organizations.* New York: Cambridge University Press.

Buchanan, James M. 1965. "A Economic Theory of Clubs." *Economica* 32: 1–14.

Clapp, J. 1998. The Privatization of Global Environmental Governance: ISO 14000 and the Developing World. *Global Governance:* 4: 295–316.

Coase, R.H. 1960. "The Problem of Social Cost." *Journal of Law and Economics* 3: 1–44.

Cornes, R., and T. Sandler. 1996 [1986]. *The Theory of Externalities, Public Goods, and Club Goods.* 2d ed. Cambridge, UK: Cambridge University Press.

Dahlstrom, K., C. Howes, O. Leinster, and J. Skea. 2003. "Environmental Management Systems and Company Performance." *European Environment* 13 (July): 187–203.

Darnall, Nicole, and Joann Carmin. 2005. "Greener and Cleaner? The Signaling Accuracy of U.S. Voluntary Environmental Programs." *Policy Sciences* 38 (1): 71–90.

Dasgupta, S., H. Hettige, and D. Wheeler. 2000. "What Improves Environmental Compliance? Evidence from Mexican Industry." *Journal of Environmental Economics and Management* 39: 39–66.

Delmas, M. 2001. "Stakeholders and Competitive Advantage: The Case of ISO 14001." *Production and Operation Management* 10 (3): 343–58.

Delmas, M., and A. Keller. 2005. "Strategic Free Riding in Voluntary Programs: The Case of the US EPA Wastewise Program." *Policy Sciences* 38: 91–106.

Dubnick, Melvin. 2005. "Accountability and the Promise of Performance: In Search of the Mechanisms." *Public Performance and Management Review* 28 (3): 376–416.

Fox, Jonathan A., and L. David Brown, eds. 1998. *The Struggle for Accountability: The World Bank, NGOs and Grassroots Movements*. Cambridge, MA: MIT Press.

Grant, Ruth W., and Robert O. Keohane. 2005. "Accountability and Abuses of Power in World Politics." *American Political Science Review* 99: 29–43.

Gunningham, N., R. Kagan, and D. Thornton. 2003. *Shades of Green: Business, Regulation, and Environment*. Stanford, CA: Stanford University Press.

International Organization for Standardization. 2002. *Environmental Management: The ISO 14000 Family of Iinternational Standards*. Available at http://www.iso.ch/iso/en/prods-services/otherpubs/iso14000/index.html, accessed June 6, 2003.

———. 2004a. *ISO, The Founding of ISO 9000 and 14000 Certificates: Twelfth Cycle*. Available from wysiwgy://10/http:/www.iso.ch/iso/en/aboutiso/introduction/fifty/pdf/foundingen.pdf, accessed July 19, 2004.

———. 2004b. *Frequently Asked Questions on ISO 14001*. Available from http:/www.iso.ch/iso/en/aboutiso/introduction/index.html, accessed July 19, 2004.

———. 2005. *ISO 9000 and ISO 14000–In Brief*. Available from http:/www.iso.ch/iso/en/ISO9000–14000/index.html, accessed July 19, 2004.

———. 2010. *General information on ISO*. Available from http://www.iso.org/iso/support/faqs/faqs_general_information_on_iso.htm, accessed July 20, 2010.

Khanna, M., and L.A. Damon. 1999. "EPA's Voluntary 33/50 Program: Impact on Toxic Releases and Economic Performance of Firms." *Journal of Environmental Economics and Management* 37: 1–25.

King, A., and M. J. Lenox. 2000. "Industry Self-Regulation without Sanctions: The Chemical Industry's Responsible Care Program." *Academy of Management Journal* 43: 698–716.

Kolk, A. 2000. *The Economics of Environmental Management*. Essex, UK: Prentice Hall/Pearson Education.

Kollman, K., and A. Prakash. 2001. "Green by Choice? Cross-National Variations in Firms' Responses to EMS-Based Environmental Regimes." *World Politics* 53 (April): 399–430.

Kotchen, Matthew. 2006. "Green Markets and Private Provision of Public Goods." *Journal of Political Economy* 114 (4): 816–34.

Kotchen, Matthew J., and Michael R. Moore. 2007. "Private Provision of Environmental Public Goods: Household Participation in Green-Electricity Programs." *Journal of Environmental Economics and Management* 53 (1): 1–16.

McGuire, M. 1972. "Private Good Clubs and Public Goods Club." *Swedish Journal of Economics* 74: 84–99.

Nielson, Daniel, and Michael J. Tierney. 2003. "Delegation to International Organizations: Agency Theory and World Bank Environmental Reform." *International Organization* 57 (2): 241–76.

Olson, M., Jr. 1965. *The Logic of Collective Action*. Cambridge, MA: Harvard University Press.

Pfaff, A., and C.W. Sanchirico. 2000. "Environmental Self-Auditing: Setting the Proper Incentives for Discovery and Correction of Environmental Harm." *Journal of Law, Economics and Organization* 16 (1): 189–208.

Pitkin, Hanna. 1967. *The Concept of Representation*. Berkeley: University of California Press.

Potoski, M., and A. Prakash. 2004a. "Green Clubs and Voluntary Governance: ISO 14001 and Firms' Regulatory Compliance." *American Journal of Political Science* 49 (2): 235–48.

———. 2004b. "The Regulation Dilemma and US Environmental Governance." *Public Administration Review* 64 (2) (March/April): 137–48.

———. 2005a. "Covenants with Weak Swords: ISO 14001 and Firms' Environmental Performance." *Journal of Policy Analysis and Management* 24 (4): 745–69.

———. 2005b. "Green Clubs and Voluntary Governance: ISO 14001 and Firms' Regulatory Compliance." *American Journal of Political Science* 49 (2): 235–48.

Prakash, A. 2000. *Greening the Firm*. New York: Cambridge University Press.

Prakash, A., and M. Potoski. 2006a. *The Voluntary Environmentalists*. New York: Cambridge University Press.

———. 2006b. "Racing to the Bottom? Globalization, Environmental Governance, and ISO 14001." *American Journal of Political Science* 50 (2): 347–61.

———. 2007. "Collective Action through Voluntary Environmental Programs: A Club Theory Perspective." *Policy Studies Journal* 35 (4): 773–92.

Ramus, Catherine A., and Ivan Montiel. 2005. "When Are Corporate Environmental Policies a Form of Greenwashing?" *Business and Society* 44 (4): 377–414.

Registrar Accreditation Board. 2004. *Frequently Asked Questions About ISO 14001 EMS CRBs.* Available from http://www.rabnet.com/er_faq.shtuml, accessed on July 24, 2004.

Rivera, Jorge, and Peter deLeon. 2004. "Is Greener Whiter? The Sustainable Slopes Program and the Voluntary Environmental Performance of Western Ski Areas." *Policy Studies Journal* 32 (3): 417–37.

Russo, M.V. 2001. *Institutional Change and Theories of Organizational Strategy.* Available from http://www.chron.com/content/chronicle/page1/92/10/23/trmain23.html, accessed November 7, 2003.

Scholz, John T. 1991. "Cooperative Regulatory Enforcement and the Politics of Administrative Effectiveness." *American Political Science Review* 85: 115–36.

Terlaak, Ann, and Andrew A. King. 2005. "The Effect of Certification with the ISO 9000 Quality Management Standard." *Journal of Economic Behavior and Organization* 60: 579–602.

PART VI

RETHINKING ACCOUNTABILITY

The recent attention given to accountability in all its various forms has created an interest in—and demand for—a more basic rethinking of how accountability relates to political and social life in general. In this section we offer four works that explore some of the fundamental questions raised by our increasing obsession with accountability.

In her examination of "Accountability in Two Non-Western Contexts," Sara Jordan notes the universal desire for accountability, but demonstrates that this "does not translate automatically into a universal definition of accountability or universal approval of the methods of exacting accountability." Her exploration begins with a distinction among the major variants (liberal, liberal-communitarian, and communitarian) of the Western tradition and then proceeds to describe two non-Western perspectives (ritual and affective accountability) drawn from east Asia and central-west Africa. The contrasts are striking, and their implications for a increasingly global perspective on accountability are significant.

In "Accountability and the Theory of Representation," Ciarán O'Kelly considers the underlying views of representation that underpin the principal-agent relationships informing most of our thinking about accountability. Focusing on the example of corporate governance, his analysis highlights the fact that issues of accountability transcend sectoral boundaries and deal with problems a good deal more substantial than those of managerial or democratic (e.g., shareholder) control. Viewing accountability as mechanisms of representation, O'Kelly argues, alters our understanding of the current scandals and crises plaguing our globalized corporate economy.

While O'Kelly's efforts are aimed at reconsidering accountability within the context of the political theory of representation, Kaifeng Yang offers a different approach that generates insights about accountability from within the social meta-theory of structuration. Relying primarily on the widely cited work of Anthony Giddens, Yang deals with the limited view of accountability as a principal-agent relationship by highlighting the complex roles and functions accountability plays in simultaneously regulating and constituting accountable behavior. Operating as both means and ends, accountability within the context of the Giddens's structuration framework is an ever "emergent" factor in social and political relationships. Viewed in this light, we gain a greater appreciation of both the growing significance and complexity of our subject.

With accountability becoming so pervasive in the world of governance (public, private and nonprofit), Dubnick and O'Brien focus attention on our collective "obsession" per se. Why are we so preoccupied with accountability as either (or both) the cause or cure of our policy and governance problems? What does this obsession tells us about how we think about—and what we expect from—greater or enhanced accountability? What are the implications of this general obsession when applied to policy design—and specifically to the efforts to reform financial markets in light of the recent (2007–2010) economic problems?

239

For those concerned with making practical sense of accountability and the challenges it poses for the day-to-day work of governing, the chapters in this section might initially seem overly abstract and of questionable "practical" value. And yet such efforts to theorize about and rethink accountability have already paid dividends, for only by constantly framing and reframing this salient feature of modern governance are we able to enrich the understanding of those who daily face the challenges posed by the promises of accountability.

15

ACCOUNTABILITY IN TWO
NON-WESTERN CONTEXTS

Sara R. Jordan

The theme of this chapter is that accountability is a universal desire of citizens. According to the logic of so many philosophers of politics, acknowledging the power of others or appreciating the threat that other beings may use their power over us is what terrifies the rational human being the most. It is a natural part of the human psyche to inquire after the sources and the depth of power, particularly if these things are unknown to us (Burke [1759] 2004, 101–28). Whether we refer to our desire to reckon with the power of the unknown as curiosity or intelligence, rationality or inquisitiveness, at the root our desire is for an account, a rendering of what is or what was, whether from other people or from nature itself.

Yet, the universal desire does not translate automatically into a universal definition of accountability or universal approval of the methods of exacting accountability. Insisting upon liberal, democratic accountability mechanisms in civil-service organizations around the globe is inconsistent with the goal of achieving meaningful accountability. Just as practices of electoral democracy cannot be grafted successfully onto nations with an alternative tradition of government, even a nominally democratic one, attempts to append democratic accountability mechanisms upon nations with a political and philosophical tradition inconsistent with state neutrality, state-centered loyalty, and an individualist notion of political responsibility are likely to be wasted or rejected. How much does a philosophical tradition of government determine accountability for a nation's civil servants? This argument begins with the contention that the differing traditions of philosophy play an important role in determining patterns and practices of accountability within a particular tradition. As a matter of describing accountability practices, local knowledge matters.

ACCOUNTABILITY WITHIN WESTERN TRADITIONS

To begin with, accountability in the Western tradition is a characteristic attached to an office indicating that the specific office holder has a moral obligation to explain her actions upon demand from a relevant party (e.g., of an Inspector General or media outlet). Others have described accountability at "punishment," "answerability," "responsibility," or what the "accountability holder" does to the "accountability holdee" (Behn 2001, 3–8). These definitions each take as given an individual or set of individuals, grouped together functionally according to their responsibilities, operating in an adversarial social environment. As Behn (2001) suggests repeatedly, accountability is about one individual or group extracting compliance from another (Burke 1986).

Liberalism and Communitarianism as Bases for Accountability Concepts

In his well-known book, *Political Ethics and Public Office,* Dennis Thompson (1987, 22–29) elaborates on a well-known definitions of individual accountability in government. Due to the problem of multiple [and] dirty hands, we cannot easily hold groups of individuals accountable. Given the tendency of modern bureaucracies to move toward interdependent specializations, the best accountability holding possible is to ferret out which specialist is the origin or at least the authorizer of the wrongdoing, and hold that person accountable. Thompson's assertion that we ought to punish only individuals as accountability holders makes sense in the context of the liberal philosophy underpinning his work.

According to the basic tenets of liberalism, the rational individual chooses his political affiliation through the mechanism of a social contract. The continued, contractual consent to the groundwork of that affiliation supports the individual's description of political or private actions taken in response to this earlier choice. Any good or malicious course of action is a discrete choice made by an individual who, if he is a rightly acting, enlightened individual, has chosen by the processes of independent reasoning. As an individual who has rationally chosen to take up the mantle of public service, the public administrator has not forfeited any of his powers of individual reasoning, nor has he forfeited the possibility of exercising the liberal privilege of exiting from the social contract. He may select for self-interest alone in decision making, or for the interests of the agency he works for, or for a set of constitutional principles. Yet, the choice of which moral compass is the individual's alone.

Liberalism as a theory of political ontology collides with the task of social organization necessary to maintain the sanctity of the individual. Two characteristics of liberalism make this the case. The first is, as Berlin (1969) suggests, the notion of liberal rights as positive liberties of the individual to act upon his wishes and the corresponding liberal obligations to protect other individuals through negative rights to prevent harm. The individual is, as Rousseau famously suggested, "born free, but everywhere in chains." These chains importantly include the obligation to account for one's actions vis-à-vis the language of other's rights. The second problem of squaring liberalism with social organization is the tendency, as Walzer suggests, for the state to become the central arbitrator of free liberal associations; the state must contend with the free-rider problem inherent in liberalism:

> Liberalism is distinguished less by the freedom to form groups on the basis of these identities than the freedom to leave the groups and sometimes the identities behind. Association is always at risk in a liberal society. The boundaries of the groups are not policed; people come and go, or they just fade into the distance without ever quite acknowledging that they have left. That is why liberalism is plagued by free-rider problems—by people who continue to enjoy the membership and identity while no longer participating in the activities that produce those benefits. . . . But if all the groups are precarious, continually on the brink of dissolution or abandonment, then the larger union must also be weak and vulnerable. Or, alternatively, its leaders and officials will be driven to compensate for the failures of association elsewhere by strengthening their own union, that is the central state, beyond the limits that liberalism has established. (Walzer 1990, 15–16)

The liberal public administrator taking up the model of positive and negative rights and associated responsibilities also commits himself implicitly to the strong-state model as foundation for such rights.

Alas, the conundrum of the public administrator operating under a system expecting a strong liberal notion of accountability is that she must accept demands that she account for her choices, and actions to those whose choices and actions her forfeiture of complete decisional freedom protects. However, as all individuals are atomic and the preferences of others are objects of supposition alone, the only method available to reconcile the competing commitments is through creating and enforcing procedures that are ever more elaborate. Such is the contradiction of philosophical liberalism and liberalism in practice; the necessary choice to protect community as more than a procedural entity shows the communitarian (soft) underbelly of liberalism.

LIBERAL-COMMUNITARIAN ACCOUNTABILITY

Liberalism, as Walzer points out, requires two pictures of the self that are contradictory. First, the atomized self, described above, is dependent on the second community—dependent self, described below. Under liberal communitarian (or weak communitarian) thought, the importance of social organization for the prosperity of the individual self becomes apparent. For example, even the most strongly worded descriptions of libertarianism, such as those offered by Nozick (1974) require the socially intervening organization of the market for creating a minimal community of meaning necessary. From attempts to resolve the issue of the individual's dependence on the community comes this notion of liberal communitarianism—the idea that the liberal self is free to choose among values represented by various communities of meaning, which he helps to craft through autonomous participation in the dialogue of meaning making (Taylor 1989). As a practical matter, it is the liberal-communitarian individual, more than the purely liberal or purely communitarian individual, that is important for understanding responsibility and accountability in politics.

Accountability in its full form, like the political self in its full form, must be liberal and communitarian, implicit and explicit, or as Etzioni puts it, operating with a reference to the "I&We."

> The 'I' stands for the individual members of the community. The 'We' signifies social, cultural, political, and hence historical and institutional forces that shape the collective factor—the community. The concept of I&We highlights the assumption that individuals act within a social context, that this context is not reducible to individual acts, and, most significantly, that the social context is not necessarily imposed or derived from voluntary or conscious transactions among individuals. Instead, the social context is to a significant extent perceived as a legitimate and integral part of one's existence, as a "We" rather than a "They." (Etzioni 1996, 157)

Without the "I&We," we find ourselves in a disenchanted polity, one where procedural compliance becomes the dominant moral metric for public life:

> The American welfare state is politically vulnerable because it does not rest on a sense of national community adequate to its purpose. As the welfare state developed, it drew less on an ethic of social solidarity and mutual obligation and more on an ethic of fair procedures and individual rights. But the liberalism of the procedural republic proved an inadequate substitute for the strong sense of citizenship the welfare state requires. (Sandel 1998, 346)

The proposed corrective for liberal-communitarian accountability encourages personal responsibility for one's role in organizations and institutions. Individuals are not required to account for their original choices, but must account for their choices, intentions, and actions within their social milieu. Liberal-communitarian accountability works on two registers: (1) the explicitly procedural accountability associated with audits and the offices of the inspector general and (2) the implicit answerability for values that gives procedural accountability meaning within the community. That liberal-communitarianism offers a "thicker" description of the political self is undeniable, but the consequences of such a description for accountability are important for understanding the deployment of the concept in present scholarship. Discussions of this explicit register of liberal accountability come from scholars of procedural styles of bureaucratic accountability such as Light (1993) and Behn (2001). Discussions of the implicit register come from scholars of public administration ethics, particularly of the constitutional stripe, such as Rohr (2002) and Rosenbloom (2002).

Liberal-communitarian accountability, more than just liberal or procedural accountability, meets the conditions of performance-based accountability popular within the present public-management literature. Performance-based accountability, or accountability for results, is more than mere procedural compliance and requires measurable outputs of goods and services, adherence to standards of moral competence, and attention to the performative dimensions of public service—"fulfilling norms" in many senses of the phrase.

The philosophical basis of liberal communitarianism is evident in Behn's (2001) concept of "360-degree accountability for performance" in his call for a "new mental model of accountability" (210–11). Under this new model, a rethinking of democratic accountability means multiplying accountability holders by creating reflexive accountability at all layers through a pattern of reciprocal accountability holding, and safeguarding or increasing the mechanisms for transparency throughout the accountability process. In describing the practice of 360-degree accountability for performance, Behn relies on the language of individual accountability primarily but also emphasizes the role of multiple, related individuals—a feedback community—for the practice of holding others accountable:

> If we had true 360-degree accountability, each individual who is part of a public agency's accountability environment would be accountable to all the others. Each individual would have an opportunity to provide accountability feedback to every other person in the accountability environment. Each individual would be answerable to every other individual. Each individual could call another individual to account. Each individual could ask another to explain his or her behavior. . . . Why should anyone be unaccountable? (Behn 2001, 199–200)

Through the creation of a network, or an environment of reciprocal accountability based upon a communal ethic of feedback, we can create a fuller definition of liberal-communitarian accountability.

Republican Communitarian Accountability and Functional Communitarian Accountability

We can define communitarian accountability of the American civic-republican strain, at least, as direct accountability holding for the purposes of interest representation and virtuous conduct. Like other forms of philosophical communitarianism, civic republicanism assumes a political self that is deeply situated through a process of acculturation and habituation (in the Aristotelian sense of a lifetime of instruction for virtues essential to living the good life in common with others). In an ideal situation, this process occurs in a small, relatively homogenous community not unlike the wards described by Jefferson or the New England townships lauded by de Tocqueville. The consequences of such habituation include the production of citizens with an appreciation of their intimate role in the community and the foundation of a community of proximity. This community of proximity allows citizens to "keep watch over" their representatives/public servants and to ensure, through the continual process of habituation, conformance with community interests and norms.

Second, as with other forms of communitarianism, civic republicanism demands a notion of accountability that preserves the values embedded in procedures rather than merely procedural norms. In the strong civic-republican tradition, perhaps best embodied in the thought of the antifederalists, where there are no gaps between the ruler and the ruled, accountability becomes an issue of synchronizing the values of the ruled with those of the ruler. In other words, the civic-republican variety of accountability is a model of prospective rather than retrospective accountability. Rather than placing faith in audit mechanisms, the ruled place their faith in the schooled belief in a common destiny for all community members regardless of their station.

A related notion of accountability tied to the civic-republican strain of communitarianism is functional accountability:

> At the heart of communal functionalism is the claim that the community is, in the first instance, composed neither of individuals nor of citizens, but, rather, of functional groupings or parts, arranged according to the nature of their contribution to the communal whole. This is essentially an organic conception of social life but one with certain distinctive features; for it defines membership in the community as a direct result of one's contribution, though the performance of a given function to the well-being or health of the whole . . . any person from any segment of society that contributes in any way to the welfare of the communal unit is thereby accorded an equal capacity to gauge the needs of the community and to perform one's functions accordingly. (Nederman 1992, 978)

Deriving some strength from the body metaphors used to describe the functionalist orientation, this viewpoint suggests that all parts of the polity are essential for ensuring its optimal state. With regard to public service, those who take up the task of public employment do so from the antecedent position that it is their natural inclination to do so, as well as the belief that this inclination is something that is emblematic of the person's moral worth to the society. A civil servant is a civil servant because that profession creates the best possible version of the self, and best serves the needs of one's community.

TWO NON-WESTERN FORMS OF ACCOUNTABILITY

The Western tradition of philosophy is not singular for its emphasis on accountability for political leaders. Extant within multiple non-Western traditions of political philosophy we find extensive descriptions of various nondemocratic mechanisms of accountability. For example, in the formation of ritual accountability in East Asia or affective accountability in central-west Africa, accountability is a product of communal moral production and face-to-face accounts of the accountable individual's behavior, not the implementation of anonymous voting procedures.

Ritual Accountability

The origins of ritual accountability lie in the historical versions of Confucianism in East Asia.[1] Combined with the extensive interpenetrations of Ch'an (Zen) Buddhism, Confucian philosophy is the major source of prerevolutionary Chinese, Japanese, and (South) Korean political values. Within this section, I assess the relationship between the concepts *li* and *ren* as foundational for notions of ritual accountability in civil service.

In its fullest form, ritual accountability is answerability for performance. Ritual accountability is answerability for one's capable performance of *li* as part of the necessary evolution of *ren* in one's self and the community. *Li* are the rituals that one performs as part of one's role in the community. Rituals, in this case, mean a set of practices that, taken as a whole, demonstrate appropriate deference to the mastery of a particular role. The proper performance of the rituals represents the individual's continued effort to develop a reciprocal relationship with that role and those community members dependent upon that role. The ritual practices are not merely technical maneuvers but are expressions of a particular social praxis that is symbolic of the relationship of the individual's actions to the unity of the whole universe (*ti'en*). Fox elaborates upon this in the following way:

> As participants [in the righteous community], however, it was acknowledged that there was a superior—a moral—way of living and participating in the world which could be known and would be made manifest through ritual activity. These li, which included different creative arts, music and poetry, various standards of decorum and acts of reverence and propriety. . . . Depending on the social role one inhabited—father, son, ruler, minister, and so forth—a different set of rituals would be appropriate. (Fox 1997, 573)

In this tradition, the surrounding, attentive, and expectant community reinforces ritual competence. The expectation to comply with rules and laws is an expectation that the good representative of the righteous community will see herself as duty bound to meet communal standards of attentiveness, rigor, and reverence. Given the highly social nature of ritual performances, the fear of disappointment and dishonor, not the fear of punishment for procedural noncompliance, is paramount as an accountability-holding mechanism.

One's failure to learn of and adhere to the rites is not merely a performative failure of noncompliance, but constitutes a moral failure as well. Failure is not merely a refusal to perform one's duties, nor is those actions doing badly emblematic of one's *li;* failure indicates inattention to the interconnections between one's self and the community, between the *li* and the *ren.* If a person does not perform the rites with a whole heart, he can be neither a person nor a part of the communal, physical, and moral universe. Thus if a particular individual suffers a moral failing, it is more than merely his failure; it is the failure of his teachers and the other members of his community.

According to the ontological assumptions of this system, just as one individual cannot be reared alone, nor be moral alone, one individual, no matter her station, cannot be punished alone (Nosco 2008, 22–5). Even the moral recluse or the highest authority in the land cannot escape sanction. This does not mean that punishment does not come only to a single violator, but it does mean that punishment is believed to function as a sanction of the whole community through the proxy of the person. For example, natural disasters (i.e., famines, floods, droughts) are perceived to signal the revocation of the ruler's mandate (from heaven) to have that office.

It is in the realm of government we find particular individuals held up as models of the role of authority figure. The authoritative person is an authority because the remainder of the community knows her to be a careful steward of the common good (*ren*). The authoritative person must be careful with the stewardship of the common good and common knowledge of morals; no one arises to a position of authority or expertise through deployment of her skills for herself alone. It is the devotion that the authoritative person shows in using her technical skills for the common good that makes her worthy of esteem and authority (Fox 1997, 585).

It is by failing to demonstrate a sense of deep moral responsibility to the preservation of the common good that one can be stripped of authoritative power—that is, called to account. Yet in this system the interconnections the community depends on require a more advanced form of punishment than mere procedural accountability. For rulers in particular, punishment for accountability failures requires the ex-communication of the offending person. Mencius describes the imperative for excommunication as punishment:

> "He who injures humanity is a bandit. He who injures righteousness is a destructive person. Such a person is a mere fellow. I have heard of killing a mere fellow [like wicked King] Zhou, but I have not heard of murdering [him as] the ruler." In other words, a wicked king who injures humanity or righteousness has failed to create the moral environment requisite to his people's own growth in the direction of moral goodness and is for this very reason in default of the definition of a true king, making him eligible for replacement even through violence. (Mencius 1B:8; quoted in Nosco 2008, 31)

To the extent that a ruler or a minister fails to act in a way conducive to his role as moral paragon in the community, he abjures his right to his authority and status, becoming a "mere fellow" outside of the system of necessary relationships for the right ordering of the world.[2]

In this traditional Confucian society, as opposed to a liberal-democratic society, there are no gaps between the leaders of the community and the community itself. A leader does not lead the community as such, but guides it from within, as a father does his sons. By "rectifying names," or ensuring the right ordering of relationships all around, the ruler moves the community as a unit, not piece by piece, interest by interest, toward a common good. Without a system of categorization of roles and responsibilities, and the clarification of associated relationships between the roles, the state will not function. Mencius says, "Indeed when the ruler is not a ruler, the minister is not a minister, the father not a father, and the son not a son, although I may have all the grain, shall I ever get to eat it?" (quoted in Nosco 2008, 30).

The rectification of names and the categorization of relationships are done in order to establishing demarcations of whom may call who into account for what. If the ruler makes it clear, through the heartfelt performance of his associated *li*, that he is the ruler, the reciprocal side of the relationship—the subject or "ruled"—is certain of the boundaries of his own role as ruled and as accountability holder for the ruler. Just as if a son's appeal to his father is rebuked, the son must abide by his father's decision, the ruled must abide by the decision of the ruler. In the Confucian cosmology, the role of one part of the relationship is to ensure that the other is continuing along the path of moral goodness. It is not, however, the chore of either reciprocal side to attempt to coerce the other. Rather, the chore was to represent moral goodness to the reciprocal side of the relationship. The ruled are to represent their side with obedience to the ruler and the cosmic order that stipulates their role, and the ruler is to represent the moral goodness inherent in the cosmic order to the ruled. As each is joined to the same cosmic order and the same community, no one can exit the community except through a choice to reject the natural order of things, shown in the ordering of the five relationships, prescribed and maintained by the *dao*. In this system, there are no "gaps" between the rightly oriented ruler and the rightly obeying ruled and no space between the accountability holder and the one to whom she is accountable. The glue of an encompassing cosmology and community-based ontology, replicated continually through adherence to rites, holds the moral universe together.

Affective Accountability

In his work *Political Domination in Africa*, Chabal (1986) offers the following definition of accountability that takes into account the more expansive notions of social responsibility and social ties within the African context:

> Political accountability lies not just in the constitutional and institutional devices which formally hold rulers to account for their deeds. It is also part of the wider fabric of society in relations between patrons and clients, ethnic leaders and their kin, party bosses and party members, bureaucrats and citizens, employers and employees, mullahs and believers, military and civilians. Above all else, it is embodied, symbolized in the relation between state and civil society. (quoted in Moncrieffe 1998, 393)

The nature of politics, epistemology, and social ties in some parts of central and western Africa suggests a different notion of accountability than the individualized, punitive concept common in the west. Following the conceptual groundwork laid by scholars such as Hyden (2006), I call this "affective accountability." Affective accountability is the idea that public figures are responsible for, and thus answerable for, actions that protect the good of the leader's community. Rooted in a strong tradition of communitarian ontology and epistemology, along with what Hyden (2006) calls the tradition of an "economy of affection," affective accountability is a concept that is largely alien to the Western traditions. Indeed, this form of accountability often goes by another, derogatory label—patronage—in Western parlance. What differentiates affective accountability from patronage are the political ontology, communal epistemology, and economic tradition that justify the former but not the latter.

We can locate the importance of association in elaborations on ontology in some of the philosophical traditions of central and west Africa. In contradistinction to the Western, liberal, model, the notions of ontology present in communities prizing affective accountability are of a fully situated self. Affective accountability relies on a deeper notion of personhood than found in the Western communitarian traditions. In a number of African systems (notably the Akan, Bantu, Igbo, and Yoruba) an individual is not born into a community but is born of a community. Gbadegesin synthesizes much of this idea in the following passage:

> Growing children are able to see themselves as a part of a household, not as atoms. They see their intrinsic relation to others and see the interdependent existence of their lives with others. Here is the limit of individualism. Not that the community forces itself on an unyielding individual; rather the individual, through socialization and the love and concern which the household and community have extended to him/her cannot now see himself or herself as anything apart from his/her community. Interest in his/her success is shown by members of the extended family who regard him/her as their 'blood' and the community are also able to trace their origin to a common even if mythical ancestor. There is therefore a feeling of solidarity among its members and this is neither forced nor solicited. It develops naturally as a result of the experience of love and concern which the growing child has been exposed to. (1998, 131)

While liberal individuals can, theoretically at least, extricate themselves from a community or switch communities at will, those born into a system based upon this form of strong communitarianism cannot. Even through multiple efforts at "relocation," the fully situated and communally constituted individual cannot "unbecome" what she is. This ontological position places a different and characteristic set of moral and practical demands on the responsible individual in this community. In the African or affective tradition, due largely to the social nature of epistemology discussed below, accountability is extracted through face-to-face interaction.

In many African communities, as Masolo makes clear, the kinship unit (nuclear and immediate extended family) forms the primary basis of all political organizations (2006, 483–99). The secondary kinship unit is the extended group—a homestead or sub-village cooperative group. The second level, importantly, is not a "tribe." The tribal level—that of a sociopolitical unit that recognizes through relations to other similarly constituted, competitive or cooperative groups—is the third significant level of political expression of African modes of community. Within this communitarian system, one does not have anomic self-interests but only interests gained from a life in the community. As Gbadegesin suggests,

> From this it follows that there need not be any tension between individuality and community since it is possible for an individual to freely give up his/her own perceived interest for the survival of the community. But in giving up one's interests thus, one is also sure that the community will not disown one and that one's well being will be its concern . . . The idea of individual rights, based on a conception of individuals as atoms, is therefore bound to be foreign to this system. For community is founded on notions of an intrinsic and enduring relationship among its members. (1991, 66–7; quoted in Isola Bewaji 2006, 397)

A concept of individuality or an individual interest does exist in African philosophy. But even within the Igbo cosmology of "chi," wherein a person is not only a unique individual but is created by an individual force, the individual cannot be socially anomic. Such an interesting idea, that of the utterly unique, originally independent individual who is nonetheless constituted as a person through his relation with others, is captured in the proverb, "For wherever Something stands, no matter what, Something Else will stand beside it" (Achebe 1998, 70).

Being of the community does not mean that one does not have moments of desire that override the continued expression of community interests. The communal self can be overcome by the disorderly desires of the willful person. For example, within the Yoruba concept of destiny, even though one's destiny is (weakly) predetermined and also shaped by the community, an individuals' destiny (personality and potential) and his use of his potential is partly his responsibility. Destiny, cosmology, and community can go only so far—an individual does (latently) choose to adopt or reject the community stance (Gbadegesin 2006, 318–19). One's self is a product of the community and any "self" interests are reflections of desires already extant in the community. No one person's strengths (or weaknesses) are meaningful without the interaction of that person with other members of the community.[3]

In practice, what cements the individual to his or her community, what gives the community its transformative power and transformative claim upon the individual is affect. Affect is the ties of love, friendship, respect, and kinship—fellow feeling that comes from the experience of living together in common. Similar to Adam Smith's notion of sympathy or fellow feeling (Broadie 2006, 168–70), this notion of affect requires trade, though not in the economic sense exclusively. Rather, trades or the face-to-face exchange of information provides the foundation of what one knows. In other words, narrative sharing creates the ties that bind. As Hallen (2006) makes clear in his analysis of Yoruba moral epistemology,

> . . . the primary source of propositional or secondhand knowledge in an oral culture is other persons. For, if that is the case, knowledge of those other persons' moral characters—their honesty, their reliability as sources of information—becomes a fundamental criterion to

evaluating the reliability of secondhand information obtained from them. Knowledge of another person's moral character is said to be obtained, most reliably from observing (first-hand) their behavior. And in Yoruba discourse behavior conventionally extends to "what they say" and "what they do." . . . But what is again in evidence here is the priority the Yoruba place upon hard evidence, upon only being able to "know" what you witness in a first-hand manner. For the point is that a person's verbal and non-verbal behavior are construed as firsthand evidence of their moral character. (Hallen 2006, 301)

Through direct exchange of knowledge, and through reiteration of the moral stories of the "in common," comes the necessity of deliberative and consensus-based protection of the community (Wamala 2006, 435–38).

The modes of community protection are often economic in nature. Despite the insistence of some African Marxists-Socialists, such as Senghor and Nkrumah, the traditional African economy does not follow the rules of Western capitalism or Western Marxism. Senghor's attempt to transform African community economics into a proto-Marxist strain shows this clearly,

I would say that the latter [the collectivist European society] is an assembly of individuals. The collectivist society inevitably places the emphasis on the individual, on his original activity and his needs. In this respect, the debate between "to each according to his labor" and "to each according to his needs" is significant. Negro-African society puts more stress on the group than on the individual, more on solidarity than on the activity and needs of the individual, more on the communion of persons than on their autonomy. Ours is a community society. This does not mean it ignores the individual, or that collectivist society ignores solidarity, but the latter bases this solidarity on the activities of individuals, whereas the community society bases it on the general activity of the group. (Senghor 1964, 93–4; quoted in Masolo 2006, 489)

As Hyden further points out, the expectations of formal institutions and economizing rationality do not conform to African worldviews. Instead,

Rationality in the economy of affection is socially embedded in the sense that it presupposes personal interdependence. For instance, A seeks out B as a shortcut to obtain a good otherwise out of reach. But it is also rational for B to accept the request, because B gains influence over A (or a credit that can be called upon in the future). An informal deal is often preferable because it does not entail the wait and uncertainty associated with formal collective action. Nor does it carry the threat of a free ride. . . . It rests on the assumption of shared expectations, not the maximization of a particular goal that relies on the organizational reconciliation of an N range of individual preferences. (Hyden 2006, 83)

Further, many communities abide by a functionalist interpretation of the purpose of each member of the community. One is destined or designed purposefully for a particular station (Gbadegesin 2006; Menkiti 2006; Teffo 2006). Community protection in this affective sense parlays into a few of the criticisms that liberal political theorists and accountability scholars suggest necessarily arise from a communitarian framework. First, this type of affective accountability does tend to lead to an exclusive community, protective of its rights and benefits to the exclusion of others. In the practice of government, this amounts to acts of "Big Man Rule" a form of personal, charismatic leadership characterized by nepotism or placement of one's kinship group members into positions of power and the elimination of rival group members' previous positions (Hyden 2006, 94–114). Such is the path to widespread, endemic patronage, recognized as that particularly vile form of "African" corruption.

Second, the affective networks are not always responsive to concerns for expertise in technical, rather than social or political, matters. In addition to patronage, conservatism, and corruption, critics charge that an affective notion of accountability also leads to widespread incompetence. According to the informal rules of the economy of affection, an individual who rises to power does so with the assistance of his or her community, which she must pay back. A frequent mode for repaying the debt of success is by bringing one's creditors along with one, or in other words, patronage in the strongest sense of the term. As the full economy is dependent upon such informal structures and ties, attempts to sever these through merit-based appointment structures will likely fail. In terms of the present accountability discussion, fulfilling the terms of accountability to the community has the unintended effect of making one appear irresponsible to those outside the community, particularly those outside of the philosophical tradition that founds affective accountability to begin with (Wamala 2006, 438–40).

Affective accountability does entail a strong degree of accountability for morality, community, and performance. Members of a particular community may call others directly to account, often through traditional means strongly reminiscent of contemporary deliberative democracy, for the ways in which their actions have (or have not) supported their community. This goal, we should hope, is part of the process of democratic accountability or any of the other forms of accountability already discussed. Those participants in the affective network work against the centripetal forces of liberal transgression and thus stabilize communities of meaning. The performance of concern may not be measured in terms of improved output of products or service unity, but if performance means satisfying the humanist norms of the population and reifying those norms that underpin the procedures that do exist, then affective accountability may be a viable, culturally specific alternative.

COMPARATIVE ACCOUNTABILITIES

What additional theoretical weight do the two non-Western models of accountability discussed add to the project of developing a global definition of accountability? The next section explores the possibility of a unified form of accountability that accounts for the two non-Western and Western models.

"No-gaps" Accountability as the Global Accountability

One of the key problems of prescribing Western mechanisms for accountability holding is that these are not grounded in a philosophical tradition that is truly global. While the march of globalization indicates (to those in globalized societies) that values are universal, these values are still only superficially related. When it comes to imposing norms of behavior rooted in a fundamental aspect of human nature, such as the desire for calling the powerful unknown into account, the imposition of superficial values will not do. What is needed is an answer that plays on the constants between the east and the west, north and south. The answer, I suggest, is a form of accountability described best as "no-gaps accountability."

The sentiment of no gaps between the ruler and the ruled is not foreign to either the Western or the Eastern traditions.[4] Specifically, I suggest that similar sentiments to the ritual and affective modes of accountability found in these two cases are also expressed in the writings of the anti-federalists. Michael Zuckert advances the thesis that the anti-federalists advocated for a morally accountable, morally responsible government in America. In what Zuckert calls the "no-gap" idea, he shows that the anti-federalists expected the true Republic to be a morally virtuous polity where the people could ensure moral symmetry and moral responsibility (as answerability) from their leaders through direct selection and supervision.

> For the Anti-Federalists, republicanism is essentially responsibility (i.e., answerability) of rulers to the ruled, and control of rulers by the ruled—and not merely ultimate control, as in Madison's definition, but a much more ongoing and regular form of control. The Anti-Federalists aimed at what we might call a "no gap" policy—no distance between rulers and ruled. (Zuckert 1992, 131)

These sentiments are familiar to the two traditions reviewed above. To ensure that the morality and will of the ruled was also that of the ruler, the original Confucians or Nso people of Cameroon or the Asante each expressed a remarkably similar set of proposals for "checks." Stipulating expectations that rulers serve as the embodiment of the people as their moral exemplars—responsive to deliberation, relationships, and tradition—the sentiment of the Confucians, the Nso, the Asante, and the anti-federalists are remarkably similar.[5] The notions of Yoruba moral epistemology and the anti-federalists' insistence on direct, community-based supervision of rulers are also quite similar. If the rulers and the people are of the same mind, borne of and by the same community, then there will be no need for a heavy-handed state. Further, if responsibility is programmed into the rules, there will be no need for elaborate procedures to ensure accountability for fairness or finances.

Proximity between the ruler and ruled—a no-gap policy—would resolve the conundrum of accountability for performance. That is, by working within and of the people, rulers rise to a position in which they can build the capacity of the whole polity and produce what is the true good of the people with little potential error (see also Johnson 2004, 652–55, 667). The comparison between the communitarian strains of Confucian, African, and anti-federalists' notions of no gaps in representative responsibility begs the question: Can we look to the anti-federalists' work as a starting point for a further project of comparative accountabilities? The answer, tentatively, is yes.

The constant theme in the two non-Western forms of accountability as well as in the anti-federalists' writings is the requirement of proximity for accountability. Unlike liberal notions of political accountability that require an abstraction of the individual to a social atom, anti-federal communitarian notions of political accountability require a deeply social self. Liberal notions of the political, as Walzer, Etzioni, and Sandel point out, require an emphasis on proceduralism as the only reasonable way to arbitrate between anomic interests. Procedures, procedural language, and ultimately, procedural compliance become the medium through which such individuals negotiate their responsibilities to one another. Thus it is only through the language of procedures that they may meaningfully call one another to account. By contrast, communitarian notions require an emphasis on community capacity building and reinforcement of communal expectations. While procedures are necessary under a communitarian system, they are not substitutes for contact between political selves.

In closing, returning to Behn's (2001) argument for 360-degree accountability for performance, I offer that reinvigorating and networking together small, proximate communities of accountability is the only workable path to meaningful accountability on a global scale. Nevertheless, apropos of the work presented here, these communities must be founded on traditions of political philosophy meaningful to the people that tradition governs. Exploring more deeply the overlaps between these traditions and mining them for workable statements of norms and rules is the project left undone for now.

NOTES

1. While most Americans and British only know of Confucius's work the *Analects* and Mencius's *Mencius,* there are multiple works and fragments from other Confucian followers, including a number of schools of thought, ranging from the Legalists to the Logicians. Much of the Confucianism offered up by proponents of "Asian values" is naively Legalist and is not "original" Confucianism. Here I interpret Confucius's works in their own right, rather than through the lens of "Asian values" or "Democracy with Chinese characteristics." For more on the variants of Confucianism, see Fung Yu-lan's (1976) *A Short History of Chinese Philosophy.*

2. There are five relationships in the Confucian system: ruler/subject, parent/child, husband/wife, elder brother/younger brother, and friend/friend.

3. This is the Communalism Thesis of Tempels ([1959] 1998, 432–34) in a nutshell. Ontologically, individuals are distinct, but epistemically they are united.

4. The two non-Western traditions elaborated upon, particularly the African traditions, ought to be recognized as philosophies in their own time and own right. By this, I suggest, following Wiredu (1998, 193–99), that we must compare these two traditions to the older, foundational traditions in the West. In this particular case, considering not only the role of American constitutional rule of law as normative in the international sphere, but also the interesting synthesis of much previous Western philosophy in the debate, I offer that we ought to look to the literature of the American founding.

5. For details on the comparison of Chinese and African (Nso) expectations, see Wingo 2006. For more on the Asante form of accountable leadership, see Davidson 1992, 53–55 or Busia 1951.

REFERENCES

Achebe, C. 1998. "'Chi' in Igbo Cosmology. In *African Philosophy: An Anthology,* ed. Emmanuel Chukwudi Eze. Malden, MA: Blackwell Publishers, 67–73.

Behn, R. 2001. *Rethinking Democratic Accountability.* Washington, DC: Brookings Institution Press.

Berlin, Isaiah. 1969. *Four Essays on Liberty.* Oxford, UK: Oxford University Press.

Bewaji, I., and J. Ayotunde. 2006. "Ethics and Morality in Yoruba Culture." In *A Companion to African Philosophy,* ed. Kwasi Wiredu. Malden, MA: Blackwell Publishing, 396–403.

Broadie, A. 2006. "Sympathy and the Impartial Spectator." In *The Cambridge Companion to Adam Smith,* ed. Knud Hakonssen. Cambridge: Cambridge University Press, 158–88.

Burke, E. 2004 [1759]. *A Philosophical Enquiry into the Sublime and the Beautiful.* London: Penguin Books.

Burke, J. P. 1986. *Bureaucratic Responsibility.* Baltimore: The Johns Hopkins University Press.

Busia, K.A. 1951. *The Position of the Chief in the Modern Political System of the Ashanti.* Oxford: Oxford University Press.

Chabal, P., ed. 1986. *Political Domination in Africa: Reflections on the Limits of Power.* Cambridge, UK: Cambridge Press.

Davidson, B. 1992. *The Black Man's Burden.* Trenton, NJ: Africa World Press.

Etzioni, A. 1996. "A Moderate Communitarian Proposal." *Political Theory* 24 (2): 155–71.

Fox, R.A. 1997. "Confucian and Communitarian Responses to Liberal Democracy." *Review of Politics* 59 (3): 561–92.

Fung, Yu-lan. 1997. *A Short History of Chinese Philosophy: A Systematic Account of Chinese Thought from Its Origins to the Present Day,* ed. Derk Bodde. New York: Free Press.

Gbadegesin, S. 1991. *African Philosophy: Traditional Yoruba Philosophy and Contemporary African Realities.* New York: Peter Lang.

———. 1998. "Yoruba Philosophy: Individuality, Community and the Moral Order." In *African Philosophy: An Anthology,* ed. Emmanuel Chukwudi Eze. Malden, MA: Blackwell Publishers, 130–42.

———. 2006. "Toward a Theory of Destiny." In *A Companion to African Philosophy,* ed. Kwasi Wiredu. Malden, MA: Blackwell Publishing, 313–23.

Hallen, B. 2006. "Yoruba Moral Epistemology." In *A Companion to African Philosophy,* ed. Kwasi Wiredu.

Malden, MA: Blackwell Publishing, 296–304.

Harding, S. 1998. "The Curious Coincidence of Feminine and African Moralities." In *African Philosophy: An Anthology,* ed. Emmanuel Chukwudi Eze. Malden, MA: Blackwell Publishers, 360–70.

Hyden, G. 2006. *African Politics in Comparative Perspective.* Cambridge, UK: Cambridge University Press.

Johnson, J. 2004. "Disposed to Seek Their True Interests: Representation and Responsibility in Anti-Federalist Thought." *Review of Politics* 66 (4): 649–73.

Light, P.C. 1993. *Monitoring Government: Inspectors General and the Search for Accountability.* Washington, DC: Brookings Institution Press.

Masolo, D.A. 2006. "Western and African Communitarianism: A Comparison." In *A Companion to African Philosophy,* ed. Kwasi Wiredu. Malden, MA: Blackwell Publishing, 483–98.

Menkiti, I.A. 2006. "On the Normative Conception of a Person." In *A Companion to African Philosophy,* ed. Kwasi Wiredu. Malden, MA: Blackwell Publishing, 324–31.

Moncrieffe, J.M. 1998. Reconceptualizing Political Accountability. *International Political Science Review* 19 (4): 387–406.

Nederman, C.J. 1992. "Freedom, Community and Function: Communitarian Lessons of Medieval Political Theory." *The American Political Science Review* 86 (4): 977–86.

Nosco, P. 2008. "Confucian Perspectives on Civil Society and Government." In *Confucian Political Ethics,* ed. Daniel A. Bell. Princeton: Princeton University Press.

Nozick, R. 1974. *Anarchy, State and Utopia.* New Edition. New York: Basic Books.

Roberts, N.C. 2002. "Keeping Public Officials Accountable through Dialogue: Resolving the Accountability Paradox." *Public Administration Review* 62 (6): 658–69.

Rohr, J.A. 2002. *Civil Servants and Their Constitutions.* Lawrence: University Press of Kansas.

Rosenbloom, D. 2002. *Building Legislative-Centered Public Administration: Congress and the Administrative State, 1946–1999.* Tuscaloosa: University of Alabama Press.

Sandel, M. 1998. *Democracy's Discontent: America in Search of a Public Philosophy.* Cambridge, MA: Harvard University Press.

Senghor, L.S. 1964. *On African Socialism,* trans. M. Cook. New York: The Free Press.

Taylor, C. 1989. *Sources of the Self: The Making of Modern Identity.* Cambridge, MA: Harvard University Press.

Teffo, J. 2006. "Democracy, Kingship and Consensus: A South African Perspective." In *A Companion to African Philosophy,* ed. Kwasi Wiredu. Malden, MA: Blackwell Publishing, 443–49.

Tempels, P. 1998 [1959]. "Bantu Ontology." In *African Philosophy: An Anthology,* ed. Emmanuel Chukwudi Eze. Malden, MA: Blackwell Publishers, 431–34.

Thompson, D.F. 1987. *Political Ethics and Public Office.* Cambridge, MA: Harvard University Press.

Walzer, M. 1990. "The Communitarian Critique of Liberalism." *Political Theory* 18 (1): 6–23.

Wamala, E. 2006. "Government by Consensus: An Analysis of a Traditional Form of Democracy." In *A Companion to African Philosophy,* ed. Kwasi Wiredu. Malden, MA: Blackwell Publishing, 435–42.

Wingo, A.H. 2006. "Fellowship Associations as a Foundation for Liberal Democracy in Africa." In *A Companion to African Philosophy,* ed. Kwasi Wiredu. Malden, MA: Blackwell Publishing, 450–59.

Wiredu, K. 1998. "How Not to Compare African Philosophy with Western Thought." In *African Philosophy: An Anthology,* ed. Emmanuel Chukwudi Eze. Malden, MA: Blackwell Publishers, 193–99.

Zuckert, M.P. 1992. "The Virtuous Polity, the Accountable Polity: Liberty and Responsibility in 'The Federalist.'" *Publius* 22 (1): 123–42.

16

ACCOUNTABILITY AND A THEORY
OF REPRESENTATION

Ciarán O'Kelly

A theory of accountability is necessarily a theory of representation. The rituals (and promises) of reporting, justification, or simple availability for punishment are shaped not only by opaque lines of corporate and individual responsibility in complex organizations (Bovens 1998, 4), but by the claim that organizations and the individuals who work in them subordinate their own interests and agendas in preference to the interests and agendas of others. Indeed, accountability mechanisms are driven by the claim that organizations and individuals *ought* to subordinate their interests to those of principals. Procedures are required to ensure that everyone remains on the straight and narrow; that they pursue the will or interests of their principals. Political and scholarly invocations of performance (Dubnick 2005) or of "best value" (Boyne et al. 2002) or of prosperity (Dignam 1998) not only constitute attempts to define organizational goals (though they are that), but also demand that organizations work in their principals' names. In other words, accountability is a matter of representation.

In approaching the issue of accountability as a matter of representation, representation becomes a primary object of study. Moreover, the complex organizations that are subject to accountability mechanisms are in practice conduits for representation—institutions through which ideas of representation are negotiated and defined. This chapter begins with a discussion of representation as a particular, institutionally bound form of a "second-person standpoint" (see Darwall 2006) and then goes on to discuss the development of the theory of representation, particularly in the works of Thomas Hobbes and Edmund Burke, and points to two key problems/distinctions that continue to characterize discussions of representation. These distinctions are described as the problem of *personhood* and the problem of *nomination*. These key distinctions are crucial to an understanding of how ideas of accountability are formed. They are also very often at the heart of problems encountered when we speak of accountability. More distant forms of representation bring with them serious questions about responsiveness to principals. Very often, it seems, accountability mechanisms are invoked in the hope that rituals might tip the political balance within the institution toward either the principal's demands or at least toward their inferred principal interests. Often it is unclear, however, how specific accountability mechanisms might have a transformative effect on the representative character of targeted institutions. That is, while it is tempting to adopt an "if they won't represent us on their own we'll force them to represent us" approach, it may well be that the character of representation in any given institution is more fixed, less amenable to change, and far more systematic than demands for greater accountability would have us believe. The risk is that accountability mechanisms will be incorporated without significantly shifting the flow of power (a problem set out, for instance, by Christopher Hood; 2002).

These kinds of dynamics surrounding notions of accountability and representation are nowhere more obvious or important than in the area of corporate governance. Despite its basic architecture having persisted more or less unchanged for 150 years, the corporation is still the subject of debate with regard to precisely what kind of institution it is. Having set out the theory of representation, the chapter then introduces elements in this debate that highlight the structures of representation within British company law. Ideas of representation have driven the debate over corporate accountability, and these debates very often replicate the misconception that representative institutions are amenable to wholesale transformation through coercive rituals.

A THEORY OF REPRESENTATION

A conduit for representation is an institution that embodies a second-person standpoint, transforming it into representation. It constructs an environment where a person can be publicly acting in another's name, whether that other be a natural or collective person. The institution's character is defined by the negotiation between principals and agents: the problems of personhood and of nomination point to the degree to which, following Hobbes as we see below, the agent has power to define and redefine his remit. As such, representation must involve a high degree of negotiation and dialogue, not just at the institution's inception (although that would be crucial) but as the environment, motivations, and circumstances change. Accountability is more than simply a crucial element in the institution as defined here, although, given the role of mechanisms in negotiating power between players, it certainly is that.

Accountability is the institutional vocabulary through which ideas of representation, legitimacy, and authorization are presented. That is not to say that we ought simply to conclude that accountability mechanisms are the same as representativeness. Rather, the politics of accountability, the invocation and circumvention of rules, is the struggle to achieve and maintain control over an organization for one person or other. This struggle is very often heightened because of the lack of recognizable principals, and the ambiguity of the bounds of authorization means that the politics of accountability will always involve some sort of political or even personal struggle.

Drawing from Stephen Darwall's work, we begin with a general discussion of representation as a specific kind of "second-person standpoint" (Darwall 2006; see also Korsgaard 2007; Wallace 2007; Watson 2007; Darwall 2007).[1] This standpoint ought to be understood within an organizational context, and it is within this context that the idea of accountability prevails. In other words, the architectures of public and private administrative organizations transform everyday moral authority into enforceable political, bureaucratic, legal, or professional authority (see Romzek and Dubnick 1987). Accountability mechanisms—the rituals surrounding the enforcement of those authorities—very often make up the vocabulary through which the organization's specific character of representation is negotiated and defined. As such, these mechanisms are useful not just for their effects on performance or efficiency or the like, but because they serve as claims on the organization's work.

The second-person standpoint is, for Darwall, an acknowledgement of the equal authority of the other as a member of a moral community, a community of understanding on questions of the good. "Just as a right involves an authority to claim that to which one has a right," Darwall writes, "so also is moral obligation conceptually tied to what the moral community can demand" (Darwall 2006, 20). Second-personal obligations arise when we are called upon to act as equal members of a moral community by others whom we recognize as equal members of the same moral community in turn. For Darwall, an obligation can exist only if one is undertaking the obligation as a free agent and if one is (publicly) taken to be competent to take on the obligation (these are "Fichte's Point" and "Pufendorf's Point." See Darwall 2006, 20–23, 70ff).

Therefore, as Darwall has it, a platoon sergeant who calls her platoon to attention is not obeyed simply because she is in a position of institutional authority over the platoon.[2] She is obeyed because both she and the members of the platoon are equal members of a moral community in which the obligation she puts the soldiers under is coherent and understood. There are agent-neutral reasons for obedience here (the sergeant being a superior officer), but any moral obligation has to be rooted in the adherence to a mutually held normative scheme (see the discussion between Wallace and Darwall in Wallace 2007, 26–27; Darwall 2007, 61).

The important point that Darwall wants to put across is that moral obligation is rooted in this equal accountability, itself a function of an intersubjective moral community. Morality is therefore rooted in an egalitarian and commonly generated substrate. Naturally, there is a range of other obligation-generating reasons that one might encounter (Darwall 2007, 60). Darwall's point is that voluntary adherence to those reasons—the sense that one ought to adhere to them and be held to account for them—must be rooted in a second-personal standpoint, a recognition that these obligations are legitimate within the context of the moral community. That the sergeant's role is not subject to negotiation is testament to the fixed nature of the martial hierarchy within this moral community. Very many institutions, on the other hand, are less fixed and more subject to explicit and implicit negotiation (which, as Runciman 2007 points out, is not necessarily a bad thing).

People who work within specific organizational settings are in a position similar to Darwall's platoon sergeant. Her instructions are understood by everyone as having moral force because she and her subordinates share equal membership in a moral community, but they are also backed up with coercive force by virtue of their institutional setting. The moral community makes her instructions legitimate (a necessary component for her being an authority in a representation relationship), but importantly it is the formal institution that underpins her instructions. Formal institutions are required for a second-person standpoint to be transformed into representation (in this example, complete with inbuilt, onerous accountability rituals). That is to say, for one to act in another's name requires a publicly recognized procedure through which agency can be conferred. Moreover, the defining of that agency requires an institutional setting through which a predictable and mutually binding mode of representation can be set.

A theory of representation requires those formal organizational elements—most importantly accountability rituals—for it to be coherent. The institutional environment or the office establishes the architecture through which both authority and agent can mutually acknowledge the representative relationship and can agree on the agent's freedom to act, the distribution of responsibility, the bounds of authorization and the like. Institutions also give fellow members of the moral community the reassurance that the agent is a representative, and how that is so, with the various implications for responsibility that entails. Representation is a formal and public acknowledgement and guarantee that one person has leave to act in the name of another. Formal institutions that facilitate representation rely upon the kinds of moral communities of which Darwall speaks.

Moreover, both institutions and communities of understanding are required for the emergence of an environment within which ideas of action, responsibility, and authority can be separated out and negotiated.[3] The negotiation of these ideas is required because it informs the mechanisms through which representation is to be enforced. Calling to account in organizations differs markedly from calling to account in moral relationships not defined by organizations. Organizational accountability is part of what makes the organization a conduit for representation. The rituals, expectations, and promises that characterize accountability are the tangible manifestation of the negotiation and competition—the politics—that take place between principals and agents over how representation can be defined. They are the weapons either of existing principals or of aspiring principals as they seek to shape modes of behavior. The accountability mechanisms will themselves define the means by which representation is to be controlled.

Two Key Distinctions

The remainder of this section is divided into two parts. First, we examine each of the problems of representation presented above in more detail through an analysis of some original steps in the development of theories of representation, specifically through discussions of Thomas Hobbes and Edmund Burke. Second, we discuss representation and accountability in the light of these distinctions. If we are to imagine institutions as providing a conduit through which representation is defined, we have to face the challenges set down by Hobbes and Burke: these challenges help explain why representation is never settled and, because of this, help explain the role of accountability mechanisms in the political struggles over representation that take place in organizations. This struggle is of crucial importance to debates over corporate governance; for instance. Hobbes's and Burke's ideas show us why equilibrium positions are hard to find or maintain and, following from that, why notions of accountability are constantly invoked.

To reiterate, the theory of representation in an institutional environment has at its core two distinctions. First, a theory of representation ought to distinguish between the representation of natural persons and the representation of artificial persons. It is the distinction between persons who are in a position to express their will toward the nomination and conduct of representatives and persons—perhaps collective or corporate persons—and those who are not possessed of a will or intentionality in an ordinary sense.[4] Rather, will and intentionality either have to be derived from procedural mechanisms or have to be inferred. This is the "problem of personhood."

Second, we ought to have regard for a distinction in philosophical discussions of representation between "actual" and "virtual" representation in Edmund Burke's writing (see Pitkin 1968).[5] This "problem of nomination" denotes the distinctive ways in which agents might be chosen by principals in the first place. Actual representation suggests that principals nominate agents directly. Virtual representation, on the other hand, denotes a situation in which, although principals had no role in nominating agents, the agents nevertheless attend to their interests. These two distinctions run to the heart of the key role of accountability in institutions: it helps mediate and articulate various claims between possible power-holders. As well as being about discipline, accountability mechanisms are about articulating the principal's claims over the agent's will.

The Problem of Personhood

Thomas Hobbes was one of the first modern thinkers to address problems of representation by recognizing the centrality of institutions to the working of representation relationships. Hobbes sought to answer the problems posed by political pluralism in an environment where the polity was characterized by irredeemable disagreement on political and moral questions. The solution to irredeemable disagreement, as Hobbes saw it, was to have the individual entirely subsume his will to a corporate person—the Commonwealth—who would defer in all matters to Leviathan. The office of Leviathan is, as a result, both the author of the Commonwealth's actions and, originally at least, the agent of each individual's will (Hobbes 1996, chap. XVI).[6] While Hobbes is interested in how Leviathan might authorize agents' actions, his primary (and most problematic) discussion concerns how we are to think of Leviathan as an agent of a will that Leviathan himself defines. How, in short, can one be an agent of a purely artificial corporate or collective person without mechanisms for articulating its will or that entirely lacks will in any conventional sense? (See Skinner 1999). The problem, as Hobbes has it, relates to how, in the struggle to define the content of representation, and given that we are not even sure what kind of person it is, are we to figure out what the corporate or collective principal wants?

For Hobbes, personhood is a function of authority. Those whose are competent and in a position to exercise their will are natural persons. Those, on the other hand, who act at the behest of natural persons are artificial persons, in the sense that "when you serve as a representative, you act not as an individual but rather as the player of a legally or socially recognized role" (Skinner 2005, 12).[7] Hobbes is quite sure about where responsibility lies in a representation relationship: if you authorize some action, then it is attributed to you, even though your representative is the one who acts in the conventional sense. Rather than following the act, responsibility follows the authority (Hobbes 1996, 111f; Skinner 1999, 11f). Moreover, "when the Actor maketh a Covenant by Authority, he bindeth thereby the Author, no lesse than if he had made it himselfe; and no less subjecteth him to all the consequences of the same" (Hobbes 1996, 112; quoted in Skinner 1999, 8).

One of the most important elements for our purposes in this chapter is that, for Hobbes, representation must be rooted in some sort of institutional understanding. The agent must have legal standing or some sort of conventional claim (through ownership, office, etc.) to being an agent of the purely artificial person (Skinner 1999, 17). This is a major innovation in the theory of the state. For the first time we see the important recognition of the centrality of institutions to notions of representation. It is meaningless to talk of any sort of public (as in commonly recognized, endorsed, and adhered to) representation without this institutional context. The Hobbesian scheme establishes the centrality of conventions and rules to the working of authority and responsibility. Authority (in this case the authority of a purely artificial person), the actions carried out in the name of that authority, and the fiction of a representation relationship authorizing the actions, is a matter of institutional architecture. In contemporary parlance, it is a matter of governance.

As significant as this move is, it immediately throws up the problem of personhood. We need to have a theory of how the representation of purely artificial persons, including corporate bodies, buildings, or establishments, or even the state or polity itself, comes into being. These entities are logically incapable of exercising will toward the granting authority to an agent, and yet in Hobbesian terms we must recognize them as exercising that will. Otherwise it would make absolutely no sense to speak, as Hobbes does, of Leviathan representing the commonwealth or of lesser agents representing churches, children, and the like.

For Hobbes, the problem of personhood—the representation of purely artificial persons—requires the maintenance, through a commonly recognized institutional architecture, of a key fiction. That is, that we can disregard the agents' *actual* authority and responsibility (in that they actually are the decision makers) because they are *imagined,* through the institution, as acting in another's name.[8] Even Leviathan is a fictional representative in this sense, or might perhaps be seen to represent the people by attending to their interests and needs, but at the same time Leviathan need display no signs of an agreement between representative and "representee" (Pitkin 1967, 35). There are no accountability mechanisms available that might either constrain or punish in such a way that the representative might become more responsive.[9]

While Hobbes establishes the context through which representation might occur, he does not succeed in explaining how institutions might be established in such a way that they allow indirect representation to be representation at all. He doesn't explain where—within the bounds of commonly understood norms of authorization, responsibility and control—we can maintain the fiction that purely artificial persons are being represented by their agents. Hobbes does not provide a satisfactory explanation of how accountability might form in any situation that is more complicated than a specific human agent following a specific human author's will.

It is not satisfactory that Leviathan is an agent of interests that he effectively defines.[10] Yet Hobbes's solution to the problem of personhood is to have the content of representation within the commonwealth defined by the natural person who is the agent of that representation relationship. All Hobbes leaves us with is a notion that the representation of purely artificial persons can be held to the same standards of conduct as the representation of natural persons. A natural person has various means at her disposal for oversight of her agents, not least being direct questioning. The problem is that complex organizations are less characterized by this sort of representation and more by representation at a great distance and of corporate, collective, or entirely fictional persons such as shareholders, parliaments, or even nations. So the problem of personhood—and how we can be said to represent these kinds of persons—is not a semantic problem: it goes to the heart of how complex organizations and their accountability mechanisms are negotiated and defined.

The Problem of Nomination

The Enlightenment saw this sense of representation, where it was is negotiated and established through institutions, being reinterpreted to fit with philosophies of the rational public. Early modernity brought with it new attempts to answer the question of how representation might be understood in the context of collective or corporate authority, i.e., where there is no actual will to be represented. The answer was to be found, Enlightenment philosophers had it, in a new sense of how representation might be understood. Instead of requiring direct, almost person-to-person authorization, the important thing was for agents to reflect the discourse of a rational public. This understanding of representation sees representative institution redefined in the context of rationality although, as we shall see, it did not evolve in a manner that would circumvent the need for a politics of representation (and attendant accountability mechanisms).

The rationalist formulation of corporate and collective representation was derived from the notion that discourse between private individuals could be held to the universally acceptable standard of reason (Habermas 1989). The public, by these lights, was not merely to be seen as being in authority (where it was). It was, by virtue of deliberation, an authority. It can formulate proper ends through discourse (on these senses of authority, see Friedman 1990). Public control of the political sphere was deemed not simply to be legitimate because of any increase in the franchise. Its legitimacy came from a qualitative difference between authoritarian domination and "rational-critical public debate" (Habermas 1989, 28). Through public discourse, private opinion becomes an articulation of enlightened rationality. Legitimate politics, especially in the British political sphere, was rooted in the discourse of the public sphere. Rational outcomes for the state can no longer be rooted in mere authority. Rather, through publicity, the aggregation of multiple private opinions was transformed into public opinion.

This is of enormous import for the concept of representation because it posits a way out of the Hobbesian dilemma. Representation of collectivities can reflect rational discourse. A moral community can emerge through discourse, and its will can be articulated through a rationally and intersubjectively developed public opinion. The key here is emergence: public reason, as this philosophy is imagined, emerges from the constant presentation of acceptable reasons between rational persons. So a corporate body can be guided by discourse, and the individual is represented through the body's translation of discourse into action.

This notion of the representation of rational publics in a corporate body presents an answer to the problem of nomination at least in the sense that it sidesteps the problem altogether. Responsivity, as the discursive theory would have it, involves institutions that are built and whose members act in a manner that is driven by rational public opinion formulated in open-ended critical debate. Interestingly, it is possible to imagine a situation where institutions do not have procedures in place for testing public opinion (say through elections), but rather where they simply emerge as extensions of discourse.

Of course, such obviously naïve institutions would be both difficult to construct and—perhaps more importantly—easy to manipulate. Nevertheless, this answer to the problem of nomination is at the heart of the representation modes of the modern state and of complex institutions, as well as at the heart of the development of accountability mechanisms.

Answering Hobbes's dilemma by talking of emergent rationality can imply two different characters for institutions. We might imagine institutions adopting procedures that explicitly harness rational discourse with an aim toward having a representative character. By these lights, institutions are, to an extent, actually representative. Alternatively, we might imagine institutions seeking out the leadership of men who, through their own enlightened rationality and discourse, can literally reflect public reason. As Edmund Burke recognizes, private reflection on public affairs is the first component in the development of public opinion. After all, public opinion arises from the airing of those private reflections. Burke points to the beneficial effects of a polity where discourse is free, as opposed to one where the domination of the prince extends to restrictions on discourse. He regards public opinion as "the vehicle and organ of legislative omnipotence" (quoted in Habermas 1989, 94, and in a discussion of parallels in the world of business, in Pearson 2002, 865). Nevertheless, Burke's primary appreciation of public discourse is that it will improve private reflections of an elite of able deliberators. By these lights, the job of the public representative is not to adhere to the collective will of his constituents. Rather, it is to represent constituents' interests by partaking in elite discourses from which their representative—rational and enlightened—will derive and articulate their interests as he sees fit (Burke 2000; see also Conniff 1977; Eulau et al. 1959; Pitkin 1967, 168–89).

As such, we have the adoption of the rational and of public reason in the development of a scheme that does not look entirely dissimilar to the Hobbesian conception of representation. Institutions are, in a modern manner, founded when private persons "come together as a public" (Habermas 1989, 27), but we have a return to representation without necessary responsivity. The Burkian scheme relies on our dispensing with general public opinion and nominates a narrower decision-making public to positions of power. This public represents and yet, returning to Hobbes, they are not in any recognizable way the authors of the will that they represent. Burke's scheme emphasizes the separation of representation of others and reflection of their will, at least not as ordinarily understood. Certainly interests are formulated and problems are solved through discourse, but the link between a specific person being party to the discourse and that person being represented is broken.

For Burke this is partly articulated as a distinction between the representation of actual constituents who have a direct role in nominating their members of Parliament (MPs) and the representation of interests in general (Burke 2000; see also Conniff 1977; Eulau et al. 1959). The drive here is the separation of the representative from having to act as a mere delegate for constituents. Burke is also skeptical of the idea that all possible stakeholders must have a role in nomination if representatives are to truly represent. The representative's job is not simply a matter of subordination to every articulation of the principal's will.

The final interesting move in the development of modern representation comes from the end of optimism about enlightened public reason. The transformation of the public sphere, according to Habermas, is sustained on the basis of a rather limited franchise. The domination of older aristocratic elites is set aside in exchange for the qualitatively different discourse-orientation of the bourgeois public. That said, it is obvious that this new public, though universalist in its self-conception, is far from universalist in practice. As both the franchise and access to public debate expanded, the club atmosphere of public debate faded, and the idea of how representation might reflect public opinion changed.

For some, the extension of the boundaries of the public sphere led to a suspicion of the body politic as manifested in the newly empowered mass (see Bellamy 2003). For others, theories of public rationality were displaced by conceptions of competing private interests. Discourses about politics were reformulated as being more about Joseph Schumpeter's mutually antagonistic interest groups (1994) than about the development of legitimate outcomes through rational discourse.

Toward Accountability

Although the discussion above can be read as a theoretical journey from first principles, these three philosophers—Darwall, Hobbes, and Burke—attempt to develop a sense of how obligations toward others might be constructed in such a way that they are public and both mutually and voluntarily acknowledged—and thus legitimate. Hobbes and Burke attempt to show how these obligations are conceived within the context of complex organizations. Darwall's theory, though oriented to interpersonal relationships, provides an important insight into the imperative for second-person relationships to be founded on a moral community—that is, on an intersubjectively produced vocabulary that promotes mutual understanding about rights and obligations. The stability of institutions in both Hobbes and Burke are founded on the assumption that such a moral community can be brought into existence but the crucial flaw with Hobbes's and Burke's work is that their attempts to reconstruct moral communities does not recognize the role that accountability mechanisms play in both stabilizing relationships and in attempts to impose specific interpretations of representation onto institutional arrangements. While both Hobbes and Burke are at base concerned with legitimacy—with formulating the most acceptable balance between usefulness and responsiveness possible—they do not recognize the manner in which struggles to tip the balance in one direction or the other are articulated through the institutional architecture (by virtue of accountability mechanisms) rather than through the formation of the institutions in the first place. Complex institutions are, in this light, the beginning of politics, not the end of politics.

We have now outlined a general theory of representation that focuses on the institutional problems associated with representation. Before moving on to the discussion of corporate governance, it is important to reiterate the importance of the moral content of representation. This is crucial because the moral underpinning to representation theory, derived here from Darwall's work, provides the impetus to get representation right. It is a crucial part of the system of argumentation that drives people to claim principal status or to demand that the will of others be subordinated to their will. Hobbesian and Burkian notions of representation are attempts to balance out the requirements for subordination in representation with the maintenance of useful and effective organizations. The problem is, as many people have pointed out regarding both Hobbes and Burke, that many persuasive arguments and claims concerning the content of both authority and agency are possible in a complex organization. Certainty is in short supply where principals or even agents are not natural persons.

It is no surprise that accountability mechanisms act not just to enforce reporting and so forth, but as political symbols of authority within organizations. They are, in a sense, conversation stoppers: invocations of coercive force designed to stabilize representation relationships in one form. Strangely, accountability mechanisms simply highlight the ambiguous content of any representation relationship. If the relationship were simple, then mechanisms might not be necessary. As such accountability is invoked where the trend is precisely away from the power distribution that the principals want.

THE CORPORATION AS A REPRESENTATIVE INSTITUTION

We now turn to how the character of representation as outlined above manifests itself in the modern company. The company provides an interesting instance for a study of representation and account-ability for two reasons. First, the company, as imagined in British company law, is explicitly a conduit for representation. That is, rather than settling questions of authority and agency in the corporation—that is, rather than answering the problems set up by Hobbes and Burke—British company law simply facilitates the politics of representation within the company. Second, the resulting politics of representation has an immeasurable effect on contemporary society. When the corporate environment shifts in response to the production of any set of accountability mecha-nisms (themselves driven by the negotiation of representation relationships), the effect goes well beyond the institution.

British company law (as well as its American equivalent) is itself politically and philosophically interesting because, rather than regulating some activity or institution that exists already, it actually imagines the limited-liability company into being. Although his writing preceded the emergence of the company by three centuries, British company law reflects Hobbes's sense of representation happening "by fiction" (Hobbes 1996, 111). The company's personhood, the manner in which it can be represented, and the manner in which it can represent are all bounded not only by law but by a variety of softer codes. Adherence to these codes is driven by market-based considerations and stock-market listings obligations (for discussions of ideas of corporate personality in the United Kingdom, especially regarding the landmark *Salomon* ([1897] AC 22) ruling, see essays in Rickett and Grantham 1998). That said, company law, at least in the "Anglo" portion of the Anglo-American corporate sphere,[11] gives the founders of companies and subsequently the various parties involved with them significant latitude in how they define the manner in which representa-tion is negotiated in their own particular manifestation of the corporate form.

In discussing the corporation as a conduit for representation, we will take two approaches. First we will look at some aspects of the origins of the corporation, chiefly to highlight the parallels in the emergence of the corporation with the development of representation theory as outlined above. Historical context is also important in establishing the fundamentals of corporate law, fundamentals that have remained more or less unchanged for the last 150 years. Second, we will look at Brit-ish company law as it is now, especially in the context of debates over ownership and directorial independence. These debates are about representation, and the accountability mechanisms that have been invoked in the wake of scandals on both sides of the Atlantic ought to be understood in the context of the politics of representation within the corporation.[12]

Developed out of unlimited-liability partnerships, the company as originally conceived was for many analysts originally imagined as a "voluntary association of respectable individuals," (Pearson 2002, 845), a company of men in the theatrical sense. That is to say, it was imagined as a publicly licensed forum for a group to act toward a common purpose. (For some analyses of the rise of the joint-stock company, see Alborn 1998; Pearson 2002; Freeman, et al. 2007; Dunlavy 2006; for some interesting discussions of the origins of limited liability, see Hickson and Turner 2005; Forbes 1986; Lobban 1996; Miller 1994; Blumberg 1985). While for others the company was always an economic vehicle through which entrepreneurs might raise capital without loosening their grip on the company's activities (see for instance Ekelund and Tollison 1980; Smythe 2006), the company was conceived as a publicly defined institution that had a "little republic" (Gamble and Kelly 2001, 111) at its core. Whatever the motives behind the formation of the company, it is important to remember that the corporation with power structures as currently conceived was not inevitable. Rather it is a result of struggles over how it ought to be conceived (see for instance

Dunlavy [2006] on the switch from corporations as one-shareholder-one-vote to one-*share*-one-vote institutions).

Private or public, corporations were and are imagined in law as offices that could provide an environment within which moral communities could collaborate toward commercial ends. How this environment is defined is down to the manner in which procedures and accountability rituals are manipulated. The company, either as a public-representative institution as it was and is imagined by many theorists or as a purely private organization, encounters many parallels with the issues raised by Hobbes and Burke. Even if we regard it as little more than a "nexus-of-contracts" confection (see Jensen and Meckling 1976; Fama and Jensen 1983a; Fama and Jensen 1983b; Dallas 1988), it seems that we cannot escape the representation issue. Although nexus-of-contracts theorists see the company's personality as a fiction (i.e., as nothing more than a semiotic device that denotes a coordinated series of contractual relationships), they still need to explain the character and extent of shareholder power within the company. Moreover, while in law a company's directors represent the company and the company alone (Companies Act 2006, s. 170 (1); for an introductory discussion, see Davies et al. 2008; see also Keay 2007a, 2007b for analysis), in practice we must recognize that, at least in terms of a representation relationship between them and the company, shareholders have substantial (and perhaps) growing power in the firm.[13] As such, the firm is a venue for major struggles over the problems of personhood and nomination. And, as we shall see, the invocation and/or rejection of accountability mechanisms is a key component of that struggle.

While it is of course possible to have duties without representing, complex organizations require that individuals subordinate their own will to that of others, that they act in the other's name. British company law mandates that directors owe their duties to the company. It thus follows that they represent the purely artificial person of the company when they act, but the situation is somewhat more complex than that.

The directors' duty to "promote the success of the company for the benefit of its members as a whole" (Companies Act 2006, sec. 172 [1]) certainly precludes directors' orienting their effort toward individual shareholders or toward factions of the shareholders, but the Act also points to the central role that shareholders have in the organization. The company should be seen here as a literal conduit for representation: the directors represent the company and the company represents the members.

Moreover, the company's articles and constitution have more or less full scope for setting out the balance of power within the corporation among managing directors, shareholders, and the board. That said, it is unlikely that the founders of companies would entirely exclude shareholders from having a say in governance, at least through the general meeting. To do so would be to exclude the possibility of investment from institutional shareholders (as not attending to the combined code), so the market drives the institution toward a constitution that mandates shareholders to have a say.

After a century of directorial power, in fact, the balance of power within the company is shifting somewhat back toward the shareholder. This is driven not by institutional change but by the concentration of shareholdings in the hands of large, institutional investors. Now, rather than simply relying on exit as a signal of dissatisfaction with the governance of a company (a signal that does not benefit those who leave), investors are able to use investor meetings and day-to-day contact with directors to exercise voice in attending to their interests (see Hirschman 1970). An unresponsive board risks the mobilization of shareholders in or out of the general meeting if shareholders are not satisfied with them (see Roach 2006; Gillan and Starks 2000).

CONCLUSION: ACCOUNTABILITY MECHANISMS AS TOTEMS OF CONTROL

So what of accountability mechanisms? While following Dubnick we can say that "accountability is a general strategic approach to the management of expectations," we ought also to recognize that "that observation does not clarify what the term means" (Dubnick 2005, 380). Part of the clarification for what accountability might mean is that we must see it in the context of struggles over representation.

Dubnick's series of systematizations of accountability mechanisms and relationships (Romzek and Dubnick 1987; Dubnick 2003; Dubnick 2005; O'Kelly and Dubnick 2006) provide us with a crucial insight into the diverse expectations under which people work in complex organizations. Administrators, whether they be in public or commercial organizations, are pulled in a number of not altogether compatible directions because their institutions are subject to an ongoing struggle over who has authority over them. That is, accountability mechanisms are a manifestation of the struggle to resolve this question: Whom do the administrators represent and how do they represent them? In this context, while specific accountability mechanisms might in practice be ineffective or might even backfire, they may serve a very useful purpose for their proponents. They may act as signifiers that the organizations work in their name.

NOTES

My thanks to the editors, Melvin Dubnick and H. George Frederickson, for helpful comments on an earlier draft. I am also grateful to participants at the Kettering Symposium on accountability in May 2008, and especially to Sally Wheeler and Justin O'Brien for their helpful remarks.

1. My thanks to Melvin Dubnick for many conversations on this and other points. On Dubnick's thinking about Darwall, see Dubnick 2008.

2. Darwall's other example is drawn from David Hume and relates to the claims that underpin protests when one person places their foot upon the toes of another.

3. Arguably, certain representative relationships might be commonly recognized and developed solely through convention and without the need for formal institutions at all. For instance, a parent's representing her child, or one spouse representing another who is incapacitated, seem to be underpinned by convention alone. Nevertheless, the general point still stands that institutions are required for any representation relationships beyond the intimate to be guaranteed and sustained.

4. As Philip Pettit has pointed out in recent work, this is different from saying that they are not possessed of a will at all (Pettit 2002; Pettit 2007a; Pettit 2007b; see also Mäkelä 2007).

5. I am extending the Burkian outlook a little bit with this distinction. Burke was speaking specifically of parliamentary representation. Nevertheless, the basic principal holds across administrative representation in general.

6. Originally in the sense that Leviathan is created when all sign a covenant with all to enter the Commonwealth.

7. It is entirely possible that one individual could be a natural person in some respects and an artificial person in others. Moreover, a fictional person, in Skinner's terminology, can be either a natural or artificial person.

8. Importantly for Hobbes, Leviathan makes just such a move: Leviathan is both the author of specific actions and the agent of the people through the mutual covenant they devise. Skinner goes on to discuss this at length (Skinner 1999, 18f). See also Pitkin's discussion of the difficulties that arise when we consider Leviathan to be both authority and agent (Pitkin 1967, 31f). As Pitkin points out, Leviathan is taken by Hobbes to be a representative of the people and of the mutual covenant. He is, in a sense, the office not the man. At the same time, Leviathan's power to act or to authorize action is virtually unlimited (constrained by the laws of nature alone), so he is not constrained by his being a representative.

9. In fact, there is only one accountability mechanism in *Leviathan:* the Commonwealth might be dis-

solved through revolution, or Leviathan might be overthrown if life has deteriorated to a point that it is worse than the state of nature.

10. Or, to put it differently, while individuals might find some action of Leviathan's abhorrent, the collectivity as a whole only exists as a collectivity by virtue of the institution of Leviathan. Since Leviathan defines that institution's will at any moment, the purely artificial, collective person must necessarily approve of Leviathan's will even if every individual that Leviathan represents is appalled by him.

11. That is, the law in the United Kingdom, Ireland, South Africa, and elsewhere allows for more principals-based regimes, as opposed to the more rules-based regimes that characterize corporate law in the United States.

12. The latest wave of scandals at the beginning of the 2000s not only drove the Sarbanes-Oxley Act in the United States, but they provoked the Higgs review of the British corporate-governance model. Previous scandals, primarily in the Mirror Group and Poly Peck, had led to the formal development of a governance code for British public companies in the early 1990s.

13. Directors' duties tend to be divided roughly between duties of loyalty and duties of care, where duties of loyalty demand the board's directing themselves to the success of the company (as opposed, say, to their own enrichment) and where duties of care demand a basic level of competence from directors. The codification of directors' duties in sections 170–77 of the Companies Act 2006 marks a departure for British law. Duties were hitherto generally defined through the courts.

REFERENCES

Alborn, Timothy. 1998. *Conceiving Companies: Joint-Stock Politics in Victorian England.* London: Routledge.

Bellamy, Richard. 2003. "The Advent of the Masses." In *The Cambridge History of Twentieth Century Political Thought,* ed. Terence Ball and Richard Bellamy. Cambridge, UK: Cambridge University Press, 70–103.

Blumberg, Phillip. 1985. "Limited Liability and Corporate Groups." *Journal of Corporation Law* 11: 573.

Bovens, Mark. 1998. *The Quest for Responsibility: Accountability and Citizenship in Complex Organisations.* Cambridge, UK: Cambridge University Press.

Boyne, George, Julian Gould-Williams, Jennifer Law, and Richard Walker. 2002. "Plans, Performance Information and Accountability: The Case of Best Value." *Public Administration* 80 (4): 691–710.

Burke, Edmund. 2000. "Speech at the Conclusion of the Poll," 3 November 1774. In *On Empire, Liberty, and Reform: Speeches and Letters,* ed. David Bromwich. New Haven: Yale University Press, 50–57.

Companies Act 2006. UK Stationery Office, Office of Public Information, London, United Kingdom. http://www.opsi.gov.uk/acts/acts2006/ukpga_20060046_en_1.

Conniff, James. 1977. "Burke, Bristol, and the Concept of Representation." *Political Research Quarterly* 30 (3): 329–41.

Dallas, Lynn. 1988. "Two Models of Corporate Governance: Beyond Berle and Means." *University of Michigan Journal of Law Reform* 22 (1): 19–116.

Darwall, Stephen L. 2006. *The Second-Person Standpoint: Morality, Respect, and Accountability.* Cambridge, MA: Harvard University Press.

———. 2007. "Reply to Korsgaard, Wallace, and Watson." *Ethics* 118 (1): 52–69.

Davies, Paul L., Sarah Worthington, and Eva Micheler. 2008. *Gower and Davies' Principles of Modern Company Law.* 8th ed. London: Sweet and Maxwell.

Dignam, Alan. 1998. "A Principled Approach to Self-Regulation? The Report of the Hampel Committee on Corporate Governance." *Company Lawyer* 19 (5): 140–54.

Dubnick, Melvin. 2003. "Accountability and Ethics: Reconsidering the Relationships." *International Journal of Organization Theory and Behavior* 6 (3): 405–41.

———. 2005. "Accountability and the Promise of Performance." *Public Performance and Management Review* 28 (3): 376–417.

———. 2008. "Accountability, Adam Smith and Policy Choice in World Financial Markets." Paper presented at the WEF/ESRC Workshop on Incentives and Governance in Global Finance, July 18–20, Radcliff House, University of Warwick, Coventry, UK.

Dunlavy, Colleen. 2006. "Social Conceptions of the Corporation: Insights from the History of Shareholder Voting Rights." *Washington and Lee Law Review* 63 (4): 1347–88.

Ekelund, Robert B. Jr., and Robert D. Tollison. 1980. "Mercantilist Origins of the Corporation." *Bell Journal of Economics* 11 (2): 715–20.

Eulau, Heinz, John C. Wahlke, William Buchanan, and Leroy C. Ferguson. 1959. "The Role of the Representative: Some Empirical Observations on the Theory of Edmund Burke." *The American Political Science Review* 53 (3): 742–56.

Fama, Eugene F., and Michael C. Jensen. 1983a. "Separation of Ownership and Control." *Journal of Law and Economics* 26 (2): 301–25.

———. 1983b. "Agency Problems and Residual Claims." *Journal of Law and Economics* 26 (2): 327–49.

Forbes, Kevin. 1986. "Limited Liability and the Development of the Business Corporation." *The Journal of Law, Economics, and Organization* 2 (1): 163–77.

Freeman, Mark, Robin Pearson, and James Taylor. 2007. "'Different and Better?' Scottish Joint-Stock Companies and the Law, c. 1720–1845." *English Historical Review* CXXII (495): 61–81.

Friedman, R.B. 1990. "On the Concept of Authority in Political Philosophy." In *Authority,* ed. Joseph Raz. Oxford, UK: Basil Blackwell, 56–91.

Gamble, Andrew, and Gavin Kelly. 2001. "Shareholder Value and the Stakeholder Debate in the UK." *Corporate Governance: An International Review* 9 (2): 110.

Gillan, Stuart, and Laura Starks. 2000. "Corporate Governance Proposals and Shareholder Activism: The Role of Institutional Investors." *Journal of Financial Economics* 57: 275–305.

Habermas, Jürgen. 1989. *The Structural Transformation of the Public Sphere: An Inquiry into a Category of Bourgeois Society.* Cambridge, MA: The MIT Press.

Hickson, Charles R., and John D Turner. 2005. "Corporation or Limited Liability Company." In *Encyclopedia of World Trade Since 1450,* ed. John McCusker, Stanley Engerman, Lewis Fischer, David Hancock, and Kenneth Pomeranz. New York: Macmillan.

Hirschman, Albert. 1970. *Exit, Voice, and Loyalty: Responses to Decline in Firms, Organizations, and States.* Cambridge, MA: Harvard University Press.

Hobbes, Thomas. 1996. *Leviathan,* ed. Richard Tuck. Cambridge, UK: Cambridge University Press.

Hood, Christopher. 2002. "The Risk Game and the Blame Game." *Government and Opposition* 37 (1): 15–37.

Jensen, Michael C., and William H. Meckling. 1976. "Theory of the Firm: Managerial Behavior, Agency Costs and Ownership Structure." *Journal of Financial Economics* 3 (4): 305–60.

Keay, Andrew. 2007a. "Section 172(1) of the Companies Act 2006: An Interpretation and Assessment." *Company Lawyer* 28 (4): 106–10.

———. 2007b. "Tackling the Issue of the Corporate Objective: An Analysis of the United Kingdom's 'Enlightened Shareholder Value Approach.'" *Sydney Law Review* 29 (4): 577–612.

Korsgaard, Christine M. 2007. "Autonomy and the Second Person Within: A Commentary on Stephen Darwall's *The Second-Person Standpoint.*" *Ethics* 118 (1): 8–23.

Lobban, Michael. 1996. "Corporate Identity and Limited Liability in France and England 1825–67." *Anglo-American Law Review* 25 (4): 397–440.

Mäkelä, Pekka. 2007. "Collective Agents and Moral Responsibility." *Journal of Social Philosophy* 38 (3): 456–68.

Miller, Andrew H. 1994. "Subjectivity Ltd: The Discourse of Liability in the Joint Stock Companies Act of 1856 and Gaskell's Cranford." *ELH* 61 (1): 139–57.

O'Kelly, Ciarán, and Melvin Dubnick. 2006. "Ethical Relationships and Moral Principles in Public Administration." *Journal for Public Administration Research and Theory* 16 (3): 393–415.

Pearson, Robin. 2002. "Shareholder Democracies? English Stock Companies and the Politics of Corporate Governance During the Industrial Revolution." *English Historical Review* 117 (473): 840–66.

Pettit, Philip. 2002. "Collective Persons and Powers." *Legal Theory* 8 (4): 443–70.

———. 2007a. "Responsibility Incorporated." *Ethics* 117 (2): 171–202.

———. 2007b. "Rationality, Reasoning and Control." *Dialectica* 61 (4): 495–519.

Pitkin, Hanna. 1967. *The Concept of Representation.* Berkeley: The University of California Press.

———. 1968. "Commentary: The Paradox of Representation." In *Representation-Nomos X,* ed. John W. Chapman and J. Roland Pennock. New York: Atherton Press.

Rickett, Charles, and Ross Grantham, eds. 1998. *Corporate Personality in the 20th Century.* Oxford, UK: Hart.

Roach, Lee. 2006. "CEOs, Chairmen and Fat Cats: The Institutions are Watching You." *Company Lawyer* 27 (10): 297–304.

Romzek, Barbara, and Melvin Dubnick. 1987. "Accountability in the Public Sector: Lessons from the Challenger Disaster." *Public Administration Review* 47 (May/June): 227–38.

lenger Disaster." *Public Administration Review* 47 (May/June): 227–38.

Runciman, David. 2007. "The Paradox of Political Representation." *Journal of Political Philosophy* 15 (1): 93–114.

Schumpeter, Joseph. 1994. *Capitalism, Socialism and Democracy.* London: Routledge.

Skinner, Quentin. 1999. "Hobbes and the Purely Artificial Person of the State." *The Journal of Political Philosophy* 7 (1): 1–29.

———. 2005. "Hobbes on Representation." *European Journal of Philosophy* 13 (2): 155–184.

Smythe, Donald. 2006. "Shareholder Democracy and the Economic Purpose of the Corporation." *Washington and Lee Law Review* 63 (4): 1407–21.

Wallace, R. Jay. 2007. "Reasons, Relations, and Commands: Reflections on Darwall." *Ethics* 118 (1): 24–36.

Watson, Gary. 2007. "Morality as Equal Accountability: Comments on Stephen Darwall's The Second-Person Standpoint." *Ethics* 118 (1): 37–51.

17

EMERGENT ACCOUNTABILITY AND STRUCTURATION THEORY: IMPLICATIONS

KAIFENG YANG

Accountability is a fundamentally important but considerably ambiguous and murky concept—particularly so in an administrative environment that is characterized by globalization, decentralization, privatization, and networks. Despite its elusive meaning, organizations—governmental or nongovernmental—are constantly called to be more accountable. But what exactly does this accountability expectation mean? How can managers effectively deal with the cross-pressures of multiple accountabilities? Why do many citizens still distrust government when many sophisticated accountability tools are being used? While public administration research on accountability has made significant progress and contributions (e.g., Behn 2001; Kearns 1996; Roberts 2002; Romzek and Dubnick 1987), it falls short of helping organizations and managers when accountability problems become more challenging in the new governance environment.

Part of this problem is a lack of conceptual clarity at a basic level—a lack of a unified framework. Is accountability the means or the ends? How can it be measured? Does it necessarily lead to beneficial consequences? It is not clear whether we will ever be able to find "the" meaning, "the" framework, or "the" solution to the problem of accountability, but it seems we need a notion of accountability that is broader, more realistic, and that has greater conceptual clarity. To get closer to that notion, it is helpful to rethink our ontological, epistemological, and methodological assumptions about accountability. This chapter argues that we should depart from dichotomist logic and embrace non-dichotomist perspectives of accountability: accountability as both means and ends, with both positive and negative consequences, and being both enabling and constraining. This will allow scholars with competing perspectives to enter into some degree of dialogue. But since any such attempt to integrate competing ideas is likely to be limited and controversial, this chapter does so by using Anthony Giddens's structuration theory to shed light on the conceptual questions raised above.

ANTHONY GIDDENS AND STRUCTURATION THEORY

In a number of texts published in the late 1970s and early 1980s, particularly *The Constitution of Society: Outline of the Theory of Structuration,* Anthony Giddens developed his theory of structuration, which challenged then dominant theoretical traditions (e.g., functionalism and structuralism) on explaining the constitution of social life. Giddens attempts to bridge micro and macro levels of social analysis by reconciling the theoretical dichotomies between agency and structure and between subjective and objective. Although structuration theory is not without its critics, it has become one of the most influential modern social theories. Below is a brief introduction of the major concepts of the theory.

Knowledgeable Agents and Action

Giddens emphasizes that all human beings are autonomous and knowledgeable agents or actors who know a great deal about the conditions and consequences of what they do in their daily lives—and know much more than sociologists normally think they know. Actors have three types of consciousness: discursive (able to be articulated), practical (routinized into the background and out of discursive consciousness), and unconscious. Among the three, practical consciousness is a fundamental feature of the structuration theory, since "much of what actors know about their world is part of their practical consciousness—it is known without being articulated as such" (Giddens 1979, 2).

With their knowledge, actors engage in actions. Giddens (1984) defines action as a continuous flow of interventions, not discrete acts. Such actions are "motivated" in the sense that they may not be "purposeful," but are mostly "purposive"—monitored by actors who continually reflect on what they are doing, how others react to what they are doing, and the circumstances in which they find themselves. That is, actors are capable of accounting for their actions, both to themselves and to others. When they are asked by others why they acted as they did, they will rationalize their actions. Moreover, actors are not merely passive or "cultural dopes" of institutional or structural arrangements; they can transform situations and make choices. In the meantime, agency does not mean that actors can create structures or social realities at will because actors are bounded by unacknowledged conditions of action (e.g., unconscious sources of motivation) and by unintended consequences of action that become unacknowledged conditions in the future. Thus actors use interpretive schemes to constitute and communicate meaning and then take action with intentional and unintended consequences.

Systems and Structures

According to Giddens (1984), systems are "patterns of relations in groupings of all kinds, from small, intimate groups, to social networks, to large organizations" (131). Systems should be viewed as the patterning of social relations across space-time, understood as reproduced practices. Systems can be, for example, families, peer groups, communities, or cities, either at the face-to-face level or existing via networks over space and time. Structures, on the other hand, are "rules and resources, recursively implicated in the institutional articulation of social systems" (Giddens 1984, 6). To study structures and structural principles is to study major aspects of the transformation/ mediation relations that influence social and system integration. Structures do not just exist in and of themselves—they cannot exist without enacted conduct, and they are both the medium and outcome of action. While people usually think of structures as large-scale entities or practices that affect us, Giddens forces us to consider how structures are reproduced: through enacted human conduct in the form of structured practices that maintain and reproduce these structures.

Giddens identifies three types of structures in social systems:

- Rules of signification: relate to the theory of coding and produces meaning through discursive practices or organized webs of language. "They restrict and enable actors to make sense of the context they act in and to communicate this meaning and their views of ongoing practices to others" (Sydow and Windeler 1998, 271).
- Rules of legitimization: relate to theories of normative legitimization and produce moral order via societal norms, values, and standards. When actors apply sanctions in interactions they draw upon such norms and rules.

Figure 17.1   **The Duality of Structure**

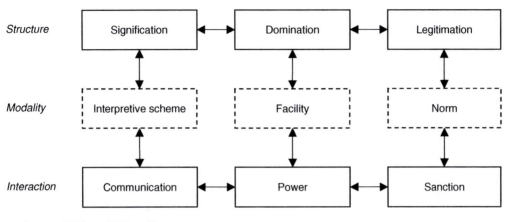

Source: Giddens, 1984, p. 29.

- Rules of domination: relate to theories of resource authorization/allocation and produce power, originating from the control of resources. To secure specific outcomes, actors influence others with their power, which is based on resources.

Duality of Structure

To bridge the dualism between structure and agency, Giddens (1984) argues that structure should not be taken as having some given or visible form external to people. Rather, structure exists only in and through the activities of human agents: "analyzing the structuration of social systems means studying the modes in which systems . . . are produced and reproduced in interaction" (Giddens 1984, 25). Structure gives form and shape to social life but it is not itself that form and shape. Actors refer to structures in their social practices and reproduce them recursively. That is, structures "are not brought into being by social actors but continually recreated by them via the very means whereby they express themselves as actors. In and through their activities agents reproduce the conditions that make these activities possible" (Giddens 1984, 2).

Structuration means the interplay between structure and agency (Figure 17.1). The duality of structure differentiates a structural dimension that involves aspects of signification, domination, and legitimation, and an interactional dimension that includes communication, power, and sanction. The two dimensions are linked by modalities of structuration such as interpretive schemes, facilities, and norms (see Giddens 1984, pp. 28–32). For example, in communicating meaning in interaction, actors draw upon interpretative schemes, which can be analyzed as rules of significance (such as semantic rules) at the level of structure.

The three types of modalities (interactions or structures) are interrelated. They are analytically distinctive but mobilize and reinforce one another. In any concrete situation of interaction, Giddens (1976) writes, "members of society draw upon these as . . . an integrated set rather than three discrete components" (124). For example, the communication of meaning cannot be substantively separated from the application of sanction or the use of power, and vice versa. As Thompson (1989) puts it, "these different modalities are woven together in social practices, so that even the most mundane action or interaction expresses overlapping aspects of the structural whole" (61).

Social Praxis

Praxis can be defined as regular patterns of enacted conduct by actors who interact with one another in habitual, reflexive, reflective, and conscious ways. Instead of treating agency as people's intentions, Giddens (1984) defines agency as the flow of actions that are path dependent, contextually bound, and embedded in social practices. The idea of praxis emphasizes the role of time and space—not as boundaries within which social life takes place, but as "distanciation," where the interaction takes place in a definite setting for a definite period, and where actors typically employ the spatial and temporal features of the interaction as a means of organizing their exchange (Thompson 1989). In summary, Giddens (1984) argues:

> The basic domain of study of the social sciences, according to the theory of structuration, is neither the experience of the individual actor, nor the existence of any form of social totality, but social practices ordered across space and time. Human social activities, like some self-reproducing items in nature, are recursive. That is to say, they are not brought into being by social actors but continually recreated by them via the very means whereby they express themselves as actors. In and through their activities agents reproduce the conditions that make these activities possible. (2)

Giddens's structuration theory operates at a high level of abstraction. It is not intended to be a guide for empirical study, but to be an ontological theory or a meta-theory. Despite the difficulty in applying it to empirical testing, structuration theory has been operationalized to study organizations, institutions, and technology (DeSanctis and Poole 1994). Jones (1997) develops four ways to use the theory: reconstructing it to accommodate a topic, applying it as an analytical tool, treating it as meta-theory, and using its concepts to inform research. This chapter borrows the theory of structuration to illustrate the emergent and power-dependent nature of accountability.

STRUCTURATION THEORY AND ACCOUNTABILITY

Accountability can be generally defined as "a social relationship in which an actor feels an obligation to explain and to justify his or her conduct to some significant other" (Bovens 2005, 84). Such a relationship can be viewed as a type of interaction and structure as defined by Giddens. That is, accountability can be viewed as the structural properties of the governance system. Lynn et al. (2001) define governance "as regimes of laws, rules, judicial decisions, and administrative practices that constrain, prescribe, and enable the provision of publicly supported goods and services" (7). Governance itself is not structure, but it has structural properties. As Giddens (1976) writes, "a structure is not a 'group,' 'collectivity,' or 'organization': these have structures. Groups, collectives, etc., can and should be studied as systems of interaction" (121).

The structural properties of accountability affect the reproduction of the governance system it is attached to or embedded in. As Cohen notes, "Structural properties in social systems may not reproduce systems, but they shape, channel, and facilitate system reproduction whenever it occurs by providing agents with the practical awareness of the practices, relations, and spatial-temporal settings they require in order to participate in the reproductive process" (1989, 201). Expressing a similar view, Brown (2007) sees that accountability has regulative and constitutive aspects. The regulative aspect means that accountability models constrain individual behaviors; the constitutive aspect suggests that accountability models give life to the experience of actors and the social system. For example, for accountability based on principal-agent theories, "the combination of

Figure 17.2 **The Recursive Interplay between Accountability and the Duality of Structure**

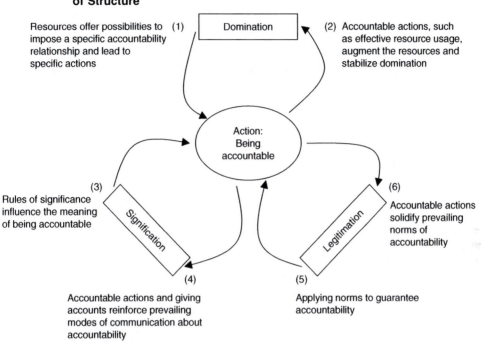

regulative and constitutive impacts can strengthen the effectiveness of principal-agent relations, but it can also create overreliance on the model" (Brown 2007, 107). For accountability based on mutual responsibility, the regulative aspect creates agreements about values and visions that emphasize operations based on trust; the constitutive aspect creates the experience and expectations of interdependence across a community of autonomous actors.

According to Giddens (1984), structure is constituted by rules and resources governing and available to agents. Accountability comes with expectations that are manifested in rules—the patterns people follow in organizational life—and it brings resources with itself. For example, politics, administration, and markets, as three sources of accountability pressure (Klingner et al. 2002), can be treated as three structural forces that have legitimation, signification, and domination implications. Politics, administration, and markets have different rules of legitimation, or what Klingner et al. (2002) call sources of control: elections, law, and discipline of markets. These three also have different communication patterns that are based on stories, reports, and contracts, respectively. And they involve different rules of domination: power and budgets, knowledge and deeds, and money and profit, respectively.

Figure 17.2 shows how accountability can be understood as structures in terms of the duality of structure. The circle in the middle represents accountable action that includes the flow of activities such as communication, use of power, application of sanction, and giving accounts. Accountable action or being accountable cannot be understood clearly without linking it to the three structural forces shaping the system. The three types of structures enable and constrain actors' actions and at the same time are reproduced by the actions.

For example, the link from domination to accountable action (Link 1) indicates that power based on resources offers possibilities to impose a specific accountability relationship and leads to specific actions of being accountable. Accountability as a domination structure is analytically treated as the means, in that power relationships of the current system determine what action is considered desirable and shapes actors' behavior. This power perspective reflects the resource-dependency theory and suggests that actors who have the dominant political influence are more likely to define the meaning of accountability, the interaction landscape, and the desirable outcome. At the same time, the link from being accountable to domination (Link 2) indicates that actions centered on accountabilities, including the use of resources as planned or promised, reinforce the current dominant relationship or accountability structure. Here accountability is implicitly treated as the ends, in that accountable actions reproduce the current social practice and system that are considered acceptable or desirable by most actors. Links 1 and 2 together indicate that accountability can be both the means and the ends.

Accountability can also be viewed as the rules of signification. The link from signification to accountable action (Link 3) suggests that rules of significance, such as cultural values and ideologies, affect what it means to be accountable, to whom, and for what. In discussing education accountability, Kuchapski (1998) contends that "in the underbelly of seemingly neutral technical processes . . . lie beliefs about how 'education' and society 'ought' to work. What public education is to be held accountable for is critically dependent on educational aims, and 'questions about the aims and content of education are intimately connected with views about the kind of society we wish to live in' (White, 1990, 16)." Here accountability is analytically the means, in that actors in the interaction follow these rules or interpretive schemes. At the same time, when they follow these rules and perform related actions, they are actually reinforcing the legitimacy and relevance of the rules (Link 4). Again, accountability as the structure of signification is both the means/medium and the ends/outcome of actions.

Similarly, accountability can be conceived of as the rules of legitimation. This conception is probably closer to what accountability is normally thought to be—sanctions and rewards based on actors' past performance. Link 5, the application of norms and sanctions to affect individual actions, is a common theme in accountability research. However, prior research does not equally emphasize the recursive aspect of Link 6, which suggests that being punished, taking sanctions, learning from mistakes, and other related activities will strengthen the currently prevailing norms. Again, accountability is taken as both the means and the ends.

Consistent with Giddens' perspective, the three aspects of accountability structures are interdependent. The interaction between political action, material change, and discursive practice greatly helps us understand accountability politics (Newell 2006). For example, the exercise of power in accountability relationships is justified and advanced by prevailing constructions and narratives of accountability. As the product of a particular set of historical and material circumstances, these constructions presume certain entitlements and validate some forms of power while delegitimizing others. This perspective helps "provide the basis for understanding the place of accountability in broader constructions of citizenship and discourse around rights, who gets to define these, and the implications of this for the poor" (Newell 2006, 39).

If we consider accountability as structural forces or rules, the public-administration literature has largely focused on how actions and consequences flow from these structures. Much has been written about the fact that accountability pressures are sometimes conflicting, and conflicts lead to problems such as disasters, crises, and mismanagement (Koppell 2005; Romzek and Dubnick 1987). It is also observed that overreliance on a particular type (or particular types) of accountability leads to problems (Romzek and Ingraham 2000; Schwartz and Sulitzeanu-Kanan 2004). In comparison, little has been written about the production of accountability structure via actions, and still less has been written on power, cognition, and legitimacy issues as interrelated aspects of the recursive accountability process.

From a structuration perspective, accountability is an emergent property, not a given set of rules or tools. And accountability is constantly changing and shifting as actors—politicians, bureaucrats, citizens, businesses—act and interact. This idea has appeared in the recent accountability literature. For example, Kearns (1996) proposes that accountability can be negotiated between actors. Roberts (2002) advises that when there are wicked problems and when traditional problem-solving methods have failed, dialogue is a good alternative as a mechanism of accountability. More similar to the idea expressed in this chapter is O'Connell's (2005) study that concludes "program accountability can be an emergent property arising from the actions of the major actors in a program's field" (85).

The accountability literature has also emphasized the role of agency. Acar et al. (2006) conclude that "the accountability-performance link may have something to do with how managers respond to accountability pressures and transform the pressures into management strategies" (17). Dubnick and Justice (2006) discuss the importance of individual moral agency. Jos and Tompkins (2004) discuss the paradox of accountability: "responsible interpretation and application of legitimate external accountability demands depends [sic] on the cultivation of the virtues that support good administrative judgment, but the institutions and mechanisms that are used to communicate these external standards, and that monitor compliance with them, often threaten the very qualities that support responsible judgment" (256).

However, except for Roberts (2002), who borrows from Harmon's (1995) idea of responsibility, paradox-rationalist discourse on government neglects the idea of agency and public officials' personal responsibility. The prior studies emphasizing emergent accountability do not rely on the idea of human agency, and the studies stressing human agency do not discuss the flux and transformability of accountability. Almost none of the prior studies emphasize that accountability structures are produced and reproduced by actions in a recursive manner. Missing from much of the literature is systematic studies of how individual actors influence the structural forces and how they enact or reproduce the social structures. For example, it would be important to examine which domination, signification, and legitimation structures an accountability system reflects, and how different groups of actors perceive and communicate through these structures. This requires studying how accountability tools and procedures are embedded in and manifested as cultures, norms, resources, and values.

The absence of transformative agency reduces the rigor of theorizing about accountability. We all complain that in practice bureaucrats are rarely held accountable for what they do. If bureaucrats know they are unlikely to be punished, how would they react to the accountability systems and relationships? Will they behave as expected by the designers of the accountability system? The assumption that bureaucrats respond only passively to external accountability systems is unrealistic and unfounded (Krause 1999; Meier and O'Toole 2006). March (1981) succinctly points out that "any system of accounts is a road map to cheating on them" (22)—that is, rule setters and rule followers are always involved in information manipulation and strategic maneuvering.

The lack of explicit and systematic attention to the agency issue is likely due to the fear that allowing more flexibility to bureaucrats may lead to irresponsible government. The contention that accountability is negotiated and reproduced through the interaction among actors such as bureaucrats and elected officials may seem undemocratic and illegitimate for those who believe in less bureaucratic power. In criticizing accountability as "managing expectations," O'Loughlin (1990) fears that this conception "shifts the emphasis from outside control over bureaucracies to administrative control and management of outsiders" and that "they [bureaucrats] can effectively fend off any potentially disruptive influence that we may try to exercise" (281).

O'Loughlin's fear is reasonable, and we should not allow bureaucrats to run out of control.

However, agency "doesn't mean that the world is plastic to the will of the individual" (Giddens and Pierson 1998, 80). The literature of bureaucratic politics shows that even when bureaucrats have high levels of power, elected officials have substantive control over such power. Recent studies emphasize a balanced view and demonstrate that bureaucratic decision making is determined by both external political controls and internal bureaucratic values (Krause 1999; Meier and O'Toole 2006). Accountability relationships are a two-way street, and we need to allow those being held accountable to exercise flexibility and discretion. Without recognizing public managers' legitimate discretion to manage and to reason, accountability is a baseless term. As Wang (2002) finds, "accountability appears to be promoted by government workers' willingness, support, and action in accountability . . . the real challenge in accountability enhancement . . . is to win government workers' support in accountability action" (366).

Moreover, when human agency is emphasized, agency refers not only bureaucrats, but also to politicians, citizens, and other stakeholders. From a governance perspective, all those actors or groups should be accountable for the overall performance of the governing system and for making collaborative governance work. Even the principals should be accountable to their agents; otherwise, credible commitment will be absent, and cooperation will be difficult. For example, politicians in accountability relationships are often considered principals, and bureaucrats agents. Accordingly, the typical question is how to make bureaucrats accountable to politicians. But politicians should be also held to account—"true accountability can be achieved only if sufficient information is provided on the activities of both elected principals and their bureaucratic agents" (Wood and Waterman 1994, 130). Similarly, governments should be accountable to nonprofit organizations (Whitaker et. al 2004), and governments and corporations should be accountable to citizens and the poor (Goetz and Jenkins 2004).

IMPLICATIONS FOR RESEARCH AND PRACTICE

With regard to the important questions raised by the contributors to the book, what can we learn from the structuration perspective outlined above? The first implication is that accountability should be treated as both means and an end. A typical justification for this treatment is a sequential or hierarchical one: accountability mechanisms lead to desirable ends at one level, which in turn serve as a means and help achieve the ends at a higher level. The structuration perspective takes a recursive approach: the means and ends interact simultaneously.

Looking at accountability only as means ignores the fact that in every interaction actors should or ought to be accountable to themselves and to others. Looking at accountability only as an end encounters the difficulty that actors have different opinions on what action is desirable and that accountability mechanisms are often used to promote a specific goal or objective. Even the concept of democratic accountability can be used to advance different goals or values, since democracy has various meanings. When accountability is taken for granted as only an end, it actually becomes an institutionalized myth. As a structural aspect of governance, accountability is not necessarily good or bad in and of itself. We should not trivialize accountability as simple managerial tools, nor should we idealize it as something we should uncritically pursue.

Second, the emergent nature of accountability indicates that accountability is context-specific and, therefore, the attempt for a unified definition may be asking too much. When accountability is treated as an end, then what exactly is deemed desirable, virtuous, or righteous depends on a specific community's (nation, city, neighborhood, organization, etc.) consensual or dominant understanding, cultural norm, or ideology. When accountability is viewed as means, it is clear that the tools and mechanisms are different—or interpreted differently—across contexts. As Giddens

(1984) emphasizes, "structure, or structural properties, or structural parameters, exist only in social reproduction across time and space" (212). This can be understood in two ways: accountability differs across cultures and evolves as environment changes.

While accountability is increasingly a global phenomenon, its impacts differ across localized social structures. For example, Considine (2002) studies accountability in Australia, the Netherlands, New Zealand, and the United Kingdom. He finds that frontline government employees from the four countries have different rankings of four types of accountability—vertical and top-down, vertical and bottom-up, horizontal, and reflexive. Tsai (2007) studies the behavior of government officials in Chinese rural areas and finds that there is accountability without democracy because the officials are subject to informal rules and norms that are unwritten and unauthorized by the state, yet established by social groups and enforced by the communities of which they are members. Brown (2007) concludes that different accountability models may resonate differently with different cultural contexts: accountability based on agency theory fits the United States' individualism and free market, while accountability based on mutual trust is more resonant with Japan's cultural values, which stress cooperative relationships and collective responsibility. As a result, "choosing among the models may turn in part on the cultural contexts in which the actors operate" (Brown 2007, 107). Indeed, "there is no global grammar of accountability that makes sense across settings" (Newell 2006, 40).

Accountability evolves and adapts. Traditional definitions of accountability have been expanded to adjust to new realities. For example, political accountability is no longer provided within the state but increasingly also by civil-society actors functioning as watchdogs of state action (Fox 2007; Goetz and Jenkins 2004). The New Public Management (NPM) reforms have made traditional accountability systems and philosophies plainly inadequate. As Considine (2002) writes, given the emergence of networks, "definitions of accountability might be extended to explicitly include the form and extent of double-loop, or improvisation . . . traditional line accountability must be accompanied by a cultural framework of obligations" (30).

Third, when accountability is seen as structures of signification, domination, and legitimation, its focus should not be solely on measuring and reporting. What about sanctioning, rewarding, and giving accounts? Focusing on measuring and reporting assumes that transparency will lead to accountable behavior. However, transparency without consequences only leads to "soft" accountability—answerability without sanctions. Transparency is a necessary but insufficient condition to accountability: "If the power of transparency is based on the 'power of shame,' then its influence over the shameless may be quite limited" (Fox 2007, 351). Many factors other than measuring and reporting affect accountability. For example, in many developing countries, the lack of accountability may be due to weak civil society and undemocratic elections. In addition, if only measuring and reporting are emphasized, would bureaucrats always be honest and never try to game the system? Under which conditions will transparency lead to accountability? What is the role of culture building?

Even when measuring and reporting are emphasized, a broader framework should be embraced to include all components of inputs, processes, outputs, outcomes, and beyond. Because multiple and competing actors have different expectations, they need different kinds of information and feedback. Therefore, accountability is necessarily contingent upon both the demander and the context of the demand (Bryant 2007), and any accountability designed to promote reform must rest on multiple indicators. NPM reforms emphasize the supremacy of outcome measures, but outcome measures are also limited—they help identify effective or ineffective practices, but they cannot necessarily translate that information into systematic changes in organizational routines and behavior (Ebrahim 2007). Yang and Holzer (2006) argue that a broader framework of performance measurement should link inputs/outputs/outcomes to measures of organizational effectiveness and management quality. In education, for example, test-based accountability has been widely criticized; instead, a comprehensive accountability system is often proposed to measure not only outcomes, but also the enabling process and context, using qualitative data derived from ethnographic studies, case studies, and surveys of students, teachers, and parents (Wheelock 2000).

Another important but also neglected factor in performance measurement is learning, particularly double-loop policy learning. Considine (2002) argues that in a governance system characterized by networks, making accountability judgments based solely on whether predetermined targets are met ignores the highly dynamic and interdependent nature of vertical and horizontal relationships. He points out that we must place performance measurement within a larger theory of agency that can accommodate organizational learning. In addition to showing that resources are accounted for, accountability processes should also involve acts of creativity and innovation.

Fourth, when accountability is understood as part of the process that is reproducing the social system, its promise for performance—or any other positive benefits—should be reconsidered in relation to power and struggle. Accountability should be understood not in terms of its functional consequences, but in relation to the conflicts and struggles it is being used to describe. For example, Fox (2007) observes a "low-accountability trap" in Mexico that is created by mutually reinforcing interaction between weak oversight and flawed election. It is difficult to break this self-reinforcing equilibrium because there are struggles between pro-accountability forces and their opponents: "the problem is caused in large part by the political weakness of civic, social, and political forces that favor public accountability: how can they be empowered when their opponents have so much to lose?" (337).

Newell (2006) clearly explains that "the ability to demand and exercise accountability implies power [,]" and "the right to demand and the capacity and willingness to respond to calls for accountability assume relations of power" (38). While this may seem obvious, much of the literature tends to reduce accountability pressures to improved management and auditing systems while ignoring that accountability is embedded in power relations in a state of flux that reflects the contested basis of relations among actors. Newell (2006) argues that "these relations both create and restrict the possibilities of new forms of accountability by generating novel dynamics of power through material change and changes in the organization of political authority" (38).

We should be cautious not only about the claims of performance from accountability (Dubnick 2005), but also about the possibility that accountability may lead to unintended consequences. Actions create unintended consequences (Giddens 1984) and a society of risk and side effects. Procedural accountability has dark sides as it creates red tape, stifles innovation, and reduces risk-taking (Behn 2001). Production-oriented accountability leads to disaster and impedes change (Schwartz and Sulitzeanu-Kanan 2004). Too much political and hierarchical accountability damages professional accountability (Romzek and Dubnick 1987; Romzek and Ingraham 2000). Even mutual accountability has its dark side: in-group trust among group members may create undue distrust toward actors outside the group. As Brown (2007) cautions, "the emphasis on constituting communities of mutually accountable members may also encourage framing nonmembers in negative terms and so foster conflict with outsiders even while community members are embracing interdependence with insiders" (108).

Finally, from the structuration perspective, the traditional notions of accountability that emphasize controlling behaviors via sanctions and rewards neglect the transformative role of actors. The traditional state-centered system of accountability serves to strengthen and reproduce the existing governance system. But how can we make changes and improve the current system? Macdonald (2007) considers this to be an issue of "transformative accountability": how can we transform the existing governance system and reject the existing core principles through which power is distributed and legitimized? In particular, as Newell (2006) contends, "the question for many of the actors engaged in the accountability struggles . . . is not what accountability does for those institutions that already wield power, but what it can do for the victims of institutional inaction, political oversight, economic marginalization and overt repression" (39).

Transformative accountability is certainly a challenging task as it indicates holding powerful actors accountable to the rules of a transformed governance system that does not yet formally exist (Macdonald 2007). Macdonald is hopeful in observing that, for example, anti-sweatshop campaigns in many developing countries have established independent information-transmission and sanctioning mechanisms, through which powerful multinational corporations are pressured to accept increased responsibility for their actions (2007). From the perspective of structuration theory, change is possible because actors are knowledgeable and transformative. The duality of structure suggests that accountability as exogenous control and responsibility as endogenous action are interdependent: the success of the former relies on the success of the latter, and vice versa.

CONCLUSION

Accountability research in public administration has generated many significant findings, but many hard questions remain unresolved. This chapter offered an alternative perspective to the study of accountability. Based on Anthony Giddens's structuration theory, this perspective considers accountability as structural properties of governance systems. Consistent with the ideal of the duality of structure, accountability is viewed as both the medium and outcome of action. Accordingly, this chapter submits that accountability is both means and ends, context-specific and emergent. Moreover, accountability (as structures) has aspects of legitimation, domination, and signification. This broader notion requires a focus that is beyond measuring and reporting inputs, outputs, and outcomes. It also indicates that accountability cannot be understood without considering power relations.

The perspective outlined here helps clarify the issues raised by many participants in the Kettering sessions, but it also opens new questions. Under which conditions will accountability make a difference, how much, and for whom? Under which conditions can actors be transformative, and under which conditions may policy learning be achieved? What are the social costs associated with accountability struggles? And what new accountability forms can help us build an effective governance system to deal with emerging challenges?

REFERENCES

Acar, Muhittin, Chao Guo, and Kaifeng Yang. 2008. "Accountability When Hierarchical Authority Is Absent." *American Review of Public Administration* 38 (1): 3–23.

Behn, Robert. 2001. *Rethinking Democratic Accountability.* Washington, DC: Brookings Institution Press.

Bovens, Mark. 2005. "Public Accountability." In *The Oxford Handbook of Public Management,* ed. E. Ferlie, L. Lynn, and C. Pollitt, 182–208. New York: Oxford University Press.

Brown, L. David. 2007. "Multiparty Social Action and Mutual Accountability." In *Global Accountabilities: Participation, Pluralism, and Public Ethics,* ed. Alnoor Ebrahim and Edward Weisband, 89–111. New York: Cambridge University Press.

Bryant, Coralie. 2007. "Evaluation and Accountability in Emergency Relief." In *Global Accountabilities: Participation, Pluralism, and Public Ethics,* ed. Alnoor Ebrahim and Edward Weisband, 168–92. New York: Cambridge University Press.

Cohen, Ira J. 1989. *Structuration Theory: Anthony Giddens and the Constitution of Social Life.* London: MacMillan Education.

Considine, Mark. 2002. "The End of the Line? Accountable Governance in the Age of Networks, Partnerships, and Joined-Up Services." *Governance* 15 (1): 21–40.

DeSanctis, Gerardine, and Marshall Poole. 1994. Capturing the Complexity in Advanced Technology Use: Adaptive Structuration Theory. *Organization Science* 5 (2): 121–47.

Dubnick, Melvin. 2005. "Accountability and the Promise of Performance." *Public Performance and Management Review* 28 (3): 376–417.

Dubnick, Melvin, and Jonathan Justice. 2006. "Accountability and the Evil of Administrative Ethics." *Administration and Society* 38 (2): 236–67.

Ebrahim, Alnoor. 2007. "Beyond Dependence: Conceptualizing Information and Accountability in NGO-Funder Relation. In *Reconceptualizing NGOs and Their Roles in Development*, ed. by Paul Opoku-Mensah, David Lewis, and Terje Tvedt, 119–59. Aalborg, Denmark: Aalborg University Press.

Fox, Jonathan. 2007. *Accountability Politics: Power and Voice in Rural Mexico.* New York: Oxford University Press.

Giddens, Anthony. 1976. *New Rules of Sociological Method: A Positive Critique of Interpretative Sociologies.* New York: Basic Books.

———. 1979. *Central Problems in Social Theory: Action, Structure, and Contradiction in Social Analysis.* London: Macmillan.

———. 1984. *The Constitution of Society: Outline of the Theory of Structuration.* Berkeley: University of California Press.

Giddens, Anthony, and Christopher Pierson. 1998. *Conversations with Anthony Giddens: Making Sense of Modernity.* Stanford: Stanford University Press.

Goetz, Anne Marie, and Bob Jenkins. 2004. *Reinventing Accountability: Making Democracy Work for the Poor.* London: Palgrave.

Harmon, Michael M. 1995. *Responsibility as Paradox.* Thousand Oaks, CA: Sage Publications.

Jones, Matthew. 1997. "Structuration Theory and IT." In *Rethinking Management Information Systems,* ed. W. Currie and B. Galliers, 103–35. Oxford: Oxford University Press.

Jos, Philip, and Mark Tompkins. 2004. "The Accountability Paradox in an Age of Reinvention." *Administration and Society* 36 (3): 255–81.

Kearns, Kevin. 1996. *Managing For Accountability: Preserving the Public Trust in Public and Nonprofit Organizations.* San Francisco: Jossey-Bass.

Klingner, Donald, John Nalbandian, and Barbara Romzek. 2002. "Politics, Administration, and Markets: Conflicting Expectations and Accountability." *American Review of Public Administration* 32: 117–44.

Koppell, Jonathan. 2005. "Pathologies of Accountability." *Public Administration Review* 65: 94–108.

Krause, George. 1999. *A Two-Way Street: Institutional Dynamics of the Modern Administrative State.* Pittsburgh: University of Pittsburgh Press.

Kuchapski, Renee. 1998. "Conceptualizing Accountability: A Liberal Framework." In *The Politics of Accountability: Educative and International Perspectives,* ed. Reynold Macpherson, 185–96. Thousand Oaks, CA: Corwin Press.

Lynn, Lawrence, Carolyn Heinrich, and Carolyn Hill. 2001. *Improving Governance: A New Logic for Empirical Research.* Washington, DC: Georgetown University Press.

Macdonald, Kate. 2007. "Public Accountability Within Transnational Supply Chains: A Global Agenda For Empowering Southern Workers?" In *Global Accountabilities: Participation, Pluralism, and Public Ethics,* ed. Alnoor Ebrahim and Edward Weisband, 252–79. New York: Cambridge University Press.

March, James. 1981. "Decision Making Perspective." In *Perspectives on Organizational Design and Behavior,* ed. A. Van De Ven and W. Joyce. New York: Wiley.

Meier, K., and O'Toole, L. 2006. "Political Control Versus Bureaucratic Values: Reframing The Debate." *Public Administration Review* 66: 177–92.

Newell, Peter. 2006. "Taking Accountability into Account: The Debate So Far." In *Rights, Resources and the Politics of Accountability,* ed. Peter Newell and Joanna Wheeler, 37–58. New York: Zed Books.

O'Connell, Lenahan. 2005. "Program Accountability as an Emergent Property: The Role of Stakeholders in a Program's Field." *Public Administration Review* 65: 85–93.

O'Loughlin, Michael G. 1990. "What Is Bureaucratic Accountability and How Can We Measure It?" *Administration and Society* 22 (3): 275–302.

Roberts, Nancy. 2002. "Keeping Public Officials Accountable Through Dialogue: Resolving the Accountability Paradox." *Public Administration Review* 62 (6): 658–69.

Romzek, Barbara, and Melvin Dubnick. 1987. "Accountability in the Public Sector: Lessons from the Challenger Tragedy." *Public Administration Review* 47 (3): 227–38.

Romzek, Barbara, and Patricia Ingraham. 2000. "Cross Pressures of Accountability: Initiative, Command, and Failure in the Ron Brown Plane Crash." *Public Administration Review* 60 (3): 240–53.

Schwartz, Robert, and Ranna Sulitzeanu-Kenan. 2004. "Managerial Values and Accountability Pressures: Challenges of Crisis and Disaster." *Journal of Public Administration Research and Theory* 14 (1): 79–102.

Sydow, Jorg, and Arnold Windeler. 1998. "Organizing and Evaluating Interfirm Networks: A Structurationist Perspective on Network Processes and Effectiveness." *Organization Science* 9 (3): 265–84.

Thompson, John. 1989. "The Theory of Structuration." In *Social Theory of Modern Societies: Anthony Giddens and His Critics,* ed. David Held and John Thompson, 56–76. New York: Cambridge University Press.

Tsai, Lily. 2007. *Accountability Without Democracy: Solidary Groups and Public Goods Provision in Rural China.* New York: Cambridge University Press.

Wang, Xiaohu. 2002. "Assessing Administrative Accountability: Results from a National Survey." *American Review of Public Administration* 32: 350–70.

Wheelock, Anne. 2000. "A New Look at School Accountability." In *Accountability, Assessment, and Teacher Commitment,* ed. Betty Lou Whitford and Ken Jones, 179–98. Albany, NY: State University of New York Press.

Whitaker, Gordon, Lydian Altman-Sauer, and Margaret Henderson. 2004. "Mutual Accountability between Governments and Non-Profits: Moving Beyond 'Surveillance' to 'Service.'" *American Review of Public Administration* 34 (2): 115–33.

White, J. 1990. *Education and the Good Life: Beyond the National Curriculum.* London: Kogan Page.

Wood, Dan, and Richard Waterman. 1994. *Bureaucratic Dynamics.* Boulder, CO: Westview Press.

Yang, Kaifeng, and Marc Holzer. 2006. "The Performance-Trust Link: Implications for Performance Measurement." *Public Administration Review* 66 (1): 114–26.

18

RETHINKING THE OBSESSION

Accountability and the Financial Crisis

MELVIN J. DUBNICK AND JUSTIN O'BRIEN

The introductory chapter of this volume began with an observation: In listening to the rhetoric surrounding discussions of government in its various forms, one soon becomes aware of a collective obsession with accountability. The contributions to the Kettering Symposium represent just a small part of the greater effort among students of governance to explore the subject of that obsession. Yet reflecting on the work presented in this volume and elsewhere, we note that one central aspect of that opening observation has been left unexplored: the obsession itself.

Two general issues arise when we focus on the current obsession with accountability. First, what is it about accountability and account-giving mechanisms that we find so critical and attractive in our search for improved governance? And second, what are the impacts and implications of our collective preoccupation with this amorphous yet pervasive idea that has become so central to our approaches to public problems? After briefly exploring possible answers to the first issue, we examine the implications of the obsession on efforts to design policy solutions to the financial crises associated with the Great Recession of 2007–2010.

THE POWER OF PROMISES

Possible answers to the first question ("Why are we obsessed with accountability?") can be found in a number of explanations drawn from the critical examination of similar governance-relevant obsessions. Students of American public administration are well versed in the Progressive Era's obsession for business approaches to efficiency (see Waldo 1984), and the preoccupation with leadership among students and practitioners of management is pervasive and rarely challenged (see Meindl, Ehrlich, and Dukerich 1985, 1987). Henry Mintzberg has taken a critical approach to these and related obsessions (e.g., strategic management) over the years (Mintzberg 1982, 1987, 2004), often highlighting the fact that while each has a place in the practice of management, there is a tendency to overestimate their value and relevance to successful organization governance. Such obsessions can range from a mere fad to a firm commitment to an explicitly articulated ideology (Williams 1961) or to a more subtle and tacit "logic" or rationale uncritically adopted and applied to matters of governance in general (i.e., what Foucault [1991] termed "governmentality"; see Burchell et al. 1991; Rose and Miller 1992; Cawley and Chaloupka 1997).

Accountability does not fall at either extreme. It reflects neither a coherent ideology nor a logic of "governmentality." Rather, accountability seems best understood as a formidable and pervasive legitimizing standard for modern governance. Thomas Nagel (1987) defines legitimacy—and specifically political legitimacy—as the process of "justifying coercively imposed political and social institutions to the people who have to live under them, and at the same time discover what those institutions must be like if such justification is to be possible" (218). Legitimacy, Nagel observes, derives from two sources: either a Hobbesian-like convergence of motives or interests generating "rational support for certain institutions from the separate motivational standpoints of distinct individuals" or a "common standpoint" (e.g., moral standard) that exists distinct and above individual motives or interests (218–219). For accountability, these two positions—convergence and common standpoint—mirror the earlier distinction (pp. xv–xviii) between those who perceive the promises of accountability in instrumental (convergence) or intrinsic (common standpoint) terms. We posit that the grounds for accountability's role as legitimizing standard fall somewhere in between the two extremes.

Highlighting the role that the instrumental and intrinsic "promises of accountability" (see Introduction, this volume) play as a contemporary standard of legitimacy begs many questions, including those related to the significant power of the concept in political rhetoric and policy discourse. Accountability has reached iconic status within epistemic and discourse communities (see Dubnick 2002), where it is treated as the holy grail of political action, the normative embodiment of what is frequently termed today "good governance."[1] Its role as a standard of governance is so widely accepted that anyone who questions its provenance or legitimacy is regarded as a radical, and his or her participation in political discourse is effectively marginalized. As important, accountability is a concept or term that has rhetorical power and can be used to either mobilize or subdue political reaction and reflection.

Historically, perhaps the concept most similar in weight to the term "accountability" was the broadly conceived notion of "planning" that emerged from the Enlightenment and reached its most influential position as a contemporary legitimizing standard in the 1960s. Aaron Wildavsky's (1973) two-paragraph description of the role planning played in contemporary governance can just as easily be applied to the concept of accountability today:

> The concept of planning stands between actors and their societies. It conditions the way they perceive social problems and it guides their choice of solutions. Their understanding of planning helps them to choose the questions they ask and the answers they find. It leads them to evaluate their experience, including their attempt to plan, in certain ways rather than others. The difficulties they experience in society are related to their understanding of the mechanism—planning—they believe will help them solve its problems.
>
> Men think through language. They can hardly conceive of phenomena their words cannot express. The ways in which men think about planning affect how they act just as their attempts to plan affect how they think about it. The problems they have with the word mirror their problems with the world. (pp. 127–28)

The lens and language of planning became so pervasive and powerful during the first half of the twentieth century that it achieved the iconic status we can now attribute to accountability (cf., Hoover 1934).[2] Despite the strong challenges of critics (e.g., Hayek 1944; cf. Dahl and Lindblom 1953), planning retained its hold on the methodology of governance for decades and remains influential in a number of fields, from city planning to strategic management (see Beauregard 1989). What gave the promises of planning its empowering legitimacy? Was it its strength as an ideology (Guttenberg 2009)? Was it the strength of the modernist governmentality that sustained it (see Scott 1998)? Or was it the practical value it had during a time when market approaches required supplementation (e.g., Stiglitz 1989)? Seeking answers to those same questions for accountability should be high on the agenda of those analysts who study this increasingly pervasive concept. What empowers the current obsession with accountability?

One answer is that the turn toward accountability reflects the challenging and complex realities of modern governance. Multiple accountabilities (see Part I, this volume), for example, can be explained as the product of a pluralist politics where the structure of governance and oversight is part of the bargains and compromises struck during the policy-formulation and program-implementation stages. The importance of public support and legitimacy (e.g., Pollitt, Chapter 5) and institutional factors (e.g., Radin, Chapter 6) in determining the form and relative success of policies are reasonable themes in several chapters. Rational-choice models are implied in Hood's earlier discussion of blame avoidance (Chapter 10), and Posner and Schwartz (Chapter 8) explicitly address the presence of account-giving mechanisms as "solutions" in the widely used policy-streams model. But while these and similar theories can be used to inform us about the adoption, form, and effectiveness of accountability, none approaches the issue of why this (or any other governance concept) holds such a powerful sway within the policy community.

Implied in the promises-of-accountability perspective, however, is an alternative set of theories that focus attention on the power of collective beliefs. Inherent in the promises perspective is the idea that assumptions we make about the appropriateness of certain institutional and policy choices are self-empowering (March and Olsen 2006). The power of those promises can be attributed to a number of factors and theories, from the relatively simple notion of the normative "power of ideas" (Reich 1988; Jacobsen 1995; Yee 1996) to social constructionism (Gergen and Thatchenkery 1996; Hacking 1999) and the empirical effort to understand the role that "folk psychology" plays in how we approach the world (Bruner 1990; Malle 2004).

Among these, the work of social (folk) psychologists on the role of internalized theories or assumptions of human behavior is most compelling, with three major attractions. First, with its roots in experimental attribution studies and recent extension through advances in cognitive science and neuropsychology, folk psychology provides empirically testable explanations for the power of the promises of accountability that go beyond views relying on the rationality, reasonableness, or moral force of those promises (see Churchland 1989). A second attraction is that this folk-psychology explanation for the power of the promises of accountability is compatible with (and complementary to) the theories of administrative behavior, organizational decision making, and democratic institutions that emerged from the works of Barnard (1968), Simon (1957), and March and Olsen (1989, 1995). The power of the promises, in short, lies in the power of the decision premises they occupy. Third, beyond the question of its credibility as a source of explanations for the power of the promises of accountability, folk psychology models help us make sense of a wide range of cases in which accountability has become a central issue of governance.

In that last regard, these models enhance our ability to deal with the second question raised by the promises framework: what are its impacts and implications for the use and role of accountability within the governance and policy-making arenas? We consider that question in the following section where we apply a variation on the "promises" theme to recent events in the global financial markets that brought the major world economies to the brink of disaster—and which generated a great number of calls for "greater accountability."

FINANCIAL MELTDOWN AND THE CALLS FOR REFORM

We previously took note of the iconic status of accountability as a source of its power, and the extent of that power was recently demonstrated in the political rhetoric, policy analysis, and reform proposals emerging from the financial crisis that began in 2007 and continues to dominate the global agenda. That crisis is perfectly suited as a case study highlighting the impact and implications of the accountability icon as well as the power of the promises that underpin it.

We begin by noting that iconic terms such as accountability are part of a larger class of concepts that cultural theorists call "keywords." The study of keywords can be traced to the work of Raymond H. Williams, a British scholar who, upon returning to academe after World War II, realized that there were certain words and phrases that played special roles in discussions about culture and society. In 1976 (and again in 1985), Williams published a book (*Keywords: A Vocabulary of Culture and Society*) building on that observation and noting that such words and phrases were more than merely terms reflecting some "meaning" that can be defined through application of its sometime complex and divergent etymological roots. These keywords were meaningful in a broader and more contextualized sense and constituted a distinct vocabulary (a "shared body of words and meanings") we apply "in our most general discussions, in English, of the practices and institutions which we group as *culture* and *society*." In *Keywords*, Williams collected relevant examples for the usage of about 100 terms. The rationale for inclusion centered on the fact that each term "has at some time, in the course of some argument, virtually forced itself on my attention because the problems of its meanings seemed to me inextricably bound up with the problems it was used to discuss" (Williams 1985, 15).[5]

Viewed through the lens of political science, Williams's list of culture-and-society keywords seems remarkably "politicized" in the sense of containing words (e.g., democracy, equality, class, bureaucracy) that would certainly be core to discussions of politics and governance. Were we to develop a more focused list used to discuss politics and governance today, there would be considerable overlap with many of Williams's culture-and-society keywords. More important, such a list would no doubt give a prominent place to the word "accountability."

Williams's keyword approach to our everyday discourses have special meaning in the politics and governance arena where words do more than merely "represent" and shape meaningful discussions. In the politics and governance arena, words are linked to power relationships (see Edelman 1964, 1971, 1977). As such they shape policy as well as conversations. Moreover, the difficulty in divining an exact meaning intentionally or otherwise serves an exceptionally useful purpose. Creative ambiguity not only masks divisions, but also facilitates the transformation of the symbolic into the substantive.

The keyword and iconic stature of accountability has been most evident in the rhetoric surrounding debates about the recent collapse of global financial markets. While explanations for the crisis have ranged from the narrowly technical to the broadly systemic,[6] much of the policy debate has focused on the role of governance as both the source of and solution to the market's problems. It is in the context of that discussion that accountability plays a central role, and it is within the scholarly literature and political rhetoric that we find the active meanings for this keyword. To uncover those active meanings and their implications for understanding and dealing with the financial crisis, we need to analytically put aside the iconic status of keywords as "affective symbols"—words that are associated with human reactions ranging from quiescence to arousal—and instead focus on how keywords impact policy issues and the ways in which solutions are developed.

Accountability as Cause and Cure

Consider, for example, the role that accountability played in efforts of commentators and analysts to "make sense" of the 2007 crisis. Explanations varied dramatically. Some accounts highlight narrowly technical considerations, such as expansive monetary policy and excessive levels of leverage (Reinhart and Rogoff 2008, 2009). Others focus on flawed incentives that were exacerbated by tacit official support for the rational actions of institutional actors in sidestepping regulation (e.g., Calomiris 2009; Ely 2009). Others still focus on the broadly systemic nature of the crisis on either practical (e.g., Posner 2009) or normative grounds (e.g., Stiglitz 2009). Much of the policy debate coalesces, however, around the role of governance and ways of making it more effective as both the source of and solution to the intractable problems in capital markets.

It is in the context of that discussion that "accountability" plays a central role. Figure 18.1 posits two critical dimensions accountability plays in the discourse surrounding the financial markets crisis. Each reflects significant but relatively obscure distinctions. Along one dimension, account-ability is often noted as either the cause and/or cure for the market's problems. As a causal factor, it is the absence or failure of effective accountability that provides the focus of the discourse. In contrast, accountability is also central to many discussions on how to deal with specific failures, including but not limited to manifestations of malfeasance and misfeasance such as deceptive or misleading conduct, unethical conduct linked to defective internal corporate codes of conduct or governance arrangements, and/or the operation of the external regulatory architecture. Account-ability can also be deployed as a counter to the overall conditions that caused the crisis, for ex-ample the need to respond to the danger posed by technical compliance within specific epistemic communities, such as lawyers, auditors, rating-agency professionals, investment bankers, or other groupings that play a gatekeeping function in contemporary markets (see Coffee 2006; McBarnet and Whelan 1999; McBarnet 1991, 2006).

The second dimension highlights another, often overlooked, distinction within the general discourse in which accountability is referred to in either mechanistic or normative terms.[7] In the former sense, being accountable means being subject to those mechanisms that are designed to impose some form of control or guidance. It means being answerable, liable, legally obligated, and so forth. Alternatively, accountability is also treated as a manifestation of the normative condition of "being accountable"—as something an agent is or ought to be. Here we associate accountability with the concepts of integrity, trustworthiness, blameworthiness, and so forth. In Figure 18.1 we note this distinction as "accountability as mechanism" in contrast to "accountability as [norma-tive] setting." In the following section we test the relevance of this framing of accountability's "active meanings" by examining how that keyword has been applied in the discourse emerging out of the recent global financial crisis.

In the general blame game (Knobloch-Westerwick and Taylor 2008; cf. Davies 2010) that has characterized much of the debate over the collapse of global financial markets, considerable attention has been paid to the failure of accountability within specific firms or institutions: those who ought to have been in control were not; those who should have known better did not. The first implies an accountability-as-mechanism approach, albeit one in which the emphasis on culpabil-ity is both wide-ranging and dependent on the particular reform agenda proposed. At times these interpretations focus on the lack of internal controls that would have prevented some of the most flagrant risk taking; at other times they focus on the failure of external control mechanisms (i.e., regulatory agents and agencies) to do their job.

The Obama administration's diagnosis, for example, combines both, citing the accountability deficit as a key common factor. Announcing a blueprint for more accountable regulatory reform (discussed in detail below), President Obama commented on June 17, 2009: "The actions of many firms escaped scrutiny. In some cases, the dealings of these institutions were so complex and opaque that few inside or outside these companies understood what was happening. Where there were gaps in the rules, regulators lacked the authority to take action. Where there were overlaps, regulators lacked accountability for their inaction" (U.S. Department of the Treasury

Figure 18.1 **Accountability's Discursive Roles**

		FOCUS ON	
		Cause	Cure
PERSPECTIVE	Accountability-as-Mechanism (i.e., control)	Failure of instrument	Reform, replace, repair the instrument
	Accountability-as-Setting (i.e., normative infrastructure)	Absence or collapse of norms, mores, standards	Reestablishing, rebuilding moral community based on effective norms/standards

2009). The European Commissioner for Internal Markets, Charlie McCreevy, by contrast, refers to the consequences of imbibing with abandon a toxic cocktail of "stupidity, ignorance and misplaced optimism" (O'Brien 2009, 33). For Commissioner McCreevy, the failure of internal risk-management systems derives from the fact that senior corporate executives "of large financial institutions have admitted in their more candid moments that they did not understand many of the new products that their firms were designing, underwriting and trading" (O'Brien 2009, 33).

At the practitioner level in London and New York, corporate executives expressed regret for what happened but denied personal responsibility. In the United Kingdom, bankers testifying before the influential Treasury Select Committee failed to provide a convincing explanation for their failures. McCreevy's concern at the levels of recklessness, noted above, was exposed in particularly acute form in the revelation that the two most senior executives at Halifax Bank of Scotland (HBOS) had little banking experience. They testified that this was unnecessary because they were surrounded by people with broad experience, a defense undermined by evidence from the bank's former head of risk and compliance.[8] Similarly, in the United States, the multifaceted ethical problems besetting Citigroup are indicative of both the paucity of institutional memory within the banking sector and the reliance on technical compliance with corporate governance norms, rules, and standards (for discussion, see O'Brien 2009, 42–44).

The major alternative to the blame game approach has been to focus on systemic causes for the crisis. Here the ambiguity over the nature of accountability plays a secondary but still significant framing role. On the one hand, to see the cause of the collapse as systemic is to imply that there is no specific blame to be apportioned; no one agent or group of agents can really be held to account for institutional-level faults. This was indeed the defense offered at congressional and parliamentary hearings. On the other hand, systemic defects also reflect the fact that flaws embedded in the very structure of financial capitalism were reinforced. It is not so much that the crisis was a result of unbridled greed; rather, it resulted from structural changes to the operation of the market that lowered the material and reputational opportunity costs for engaging in risky practices that proved unsustainable and indefensible in the long run. In both cases accountability is brought into the narrative as part of the "system."

In the former (no one is to blame), accountability is used as a defense (i.e., the crisis was the result of a confluence of factors in which none was immediately culpable). It is a perspective that allows those corporate and regulatory actors who face accusations of blameworthiness for the crisis to defend themselves on grounds that the acts they engaged in were not merely legal at the time, but also widely accepted and at times even rewarded. In the latter (systemic defects), accountability serves an offensive function (i.e., the crisis was the result of the degradation of embedded norms, values, and standards, which as a consequence of compartmentalized views of responsibility were present only in symbolic terms). Here Citigroup provides a telling example. Until his departure from the organization, Robert Rubin denied any responsibility for either the failings within the conglomerate or within the integrated banking model he helped create and sustain, as both a leading practitioner and as a policy maker serving in the Clinton administration as Treasury Secretary. In an interview with the *New York Times* (Dash and Creswell 2008), Rubin argued, "in hindsight there are a lot of things we'd do differently. But in the context of the facts as I knew them and my role [as Vice Chairman of Citigroup] I'm inclined to think probably not." Moreover, some senior chief executives went so far as to blame ex post facto government intervention (e.g., Steel 2010).[9]

In hindsight, most analysts now believe the decision to allow Lehman Brothers to fail turned the subprime housing scandal into a major global catastrophe. Belated recognition of market panic forced the U.S. federal authorities into a series of immediate policy reversals. In such circumstances, it was not surprising that the Lehman CEO, Richard Fuld, would be unapologetic. In written testimony to the House Oversight and Government Reform Committee he maintained that Lehman Brothers, as the smallest investment bank, could not withstand a "financial tsunami" that had generated "a storm of fear" (U.S. Congress 2008c; also Fuld 2010).[10] No one institution could be held responsible for the unintended consequences of belatedly recognized deleterious market and policy choices. Rather, Lehman was "overwhelmed, others were overwhelmed and still other institutions would have been overwhelmed had the government not stepped in to save them" (U.S. Congress 2008c). Accordingly, Lehman was to be regarded as an innocent victim of a collective failure to foresee a once-in-a-lifetime crisis. This argument failed to impress the U.S. House of Representatives Committee on Oversight and Government Reform. Representative Waxman, chair of that body, castigated Lehman Brothers as "a company in which there was no accountability for failure" (U.S. Congress 2008a). This was true, but it was also true that there was very little accountability within any major institutional actor on Wall Street and the City of London.

The collapse of Lehman Brothers, the forced sale of Bear Stearns and Merrill Lynch, and the calamitous failure of Royal Bank of Scotland and HBOS reflected grossly deficient internal risk-management systems, cosmetic compliance, poor ethical training, and exceptionally weak external oversight at both individual firm and on the wider systemic level.[11] This failure destroyed not only the corporate reputation of many storied firms and individual financiers but also the trust on which a credible banking system is founded. It is important to emphasize that while there was undoubtedly criminal activity on the margins—such as Bernie Madoff's Ponzi-style investment scam—the vast majority of the crisis can be traced to collective misjudgment about the capacity of markets to price information effectively and to be self-correcting. From this perspective, the critical significance of the global financial crisis lies in the fact that the norms and values of the banking community disappeared or were insufficient; assumed to be relatively stable after having accreted over centuries, they were in fact seriously degraded.

As Joseph Stiglitz put it in evidence to Congress, "securitization was based on the premise that a fool was born every minute. Globalization meant there was a global landscape on which they could search for these fools and they found them everywhere" (U.S. Congress 2008d; cf. Tett 2009). There is nothing unethical about securitization per se, but rather its reckless deployment. The compartmentalization of responsibility—through the originate-rate-distribute model and a comprehensive failure to calculate systemic risk—provided both the opportunity and justification for this kind of behavior. The unresolved question is whether these normative issues would be addressed in the reform agenda. As will be explored below, accountability played a central role in shaping the answer to that question.

Accountability and the Design of Reforms

In response to the idea that the industry's norms and values did not foster appropriate behavior, there was a general call for reforms that would enhance accountable actions. This was most notably reflected in the political rhetoric of national leaders, but it also reflects a long-standing view that markets are indeed civilizing institutions with moral foundations (Hirschman 1982; cf Fourcade and Healy 2007; Boltanski and Chiapello 2005). Financial markets would operate well, it is assumed, if only the trust and moral commitment to responsible action can be assured, a central if overlooked preoccupation of Adam Smith in *The Theory of Moral Sentiments* (1759; see also Mason 1958; Stiglitz 2001; Sen 2009)—a work that philosophically informs the later (and more often cited) *Wealth of Nations*. A moral commitment to responsible action, in turn, may require reforms that would promote a more normative perspective on what constitutes accountable behavior.

Following this well-developed narrative path, President Obama's Inaugural Address emphasized the need for the inculcation of a new "ethics of responsibility" in corporate governance, echoing earlier calls by then British Prime Minister, Gordon Brown (2008), for moral restraint within financial centers (if only for instrumental reasons). Beyond London and New York, however, the extent to which the crisis metastasized with such ferocity has substantially strengthened calls for an integrated response to nullify what then Australian Prime Minister, Kevin Rudd (2008), called "extreme capitalism." Although many would disagree with such polemical framing, there can be no question that the policy discourse reached an inflection point for both the theory and practice of regulation through enhanced accountability. The critical question is what constitutes or should constitute accountable governance? In this context we again find advantage in pursuing the "promising" nature of accountability as a variable keyword in regulatory dynamics.

The rhetoric of reform, for example, focused on the need for changes in the normative infrastructure to enhance the responsibility, ethics, and integrity in governance of the financial markets. However, when the specific proposals for reform are examined, there is little doubt that the dominant approach has been to establish or revitalize the mechanisms of accountability—mainly regulatory— that have been at the heart of market-reform agendas for decades (see O'Brien 2007a).

The proposed reform of the U.S. regulatory system is a case in point. On June 17, 2009, the White House officially launched its proposals for reforming the federal government's approach to reform oversight of the banking industry and financial markets (U.S. Department of the Treasury 2009). It was billed as the most significant overhaul of any U.S. regulatory system in nearly eighty years. It involved structural and jurisdictional changes that (if passed and implemented) would, it was claimed, transform the way both government and the entire financial sector conducted business in the United States and globally. Reflecting the strategic and politically pragmatic orientation of the Obama administration, the concerns and/or displeasure of potential opponents from most quarters had been considered, and few if any of the main players complained that they had not been consulted or their ideas not given serious consideration. Throughout the process of developing these reform proposals, President Obama made clear that a normative dimension had to be considered and rendered operational.[12]

Although many of the specifics of the Obama plan for reform were likely to be modified as proposals wended their way through the policy-making process, few doubted or challenged the basic stated premise of the effort: the regulatory system of the U.S. financial sector was broken to an extent that it required major repairs; an overhaul was needed that would prevent a recurrence of the global financial crisis and its impact on the operation of credit markets, which, in turn, converted an emerging recession into what many analysts termed an economic depression. Despite the alteration of the U.S. regulatory regime that might have emerged from these proposals, there was little in the details that addressed the often-stated need for promised changes in the normative setting of corporate governance in the banking industry to accompany the soaring rhetoric.

The stress on mechanistic cures to solve the accountability problem was also evident globally. There was, of course, recognition that reform required much greater coordination and integration of accountability at the global level, if only for protection of national self-interest. The Group of Twenty Finance Ministers and Central Bank Governors (G20) began to lay the foundations for a new international regulatory architecture covering all systemically important financial institutions and markets (including hedge funds which, through judicious structuring, had been effectively unregulated), as well as systemically important financial instruments (such as securitization and credit derivatives). The European Union proposed the establishment of the European Systemic Risk Council, headed by the president of the European Central Bank, and much greater coordination of securities-market regulators through the formation of a European System of Financial Supervisors. Both initiatives eventually secured the requisite approvals with the European Union. The question is whether concentrating power among those who have demonstrably failed in the past will work. The United Kingdom, which had gone further than most in proposing limitations to executive pay, put a sunset clause in its operation, mainly because of fear that global coordination would not gel. The failure of the G20 finance ministers' meeting in London in September 2009 to agree to a cohesive framework, combined with the decision by the Obama administration to release major banks from congressional oversight, appears to justify British caution.

The gap between reform rhetoric and the actual proposals for reform of the financial markets can be traced to both the treatment accountability receives as a keyword in our discourse on policy and governance and the various promises it generates. Regulatory reform discourse and proposals can be seen as manifestations of both the instrumental and intrinsic promises of accountability. In the discourses surrounding reform of financial markets, accountability is articulated as either a means to some desirable end (i.e., accountability valued for its instrumental functionality) or as a good unto itself (i.e., intrinsically valued). Instrumentally, accountability-based reforms promise to enhance control over resources (e.g., through strengthening accounting and reporting requirements); to ensure proper behavior and actions by agents (e.g., through enhancing both hierarchical responsibility and shareholder governance); and to promote and enhance improved performance (e.g., through external auditing requirements and oversight of compensation contracts). Intrinsically, many of the reform proposals promise to render regulated actors (or regulatory agencies) more trustworthy while enhancing their integrity and promoting the legitimacy of the process as well as the fairness and justness of the decisions generated by the agency, firm, or market.

The evident bias toward mechanistic proposals reflects a strong indifference to the political rhetoric of reform in the deliberations taking place at the proposal-formulation stages. We contend that much of this bias can be attributed to a tendency at that stage to view accountability-based policy options as a response to two questions: to whom is the accountable party to be accountable, and for what? While often a convenient approach, efforts to reduce accountability to simply

Figure 18.2 **Accountable Strategies**

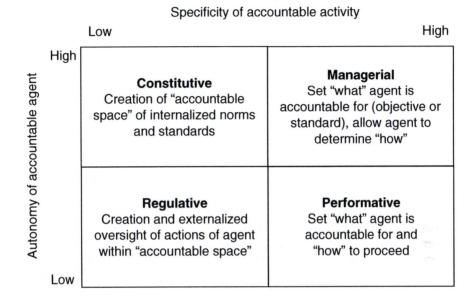

Specificity of accountable activity

the governance and policing of principal-agent relationships (through either prescriptive rules or agreed-upon principles) perhaps too narrowly defines both the functions and forms of accountability as it operates within real governance systems.

To put the bias of the current reform agenda in perspective, consider the two major issues that could be the focus of accountability-based reform proposals: (1) how specific or detailed should the scrutiny be of the activity or behavior subject to account-giving, and (2) how much autonomy does the accountable party have in the fulfillment of his or her required behavior. As illustrated in Figure 18.2, four general strategic types of reform can emerge in response.

Performative Reform

In the financial services market, for example, there are state, national, and regional regulatory regimes where banks falling under certain jurisdictions are obligated to issue intermittent but time-specific (e.g., quarterly, annual) reports to oversight agencies or make public statements that are to include detailed information that is standardized by rule or agreement. As a strategic approach, this form of accountability integrates accountable governance with the very definition of "doing business," and failure to perform the required account-giving frequently requires sanctions. We consider these performative strategies of accountable governance.

Performative forms of accountability are commonplace in even the most mundane regulatory contexts (e.g., Bardach and Kagan 1982), but they also play major and more visible roles in broader markets as well. Crucial to the use of the strategy, however, is the fact that the capacity of regulatory agencies to engage in performative exercises is usually time-limited (this has been empirically demonstrated) to a period in the immediate aftermath of scandal, where political appetite for enforcement trumps concern that excessive regulation may curb innovation (O'Brien 2007b). Consider, for example, the pervasive use of negotiated prosecutions in the aftermath of Enron and related accounting scandals in which invasive and ongoing external monitoring of compliance programs was conceded to by individual corporations in exchange for an agreement not to proceed with civil or criminal prosecution. These are examples of both the power and limitations of such a performative-based approach (see O'Brien 2009, 48–56). Its efficacy was contingent on acquiescence by all concerned to the legitimacy of the mechanism. Injudicious use and a changed business and political climate demonstrated all too clearly the contingent and, therefore, suboptimal nature of the mechanism.[13]

Managerial Reform

The managerial approach involves an articulation of accountability that provides considerable discretion in meeting some standard of behavior set by oversight or regulatory bodies. A simple example drawn from city building codes can serve to illustrate: traditionally, builders and landlords are held accountable for meeting standards that get to the detail of the type of wiring to be used or the placement of exits, and even the material composition (e.g., steel, oak) of doors. In some jurisdictions, however, those performative requirements are replaced with more a managerial approach based on general standards, and the burden falls to the accountable party to demonstrate to the building-code authority that their plans and material meet or exceed the objectives of the code. In financial markets, the distinction between performative and managerial accountability is manifest in the debate between those advocating rules-based (i.e., performative) versus principles-based (managerial) regulation (Kaplow 1992; Ford 2008; Surowiecki 2008). Traditionally, U.S. regulatory regimes have tended to be rules-based, while in the United Kingdom and elsewhere the stress has been on principles-based regulation.

The managerial approach has its benefits in allowing the accountable party a greater degree of freedom in meeting the demands of an accountant, but the strategy has proven problematic in practice. In its annual report for 2007–2008, for example, the UK's Financial Services Authority admitted it failed in its oversight of the market but claimed this derived not from a flaw in the logic of principles-based regulation, but rather in a failure to apply it.[14] Problems also arose when the U.S. Securities and Exchange Commission (SEC) attempted to rely on a managerial approach in its short-lived experiment with regulating U.S.-based global investment banks. In 2004, the SEC established a Consolidated Supervised Entity (CSE) program to fill a regulatory gap in U.S. law regarding large investment-bank holding companies such as Goldman Sachs, Lehman Brothers, Bear Stearns, and others. The program was voluntary for those firms, but they opted into it once an understanding had been reached with EU banking regulators who were willing to accept the SEC (through the CES program) as a legitimate "regulatory supervisor" in lieu of the more burdensome European options. This arrangement provided those U.S. firms with a competitive advantage, not merely because it helped them avoid the more stringent EU regulators, but also because of the managerial approach taken by the SEC. The CSE was attractive to the investment banking firms precisely because "under [its] alternative capital computation method, the broker-dealer will be allowed to compute certain market and credit risk capital charges using internal mathematical models" (SEC 2008a).

The decision to take this approach represented transference of control over accountability to the firms themselves. SEC commissioners were not unaware of the risks involved in this approach. One commissioner at the time commented, "if anything goes wrong, its going to be an awfully big mess"; a second commented that he was "very happy to support it and I keep my fingers crossed for the future" (Labaton 2008, p. A1). As it turns out, the SEC was at best naïve in relying on the internal mathematical modeling provided by the investment banks. Moreover, an investigation by the inspector general for the agency revealed that responsibility for managing a combined $5 trillion asset portfolio was delegated to a team comprising just seven staff members, which had functioned without a director since March 2007. The SEC instead relied upon the market to provide an early warning system. The SEC abolished the initiative in September 2008 as a consequence of recognition from its then chairman, Christopher Cox, that "voluntary self-regulation does not work" (SEC 2008b).[15]

Regulative Reform

The regulative and constitutive strategies rely less on the specificity of actions to be held to account and more on the creation of a jurisdictional "accountable space" within which the accountable agent is expected to act in an appropriate or reasonable fashion. This space can be regarded as a normative setting—an arena in which trustworthiness is a central feature, and where accountability is intended to foster integrity. What differentiates these two strategies is the regulative reliance on some external or independent oversight body that has as its prime mission the monitoring of what takes place in the accountable space. Here the classic examples are found in the broad and ambiguous legislative mandate originally given to many U.S. regulatory commissions to ensure that the enterprises under their purview (e.g., in transportation, power generation, communications, and other utilities) operated "in the public interest." As demonstrated by several well known cases (e.g., the Interstate Commerce Commission, the Civil Aeronautics Board), three factors worked against this approach in practice: the ambiguity of what constitutes "the public interest"; the inclination of those agencies to rely on narrow performative and managerial approaches in pursuing their mission; and the inability of the oversight agencies to sustain their independence from those being held to account (i.e., agency capture).

To some degree, central banks were originally designed to act primarily (if not exclusively) through a regulative strategy. Typically they are provided with broad missions. The European Central Bank declares that its "main objective" is to "maintain price stability: safeguarding the value of the euro" (http://www.ecb.int/ecb/html/mission.en.html). Referring to its 1913 founding authorization, the U.S. Federal Reserve System notes its mission as "to provide the nation with a safer, more flexible, and more stable monetary and financial system" (http://www.federalreserve.gov/aboutthefed/mission.htm). The Central Bank of Indonesia's objective is to "achieve and maintain rupiah stability by maintaining monetary stability and by promoting financial system stability for Indonesia's long term sustainable development" (http://www.bi.go.id/web/en/Tentang+BI/Fungsi+Bank+Indonesia/Misi+dan+Visi/). These broad mission statements establish the accountable space within which those banks under their jurisdiction operate. To carry out those missions, these and other central banks typically have significant discretion and/or autonomy (Acemoglu et al. 2008; Keefer and Stasavage 2003, 2000; Magnette 2000). Moreover, the actions they take in response to some problem or need will require them to rely in part on performative and managerial forms of accountability. A similar dynamic informs many of the functions and operations of securities regulators, such as the UK's Financial Services Authority and the U.S. Securities and Exchange Commission.

In the recent financial market crisis, however, a critical flaw in the logic of this regulative approach became evident. Those who sit in key positions in those agencies designed to make certain that accountable space is generating appropriate and accountable behavior often do so with a bias, sometimes subtle and at other times explicitly ideological. The choices they make in this regard are usually informed by an ideationally driven belief in the self-correcting power of the markets. There is perhaps no better case study of what can happen than the story of Alan Greenspan's fall from grace following this extraordinary admission: "I found a flaw. That is precisely the reason I was shocked because I had been going for 40 years or more with very considerable evidence that it was working exceptionally well." The mea culpa that followed marked the moment when the intellectual edifice governing financial capitalism crumbled. Greenspan's testimony before an exceptionally hostile congressional committee October 2008 was one of the most memorable moments in the drama associated with the implosion of global capital markets (see O'Brien 2009). It might also prove to be one of the most significant from the perspective of regulatory theory:

> A Nobel Prize was awarded for the discovery of the pricing model that underpins much of the advance in derivatives markets. This modern risk management paradigm held sway for decades. The whole intellectual edifice, however, collapsed in the summer of last year because the data inputted into the risk management models generally covered only the past two decades, a period of euphoria. Had instead the models been fitted more appropriately to historic periods of stress, capital requirements would have been much higher and the financial world would be in far better shape today, in my judgment. (U.S. Congress 2008b)

The failure of the regulative approach was evident to all. The extent of government intervention required to stabilize financial markets across the world after the financial crisis of 2007 temporarily transformed the conceptual and practical dynamics of capital-market regulation. The power and influence of government has been augmented considerably. In the short term, the Federal Reserve (and other U.S. agencies) has turned to managerial and performative approaches to contend with the emergency conditions in the United States. The issue is whether that can return to the regulative approach that is inherent in their original mandate (see Mariani 2009) and whether this is, on its own, going to be sufficient to deal with the normative failure of regulatory policy.

Constitutive Reform

In contrast to the regulative option, the constitutive approach relies on the development of governance norms and standards within the accountable space and reflects a classic political-economy approach most often (and mistakenly) associated with free-enterprise capitalism. Here the emphasis is on the design and maintenance of institutional arrangements that foster accountable behavior without the monitoring and oversight of the regulative approach or the specificity of actions of the performative and managerial strategies.[16] Perhaps the best examples come from the use of the legal system to structure (or restructure) a dysfunctional market. Markets already operate within established legal environments that set parameters and rules around behaviors. The influence of the legal context goes well beyond its having a direct impact on behavior. Legal scholars and economists have long been aware of the impact the "shadow of the law" has on individual and corporate behavior (Stevenson and Wolfers 2006; Jacob 1992; Cooter et al. 1982; Bagley 2008; Dixit 2004).

Several prominent analysts of the current economic crisis believe that financial markets can be made more accountable through institutional reforms rather than more explicit regulative, managerial, or performative interventions (e.g., Shiller 2008). On the surface, advocates of this approach to reforming accountability seem to be engaged in an updated version of deregulation. The difference, however, is in the emphasis on purpose and intent, with the goal being to reconstitute markets so that institutional incentives and pressures will promote greater accountability.[17] Consider, for example, the case of Sarbanes-Oxley. While it hardly stands as a model for effective regulation, the basic logic was an approach that would create the legal context in which specific corporate actors (chief executive officers and chief financial officers) were on notice that they could no longer hide behind the fiction of the corporate "person" and were now going to be held criminally accountable for their actions as corporate officers.

On a more abstract level, academics such as Oliver Williamson have been pursuing studies that can provide a coherent positive theory to support a more constitutive approach—one that views financial markets as dynamic arrangements of incomplete and imperfect contracts. Combining the logic of economics with the design imperatives of organization theory, Williamson has already addressed the possibility of reforming corporate governance (Williamson 2008). Constituting through laws and other devices a financial marketplace characterized by integrity and worthy of trust (i.e., an accountable market) requires a strategy based on design rather than deregulation. Accountability is therefore a design question at both corporate and regulatory levels, which to be effective needs to be mutually reinforcing and address dynamically the calculative, social, and normative reasons for behaving in a more (or less) ethically responsible manner. Ironically, such an approach would be the fulfillment of Adam Smith's vision of the marketplace as a venue in which our all-too-human moral sentiments can be allowed to play themselves out.

INSIGHTS AND LESSONS

As is evident to anyone tracking the proliferating literature on the subject, many lessons can be drawn from the global financial crisis of 2007. We make no claims that the present work adds anything of value to those analyses. Rather, the crisis was used here as a case study demonstrating the impact and implications of our collective obsession with accountability and the influence it wields in our political and policy discourses. What has emerged is strong evidence supporting the view that accountability deserves the designation of a "keyword" according to Raymond Williams's definition of the term. Moreover, accountability's central role in the crisis—as a core concept in discussions of what caused and what can cure the crisis, as well as the basis for deliberations regarding potential reforms of the domestic and global financial marketplace—gives credence to the view that a degree of power can be attributed to some keywords and other symbolic language that explicitly or subtly shape and direct political action and governance.

In addition, our analysis gives some support to the contention that the influence of accountability as a keyword is derived from the power of its various promises—promises that are themselves derived from belief systems rooted in our folk psychology. This perspective on accountability warrants further exploration and application in the study of governance and policy making.

NOTES

1. For example, Both the World Bank (www.worldbank.org/wbi/governance) and the International Monetary Fund (http://www.imf.org/external/np/exr/facts/gov.htm) have made good governance a major component of their long-term agendas.

2. "To plan or not to plan is no real issue," declared Charles E. Merriam. "Planning even of economic affairs has existed at all levels of our national life, both public and private, since the beginning of our history. The only issue is who shall plan for what ends" (1944, 397). In this regard, Merriam was echoing the words of Herbert Hoover, who observed a decade earlier that the United States "have been engaged in planning, and the execution of plans, within the proper functions of government ever since the first days of George Washington's Administration.

> No civilization has hitherto ever seen such a growth of voluntary associative activities in every form of planning, coordination and cooperation of effort, the expression of free men. It comes naturally, since the whole system builded on liberty is a stimulant to plan and progress. The unparalleled rise of the American man and woman was not alone the result of riches in lands, forests or mines; it sprang from ideals and philosophic ideas out of which plans and the execution of them are stimulated by the forces of freedom. (Hoover 1934, 6)

3. For a critical and useful overview, see John 2003; cf. Wedel et al. 2005.

4. Much of what follows in the next two sections is drawn from Dubnick and O'Brien 2009.

5. For Williams, keywords have two major (and intertwined) functional characteristics. First, they are "significant, binding" terms that are "indicative" of the meanings and interpretations of the discourse; at the same time these same words were "elements of the problems" the very discourse they addressed had generated (Williams 1985, 15–16). He observed that we typically become aware of keywords only after the discourse in which they played such a significant role had passed. But what if we were to become more "aware" of the keywords that are dominating our ongoing discourse community? That was Williams's project in *Keywords,* where he focused attention on some of those words that are at the heart of our contemporary discussion of culture and society; and in his two editions (the second was published in 1983) these included terms such as literature, unconscious, evolution, liberal, empirical, equality, etc.

6. See the recent collection of articles focused mainly on the causes of the 2007 crisis—the June 2009 issue of *Critical Review,* esp. Bhidé 2009; Acharya and Richardson 2009; Friedman 2009; Jablecki and Mateusz 2009; Stiglitz 2009; Wallison 2009b, 2009a; and White 2009; see also Posner 2009 and the online and ongoing analyses by Paul Krugman, Simon Johnson, and others.

7. This distinction has its roots in one of the foundational debates of modern governance studies that took place in the early 1940s between Carl J. Friedrich (1940) and Herman Finer (1941). Friedrich regarded accountability as a condition instilled in public officials as they become more professional; Finer insisted that the only way to ensure accountability was through institutions and mechanisms that constantly check on the exercise of public authority.

8. The executive, Paul Moore, noted that "my personal experience of being on the inside as a risk and compliance manager has shown me that, whatever the very specific, final and direct causes of the financial crisis, I strongly believe that the real underlying cause of all of the problems was simply this—a total failure of all key aspects of governance" (cited in O'Brien 2009, 36).

9. For overview of steps taken in response to the crisis as it emerged, see Broome 2009.

10. This choice of metaphor was also deployed by Alan Greenspan to deflect responsibility two weeks later (U.S. Congress 2008b).

11. For wider problems and lack of oversight on Wall Street, see Morris 2008 and Soros 2008; for lack of political oversight in the United States, more generally, see Milhaupt and Pistor 2008, 47–66, and Galbraith 2008. For problems in the British banking sector, see UK Parliament 2009a. Paul Moore, the author of that memorandum, is former head of regulatory risk at HBOS. He argued (at section 4.3) that there was a need for more detailed policy guidance from the Financial Services Authority (FSA) on the form and content of ethics training within banking corporations. He says it is essential to introduce "a more detailed policy and rules which allows the FSA to test the cultural environment of organizations they are supervising e.g., tri-annual staff and customer survey. There is no doubt that you can have the best governance processes in the world but if they are carried out in a culture of greed, unethical behavior and indisposition to challenge, they will fail. I would now propose *mandatory* [emphasis in original] ethics training for all senior managers and a system of monitoring the ethical considerations of key policy and strategy decisions within the supervised firms."

12. In remarks at release of the reform proposals on June 17, 2009, President Obama said:

> "There's always been a tension between those who place their faith in the invisible hand of the marketplace and those who place more trust in the guiding hand of the government—and that tension isn't a bad thing. It gives rise to healthy debates and creates a dynamism that makes it possible for us to adapt and grow. For we know that markets are not an unalloyed force for either good or for ill. In many ways, our financial system reflects us. In the aggregate of countless independent decisions, we see the potential for creativity—and the potential for abuse. We see the capacity for innovations that make our economy stronger—and for innovations that exploit our economy's weaknesses. We are called upon to put in place those reforms that allow our best qualities to flourish—while keeping those worst traits in check. We're called upon to recognize that the free market is the most powerful generative force for our prosperity—but it is not a free license to ignore the consequences of our actions." (Obama 2009)

13. It is instructive that negotiated prosecution, which was predicated on the assumption that the formal existence of a performative compliance program was in itself insufficient to address the risk of inappropriate behavior, was subject to an increasingly vocal and effective campaign of corporate and political vilification from 2004 onwards—precisely the same time as the expansion of securitization magnified the risk of defective risk-management systems. Policy makers such as the Treasury Secretary Hank Paulson, along with influential academics, advocated the expansion of a principles-based (i.e., managerial) regulatory regime,

which transferred the exercise of discretionary power from the regulator to the regulated (see U.S. Department of the Treasury 2008).

14. Responding directly to criticisms from Parliament, the FSA offered the following self-assessment:

> The regulatory philosophy which we pursued in the past focused on ensuring that firms had the appropriate systems and controls in place and relied on the senior management of firms to make the right judgments. We did not see it as a function of the regulator to question the overall business strategy of the institution or more generally the possibility of risk crystallising in the future.
>
> Our approach has now changed. We now expect firms' management to make decisions knowing they will be judged on the ultimate consequences of those actions. In our supervision we will judge firms on those outcomes and on the consequences of their actions, not on the compliance with particular rules. We will apply this outcomes-based approach through our new intensive supervisory model, which is underpinned by our focus on credible deterrence. (UK Parliament 2009b)

15. Cox was also under considerable pressure to do so from Treasury Secretary Paulson and Federal Reserve Chairman Bernanke as the looming financial crisis worsened and the need to impose more stringent controls on those banks became increasingly urgent.

16. The contemporary academic view most closely identified with this perspective is the public choice school of political economy most often identified with James Buchanan and Gordon Tullock (see, for example, Buchanan and Tullock 1962).

17. In a very real sense, all regulatory regimes are constitutive to the extent that the state acts as an autonomous actor in pursuing the redesign of the marketplace (Vogel, 1996; Shearing, 1992).

REFERENCES

Acemoglu, Daron, Simon Johnson, Pablo Querubin, and James A. Robinson. 2008. "When Does Policy Reform Work? The Case of Central Bank Independence." In National Bureau of Economic Research Working Paper Series. Cambridge, MA: National Bureau of Economic Research.

Acharya, Viral V., and Matthew Richardson. 2009. "Causes of the Financial Crisis." *Critical Review: A Journal of Politics and Society* 21 (2): 195–210.

Bagley, Constance E. 2008. "Winning Legally: The Value of Legal Astuteness." *Academy of Management Review* 33 (2): 378–90.

Bardach, Eugene, and Robert A. Kagan. 1982. *Going By the Book: The Problem of Regulatory Unreasonableness.* Philadelphia: Temple University Press.

Barnard, Chester I. 1968. *The Functions of the Executive.* Cambridge, MA: Harvard University Press.

Beauregard, R. A. 1989. "Between Modernity and Postmodernity: The Ambiguous Position of U.S. Planning." *Environment and Planning D: Society and Space* 7 (4): 381–95.

Bhidé, Amar. 2009. "An Accident Waiting to Happen." *Critical Review: A Journal of Politics and Society* 21 (2): 211–47.

Boltanski, Luc, and Eve Chiapello. 2005. *The New Spirit of Capitalism.* London: Verso.

Broome, Lissa L. 2009. "Extraordinary Government Intervention to Bolster Bank Balance Sheets." *North Carolina Baning Institute Journal* 13:137–55.

Brown, Gordon. 2008. "The Global Economy." Speech Delivered at Reuters Building, London, October 13.

Bruner, Jerome. 1990. *Acts of Meaning.* Cambridge, MA: Harvard University Press.

Buchanan, James M., and Gordon Tullock. 1962. *The Calculus of Consent: Logical Foundations of Constitutional Democracy.* Ann Arbor: University of Michigan Press.

Burchell, Graham, Colin Gordon, and Peter Miller, eds. 1991. *The Foucault Effect: Studies in Governmentality: With Two Lectures by and an Interview with Michel Foucault.* Chicago: University of Chicago Press.

Calomiris, Charles W. 2009. "Financial Innovation, Regulation, and Reform." *Cato Journal* 29 (1): 65.

Cawley, R. McGreggor, and William Chaloupka. 1997. "American Governmentality: Michel Foucault and Public Administration." *American Behavioral Scientist* 41 (1): 28–42.

Churchland, Paul M. 1989. "Folk Psychology and the Explanation of Human Behavior." *Philosophical Perspectives* 3: 225–41.

Coffee, John C. 2006. *Gatekeepers: The Professions and Corporate Governance.* New York: Oxford University Press.

Cooter, Robert, Stephen Marks, and Robert Mnookin. 1982. "Bargaining in the Shadow of the Law: A Testable Model of Strategic Behavior." *Journal of Legal Studies* 11 (2): 225–51.

Dahl, Robert A., and Charles E. Lindblom. 1953. *Politics, Economics, and Welfare: Planning and Politico-Economic Systems Resolved into Basic Social Processes.* New York: Harper Torchbooks.

Davies, Howard. 2010. *The Financial Crisis: Who Is to Blame?* Cambridge (UK): Polity.

Dixit, Avinash K. 2004. *Lawlessness and Economics: Alternative Modes of Governance.* Princeton, NJ: Princeton University Press.

Dubnick, Melvin J. 2002. "Seeking Salvation for Accountability." Paper read at American Political Science Association, August 29–September 1, Boston.

Dubnick, Melvin J., and Justin P. O'Brien. 2009. "Retrieving the Meaning of Accountability in Financial Market Regulation." Paper read at American Political Science Association, September 3–6, Toronto, Ontario.

Edelman, Murray. 1964. *The Symbolic Uses of Politics.* Urbana: University of Illinois Press.

———. 1971. *Politics as Symbolic Action: Mass Arousal and Quiescence.* Chicago: Markham Publishing.

———. 1977. *Political Language: Words that Succeed and Policies that Fail.* New York: Academic Press.

Ely, Bert. 2009. "Bad Rules Produce Bad Outcomes: Underlying Public-Policy Causes of the U.S. Financial Crisis." *Cato Journal* 29 (1): 93.

Finer, Herman. 1941. "Administrative Responsibility in Democratic Government." *Public Administration Review* 1 (4): 335–50.

Ford, Cristie L. 2008. "New Governance, Compliance, and Principles-Based Securities Regulation." *American Business Law Journal* 45 (1): 1–60.

Foucault, Michel. 1991. "Governmentality." In *The Foucault Effect: Studies in Governmentality: With Two Lectures by and an Interview with Michel Foucault,* ed. G. Burchell, C. Gordon, and P. Miller. Chicago: University of Chicago Press.

Fourcade, Marion, and Kieran Healy. 2007. "Moral Views of Market Society." *Annual Review of Sociology* 33 (1): 285–311.

Friedman, Jeffrey. 2009. "A Crisis of Politics, Not Economics: Complexity, Ignorance, and Policy Failure." *Critical Review: A Journal of Politics and Society* 21 (2): 127–83.

Friedrich, Carl J. 1940. "Public Policy and the Nature of Administrative Responsibility." In *Public Policy: A Yearbook of the Graduate School of Public Administration, Harvard University,* ed. C. J. Friedrich and E. S. Mason. Cambridge, MA: Harvard University Press.

Fuld, Kenneth S., Jr. 2010. Testimony of Kenneth S. Fuld, Jr., Former Chairman and Chief Executive Officer of Lehman Brothers, September 1, before the U.S. Financial Crisis Inquiry Commission.

Galbraith, James K. 2008. *The Predator State: How Conservatives Abandoned the Free Market and Why Liberals Should Too.* New York: Free Press.

Gergen, Kenneth J., and Tojo Joseph Thatchenkery. 1996. "Organization Science as Social Construction: Postmodern Potentials." *Journal of Applied Behavioral Science* 32 (4): 356–77.

Hacking, Ian. 1999. *The Social Construction of What?* Cambridge, MA: Harvard University Press.

Hayek, Friedrich A. 1944. *The Road to Serfdom.* Chicago: University of Chicago Press.

Hirschman, Albert O. 1982. "Rival Interpretations of Market Society: Civilizing, Destructive, or Feeble?" *Journal of Economic Literature* 20 (4): 1463–84.

Hoover, Herbert. 1934. "Consequences to Liberty of Regimentation." *Saturday Evening Post* (September 15): 5–89.

Jablecki, Juliusz, and Machaj Mateusz. 2009. "The Regulated Meltdown of 2008." *Critical Review: A Journal of Politics and Society* 21 (2): 301–28.

Jacob, Herbert. 1992. "The Elusive Shadow of the Law." *Law and Society Review* 26 (3): 565–90.

Jacobsen, John Kurt. 1995. "Review: Much Ado About Ideas: The Cognitive Factor in Economic Policy." *World Politics* 47 (2): 283–310.

John, Peter. 2003. "Is There Life After Policy Streams, Advocacy Coalitions, and Punctuations: Using Evolutionary Theory to Explain Policy Change?" *Policy Studies Journal* 31 (4): 481–98.

Kaplow, Louis. 1992. "Rules versus Standards: An Economic Analysis." *Duke Law Journal* 42 (3): 557–629.

Keefer, Philip, and David Stasavage. 2000. "Bureaucratic Delegation and Political Institutions: When Are Independent Central Banks Irrelevant?" In *Regulation and Competition Policy,* Development Research Group, Policy Research Working Paper No. 2356. Washington, DC: World Bank.

———. 2003. "The Limits of Delegation: Veto Players, Central Bank Independence, and the Credibility of Monetary Policy." *American Political Science Review* 97 (3): 407–23.

Knobloch-Westerwick, Silvia, and Laramie D. Taylor. 2008. "The Blame Game: Elements of Causal Attribution and Its Impact on Siding with Agents in the News." *Communication Research* 35 (6): 723–44.

Labaton, Stephen. 2008. "Agency's '04 Rule Let Banks Pile Up New Debt." *New York Times,* October 2, 2008.

Malle, Bertram F. 2004. *How The Mind Explains Behavior: Folk Explanations, Meaning, and Social Interaction.* Cambridge, MA: MIT Press.

March, James G., and Johan P. Olsen. 1989. *Rediscovering Institutions: The Organizational Basis of Politics.* New York: Free Press.

———. 1995. *Democratic Governance.* New York: Free Press.

———. 2006. The Logic of Appropriateness. In *The Oxford Handbook of Public Policy,* ed.M. Moran, M. Rein, and R. E. Goodin. New York: Oxford University Press.

Mariani, Pierre. 2009. "Ways Towards a More Stable and Credible Financial Sector." *European View* 8: 65–72.

Mason, Edward S. 1958. "The Apologetics of 'Managerialism.'" *Journal of Business* 31 (1): 1–11.

McBarnet, Doreen. 1991. "Whiter Than White Collar Crime: Tax, Fraud Insurance and the Management of Stigma." *British Journal of Sociology* 42 (3): 323–44.

———. 2006. "After Enron Will 'Whiter than White Collar Crime' Still Wash?" *British Journal of Criminology* 46 (6): 1091–09.

McBarnet, Doreen J., and Christopher J. Whelan. 1999. *Creative Accounting and the Cross-Eyed Javelin Thrower.* Chichester, UK: Wiley.

Meindl, James R., Sanford B. Ehrlich, and Janet M. Dukerich. 1985. "The Romance of Leadership." *Administrative Science Quarterly* 30 (1): 78–102.

Meindl, James R., and Sanford B. Ehrlich. 1987. "The Romance of Leadership and the Evaluation of Organizational Performance." *Academy of Management Journal* 30 (1): 91–109.

Merriam, Charles E. 1944. "The Possibilities of Planning." *The American Journal of Sociology* 49 (5): 397–407.

Milhaupt, Curtis J., and Katharina Pistor. 2008. *Law and Capitalism: What Corporate Crises Reveal about Legal Systems and Economic Development around the World.* Chicago: University of Chicago Press.

Mintzberg, Henry. 1982. "A Note on That Dirty Word 'Efficiency'." *Interfaces* 12 (5): 101–05.

———. 1987. "The Strategy Concept II: Another Look at Why Organizations Need Strategies." *California Management Review* 30 (1): 25–32.

———. 2004. "Enough Leadership." *Harvard Business Review,* 22.

Morris, Charles R. 2008. *Trillion Dollar Meltdown: Easy Money, High Rollers, and the Great Credit Crash.* New York: Public Affairs.

Nagel, Thomas. 1987. "Moral Conflict and Political Legitimacy." *Philosophy and Public Affairs* 16 (3): 215–40.

Dash, Eric, and Julie Cresswell. 2008. "Citigroup Saw No Red Flags Even as It Made Bolder Bets." *New York Times,* November 23.

Obama, Barack. 2009. President Obama's prepared remarks on the proposed financial regulatory reform plan, June 17. The White House.

O'Brien, Justin. 2007a. *Redesigning Financial Regulation: The Politics of Enforcement.* Chichester, England: Wiley.

———. 2007b. "Managing Conflicts: The Sisyphean Tragedy (and Absurdity) of Corporate Governance and Financial Regulation Reform." *Australian Journal of Corporate Law* 20 (3): 317–42.

———. 2009. *Engineering a Financial Bloodbath.* London: Imperial College Press.

Ostrom, Vincent. 1974. *The Intellectual Crisis in American Public Administration.* Rev. ed. Tuscaloosca: University of Alabama Press.

Posner, Richard A. 2009. *A Failure of Capitalism: The Crisis of '08 and the Descent into Depression.* Cambridge, MA: Harvard University Press.

Reich, Robert B., ed. 1988. *The Power of Public Ideas.* Cambridge, MA: Ballinger Publishing.

Reinhart, Carmen M., and Kenneth S. Rogoff. 2008. "Is the 2007 U.S. Sub-Prime Financial Crisis So Different? An International Historical Comparison." In National Bureau of Economic Research Working Paper Series. Cambridge, MA: National Bureau of Economic Research.

———. 2009. *This Time Is Different: Eight Centuries of Financial Folly.* Princeton, NJ: Princeton University Press.

Rose, Nikolas, and Peter Miller. 1992. "Political Power Beyond the State: Problematics of Government." *British Journal of Sociology* 43 (2): 173–205.

Rudd, Kenneth. 2008. "The Children of Gordon Gekko." *The Australian* (6 October): 12.

Scott, James C. 1998. *Seeing Like a State: How Certain Schemes to Improve the Human Condition Have Failed.* New Haven: Yale University Press.

Securities and Exchange Commission. 2008a. Press Release, 28 April.

———. 2008b. Press Release, 28 September.

Sen, Amartya. 2009. *The Idea of Justice.* Cambridge, MA: Belknap Press of Harvard University Press.

Shearing, Clifford D. 1992. "A Constitutive Conception of Regulation." In *Business Regulation and Australia's Future,* ed. P.N. Grabosky and J. Braithwaite. Canberra: Australian Institute of Criminology.

Shiller, Robert J. 2008. *The Subprime Solution: How Today's Global Financial Crisis Happened and What to Do About It.* Princeton, NJ: Princeton University Press.

Simon, Herbert A. 1957. *Administrative Behavior: A Study of Decision-Making Processes in Administrative Organization.* 2d ed. New York: Free Press.

Smith, Adam. 1759. *The Theory of Moral Sentiments.* London: A. Millar.

Soros, George. 2008. *The New Paradigm for Financial Markets: The Credit Crisis of 2008 and What It Means.* New York: Public Affairs.

Steel, Robert K. 2010. Testimony of Robert K. Steel, Former CEO of Wachovia Corporation, September 1, before the U.S. Financial Crisis Inquiry Commission.

Stevenson, Betsey, and Justin Wolfers. 2006. "Bargaining in the Shadow of the Law: Divorce Laws and Family Distress." *Quarterly Journal of Economics* 121 (1): 267–88.

Stiglitz, Joseph E. 1989. "Markets, Market Failures, and Development." *The American Economic Review* 79 (2): 197–203.

———. 2001. "Principles of Financial Regulation: A Dynamic Portfolio Approach." *World Bank Observer* 16:1.

———. 2009. "The Anatomy of a Murder: Who Killed America's Economy?" *Critical Review: A Journal of Politics and Society* 21 (2): 329–39.

Surowiecki, James. 2008. "Parsing Paulson." *New Yorker,* April 28.

Tett, Gillian. 2009. *Fool's Gold: How the Bold Dream of a Small Tribe at J.P. Morgan Was Corrupted by Wall Street Greed and Unleashed a Catastrophe.* New York: Free Press.

UK Parliament. 2009a. HC. "Memorandum to the Treasury Select Committee," from Paul Moore, ex-head of Group Regulatory Risk, HBOS Plc Westminster.

———. 2009b. HC. "Response to the House of Commons Treasury Committee"—Seventh Special Report from the Financial Services Authority. Westminster.

U.S. Congress. 2008a. House Committee on Oversight and Government Reform. *Opening statement, Representative Henry Waxman, Hearing on the Causes and Effects of the Lehman Brothers Bankruptcy.* October 6.

———. 2008b. House Committee on Oversight and Government Reform. *Testimony of Alan Greenspan, Hearing on the Role of Federal Regulators in the Financial Crisis.* October 23.

———. 2008c. House Committee on Financial Services. *Testimony of Joseph Stiglitz, Hearing on the Regulatory Restructuring of the Reform of the Financial System.* October 21.

———. 2008d. House Committee on Oversight and Government Reform. *Testimony of Richard Fuld, Hearing on the Causes and Effects of the Lehman Brothers Bankruptcy.* October 6.

U.S. Department of the Treasury. 2008. *Blueprint for a Modernized Financial Regulatory Structure.* Washington, DC: U.S. Department of the Treasury.

———. 2009. *Financial Regulatory Reform: A New Foundation.* Washington, DC.

Vogel, Steven Kent. 1996. *Freer Markets, More Rules: Regulatory Reform in Advanced Industrial Countries.* Ithaca, NY: Cornell University Press.

Waldo, Dwight. 1984. *The Administrative State: A Study of the Political Theory of American Public Administration,* 2d ed. New York: Holmes and Meier Publishers.

Wallison, Peter J. 2009. "Cause and Effect: Government Policies and the Financial Crisis." *Critical Review: A Journal of Politics and Society* 21 (2): 365–76.

———. 2009. "Credit-Default Swaps Are Not to Blame." *Critical Review: A Journal of Politics and Society* 21 (2): 377–87.

Wedel, Janine R., Cris Shore, Gregory Feldman, and Stacy Lathrop. 2005. "Toward an Anthropology of Public Policy." *The Annals of the American Academy of Political and Social Science* 600 (1): 30–51.

White, Lawrence J. 2009. "The Credit-Rating Agencies and the Subprime Debacle." *Critical Review: A Journal of Politics and Society* 21 (2): 389–99.

Wildavsky, Aaron. 1973. "If Planning Is Everything, Maybe It's Nothing." *Policy Sciences* 4 (2): 127–53.

Williams, Bernard. 1961. "Democracy and Ideology." *The Political Quarterly* 32 (4): 374–84.

Williams, Raymond. 1985. *Keywords: A Vocabulary of Culture and Society.* Rev. ed. New York: Oxford University Press.

Williamson, Oliver E. 2008. "Corporate Boards of Directors: In Principle and in Practice." *Journal of Law and Organization* 24 (2): 247–72.

Yee, Albert S. 1996. "The Causal Effects of Ideas on Policies." *International Organization* 50 (1): 69–108.

CONCLUSION

Taking Stock and Moving Forward

In history's best known symposium, Plato (in the personage of Apollodorus) speaks third hand of what Socrates and others have told him transpired at a dinner gathering of Athenians who fell into a discussion about a topic that fascinated each of them: love. As related by Plato in *The Symposium,* both the gathering and the debate that ensued were happenstance, an event not unlike others (fictitious we assume) used by Plato to present the multiplicity of views on intellectually challenging issues (Plato 2006). Today, the convening of a symposium is a more formalized and intentional endeavor, but the hoped-for outcome remains the same, that is, to facilitate the advancement of knowledge through an exchange of views on a very challenging topic. In our case, the subject was accountability.

Contemporary symposium conveners have two strategic options when developing the agenda for a meeting such as this. One approach is to provide participants with a predefined framework or theme, which they are asked to apply from their distinct perspectives (e.g., Castells and Cardoso 2005). The other option attempts to replicate Plato's implied ideal by bringing together a variety of analysts who have common interest in some particular subject or issue, and to operate under the speculative assumption that relevant themes and important frameworks will emerge from the presentations and the interaction of participants.

The Kettering Symposium was convened applying the latter model under the added rationale that after at least two decades of scrutiny by scholars from various disciplines from around the world, it was time to take stock of what we had learned from our own work and those of our colleagues. Despite efforts made to invite presentations reflecting the wide range of perspectives on (and approaches to) accountability, there were admittedly notable gaps in coverage. Nevertheless, from the conveners' perspective this Symposium succeeded in bringing attention to several important research themes and practical lessons.

First, if there is a major challenge posed by accountability for those engaged in governance, it is the need for them to realize that they operate in a world of multiple, diverse, and often conflicting accountabilities. Unless you are a Kafkaesque warder at the bottom of some formidable hierarchy who lacks discretion of any sort, there is no escaping that condition. Rather, you must learn to live—and perhaps to thrive—within the constraints and parameters established by multiple accountabilities. The exploration of the redundancies (Schillemans and Bovens), complexities (Romzek; Brown, Potoski, and Van Slyke), and dilemmas (Koppell) of multiple accountabilities remains a fruitful enterprise that enhances our growing knowledge of modern governance.

A second insight drawn from these chapters is that context matters. There are two lessons to be drawn here. The first is that the effectiveness of accountabilities is contingent on a range of factors, from public awareness and support (Pollitt) to the institutional settings in which they are applied (Radin; Johnson, Pierce, and Lovrich). At the same time, accountability mechanisms generated and "enact" their own contingencies, which have an impact upon policy making (Posner

302

and Schwartz) and institutions (see Ghere), as well as behavior and choices of those being held to account (e.g., Hood; Karns, Shaffer, and Ghere; Kearns).

A third lesson follows: strategies designed to enhance accountability are going to be difficult at best. This is most evident in the two examples of efforts to enhance accountability in the corporate sector (Wheeler; Potoski and Prakesh).

Finally, it is also evident that, despite at least two decades of substantial advances in our understanding of accountability, we have a great deal more to learn about this fascinating subject. Among other things, we need to break free of our cultural blinders and broaden our perspective on what it means to be accountable in other social contexts (Jordan). We also need a greater appreciation of the philosophical (O'Kelly), social (Yang), and cognitive (Dubnick and O'Brien) foundations of our own approaches to accountable governance.

There are no doubt many other (and more specific) lessons to be culled from the growing literature on accountability. While this volume offers a general survey of a wide range of research and writing on accountability, the fruits of the Kettering Symposium should be regarded only as a "sampler" that offers a taste of things to come. The effort of building a useful knowledge base continues.

REFERENCES

Castells, Manuel, and Gustavo Cardoso, eds. 2005. *The Network Society: From Knowledge to Policy.* Washington, DC: Johns Hopkins Center for Transatlantic Relations.
Plato. 2006. *Symposium.* Fairfield, IA: World Library-Literary Society.

ABOUT THE EDITORS AND CONTRIBUTORS

Editors

Melvin J. Dubnick is Professor of Political Science at the University of New Hampshire and Professor Emeritus of Political Science and Public Administration at Rutgers University-Newark. He served as managing editor of *Public Administration Review* from 1991 to 1996 and co-editor in chief of the *Policy Studies Journal* from 1985 to 1990. In 2003–2005 he held senior research fellowships at the Institute of Governance at Queen's University, Belfast, and has also served on faculty and adjunct appointments at the University of Kansas, Baruch College/CUNY, Columbia University, and the University of Oklahoma. The author of numerous articles on accountability, he has also co-authored textbooks on American government, public administration, and policy analysis.

H. George Frederickson is the Edwin O. Stene Distinguished Professor of Public Administration at the University of Kansas. In 2003–2004 he served as the Winant Visiting Professor of American Government at the University of Oxford, and as a Fellow of Balliol College, Oxford. He is the author of *The Spirit of Public Administration* and *Social Equity and Public Administration: Origin, Developments and Applications*. He is a co-author of both *The Public Administration Theory Primer* and *The Adapted City: Institutional Dynamics and Structural Change*. He is the editor-in-chief of the *Journal of Public Administration Research and Theory*. He received the John Gaus Lecturer Award from the American Political Science Association in 1999.

Contributors

Mark Bovens is professor of public administration and research director at the Utrecht University School of Governance, and adjunct professor at the Australian National University. His research interests include public accountability, success and failure of public governance, democracy and citizenship, and political trust. He has published approximately 15 monographs and edited volumes in the areas of politics, government, and legal theory. His present research interests include accountability and governance, citizenship and democracy in the information society, success and failure of public governance, and trust in government. He is a member of the Royal Dutch Academy of Sciences.

Trevor L. Brown is associate professor and associate director for academic affairs and research at the John Glenn School of Public Affairs at the Ohio State University. He teaches courses on public management, public sector strategy, and organizational theory. His research examines why governments elect to make some goods and services internally, while contracting for others. When governments elect to contract, Dr. Brown's research has examined the investments governments make in contract management capacity to deliver desired outcomes. This research has been published in such journals as *Public Administration Review*, *Journal of Public Administration Research and Theory*, and *Journal of Policy Analysis and Management*.

Richard K. Ghere is associate professor of political science at the University of Dayton and is a core instructor in the Master of Public Administration Program there. He is an author of articles on public-sector ethics and private-public partnerships and is coeditor of *Ethics in Public Management* (M.E. Sharpe, 2005).

Christopher Hood is Gladstone Professor of Government and Fellow of All Souls College Oxford, and a Fellow of the British Academy and Academician of the Academy of Learned Societies of the Social Sciences. He specializes in the study of executive government, regulation and public-sector reform. In the past he held chairs at the London School of Economics, the University of Sydney, NSW, and worked at the universities of Glasgow, York, Bielefeld, the National University of Singapore and the City University of Hong Kong. His publications include *The Limits of Administration* (1976), *The Tools of Government* (1983) (updated as *The Tools of Government in the Digital Age* [2007] with Helen Margetts) and *The Art of the State* (1998 and 2000) for which he was awarded the Political Studies Association's Mackenzie Book Prize in 2000. He is the recipient of numerous other honors, including the Public Management Research Association's H. George Frederickson Award for Career Contributions to Public Management Research. In 2008, a prize for political theory at the University of Sydney was named in his honor. In February 2010, Professor Hood presented "Risk and Government: The architectonics of blame-avoidance" as part of the Darwin College Lecture Series.

Bonnie J. Johnson is assistant professor in the urban planning department at the University of Kansas. She teaches planning theory, land use, and politics and planning courses. Research interests include how planners communicate, civic bureaucracy, and sustainability. Before getting her doctorate, Professor Johnson was a practicing city planner for eight years.

Sara R. Jordan is assistant professor of politics and public administration at the University of Hong Kong. Her major research interests include the intersections between normative theories of politics and public administration theory and practice, the administrative thought of Continental political philosophers (specifically Jürgen Habermas) and modern American political thinkers (specifically John Dewey), and the tension between liberal democratic theories of politics and emerging problems in health care research and practice. Her work appears in *Public Administration*, *Review of Policy Research*, and *Administrative Theory and Praxis*.

Margaret P. Karns is professor emerita of political science at the University of Dayton and its first director of the university's Center for International Programs. She specializes in international politics and organizations, with a particular emphasis on U.S. foreign policy and multilateral institutions. She has coauthored three books: *The United States and Multilateral Institutions: Patterns of Instrumentality and Influence* (1990), *The United Nations in the Post–Cold War Era,* 3d ed. (2006), and *International Organizations: The Politics and Processes of Global Governance*, 2d ed. (2010), as well as numerous articles on UN peacekeeping, global governance, and the future of the UN system. Professor Karns is a past vice president of International Studies Association, a member of the Council on Foreign Relations, and a long-time board member and past president of the Dayton Council on World Affairs.

Kevin P. Kearns is professor at the Graduate School of Public and International Affairs at the University of Pittsburgh. He has published widely on nonprofit managers including accountability in nonprofits, strategic planning, board development, and general management. He is the author of *Private Sector Strategies for Social Sector Success*, which was honored with the Best Book Award by the Alliance for Nonprofit Management. Dr. Kearns has held a variety of leadership positions in higher education and philanthropy, including serving on the boards of directors of numerous nonprofit organizations and as president of The Forbes Funds, an organization devoted to capacity-building in nonprofit organizations.

Jonathan Koppell holds the Lattie & Elva Coor presidential chair at Arizona State University and is director of the School of Public Affairs. He is former director of the Millstein Center for Corporate Governance and Performance at Yale University. His research concerns the design and administration of complex organizations, particularly entities that hover at the intersection of politics and markets. He has examined global governance organizations that promulgate international rules as well as public-private hybrid entities that operate in the marketplace to achieve public policy goals. He is the author of *The Politics of Quasi-Government: Hybrid Organizations and the Dynamics of Bureaucratic Control* (2003), and *World Rule: Accountability, Legitimacy, and the Design of Global Governance* (2010).

Nicholas P. Lovrich, Jr. has been director of the division of governmental studies and services at Washington State University since 1977. Lovrich holds the rank of regents professor in the department of political science and criminal justice program, and the honor of a Claudius O. and Mary W. Johnson Distinguished Professorship in Political Science.

Justin O'Brien is professor of law at the University of New South Wales. He specializes in the dynamics of financial regulation and capital market governance. The author of a trilogy of books on regulatory politics (*Wall Street on Trial* [2003]; *Redesigning Financial Regulation* [2007]; and *Engineering a Financial Bloodbath* [2009]) and has edited volumes on corporate governance, including *The Future of Financial Regulation* (2010).

Ciarán O'Kelly is coordinator of the LLM corporate governance program and lecturer in law at the Institute of Governance, Queen's University, Belfast. His research focuses on the ethics of public administration, corporate governance in the regulatory state, and the politics of identity in divided societies.

John C. Pierce is research associate and affiliate faculty in the public administration department at the University of Kansas and research professor in political science at Washington State University at Vancouver. Pierce is the author or coauthor of numerous books and journal articles on American politics and political culture.

Christopher Pollitt is research professor of public management at the Public Management Institute, Katholieke Universiteit Leuven. Previously he has held full professorships at Erasmus Universitiet Rotterdam and Brunel University (UK). Author of more than a dozen book and 60 articles in scientific journals, his most recent works are *Time, Policy, Management: Governing with the Past* (Oxford University Press, 2008) and *Continuity and Change in Public Policy and Management* (Edward Elgar, 2009). Christopher was president of the European Evaluation Society, 1996–98, and scientific director of the Netherlands Institute of Government, 2004–2006. He has also worked in advisory roles for the World Bank, OECD, European Commission, Finnish Ministry of Finance, Danish Top Executive's Forum, and several UK central government bodies.

Paul L. Posner is the director of the public administration program at George Mason University, chair of the Federal Systems Panel of the National Academy of Public Administration, and former president of the American Society for Public Administration. The author of numerous articles on budgeting and federalism, his book *The Politics of Unfunded Mandates* received the award for best book on federalism from the American Political Science Association. Before his current position, he was with the GAO, serving as managing director for federal budgeting and intergovernmental management.

Matthew Potoski is a professor in the department of political science at Iowa State University where he teaches courses on public management and policy. He has received Iowa State University LAS awards for Early and Mid-Career Achievement in Research. He is coeditor of *Journal of Policy Analysis and Management* and *International Public Management Journal.* His research investigates public management and policy in domestic and international contexts, including public sector contracting and service delivery, environmental policy, and voluntary regulations. He is coauthor with Aseem Prakash of *The Voluntary Environmentalists* and coeditor of *Voluntary Programs: A Club Theory Approach.* He is author or coauthor of over 30 articles appearing in journals such as the *American Journal of Political Science, Journal of Policy Analysis and Management*, and *Public Administration Review*.

Aseem Prakash is the Walker Family professor for the arts and sciences at the University of Washington-Seattle. His research examines core issues in the study of governance, especially the complex relationship of businesses with governments and nongovernmental organizations. He has published over 40 articles in refereed journals including *The American Political Science Review, The American Journal of Political Science, The Journal of Politics, World Politics, International Studies Quarterly, Journal of Policy Analysis and Management, J-PART*, and *Public Administration Review*. He is the author of *Greening the Firm*, coauthor of *The Voluntary Environmentalists*, and the co-editor of *Advocacy Organizations and Collective Action, Voluntary Regulations of NGOs and Nonprofits: An Accountability Club Framework, Voluntary Programs: A Club Theory Perspective* (The MIT Press, 2009), *Coping with Globalization, Responding to Globalization*, and *Globalization and Governance*.

Beryl A. Radin is scholar in residence in the department of public administration and policy at American University. She has published books and articles that deal with federal management issues, particularly performance measurement and intergovernmental relations. She was the recipient of the 2009 H. George Frederickson Award for Career Contributions to Public Management Research, and is a fellow of the National Academy of Public Administration.

Barbara S. Romzek is professor of public administration at the University of Kansas and interim vice provost for academic affairs. She has published three books and scores of research articles and book chapters on public management, with an emphasis on accountability, government reform, and contracting. Dr. Romzek is a fellow of the National Academy of Public Administration and has received research awards from the American Society for Public Administration and the American Political Science Association. She currently serves on the board of the Public Management Research Association.

Thomas Schillemans is assistant professor at the Utrecht School of Governance, Utrecht University. He received his PhD with honor in 2007 for his thesis on "horizontal accountability in the shadow of hierarchy." He has published substantially on accountability in a context of changing governance structures, executive agencies, social policy, and the role of the media.

Robert Schwartz is director of evaluation and monitoring for the Ontario Tobacco Research Unit and associate professor at the University of Toronto. He has extensive training in public policy and administration, program evaluation, public oversight, and state audit. In recent years, he was a tenured faculty member at the University of Haifa where he was involved as an auditor and evaluator in many international projects, most recently as a performance monitoring and evaluation consultant for the World Bank. From 1987 to 1997, he worked in the state comptroller's office in Israel, serving as an expert in program evaluation. In addition to his work on public health policy, his research focuses on accountability mechanisms, performance measurement, balanced scorecards, and program evaluation. He has published in a wide range of journals, including *J-PART, Public Money and Management, Public Integrity, Canadian Public Administration*, and *Journal of Public Policy.*

Timothy J. Shaffer is a graduate of the MPA program at the University of Dayton and is currently a PhD student at Cornell University. His research focuses on civic engagement, democratic theory, and ways that professionals and citizens engage in collaborative public work.

David M. Van Slyke is an associate professor of public administration and senior research associate in the Campbell Public Affairs Institute at Syracuse University's Maxwell School. A recipient of the best article award from the *Journal of Public Administration Research and Theory*, his research has also appeared in *Public Administration Review* and *Organization Science*. His work focuses on government contracting, public-private partnerships, strategic management, government-business relations, and policy instruments.

Sally Wheeler is professor and director of Queen's University, Belfast's Institute of Governance. Currently serving as chair of the Socio-legal Studies Association, she is a noted specialist on company and corporate governance in the United Kingdom and has held chairs in the law faculty at the University of Leeds and at Birkbeck College, University of London. She joined the law school at Queen's University as chair of law, business, and society in 2004.

Kaifeng Yang is associate professor and MPA director at Florida State University's Askew School. His research and teaching interests are in public and strategic management, organizational theory and behavior, performance measurement, and e-government. He holds PhD degrees in both business administration (Renmin University) and public administration (Rutgers-Newark), and has engaged in consulting for a number of international companies on strategic management and organizational change. He is a senior research associate of the National Center for Public Productivity at Rutgers-Newark, and a research affiliate of the DeVoe Moore Center at FSU. His work has appeared in *J-PART, Public Administration Review*, and *Public Performance & Management Review.*

NAME INDEX

Acar, Muhittin, 32, 275
Acemoglu, Daron, 293
Acharya, Viral V., 296n6
Achebe, C., 249
Adelberg, S., 4
Agranoff, Robert, 22, 27
Ahmad, Mokbul M., 183, 188, 190,
    191–192, 194
Ahmed, Qazi Faruque, 194
Akerloff, G., 53n1, 53n2
Alborn, Timothy, 263
Alford, J., 141
Alkin, M., 142
Anderson, D., 218
Anderson, J.L., 131
Anechiarico, F., 129
Antöv, Hans, 183
Apple, R.W., Jr., 63
Aramony, William, 197
Arens, Sheila A., vii
Argyris, Chris, 204
Armstrong, Mary I., 25
Arndt, C., 89, 90, 91, 93
Austin, Michael J., 36
Avina, Jeffrey, 182
Axelrod, R., 53

Bagley, Constance E., 294
Baird, J., 141
Bajari, P., 43, 53n3
Bal, Roland, 94
Balla, S., 82, 83
Balla, S.J., 112
Banfield, Edward C., xvi
Bardach, Eugene, 28, 29, 32, 291
Barker, Richard A., xvii
Barnard, Chester I., xvi, xvii, 284
Baron, David, 228

Baron, J., 116
Barzelay, Michael, xxiv, 133
Bass, xviii
Baston, C.D., 4
Baumeister, Roy F., 177n1
Baysinger, B., 218
Beam, David R., 104, 134
Beauregard, R.A., 283
Behn, Robert, 4, 7, 14, 18, 31, 83, 87, 129,
    225, 227, 241, 244, 252, 269, 278
Bellamy, Richard, 262
Bendor, J., 17, 18, 19
Benoit, William L., xiv
Bentham, Jeremy, 178n4
Benton, J.E., 111, 112, 119, 124
Benveniste, Guy, xvii
Berle, Adolf Augustus, xi
Berlin, Isaiah, 242
Bernanke, Ben, 297n15
Bernstein, D.J., 141
Bertelli, Anthony M., xi
Besley, Timothy, xvi
Bessen, S.M., 231
Bevan, G., 81, 84, 87, 88
Bewaji, Isola, 249
Bezdek, Barbara L., xix
Bezemer, P., 219
Bhagat, S., 218
Bhidé, Amar, 296n6
Biggs, Stephen D., 181, 182, 185
Black, B., 221
Blair, Tony, 172, 173, 176
Blumberg, Phillip, 263
Boettger, Richard, xxiii
Boltanski, Luc, 289
Bolton, B., 218
Bond, M., 220, 221
Boonstra, Albert, 154, 155

Borgada, E., 113
Bottom, William P., 32
Bouckaert, G., 82
Boudieu, Pierre, xxiii
Bovaird, T., 90
Bovens, Mark, xii, xiii, xiv, xvi, xviii–xix, 3, 5, 7, 23, 35, 55, 58, 142, 167, 255, 272
Boyne, G., 82, 93, 255
Bozeman, Barry, xvii
Brainard, Lori A., 149, *149,* 160n2
Braithwaite, John, xiv–xv, 4, 17, 18
Brehm, John, xvi, 23
Brinkerhoff, Jennifer M., 149, *149,* 160n2
Broadbent, Jane, xvi, 133
Broadie, A., 249
Brown, Gordon, 289
Brown, L., 133, 134
Brown, L. David, xvii, 225, 272–273, 277, 278
Brown, Trevor L., xx, 42, 53n3
Bruner, Jerome, 284
Bryant, Coralie, 277
Buchanan, Allen, xvii
Buchanan, James M., 228, 297n16
Burchell, Graham, 282
Burke, Edmund, 241, 255, 258, 261, 262
Bush, George W., 63, 102
Busia, K.A., 253n5
Butler, H., 218

Cadbury, Adrian, 214, 216
Calomiris, Charles W., 286
Campbell, David, 203
Canally, Greg, 157
Cardoso, Gustavo, 302
Carmin, Joann, 234
Carroll, J.S., 17, 18
Castells, Manuel, 302
Cavalluzzo, K.S., 141
Cawley, R. McGreggor, 282
Cecchini, Simone, 157
Cerny, Philip G., xvii
Chabal, P., 248
Chaloupka, William, 282
Chambers, Robert, 182
Chen, Don-yun, *149*
Chiapello, Eve, 289
Cho, Yong Hyo, 157
Choi, Byung-Dae, 157

Choi, Youseok, 25, 31
Churchland, Paul M., 284
Claibourn, M., 114
Clapp, J., 231
Clark, Kathleen, xi
Clarke, J., 84, 85
Clarke, T., 217
Clinton, Bill, 172, 173
Cloward, Richard A., 60
Coase, R.H., 227
Coffee, John C., 286
Cohen, Ira J., 272
Coleman, J.A., 116
Coleman, J.S., 113
Confucius, 245–246
Conlan, Timothy J., 104
Conniff, James, 261
Considine, Mark, xxiv, 4, 22, 34, 277, 278
Cook, Brian J., ix
Cooter, Robert, 294
Corell, Chuck, 236n14
Cornes, R., 228, 231
Coulter, A., 88
Cousins, J.B., 142
Cox, Christopher, 293
Creswell, Julie 288

Dahl, Robert A., xvii, 56, 66, 283
Dahlstrom, K., 234
Daily, C., 218
Dallas, Lynn, 264
Dalton, C., 215, 218
Dalton, D., 215
Damon, L.A., 235
Danziger, Sheldon, 130
Darnall, Nicole, 234
Darwall, Stephen L., 255, 256–257, 262
Dasgupta, S., 234
Dash, Eric, 288
Daudi, P., 219
David, P.A., 53n1
Davidson, B., 253n5
Davies, Howard, 286
Davies, Paul L., 264
Davis, G.F., 214, 216, 218
Davis, J., 218
Day, Patricia, xiii, 3, 5, 8
De Bruijn, H., 81, 84
de Vreede, Gert-Jan, 157

deLeon, Peter, 235
Delmas, M., 233, 235
DeSanctis, Gerardine, 272
Dicke, Lisa A., 23, 29, 205
Dignam, Alan, 255
DiIulio, John D., Jr., 60
Dixit, Avinash, 294
Dobel, J. Patrick, xvii
Doble Research Associates, vii
Dodd, E. Merrick, Jr., xi
Dowdle, M., 4
Dowswell, George, 94
Drahos, Peter, xiv
Dubnick, Melvin J., xi, xii, xiii, xvii, xviii, xx, xxi, xxiii, 3, 4, 5, 6, 23, 24, *26,* 27, 29, 60, 98, 99, 100, 105–108, 111, 112, 124, 129, 147–148, 150, 152, *153,* 158–160, 181, 183–185, *186,* 192, 198, 225, 227, 255, 256, 265, 269, 274, 275, 278, 282, 283
Dukerich, Janet M., 282
Dunlavy, Colleen, 263
DuPont-Morales, M. A., xi
Durant, Robert F., xvii

Ebrahim, Alnoor, xiii, xxiii, xxv, 4, 198, 277
Edelenbos, Julian, 27
Edelman, L., 214
Edelman, Murray, 285
Edwards, Michael, 181, 182, 183, 188
Ehrlich, Sanford B., 282
Eikenberry, Angela M., 200
Eisenhardt, Kathleen M., xvi, 218
Eisenhower, Dwight D., xx
Ekelund, Robert B., Jr., 263
Elazar, Daniel, 113, 120
Ellerman, David, viii
Ely, Bert, 286
Entwistle, Tom, 22
Epstein, P., 83
Ester, Jon, xiv
Etsy, D.C., 62
Etzioni, A., 112, 243, 252
Eulau, Heinz, 261

Falk, R., 55
Fama, E., 215, 264
Fearon, James D., xxiii
Feldstein, L.M., 113

Ferlie, Ewan, 174
Filatotchev, I., 218
Fine, Allison H., 203
Finer, Herman, xi, 3, 5, 296n7
Finnemore, Martha, 158–160
Fletcher, Patricia D., 157
Flinders, M., 9
Flono, Fannie, ix
Florini, Ann, xvii
Flynn, Paul, 176
Folbre, N., 116
Forbes, D., 219
Forbes, Kevin, 263
Ford, Cristie, 292
Foucault, Michel, xviii, 282
Fountain, Jane, xxi, 147–148, 149, 155, 158, 160n3
Fourcade, Marion, 289
Fox, Jonathan A., 225, 277, 278
Fox, R.A., 246, 247
Franz, Douglas, 64
Frederickson, David G., xviii, 23, 28, 31, 36n3, 98
Frederickson, H. George, viii, xviii, 23, 28, 31, 36n3, 90, 98, 112
Freeman, Mark, 263
Freundlich, Madelyn, 22
Fried, Robert C., xx
Friedman, Jeffrey, 296n6
Friedman, R.B., 260
Friedrich, Carl J., xi, 3, 5, 296n7
Froud, J., 221
Fuld, Richard, 288
Fung, Archon, xvii
Fung Yu-lan, 253n1

Gaebler, Ted, xix, 61
Galbraith, James K., 296n11
Galtung, Fredik, 154
Gamble, Andrew, 263
Garfinkel, Harold, xiv
Gates, Scott, xvi, 23
Gawthrop, Louis C., 99
Gbadegesin, S., 248, 249, 250
Gelman, Sheldon, 197
Gergen, Kenneth J., 284
Gertzenzang, Sarah, 22
Ghere, Richard K., xxi, xxii, 146, 180

Gibbons, James Howard, 64
Gibelman, Margaret, 197
Giddens, Anthony, xiv, xxiii, 269–275, 276–277, 278
Gillan, S., 216, 264
Gilmour, Robert S., 60
Glaberson, William, 68
Glaser, John S., 197
Glasser, William, 233
Globerman, Steven, 37n11
Goddard, M., 83, 88
Goetz, Anne Marie, 276, 277
Goodin, Robert E., 59
Gore, Albert, xii
Gormley, W.T., Jr., 82, 83, 112, 138
Gournay, Vincent de, 174
Gradstein, M., 116
Granovetter, M., 220
Grant, Ruth W., 226
Grantham, Ross, 263
Grassley, Charles, 197
Gray, A., 133
Green, Ashbel S., 68
Greenbury, R., 216
Greenspan, Alan, 293–294, 296n10 (288)
Greve, Carsten, 22
Greve, H.R., 216
Gruber, Judith, 99
Grumman, Northrop, 47, 51
Guha, K., 92
Gunningham, N., 226
Gupta, V., 81
Guttenberg, 283

Habermas, Jürgen, xiv, xxiii, 260, 261
Hacking, Ian, 284
Halachmi, A., 7, 8, 129
Hallen, B., 249–250
Halligan, J., 82
Halpern, D., 113
Hammond, K., 81, 84
Hampel, R., 216
Haque, M. Shamsul, 35, 187, 188, 191
Harmon, Michael M., xi, 275
Harris, D., 220
Harris, Jean E., xii
Harrison, Steve, 94
Hart, H.L.A., xviii
Hart, O., 43

Harwood, Richard C., viii
Harwood Institute for Public Innovation, viii
Hasenfeld, Yeheskel, 204
Hayek, Friedrich A., 283
Heald, David, xvii
Healy, Kieran, 289
Healy, Melissa, 59
Heclo, H., 132
Hedström, Peter, xiv
Hegel, Georg W.F., 173
Heide, J., 45, 53
Heinrich, Carolyn, 25, 31, 43
Held, David, xvii
Helfat, C., 220
Hellwig, Timothy, xxiii
Henry, G.T., 142
Hero, R.E., 116, 118–119, 120
Hibbard, J., 81, 83, 84
Hibbert, Christopher, xviii
Hickson, Charles R., 263
Higgs, D., 216, 217, 221
Hill, K.Q., 116, 118, 124
Hiller, John R., xx
Hilzenrath, David S., 70
Hird, J.A., 133
Hirschman, Albert, 264, 289
Hirshhorn, Ronald, xvii
Hobbes, Thomas, 255, 256, 258–260, 262, 263
Hodge, Graeme, 22
Hoefer, Richard, 203
Hofstetter, C.H., 142
Holden, Stephen H., 157
Holzer, Marc, xx, 141, 277
Hood, Christopher, xvii, xix, xxii, 5, 7, 81, 84, 87, 88, 167, 168, *169,* 172, 255, 284
Hood, John, 173
Hooghiemstra, R., 219
Hoover, Herbert, 283, 295n2
Huang, Kun, 32
Hughes, E.F.X., 142
Hulme, David, 181, 182, 183, 188
Hume, David, 265n2
Hummel, Ralph P., 60
Humphrey, Kristen, 32
Huo, Yuen J., xviii
Hutton, J., 42
Hyden, G., 248, 250, 251

Ingraham, Patricia Wallace, 60, 274, 278
Isett, Kimberley Roussin, 32
Ittner, C.D., 141

Jablecki, Juliusz, 296n6
Jackson, Dan, 64
Jacob, Herbert, 294
Jacobs, J., 129
Jacobsen, John Kurt, 284
James, Estelle, 200
Jeffrey, B.R., 121
Jenkins, Bob, 276, 277
Jensen, M., 214, 215, 264
Jerak, Sonja, 94
Johnes, Martin, 178n7
Johnson, Bonnie J., xxi, 111, 117, 118
Johnson, C., 83
Johnson, D., 89, 93
Johnson, J., 252
Johnson, R.B., 142, 218
Johnson, Simon, 296n6
Johnson, Tana, 185
Johnston, Jocelyn M., 22, 24, 25, 26, 29, 31, 32, 34, 37n8
Jones, I., 214, 216
Jones, Matthew, 272
Jones, Nicholas, 170
Jordan, Lisa, xvii, 185, 186, 192
Jordan, Sara R., xiii, xxiii, 241
Jorna, Frans, 156
Jos, Philip, 275
Josling, T.E., 55
Julnes, P., 141
Justice, J., 129, 275

Kagan, Robert A., 291
Kahneman, D., 84
Kant, Peter A., 31
Kaplan, Robert S., xviii
Kaplow, Louis, 292
Karim, Mahbubul, 180, 183, 187, 188, 189, 193
Karns, Margaret P., xxii, 180
Karpoff, Jonathan M., xx
Katchanovski, Ivan, 146
Kaufman, Herbert, xvii, xx, 99
Kaufmann, Daniel, 89, 90, 91, 92, 93, 150, 153

Kearney, Richard C., 60
Kearns, Kevin P., xxi, xxii, xxiv–xxv, 23, 111, 112, 113, 124, 197, 199, 206, 269, 275
Keay, Andrew, 264
Keefer, P., 116, 293
Keenan, J., 215
Keller, A., 235
Kelly, Gavin, 263
Kelman, S.J., 42
Kenis, Patrick, 27, 28, 36n4
Keohane, Robert O., 8, 55, 56, 226
Kershaw, D., 214
Kesner, I., 218
Kettl, Donald, 28, 31
Khanna, M., 235
Kim Jong Il, 167
King, Andrew A., 225, 235
Kingdon, John, xxi, 130, 143
Kirkhart, K.E., 142
Klein, Rudolf, xiii, 3, 5, 8
Klijn, Erik-Hans, 27, 28
Klingner, D.E., 6, 23, 273
Kluver, Jody D., 200
Knack, S., 113, 114, 115, 116
Knobloch-Westerwick, Silvia, 286
Koch-Mehrin, Silvana, 63
Koppell, Jonathan, xx, 4, 7, 16, 55, 57, 58, 62, 73, 274
Koppenjan, Joop F.M., 28
Korsgaard, Christine M., 256
Kotchen, Matthew J., 229
Kraemer, Kenneth, 146
Krause, George, 275, 276
Krishna, S., 157
Krislov, S., 111
Krueger, A.O., 116
Krugman, Paul, 296n6
Kuchapski, Renee, 274
Kulchitsky, D. Roman, 156
Kurtz, Howard, 170, 172, 178n7

La Porte, Todd, 146
Labaton, Stephen, 292
Lamothe, Meeyoung, 22, 24, 27
Lamothe, Scott, 22, 24, 27
Lan, Z., 146
Landau, M., 17, 18
Landau, Martin, 99

Lau, Richard R., 177n1
Laughlin, Richard, 133, 178n5
Lavis, J.N., 131
Leazes, Francis J., Jr., 60
Leblanc, R., 218
Lee, Julian, 180
Leithwood, K.A., 142
Leland, S., 111
Lenox, M.J., 235
Lerner, Jennifer S., xiv, xxiii, 4
Lesser, Cara, 28, 29, 32
Leviton, L.C., 142
Levy, Amir, 178n5
Lewis, Jenny M., xxiv
Li, X., 215
Lichbach, M.I., 46
Light, Paul, 24, 99, 244
Lindblom, C.E., 132, 283
Lipsky, Michael, 205
Lobban, Michael, 263
Löffler, E., 90
London, Scott, viii
Lonsdale, J., 139
Lovrich, Nicholas P., Jr., xxi, 111, 112
Lowi, Theodore, 131
Lynn, Laurence E., xi, 31

Macdonald, Kate, 278, 279
Machiavelli, Niccoló, 168
MacNeil, I., 215
Madoff, Bernie, 288
Magnette, 293
Majone, Giandomenico, xvii
Malek, Frederick, 99
Malle, Bertram F., 284
Mannion, R., 83, 88
March, James, 275, 284
Margolis, Joshua D., xvii
Mariani, Pierre, 294
Mark, M.M., 142
Marshall, M., 83, 88, 94
Martin, J., 216
Martin, L.L., 43
Martin, P.S., 114
Martin, Steve, 22
Masolo, D.A., 249, 250
Mason, Edward S., 289
Mateusz, Machaj, 296n6
Matheson, Craig, xvii

Mathews, David, vii, viii
Matsubayashi, T., 116, 118, 124
Maxwell, Robert, 217
McBarnet, D., 217, 220, 286
McCreevy, Charlie, 287
McCubbins, Matthew, 135, 167
McDermid, Mark, 233
McEwan, William J., 187
McGivern, Gerry, 174
McGregor, R., 92
McGuire, Michael, 22, 27, 231
McKinney, Jerome B., 60
McLean, Iain, 178n7
McNamara, Robert, 137
McNulty, T., 219, 221
Means, Gardiner Coit, xi
Mechanic, D., 197
Meckling, W., 214, 264
Meier, Kenneth J., 23, 27, 28, 275, 276
Meindl, James R., 282
Melkers, J., 141
Mencius, 247
Menkiti, I.A., 250
Merriam, Charles E., 295n2
Meyer, J., 81
Meyers, Marcia K., 22, 28
Milhaupt, Curtis J., 296n11
Miller, Andrew H., 263
Miller, Arthur S., xx
Miller, D.Y., 113
Miller, G.J., 8
Miller, Peter, 282
Miller, Trudi C., xx
Milliken, F., 219
Mills, C., 221
Milward, H. Brinton, 22, 27, 35
Miner, A., 45, 53
Minow, Martha, xviii
Mintzberg, Henry, 282
Mirabella, Roseanne, 200
Mitchell, L., 213
Mizruchi, M., 220
Mladenka, Kenneth R., 60
Moe, Ronald C., 60
Moe, T., 8
Mohmud, Dahlina D., 157
Moncrieffe, J.M., 248
Monteil, Ivan, 235
Moon, C.D., 112

Moon, M. Jae, 29
Moore, J., 43
Moore, Mark H., xvii, 99
Moore, Michael R., 229
Moore, Paul, 296n8, 296n11
Morris, Charles R., 296n11
Morris, Phillip, 64
Morse, Suzanne, viii
Moulder, E.R., 112
Mucciaroni, Gary, xxi
Mulgan, Richard, xiv, 4, 5, 7, 8, 9, 18, 22,
    198–199
Murphy, Craig N., 63
Musso, Juliet A., 156

Nagel, Thomas, 282
Neame, Arthur D., 181, 182, 185
Nederman, C.J., 245
Neitsch, Bruce, 157
Nelson, J., 116
Newell, Peter, 274, 277, 278, 279
Nielson, 226
Niland, Carmel, xvii
Niyazov, Saparmurat, 167
Nkrumah, 250
Noble, Alice, 197
Nordheimer, Jon, 64
Nosco, P., 246, 247
Nozick, R., 243
Nye, Joseph S., 55

Obama, Barack, 286, 289, 290
Oborne, Peter, 170
O'Brien, Justin P., xxiii, 282, 287, 289, 291–
    292, 294
O'Connell, L., 4, 275
O'Donnell, Guillermo A., xvii
Oh, C.H., 131
O'Kelly, Ciarán, xiii, xxiii, 158, 255, 265
O'Leary, Rosemary, xvii
O'Looney, J.A., 43
O'Loughlin, Michael G., 275
Olsen, Johan P., 284
Olson, M., Jr., 229
Oman, C., 89, 91, 93
O'Neill, Onora, 174, 175
O'Neill, R.J., Jr., 112
O'Rourke, R., 50
Osborne, David, xii, xix, 61

Ostrom, Elinor, xiv
O'Toole, Laurence J., Jr., 22, 23, 27, 28, 35,
    275, 276
Ott, J. Steven, 23, 29, 205
Ott, Steven, 205
Ouchi, William G., xvi

Padgett, C., 215
Page, Stephen, 32
Park, Stephen Kim, xviii
Paulson, Hank, 296n13, 297n15
Pearson, Robin, 263
Peck, Polly, 214, 266n12
Peel, Michael, 73
Petersen, Trond, xvi
Pettigrew, A., 218, 219
Pettit, Philip, 265n4
Pfaff, A., 227
Phillips, Robert A., xvii
Pierce, John C., xxi, 111, 112, 113
Pierson, Christopher, 276
Pistor, Katharina, 296n11
Pitches, D., 88
Pitkin, Hanna, 225, 258, 265n8
Piven, Frances Fox, 60
Plato, 302
Poister, T.H., 132, 141
Pollitt, Christopher, xx–xxi, 5, 7, 9, 18, 82,
    84, 85, 133, 284
Pollitt, M., 214, 216
Poole, Dennis L., 203
Poole, Marshall, 272
Porter, Michael, 66
Posner, Elliot, 70
Posner, Paul L., xxi, 3, 31, 32, 129, 284
Posner, Richard A., 286, 296n6
Potoski, Matthew, xx, xxii, 42, 225, 226, 228,
    229, 233, 234, 235
Potter, David M., 188
Power, Michael, 129, 139
Prager, Jonas, 24
Prakash, Aseem, xxii, 225, 226, 228, 229,
    233, 234, 235
Prat, Andrea, 168
Predash, Andrah, 157
Price, B., 114
Propper, Carol, xviii
Provan, Keith G., 22, 27, 28, 32, 35, 36n4
Przeworski, A., 9

Purchase, Bryne, xvii
Putnam, R.D., 113, 114, 121

Qiao, Zhigang, 157

Radin, Beryl A., xviii, xxi, 24, 27, 60, 81, 84,
    98, 99, 107, 284
Ramus, Catherine A., 235
Reich, Robert B., 284
Reinhart, Carmen M., 286
Rethemeyer, R. Karl, 157
Rhodes, R. A. W., xii
Riccucci, Norma M., xvii
Richardson, Matthew, 296n6
Rickett, Charles, 263
Rivera, Jorge, 235
Roach, Lee, 264
Robbins, G.E., 214
Roberts, J., 219
Roberts, Nancy C., 27, 111, 112, 269, 275
Roberts, S., 133
Roche, Declan, xviii
Rogoff, Kenneth S., 286
Rohr, John A., xvii, 244
Romzek, Barbara S., xi, xiii, xix, xxi, 3, 5, 6,
    22, 23, 24, 25, *26*, 27, 28, 29, 31, 32, 34,
    36, 37n8, 60, 61, 82, 98, 99, 100, 105–
    108, 111, 112, 124, 181, 183–185, *186,*
    192, 198, 256, 265, 269, 274, 278
Ronald, David, 233
Rooney, Patrick, 200
Roothaan, Susan, 233
Rose, Nikolas, 282
Rose, Richard, 170
Rosen, Bernard, 61, 99, 131
Rosenbloom, David H., xvii, 106, 111, 244
Ross, Stephen A., xvi
Rothstein, B., 90
Rourke, Francis E., 61
Rubin, Robert, 288
Rudd, Kevin, 289
Rugeley, Cindy, xvii
Runciman, David, 257
Rupasingha, A., 112, 115, 116
Russo, M.V., 234

Sabatier, P., 130
Sackett, Peter, 157
Salamon, Lester, 3, 199

Salem, Joseph A., 157
Saloner, G., 231
Samuels, David, xxiii
Sanchirico, C.W., 227
Sandel, M., 243, 252
Sandler, T., 228, 231
Sanger, Mary Bryna, 31
Sarkin, Jeremy, xviii
Satkunandan, Shalini, xvii
Schattschneider, E.E., 118
Schelling, Thomas C., xiv
Schillemans, Thomas, xiii, xiv, xviii–xix, 3,
    9, 58
Schmid, Hillel, 204
Schmidt, Steve, 63
Schmidt, Vivien A., xvii
Schneider, Jo Anne, 116
Scholz, John T., 229, 235n1
Schumpeter, Joseph, 262
Schwartz, M., 218
Schwartz, Robert, xxi, 31, 129, 131, 133, 137,
    139, 140, 141, 274, 278, 284
Schwartz, Thomas, 135, 167
Sclar, Elliott, 24, 31, 42
Scott, Austin W., xi
Scott, Christopher, 4, 5, 17, 18, 19, 157
Scott, James C., 283
Scott, John, 220
Scully, Patrick L., viii
Sen, Amartya, 289
Senge, Peter, 204
Senghor, L.S., 250
Sennott, Charles M., 197
Sensenbrenner, Jospeh, 61
Shabbir, A., 215
Shaffer, Timothy J., xxii, 180
Shafritz, Jay M., 198
Sharkansky, I., 133
Sharp, E.B., 113
Shearing, Clifford D., 297n17
Shiller, Robert J., 294
Shleifer, A., 215
Shrader-Frechette, Kristin, 173
Shulha, L.M., 142
Sikka, Premm, 73
Sikkink, Kathryn, 158–160
Simon, Herbert A., xvii, 284
Sinha, Chandan, 60
Skinner, Quentin, 258, 259, 265n8

Smith, Adam, 249, 289
Smith, Bruce L.R., xix
Smith, Doug, 233
Smith, Peter, xii, 81, 84, 129
Smith, Steven Rathgeb, 205
Smoller, Jeff, 233
Smythe, Donald, 263
Soros, George, 296n11
Starks, Laura, 264
Stasavage, David, 293
Steel, Robert K., 288
Stein, J.G., 18
Stern, I., 221
Stevenson, Betsey, 294
Stiglitz, Joseph, 92, 283, 286, 288–289, 296n6
Stoker, Gerry, xii
Stokes, Susan C., xxiii
Stone, Deborah, xiii, 130
Stout, Russell, Jr., 99
Strauss, A., 55
Streib, G.D., 111, 120, 132, 141
Strøm, K., 9, 18
Sulitzeanu-Kenan, Raanan, 139, 168, 274, 278
Sunstein, Cass R., xvi
Surowiecki, James, 292
Sutherland, S., 133
Svennson, Jorgen, 28
Swedberg, Richard, xiv
Sweet, A.S., 7
Sydow, Jorg, 270
Syring, Tom, xviii

't Hart, Paul, 23
Tadelis, S., 43, 53n3
Talbot, C., 83
Taylor, C., 243
Taylor, Laramie D., 286
Teffo, J., 250
Teorell, J., 90
ter Bogt, H.J., 83
Terlaak, Ann, 225
Tetlock, Philip E., xiv, xvi, xxiii, 4
Thaler, Richard H., xvi
Thatchenkery, Tojo Joseph, 284
Thatcher, M., 7
Thiel, S. van, 9
Thompson, Dennis, 23, 242

Thompson, Frank J., xi
Thompson, James D., 187
Thompson, John, 272
Thompson, Victor A., xvii
Thurmaier, K., 111
Tierney, 226
Timmons, Stephen, 156
Tirole, Jean, 43
Toffel, 234
Tollison, Robert D., xx, 263
Tompkins, Mark, 275
Trailer, Jeff W., 23
Tsai, Lily, 277
Tsoukas, H., 81, 83, 84–85, 88, 92
Tuijl, Peter van, xvii, 185, *186*, 192
Tullock, Gordon, 60, 116, 297n16
Turnbull, N., 216
Turner, John D., 263
Tversky, A., 84
Twarowski, Christopher, 73
Tyler, Tom R., xviii
Tyrall, David, 73

Useem, M., 220

Van de Walle, S., 89
van Manen, J., 219
Van Roosbroek, S., 89
Van Ryzin, G., 84
Van Slyke, David M., xx, 22, 24, 31, 32, 35, 42
Van Thijn, Ed, 177
Van Wart, Montgomery, xvii
Verweij, M., 55
Vining, Aidan R., 37n11, 53n1
Vishny, R., 215
Vogel, David, xvii
Vogel, Stephen Kent, 297n17

Wagenaar, Pieter, 156
Waldman, Amy, 180
Waldo, Dwight, xii, 282
Wallace, R. Jay, 256, 257
Wallach, Lori M., xxiv
Wallison, Peter J., 296n6
Walsham, Geoff, 157
Walzer, Michael, 66, 242, 243, 252
Wamala, E., 250, 251
Wang, X., 111, 112, 141, 276

Waterman, Richard, 111, 276
Watson, Gary, 256
Waugh, W.L., Jr., 120
Weare, Christopher, 156
Weaver, Gary R., xvii
Weaver, Kent, 167, 170–171
Weber, Edward P., 23, 198
Weber, Max, 63
Weimer, David, 53n1, 155, *156*
Weisband, E., 4
Weiss, Carol, 129–130
Weiss, Thomas G., xvii
Welch, Eric W., 29
Wellman, J.K., 123
West, W.F., 111
Westphal, S., 221
Wheeler, Sally, xxii, 213
Wheelock, Anne, 278
Whelan, C., 217, 220, 286
Whitaker, Gordon P., 27, 28, 32, 276
White, J., 274
White, Lawrence J., 296n6
Whiteman, David, 143
Whitley, Richard, 220
Wholey, Joseph S., xx
Wiemer, David L., 138
Wildavsky, Aaron, xii, 17, 18, 132, 283
Williams, Bernard, 282

Williams, Raymond H., 285, 295
Williamson, Oliver E., xiv, xx, 43, 44, 215, 295
Willoughby, K., 141
Willoughby, W.F., 111
Wilson, C., 130
Wilson, Deborah, xviii
Windeler, Arnold, 270
Wing, Kennard, 202
Wingo, A.H., 253n5
Wish, Naomi, 200
Wolfers, Justin, 294
Wood, B.D., 111
Wood, Dan, 276
Woodlief, Wayne, 63
Woods, N., 92
Wuthnow, R., 123

Yang, Kaifeng, xiii, xiv, xx, xxiii, 146, 269, 277
Yee, Albert S., 284
Young, Dennis, 22, 200
Yunis, Mohamed, 191

Zajonc, T., 89, 93
Zaman, Hassan, 188
Zauderer, Donald G., xvii
Zuckert, Michael, 252

SUBJECT INDEX

Italicized locators indicate charts and illustrations.

accountability
  consequences phase of, 5, *10,* 15–17, 247
  debating phase of, 5, *10,* 13–15
  desire for, 227, 241
  information phase of, 5, *10,* 11–13
  national views of, differing, 4–5
  as normative concept, 4, 214
  performance measurement, tension with,
    83–85, 93–94
  performance measurement promoting,
    82–83
  redundant, 17–19
  research trends in, xi–xii
  structuration theory of, 272–276, *273*
  varied definitions of, 4, 5, 57, 58–61,
    198–199
  as virtue, 4, 214
accountability dilemma, 6
Accountability Hot Zone, 70–72
accountability institutions
  collaboration in, 138
  competition in, 137–138
  conflict management in, 138
  contingent nature of impact, 138–140
  performance measurement of, 140–141,
    141–142, 203–204, *206–207*
  principal agency in, 138
  program evaluation, 142
  shame in, 137
accountability mechanisms, 5–6, 99–101,
    100, 105–108. *See also* accountability
    institutions
  as political symbols of authority, 262
  research focus on, xiii
  and voluntary codes of conduct, 226–230
accountability relationships
  formal, 29, 31–32, *33*
  informal, 32, *33,* 34

accountability relationships *(continued)*
  vertical and horizontal structures for, 28–29,
    30, 32, *33,* 34
accreditation authority in voluntary programs,
    232
Administrative Procedures Act (1946), 61,
    155
advanced performance measurement regimes.
    See performance measurement
advertising, social case for, 173
affective accountability, 248–251
African systems of accountability, 248–251
agency strategies of blame avoidance, 168,
    169, 170–171
agency theory and structuration, 270, 275
agentification, 9
Airline Stabilization Board, 130
American Society for Public Administration,
    146
Amnesty International, 154
appropriate behavior, *xv,* xvii
Arthur Andersen, 59
asset specific investments, 44–45, 47–48
Association of Development Agencies in
    Bangladesh (ADAB), 193
Austin, Texas, IT systems in, 156, *164*
authority
  accountability mechanisms as political
    symbols of, 262
  and constrictiveness, 65–69
  in global governance, 57–58, 62
  moral obligation in, 257
  and problem of personhood, 259
  salience of, 63
autonomy of agents, 8

Bangladesh
  external aid to, *189*

Bangladesh *(continued)*
  historical background, 187–188
  nongovernmental organizations in, 180, 181
  PROSHIKA in, 188–195
  and stakeholder concerns, 191
Bank of Credit and Commerce International
    (BCCI), 214
BCCI (Bank of Credit and Commerce
    International), 214
Bear Stearns, 288, 292
Better Business Bureau, 198, 203
Beyond the Magic Bullet (Edwards and
    Hulme), 181
"Big Man" rule, 250–251
bilateral accountability, 45–46, 50–52
blame avoidance
  and accountability in executive government
    (AEG), 167–168
  agency strategies of, 168, *169*, 170–171
  blame games and multiple accountability, 7,
    14–15
  as defensive approach, 176, 288
  and global financial markets in Great
    Recession, 286–289
  hard delegation, *175*, 175–176
  and human behavior, 167
  negative effects of, 173–176, *175*, 177
  neutral effects of, 171–172, 174–176, *175*
  policy strategies of, 168, *169*, 170–171
  positive effects of, 172–173, 174–176, *175*,
    177
  presentational strategies of, 168, *169*,
    170–171
  soft/complex delegation, *175*, 175–176
  and spin, 170
  for winning arguments, 176
boards of directors
  in Dutch agencies study, 8–17
  as early warning systems, 18–19
  interlocked boards, 220
  outside directors, 216–217, 218–222
  and phases of accountability, *10*
  and representation, 264
  retirement of personnel, 221
  risk-monitoring role, 213
  structure of, 214
Building the Virtual State (Fountain), 147–148
bureaucratic accountability mechanisms, 99,
    100, 101, 106
Burke, Edmund, 261–262

Cadbury-Schweppes PLC, 214–215
California, political accountability in, 121,
    121, 122
Canada, performance measurement in, 83
Canadian Auditor General, 143
Catholic charities, 197
CBO (Congressional Budget Office), 133
Central Bank of Indonesia, 293
Centre for Work and Income, 9–17
"chains of accountability," 226
Challenger space shuttle tragedy (1986),
    181
charitable sector, naming of, 200
child welfare services, 24, 32, 36n2, 36n6
China
  IT systems in, *149*, 152, *153*, 154, *156*, 157,
    163
  ritual accountability in, 246
Citigroup, 288
"City" figure in governance, 214, 215–216
collaboration in accountability institutions,
    138
collective beliefs, 284
collectivist society, 250
communal functionalism, 244–245
communitarianism as basis for accountability
    concepts, 242–244
community in African systems of
    accountability, 248–251
Community Development Block Grant
    program, 107
competition in accountability institutions,
    137–138
competitive elections and political
    accountability, 118–119, *119*
complex contracting game, 44–46, 46–52
complex products, 42–44
conflict management in accountability
    institutions, 138
conflicting expectations, 6, 14–15
Confucian philosophy, 245–247
Congressional Budget Office (CBO), 133
consequences phase of accountability, 5, *10*,
    15–17
Consolidated Supervised Entity (CSE), 292
Constitution of Society (Giddens), 269
constitutive reform, *291*, 294–295
constrictiveness
  and authority, 65–69
  in global governance, 58

constrictiveness *(continued)*
  mapping degree of, *69,* 69–70
  in sample organizations, *67, 68, 69, 72*
Consumer Product Safety Commission
    (CPSC), 108
consumers as force for governance, 228
consummate behavior, 43–44, *45,* 46, 49
context-specific accountability, 276–277
contract completeness, 43–44, 48–49
contract monitoring, 31–32
contract networks. *See also* accountability
    relationships
  clarity of contract design, 25
  and "many-hands" problems, 23–24
  market conditions for, 24
  multiple key actors in, 25
  multiple stakeholders and diverse
      expectations in, 25–27
  and principal-agent accountability, 23
  structure of, 27
  tangled nature of, 23, 28–29, 34–36
  trust in, 27
  and variety of institutional contexts, 23–24
  and welfare reform, 22–23
contracting accountability challenges
  asset specific investments, 44–45
  bilateral and vertical accountability, 45–46
  complex products, 42–44
  future uncertainty, 45
  prisoner's dilemma, 44, *45*
controllability, *xv,* xvi, 60
conventional approach to accountability, 3
corporation as representative institution,
    263–264
cost-reimbursement contracts, 53n3
counties, political accountability of
  and competitive elections, 118–119, *119*
  and diversity, 118–119, *119*
  and forms of government, 119–120, *120*
  measures for, 112–113
  and political culture, 113–117, 122–124
  services provided by, 111
  state influence on, 120–122, *121, 122*
CPSC (Consumer Product Safety
    Commission), 108
CSE (Consolidated Supervised Entity), 292

Darwall, Stephen, 256–257
debating phase of accountability, 5, *10,* 13–15
Deepwater program. *See* Project Deepwater

delegation as blame shifting, 7
Department of Defense, 137
Department of Energy (DOE), 157
*Dictionary of American Politics and
    Government* (Shafritz), 198
discursive roles of accountability, *287*
disinterestedness, 61
diversity and political accountability,
    118–119, *119*
Doble Research Associates, vii
DOE (Department of Energy), 157
domination, rules of, 271, *273*
double-layered accountability, 216–217,
    218–222
double-loop policy learning, 278
duality of structure, 271, *271*
Dutch agencies
  consequences phase of accountability, 15–17
  debating phase of accountability, 13–15
  information phase of accountability, 11–13
  multiple accountabilities through boards of
      commissioners, 8–11
Dutch Land Registry Office (Kadaster), 9–17

Easy Innovation and the Iron Cage
    (Frederickson), viii
Economic and Social Research Council, 85
Educational Testing Service (ETS), 64
Egypt, IT systems in, *149, 163*
Enlightenment
  planning as forerunner of accountability,
      283–284
  and the problem of nomination, 260
Enron, 59, 216, 291
environmental management system (EMS), 232
Environmental Protection Agency (EPA), 229
environmental standards. *See* ISO 14001
    program
equality before the law, 61
ETS (Educational Testing Service), 64
European Central Bank, 293
executive and legislative branches, conflict
    between, 103–105
executive government and blame avoidance,
    167–168, 171–174
executive power and political accountability,
    119–120, *120*

fairness as promise of accountability, *xv,* xviii
familiarity, need for, 114–118

Fannie Mae, 70
federal spending, 42–43
financial crisis. *See* Great Recession of
    2008–2010
Financial Services Authority, 292, 293
"fire alarm" legislative strategies, 167
fixed-price contracts, 53n3
Florida
    child welfare services in, 24, 32, 36n2, 36n6
    political accountability in, 121, *121, 122,
        123*
folk-psychology and promises of
    accountability, 284
Forest Stewardship Council, 62
form of government and political
    accountability, 119–120, *120*
formal accountability relationships, 29,
    31–32, *33,* 136, *136*
forums in accountability process, 5
free discourse and representation, 261
free rides, perception of, 114–118
Friedrich-Finer debate, 3, 5
functional communitarian accountability,
    244–245
functional *versus* strategic accountability, 182,
    184
future uncertainty, 45

G-20, 290
GAO (Government Accountability Office),
    133, 136–137
GGOs. *See* global governance organizations
Giddens, Anthony, 269–275
global financial markets in Great Recession,
    286–289
global governance organizations (GGOs)
    choosing responsiveness and/or
        responsibility, 74–75
    constrictiveness in, 58
    criticism of, 55–56
    legitimacy-authority tension, 57–58
    mapping degrees of publicness and
        constrictiveness, 74
    publicness in, 58
    responsibility in, 58
    responsiveness in, 58
    specific organizations studied, 56, *57*
goal congruence, 28
Goldman Sachs, 292
golf and social capital measures, 115, *115*

goodness, desire for, 227, 247
governance
    accountability as standard of, 283
    "chains of accountability," 226
    "City" figure in, 214, 215–216
    consumers as force for, 228
    double-layered accountability, 216–217,
        218–222
    government regulations for, 228
    the Maxwell test, 217
    measured by World Bank, 90–92
    need for, 213
    Northern Rock example, 217
    private politics as force for, 228
    and public welfare, 227
    voluntary codes of corporate conduct,
        214–217
Government Accountability Office (GAO),
    133, 136–137
Government Performance and Results Act.
    See GPRA
government regulations for governance, 228
GPRA (Government Performance and Results
    Act), 136
    and intergovernmental relationships, 104–
        105
    legislation of, 101–102
    legislative and executive conflict, 103–104
    and limitations of federal measurement,
        105–108, 109
Great Recession of 2007–2010
    accountability as cause and cure, 285–289
    and calls for reform, 284–285
    reform designs of, 289–295
Gulf War, 131–132

Halliburton, 64
health care systems, 152, *164,* 171, 197
Hero diversity formula, 118–119
hierarchical accountability, 29
Higgs Report, 216–217
Hobbes, Thomas, 258–261
home-rule authority in states, 121
horizontal structures for accountability,
    28–29, 30, 32, *33,* 34, 35
human behavior
    and blame avoidance, 167
    desire for accountability, 227, 247
    and promise of accountability, 284
Hurricane Katrina, 51

IASB (International Accounting Standards Board), 73–74

ICANN (Internet Corporation for Assigned Names and Numbers), 62, 71, 73

ICGS (Integrated Coast Guard Systems), 47, 48, 49–50

ICMA (International City/County Management Association), 112–113, 119–120, *120*

IDIQ (indefinite delivery, indefinite quantity) contract, 48

IFRS (International Financial Reporting Standards), 73

Igbo cosmology, 249

Illinois, political accountability in, 121, *121, 122, 123*

ILO (International Labor Organization), 71

indefinite delivery, indefinite quantity (IDIQ) contract, 48

independent/third sector, naming of, 201

India, IT systems in, *149,* 152, *153, 156, 164*

individual administrative responsibility, 3

informal accountability relationships, 32, *33, 34,* 136, *136*

information
  information phase of accountability, 5, *10,* 11–13
  informational terms of accountability, ix
  needed for governance, 226–228
  voluntary clubs as source for, 228–230

institutional legitimacy, 132–133

Integrated Coast Guard Systems (ICGS), 47, 48, 49–50

Integrated Product Teams (IPTs), 48, 49

integrity, *xv*

intergovernmental relationships, 104–105

interlocked boards, 220

Internal Revenue Code for nonprofits, 201

International Accounting Standards Board (IASB), 73–74

International City/County Management Association (ICMA), 112–113, 119–120, *120*

international comparison of systems enactments, 152, *153,* 154–158, *156, 163–164*

International Electrical Commission, 66

International Financial Reporting Standards (IFRS), 73

International Labor Organization (ILO), 71

International Maritime Organization, 71

International Organization for Standardization (IOS), 66, 71, 225, 230–231

International Telecommunications Union (ITU), 66, 71

Internet Corporation for Assigned Names and Numbers (ICANN), 62, 71, 73

IOS. *See* International Organization for Standardization

Iowa, political accountability in, 121, *121, 122, 123*

IPTs (Integrated Product Teams), 48, 49

ISO 14001 program
  accreditation authority in, 232
  as example of voluntary program, 225
  institutional design of, 231–232
  as signaling device, 233–235
  stakeholder's view of, 232–233

Israel Defense Force, 131–132

Israel State Comptroller's Office, 139

IT in government. *See* virtual state

ITU (International Telecommunications Union), 66, 71

Japan, ritual accountability in, 246, 277

Jordan, IT systems in, *153, 156, 164*

justice as promise of accountability, *xv,* xviii

Kansas, child welfare services in, 23–24, 25, *26,* 32, 34, 36n2, 37nn9–11

Kentucky, political accountability in, 121, *121, 122*

Kettering Symposium, vii, xii–xv, 302

keywords and stature of accountability, 285

Keywords (Williams), 285

kinship units, 249

legal accountability mechanisms, 29, *100,* 100–101, 108

legislative and executive branches, conflict between, 103–105

legitimacy
  of elected officials, 63
  in global governance, 57–58, 61–62
  of institutions, 132–133
  and nongovernmental organizations, 185, *186,* 192
  planning as standard for, 283–284
  as promise of accountability, *xv,* xvii
  and publicness, 63–65
  salience of, 63

legitimization, rules of, 270, *273, 274*
Lehman Brothers, 288, 292
Leigh Stowell & Company, 114–115
liability, 59
liberalism as basis for accountability
    concepts, 242–244
life-cycle of nonprofits, 204–208, *206–207*
lock-in risks, 47–48
Los Angeles, Calif., IT systems in, *163*
loss of control of agents, 8, 16–17

MAD (multiple accountabilities disorder),
    7–8, 57, 75
Malaysia, IT systems in, *149, 153, 156, 164*
malpractice suits, 171
managerial reform, *291,* 292–293
Manhattan project, 18
Marks and Spencer PLC, 215
Maryland, political accountability in, 121,
    121, 122
Maxwell test, 217
mechanisms for accountability, 5–6, 99–101,
    100, 105–108
Merrill Lynch, 288
Mexico, "low-accountability trap" in, 278
microcredit, in Bangladesh, *190,* 191–192
Microsoft, 66–67, 70, 214
money interests among public officials,
    114–118
moral obligation and authority, 257
Mozambique, IT systems in, *149,* 152, *153,*
    164
multiple accountabilities disorder (MAD),
    7–8, 16–17, 57, 75
multiple accountability
    for agencies, *9*
    balancing overloads, 19
    versus conventional model, 3–4
    Dutch agencies study, 8–17
    negative expectations for, 6–8, *8,* 12–13,
        14–15, 16–17
    and promises of accountability, 284
    and redundancy, 17–19

NASDAQ, 70
National Center for Charitable Statistics,
    201
National Committee for Responsive
    Philanthropy, 198
National Institutes of Health (NIH), 107

National Taxonomy of Exempt Entities
    (NTEE), 201–202
negative externalities and overproduction, 227
negativity, 7, 14–15, 171
Netherlands
    blame avoidance in, 177
    Dutch agencies study, 9–17
    IT systems in, *149, 152, 153,* 154, *156, 164*
Netherlands Vaccine Institute, 9–17
network-based social capital, 115, *115, 118*
network collaboration goals
    in, 28
    management of behaviors, 27–28
network structures for social services, 22–23
New Labour Party, 82
New Policy Agenda (NPA), 183, *184*
New Public Management (NPM), 81,
    146–147
NGO Accountability (Jordan and van Tuijl),
    185
NGOs. *See* nongovernmental organizations
NHS. *See* UK National Health Service
No Child Left Behind Act, 82, 107
"no-gaps" accountability, 247, 251–252
nomination, problem of, 255, 260–262
nongovernmental organizations (NGOs)
    accountability expectations for, 181–183,
        184, 185, 192
    in Bangladesh, 188
    examples of, 180
    expectations of, 192
    function of, 180–181
    functional *versus* strategic accountability in,
        182, *184*
    internal structures and roles, 183, *184*
    in International Organization for
        Standardization, 230–231
    legal accountability of, 192
    legitimacy issues in, 185, *186*
    New Policy Agenda (NPA) influence, 183,
        184
    Northern and Southern hemispheric
        differentiations, 182, *184*
    performance accountability for, 193–194
    performance criteria in, 182, *184*
    professional accountability mechanisms for,
        193
    PROSHIKA example, 188–195
    self-regulation, 183, *184,* 185
    stakeholders in, 182, 193–194

non-mandatory spending, decline in, 170–171
Nonprofit Almanac (Wing), 202
nonprofit sector
  accountability defined for, 198–199
  accountability standards, challenges in
    setting, 203–204
  charitable sector, naming of, 200
  growth of in United States, 197–198
  Internal Revenue Code for, 201
  life-cycle approach for accountability,
    204–208, *206–207*
  limited/asymmetric capacity of, 202–203
  naming of causing confusion, 199–201
  third/independent sector, naming of, 201
  variability of missions, 201–202
  voluntary sector, naming of, 200
non-rent-seeking organizations and social
  capital, 116, 124
non-western forms of accountability
  affective, 248–251
  ritual, 245–247
  in specific social structures, 277
norms development ("oughtness") in virtual
  states, 158–160, *159*
North Dakota, political accountability in, 121,
  121, 122
Northern Rock, 217
NPA (New Policy Agenda), 183, *184*
NPM (New Public Management), 81,
  146–147
NTEE (National Taxonomy of Exempt
  Entities), 201–202
nuclear plants, 17

objectivity, 61
OECD (Organisation for Economic co-
  operation and Development), 129
Office of Management and Budget (OMB),
  101, 105, 107
OMB (Office of Management and Budget),
  101, 105, 107
opinions not taken seriously, perception of,
  114–118
opportunity costs, 6–7, 12–13
Oregon, political accountability in, 121, *121,
  122, 123*
Organ Procurement and Transportation
  Network, 155
Organisation for Economic co-operation and
  Development (OECD), 129

organization-governed networks, 36n4 (27)
"oughtness" (norms development) in virtual
  states, 158–160, *159*
outside directors, 216–217, 218–222, 229
overloads, balancing, 19
overproduction with negative externalities,
  227

PART (Program Assessment Rating Tool)
  legislation of, 101, 102–103
  legislative and executive branches, conflict
    between, 103–104
  and limitations of federal measurement,
    105–108, 109
  in politics stream of accountability, 136, 137
passive accountability, 5
"pathways" of power, *134,* 134–135
Pennsylvania, political accountability in, *122*
performance accountability for
  nongovernmental organizations, 193–194
performance audit for accountability
  institutions, 141–142
performance measurement
  accountability, promoting, 82–83
  accountability, tension with, 83–85, 93–94
  defined, 150
  double-layered accountability, 218–222
  federal limitations, 105–108
  federal requirements, 101
  gaming or cheating by subjects, 84
  impact on accountability institutions, 140–
    141
  learning in, 278
  literature on, 98–99
  in nongovernmental organizations, 182, *184*
  power and struggle in, 278–279
  as promise of accountability, *xv,* xvii–xviii
  skepticism in literature regarding, 81–82
  in structuration theory, 277–278
  "tyranny of the light," 81, 84–85, 88
  UK National Health Service example, 85–88
  virtual states, applied to, 152, *153,* 154–158,
    156, 163–164
  World Bank example, 89–93
performative reform, *291,* 291–292
perfunctory behavior, 43–44, *45*
personhood, problem of, 255, 258–261
planning as legitimizing standard, 283–284
policy strategies of blame avoidance, 168,
  169, 170–171

policy streams
  and institutional legitimacy, 132–133
  overview of, 130
  politics stream, 135–140
  problem stream, 130–133
  solutions stream, 133–135
political accountability
  and competitive elections, 118–119, *119*
  and diversity, 118–119, *119*
  and form of government, 119–120, *120*
  home-rule authority in states, 121
  self-rule authority in states, 121
  state influence on counties, 120–122, *121, 122*
political accountability mechanisms, 29, 100,
    100, 106–107
  in counties, 111–113, 122–124
  familiarity, need for, 114–118
  free rides, perception of, 114–118
  money interests among public officials,
    114–118
  opinions not taken seriously, perception of,
    114–118
  risk-taking, tolerance of, 114–118, 124
  social capital affect on, 113–117, *115, 118*
political culture
  accountability affected by, 113–117, 122–124
  and social capital, 113–117, *115, 118*
Political Domination in Africa (Chabal), 248
politics stream, 135–140
positive externalities and underproduction,
    227
postal service in United States, 58
power and struggle in performance, 278–279
PPBS system, 137
predictability, 61
presentational strategies of blame avoidance,
    168, *169,* 170–171
principal agency in accountability institutions,
    138, 226–227
prison system in United States, 58, 64
prisoner's dilemma, 44, 45
private politics as force for governance, 228
privatization as government reform strategy, 22
problem stream, 130–133
professional accountability mechanisms, 29,
    100, *100,* 107–108, 193
professional norms, 3, 61, 133
Program Assessment Rating Tool. *See* PART
program evaluation and impact on
    accountability institutions, 142

Project Deepwater, 46–52
  asset specific investments, 47–48
  contract completeness, 48–49
  lock-in risks, 47–48
promises of accountability, *xv,* xv–xviii,
    282–284
PROSHIKA
  accountability issues of, 191, 192–194,
    194
  government concerns regarding, 191
  inception of, 188–189
  internal structure of, 189–191
  legal accountability of, 192
  and microcredit, *190,* 191–192
  programs of, *190*
public opinion and representation, 261
public welfare and governance, 227
publicness
  in global governance, 58
  and legitimacy, 63–65
  mapping degree of, *69,* 69–70
  of sample organizations, *65, 68, 69, 72*

rationalist formula of representation, 260
rationality, 250
redundancy, advantages of, 17–19
regulative reform, *291,* 293–294
relational terms of accountability, ix
religious networks and social capital
    measures, 115, *115,* 116, 122–124
rent-seeking organizations and social capital,
    116, 124
representation
  accountability as, 255–258
  and boards of directors, 264
  Burke on, 261–262
  corporation as institution of, 263–264
  Hobbes on, 258–261
  and moral obligation, 257
  nomination, problem of, 255, 260–262
  personhood, problem of, 255, 258–261
  public opinion and free discourse, 261
  rationalist formula of, 260
  second-person standpoint, 256–257
  stakeholders in, 261
republican communitarian accountability,
    244–245
responsibility
  as accountability type, 60–61
  in global governance, 58, 61–62, 74–75

responsiveness
  as accountability type, 62
  in global governance, 58, 62, 74–75
retirement of board personnel, 221
risk-monitoring, 213
risk-taking, tolerance of, 114–118, 124
ritual accountability, 245–247
Royal Bank of Scotland, 288
rules, fidelity to, 61

sanctions (consequences) phase of
    accountability, 5, *10*
Sarbanes-Oxley Act, 197, 216, 217, 294
SARS epidemic, 71
school superintendents, 59
Scotland, blame avoidance in, 172
SEC (U.S. Securities and Exchange
    Commission), 292, 293
second-person standpoint, 256–257
self-rule authority in states, 121
September 11 attacks, 18, 51, 130
shame in accountability institutions, 137
shareholders, directorial power of, 264
signaling device, voluntary clubs as, 233–235
signification, rules of, 270, *273*, 274
simple products, 43
social capital
  golf and, 115, *115*
  network-based, 115, *115*, *118*
  and political accountability, 113–117, *115*,
    118
  religious networks and, 115, *115*, 116,
    122–124
  and rent-seeking/non-rent-seeking
    organizations, 116, 124
  trust-based, 114, *115*, *118*, 122
social life, structuration theory for, 269
social praxis, 272
Social Security Agency (UWV-Netherlands),
    9–17
social systems, structures of, 270–271, *273*
solutions stream, 133–135
South Africa, IT systems in, *149, 153, 156, 164*
South Korea
  IT systems in, *149*, 152, *153, 156*, 157, *164*
  ritual accountability in, 246
spin and blame avoidance, 170
stakeholders
  in nongovernmental organizations, 182, 191,
    193

stakeholders *(continued)*
  and performance accountability, 193–194
  and representation, 261
  view of ISO 14001 program, 232–233
State Forest Authority, 9–17, 19
state influence on county political
    accountability, 120–122, *121, 122*
Stowell survey, 114–115
strategic *versus* functional accountability, 182,
    184
structuration theory
  of accountability, 272–276, *273*
  and agent theory, 275
  context-specific accountability, 276–277
  duality of structure, 271, *271*
  knowledgeable agents and action, 270
  performance measurement in, 277–278
  and responsibility of all actors, 276
  rules of domination, 271, *273*
  rules of legitimization, 270, *273*
  rules of signification, 270, *273*
  social life, for explaining structure of, 269
  social praxis, 272
  and social systems, 270–271
  systems and structures in, 270–271, *273*
symbolic accountability, 8, 16–17
systems enactments by country, 152, *153*,
    154–158, *156, 163–164*

Taiwan, IT systems in, *149*
Tanzania, IT systems in, *149, 153, 156, 164*
Theory of Moral Sentiments, The (Smith), 289
third party monitoring. *See* outside directors
third/independent sector, naming of, 201
TI (Transparency International), 154
transaction costs, 6–7, 12–13
transparency
  insufficiency of, 277
  necessary for accountability, 59, 61
  and "tyranny of the light," 88
Transparency International (TI), 154
tribal levels of community, 249
trust, in contract networks, 27
trust-based social capital, 114, *115, 118*, 122
Tyco, 216
"tyranny of the light," 81, 84–85, 88

UCAs (Undefinitized Contract Actions), 48
UK National Health Service (UK NHS),
    85–88

Undefinitized Contract Actions (UCAs), 48
underproduction with positive externalities, 227
UNICEF (United National Children's Fund), 69
unintended consequences, viii–ix, 278
United Kingdom
  blame avoidance in, 172, 173
  corporation as representative institution in, 263–264
  define-contribution pension plans in, 213
  IT systems in, *149,* 152, *153, 156, 164*
  performance measurement in, 82, 83–84
  utilization of reports, 139
  voluntary codes of corporate conduct in, 214–217, 221
United National Children's Fund (UNICEF), 69
United Nations Conference on Trade and Development, 231
United States
  blame avoidance in, 172, 173
  define-contribution pension plans in, 213
  interlocked boards in, 220
  IT systems in, *149,* 152, *153, 156, 164*
  performance measurement in, 82–83
  voluntary codes of corporate conduct in, 216
United States Postal Service (USPS), 67–68
United Way of America, 197
universal desire for accountability, 241
Universal Postal Union (UPU), 71
University of Electronic Science and Technology of China, 146
UPU (Universal Postal Union), 71
U.S. Coast Guard, 46–52
U.S. Federal Reserve System, 293
U.S. House of Representatives Committee on Oversight and Government Reform, 288
U.S. Securities and Exchange Commission (SEC), 292, 293
USPS (United States Postal Service), 67–68

vertical structures for accountability, 28–29, 30, 32, *33,* 34, 45–46
Virginia, political accountability in, 121, *121, 122*
virtual state (IT in government)
  accountability in, 147–148
  norms development ("oughtness") in, 158–160, *159*
  specific counties studied, *149*
  study methods, 148–152

virtue, accountability as, 4, 214
voluntary clubs
  crowding in, 231
  as signaling device, 233–235
  as source for information, 228–230
voluntary codes of conduct. *See also* ISO 14001 program
  as accountability mechanisms, 226–230
  evaluating, 225
  failure of, 293
  Higgs Report, 216–217
  importance of, 225–226
  principal-agent theory, 226–227
  reason for studying, 226
  in United Kingdom, 214–217, 221
  in United States, 216
voluntary sector, naming of, 200

Wal-Mart, 70
Washington, political accountability in, 121, *121, 122*
WCO (World Customs Organization), 62
welfare accountability
  and liberalism, 243
  tangled nature of, 34–36
welfare services. *See also* contract networks
  in Florida, 24, 32, 36n2, 36n6
  in Kansas, 23–24, 25, *26,* 32, 34, 36n2, 37nn9–11
  reform in, 22–24
western traditions of accountability, 241–245, 277
WGIs (World Governance Indicators), 89–93
WHO (World Health Organization), 71
win-win outcomes, 43, 45, 46
WIPU (World Intellectual Property Organization), 71
World Bank, 89–93
World Customs Organization (WCO), 62
World Governance Indicators (WGIs), 89–93
World Health Organization (WHO), 71
World Intellectual Property Organization (WIPU), 71
World Trade Organization (WTO), 66, 71
WorldCom, 216
WTO (World Trade Organization), 66, 71

Yahoo!, 214